Mission to Pakistan

An Intelligence Agent in Pakistan

Attention Authors

Manas Publications is fighting a war to tell the world that India can win the battle not only by the bullet but also by pen. We are converting fighters into writers. There is no dearth of intellectuals in our country, however, their knowledge is confined to them only. No sincere effort has been made by any other publisher to channelise their knowledge, that is why the talent of every intellectual remains latent. An author always presents the raw material in the shape of a manuscript and it is the job of the publisher to convert it into a finished product. Manas has been continually motivating intellectuals and publishing their manuscripts for more than three decades and would like to publish your manuscript too. If you or your colleagues have a manuscript ready for publication or are working on it, contact us with a detailed synopsis and list of contents. Manas can also suggest you a suitable title for writing related to your area of expertise. Manas is known for its publishing quality. We take utmost care in production and also give wide publicity to the book and its author through our national and international distribution network.

Mission to Pakistan

An Intelligence Agent in Pakistan

Maloy Krishna Dhar, IPS (Retd)
Former Joint Director : Intelligence Bureau

Manas Publications
(We Convert Fighters into Writers)
New Delhi-110 002 (INDIA)

MANAS PUBLICATIONS
(We Convert Fighters into Writers)
(Publishers-Library Suppliers-Importers & Exporters)
4402/5-A, Ansari Road (Opp. HDFC Bank)
Darya Ganj, New Delhi - 110 002 (India)
Phones: Off.: 011-23260783, 23265523, Res.: 011-23842660
E-mail: manaspublications@gmail.com
manaspublications@yahoo.com
Website: www.manaspublications.in

New Impression 2016

ISBN: 978-81-7049- 148-4 (13 Digits)
81-7049- 148-7 (10 Digits)

Rs. 795/-

Designed at
Manas Publications

Printed in India at
RK Print Services, Delhi
and published by Mrs Suman Lata for
Manas Publications, 4402/5-A,
Ansari Road, (Opp HDFC Bank),
Darya Ganj, New Delhi - 110002 (INDIA)

Contents

Dedication

Mission to Pakistan is dedicated to Sunanda Dhar, my wife and life partner. She helped me all the way in collating the research materials and developing the story line, till the nagging cancer, against which she fought valiantly, defeated her body and spirit on September 1, 2001.

To honour her expressed wish the author's share from the proceeds of this book will be donated to research work on Breast Cancer

Acknowledgement

My past and present colleagues in the intelligence fraternity and my nameless and faceless professional friends are the real heroes of Mission to Pakistan. I salute them.

I am grateful to a mother, whom I cannot name, for giving me the opportunity to pursue some of the communications she and her son, an Indian intelligence agent incarcerated in Pakistan, had exchanged till the channel finally dried out. I have tried to share with my readers some of the sentiments expressed in their communications. *Mission to Pakistan* would have remained incomplete without the anonymous mother's generous help.

I am grateful to Smt. Sangeetha Chengappa for meticulously scanning the text and making valuable suggestions.

My son Mainak Dhar stood like a rock behind my wife and me, when we were grappling with the research materials and the text. It would have been impossible for me to successfully ground my shattered emotions and complete the Mission without his unflinching support.

List of Acronyms

AEC	Atomic Energy Commission
AHQ	Army Head Quarters
ATC	Air Traffic Control
BHC	British High Commission
CCSA	Cabinet Committee on Security Affairs
CFL	Cease Fire Line
CHQ	Command Head Quarters
CIA	Central Intelligence Agency
CMLA	Chief Martial Law Administrator
COAS	Chief of Army Staff
CRISMAS	Crisis Management Station
DBN	Dera Baba Nanak
DCM	Deputy Chief of Mission
DF	Direction Finder
DINASIA	Director Natioanal Security India
DLB	Dead Letter Box
DMI	Director Military Intelligence
DMO	Director Military Operations
ELINT	Electronic Intelligence
EPABX	Electronic Private Automatic Branch Exchange
FIB	Federal Intelligence Bureau
Fosur	Foot Surveillance
FUZ	Field Unit Zebra
GHQ	General Head Quarters
GREG	Global Research Group
GREG	Special Services Group
GSO	General Staff Officer
HF	High Frequency
HoM	Head of Mission
HUMINT	Human Intelligence
ICC	Integral Command Centre
IMINT	Imagery Intelligence
ISI	Inter Services Intelligence
JCMM	Joint Crisis Management Committee
JCO	Junior Commissioned

JIM	Joint Intelligence Miscellaneous
JIN	Joint Intelligence North
JIS	Joint Intelligence Signals
LLB	Live Letter Box
MCD	Municipal Corporation of Delhi
Mosur	Mobile Surveillance
NSI	National Security India
OBR	Operation Briefing Room
OTP	One Time Pad
PFLP	Peoples Front for Liberation of Palestine
PIB	Pakistan Intelligence Bureau
PLA	Palestinian Liberation Army
PLO	Palestinian Liberation Organisation
PSO	Personal Staff Officer
PSTN	Public Service Telephone Network
PTDC	Pakistan Tourism Development Corporation
RAX	Restricted Area Exchange
SAAD	Safe Accommodation Address
SAF	Special Aviation Force
SAM	Surface to Air Missile
SCSB	Signal Communication Security Bureau
SIB	Signals Intelligence Bureau
SIGINT	Signal Intelligence
SUCSON	Supreme Command Station
SVF	Special Volunteer Force
TECHINT	Technical Intelligence
Tesur	Technical Surveillance
UHF	Ultra High Frequency
VHF	Very High Frequency
VLF	Very Low Frequency

Chapter 1

Nakshatra Lok (galactic abode), the awesome structure that carried an audacious name, housed India's super-secret spy agency, the National Security India (NSI). Located at a remote corner of Delhi, bordering the wooded banks of the river Yamuna, alongside the grave of Humayun, the second Mughal emperor, it presented the eerie spectre of a spiraling space station. Its architectural marvel created an illusion of amorphous and ethereal awe. It copied a star-war concept, stolen from the neurons of science fiction scribblers. The architect had translated the geometric designs and aesthetic concepts of a space station, envisioned by the chief of the NSI, Balachandran Nampoothiri.

Nakshtra Lok's structural ingenuity was craftily synthesized with its functional ethics. It was meant to be a business place, serious business of national security and external intelligence affairs. Specially designed glass-encased tubular elevators, controlled by a master computer connected the functionally and intrinsically independent modules.

The reception area, designed after modern business-house front offices, offered soothing ecological delight. Green tropical plants, arranged with poetic imagination created a mirage of cool environs, far removed from the heat and dust outside and webs of intrigues and guile spun by the intelligence community inside. Casual visitors, once inside the reception module, felt suddenly transported to an encapsulated greenhouse. Their discerning minds were reminded of the flavors of the exotic forests of the misty Himalayas. But ***Nakshtra Lok*** was far from a cool niche.

Exceptionally beautiful women, all in the age group of twenty to twenty five, manned the geometrically designed front reception cubicles. Glued to their chairs and specially designed desks they presented a monotonously titillating sight. Soft indirect azure lights, embedded below desk panels, scattered the illumination evenly, creating a fairy tale effect. It added a pre-dawn charm on the faces of the women, draped in floral designer print ***saris.***

They were, however, not clones. Each one of them, fabulously charming, presented a cool impersonal appearance, distinct from their surrounding. Their chiseled features, sculpted frames and honey-laced impersonal looks created a clone syndrome.

Monogrammed plastic boards, hung in front of each desk, proclaimed the names and logos of the companies they pretended to represent. These front decoys were wired to the access control system of the National Security India and entry to the surreal front reception was routed through basement parking bays, which were controlled by laser-hologram identity cards. Hidden close circuit television cameras concealed beneath fancy lighting props monitored front desk and peripheral bays. These were, in turn, connected to the master consoles of the security terminals, located in the basement backrooms.

The charming dames mechanically placed the cards under scanning beams connected to a mainframe computer. A green flash elicited melted smiles and programmed welcome greetings. A flicker in red meant trouble, leading to segregation and polite but uncomfortable questioning and an occasional journey to a safe house for thorough screening and decontamination.

This nimble façade, a unique concept of the National Security India Chief, Balachandran Nampoothiri symbolized with great success the good, the bad and the ugly features and functions of the reputed, ridiculed and often cursed external intelligence agency of India.

One of the front desks, farthest from the right, displayed a miniature signboard, 'World Vision Infotech'; proclaiming supposed commercial activity in information technology carried out from the fourth tower of the seemingly galactic complex.

That tower terrace housed the global communication network of the National Security India, connecting its stations in world capitals as also the capitals of Indian provinces and district detachments. An intricate Compact Communication Module (CCM), hooked to a supercomputer, handled digitally secured data and voice communication that poured in over line, radio and satellite facilities.

The super secret communication monitoring facility, with an installed capacity to hook 10,000 inland and overseas telephone lines, was housed in the top two floors. The satellite communication-tapping hub, hooked to the major Foreign Transmission Gateways and wired to the hubs, which encompassed the footprints of the Chinese and the Pakistani satellite communication systems, supplemented the traditional physical line monitoring consoles.

Arrays of antennae, dispersed over two separate funnels, facilitated the reception and transmission modules for High (HF), Very High (VHF), Very Low (VLF) and Ultra High Frequency (UHF) radio stations. Radio wizards handled all secret and top-secret communications and trained mathematicians and computer buffs manipulated the complicated computer generated cipher traffic.

Internal communication linkages were skilfully segregated from the Public Service Telephone Network (PSTN). A nine hundred-line Electronic Private Automatic Branch Exchange (EPABX) system with automatic patching facility with the PSTN system handled the internal traffic.

Two dedicated lines connected the office of the ***DINASIA,*** Director National Security India. Ten exclusive lines were extended to an underground bunker complex, spread below the Raisina Hills. These arrays of bunkers housed the Crisis Management Station (CRISMAS) and the Command Head Quarter (CHQ), two super secret entities, which were designated to be activated in the event of a nuclear war.

The special NSI exchange wires were extended to another super-secret underground complex, located somewhere in Lutyens' Delhi that accommodated the Supreme Command Station (SUCSON); the emergency functional head quarters for the President, the Prime Minister and his Cabinet besides, the Chiefs of the Armed Forces.

Somewhere in the maze of rooms and cubicles in the fourth tower, was housed the super-secret Technical Division. Here highly trained experts in Electronic, Signals and Technical Intelligence, toiled incessantly to keep the company going strong.

Balachandran Nampoothiri had segregated, by deliberate design, the general intelligence branches from the TechInt (Technical Intelligence), SigInt (Signal Intelligence), ImInt (Imagery Intelligence-satellite input) and ElInt (Electronic Intelligence) divisions. Even senior officers of the NSI were required to take clearance from the boss for accessing the super-secret holy ghosts of the NSI, strictly on a need to know basis.

Tower Four was very close to Mr. Balachandran Nampoothiri's heart tissues. He designed and created it from the scratch, collecting the most sophisticated gadgetry and equipments from Western and Southeast Asian markets. A legendary TechInt buff, Nampoothiri wasn't less immersed in intelligence operations, analysis and human resources management. But the first and reigning Chief of the NSI preferred the glamorous cocktail of Human Intelligence (HumInt) and technical operations. He was an acknowledged master in both crafts of the oldest trade.

The Chief of the Director National Security India, designated ***DINASIA***, occupied the fabled room number 0003, at the eleventh level of the fourth tower. Mr.Balachandran Nampoothiri, fondly called Balu and Balls by acquaintances and golf turf buddies, was born in an orthodox Malayali Brahmin family. By training a policeman, he was inducted into the Federal Intelligence Bureau (FIB) soon after independence, by his uncle, a senior minister in the Union Cabinet.

A dedicated professional, Nampoothiri worked his way up, much to the envy of colleagues and Delhi's bureaucrat watchers, nicknamed ***beauronthologists,*** seemingly the first cousins of ornithologists. A glib talker and a social livewire he had endeared himself to the top politicians and famous parlour femme fatales, who normally seeded India's political and economic clouds over soothing drinks and warm beds.

Nampoothiri's thirst for the top intelligence slot, a lonely place at the pinnacle of the pyramid, had propelled him into a fiery race against another powerful contender. His colleague in the undivided Federal Intelligence Bureau, Kumar Anand Prasad, a wily Bihari ***kayasth*** (intermediate caste) didn't dither in mustering more potent propellants for out-racing Nampoothiri. This was a bitter blazing fight, a razing fire that refused to be extinguished by soothing Scotch on the rocks and contrived manipulation of facial muscles, often described as smiles.

Kumar had secured the top FIB slot; the alley cats whispered, through the courtesy and influence of another powerful minister, Ram Karan Prasad. Both hailed from ***Pataliputra,*** the nerve centre of an ancient empire, associated with the name of ***Chanakya,*** the acknowledged Indian spymaster. What better credential could Kumar Anand claim?

But, a Nampoothiri, according to Hindu tradition cannot be wished away as a lesser ***Chanakya***. In Kerala, where the Namboodris hail from, people preferred to kill a Namboodri first before smothering a menacing hooded cobra.

Balachandran, friends and foes vouchsafed, wasn't as malevolent as his legendary caste kinsmen were portrayed to be. He used his own brand of lubricants, which Kumar Anand jokingly described as coconut butter, and polished his way up the critical cone of the external intelligence outfit. The reference to coconut butter critically reflected the NSI chief's glorious roots in the coastal state of Kerala.

Then there was Mandira, the third Prime Minister of India who had rescued Nampoothiri, otherwise left out in Delhi's bureaucratic rat race. She had carved out the NSI niche by truncating the FIB monolith and offered the new peak to her favourite sleuth. So, Kumar Anand Prasad continued to lord over what was left of the erstwhile second pivot of power in Delhi, the Federal Intelligence Bureau of India.

Neither Kumar Anand nor Nampoothiri was ashamed of using his own brand of lubricants. The use of lubricant was an integral part of the Indian system; prescribed by Manu, the Hindu social-law dispenser and copied lock stock and barrel from the imperial masters. The lubrication process helped in overlooking merit and seniority and in playing footsy to the idiosyncrasies of the bosses. What could be wrong with Nampoothiri, if he did at all apply some grease somewhere?

Nampoothiri, his friends and foes agreed, was an accomplished spymaster, with well-greased exclusive tunnels to the minds, thoughts and perceptions of leading politicians. It was no mean achievement. With the advent of Mandira, after the tragic death of her predecessor, Jung Bahadur Sharma, the appointment to higher government slots depended on a single cardinal principle-loyalty to the throne. She preferred a committed bureaucracy. She herself claimed to be committed to the mission of rescuing India, a task she feigned to have inherited from her father.

Nampoothiri was a different piece of blade, adept in a fencing game of the highest order. His opponents didn't even winch after their heads were severed from their torso. It required a whiff of Virginia snuff to make the severed crown sneeze and fall apart.

The capital's bureaucrats maintained a fearful proximity and distance from Nampoothiri for his alleged capability of staging a coup at the most unexpected moment. That was the precise reason why some of them preferred to call him Balls. They were not referring to the balls used for golf. They meant, the parts of the sex organs of the politicians, to which, they alleged, Nampoothiri preferred to attach himself.

He was by far the coolest cat in Delhi's power alley.

****

However, on this cool November day Balachandran Nampoothiri alias Balls alias Balu, the Chief of the National Security India, was sweating profusely and uncomfortably in his den, room number 0003.

A special thick inner lead casing, for denying access to invasive electronic snooping, protected the dreaded and coveted room. The lead coating supplemented by soundproofing materials made the room impregnable. Nampoothiri was fond of opening windows, both of his habitat and mind. But the intelligence bug in him had prompted the redesigning of his office room window. The only window of the room was treated with chemical absorbents for deflecting snooping laser beams. Besides the air-conditioning, a special air outlet, in the form of a sophisticated exhaust fan, which operated silently, helped circulation of fresh air. This was a necessary prop to allow Nampoothiri to have his occasional puff from imported Havana.

The two other integral fixtures of his office were Jatadhari Garo, Nampoothiri's Man Friday and Amrita Bhalla, his secretary cum alter ego.

Nampoothiri could perhaps not be a complete intelligence boss without his shadow, Jatadhari Garo. In real life Jatadhari held the rank of a junior superintendent of police. Nampoothiri picked up this tribal of Tibetan stock, six feet two inches tall, all muscle and no fat, soon after his recruitment as a junior intelligence officer, way back in the mid-fifties.

A strange accident at Nathu La pass, one of the frontier outposts on Sikkim China borders, brought them together. Balachandran Nampoothiri was on one of his many trips to Nathu La, heading a group of electronic specialists, for the installation of directional microphones and a Very High Frequency (VHF) radio-monitoring centre. Directional microphones were designed to pick up conversations of the Chinese army contingents, which occupied a lower shoulder, barely 300 metres below the ridge. Howling winds rolled up from the Chumbi valley below and thrashed against the peaks on the Indian side with wailing and roaring sounds. The windy pass frustrated all the HumInt and TechInt efforts of the FIB from recording conversations of the inscrutable Chinese troops.

Challenges never disheartened Nampoothiri. He worked on the idea of installing directional microphones, drawing inspiration from similar CIA operations on the North Korean borders.

That January morning Nampoothiri stood facing the Chinese formations. Snowfall had come early that year. The water in Changu Lake, on Indian side of the valley, was still full of rainbow trout and the grazers were yet to move down to the lower reaches of the rippling pastures. The Yak herds were still roaming in the green patches dotted with Dandelion, Iris and Tiger lilies. The ***Bhutia*** and ***Lepcha*** herd-tenders were busy cooking barley meals, roasting dry meat and melting frozen cheese, in their Yak-skin tents. Fresh coats of powdery snow covered the Rhododendron bushes that were trying to burst out of their wet white burial.

It happened suddenly, the soft snow beneath his feet gave way and Balachandran Nampoothiri slithered down the precipices, a sheer fall of 500 feet. By instinct he grabbed a Rhododendron bush and managed to hang on to that precariously.

Before anyone could react, Jatadhari, all six feet of himself, clutched at another Rhododendron bush, stretched down long arms and jerked up Nampoothiri, as if he was tossing a tiny basketball up. Nampoothiri fell on soft snow with a thud. The Rhododendron bushes wilted under his weight and his bulky figure skidded down to a grassy patch, a good 20 feet below.

In the process Jatadhari slipped down the slope into a deep crevice.

Jatadhari, a trained mountaineer, was finally rescued with one leg and three broken fingers. The operation was temporarily abandoned and Nampoothiri airlifted the junior officer for treatment to the Siliguri army base hospital. After eight weeks of hospitalisation, Jatadhari was flown to Delhi from Bagdogra in a special AN 26, owned by Kalyani Air Lines, another super-secret adjunct of the Federal Intelligence Bureau. Nampoothiri himself was in the flight. He owed his life to the valiant tribal officer.

From that fateful day onwards, he and Jatadhari became inseparable and emotionally interdependent. They were made for each other, the bond of trust between them more sacrosanct than the holy vow of a Hindu marriage in front of a sacrificial fire.

The heavy door slightly opened up, noiselessly, and Jatadhari, like a silent ***cheetah***, glided in. Nampoothiri, busy reading a despatch from his station chief in Rawalpindi, looked up, almost as if he could scent his shadow.

"What's the matter? "

"Sir, Mr. Achariya is at the front desk. He wants to see you urgently. "

Balchandran Nampoothiri wasn't pleased. Achariya, he presumed was on a panic trip over the mysterious loss of contact with Harfan Bukhari, NSI's Operation Triple X and Alamgir, India's most valuable long-term intelligence anchor inside Pakistan. He had expected his desk chief to rush up with the bad news.

But the NSI boss wasn't in a mood to share his concerns with his desk chief. He was immersed in problems of greater significance. Triple X had mysteriously landed in an Air Force base near Delhi, in an aircraft piloted by a South African mercenary, hired by Islamabad for ferrying weapons to East Pakistan. Only Nampoothiri and the Case Officer of Operation Triple X, Dhiren Bhagat, were aware of the hideout where Harfan Bukhari was housed.

Nampoothiri didn't like sparrow-flight by his officers to his den. He was a stickler for formally appointed meetings. Even the senior analysts and veteran desk officers were required to come through his special assistant, Amrita Bhalla.

She was there, not because of her stunning aquiline Greek features and Aphrodite like intense sensual beauty. She was the daughter of a trusted former colleague, who was killed by the advancing Chinese troops at Bomdi La, a remote post in the North East Frontier Agency (NEFA), during India's border skirmishes with the Chinese Communist regime in 1962.

Amrita Bhalla, behind her ***sari***-clad chiselled body was a black belt in judo and trained in unarmed combat from the Royal Canadian

Mounted Police Academy, Winnipeg, Manitoba. Early in her career in the NSI she had earned the distinction of representing the country in the Commonwealth Games.

Robin Achariya frequented the front desk of his boss with tonnes of sighs and aches inside his chest cavity. His hungry imagination liked to fly above cloud nine with Amrita Bhalla by his side. He liked to imagine that his eyes were X-ray machines and he could see the flesh and bones of the lady behind her apparel.

Amrita Bhalla discreetly appreciated the hungry looks of her male colleagues. A thing of beauty, as she was, Amrita recognised her admirers. She often reflected back their hungry looks with stony silence, and derived a rare impish delight by accepting odd invitations to dinner. That she did selectively, with Nampoothiri's knowledge, only to pump out information about gurgling rumblings in the organisation and to fathom the depth of factionalism. Such selective favours had created a clientele of informers, useful to boss Nampoothiri and essential for her survival in the male dominated organisation. Robin Achariya, the Pakistan desk analyst, had unwittingly become an informer of Amrita Bhalla. She knew it and used her tricks deftly.

"How're you Robin?" Amrita asked smilingly, "Anything gone wrong?"

"Big problem dear," Robin drew in a chair, "Triple X has disappeared."

"Oh dear!" Amrita started with a pout, "Don't get worked up, agents come and go like monsoon clouds."

"He was important, dear to the boss." Robin smiled back, hoping to prolong the dialogue.

A faint blue light momentarily glowed on a screen hidden under the wooden panel of her table and Amrita stood up with a courteous gesture.

"You can go in sir." She cleared the way for Achariya with a naughty twinkle.

She always spoke these last words with a lilting and slurring accent. Some visitors interpreted it as a deliberate sexy finale. Others digested it as an expression of arrogance of a junior officer, with a bloated ego, because of her physical intimacy with the top man; a perception not based on fact.

Achariya threw a smile at her with a wink and entered the room closely on Jatadhari's heels. As he occupied a thick cushioned moccasin upholstered chair, Jatadhari drew the heavy curtains on the window

Nampoothiri switched on his music system at low bass. This was a normal practice, to create noise pollution, making it difficult for hostile snooping operations.

"What brings you here this morning Achariya?" Nampoothiri looked up at his subordinate, whose face presented an anguished look.

"We appear to have run into problems with Operation Triple X., our man in Pakistan. We're cut off from him for last couple of days He should've been in London by this time, following your final instructions. Our efforts to activate the communication channels have failed? Agent Double X, I mean Qurban, is silent too." Achariya blurted out rapidly, his panic apparent.

"Where is Alamgir?" Nampoothiri enquired about India's most valuable long-term resident anchor in Pakistan.

"He's silent too. Kabul isn't able to raise him, and we haven't heard from him since he left London for Islamabad. His silence is ominous."

"Have you checked with his family in Berne?"

"Not yet."

"Has there been any distress signal at the pre-fixed radio band?"

"No sir. Our boys have been scanning all the three channels assigned to Alam." Achariya kept on staring at his boss, "As you're aware Triple X's radio was earlier decommissioned."

"That's correct. Have you checked with our man in Peshawar?"

"Peshawar is unaware of his whereabouts. Alam and Harfan have simply disappeared, it seems. I'm afraid, they may have fallen into the ISI trap."

Nampoothiri felt uncomfortable. Small drops of sweat appeared on his forehead. He wiped the back of his neck and forehead in repeated motions with a silk handkerchief and pressed the buzzer.

His cause of anxiety wasn't for Triple X, who had appeared in Delhi, just a few hours ago, like a comet. He was yet to spill the beans and the NSI chief had not quiet comprehended the circumstances that compelled the prized resident agent in Pakistan to defy his disengagement order.

Nampoothiri did never feel any positive vibe for Robin Achariya and today he did not require his input to order a fresh hunt for Triple X. But he did not like to be trapped by his desk chief. Nampoothiri played for time. He tried to acquire as well as deny information to his junior. His eyes summarily mapped up the facial contours of Achariya. Was he playing a subtle game of drawing out vital information from the boss? Crafty subordinates were capable of casting invisible nets for trapping their seniors.

Nampoothiri drew a safe conclusion over a few silent puffs of Havana. Achariya was genuinely concerned. Nampoothiri was worried too, about Alamgir's silence. India's intelligence anchor in Pakistan had become mysteriously incommunicado.

Nampoothiri's thought waves made a sharp inward trip.

Yes, he had spent two crucial hours with Harfan Bukhari and had pumped out sensitive intelligence about Pakistani plans of an aerial blitzkrieg against Indian targets. Triple X was dead accurate on that count. He was informed, minutes ago, by Major General Gandhi, the Director of Military Intelligence (DMI), about the strafing of Indian airbases by Pakistani Sabre jets in the volatile western sector. But Harfan persistently dodged the Alamgir issue. Nampoothiri didn't press either. The Prime Minister had placed an embargo on unnecessary needling with Triple X and the South African pilot.

It suited Nampoothiri. The NSI, at this point of crisis, when Indian and Pakistani forces were in active engagement in the eastern and western theatres, was more interested in a post-mortem of the spectral collapse of its intelligence network inside Pakistan. The job required a levelheaded approach and calm analysis. No rush action, Nampoothiri agreed with the Prime Minister. In any case he wasn't keen to share the nuts and bolts of the foxy riddle with Achariya. Pakistan related intelligence was his special turf and Operation Triple X was his own baby and he'd like to carry out a leisurely post-mortem.

But the Alamgir affair puzzled him and rang an ominous bell.

Nampoothiri pressed the buzzer. Jatadhari entered silently, fleeting like a water-walking yogi. Nampoothiri pointed his finger at a glass. Jatadhari poured water out from an eagle shaped bottle and offered to his master. Nampoothiri still felt the thirst gnawing at his windpipe.

The pre-emptive Pakistani air strike had triggered off cloudbursts of another ghastly spectre of war. The western theatre had become extremely vulnerable. The KGB had supplemented the NSI and DMI reports about pumping of Chinese and American weapons to Islamabad through Jordanian, Saudi and Turkish pipelines.

The eastern sector too was clouded with war fumes. The brave Bengalis had unfurled the banner of independence and unexpected circumstances had sucked India into the eye of another devastating storm.

Nampoothiri licked his parched lips and looked towards Jatadhari.

Jatadhari knew the drill well. The sweating forehead of the boss told him that something was cooking inside Nampoothiri's tossing mind. He switched on the exhaust, picked up a Havana from a silver casket and flicked open a blue flame by pressing the Ronson lighter.

Nampoothiri inhaled the smoke with a relish, like a fish starved of oxygen and looked up at Achariya.

"What about your Quetta Listening Post?"

"The Quetta LP and our observation post at Chaman haven't been able to contact Alamgir." He hinted at a top-level Afghan trader, who operated dozens of loan sharks in the Indian states of Bengal and Bihar.

"What about your auxiliary channel at Tashkent?"

"They're dry too. I'm afraid," Achariya blinked peevishly with a naughty smile, "Triple X may have defected to Pakistan."

"I don't think so." Nampoothiri looked up with a stony gaze and mildly shook his head.

Robin Achariya nervously rattled his throat and explained that the prolonged silence of Triple X, located at Jhumra near Faisalabad worried him. This particular asset, turbulent and irrepressible, had the potential of exploding into a self-destructing blast. In the process he could trigger off an avalanche of exposure, burying other intelligence operations in Pakistan.

"I can't agree more," Nampoothiri looked squarely into Achariya's eyes, "Raise our MI6 liaison channel in Cairo. Not the River one. They may have some clue."

Nampoothiri waived him off and picked up a yellow phone, part of the exclusive in-house communication network and asked Krishna Kumar, Chief of the cryptographic division to rush in.

****

Nampoothiri lapsed back into his memory lane.

Alamgir was a unique asset, from day one.

He was an antithesis of the copybook low-key resident agent. His flamboyance coupled with the traits of a bullfighter had created an aura of dubious reputation with wide spectrum acceptability in the Pakistani establishment. He owned several business establishments at Peshawar Fort market, ostensibly selling dry fruits and assorted merchandise.

Alamgir owned another establishment, an under-cover one, better known in Pakistan as GREG (Global Research Group). The shady outfit had levelled up deals with the high and mighty in the Pakistani armed forces. In simple language, Alam Khan, a patriotic Pathan and his honourable associates scouted around for and procured arms and ammunition from world arms bazaars for the military regime. His marketing networks were spread over Afghanistan and the Central Asian Soviet Republics, besides the lucrative arms bazaar in Europe and South American countries. The arrangement kept everybody happy. The reward packet was fat.

His dry fruit business had, over the years, metamorphosed into a convenient cover operation for international drug trafficking from the Golden Crescent to the dark alleys of Europe and USA. The uniformed bosses and fringe politicians had found a convenient fall guy in the daredevil Pathan. They thrived merrily on human miseries and Alamgir craftily used the cover for deeper infiltration into the system. Delhi turned a blind eye at his cover operations. What he did hardly mattered to them as long as their bird laid golden eggs.

Besides catering very high-level intelligence on Pakistan, Alam acted as Nampoothiri's personal emissary and handled shallow penetration Indian intelligence assets in Pakistan. New talents infiltrated by the Federal Intelligence Bureau, now the NSI, were supposed to go through the grilling sieve of this master spy. He enjoyed the total trust of the organisation, especially its boss, Nampoothiri.

The discreet blue lamp glowed instantly and vivacious Amrita silently and respectfully ushered in Krishna Kumar.

A dry and matter of fact person, Krishna Kumar had no other interest in life, except sitting before computers and playing around with intercepted coded messages. To him breaking enemy codes was as exotic and erotic as exploring the creases and contours of a beautiful woman.

"Transmit this immediately to Kabul, Tashkent and Moscow." Nampoothiri passed on a slip to Krishna Kumar.

The chief cryptologist glanced at the paper, brought out a compact briefcase from a cupboard, a High Frequency trans-receiver connected to the main transmission tower.

The simple message asked the tertiary station chiefs to immediately direct Alam to get in touch with Sparrow, one of the several code names of Nampoothiri. The auto-encrypted message was burst transmitted in less than 3 seconds. Krishna Kumar received the 'roger' protocol and switched off.

"I want quick confirmation." Nampoothiri extinguished the cigar and sipped water leisurely.

"No problem sir, if the receiving stations have none."

Krishna Kumar replaced the trans-receiver in the cupboard, handed over the key to his boss and left without even exchanging the usual mandatory greeting.

Agent Taqdeer from Kabul reacted after 4 hours, via a special communication hub in Moscow. Operation Triple X wasn't traceable. His wife and child at Lahore were missing as well. The Lahore police didn't confirm his death or arrest. He had simply vanished into thin air. Alamgir's usual communication hubs were silent. Crucial channels assigned to the top agent failed to raise him and his Peshawar den maintained a mysterious silence.

The Taqdeer input unnerved Nampoothiri. He had reasons to be. Alamgir wasn't a dime of an intelligence agent. He alone could demystify the riddles of the suspected busting of the Indian network inside the hostile country.

The blue lamp on Amrita's desk glowed and Nampoothiri's voice came in.

"Can you come in for a minute?"

"Yes sir."

"What do you think of this Operation Triple X affair and Alamgir's silence?" Nampoothiri tried to pick fresh ideas from his secretary.

"Harfan must have been pushed to the wall," Amrita spoke in soft measured words, "I'm not sure how Alam handled the final disengagement ritual."

"Do you doubt Alam's integrity?"

"Pardon me sir," Amrita continued, "His latest reports on Triple X weren't unbiased. I've a feeling that they had developed incurable empathy."

"Yes. You're correct dear. Perhaps I should've intervened." Nampoothiri lowered his eyes, probably in retrospection; "I suspected traces of incompatibility between Alam and Harfan. Double X had also warned me. But that shouldn't trigger off a collapsing avalanche."

"I presume so. But you don't know how much they had drifted. The desk officer should've smelt a rat. But you appear to be worried about Harfan's sudden arrival in Delhi."

"Right you're dear. But I'm more worried about Alamgir. He's silent and not responding to our radio pulses." Nampoothiri picked up another Havana. Amrita flicked the lighter on.

"Thanks dear. I'm stuck in muck. Another India-Pakistan war is breathing down our neck and my top agent has disappeared. Intelligence machinery inside Pakistan has simply collapsed. That's no fun. The PM isn't going to be pleased. You know her."

Amrita knew little about the lady Prime Minister. But she knew well that the NSI would come under direct fire, if her patron and boss failed to deliver the goods.

"Better go home and relax sir."

"No dear. You call it a day. I have to wait for some urgent feedback. Tell Jata to be around."

Nampoothiri, for a change, walked up to the window and opened the glass panels and looked out at the waters of the river Yamuna. His mind was clogged like the polluted Yamuna. It wasn't moving in any direction.

What did go wrong, where and why?

Operation Triple X had made a dramatic appearance in Delhi, just 18 hours ago. His escape from Pakistan in a mercenary flight, that was designed to carry toxic nerve gas shells to East Pakistan, had rattled the government. His comet like appearance and timely tip off had no doubt saved the country from a double jeopardy, a devastating aerial blitzkrieg by the Pakistani Air Force and a holocaust of chemical warfare. But it opened up more complicated questions.

Nampoothiri had drawn a blank while quizzing Triple X on Alamgir's status. The sullen agent maintained an enigmatic silence. The refrain of his story revolved around the Inter Services Intelligence of Pakistan haunting his trail after a chance interception of signals from his clandestine HF trans-receiver. He had alleged, rather robustly, about the callous handling of sensitive intelligence handed out by him. Fatal leakages from Delhi end, he asserted, had sealed his fate.

Harfan's assertions weren't baseless. The Indian Mission in Ottawa had corroborated intelligence gathered and catered by him on the Pakistani search for nuclear know-how. It had noticed the suspicious activities of a Pakistani scientist on furlough in McGill University, Montreal. The same scientist, according to station Chicago, had visited several US nuclear facilities. Despatches from the Indian Mission at Bonn also reported about suspicious activities of another Pakistani scientist in one of the universities there, and the involvement of a German firm in selling nuclear reactor components to Pakistan.

A review meeting, conducted a few days back, at the Prime Minister's level, finally sounded the warning siren. After all, Triple X and Qurban, the Double X weren't totally off the track. The Zebra Unit of the FIB and Nampoothiri's own surveillance apparatus had confirmed that the bureaucratic poodles at higher places had developed ominous leaks. Pakistan had perilously penetrated the paper curtains of the Indian bureaucracy. India's nuclear secrets and its deep penetration sources in Pakistan had been compromised.

The Inter Services Intelligence of Pakistan must have tracked back the trails of origin of the intelligence to either Triple X or Alamgir. Intelligence tradecraft supported such a possibility. Why possibility alone? A dogged sleuth could easily slip back into the womb of the original piece of intelligence.

Nampoothiri moved closer to the window, lighted a Havana, diverted his gaze to the constellation Cancer and smiled. What a damn coincidence! Both he and Triple X were Cancerians, impulsive, sensitive and decisive!

Yes, Harfan Bukhari had hit the nail on its head. There must have been a fatal intelligence leakage. Someone, well placed in the Indian decision making structure, had traded either with the Pakistani or with a third country intelligence operative.

In all probability, the ISI might have pricked a pin in the overblown balloon of Alamgir's cover and neutralized him. The ISI had scored on two counts, Nampoothiri reasoned. It destroyed an important Indian espionage network and proved its excellent penetration inside the Indian system, presumably at a very high political level. But no tangible conclusion could be drawn before Triple X was interrogated and categorized, and he let down his veil of diffidence and indifference.

Nampoothiri stopped pacing around the room impatiently and settled on his chair. Why blame the beleaguered agent alone? The NSI had probably overstretched its manoeuvrability inside Pakistan! He had probably overexploited Triple X.

Were his cutting edges blunting out? Had he failed to protect his own turf? Had his counterpart in the FIB gone on hibernation? Kumar Anand Prasad, the recently purged FIB chief had been busy placating political bosses, particularly his Bihari compatriot, Ram Karan Prasad, a minister in Mandira's cabinet.

Kumar Anand had just closed his eyes on the professional efficacy of his counter intelligence outfit; a turf exclusively assigned to the FIB and had diverted vital resources for dogging the political opponents of the ruling party. That was the easiest way to please the bosses. Prime Minister Mandira's anxiety over her political survival had overshadowed her concern for national security. She was often scared of her own shadow and perceived presence of political ghosts even under the glow of the midday sun.

Well! Why blame Kumar Anand alone! His own boys were bogged down in the killing fields of East Pakistan, and for good reasons too. They had ignited and stirred the cauldron of discontent, in collaboration with the Peoples' League. The disenchanted Bengalis were now ready for a final war, to achieve an independent homeland, fondly called ***Sonar Bangla,*** a golden Bengal.

Yes. Both the NSI and the FIB were equally guilty of neglecting the gnawing reality of Pakistani inroads into the Indian establishment. Nuclear facilities aside, Nampoothiri thought aloud, the Inter Services Intelligence had probably infiltrated the marrow of the nation.

He closed the window and called in Jatadhari and ordered another coffee. He was unable to find an escape chute from the psychological crunch he was thrown in, by the sudden appearance of Triple X in Delhi and the disappearance of Alamgir. The events had changed the entire contour of Indian intelligence thrust in Pakistan. The NSI presence in Pakistan sans Alamgir would be next to nothing.

"Sir," Amrita Bhalla spoke on the secured intercom, "Mr. Krishna Kumar is here."

"Haven't you gone home? It's going to be ten pm."

"I can't leave you alone when you're lost in an uncertain walk inside your mind."

"How do you guess that?"

"Too much unguided walk inside yourself isn't going to help sir. You'd get lost. I think you require a focus. Shall I bring him in?"

"Perhaps you're correct dear. I'm taking a disjoined walk and I feel that I'm lost. Please bring him in."

Nampoothiri's worst fears were confirmed by reports from other sources. Krishna Kumar walked in with a few crisp decoded reports. Station Kabul reported, quoting Russian embassy sources in Islamabad, that Alam's bullet ridden body was recovered from Bhagatanwala airbase, about 150 km south-east of Chak Lala. He was killed; the report said, along with five other Pakistanis, one of them identified as Ibadat, a hotel employee. Jamant Ali, a senior ISI official was also reported seriously injured in the shootout, allegedly carried out by Indian commandos. Their target, the Russian sources added, were two squadrons of improved version Sabre jets, just flown in from Turkey, a virtual gift from Washington.

Shit! Nampoothiri scowled. He hadn't commissioned any commando raid.

The Kabul report continued that the ISI had stormed the Jhumra residence of a suspected Indian linkman and lifted some of his contacts and acquaintances, which included a few notorious and notable arms traders. The ISI was tight lipped about the entire clean up operation. There was an ominous blanket of secrecy over the whole affair.

The Pakistani media, wrapped under wartime censor, maintained a ghostly silence about the disappearance of a Pakistani charter flight with a consignment of supplies for Dacca. The media, however, blamed Indian commandos for the assassination of one of the patriotic sons of Pakistan and a few policemen. They attained martyrdom, but had succeeded in saving two squadrons of precious fighter-bombers. Some papers carried a photograph of Alam Khan, paying tribute to him in glowing words.

These reports confirmed Nampoothiri's hunch that Alamgir's cover wasn't blown up by Triple X. Harfan didn't betray India. Alam died in a shoot out.

But, who'd shot him? What was Double X doing there in the airbase? Was Ibadat helping out Alam in a super-sensitive operation? What could that be? Delhi hadn't assigned any task to its agents at Bhagantanwala.

What was Alam doing at Bhagatanwala? Was he trying to prevent Triple X from fleeing Pakistan? Did Harfan kill his tactical handler?

Fresh inputs from London surprised Nampoothiri.

One of Alam's MI6 contacts had broadly indicated his involvement with some Cyprus based mercenary flight operators. Was he commissioned by Pakistan's Chief Military Law Administrator to hire the mercenary flights? That's a big surprise! Alam hadn't kept his controlling station informed of his direct involvement in Pakistan's war efforts in its eastern wing. Was he earning money on the side? Did his greed overtake his mythical loyalty to his organisation and the country? Did he develop a vested interest in Pakistan, of which Delhi wasn't aware?

Did Triple X kill Alam?

The thought came back to Nampoothiri, as he lighted another Havana. He didn't rule out the possibility. After all, the fellow was a cold-blooded killer. His recruitment as a potential resident agent and his training process had presented plenty of pleasant and bitter surprises. Did he slip up anywhere in selecting the target and molding the raw material? Where did he, as the Chief Operations Director of the Federal Intelligence Bureau go wrong? Did he fail to assess the intrinsic deficiencies in Harfan Bukhari?

Nampoothiri tried to unfold the pages of the fascinating story, the story of his tryst with Indian intelligence and tango with a turbulent agent, Ramendra Kaushal @ Harfan Bukhari @ Operation Triple X.

"Sir it's time you went home." Amrita Bhalla reminded her boss who was ruminating over the fast-paced events that had caused the collapse of his intelligence edifice in Pakistan.

"Oh dear, you're still there! I'm confused. I don't know what to make out of all that has happened. Appears I'm caught in a witch's mirror. It's like being stuck in a tunnel with no light in sight."

"You can crack it sir. All you require is some rest."

"Perhaps you're correct. Let's call it a day dear."

Nampoothiri just about stepped out of his office around 11.30 pm, when Rajinder Singh Dewan, personal secretary to the Prime Minister came on the red Restricted Area Exchange (RAX) telephone.

"***Huzoor*** (sir), Dewan here."

"Still at work?" Nampoothiri asked.

"I'm not the lucky guy you're, sir." He replied, "Come sharp. Ma'am boss wants you and the FIB chief immediately."

"Anything special? Has it anything to do with the war."

"Looks she is trying to crack tougher nuts."

"Cough it out."

"Can't say much now. Secretary of the Atomic Energy Commission and the chief of the Bhaba Atomic Research Centre are already here. Draw your own conclusions."

Dewan disconnected. A busy man, he normally spent hours on phones, to convey, as pleasantly as possible, the most unpleasant decisions taken by the Prime Minister.

Nampoothiri was one of the fringe clients, not in the PM's direct line of fire. Yet he shivered at the idea of facing the inscrutable lady over an undefined agenda. He took the elevator down to the specially designated bay in the basement of the fourth tower of the ***Nakshatra Lok*** and asked Jatadhari to drive straight to Safdarjung Road residence of the Prime Minister.

Seated behind a rosewood table in her camp-office, Mandira was engrossed in an animated discussion over priority war matters with the Chief of Army Staff and the Air Chief.

Pakistan had, just hours ago, carried out Israeli style blitzkrieg bombing of Indian Air Force targets in the western sector. The attack didn't take India by surprise. Nampoothiri had earlier shared with the PM the contents of the last message of agent Double X, physically carried by Triple X.

The Chiefs left after half an hour. Dewan signalled in Nampoothiri and whispered in his ears that the PM wasn't in heavenly moods. That was a precious warning, more precious than the meteorological warning about another severe cyclone approaching the eastern coastal belt.

"I hope Ahooja, the country isn't wasting money in maintaining a bunch of sissies," Mandira came direct to the subject, "I thought, I took personal charge of the intelligence outfits in order to provide cutting edge to the otherwise blunt weapons of national security. Your people have failed to detect some important spies in our establishments handling nuclear research."

"Ma'am," Ahooja, the new FIB chief, who replaced Kumar Anand Prasad couple of months back, croaked out nervously, "We've primed our intelligence assets in the main nuclear establishments. But I am not aware of the latest NSI input."

"I thought you've a mechanism for exchanging notes and you two have drawn up a common meeting ground." Her voice exuded a pungent odour.

"Yes ma'am," Nampoothiri volunteered a damage controlling reply, "We meet regularly. But, as you're aware, the developments on the warfronts have kept me awfully busy."

"Better make a drill of it," Mandira threw him a vital hint, "It's a shame that I've to hear from independent sources about leakage of discussions at top-level meetings. How could Pakistan get to know about our nuclear secrets? Find out if there are any Pak moles in our nuclear facilities and among the senior echelon of the bureaucracy. Don't hesitate. Go for them and keep me informed." She referred to a Russian embassy input, which corroborated the latest Triple X information.

She dismissed Ahooja, by lifting her face and giving one final look.

That's what she normally did to express displeasure. She hardly raised her voice. Her penetrating x-ray looks were good enough to send shivers down the spines of senior bureaucrats.

A no-nonsense person, Mandira was worried. The unpatriotic acts of some whisky and whore loving scientist and bureaucrat shouldn't unsettle her own nuclear programme, which was personally nursed by her father.

She was worried too, for other flaming reasons. A mysterious blast had killed, just about a fortnight back, a senior minister in her cabinet. The perpetrators of the heinous crime had missed her by minutes. She had no doubt as to the capability of the ISI in penetrating her security rings and taking pot shots at their sweet will.

A ghastly war with Pakistan was raging on both the fronts and Peking and Washington were making ominous noises too. She could take no chance, either on the war fronts or with the security of India's nuclear establishment.

Nampoothiri should offer plausible explanations, she demanded, for the latest fiasco involving crucial intelligence operations inside Pakistan.

Mandira picked up a pencil and silently started jotting down notes on a scrap of paper. Nampoothiri waited with bated breath, not sure from which side the multi-edged sword would hit.

"I expected professionalism from you Balu, You've let me down." She stopped scratching on the paper.

"Ma'am," Nampoothiri continued, "I'm sure that something has gone wrong with our operations. Alamgir is dead, though Triple X has managed to reach Delhi with concrete proof of Pakistani involvement in a chemical warfare. I'm yet to interrogate and categorise him."

"Put it off for a few days. Divert your resources to East Pakistan, monitor the Chinese and American moves."

"Our reports from Moscow and Philippines aren't encouraging," Nampoothiri, added, "The US has put its Seventh Fleet on full alert. The Chinese too have started amassing troops in the north."

"Now that your assets in Pakistan have suffered reverses, what impact would it have on our war efforts?"

"Normally in war times we ask our agents to lie low and the usual communication channels are suspended. Our stations in Afghanistan, Tajikistan and Iran have been instructed to double up for losses inside Pakistan." Nampoothiri replied.

"Co-ordinate with Ahooja. He's made of better stuff and is a sure improvement upon Kumar Anand. Identify and neutralise all Pakistani moles. I don't want other Ram Karans to gnash their teeth inside my government and the system. No compromise of our crucial nuclear programme and, I don't want any slackening of Operation Lotus. And remember, we've lots of lessons to draw from the Ram Karan affair."

Mandira's reference to Operation Lotus was clinically linked to the on going turmoil in the eastern wing of Pakistan. It was a delicate intelligence initiative initiated by her father Amritlal, which was nursed by her as a co-ordinated intelligence thrust in East Pakistan, with intractable linkages with the sub-continent's political and diplomatic developments. The dramatis personae of the Bengali freedom movement were intricately connected with the Lotus concept, independence for the ethnic Bengali speaking East Pakistan. Her father, Amritlal and her predecessor Jug Bahadur Sharma had nursed the precious concept with admirable patience and grit.

The sub-continent was again on fire; it always was, since independence and the Great Partition. But this time around, the quake was apocalyptic. The communal Radcliffe award, which had infracted the Indian people, had virtually collapsed. The mirror of a two-nation philosophy, nursed by some political witches and the imperial masters was cracking up very fast. New realities, new identities and new consciousness were sure to emerge out of the war fumes and death pangs of the old order.

"I trust you. Pakistan must meet its nemesis in East Pakistan. Hope your boys won't let me down." Mandira looked up with a faint look of appreciation.

"My loyalties are fully with you ma'am. The Lotus will bloom very soon."

"What do I do with the mercenary South African pilot and his crew?"

"He wants to visit his roots at Uttar Pradesh. I can arrange it, if you've no objection."

"Do it on the quiet. We don't even have diplomatic relations with the Pretoria regime. And put them on a flight to Bangkok. I've spoken to the French Ambassador. They've no objection to giving him a visa."

"Thanks ma'am."

Nampoothiri stood up and left, closing the door silently behind him.

"One more point," Mandira looked up with an unusual charming glint in her eyes, " You can talk to Triple X personally. He has rendered a great service."

"Yes ma'am." Nampoothiri returned her smile with a pleasant nod and walked out of the room.

"That crook has emerged as a living martyr." He muttered under his breath as he entered Dewan's room.

"Did you say anything?" Dewan asked.

"No dear. It's my nemesis that I'm trying to figure out."

Chapter 2

The X category forward intelligence operations were special; a clever synthesis of shallow and deep penetration intelligence thrust inside Pakistan. That was the brainchild of Rabindra Narayan Dutta, chief of the Federal Intelligence Bureau, who had spun around him queer threads of history and mythology; the history of the dreaded Imperial intelligence establishment and the myth of his invincibility, which he derived from the first Prime Minister of India, Amritlal.

Simple X assets were shaped out of trans-border smugglers for gathering shallow tactical intelligence. The Double X agents were literally double edged. They were trained for penetration up to a depth of 50 miles. Some Double X talents, recruited from amongst the collaborating Pakistani nationals, offered a mixed bag of tactical and strategic intelligence. Some of the sharper talents were used for one-time dirty-trick operations; some bomb blasts, some acts of arson and mindless massacre. The messages transmitted were often brutal, matching the boorish and brutal acts of proxy war executed by the Inter Services Intelligence (ISI) of Pakistan.

The Triple X concept was born way back in late 1964, long before the NSI achieved embryonic conceptualisation. The process started soon after Amritlal, the first Prime Minister of independent India, a hotchpotch philosopher and a romantic dictator, expired barely after two years of a mismanaged war against China. The euphoria of universal friendship and the theme of ***Panch Sheela***, enunciated by Amritlal had received a white burial in the heights of the Himalayas. The heart broken messiah of world peace and a co-author of the Third World concept was afraid of anointing his daughter Mandira, as his successor. The country had virtually rejected him and he knew that the honeymoon was over. Indians were unlikely to endorse the succession of his daughter.

Jung Bahadur Sharma, a down to earth man, was installed as a stopgap arrangement. The seemingly rustic person, of sound common sense, didn't take aeons to sum up the strategic scenario. War clouds over the sub-continent were again spreading shivers of gloom. Pakistan, taking advantage of India's humiliating defeat in the China war, had started rattling its armours in the vast saltpan of Kachchh. The military junta, in search of an illusory logical conclusion to the unfinished agenda of 1948 war was piously and doggedly carrying forward their aggressive policy in Kashmir.

Rabindra Narayan Dutta, Chief of the Federal Intelligence Bureau, an impeccable British clone and an inimitable intelligence sleuth wasn't quick enough to realise that International Communism had ceased to be the prime threat to India's security. He hesitated in shifting the needle of Indian intelligence towards the umbilical twin, Pakistan. The imperial masters, just emerging out of the ashes of the Second World War, weren't eager either, to see India shifting its intelligence thrust to the new born Muslim nation that was the most willing and obliging launching pad against the northern Red Bear and the eastern Red Panda.

Jung Bahadur didn't confuse his orientation. His needles picked up the ground tremors immaculately. The turmoil over the theft and subsequent restoration of the holy relic of the Prophet in the vale of Kashmir had ingrained in his mind the paramount need (PbuH) for penetrating the Pakistani establishment. The rogue neighbour had emerged as the stormiest magnetic pole for India's internal and external security. The FIB, he argued, required a multi-pronged intelligence thrust. What prevented Dutta from generating adequate assets inside Pakistan, the new Prime Minister asked?

"I fail to understand what you people have been doing all these years? Why can't we work deep inside the Pakistani system?"

"There are problems sir," Dutta explained, "They've an advantage over us. They've easy access to a section of our population. Our boys stand up as sore thumbs in Pakistan's exclusive Islamic society. We've lost eight assets in the last three years."

"Infiltrate your boys with iron-cast Muslim covers. It shouldn't be a difficult job. Penetrate behind the enemy lines. You know the tools of the trade better than I know."

The Prime Minister didn't hide his displeasure. The short meeting, convened shortly after his accession, for a comprehensive intelligence briefing, was over in minutes. Dutta carried the fumes of the pungent encounter to his sprawling office room. And his two senior deputies were at hand to inhale the smoke.

"Sir, the idea isn't new. We've done this in Operation Alamgir," Commented Balachandran Nampoothiri, a Deputy Director in the organisation," But, to give foolproof cover to a Hindu and make him merge into the Muslim milieu isn't an easy job."

"I never said it's easy, and you can't rest on your haunches with one Alam and a couple of X and Double X talents," Dutta shot back," The job is tough. I'm just back from the PM's office. The old man is furious and wants immediate action. He wants quick results. And I agree with him. Less of golf dear, concentrate on the Pak-turf." An agitated Dutta, slighted by the PM's silent ire, screwed up his deputy, an avid golfer.

"Sir, it's easy for Pakistan to locate their agents in our country. Their pigeons can roost in sympathetic religious nests." Commented Kumar Anand Prasad, the other Deputy.

Dutta shook his head impatiently.

"We should pick up Muslim talents, especially from families having relatives in Pakistan." Prasad continued.

R.N. Dutta shook his head violently.

"No, no... You've got it all wrong." He looked at Pradumnya Karnik, Assistant Intelligence Director, handling X operations.

"I want Karnik to handle the project and you'll supervise it." Dutta pointed his finger at Nampoothiri, "I don't trust any Muslim and I can assure you, as long as this damn democracy doesn't force us, I'll oppose the induction of Muslims in the Federal Intelligence Bureau."

"But sir, we need Muslim talents."

Prasad pressed his point. Dutta smiled at the agitated suggestion of his deputy.

He knew well the niche of Kumar Anand's heart that prompted him to parrot the agenda of his political mentor, Ram Karan Prasad, a minister in Jung Bahadur's cabinet and a known friend of Pakistani stalwarts. A leader of the depressed Hindu castes, Ram Karan commanded the unstinting support of a vast Muslim vote bank. He had pioneered the formation of a United Front, way back in 1937, a coalition of Muslims and low-caste Hindus. The empire had catapulted the scion of the Mallah dynasty to a sky-skimming orbit with a view to dividing India into multiple caste and religion based nations.

"I never said no," Dutta quipped back, "You raise as many informers and agents as you can from that community. No problem. But I can't trust any Muslim with sensitive intelligence matters. The nation can't afford to have these fifth columns in sensitive areas of state activity. A minister here and a governor there are good decorative pieces... Please, no more argument. I've discussed this over with two Prime Ministers and they don't disagree with me."

Dutta momentarily closed his eyes, an indication that the point was not debatable.

"But sir, in a secular country we should have some Muslims in the organisation." Prasad reiterated.

"Over my dead body Prasad. I can't afford to induct the enemies of the nation in a top-secret organization. Let the politicians extend lip service to secularism. I have a job to do and you all play by my rules. It's an unwritten state policy. No argument." Dutta snapped back sharply, thumping a clenched fist on the table.

"Let this project be known as Operation Triple X. Draw up a comprehensive training programme. Take a few crack officers. Apply the finest of fine tradecraft. Yes, don't forget to involve Shyam Purohit, your Maulana Rizwan. I want him to convincingly convert the recruits to Islam and teach them everything that goes into the making of orthodox Muslims, out of our targets."

Dutta instructed his deputy Balachandran Nampoothiri, with a sanctified sermon from the pulpit.

"I want young, daring and daunting targets, capable of facing the impossible and living on the edge of life. The project requires young and offbeat talents with plenty of courage and a bag full of weaknesses for the good things of life."

Young minds, he elaborated, were far more resilient than ossified middle-aged professionals. The old fogies, he believed, were incapable of thinking beyond having ritual sex with their spouses once a week, preferably on a Saturday night, and sleeping out the mandatory Sunday. They were too rigid, timid and fossilised to bare any part of their brain to challenging jobs.

Nampoothiri took over from Dutta. The company, he impressed upon a select group of talent spotters, was ready to foot the bills for all the grease that were traditionally used for trapping suitable targets. The slippery tracks of the game of espionage were coated with glittering gold, to some it symbolized the gold of patriotism and to some others it was the Midas metal.

"Mount aggressive hunt", He advised the crack team, "The talents, once trapped, should not be able to escape. They should surrender to the seasoned blackmailers, their designated case officers....

"Offer them a price, each one according to his utility and corrode their original personality. Encapsulate them in an ideological cocoon. The cerebral cortices of the targets should suffer permanent lesions, changing their personality beyond redemption and restoration....

"A successful agent handler should feel happy," Nampoothiri emphasised, "Only when his target had undergone a total personality transformation; the edifices of his self-confidence sufficiently subverted. The perfect spy should be like a hypnotised zombie, a human robot....

"Any question?" He asked the assembled Operation Triple X talent spotters, who stared at him with half closed pigeon-eyes.

"Good boys, as we understand in our daily lingo, may not agree to take up challenges of trans-border operations, sir." Dhiren Bhagat, a junior intelligence officer stood up, after mustering great courage.

Son of a shoemaker, Bhagat had entered the hallowed precincts of the intelligence fraternity by dint of sheer merit. But, as was the vogue in Hindu society, Bhagat was a hated brat, catapulted to the high pedestal of a government job by virtue of the constitutional reservation policy. Caustic comments at his lowly origin and open discrimination were a part of his daily bread.

"I don't want saints," Nampoothiri smiled back, "I want boys with guts. I don't mind if they're fringe criminals. But they should be honest criminals. Not the double crossing and cross-cutting types."

"Roger sir." Bhagat replied with a dash of enthusiasm. He was happy to be tasked, for the first time, with a major operational responsibility.

****

Dhiren Bhagat's beat, Pradumnya Karnik, a Konkan Brahmin decided, should be the difficult Delhi University circuit, the hottest hub of student activities. A whole lot of them, the socialists, communists and budding pro-Chinese extremists thronged the campus, its restaurants and pubs, and of course the lovers' corners in the manicured ridge park.

It was a tough beat. The students hated the red turbaned police and the intelligence operatives, derisively called ***'chipkalis'*** (house lizards). The hatred was rooted in history. These trades represented the long and strong arms of the colonial administration. They continued to play the same role even after independence, protecting and promoting the new rulers. For them nothing had changed. Only the wordings of the choir were substituted; singing in praise of the indigenous instead of the foreign masters.

But Bhagat was lucky.

The most shining star of the campus, Ramendra Kaushal, fondly called Prince by his acolytes couldn't be missed, even by a fish-eyed mendicant. The Prince, with his wild macho personality was present everywhere. A lady-hunter and a drug pusher, Ramendra Kaushal walked the very edges of crime and politics and was a virtual terror in the campus.

The Prince honorific, his friends asserted, was a blood inheritance. He belonged to some obscure royal family of Jhun Jhunu, in the fabled land of the kings and queens of Rajasthan. And he lived the life of a giant sized prince.

Dhiren Bhagat, an intelligence ground rat, studied the susceptibilities of his strange target, Ramendra Kaushal. He trailed him for about a month and logged in a highly impressive dossier.

"Well, well." Rabindra Narayan Dutta said tapping his fingers on the table. It was pretty unusual for him to betray excitement.

"Our friend is an all rounder. Whisky, yes; women, yes; brawls, plenty and oh my!" Dutta laughed heartily, "I find he can pay simultaneous attention to scores of women."

"There are more attractive attributes, sir." Added Nampoothiri.

Dutta looked up, eyebrows squeezed in at the centre of his forehead, that formed a deep vertical furrow.

"He's a close associate of Ram Karan Prasad, the minister, and fronts a petty drug pushing chain for him. And sir," Nampoothiri halted, "There is an unconfirmed suspicion of his involvement in a gruesome murder case. He carries a gun and a couple of knives on his person."

Dutta liked the target. His guts told him that this one bastard would make a fine agent. With some fine trimmings and toppings he could be shaped up as a daredevil deep-cover resident agent, a category XXX agent.

And his parental background at Jhumra Valley in Pakistani Punjab, near Chiniot, made him especially invaluable. A real life Prince, Ramendra Kaushal was the legal successor to the throne of the tiny kingdom of Jhumra. But his mother was forced to flee Pakistan after his father; Raja Dayaram Kaushal was killed by Muslim Niazi serfs and assorted tribals for refusing to merge his sovereign kingdom with Pakistan.

The big-ego potentate of the tiny kingdom pretended that he could bargain like the Nizam of Hyderabad and dreamily vacillate like the Maharaja of Kashmir. He had adopted a tough line of bargaining and had invited the wrath of the Muslim League and the Niazi, Mazari and Khan landed gentries. They coveted the fertile Jhumra valley land and wanted the Hindu king out. The inevitable course of partition-eve holocaust overtook Dayaram's ego. He died, fighting a vain battle to protect his honour and kingdom.

"It's a good catch," Dutta passed his final verdict, " Hook him and exploit his background to weave a fine cover. Consult Shyam Purohit for developing the cover story. I think this rogue is a Triple X material."

Balachandran Nampoothiri agreed. Pradumnya Karnik didn't. Karnik, the designated supervisor of the P7 desk, which handled operations inside Pakistan, nursed different ideas. The Konkan Brahmin in him abhorred the idea of working with a shoemaker son and recruiting a rank criminal as a Triple X category agent.

Largely his moorings in the service hierarchy spiced Karnik's ideas. He had tied his ropes to the chair-legs of Kumar Anand Prasad, expecting a bonus posting to Washington. Dutta, on an extended post-superannuation tenure was sure to step down from the apex position. And Kumar Anand Prasad, with his correct political connections, was sure to climb the top cone of the pyramid. The alignment of service constellation was not conducive to the Konkan Brahmin's kowtowing to Nampoothiri, a known rival of Kumar Anand. He simply followed the behavioural furrows ploughed by his senior mentor in the service.

Nampoothiri's dislike for Karnik was obvious. A Prasad acolyte, he was sure to assist his benefactor with a spade and shovel for digging a bottomless grave for Nampoothiri. Why take a chance? Nampoothiri fretted and fumed and finally settled for a compromise. He suppressed his revolting dislike for Karnik, a rated fortune hunter and invited him to sit through the session for briefing and debriefing Dhiren Bhagat.

"Have you made direct contact? What were his responses?" Asked Nampoothiri.

"I met him twice under the cover of a bookseller, hawking books to college libraries. He didn't take interest and I didn't want to break the cover."

"What are his weak spots? Can he be blackmailed?" Nampoothiri didn't hide his impatience. This should have been examined before putting up the dossier to him.

"Sir," Replied Bhagat, "He enjoys the privilege of a free pad at Divine Inn, a shady joint in Gole Market, courtesy Ram Karan Prasad. He takes his girls to the joint. The inn manager Vidya Sagar Suri isn't happy with Kaushal, as he squeezes out weekly protection money and other frills."

"I find you've a good understanding of the target. But you didn't record these in your reports." Karnik intervened with a scowl on his face.

"Sir this is my initial target priming report. I can't record unconfirmed observations." Bhagat quipped back.

Nampoothiri felt heat building up under his skin. But this wasn't the correct time to intervene.

"Well! I think the first report is rather exciting." He looked at Pradumnya Karnik and continued, "I want an operation appraisal plan by tomorrow. I'll prefer the use of blackmail bait to hook this cute bastard."

"Pardon me sir," Bhagat submitted, "It won't be easy to hook Kaushal. He's close to the top political leaders. He has a brigade of ruffians, ready to kick up a fight at the slightest provocation, at his bidding."

"Why don't we try some other targets?" Karnik spoke in a measured voice," Blackmail isn't the best tool, I suppose."

"What brings you to that conclusion?" Nampoothiri shot back.

"A criminal like him can't make a good resident agent."

"Let's not split our hair so early in the day. You're still a kid in this profession. And you've heard the boss." Nampoothiri snapped back.

Karnik digested the dig, but could not download the idea of Bhagat stealing the show and polluting his cultural and religious ambience. How could a blue blooded Konkan Brahmin associate himself with a low caste nobody! He would have been ostracised, back in his village, if he displayed the temerity of sharing his table with a shoemaker's son.

"Have I made myself clear?" Nampoothiri asked with a touch of finality, "Show me your action plan tomorrow morning."

He pressed a button summoning Jatadhari. This was a loud signal for Pradumnya Karnik. He quietly withdrew.

Jatadhari poured out coffee from an ornate glass percolator. He sipped the black brew, simmered out of golden Brazilian seeds and looked up at Jatadhari.

"Jata, what do you think of this fellow Bhagat? Is he good? Can he be trusted with a delicate operation?"

The tribal from Garo Hills, Nampoothiri knew, carried in his genes the tributes of excellent Tibetan shrewdness.

Jatadhari knew his master well. When in confusion he preferred to consult him rather than talking to his wife and God.

"Sir, we did a stint in Manipur together. He did very well there in anti-insurgency operations. And I understand he's very good in Counter Intelligence work." Jata replied in a confident voice.

"What damn good did he do in Manipur?"

"Don't know much. But sir, he is an icon of tenacity and rational thinking. He had, all by himself, tackled the movement of a Naga insurgent gang to Pakistan and had infiltrated right up to Sylhet. He returned in one piece with the photo-evidence of training camps run by the Pakistan Intelligence Bureau (PIB)." Jata finished the sentence in one breath, and inhaled another lung full with an audible sound.

A pragmatic intelligence operative and analyst, with his ears nearer to the ground, Nampoothiri derived pleasure in discussing operational matters directly with his juniors. The lowest seam in the shaft mostly yielded the best diamond. Their raw productions usually passed through several filters and lost a lot of sheen and brilliance. Some intermediate filters were adept in credit grabbing, usurping the fine works of their juniors.

"Ask him to meet me at my residence tonight and tell the fellow to keep his trap shut."

The hint was enough for Jatadhari. He had carried out similar errands in the past. Damn lucky fellow; Jatadhari silently congratulated Dhiren Bhagat. The boss was a fussy person and it wasn't easy to please him.

****

Dhiren Bhagat, an Assistant Intelligence Officer, a veteran of 17 years, was visibly shaken by the invitation to the lion's den. It was very unusual for the number three in the Company to invite an outcast untouchable to a social evening.

In his strata of Indian society the cardinal mantra of survival included the time-tested tricks of avoiding the frontal ire of a boss and the posterior fury of a wild horse. His wise father, a cattle hide processor and dealer had survived all his seventy summers by scrupulously following the golden Indian social prescription.

The other fear that haunted him was the sacred mantra of restrictive security, which was pursued with divine doggedness in Bhagat's profession. Talking to a fellow officer was often frowned upon with suspicion. Field Unit Z, the dreaded FUZ, acted as the third eye of the organisation. Its agents microscopically examined the officers' personal lives, their alignment inside the Company and inclinations outside the organisation.

Their private friends and relatives were subjected to FUZ scrutiny. The organisation had put a complete embargo on the political entities like the Hindu Sangh and the Communists. No other political hue except the ruling one that had inherited the British mantle could claim the stamp of patriotism.

On paper the FUZ didn't exist. In reality it was the most powerful organ of the Federal Intelligence Bureau, busy in house cleaning operations.

The FIB itself was a queer place to work in. It was haunted by shadows even on shadow-less dark nights. Layers of super-secret in-house apparatus and sanctified voodoos guarded the inner core. A junior like him couldn't imagine jumping the guns and reporting directly to the boss! His upper caste seniors like Karnik would simply hang him from the nearest lamppost.

Bhagat was more worried about Karnik. The Brahmin in him had no end to the hatred for a social insect like him. His friends in the FUZ were sure to enlighten him on the odd meeting of an untouchable junior officer with the big boss. That should be provocation enough to bring down avalanches of humiliation on him.

Bhagat, immersed in his dark thoughts, walked along the pavement. The system didn't allow people like him aspire for the top. Tradition and convention inherited from mythical times had twisted the social fabric. This was his first encounter with a real big boss. And he didn't know how to face it. He prayed silently. God should see him through this ordeal.

"What do you want?" Bhagat suddenly found himself accosted by an unarmed security guard from the other side of an iron gate.

"I'm Bhagat, Assistant Intelligence Officer. I'm supposed to see the boss at 9 pm." He stood in front of the gate with excitement galloping through his veins.

"Wait." The duty officer talked on the intercom before opening the gate.

He escorted Dhiren Bhagat to a flight of stairs leading to the living room of Balachandran Nampoothiri, opened the door partially and announced the arrival of the guest.

Nampoothiri, seated in one corner of the sprawling living room was turning over the pages of the *Time* magazine, not really reading any item. He concentrated on the soft recital of ***Darbari Kanada***, a Hindustani classical ***raga***, played on the ***Sitar*** by maestro Alauddin Khan. He loved classical music, western, Hindustani and Carnatic, besides Negro spirituals and open throated North American country music.

"Yes." Responded Nampoothiri.

"Sir, the officer has come." Announced the duty officer.

"Oh yes." Nampoothiri looked at his watch. Two minutes past nine. He was impressed.

He walked up to the door, opened it fully and gestured at Bhagat to enter. Guiding him to a corner, he called for Jatadhari.

Jatadhari entered, pushing a trolley, laden with a bottle of Chivas Regal, neatly wrapped in a piece of pink cloth, a Belgian cut-glass decanter and a ice bucket, all in pink.

He poured whisky with meticulous artistry, mixed soda and dropped two cubes of ice and offered one to Nampoothiri.

"Have a drink." Nampoothiri offered the glass to Bhagat.

Dhiren hesitated; his eyes weren't meeting his boss's.

"Come'n. Have one with me. Forget office. It's my home and you're my guest." He pushed the glass into the clammy palms of the junior officer.

Jatadhari served chicken nuggets in pink bone china plates.

On Tuesdays Nampoothiri preferred everything in pink. That was based on an astrological advice, tendered by the holy saint of Sringeri temple, a shrine in the southern peninsula. Each day of the week was represented by a distinct colour code, synchronising with the colours of the planets of the solar system. He followed the code scrupulously with a view to deflecting evil designs of the malevolent stars and planets.

Though a perfect brown Brit, Nampoothiri had cultivated a fervent belief in astrology, herbal medicine, the occasional oil bath and regular sea-fish dishes, cooked with Malabar spices and coconut milk. The permissible exceptions were Brazilian instead of Malabar coffee and imported Havanas.

Dhiren Bhagat still couldn't make himself easy. He sat erect on the edge of the sofa, left hand placed on a knee joint and the whisky held in a firm grip in the right hand.

"Now tell me all about this fellow Kaushal. Am I wrong in saying that we should resort to blackmailing the guy? "Nampoothiri kept on munching chicken nuggets in between words.

Bhagat suddenly felt a surge of confidence. He sipped the golden liquid and enjoyed the warmth flowing down his throat and firing up the capillaries around his heart. He always felt confident when it came to professional matters. He started on a brief resume of the target and dwelt upon his wild sex life. The target was courageous, capable of taking on the impossible and improbable, fond of imported whisky, easy cash and women. He dwelt on the fringes of crime, drug peddling and hoped to climb the higher ladders in national politics.

"Most criminals do. Isn't it?" Nampoothiri added.

"Yes sir. His role model is Ram Karan Prasad."

"Understandable. If Ram Karan can manage to reach the top, why can't he?"

"He has access to Mandira, the junior minister."

"Don't worry. So far the criminals have been helping the politicians to rule and loot the populace and extracting their share of the spoils. Now is the time for the criminals to capture political power. They'll soon drive in direct snouts into the soul of the nation. Forget all this. Tell me if the target has any other weakness."

Nampoothiri lighted his favourite Havana and settled for another serving of fish nuggets.

"Two more points of susceptibility have been noticed. He has an admirable umbilical attachment to his mother and every Tuesday he visits the Hanuman (Hindu Monkey God) temple, exactly at 5 am."

"I see. He has a hidden streak of religious leaning too! Why do you think that his attachment to his mother is a point of weakness?" Nampoothiri pressed the calling bell.

Jatadhari entered silently, poured another drink and placed two fresh plates of fried fish nuggets and retreated.

Bhagat looked at his boss intently, slipped back on the sofa and replied, "Perhaps he can sacrifice his girls to see his mother happy."

"Here you are. Behind the whirlwind there's a placid lagoon of love. The man is capable of loving and caring. He can love and respect the job, if properly motivated." Nampoothiri grabbed pieces of fish nuggets, indulgently placed them in mouth and came up with an idea.

"Here's the spot you can hit. A Casanova like him can't be blackmailed simply for sleeping with girls. His mother is the key. His love is the key. How do you want to proceed now?"

"Sir, as I understand," Bhagat spoke in a low tone,"He has an indomitable lust for women. He is specially attracted to Hema."

"Who is she?"

"I believe she is the daughter of the health secretary."

"Keep a track."

"And sir, the target has a volcanic temper. He flares up at the slightest provocation."

"How does it help?"

"His criminality sir. That's the possible window for blackmailing. We've to send him a message, in due course, that he has reached a cul-de-sac."

"And the mother angle?"

"Once properly implicated, we can use the threat of exposing his misdeeds to his mother," Bhagat added haltingly, "One more point sir...."

"Continue."

"He often gets into violent fits, destroying everything coming his way. That's what I call a killer streak."

"I get you. Is it living by conviction rather than convention?"

"I should say more of conviction...his own brand of conviction."

"That suits me. Both conviction and convention can be manipulated, at least in our trade." Nampoothiri lighted another Havana and added its smoke with the philosophy he just enunciated.

Dhiren Bhagat sipped his whisky in silence and felt strange warmth rising up from his intestines to his front lobe. Below the scalp, warm streams of sensation stirred up his neurons, electricity travelling fast from one junction to another. The golden liquid was doing well. New neutron proteins were sending signals of innovation.

For the next one-hour Nampoothiri and his junior carried out an exercise on the multi-dimensional aspects of Operation Triple X. Over four plates of nuggets and couple of servings of Chivas Regal, Balachandran Nampoothiri felt a unique satisfaction, very rare in his profession.

He admired the professional excellence of the junior officer and silently appreciated his grasp on the subject. But for a few professionals like him, the organisation would have gone to the dogs by this time.

He felt confident that Operation Triple X should be a fabulous success story. It would be a sweet score over Kumar Anand Prasad, the nagging Bihari. The message should go louder to Rabindra Narayan Dutta too, that he, the one and only Nampoothiri was the worthiest successor to room number 308, the top-secret hole of India's intelligence chief.

"Fine," Nampoothiri stood up, "Follow up the leads meticulously, note all the details. Every bit of information counts."

"What about his cover and motivation?" Asked Bhagat.

"Let me talk to Maulana Rizwan. I've something in view. Visit Jhun Jhunu and gather all the dope on his family in pre-partition India and his relatives in Pakistan. Rizwan should be able to weave a fool-proof cover story."

Nampoothiri hinted at the training and research unit of the Federal Intelligence Bureau, headed by Maulana Rizwan alias Shyam Purohit. A career intelligence officer turned covert Islamic scholar; he was the fulcrum of FIB's super-secret grinding machine that churned out deep-cover agents for operations inside Pakistan.

"You get going. We're under pressure. This target must be prepared in record time. Good night and God bless you."

Nampoothiri felt mighty pleased. The fine evening was well spent, in good company and over good work, drink and food.

Chapter 3

Rajni Krittika Hemaprabha Rao, in short Hema, was the cutest butterfly, which fluttered around Delhi University campus, located amidst the sprawling greens of the Shivalik range that had witnessed several battles during the 1857 uprising against the rulers of the British East India Company.

Tall, slim and fair, with a Hellenic complexion, head full of curly hair and a youthful bust, Hema padded her charm consciously with a contrived Marilyn Monroe pout. A pulsating throb of the campus young hearts Hema was overtly conscious of her body and beauty and the status of her father, a secretary to the government of India. Her aloofness verged on contempt for the creatures around. A fluttering beauty like her hadn't graced the campus for the last two decades. That was the verdict of the veterans, some of them habitual students for the last decade.

Students from the post-graduate faculties drifted around the corridors and canteen of St. Stephens, to have rare glimpses of the dream girl and to steal some whiffs of her biological aroma. She ignored most of them, and at best, looked at some from the corners of her eyes, lips slightly curled in, either in contempt or wilful arrogance. The electrifying oblique looks were more devastating than the debilitating darts.

Her aroma sprayed out a loud message: touch me not. She was aware of the biological theory of intricate linkages between smell and sex. Hema used costly French perfume to camouflage her real body odour. She carried a spray in her crocodile-leather beauty pouch.

Bagging a Rhodes scholarship was a family tradition. Her father was one. Sure of flying to London in another two years, for her Masters in economics, Hema looked at the surrounding creatures as insects from wayside gutters. These baser animals weren't pedigreed enough to talk and socialise with her.

Disdainful though she was, of the crowd around, Hema liked to dress to kill. She preferred a modified version of the Punjabi ***churidar*** suit; lower portion clung to her slim legs, in cascading creases. The upper ***kameez*** (shirt) was tailored with deep cuts at the back and front, deep enough to reveal her bosom, displaying the rippling pink bulge of arrogance. Just from below the bust line it tapered down in a sharp fall, lifting the bosom provocatively. Hema didn't bother to cover her bust with a flimsy ***chunni***, a silk scarf. Her life-style logic was directly borrowed from the pages of the western magazines and periodicals. Shying away from exhibiting her assets wasn't her cup of tea. Flowers didn't cover themselves up with foliage. Did They? Didn't. They were things of beauty, to be appreciated by the connoisseurs of ethereal aesthetics.

Prince Ramendra Kaushal's philosophy of beauty was poetic, with a different connotation. A flower? It's there to be plucked, enjoyed and thrown out with the memories of the exploits of a stale night. Didn't some people enjoy flowers fried in batter and fat? And what better appreciation of a feminine beauty could one expect, rather than being pleasantly tormented under masculine muscle!

No one, not even his staunchest admirers, took him seriously when he declared his intentions to tame the bronze-beauty and pin her down under his thighs. Kaushal didn't mind swinging away minor campus girls to his secret den at the Divine Inn. That was his usual style. But roughing up Hema was a different ball game. Her father's official status, as was the wont in the city of bureaucrats, had added an almost impregnable shield around her.

However, the torrent called Prince Kaushal was equally irrepressible.

Ramendra Kaushal, the lady-killer, fondly called LBW - Ladies' ***Bawarchi*** (cook) and Waiter, by admirers and friends, was in a foul mood that morning. The Hindu Sangh candidates had defeated his boys, fronting the ruling Congress party, in the students' union elections. The scimitar of defeat had pruned down his ego by a couple of inches. It was a big slap on the big boss's face.

"Fuck the bastards, those Sanghi Nazis," Shouted Kaushal, "I must spray a few of them with bullets."

"***Ustad*** (captain) don't take it so hard. If you want, we can finish off the Sanghi bastards and go for a fresh election."

"Plan it out. I don't mind spending a little dough on bullets. But, that bitch is...." Ramendra stopped short of revealing his mind.

One of the cronies offered coffee to the boss who was in a foul mood. Another one flicked open a packet of Players. They were uneasy with the sulking and fretting captain.

Ramendra ignored the coffee, lighted the cigarette and kept on looking vacantly at a patch of sky, visible from his corner of the café. He looked somewhat pensive and withdrawn. That's what worried his cronies. His murderous mood normally witnessed broken glasses and china and splashes of blood, if the fracas happened to be a minor one. They hadn't seen him enwrapped in melancholia.

The five jewels, Kaushal's permanent companions, were piqued by their boss's unearthly mood. It was something more than just election discomfiture. The Prince, if it were, would've stabbed a few of his rivals by now, a few bombs would've gone off and a few heads crushed.

Was it a love affair? Kaushal wasn't a love loony. If he liked a girl he seldom let her go. Prince Ramendra Kaushal simply grabbed his kill. In last two years, the campus roster recorded that he had swept away eight odd girls off their feet. His fat wallet, audacious tenacity and animal machismo helped him bluff his way through. Most of them landed up in the special room, reserved for the Prince in Vidya Sagar Suri's Divine Inn.

"***Ustad***, any problem?" Asked one of his sidekicks.

"***Sali*** (an abuse) thinks she's more beautiful than Marilyn Monroe. If I don't take her to bed in the next seven days I'm not the Prince of Jhun Jhunu."

Kaushal turned the chair around and demanded another cigarette.

"Hey ***Kancha*** (a Nepali boy), get me a double chicken omelette with two toasts and lots of butter. Don't forget to spray a dash of black pepper."

Ramendra shouted at the waiter. He felt more relaxed and enthralled his gang by lighting another Player.

"***Ustad***, who's the new chic?"

"That bitch, that whore of a daughter of the secretary," Kaushal took a big bite of the omelette and continued, "She has the audacity of casting nasty glances at me! She calls me dirt, a goon. Am I a speck of dirt! No woman does that to me." Ramendra Kaushal looked up, demanding an endorsement of his special philosophy of social relationship.

"Surely not ***Ustad***," Brij, one of the tails, prodded up the spirit of his leader, "She must be humbled."

"Tell me a practical way, no film stunt. How do I get her to bed? She must pay for her arrogance and calling me names."

Kaushal expected some clever reply from Matang, his disciple from Bihar, and a habitual resident student for the last six years. Matang's cultivator father had sent him to Delhi from his remote village in north Bihar, for earning a law degree. Matang dropped three years, busy as he was in chasing girls and peddling smuggled gold and drugs. A worthy companion of the campus prince, Ramendra Kaushal, it was expected of him to flunk the exams this year as well.

Married to a daughter of the richest farmer in his village and in the process bagging a fat dowry along with the bride, Matang was expected to return to the village as a fully hatched lawyer. Though not a law graduate yet, the mere intention to become one, had bestowed excess grey matter in Matang's cranium. He was treated as the ***Chanakya*** (strategist) of the group. This was the bare minimum attribute he could attract, having hailed from the land of the fabled Indian statesman, spymaster and philosopher.

"Why are you agitated dear? Every woman has a secret door open to her heart." Commented Matang.

"I'm not bothered about her heartaches, I want her to suffer pain, for insulting me."

"Yes ***Ustad***," Matang slurred out the words while gulping down juices of ***paan*** (betel leaf) and tobacco, some rolling down the corners of his mouth.

"I've digested the essence of the problem. That ***sali's*** father happens to be a secretary to the government. I think you should go for another cow. This one's holy."

Matang passed his judgement with the air of a grave elder in wigs.

"***Sala*** (abuse)," Ramendra Kaushal exploded. He thumped the table repeatedly and kept on shouting," You Bihari ***chuha*** (rat), you're afraid of a secretary! You call her a cow! How dare you? She, this bloody Hema, must come between my thighs. I must snatch away that arrogant smile from her face."

"Do that. It's your peril you're inviting. Why the hell abuse me?" Matang, technically a senior to Kaushal, shouted back, "You asked for the advice. If it doesn't suit you, go to hell." He stood up and made a motion towards the exit.

"Me? And go to hell? How dare you Bihari rat say that? Why do you think a secretary's daughter is inviolable?" Kaushal shouted back menacingly.

"Because he can mobilise all the police machinery at the drop of a hat," Matang stuffed another betel leaf in his mouth, "They're sure to catch up with you, friend. This one may prove fatal, for all of us. You better find yourself another cow."

The modern day Chanakya replied, chewing the betel leaf and the words in a luxurious motion of his tongue and teeth.

Kaushal, in a split second whipped out a pistol from his waistband and pointed it at Matang, waiving the barrel menacingly.

"You bloody Bihari, you can't talk like that about my girl. And you can't walk out on me like this. We've been together in too many crimes and you've to be with me, in this game too. Don't ever try to be a police informer. I'll split your head apart like a rotten melon, if you ever try anything funny with me."

"Don't be funny." Replied Matang, "This cow isn't your wife. We know your worth. You can't even win a small college election and you dare to challenge the might of a secretary to the government! I don't propose to rot in jail, because of your precious fucking."

"You Bihari trash." Ramendra rushed at Matang with the cocked pistol.

"Don't call me names and remove that toy. It doesn't frighten me. If you can't wait to fuck that cow go and have a go with your mom." Matang waved his hand trying to brush aside the dangling pistol.

"You scum," Kaushal erupted like a volcano, "You dared to call my mother a whore? How dare you insulting my mother?"

He cocked the pistol in a swift move. Brij, another acolyte, stood in front of the barrel and pushed Matang back. He was privy to the weakest lesion in Kaushal's heart. A known woman eater, the Prince of Jhun Jhunu nursed a profound regard for his mother. The very mention of her name worked like the flute-tune of a snake charmer. That was a sure trick for lowering the king cobra's hood.

"***Ustad***, what's happened to you? Calm down. And Matang, have you lost your mind? Why drag his mother into this? We're one in this game and we can't afford fighting like wild roosters. We can't break up our company for a silly girl."

He turned to Matang.

"What the hell are you up to? And what's your worth minus our captain?"

Brij, son of a ***Hanuman*** (Hindu monkey god) temple priest, recited a ***Sanskrit*** couplet from the Hindu holy scripture Gita, which meant: anger generated hallucination, leading to destruction of the faculty of reasoning, finally ushering in total annihilation.

"***Sala***, don't quote from the scriptures," Kaushal threw a dirty look at Brij and took a chair, "I know, some day you scum will purify yourself with the holy water of the Ganges and occupy the chief priest's throne, in that bloody den of corruption, you call a temple. Tell that bloody Bihari to behave. Another mention of my mother's name and he's a dead rat."

"Listen carefully. There are outsiders around," Brij signalled at Dhiren Bhagat occupying a corner table, "I'm a pure Brahmin; I recite ***Gyatri*** (a sacred couplet in praise of the Sun God) five times a day. Don't breach the banks. I know that the best flower in the garden must be offered to the deity. But friend, have patience."

"Fuck you Brahmins, you ***sala,*** a boozer and whore fucker, don't daie to hurl ***mantras*** at me. I've also come from the sperms of a Brahmin and at that a king. That doesn't make me a fucking Brahmin. I have no patience and I want her quick."

Ramendra Kaushal really didn't have much patience.

That's one trait of Ramendra Kaushal's character had escaped the calibrated prism of Dhiren Bhagat. He had failed to analyse the steam of the carnal pressure that boiled inside the Prince. He had meticulously mugged up the family history of his target. Information gathered from diplomatic sources and archive records had helped him in building up a fascinating profile on Kaushal. However, the printed materials weren't the correct barometers to measure up the wild progeny of a wild king. The FIB field officer simply wasn't aware of the depth of the complex 'mother' syndrome Ramendra Kaushal suffered from. Women were playthings for him, but Kaushalya was sacrosanct. The turbulent twister of the campus was scared of the saintly lady, whose prayers flowed around him as a protective cocoon.

Bhagat concentrated on a piece of mutton cutlet garnished with garlic sauce and ruminated over the fascinating story, which was an inseparable part of India's fragmented and bloody independence.

Ramendra Kaushal, son of a Punjabi Brahmin royal, had drawn more on the gene banks of his father, Raja Dayaram Kaushal, the maverick king of Jhumra, a principality on the banks of the Chenub, below Sangla Valley, in Pakistani Punjab.

Adulated and abused for his pro-British leanings, arrogance, impatience and legendary weakness for women, Dayaram Kaushal ran his hereditary grant with a mixture of iron handedness and benevolent dispensation.

The grant, owned by a vanquished Niazi ***sultan*** (Rex), was bestowed upon Pundit Vikramaditya Kaushal, Dayaram's great-grand father, for his pioneering services to the advancing British troops to the Wild West of India, the Northwest Frontier Provinces. The British traders had grabbed India from the decomposing Muslim rulers. To stabilise the new gains they required Hindu support, starting from Bengali baboos to upcountry Brahmin and ***Kshatriya sepoys*** (warrior class soldiers).

The Kaushals, a family of brave fortune seekers didn't disappoint the British masters. Most of their kind didn't. It was a period of British bonhomie with the Hindu collaborators, against the just vanquished Muslims.

Dayaram's wife, Kaushalya, daughter of a Kanauj (city in central India) Brahmin, was given in marriage to the young king. Daughter of a blue-blooded temple priest, Kaushalya was declared barren, after she failed to bear an heir to the Jhumra throne. Dayaram direly needed an inheritor, to keep the throne to his line. The Muslim nobility, he knew, wouldn't even wait for his ashes to cool, before they petitioned the Crown to revert the Jhumra throne to its original owners, the descendants of the deposed Niazi ***sultan*** of Mianwali.

Bhagat's records were silent on the miracle of Ramendra Kaushal's birth from the womb of a barren mother. Some vague reports mentioned a Vedic sacrifice performed by the saints from the Himalayas, which helped in fertilising Kaushalya.

The events around the apocalyptic Second World War had signalled the collapse of the colonial powers. Inability of the bankrupt Buckingham Palace to keep its sprawling empire in leash had triggered off the inevitable process of chaotic transfer of power. London was in a hurry to abdicate its empire overnight, what had taken centuries to acquire and consolidate. Independence came to the sub-continent like the apocalyptic Great Flood. There was no Noah to save the millions of Hindus and Muslims, who were guillotined at the altar of political independence.

Dayaram wasn't brought up in the culture of digesting pragmatic advices. He scowled at his friends and courtiers and politely brushed aside a subtle message from the Viceroy to agree to merge his kingdom with Pakistan. No. Under no circumstances would he agree to surrender his sovereign power to either of the contending monkeys, one Hindu and the other Muslim, both busy in a tug of war over an abandoned loaf called India.

Dayaram proclaimed his sovereignty, soon after the lapse of paramountcy of the Crown. His was the second voice of defiance after that of the Nawab of Multan. The Muslim leaders, especially the inheritors of the Niazi ***sultans*** refused to allow the Hindu usurper to assert unilateral sovereignty over a predominantly Muslim population. Hindu India had denied the merger of the Muslim ruled states of Junagarh and Hyderabad with Pakistan and the fate of Kashmir was still hanging precariously on the balance.

How could they allow tiny Jhumra to fly its own flag? No. One more Hindu king couldn't be allowed to defy the wishes of the Muslims, who were waiting impatiently for the resurrection of the Crescent Nation. The British traders had cheated the Great Mughals. But the new awakened Muslims were in no mood to suffer Hindu suzerainty any more. The inheritors of the conquerors of Hindu India were simply not ready to allow the tiny ***kafir*** king to fly his flag of arrogance and defiance.

Dayaram Kaushal had closed his mind and refused to see the tsunami overwhelming his tiny principality. He decided to defend his territory, against all odds. Partition or no partition, he would defend his domain-Dayaram's telegrams to King George VI and the Viceroy was unequivocal. Not known to be a prudent judge of complicated geo-politics, Dayaram precipitated the situation by leading a hoard of horsemen and foot soldiers and burning down a few Niazi settlements.

It was meant to be a warning to all! The Brahmin king won't allow any act of stupidity by his Muslim subjects.

He was wrong.

Dayaram couldn't fight fire with fire. The sub-continental mood had changed. The seeds of two nations, sown jointly five decades ago by the kulaks on the Thames and the dreamers of resurrection of the Islamic power in India, had taken firm roots and the rupture of minds had become complete. The impatient, greedy and tired Hindu and Muslim leaders of 1947, sensing that the Crown was too eager to take out the empire-bone, stuck in its oesophagus, fought like wayside kids and settled for truncated spoils. They achieved a blood stained independence, blood of both Hindus and Muslims.

The rest of the story wasn't much too different from the fate of the Hindu gentry living in predominantly Muslim inhabited west Punjab. Fanatic gangs of Niazis, aided by northern tribals, liquidated most of his Hindu and loyal Muslim ***rayats*** (subjects). The marauding killers had accomplished, what they claimed, the holy task of cleaning up the soil of Pakistan, washing it with the blood of the Hindu ***kafirs*** (non-believers).

Dayaram vainly waited for a British contingent, promised by Delhi, to rescue him and his family. The Irish District Collector was too busy managing rivulets of blood and mountains of dead bodies, worthy offerings to the deity of political independence.

On a fateful morning Dayaram led a final valiant charge to the top of ***Jung Tikri*** (hillock of war) against the combined force of police, tribals and armed Niazi feudals and died on the back of his favorite horse. Arman Ali Niazi, son of a former scion of the buried sultanate, severed his head, with a clean mighty blow.

Queen Kaushalya and the suckling babe Prince Ramendra Kaushal were guided across to the safety of Hindu India, by the loyal ***khansama*** (cook) and a ***syce*** (horseman). Kaushalya landed up at Jhun Jhunu and took shelter with her brother, a court official in the ***durbar*** of a local potentate. Himself a childless Brahmin, Kaushalya's brother had adopted Ramendra as his son and legal heir.

With a view to giving Ramendra the best possible education Kaushalya silently and secretly encashed her gold ***mohurs*** (coins), which she had managed to bring with her from Jhumra. She wished to see him climbing the high chair of a Collector, an administrative position she understood well. That office, in her perception, controlled the lives and deaths of millions in British India. And there wasn't much of a change in the new dispensation.

****

Dhiren Bhagat's diary ended there.

His archives didn't contain the drama of charade and shame that took place behind the thick walls of the Jhumra palace.

The pious and saintly Kaushalya nursed under her bosom a big scar and a sweet secret. Subjected to total hysterectomy a few years after her marriage, in order to get rid of a multiple fibrosis, Kaushalya failed to gift her husband with an heir.

Then there was a Vedic ***yagna*** (sacrifice) and months later a royal edict was issued to declare that the queen was pregnant and was expected to deliver a child in due course. A report was also filed with the British agent and to His Excellency, the Viceroy of India. The Jhumra kingdom was on its way to receiving its heir and successor and the Doctrine of Lapse was not to be invoked.

The precise ceremony was more bizarre than the open ***yagna,*** in which 101 animals were sacrificed. A religious sanction and mutual agreement followed the gory sacrifice, offered in honour of the family deity, a bizarre stone idol of goddess ***Kali***. Kaushalya permitted the king to fertilise the wombs of her companion, Rama Bai. Ramendra Kaushal was born behind the guarded walls of the Jhumra palace and was transferred permanently to Kaushalya's lap.

The young Prince was unaware of his complicated and painful past. The secret was closely guarded even from his maternal uncle. Ramendra was vaguely aware of his royal background. Father was a distant dream. Jhumra was a mirage, never to be reached and achieved. Rama Bai had simply disappeared from his life.

Dhiren Bhagat and his information pool missed out these secrets of the Kaushal lineage. He missed out other vital inputs too.

Ramendra Kaushal believed, like his father did, that the world was there, because he wanted it to be there under his shoes. He ardently believed that political muscle and wealth alone could take him to cloud nine. That was a sure guarantee to earn respectable slots in independent India. Few dips in the pool of crime didn't matter. In feudal India it rather added a machismo image to the new political masters. Who in India didn't know that kings and princes were made of heavenly stuff? They all claimed to be direct descendent from the Gods, 330 million of them, some of the Sun and others of the Moon etc, etc.

Raping a woman here and killing a man there were special divine privileges. Didn't the Gods indulge in chasing damsels and in procreating divine bastards? Didn't they kill people at will and stamp them as ***Asuras***, the non-Aryan demons called ***Dasas***?

Bhagat ruminated over his thoughts and chewed on his mutton cutlet. But he didn't fail to capture Ramendra Kaushal puffing away cigarette after cigarette and eyeing Matang from the corners of his eyes. He wasn't exactly listening to Brij.

Ramendra Kaushal, Dhiren Bhagat was yet to discover, believed that he was a born ruler. And for a ruler the slightest act of defiance by a courtier deserved capital punishment. The tiff with Matang was, therefore, a mighty provocation. The puny Bihari shouldn't have dared to advice him on his choice of a casual bed partner. A jackal never dictated terms to a lion on the preference of the kill, it should choose for its mid-day meal.

Was he a police informer? Not unlikely. Ramendra had seen him sucking secret nectar from Vidya Sagar Suri's honey pod. And that implied a latent link with the criminal investigation department. To top all these Ramendra hadn't forgotten that this dirty Bihari had double-crossed him in a recent gold smuggling assignment.

Brij thought he had managed to diffuse the Blue Dart scuffle and that things were back on the rails. He had reasons to believe it. His captain threw up volcanic magma every second day. Such scuffles were as bitter as a few drops of Tabasco on a piece of medium cooked meat.

He helped Kaushal to gently push down the firing pin and turned on his heels at Dhiren Bhagat.

"Hey lout, who're you?"

Bhagat, in the midst of chewing his thoughts and the mutton cutlet, didn't expect the fast turn of events.

"Sir," He stammered, "I'm a bookseller, from Sterling Publication. I sell text books."

"That I can see. Are you a Commie, a Chinese ***chuha*** (rat)? What the hell are you doing here?" Kaushal joined Brij and lifted Bhagat up by his collars.

"Sir I'm a poor bookseller. I've nothing to do with Communists. I'm a regular visitor to this cafe. You can ask the people here."

"Empty your bag." Kaushal thundered.

Bhagat emptied the contents of a grey leather bag on the table, a few brand new books on English literature and economics.

"Let him go ***yar*** (friend). He's an innocent rat, not a Chinese one." Matang intervened.

"Don't interfere in my affairs. I hate the Commies. They worship either Mao or Stalin as the Chairman of India."

Ramendra pushed Bhagat back on the chair, demanded another Player from Brij and wheeled back towards Matang. His eyes narrowed down to mere slits.

Yes. He thought this one rat, Matang Singh, had exhausted his lease of life and not that rat of a bookseller. He had become too big for his boots, too uncomfortable for the reigning lion of the University campus.

"Now get lost. Remove your sticky ass from here. Don't dare sell Chairman Mao to us." He scowled at Bhagat and dismissed the meeting with warm handshakes and promised to join them later near Khalsa College.

He wheeled back on his heels just before stepping out of Blue Dart, embraced Matang and apologised for the nasty incident. He was too depressed by the insulting looks and gestures of that stupid girl. And the election humiliation hung heavily on his psyche. Such a minor tiff, Kaushal explained shouldn't spoil their camaraderie. He lighted a cigarette and put it in between Matang's lips and loudly informed his folks about his intention to take a night bus to Jhun Jhunu. He would be out for two days.

Ramendra Kaushal jumped into his Morris Minor followed by his cronies and disappeared behind the next bend.

Bhagat heaved a sigh of relief.

Thank heavens! The Prince and his cronies had failed to notice the clandestine camera tucked in a corner of the bag. The camera with an auto-switching mechanism, embedded in the leather bag, had silently snapped all the developments at Blue Dart restaurant. The concealed tape recorder had recorded the dramatic conversations faithfully.

He walked out leisurely and summoned a motorbike borne surveillance shadow, positioned outside the restaurant.

"Follow the target. Be on the air and keep reporting."

"Till what time?"

"Till I call off."

Bhagat took a bus ride to Dreamland, a cover name for FIB's Technical Laboratory, the secret hub of technical intelligence.

Bhagat's trained mind didn't fail to perceive murder in Kaushal's eyes, the reconciliation drama notwithstanding. Ramendra Kaushal couldn't be far from big mischief. His eyes had spewed fire and he had spoken in the voice of death, chillier than that of the ghosts from the depths of the black dungeon.

Matang Singh wasn't a saint. Bhagat's archive overflowed with records of his sins in tonnes, which included a couple of gold smuggling and drug pushing cases and two murders. But the budding criminal was no match for Kaushal in ruthlessness. The ruthless Prince, he thought, should be kept under constant surveillance. The killer could do anything to get his dream girl and punish a renegade collaborator.

****

At the end of the day Bhagat knocked on the doors of Pradumnya Karnik's office. He didn't choose propitious stellar configurations to send in a slip, seeking an audience. The Konkan Brahmin was in a foul mood. His name was just scratched out from the panel of officers being considered for an undercover posting at the Indian Mission in Washington.

Damn the Punjabis! He cursed a Punjabi colleague, claiming to be a sibling of some unheard of prince in Punjab, for grabbing the post. Why the Punjabi prince and not him? Karnik was busy figuring out the lay out of the hierarchical constellations. Mentor Kumar Anand Prasad had failed to protect his interest, and Chief Dutta wasn't made of stuff to take interest in the career scheme of a junior officer. He finally grabbed the handle of a sharp paper cutter and repeatedly stabbed the tabletop and the slip sent in by Bhagat. He dumped the slip in a garbage bin and re-entered his tunnel of frustration.

After another half an hour Bhagat gathered the pulps of his courage and peeped in.

"Can I come in sir?"

Karnik blew his top.

"What for? What the hell do you think you're up to?" He shouted, "I'm not interested in wasting my time, looking at some stupid photographs. Come with your report tomorrow and send it through the proper channel."

In the FIB, basically a police organisation, protesting was a blasphemous behavioural trait. Junior officers often preferred to retreat from their senior's room like earthworms recoiling from an impenetrable obstruction ahead.

Bhagat withdrew. He burnt inside and felt the churning and rumbling of acids in his stomach. This upper caste officer, he apprehended, was going to be his nemesis.

"Bloody shoemaker's son. He comes to teach me operations, as if I've been cooking trash all these years and he has been my boss. ***Lord Vishnu*** alone knows when this country would be rid of these insects!" Karnik muttered within Bhagat's hearing, as he turned his back in abject frustration.

Bhagat wasn't surprised. But he felt seriously hurt, to hear the indiscreet abuse usually heaped on low castes. It was a part of the social dispensation he was supposed to accept. God himself had ordained this in the holy scriptures. Didn't Manu the Lawgiver place his class at the bottom of the social ladder? The Saints had told his class to respect and obey the system and worship the Brahmins.

He brushed aside the abuse and turned to the room of Ramkrishna Prasanna Banerjee, in short RP, the immediate boss and his designated proper channel.

RP was in a furious hurry to take off for New Delhi ***Kali*** temple, for the special Saturday eve worship. This was a mandatory exercise, a ritual set by his mother, soon after he was born and reinforced by his wife, when he was married off at eighteen. After all, he, the only male progeny from his father's line, was born after his mother had offered special prayers at a ***Kali*** temple, presided over by a 19th century godman, Ramakrishna.

"***Ma Kali*** (mother Kali) clear my promotion case." Banerjee chanted the words like a holy ***mantra,*** as Bhagat peeped in through the curtains.

The very sight of Bhagat, at the end of the day, meant the inevitable stretching of hours beyond the needles of the clock. That low caste work-worm had perhaps no other pleasure in life. Banerjee muttered a curse. He should have taken to curing animal hides, his ancestral profession. He wondered if the shoemaker's son could snatch even a few lonely hours for copulating with his wife!

But, professional, ethnic and cultural decency prevented him from pouncing upon the gutter creature, elevated to human status after India's independence.

"What brings you so late Bhagat?"

"Sir, there are some interesting leads on the Operation Triple X target." Bhagat submitted meekly.

"You're late my friend. I'm supposed to go to the office of the Deputy Director, to pay my respects and to discuss an important operation. Come tomorrow."

Banerjee didn't wait for Bhagat's reply. He walked out and turned his bicycle towards the ***Kali*** temple. Oh holy Mother! He pedalled furtively. The most auspicious conjunction of Moon and Jupiter with constellation Virgo shouldn't pass by. The impure idiot had barged in without warning. The damn fool should perish. Oh Mother! Banerjee touched his forehead. Kill these low caste idiots, like you once killed the demons to liberate the Gods.

Bhagat felt flattened with frustration. He was anxious to file the Blue Dart report, but he was intrigued by the murderous looks in Kaushal's eyes. Something told him that the Prince of Jhun Jhunu was up to greater mischief. He had seen murder in Kaushal's eyes. That ruffian wasn't made of stuff to allow defiance and digest insult. Perhaps Matang's indiscreet use of the bovine epithet to describe Hema and the indecent dig at Kaushalya had touched off some wild chords in him.

The churning of Bhagat's intestinal acid turned to gurgling sounds. Something continued to tick away inside ringing a warning bell. He could perhaps gather valuable lead on his target by placing timely surveillance. He required support from the wizards of Dreamland, the FIB's technical intelligence wing. But that required Karnik or Nampoothiri's nod.

The thought of visiting the South Block office of Nampoothiri for consultations crossed Bhagat's mind. He abandoned the idea. It would be too much to walk straight up to the big boss. Neither Karnik nor Banerjee was going to support this. His gut feeling advised him to call it a day. Bhagat opted for a short route through a gap between South and North Blocks, which led to the bus terminus. He entered the portals of South Block, cutting across the corridors below the arches of the ornate gate. His steps were frozen by a lively reverberating shout, as he approached the exit gate, from where the long winding corridors forked out towards the Prime Minister's office.

He turned around.

It was Balachandran Nampoothiri, walking down the corridor towards his office, a smoking cigar pressed between his fingers.

"So young man, what's the news?"

Nampoothiri was in a happy frame of mind. He had had an hour-long audience with the new Prime Minister, Jung Bahadur Sharma. The formal briefing on Pakistan was prompted by the Prime Minister's concern over loud noises made by the hostile neighbour, along the Kachchh border, a new conflict theatre. The briefing session went off very well. Neither he expected the new Prime Minister to listen to the number three of the FIB with rapt attention nor did he have high opinion of the intellectual accomplishment of the seemingly rustic neighbourhood politician.

Nampoothiri's encounter with the PM changed his perception. Contrary to the allegations, made by political pundits, Jung Bahadur sure wasn't keeping the prime ministerial seat warm for Mandira, daughter of his mentor, the just deceased Prime Minister Amritlal. He had a mind of his own and he understood the intricate functioning of the military regime in Pakistan. His perception of the emerging ties between USA, Pakistan and China was clear. The White House, he felt was eager to see India as a new whipping boy, after Vietnam, Cuba and any other nation having tinge of red or rouge in their ideological coating. Washington was keener to build new bridges with China.

Why?

He had smiled over the silly question from Nampoothiri. Wooing China was a major step towards cracking the iron curtain and pumping in hot air into the Cold War balloon.

The uncanny fellow fortunately disagreed with some of his political colleagues and bureaucrats about the military intentions of Pakistan. A weak India after humiliating defeat in the Chinese war, and the sudden change in leadership held out tantalising promises to the adventurers in Rawalpindi. The men in uniform, in Pakistan, were planning dirty tricks, in tandem with China and the USA, Jung Bahadur warned his deputy intelligence chief.

He sounded a warning that India stood isolated diplomatically. The Russians had no particular love for the new Indian leadership and the Americans and allies could care less for what happened to India. India's Vietnam policy had irked Washington. Pakistan was a better client; they felt, not suffering from high and empty moral shenanigans. Their bedspread was well laid down to receive the Yankee ***humbister*** (bed partner) at any conceivable point of geo-political necessity of the newborn Islamic nation.

He advised Nampoothiri to sharpen India's intelligence tools and to build on penetrating assets. Pakistan won't allow India a long breather, he warned. He smelt burning powder in the air. The short wily fellow, Nampoothiri laughed, didn't forget to prick a pin, by adding that the FIB should've been able to convince his predecessor about the perfidious intentions of the Chinese leadership. Intelligence was supposed to tender advice without fear and favour, without caring for the idiosyncrasies of the political masters. It was a subtle dig at Amritlal; his rouge tinted maverick defence minister and Dutta, the FIB chief.

Nampoothiri was busy talking to himself. The smile hanging on his face displayed his happy frame of mind. Bhagat returned the greetings with an uncertain Japanese style bow and stood aside. The distant greeting of the boss must not be anything more than a passing formality, he presumed. Very kind of the big boss indeed!

But Nampoothiri was in a buoyant mood. He wanted to share his happiness even with the inanimate bricks of the cool South Block walls. He could sense a positive streak in the new PM. It should augur well in the forthcoming succession struggle, between him and Kumar Anand Prasad.

"So young man, what's new with your Operation Triple X target?"

"Sir, there are some interesting developments."

He tried to keep pace with Nampoothiri's brisk steps. Perhaps he could brief the top boss about his intelligent guess, probably a hunch.

Perhaps, sustained surveillance and technical coverage around the target could yield convincing leads.

"Is that so? Come up."

Nampoothiri silently climbed the stairs. He preferred to climb rather than taking the ancient elevator. Room number 187 was just around the corner, in the first floor.

"Tell me what's so interesting." Nampoothiri settled down in his chair, as Jatadhari Garo poured coffee in an ornate mug.

Bhagat narrated the story, for the next twenty minutes, in slow halting words, played the audiotape and impressed upon him the need for mounting surveillance and technical operation. Ramendra Kaushal, he said, was capable of committing any crime. Killing came naturally to him and kidnapping a girl was part of his routine.

Rajni Krittika Hemaprabha Rao was in grave danger.

Nampoothiri reached for the special red phone.

"Is it Dreamland? Hi Mitra, it's me. Do you have the night vision camera ready to move at short notice?" Nampoothiri talked to his DTL (Director Technical Laboratory).

"Yes sir. How soon?"

"In the next 20 minutes your covert surveillance van should report to me." Nampoothiri put back the handset on its cradle and gave instructions to Bhagat.

"Don't bother about the hierarchy. Get along, watch the fellow, and don't interfere. Have everything covered. This is your chance to gather materials for blackmailing your target."

Nampoothiri wished Bhagat Godspeed and reached for the red phone again. A briefing meeting with boss RN Dutta was necessary to discuss the action points along the Kachchh-Pakistan border. War clouds over the western front were not the only problems. Some southern states were burning on the language issue, and Mandira, a minister in Jung Bahadur's cabinet had rushed to Madras, to be with her people, she asserted. The PM, though highly embarrassed, couldn't afford to adopt a strong public posture against her. She was, after all, the daughter of Amritlal, who ruled India for 17 years.

And the enigmatic lady cared very little for set norms and established protocol. She was the real inheritor to the Indian throne, the acolytes claimed, passed on to her father by George VI, the King Emperor of India. A new dynasty had just taken over from the House of Windsor. And Mandira wasn't in the habit of living with interludes and regents.

Nampoothiri carried an impression that, the PM was suspicious of the commitment and impartiality of RN Dutta, hand picked by Mandira's father. He probably had the creeping feeling, under his skins, of being upstaged by Wily Mandira on the one hand and tenacious Bulabhai Khemji, the elderly Gujarati, on the other.

"Sir, the PM appeared to be highly suspicious of Mandira and Bulabhai Khemji. He didn't come out clean and spell it out, but gave me enough of a hint." Nampoothiri averred.

"The old man from Gujarat has been waiting in the wings for long. He has lost any hopes he had harboured after Jung Bahadur's succession."

Dutta spoke in impeccable Oxonian accent.

"Leave the politicians alone. Let's play our own game. I feel the country is sure to face another war, pretty soon. Let's hone up our own preparations." RN Dutta mildly cautioned his deputy.

"The PM also evinced keen interest sir. He made piercing enquiries about our assets in Pakistan."

"I know. He feels we aren't doing much. Let's settle our home first. You better pay attention to the observations of the Prime Minister." Dutta replied in a sinking tone.

He was aware of the not too mute rivalry and war of nerves between Nampoothiri and Kumar Anand. He only hoped that the two powerful and ambitious deputies would wait till he gracefully retired and his remains were cremated honourably. He wished that they wouldn't sell the highly professional organisation to the self-seeking politicians. Both of them, locked in an acrimonious battle, were capable of compromising the institution, obviously at a regrettable cost.

Balachandran Nampoothiri feigned ignorance at the tangent prick in Dutta's words. He stood at the crossroads of a succession war for the top FIB slot. Coming few months was crucial. How could he allow his Bihari colleague Kumar Anand to grab the coveted slot? He knew, Nampoothiri spoke to himself that the biggest war of his life was just ahead. What would he do in the FIB headed by that obnoxious rival?

As he left Dutta's room, after a stocktaking session on intelligence operations inside Pakistan, Nampoothiri simply forgot to call Alladi Subhash Chandra Rao, the health secretary. His daughter Rajni Krittika Hemaprabha Rao was in real danger. Ramendra Kaushal, if Bhagat was to be believed, wasn't going to digest the haughty demeanour of the impetuous fluttering Freya of the campus. He habitually managed to take his choice to bed. And the journey to his bed wasn't always strewn with rose petals. Some of them were often unloaded in Ram Karan Prasad's pleasure palaces, classy apartments, used as five star brothels. They were treated deferentially, distinct from the shanty red light shacks in India and the dusty markets in the third world countries.

But today, Nampoothiri, under tremendous pressure of his own making, simply forgot to lift the phone and alert Rao. The professional in him was under a severe tectonic crunch. The immediate task of raising deep penetration agents for Pakistan and the likely succession coup by Kumar Anand Prasad fogged out his rational thinking process. His dislike for Prasad and burning desire to step into the shoes of Dutta at the earliest opportunity had temporarily plugged the flow of signals from his neo-cortex. He was, for a few hours, being simply guided by the serpent, vainly hissing from beneath his medulla, buried deep, deep below his cranium.

His neuron signals swung like an erratic pendulum.

Who could ensure his succession to the coveted top seat? Jung Bahadur?

Perhaps not.

How long would he last! Perhaps, Mandira would protect his interest better. Amritlal's daughter had seen, from ringside seat, the serpentine political creepers around her father and grandfather. She wouldn't allow the diminutive earthy gentleman to drive down his roots deep.

It shouldn't be difficult for a wily Kerala Nampoothiri Brahmin to keep the two Prime Ministers, the incumbent one and the other impatiently biting her nails away, in good humour. As an ace intelligence operator he had mastered the art of deception very well. The time had come to put his professional expertise to test.

Nampoothiri went to bed a totally confused person. His professional bearing was lost in the storm of his career problems. Bhagat, Hema, Ramendra Kaushal simply faded out into the slippery by-lines of disturbed sleep. Liberal helpings of Chivas Regal weren't of much help.

Chapter 4

The Second World War vintage Willy's jeep, remodelled as a van, normally remained under a canvass wrap, inside a garage, at a far end of the South Sunken Road, which connected the President's Palace to Dalhousie Road.

Kunal Kaushik, an assistant with Dreamland was busy giving final touches to the vehicle and chic electronic equipments. Adhesive screen-printed stickers bearing false number plates were put on the originals. Bold adhesive stickers reading MCD (Municipal Corporation of Delhi) were put on the rear and flanks of the van. Another sticker announced that the vehicle was on Emergency service.

Nirmal Mitra, a wizard in electronics and communication technology entered the van accompanied by Bhagat for final systems check. He switched on the VHF trans-receiver and spoke to his operations control room.

"Wolf here," Mitra intoned, " How do you read me?"

"Roger sir, Lamb here. I get you five."

"All units standby, remain on air, till you hear me next." Mitra ordered.

He dialled a number and talked to the commander of the ZEBRA UNIT, the super secret arm of the FIB, deployed on selected operations.

The ZEBRAS, described as scavengers, wiped off telltale marks left behind by the vanguard operations team. They mounted counter-counter-surveillance on possible counter-surveillance measures adopted by the targets under coverage. And they performed daring rescue operations, whenever the vanguard teams ran into unexpected trouble. The ZEBRAS, well-trained commandos, were legendary sharp shooters. They didn't have the licence to kill. But they did kill, during extremely difficult rescue operations only.

"I hope you have your orders to cover my team. No communication till we're in danger. Plug in and maintain silence. I'll give two beeps at every 5-minute interval. In case I miss two laps, rush to our aid. Got it?"

"Roger sir."

"Is your GPS in position?"

"All in tops sir. My boys have charged their automatics. Give them a chance tonight." The remote voice chuckled.

"No dear. No fireworks. We're operating in the heart of the capital. Just follow my orders." Mitra sounded the final note of caution.

"Roger sir. Will comply." The ZEBRA commander switched off.

Nirmal Mitra went about checking the instrument panels. Night Video? OK. Infrared camera? OK. Night Vision Binocular? OK. Directional Microphone? OK.

"Kaushik," Mitra signalled his colleague, "Handle the video camera. I'll handle the Infra, and Bhagat you keep the binocular. Signal me when to roll the cameras."

"Copy sir." Bhagat replied.

"What's your rendezvous?"

"The target, if I'm not incorrect, should come to his hunting hole." Bhagat replied and placed the MCD Emergency service vehicle about 100 yards away from Ramjas student's hostel, the identified den of Matang Singh. He removed a manhole iron lid and hung a red lamp as a warning to drivers and pedestrians. Emergency maintenance works were on.

"Are you sure?" Mitra felt fidgety to position his chariot on a main thoroughfare.

"No problem sir. My boy is shadowing the target. I'm in radio contact with him."

Bhagat trained his binocular on the hostel gate. No. There was no sign of Kaushal. He had perhaps taken the Jhun Jhunu bus. The Rajasthan bound buses normally left around 8 p.m.

Droplets of perspiration appeared on his forehead. A misfiring at a crucial juncture like this would be devastating. It would mean a serious loss of credibility. Bhagat tried to imagine the scenario: standing with a blank face in front of Banerjee and Karnik, their eyes burning holes inside his chest and head, caste hatred dousing him with cans of incendiary liquid.

Just one adverse report from one of them would be bad enough to block his promotion for five years. The message would be sharp and clear; jumping the gun was too risky for a low caste bum like him. The sages, kings and the warriors had enough divine insight to place his caste people at the lowest ladder of the society. The low life form had no right to jump the ladder of evolution.

No. No. Bhagat nervously shuffled his position.

A motorbike suddenly zoomed passed the van. Bhagat trained the binocular again. Yes. A shadow was approaching the main hostel gate...perhaps....

Yes. The night vision binocular captured Kaushal's silhouette. Bhagat signalled Mitra and Kaushik. The reels started rolling and clicking silently.

Kaushal parked his car at a distance and approached the hostel gates on foot.

The night guard saluted him and opened the door.

The cameras stopped. Mitra switched on the directional microphone.

Kaushal talked to the night guard in his usual cool murderous voice and passed on a few crisp notes and ordered him to get lost. The directional microphone picked up some of the words.

"How much do you earn?" Kaushal asked the guard.

"Only one hundred per month, master." The night guard with an over sized belly responded.

"Here is Rupees 1000. Get lost and I don't want to see your face in Delhi any more. Look at the gun. You must comply or else die." Kaushal's voice came in clear in the powerful micro phone.

"***Huzoor mai baap*** (master is the supreme boss). I'll be happy back in my village running a grocery shop."

The night guard walked out silently, pocketing the thick wad of notes.

Mitra's face lighted up in satisfaction, the microphone was responding superbly. The first break was lucky.

In about twenty minutes Kaushal emerged out of the gate, accompanied by Matang Singh.

"You're supposed to go to Jhun Jhunu!" Matang.

"***Yar*** (friend), I missed the bus," Kaushal replied, "Let's go to Delite. They're screening Hot Hot Woman."

"I don't feel like." Matang replied.

"Come ***Yar.*** I owe you an apology. Give me a break." Insisted Kaushal.

"I don't feel like it." Matang resisted.

"Don't be silly. We're friends. You've the right to disagree and fight once in a while." Replied Kaushal.

They silently walked up to the car.

"Where did you get this Fiat? Is it stolen?" Matang.

"I borrowed it from our friend Yaseen." Kaushal mumbled.

Bhagat removed the red light and replaced the manhole cover. He winked at Mitra to follow the Fiat.

Kaushal stopped his car near the mausoleum of Mahatma Gandhi on the Ring Road.

"Why stop here?" Matang.

Mitra's microphone faithfully recorded.

"Look, the bastards are turning the city into a ***qabristan*** (burial ground). Look at the Red Fort. Who knows how many are buried there? Some tomb of some fucking idiot punctuates every nook and corner of Delhi. At this rate the entire Yamuna face will be taken over by the grave diggers." Kaushal's philosophical voice came in sharp.

"We Indians believe in necrolatry. It's strange that you're surprised. Being a Congressman you shouldn't talk like this." Matang.

"Fuck all the political climbers. Yesterday they deified Amritlal, tomorrow they'll worship his daughter." Kaushal.

"Where are we going?" Matang.

"I've scouted out a fine ***chuda*** (night soil carrier) girl. She is a damn beauty and is a game too. Let's have fun." Kaushal.

"What about Hot Hot Woman?" Matang.

"Come on ***yar***! Surely you want real kick from a warm blooded hot beauty. What's the fun in a celluloid one?"

Kaushal's vicious voice slightly turned to a whisper in the recorder, giving an impression that his beauty in bare skins was waiting in her waterfront shack.

Matang's reaction to the luscious invitation remained mute, as the duo entered a narrow alley that led to the river waters. Bhagat whispered in Mitra's ears to follow them down the narrow deserted river front road. Mitra looked out thoughtfully and negated the request. The target could look back any time, he warned.

"You take the Kodak and Kaushik'll follow with the Video. Maintain a safe distance. Cover the red indicators on your cameras with black tape." Mitra cautioned Kaushik.

Kaushal guided Matang to a cluster of shacks, occupied by migrant labours, hired for giving final touches to Shanti Vana, the cremation ground of Jawaharlal Nehru.

Kaushal suddenly turned towards Matang, little short of the cluster, whipped out a huge Swiss blade and in neat and fast moves stabbed him twice.

"This is for abusing my mother and this is for calling my girl a cow."

The powerful blows almost decapitated Matang.

Matang's burly figure didn't get chance to react to the fatal blows. His half-lifted right hand slumped and he collapsed with a dull thud. His eyes were still open, whites glistening, as if asking Kaushal: were all these violence really necessary!

Kaushal folded the Swiss blade, wrapped it in a piece of cloth and flung it with full thrust at Yamuna waters. The blood soaked knife made mild sound on impact and settled down under mud. He briskly walked through a patch of wild berry-bush and turned to the parked Fiat and drove straight to the grounds behind the Red Fort. He leisurely alighted from the car, sprinkled a canister of petrol on it and threw a matchstick, after lighting a cigarette. Fire engulfed the small buggy, followed by an explosion. Ramendra Kaushal walked fast towards a lane leading to Jama Masjid. He didn't look back. A dead Matang and an exploded stolen car didn't matter much.

He was avenged.

Nirmal Mitra and Bhagat followed the sequences from their van, taking the cover of the lush riverfront foliage. The video and still cameras rolled and clicked away merrily.

Technically the operation was a copybook success. Mitra reclined against the passenger seat, lighted a cigarette and picked up the mouthpiece of the radio set.

"Wolf calling Lamb, do you read me?"

"Yes sir. Any order?"

"Operation concluded. Returning to base. Instruct ZEBRA team to wind up." Mitra asked the driver to turn towards the Technical Laboratory.

"Sir, instruct the Lab boys to help me in processing the films and cassettes right away. The boss may like to see the inputs, first thing in the morning." Dhiren Bhagat requested.

"The rest of the night is yours. Just don't disturb me. I want a solid 6 hours of sleep. Anyway, I hope we don't have to report this to the police."

"No sir. The police will find the body any way. Our game is different."

****

Bhagat went over the events in his mind and felt happy that his target priming was progressing on the correct lines. The jackal was inevitably walking into his trap, like cosmic particles being sucked into a black hole. The first physical contact, he presumed, should take place in another fortnight.

His Mosur (mobile surveillance) boys tracked Kaushal back at the official residence of Ram Karan Prasad, a palatial bungalow at 6 Racecourse Road. He had chaperoned a young campus beauty along to plead her case for a coveted scholarship.

Ram Karan turned out in an impeccably white hand-spun dress, characteristic of a particular political creed and summoned Kaushal to a corner.

"What do I hear about the murder of Matang Singh?"

"It's a mystery sir," Kaushal spoke in a steady voice, "I'm not sure what happened."

"I believe you had a quarrel yesterday."

"Oh shit!" Kaushal exclaimed, "Who told you that? Any way it was a minor argument sir."

"Whatever it is. Hole yourself up in Divine Inn for a few hours. I'll tell Suri to cover up your trails and to provide you with an iron-cast alibi. Don't drag my name."

"I need money."

"How much?"

"Five thousand."

"That's big. Any way, Matang should receive a hero's funeral. Blame the Communists and Hindu Sanghis and gain sympathy for our party."

"Done sir. Please do something for this poor girl."

"Leave her behind. She'll leave this place none the poorer." Ram Karan summoned his Man Friday, Kalua Mushahari and ordered him to make the girl comfortable in an adjoining room.

"Spare her." Ramendra pleaded.

"Sure," Ram Karan slurped up the flowing ***paan*** (betel leaf) juices and said in a mocking tone, "She's as safe with me as she was with you."

Ramendra Kaushal took the hint and left on his motorbike after collecting a bunch of bills from Kalua. He drove straight for his sanctuary, Divine Inn, minus the campus beauty. She stayed back for deriving inspiration from the veteran politician.

Divine Inn, a seedy joint, not far from the Mughal City of Sahjehanabad, Lutyens' Viceregal palace and British Delhi's Piccadilly, the Connaught Place, was located at Gole Market, an up-beat shopping joint for the Indian baboos. The inn had lost its glamour, like most landmarks associated with the abandoned empire. The historic city was now under the occupation of a new breed of adventurers and invaders, the Punjabi refugees from Pakistan and the fortune hunters from the rest of India.

Vidya Sagar Suri fronted the pleasure spot owned by Ram Karan Prasad, the seemingly permanent minister in the Indian cabinet. Suri's father had migrated from Jhang Maghiana, in West Pakistan, with his family and exactly Rs 500 in his pocket. Dumped at King's Way Camp transit centre, the Suri family started hawking clothes on cycle back. The elder Suri, a man of indomitable courage and integrity, wanted his son Vidya Sagar to follow the footsteps of his namesake, a torchbearer of the nineteenth century renaissance in Bengal.

But the young Suri had other ideas about life. He perceived that the fuel for post-independence renaissance didn't come out from the well of knowledge. It came from the money that floated in the air of the new licence and permit raj. He believed in short-fusing his route to the top. Before his innocent adolescence could guide him through college education, Vidya Sagar had taken a fancy for red-light beauties and alcohol. He was sucked into the lucrative business of peddling charas, opium and bladder loads of contraband alley-brewed liquor.

His immediate handler, another one-eyed migrant political entrepreneur from Pakistani Multan, a budding leader of the ruling Congress party, had guided Suri to the greasy alleys of Ram Karan Prasad.

The new generation of migrants wasn't aware of the illustrious background of Ram Karan's family tree. He represented the new social forces, which gushed out of the gaping fault line of caste and communal divide, promoted and exploited by the mythological Hindu society and the British Empire.

Descendant of a fish contractor from Bhagalpur, in Bihar, Ram Karan had inherited the fishy mantle from his grandfather Rai Bahadur Durga Kiran Prasad, a ***Mallah*** (fisherman) by caste and vocation.

Rai Bahadur Durga Kiran's father, according to the East India Company's chronicled records, way back in 1857, had provided boats to their troops for crossing the mighty Ganges and remounting a strategic assault on the rebellious Indian sepoys at Kawnpore. Reoccupation of Kawnpore had changed the fortune of the British trading company. The victory march from Kawnpore to Meerut and to Delhi's Red Fort had helped the Albion to paste a new sun on the Indian firmament that shone for over two centuries. This was the second civilisational occupation of India, by a Christian power, after a few hundred years of occupation by the Islamic invaders.

Durga Kiran's father Ram Janam Mallah was, therefore, rated as not too insignificant an Indian collaborator. After the mutiny was crushed, the grateful Company Bahadur, as the de facto sovereign, had decorated Ram Janam with a Rai Bahadur title. The new sovereign had sanctioned him a ***Jagir*** (land endowment) of 160 villages and exclusive fishing right to a 150 miles stretch of the Ganges.

Durga Kiran Prasad's son Kalika Kiran Prasad had died under mysterious circumstances, in an upmarket salon at Free School Street, Calcutta, operated by a famous socialite Madame Kathleen Hepburn. An inseparable part of the moral and behavioural mural of the buccaneering British traders and fortune seekers, Madame Kathleen patronised a large clientele of rajas and maharajahs. Some of them were heirlings of the decadent kingdoms. And the indulgent new British masters created new nobles with a view to augmenting indigenous vested interests.

Their male children were sent to Kathleen's parlour, to learn English language and British and French social customs and to arm themselves with the charming ways of bowing and leading the fine ladies to the dance floors. It wasn't too poor an imitation of the salons of Paris.

Kalika had run foul of a maharajah from a West Indian princely state, on the delicate duel over owning the favours of Martha, a charming British girl and a new arrival in Kathleen's salon. He was found dead, drowned in an imported bathtub.

Ram Karan Prasad, inheritor of such blue blood and patronage of the Crown, did not only retain the Rai Bahadur title, but soon after the Second World War was decorated with the coveted award of Order of the British Empire. The reward was in recognition for the uninterrupted supplies to the beleaguered British troops in the north eastern war theatres.

His trains of trucks and mules had braved serious obstructions from rebel Bengali leaders, who supported the Empire's enemy number one, Subhash Chandra Bose. But the inveterate rice bowl revolutionaries and their copycats, some Assamese, stupid Manipuris and naked Nagas couldn't deter Ram Karan's supply trails.

Ram Karan was nominated to the Central Legislative Assembly, representing a party floated by the backward castes, with open support from the British officials. The backroom wizards of the colony, who wanted to invent a second Hindu Nation, supported him to the hilt. In due course, Ram Karan secured a seat in the Viceroy's Advisory Council. On the eve of transfer of power, he was goaded by the Home Office to align with the Muslim League.

To Hindu Congress leaders Ram Karan was too valuable a political asset to be on the loose. His induction into the Congress was prompted by the desire of maintaining the façade of Hindu solidarity. Amritlal, the first Prime Minister of India, had painstakingly applied heavy coats of patriotic paints on Ram Karan's alleged contribution to the freedom struggle. He suddenly emerged as a towering freedom fighter and secured a berth in the first cabinet of independent India. It was indeed a strange tryst with destiny.

Either by design or irony of fate Ram Karan had purchased the house at Free School Street, once a booming salon of Madam Kathleen. He started a brand new salon with Dorothy, said to be a sister of Martha, as the reigning hostess. From this amorphous nucleus, Ram Karan had built up a flourishing business of guesthouses and inns in major cities.

Divine Inn, one of the joints fronted by Vidya Sagar Suri, therefore, was an integral part of the glorious legacy of the ***Mallah*** family. It was Delhi's favourite drug and sex joint. Ram Karan's wonderful temple of pleasure also provided cover to another flourishing business, export of live flesh, not for the cooking pots, but for the boiling cauldrons of desire and damnation.

Ram Karan had taught Vidya Sagar some pragmatic business practices. Like a devout Hindu, he believed and practised the pragmatic rule of ritually offering graft and bending heads to all the conceivable deities of the system. Ram Karan, in his own turn, expected all heads to bow before him. Some heads, refusing to bend complimentarily, were often broken like over-ripe melons. He maintained a steady band of goons, under command of his private Generals like Kalua Mushahari.

Ramendra Kaushal drove straight to the Divine Inn trailed by Dhiren Bhagat's Mosur. He parked the motorbike behind a shrub and walked up to room 105, especially reserved for his pleasure breaks. Suri saluted the budding politician and followed meekly.

"I'm not here," Kaushal whispered, " Understand?"

"No problem sir." Suri replied meekly.

"Send up a Scotch and I don't want to be disturbed for next few hours."

"Anything else?" Suri asked with a grin hanging on his face.

"No thanks. Call up Prasadji. He has instructions for you."

"Some policemen had come looking for you."

"What the hell did you tell them?" Kaushal gripped Suri's collar, ready to thrash him.

"Nothing, like you said yourself, you're not here."

Kaushal banged the door on Suri's face.

The gatekeepers of sin often dare not challenge the keepers of law. Dhiren Bhagat didn't have to haggle much with Vidya Sagar Suri, when he approached the innkeeper. His FIB identity card, some photo snaps of Suri's involvement in drug dealings and a bunch of currency notes to top it all, convinced VS that he was in mighty unpleasant company. The long arm of law was just about throttling his jugular. He opened the door to the pleasure castle of Ram Karan with an obliging bow.

"What exactly do you want? " Sagar made a meek submission.

"Leave the details to me. You want to even the score with Kaushal and we want our job done. Don't drag Karan sahib into this business. My men will come to install few gadgets. No questions and no running to the minister."

"Fine. But take care of the minister. A simple goof up could mean death. The new Station House Officer already troubles me; he refuses to accept bribes."

"There're more surprises in Hindustan Mr. Suri," Bhagat consoled him, " That's why the country still breathes."

"Sir," Said Suri bringing down his incisors on his tongue, and simultaneously touching his ear lobes," By God! Mine is a honourable profession. I barely earn my family keep."

"Well, well! Let God bless your family with more progeny like you. Take care. Nobody should get any whiff of this stink; you and I are involved in. You know the consequences for a drug related offence and you know how cruel SITA is (Suppression of Immoral Traffic Act). You'll simply rot in jail for ten years."

"I'm your servant sir. Just take care of my security."

Vidyasagar bent down before Bhagat with folded hands.

He didn't feel comfortable with the idea of conniving with a FIB officer. Dhiren Bhagat, however, played the game cool, sending Himalayan chill waves inside Suri's bones. The quid pro quo was neat and brutish.

"Sir, take care that my inn isn't defamed."

"Don't worry, we do often trample on the privacy of social pirates. But we do it scientifically. Everything is top secret with us."

Bhagat and his team were trained to be discreet, and very discreet, where honey traps were involved. Nirmal Mitra and his Dreamland boys operated, for the next two days, on rooms 105 and 106. Two pinhole video cameras and radio microphones were installed and synthesised with the video and audio tracks.

The super-secret technical operation was Nampoothiri's brain wave. With powerful political mentors shielding him, the police might find the going tough in slapping a murder charge on Kaushal. The Indian political breed was adept in blunting the edges of the law and bending the judiciary. They, Nampoothiri argued, belonged to a heavenly class and considered themselves above the Constitution and the statute books. Moreover, the police and politicians were the last items in his scheme of things.

He preferred chiselled tradecraft evidence for blackmailing the target. The fear of his photographs, in compromising position with women in bed, reaching his mother could clinch the deal. Ramendra, as the records said, was more scared of his mother than himself. He didn't have, if Bhagat's archives were correct, any God to fear. His mother was his Goddess.

****

The net was cast. But the big catch was busy elsewhere, dangling tantalising baits to the stunned and stupefied student community.

The university campus was in turmoil. The recovery of Matang's decapitated body from the back alley of Raj Ghat, horrendously named in the memory of Gandhi, a person, who had little to do with any Raj, either the British or its successor, had created tumultuous commotion.

Brij, the permanent appendix of Ramendra Kaushal, led the cheer group, in a gathering of students addressed by his leader. Kaushal's fiery speech condemned the left-extremists and the Hindu Nazis for polluting the campus with nihilist culture. He blamed the Chinese agents for the gruesome murder of the popular student leader Matang Singh. The Hindu Nazis, Ramendra thundered, had entered into an unholy pact with the Commies for a second enslavement of India.

The students didn't clap. Ramendra's political filibustering was too incongruous and they were well aware of the deeds and black-deeds of the campus charlatan.

Brij and his fellow acolytes looked at the sombre crowd and raised slogans.

"***Shahid Matang amar rahe*** (martyr Matang be immortal), Chinese ***chuhas murdabad*** (death to the Chinese rats), kill the Hindu Nazis, Kaushal ***tum age chalo, hum tumhare peeche hain*** (Kaushal you advance we're behind you)."

Some students repeated the slogans and clapped indeterminately. Others walked out silently. Kaushal didn't convince them. They knew him too well, an extortionist, rapist and murderer. He could as well be behind the ghastly killing.

Brij too, couldn't drown his conscience under the din of tutored slogans, and wasn't carried away by the rhetoric. Matang, the ruffian from Bihar, was apolitical. He was deeply entrenched in criminal activities and believed that the highway of criminality was the shortest conduit to the exalted pedestal of national politics. The communists had no interest in him and the Hindu Sanghis weren't the criminal types, not as yet. He hadn't forgotten the tongues of fire in Kaushal's eyes, at Blue Dart Restaurant. He had seen that look earlier when Kaushal and Matang killed two gold smugglers from Punjab. The greedy stooges had misappropriated 50 Kgs gold and passed on the blame to a marginally corrupt police party.

Ram Karan had his unique way of reaching the bottom of such affairs. His network was wide and his penetration very deep. The concerned police officer, when placed under a roller stone in Kalua Mushahari's interrogation centre, pointed fingers at the smugglers. He had received only 5 biscuits; they had grabbed the rest. The officer was spared with a minor punishment, loss of a small finger to the knife of Kalua. This was to advise him to follow the path of honesty; re-proclaimed by the father of the nation: ***Satyameva Jayate*** (the truth shall be victorious).

Why not? The smugglers and flesh traders too observed their own code of conduct. Straight dealing was the basic code of honesty. Dishonesty, betrayal and double crossing attracted capital punishment.

Ramendra accompanied by Matang and Brij had carried out the cleanup assignment at Chuna Mandi, behind Paharganj police station. They spent only two bullets, fired at the back of the skulls of the renegade Punjab smugglers.

"Are you hiding something?" Brij gathered courage and asked. He wasn't unaware of the consequences of crossing Kaushal's path.

"Do you suspect me?" Kaushal shot back angrily.

"No. I don't. But there were other witnesses in Blue Dart. Some of them may sing under police torture."

"You bastard! Don't you dare betray me? I'll make mince meat of your dirty balls."

Kaushal slipped his hand on the cool comfort of the blue steel in his pocket.

Brij looked at the contour of the gun and softened his tone.

"Cool down boss. Sharpen your guard. You remember that communist looking book seller in Blue Dart?"

"Where's that bastard? I'll squeeze out his balls too."

"Patience captain. Just cool down. Why don't you go home for a few days?"

Kaushal took out his hand and placed it around Brij's shoulder.

"You're my best friend Brij. Matang has paid for his ***gaddari*** (act of betrayal). Do you know that he tried to woo Hema?"

"Don't tell me!"

"I'm correct. He'd even written a love letter to her. How could he dare to touch my kill?"

"You still want her? Don't you?"

"Why not? She must pay for scorning my offer of love. No girl can do that to me."

"Take care boss. Things are too hot." Brij volunteered the advice after gathering plenty of courage.

Ramendra Kaushal levelled his cool eyes with Brij's uncertain looks. Brij nodded his head vaguely. That was a sure fire way of saving his skull.

"Now leave my kill to myself. I'll take her at my own sweet will. Get busy with Matang's funeral. I want at least 30 vehicle loads of people. Get them from the nearest slums. It's politically important for us. Ram Karanji and Mandiraji have promised to come. Matang's funeral will be a major political offensive against the campus Commies and the Hindu Sanghis. We must put up a formidable show."

Matang's funeral turned out to be an impressive affair indeed. Mandira arrived in an impressive cavalcade as a special gesture of solidarity with the students. She placed an all white wreathe on the dead body and in a short and shrill speech attacked the pro-Chinese communist ultras and Hindu Sanghis for their alleged nation wrecking activities. Matang was the first victim of the communist nihilists, she claimed.

Ramendra Kaushal announced, to the accompaniment of thundering applause, Mandira's noble offer of fund for installation of Matang's bronze bust. Minister Ram Karan announced institution of a gold medal in memory of the departed student leader, to be awarded to the brightest depressed class student from Bihar.

Matang's father, a broken man, lighted the stack of sandalwood, amidst chanting of ***mantras*** by the Brahmins. Ram Karan, in a brilliant display of practiced emotion, hugged Matang's father, and promised him an allocation of 10 acres of land from the government reserve. He loudly announced that Matang's martyrdom would strengthen the nation's resolve to fight the Pakistani aggressors and Chinese betrayers.

Chapter 5

The tongues of fire from Matang's funeral pyre still licked and singed the minds of the terrified students. The glowing embers were yet to cool down in the polluted waters of the Yamuna. The campus was yet to limp back to normalcy. Fear stalked the students ominously.

But Matang's spectacular and politically correct funeral buoyed up Ramendra Kaushal's stature by a few more inches. Open shoulder rubbing with two high profile ministers injected a sense of invincibility in him. His acolytes sounded loud warnings to the Hindu Sangh controlled Students' Union that the Prince from Jhun Jhunu was still the uncrowned king of the campus.

Kaushal didn't fail to rub in the message with extra muscle flexing. His goons stormed the Hindu Sangh office and left three students with broken limbs. The message was loud and clear. It's Kaushal who ruled the campus. All dissenters and challengers were welcome to follow the Matang route-journey to nowhere.

Kaushal's inflated ego and burning sensuality didn't abate with Matang's death and the roaring flames of his funeral pyre. The fire of carnal desire became a schizophrenic vector to propel his heart muscles with spasm of craving. This wasn't a fire that he could douse with liberal servings of Scotch, philosophical buffers and cautionary signals from a balanced cerebral cortex. The captive fire continued to pour fats into Kaushal's blazing cauldron of desire. His twisted gene-cords were chemically so aligned that, a mere infatuation exploded into an infernal desire. He knew for sure that the ghost wouldn't descend from his shoulders till he mounted on Hema and punished her for her arrogance. The unseen hands of destiny engineered him like this, he knew.

"I must get her," He told Brij, while sipping coffee at Blue Dart.

"Wait. Let things cool down." The pragmatic son of a priest advised.

"What for? It's my way of life. I want her."

"It's a different case."

"What bloody difference does it make?" Kaushal grimaced with a nonchalant look.

"Wait for a few days," Brij commented, "I've to take my mom to Benaras for a pilgrimage. We shall talk again."

Brij didn't dare repeat his advice. His tactical absence from Delhi should be a better act of discretion. The Prince was in no mood to wait. Patience was not his *forte*.

Kaushal was indeed not ready to wait for Brij's return from Benaras. He preferred to enjoy his women in absolute privacy. No group sex.

Hema should be his private kill. She probably belonged to a different class altogether. Kaushal couldn't, despite best efforts, put her in any typical pigeonhole. She was unique and a live encounter could only help categorise her.

Kaushal kept on driving, rather absent-mindedly, concentrating on the likely expression on Hema's face. She might squirm and cry out in ecstasy. Some apparent cool cats often exploded on impact. A high-strung woman apparently abhorred sexual overtures. But they sure admired hot pulsating muscle. He felt sure that this one cool cat would get electrified, once she was disrobed and masculine fingers caressed her vital contours.

Screech! Kaushal suddenly applied the brake. Hema's contorted facial muscles fleeted past his mind's screen. He licked his parched lips and looked into his own eyes in the rear-view mirror.

Why not now? Yes, now. He should abduct her. This one cool cat wouldn't yield, unless she was forced to.

Kaushal parked his car near the mouth of the ridge road that faced Kashmiri Gate and lighted hashish filled cigarette. The magic-smoke electrified his neurons. He looked out impatiently for the black car that usually dropped Hema at the college gate. It should've turned up by now. Perhaps, the bitch wasn't turning up today, Kaushal thought.

The hashish started acting slowly but surely. Ramendra closed his eyes, responding to the slackening impulses of his brain. Perhaps the stars weren't propitious. Perhaps, his decision wasn't correct. Should he wait for Brij's return? What for? That son of a priest wasn't going to chant ***mantras*** while he pinned Hema down under his thighs.

Kaushal closed his eyes. The hashish had started seeping into his blood. For a split second he nearly missed noticing the black Ambassador car approaching from the opposite direction. Kaushal ignited his car engine. In a sharp swing he placed his Morris Minor horizontally on the main road and forced Hema's driver to apply the breaks.

Kaushal sprinted down to the Ambassador, dragged Hema out and shoved her inside the Morris. Hema fought back and spontaneously rained blows on Kaushal. Her fingers scratched his chest, drawing blood and flesh.

Kaushal freed his right hand and hit Hema's medulla in a swift karate chop, dumped her on the back seat and drove off at high speed. Hema's limp body writhed and convulsed for a few moments and turned still. Three vertebrae, out of the seven, of her neck had snapped under the unmeasured blow.

Kaushal pressed the accelerator, concentrated on driving and anxiously scanned the rear view mirror. He was soon out of reach of Hema's aging driver. But he failed to notice his nemesis, Dhiren Bhagat, following his Morris in a posh Ford with a fake diplomatic number plate of a West-European embassy.

An alley cat of the walled city, Kaushal avoided the main thoroughfare and drove straight to Ajmeri Gate, took a turn to Connaught Circus and swung towards Gole Market. The vehicle entered straight inside Divine Inn and came to a halt under a huge Banyan tree.

Dhiren Bhagat parked his car well away from the hotel and activated his VHF communication set.

"Tiger's in the den," He raised Mitra.

"Fine. Bait's ready." Mitra replied and activated the system.

"I'll join in soon."

"Roger, no hurry. Take your time." Mitra hung up and switched on the pinhole video cameras and concealed audio systems.

****

Kaushal's Divine Inn room was fitted with a small fridge, an air conditioner and was well stocked with the beer and whisky of his choice.

He dumped Hema's body on the bed and switched on the air conditioner. The damn compressor didn't whine.

Bloody bullshit! He summoned the room service.

"What the hell is this? Why isn't the AC working?"

"Sir I really don't know," The room boy trembled in terror.

"Go and call VS."

"Sir, he's out of Delhi."

Kaushal dialled the intercom and demanded immediate replacement of the AC. The floor manager politely informed him that, the compressor had blown off and it would take at least three days to get a replacement.

Kaushal kicked the room boy out, closed the door and gulped a stiff dose of whisky straight from the bottle. The liquid fire warmed him up as it travelled down the oesophagus, leaving a burning sensation all the way down.

The Raleigh brand ceiling fan, an ancient acquisition, rotated slowly and screwed into Kaushal's patience. Everything was going wrong.

The bloody bitch was still feigning unconsciousness.

Did he hit her very hard? Perhaps. At that anxious moment, he could probably not measure the momentum. Such a chop at the base of the neck could often lead to a fracture.

Damn, damn! Damn the whole world! Did he carry a dead body all the way?

Kaushal gulped another drink and tried pushing a few drops into Hema's mouth, parting her lips with his thick fingers. The fairy girl didn't respond. But her rouge tinted cheeks; red lips and fine folds on the eyelids provoked Kaushal. Dead flesh couldn't ignite that kind of fire in him. Her body was still warm and it was driving him mad.

He slapped Hema's cheeks gently and kissed her lips.

Unknown to Kaushal, Dhiren Bhagat and his team rolled on the video cameras. Bhagat kept on silently directing the technical team like an orchestra conductor; his eyes glued on the monitor synthesiser.

The radio microphones picked up each and every utterance of Kaushal. Noise pollution didn't hamper the operation. The air conditioner was muted under Bhagat's instructions. His boys had also de-activated three contact points of the ceiling fan regulator, compelling the ancient Raleigh machine to rotate at a fixed speed.

These were routine exercises undertaken by the backroom boys of Nirmal Mitra.

Kaushal picked a bottle of chilled water from the fridge and sprinkled some on Hema's face and eyes. Were Hema dead? The mighty karate chop might have broken her vertebrae and a piece of bone had probably punctured a few veins travelling down from the brain. Kaushal's eyes betrayed fear as he unknowingly looked into the camera. An eerie feeling gripped him.

He wasn't ready to believe that his kill was dead before he had feasted on it. Her body was still warm.

Kaushal placed his ears on Hema's breast, trying to feel the beats. The bulging sacks of membrane were still warm. He couldn't feel the heartbeats, but the dying embers of Hema's body sent shivers of warmth down his spines. Kaushal was seized by a maddening impulse that ran through his spine and travelled down to the muscles of his genital.

He kept on caressing Hema's breasts over and over again, trying to draw warmth from the taut flesh. Hema's face, a wonderful sculpture in beauty and innocence, didn't react to his paranoid touches. She couldn't. The life essence had deserted the body at least 20 minutes ago. But the neutrons of her brain still pulsated, acknowledging Kaushal's touches. But her neurone proteins weren't in position to send instructions to Hema, to react. She, the living-kicking creature was simply not there.

A strange frenzy gripped Kaushal. How could she dupe him? Nobody could.

He undressed Hema, slapped her cheeks again and failing to get a response shouted out some obscenities. Undressing himself, Kaushal mounted on the cadaver of Rajni Krittika Hemaprabha Rao and carried out the frustrating ritual of a sexual assault. A frustrating ejaculation sent a shiver of shame and guilt in him. Ramendra Kaushal, for the first time, felt that he'd wronged an innocent girl. This one murder wasn't necessary, neither for his survival nor for his pleasure. He shouted out like a deranged lunatic. The bitch had defeated him, at the final moment of his victory. She had deprived him of the pleasure of making her beg for mercy. He had gone too far. He had killed Matang not for this dead idiot woman! He wanted her alive, submitting and begging.

Kaushal ran for the toilet, collected a mug of water and sprinkled some on Hema, as if the liquid would wash away his sin. He developed a strange affection and aversion for the flesh, which used to be Hema, lying before him. He felt haunted and scared.

The face of his mother Kaushalya shot across his mind in a flash.

"No mother, no. I didn't intend to kill her." Ramendra covered his eyes and shouted. But Kaushalya's face kept on hanging.

Kaushal sprinkled some water on his face.

"How could I kill a woman?" He cried out. He couldn't kill his mother. Could he? What a damn mess! His mother wouldn't ever pardon him, for raping a dead woman. A black cloud of guilt enveloped him.

"Oh Mother!" He cried out aloud and rushing to the toilet, picked up the water jet and applied cold blast on his face and head.

Two frames started quickly zooming in and fading out on the thin film of water; Hema's and Kaushalya's. He threw down the water jet and screamed out in anguish and frustration.

This dead woman was reminding him of his mother's face. Why? What was the commonality? Why did he see the image of his mother's face whenever he was in the company of women? Kaushal couldn't make any sense of it. Did a sin syndrome strike him? What sin? It wasn't his mistake. That idiotic girl shouldn't have resisted, compelling him to use the karate chop.

Kaushal muttered few more curses and replaced Hema's clothes, as best as he could, and wrapped the body up in a bedspread. He straitened his clothes; momentarily tended to the bleeding scratches on his chest, combed his dishevelled hair and picked up Hema's limp body. He disappeared from the monitor.

Ramendra placed Hema's body in the back seat of his car and zoomed out of Divine Inn. He drove past New Delhi Kali temple, took a right turn on to a small dirt lane that disappeared into the ridge forests. He parked the car by a huge weather beaten boulder, overlooking a depression that was covered with thick flowery foliage of wild lilies.

Kaushal gently took out Hema's body and placed it on the ground.

A few red faced ***langoors*** (monkeys), expecting Kaushal to offer them eatables, like normal devotees visiting the nearby temples did, tiptoed closer to Hema's body. Taking advantage of Kaushal's pre-occupation with a cigarette, some of the daring simians pulled out the bedspread and grimaced at the bluish face of Hema.

One of the more daring, perhaps the herd leader, bent down and sniffed the cool skins of the once vibrant girl. No. It wasn't exactly an edible offering. The frustrated herd grimaced at Kaushal and climbed up the nearest Banyan tree, with loud sounds of protest. Startled by the queer behaviour of the simians, Kaushal shooed them away by hurling pieces of stone at them.

Stupid fools!

Kaushal lighted another cigarette, removed the bedspread and for the last time looked at Hema's body. His eyes moistened up and a few drops of tears rolled down his cheeks. He didn't want to kill the girl. This one accident was unintentional. In a rare gesture Kaushal folded his palms and prayed in silence, perhaps after ages.

What the hell did he do with his seeds of desire? The damn demon had sprouted into a sky piercing shadow of death. Could he, by any chance, change the shape of events that might ensue from this unintended act of wanton violence?

No, he won't be able to drown this ghastly experience even in a sea of whisky. Perhaps the seeds of his desire would be finally incinerated with the mortal remains of the girl, whom he had picked up as a sex object and ended up developing aches in his soul.

Would he be able to have sex with any other woman? Perhaps not, not in near future.

He looked deep into Hema's eyes and felt a sinking sense of guilt. He closed his eyes firmly, with a determined effort to wipe out from his memory cells the ghastly act of raping the dead girl. He lightly kissed Hema's dry blue lips.

Had he started loving Hema? He had never loved any girl. He didn't know what love was all about. That lightening had never struck him.

Ramendra stood silent for a few moments and picked up the body and rolled it down the grassy slopes. Hema's remains rested with a thud against a big stone, after rolling over few thorny bushes. The thick greens covered up Rajni Krittika Hemaprabha Rao, in a final gesture of taking the dusts back unto them. The multi-coloured wild lilies parted temporarily and sympathetically wrapped up the beautiful naked body.

It was a final flowery burial.

Kaushal stretched his neck and looked down the depression. Hema's body, covered under the thick foliage of flowering lilies, wasn't visible from his position.

A sudden burst of remorse seized him as his overflowing eyes glanced at the mocking lilies. He never had the opportunity of looking at flowers dancing under a lazy breeze. The beautiful blooms were taunting him, Ramendra Kaushal felt, by shaking their heads. The beauty, that he had wanted to torment had defeated him and had just begun a process of tossing and turning his entire existence.

As he ignited the engine, Kaushal again felt two drops of tear rolling down his cheeks. What nonsense was happening to him? He didn't have any answer to that question.

He wiped the teardrops and swore silently to atone for this ghastly mistake. This one woman had shaken his world. Hema proved in her death that muscle alone couldn't open the door to a heart. What was it? Love? But he hadn't bothered about that amorphous commodity all these years. He didn't know its meaning.

Perhaps he should really go over to Jhun Jhunu, to his mother and seek her blessings. She alone could put his mind on the rails again. Perhaps she could tell him what love was made up of. Perhaps she could transform the seeds of his desire to the seeds of creation. Only a mother could do that.

Chapter 6

Pradumnya Karnik, like most Indian mortals and deities, reserved the right to break all the rules and laws and expected others to go by the statute books. He didn't see any virtue in the operational methodology that was adopted by Balachandran Nampoothiri to hook the Triple X target. Where was the need for such wanton bloodshed, sex and excesses? The chain of events had confirmed his conviction that Kaushal was purely a mindless criminal. He wasn't made of the stuff that could qualify him for grooming as a deep penetration resident agent. The entire process smacked of unethical crudity.

He wondered why Chief Dutta was in love with the target! Why did he give carte blanche to Nampoothiri and his stooge Bhagat? Didn't the organisation have any moral obligation and accountability? At the end of the day the taxpayers footed the entire bill.

Karnik was yet to learn that the intelligence community in India still trudged along the British furrow. It framed its own rules and it wasn't accountable to any law of the land.

His anger wasn't so much with the operation as such. His anger was cooking in the cauldron of frustration and prejudice, the frustration of losing out in the race to a posting to Washington and prejudice against Bhagat. How could the bosses saddle him with an untouchable? The arrow of his ire was directed at Bhagat, an officer of the low caste. Nampoothiri shouldn't have unzipped the entire wool-ball for the untouchable junior officer. Left to himself he would've screwed and crucified him against the wall.

This was the finest opportunity to finish the fellow and put Nampoothiri in a spot. He toyed with the idea of walking into the room of Kumar Anand Prasad, Nampoothiri's bete noire and pass on the dope of the murder of Matang and Hema. Ramendra Kaushal was allowed to commit the crimes under Bhagat's indulgent nose.

Karnik paused for a while. What would he gain out of it? Could Prasad assure him of a plush foreign posting? Karnik didn't find the answer to suit his career planning.

He resisted the temptation and tinkered with the idea of tilting towards the Kerala Brahmin, changing orbit from the Bihari ***kayasth.*** A Brahmin should stand in good stead for a fellow Brahmin. Their clique and religious mumbo-jumbo had ruled over the Indian people for hundreds of centuries. Why give up on that brotherhood?

Blackmail was the prescribed bait to hook the Triple X talent. Why could he not try the same weapon, in a way, to influence Nampoothiri? A little sound with less fury should do the trick.

But that son of a low caste must be taught a lesson. The scum should be cut down to size and a few bad entries in his annual confidential report shouldn't be out of place. Why should a pure Brahmin like him allow a untouchable a free passage to the upper ranks?

"Sir," Karnik's woolly thoughts were broken by the sudden intrusive voice of Dhiren Bhagat.

"You wanted a briefing on Triple X."

"Give me the papers."

"I haven't drawn up a report yet. I thought you'd like to have a verbal report first."

"What makes you think that your verbal junk is acceptable to me?" Karnik shot back.

"There are some sensitive aspects. Perhaps, you would like to keep the technical operations out of the written report." Bhagat tried to reason out, what he thought was the normal FIB practice.

"Well, I don't want any verbal briefing," Karnik snapped at Bhagat, "I want a detailed written report, a comprehensive basic operational data-sheet, for discussion with the Deputy Director. And I want it by 5 today. No hedging and no monkey games."

"Do I put down all the details in black and white?" Asked Bhagat.

"What's your problem? As an intelligence officer you're expected to put down all the details on record."

"Fine sir, the job will be done. I just wanted to know if all the details of our technical operations are also to be incorporated."

Bhagat tried to remind his boss, that his instructions flouted a cardinal principle of the FIB. It didn't allow its deeds to be recorded in black and white.

"Yes, do as I say. Banerjee will help you." Karnik dismissed the intruder.

Banerjee was again in a dilemma. Like most Indians he was averse to catching the bull by its horns. In such delicate matters, where the bosses crossed swords he preferred not to see, hear and speak any evil.

Why should important developments take place on Saturdays alone! Oh Mother ***Kali***, why should it happen to him! And why should this son of a shoemaker be after his blood! It happened to be another Saturday and he was in no position to stay behind late. He was bound to be late for the mandatory evening ***Kali puja*** (worship of Goddess Kali). Banerjee felt he was tossing about on red-hot coal.

"To be frank, I really don't know the details. It's between you and him. If he wishes my presence, I can come in at the discussion stage. I can probably give few suggestions on tradecraft matters, at the training stage."

He walked past Bhagat and rushed for his bicycle.

Thanks Mother Kali! He didn't want to stand between Bhagat and Karnik. The Konkani officer was blatantly wrong. The company never permitted the mixing up of operations and technical reports. It was better they fought it out among themselves. Nampoothiri was sure to chew up Karnik's bones.

He should. Let Karnik go to hell! Mother ***Kali*** should ensure his promotion and the coveted Pakistan desk job. Banerjee pedalled off fast.

Bhagat looked at the fading figure of Banerjee and lighted a cigarette.

Hell and damnation! Writing down an operational report wasn't as easy as filing a heated knife through a lump of frozen butter. Bhagat couldn't get his thoughts together. He couldn't establish smooth co-ordination between his training, service ethics, gut instinct and cerebral signals. Something was amiss. Karnik wasn't acting straight. Was he trying to implicate him and Nampoothiri in criminal liability? Was he working on Kumar Anand Prasad's game of torpedoing Nampoothiri? That was the probable scenario. There was no dearth of king cobras in FIB's serpent pit. Karnik was playing a deep and dirty game.

Ramendra Kaushal was a powerful guy. For him to get past the law wasn't a big deal. In India, law was applicable in different degrees to different strata of the society. Powerful political creatures, criminals, senior bureaucrats and magnates of business and industry were obviously above the statue books.

Nampoothiri wouldn't face any turbulence either, Bhagat reasoned. A small fry like him was sure to be fried deep in the hottest pan of law and prejudice.

No. He sure won't opt for the noose. He must alert Nampoothiri. Karnik's trick was bound to jeopardise Operation Triple X and Jung Bahadur's government wasn't likely to take the developments kindly. The newspapers were sure to pick up the threads and trace out the FIB's alleged connivance with acts of wanton violence.

That would simply be a flaming iron ball to palm.

Bhagat decided to try his luck with the top boss.

But reaching him wasn't easy.

Jatadhari could help.

Room number 187, at the turn of the corridor towards the Ministry of Defence, was buzzing with activities that evening. Nampoothiri was in the midst of a meeting with Major General Naveen Sahni, Director, Military Intelligence and the intelligence chiefs of the Navy and Air Force. The Director of Military Operations, Maj. General Harbaksh was also present with his number two.

"Very difficult today. He's too busy. A Hindustan Pakistan war is about to begin. Sahibs are talking about the Rann of Kachchḥ." Jatadhari conveyed his helplessness.

Bhagat scribbled a few sentences on a slip of paper and begged Jata to show it to Nampoothiri.

"If I don't see him now, the boss is bound to face personal harm. It's more for him than for me." Bhagat threw a psychological dart.

Jatadhari went in and in a few seconds Nampoothiri came out. He advised Bhagat to go home and meet him the next day at 7.30 p.m.

Should he write the report?

No. He should sleep and rest. He deserved it. Nampoothiri rushed back and called Karnik's number.

"Pradumnya, can you ask your officer Bhagat to see me?"

"Yes sir. It's my pleasure. He should be around."

Karnik panicked. Did Bhagat directly approach the Deputy Director S—S standing for all security matters? That son of a shoemaker, Karnik calculated, was capable of elbowing past his immediate boss. Any way, this wasn't the correct time to bray for the blood of Bhagat.

The bastard! Karnik vowed to finish off the scoundrel, once Kumar Anand, the Deputy Director I—I standing for internal affairs, assumed command. He pressed the bell, rather a long one, adding his anger and frustration to the 220 volt AC current.

"You called me sir?" Bhagat entered the room peevishly.

"Is the report ready?" Karnik looked up with a flicker of a butcher's smile below his butterfly moustache.

"Not yet sir, I suppose it should take another two hours. And I'm yet to receive the technical report from Mitra sahib. Would you like to call him, sir?"

"Leave it. See the DD (S) first. Tell me if he has any new instruction."

Bhagat returned to Karnik's room in ten minutes.

"Sir, he's busy in a meeting. He just told me that you may like to see him, tomorrow at 7.30 p.m. Till than, he said, no report should be drafted. He would like to discuss some important operational aspects with you."

"Okay. you can go. Prepare a check list of points for the discussion." Karnik dismissed Bhagat.

Very clever, eh? Karnik turned and twisted his neurons again. How did that Keralite get to know his mind? That Bhagat must've short-fused him.

He should check up with Jatadhari.

****

That exercise proved futile. Jata wasn't in the habit of opening his mouth. And Nampoothiri was awfully busy. He was tasked to co-ordinate the entire intelligence input on Pakistani manoeuvres in the saltpan of Kachchh and draw up a brief for the PM.

Sources from Karachi, Hyderabad and the Gulf stations had been sending reports about a military build up along the Sind-Kachchh border. A Double X asset located at Nagar Parkar had sent a few photographs, through a trans-border smuggler, indicating a massive deployment of Pakistani cavalry, artillery and mechanised infantry units.

Intelligence inputs from the FIB, Directorates of Military, Naval and Air intelligence and reports received from Dalpat Rai Mehta, the Chief Minister of the Border State of Gujarat, helped in building up a coherent collage of Pakistani intentions.

"Are you ready?" RN Dutta spoke on the intercom, "We've to see the PM in the Army Chief's operation room, in another 15 minutes."

"We're ready sir." Nampoothiri replied.

"Stay put, I'll join you in few seconds. I need a fast capsule briefing."

Briefing Dutta wasn't a difficult job. Nampoothiri shared with him a map, detailing Indian and Pakistani troop deployments and possible points of incursion by enemy armour, artillery and infantry. The Indian side wasn't at all prepared for another skirmish over the saltpan of the Rann. Barring a few police and para-military posts, the Indian presence was deplorably poor, not capable of facing even a brigade strength push from Pakistan.

The Operations Briefing Room (OBR) of the Chief of the Army Staff (COAS) was specially decked up with two rows of sofas. Designation stickers pinned at the upper edges indicated the sitting arrangement. Everything went by rank and gradation, in pure military style.

Green folders with red stripes and 'top secret' signs in red on top and bottom gave testimony to the seriousness of the meeting.

General Arobindo Mukherjee, the COAS and the Chief of the Western Command Lt. General Ratan Sinhji ushered in the Prime Minister, who was clad in the usual ***Khadi*** (hand spun) ***dhoti-kurta*** (Indian male dress) with a light brown jacket to match.

"Our int. reports indicate that, Pakistan has raised a claim on 30,000 km. of Indian Territory in the districts of Kachchh and Banaskantha."

A Brigadier flashed his foldable steel whip-indicator and browsed over the grids claimed by Pakistan. The area comprised a big bulge in the Rann of Kachchh, dry and dusty in winter and summer and a shallow sea in the monsoon.

"There have been traditional border disputes between Sind and Kachchh, but during partition and alignment of the borders Pakistan didn't raise a claim on this territory," the Brigadier continued.

"What's your report about the presence of Pak troops?" Asked the Prime Minister.

"Sir, the FIB and DMI int reports talk of massive deployment of Pak troops and armour. Our Naval and Air int reports from Koteswar, Nalia and Bhuj have supplemented these reports. Air reconnaissance has noticed Pak patrol boats at Kati Bandar, ready to head for Sir and Kori creeks. Our radars at Sanchor and Bhuj have detected several Pak air sorties along the border."

"Anything else you want to add? Any specific input from your boys?" The PM looked at RN Dutta and asked.

The FIB chief understood the finer digs of the PM's comment about the sheer inadequacy of the Indian intelligence thrust inside Pakistan. The boss had pointed this out a few days back, while assessing the FIB's operational efficacy.

Dutta walked over to the podium and spoke in short staccato sentences.

"Kachchh is symptomatic of the overall Pak design. They call it ***Operation Hikmat.*** Attack in this sector is imminent. Pakistan is preparing for another round of conflict in Kashmir too. It has recently acquired 80 tanks, 200 armoured personnel carriers, 60 pieces of long range field guns and advanced varieties of field rifles. We've reports of the arrival of three squadrons of US fighter bombers through Iran, Turkey and Saudi circuits."

"When do you expect the attack on Kashmir?" The PM asked.

"Sir, we've noticed infiltration by trained regulars, in the guise of tribals, in the Punchch-Rajouri sectors. Some of these have been trained in the NWFP camps run by a religious leader belonging to the Hazara tribe. Pakistan feels that India is passing through internal turmoil and power struggle in the ruling party and it wasn't prepared to take them on after the Chinese war humiliation. We expect Kachchh to be followed by Kashmir, before heavy snowfall starts, say around September-October. The Pakistani thrust, code named ***Operation Gibraltar*** is in the final stages of implementation."

"What's our position in the Kachchh? "

"Militarily, I think the position is very unsatisfactory. Our presence on the ground is very thin."

"Can't we rush fresh troops and tank formations?" The PM looked anxiously at the COAS.

A wall mounted red phone rang twice sharply. A duty sergeant picked up the receiver, listened for about two seconds and turned to the COAS.

"Sir, this call's from Bhuj."

General Arobindo Mukherjee walked up elegantly.

"When?" He asked, listened for a short while and reported back to the PM.

"Sir, there has been a terrible accident. The DC3 in which Chief Minister, Dalpat Rai Mehta was flying inside our territory, along the Pak border, has been brought down by Pakistani ground fire. The wreckage has fallen in our territory and the CM is dead."

Jung Bahadur stood up, his short frame apparently agitated.

"Inform the Cabinet Committee for Security Affairs (CCSA) to assemble in ten minutes," The PM directed his personal secretary.

"And ask the Cabinet, Home and Defence secretaries, Chiefs of the Services to remain present. You also come and bring Kumar with you." The PM asked his FIB chief.

This was a clear snub to Nampoothiri. He was the master spy operator inside Pakistan and was responsible for developing all sensitive strategic and tactical intelligence. It was strange for the PM to repose trust in Kumar Anand Prasad, responsible for internal intelligence. A whirlpool of disturbance started gurgling inside his intestines. This was unfair. Kachchh wasn't a simple Ganges fish, to be hooked and cooked by the legendary fishmonger of the ***Mallah*** dynasty.

The Chief of Army Staff, General Mukherjee picked up his cap and looked at Nampoothiri.

"Aren't you coming Balls?"

"You heard the PM, he wants that fishmonger to be at the CCSA meeting."

"What's wrong?"

"Perhaps, he thinks I'm more loyal to his rival, the PM in waiting." Nampoothiri threw a meaningful smile at his golf partner.

"Best of luck. Come over after the CCSA. I'd like to have a chat on the probable scenarios. I find it difficult to digest incoherent eructation from both orifices of your colleague, Prasad. Why don't you ask him to consume less garlic?"

"He takes several concoctions of garlic to increase sexual potency." Both of them laughed heartily and left.

That night, the CCSA, after prolonged deliberations, decided to meet the Pakistani invasion with appropriate military responses. The COAS, however, declined to divert additional troops to the troubled Gujarat border. He had priority tasks to attend to in Punjab and Kashmir borders, the Defence Minister explained.

As the PM prepared for a well-deserved retreat to his residence after another round of situation briefing session with the FIB chief, Mandira stormed her way in.

"What's the matter dear Manu?" Asked a visibly annoyed Jung Bahadur.

"I want to visit Bhuj. I want to be with the people at this moment of crisis."

"It's not possible. The forces have started rolling and I can't expose you to the enemy shelling."

He spoke slowly, an innocent smile lingering on his face.

"I want to be with my people at this point of time." Mandira repeated impatiently.

"Take your turn darling. I'm still in command." Jung Bahadur replied in a flat tone and diverted his eyes to some files.

Mandira stomped out in disgust. She briskly walked down towards the room of Nampoothiri, the FIB Deputy Director.

"Mr. Nampoothiri, tell me what's happening in Kachchh."

Nampoothiri was floored by the sudden and unannounced entry of the junior minister. It was uncommon for a government minister to drop in through the roof and demand an intelligence briefing. But Mandira was different. Her father had ruled the country for good 17 years and she felt she had a right to walk into his shoes. That spoilsport Jung Bahadur was an unnecessary interlude.

Nampoothiri stood up, made her comfortable on a sofa and asked if she would care for a cup of coffee.

Mandira gave him an appreciative look and settled for black coffee. She wondered at the way this man understood her mood.

Over cups of coffee, they settled down for a long session, discussing the scenario frame by frame. She was quick on the uptake and Nampoothiri appreciated her sharpness.

"Tell me," Mandira intervened, "If I'm not over curious, are we really any match for the Pakistani intelligence penetration in India? "

"Well, there are ways to describe the situation," Nampoothiri dithered, "They've natural advantages over us."

"And how're we placed militarily?"

"They've more advanced aircraft and tanks. Our main problem is lack of preparation in the entire western front." Replied the intelligence deputy.

"Why? What prevents us?"

"Our strategic pole is still aligned to China. We've ignored the disturbing signals in Kashmir. As you're aware Pakistan has started infiltrating its irregulars in the Poonch and Uri sectors."

"Thanks Balu. I must fly to Srinagar. I must be with the people. They need me."

Mandira spoke in a soft and possessed voice and left Nampoothiri absolutely clueless. The whirlwind visit was curious and alarming. The snoopers operating on behalf of Kumar Anand were sure not to miss the private powwow and carry tales back to the PM's office.

Hell with it! Nampoothiri shrugged.

He collected the papers on the latest target-Operation Triple X and concentrated on the technical reports submitted by Nirmal Mitra.

Chapter 7

The procession arrived at 19.30 hrs sharp, strictly according to protocol, headed by Pradumnya Karnik and tailed by Dhiren Bhagat.

"Good evening sir." Karnik greeted the boss.

Nampoothiri didn't respond. His eyes were glued to copies of diplomatic telegrams from Karachi and Rawalpindi on Kachchh war situation.

"So Karnik," Nampoothiri shuffled the telegrams under a folio cover and asked,"What brings the gang here?"

"Sir, you desired a briefing on the Triple X target."

"Oh yes! What do you think? Is the target ready for recruitment?" Nampoothiri asked with a hint of a naughty smile.

"Sir, let's hear Bhagat out. He's the main handler or you may say the master chef." Karnik replied, vainly trying to hide his discordant vibe behind the raw humour.

"You should give us your impression Karnik. I depend on you totally." Nampoothiri spoke with an impish smile.

"What can I say sir?" Karnik blushed.

Was he caught, pants down by the boss? Did Dhiren Bhagat carry tales to the archrival of Kumar Anand?

"Let Bhagat speak sir." He added peevishly.

The story from the beginning to date was lengthy and intricately textured. The daring technical operation fascinated Nampoothiri. But a mist of gloom suddenly generated an ache somewhere in his heart. He rued with silent and deepest regret his colossal amnesia. He had simply forgotten to warn the health secretary, Alladi Subhash Chandra Rao, about the imminent danger to his daughter.

Nampoothiri begged to be excused and rushed into the toilet. He looked at the mirror. The wrinkled face and black shadows under the eyes reflected his tormented psyche.

Did he commit a mistake? Was it deliberate? Perhaps yes. The smoking anxiety over the succession battle had burnt out his reflexes. Yes. The fire was still raging, burning him down to ashes. What the hell was he doing in this damn FIB? That bloody Kumar Anand was sure to walk away with the cake.

What was damn Karnik up to? Was this Konkani asshole trying to implicate him in a devastating scandal!

Nampoothiri felt sorry for Hema. But wasn't perturbed over the moral implications of the operation. In his profession moral scruples normally took the back seat. It was by far the most immoral profession, a few degrees on the higher side, than professional prostitution. The latter had some occasional privilege of choosing a business partner. He didn't. To him a task was a task and no price was insurmountable. It was a war; a war of wits and prick of the conscience wasn't charted out as an ingredient of the tradecraft.

Nampoothiri momentarily paused. Hema could've been saved and she needn't have died a grisly death. He splashed his face and eyes with cool water, perhaps to wash away the momentary pangs of guilt. He re-emerged from the toilet and called in Jatadhari and ordered coffee and Havana.

"So, where were we?" Asked Nampoothiri.

Bhagat narrated the nuts and bolts of the story. But he skipped details on the Matang Singh and Hema episodes.

Karnik felt ill at ease. Bhagat was trying to protect his hide, as well as that of his super boss, Nampoothiri. Two murders and a rape had taken place with the virtual FIB collaboration. What for? Just for the sake of an idiotic operation? His eye suddenly crossed glances with Nampoothiri's eagle squint. He felt a dozen darting electrodes piercing his corneal film.

Nampoothiri didn't shift his gaze. He finished the coffee and asked Karnik in a contrived pleasant voice, "You've been looking for a posting abroad. Would you like Moscow?"

Karnik, for a while couldn't detect the catch. Was it a trap to bargain his silence? Was the foggy Balls trying to remove another prop of Kumar Anand?

"Sir, let me talk to my wife. Thanks for the offer any way."

"Let me know. We're in a hurry. You have to move immediately." He sucked the Havana with an unusual loud sound and turned to Bhagat," You can stay back for a while."

The meeting over, Karnik went out a worried man. Nampoothiri had played his trump card well to buy his silence. Well! Moscow wasn't a bad place to go to, and not too bad an incentive to keep his trap shut. Why wait for Prasad? Hema had received a nice funeral; Matang's bronze bust was soon going to decorate the University premises. And Nampoothiri was very happy with Dhiren Bhagat and his pet Triple X target.

The direct boss being visibly happy, he could now afford to offer a few flowers less, to his former godfather, Kumar Anand Prasad. It wasn't unusual in Hindu practice to shift loyalty from one deity to another. They interchanged positions at regular intervals. Some days Shiva took precedence over Vishnu, some days Hanuman over Rama.

So, Nampoothiri, the present presiding deity was okay. Moscow was fine, so was his golden silence!

"What do you feel?" Asked Nampoothiri, "Is Karnik serious with the operation?"

"You know better sir." Bhagat parried the embarrassing question.

"Fine. I don't want any more intermediary. Report to me directly. I want all the video and audiotapes and the still positives and negatives. Seal them in a cover and hand them over to me by 9 p.m. tonight. Understood?" Nampoothiri directed Bhagat.

"Yes sir, the job will be done." Bhagat got the message straight. The boss was building up defences.

"And no one moves about in the organisation with leaking cans. There should be no juicy story about Triple X going about the place."

"No problem sir. But how do we accost him now?"

"Use the direct approach. He's now a cornered scarecrow. Take precautions. I expect him to behave like a coward. A bully can't stand up to crisis. He generally fumbles and caves in."

"What about his political clout? Ram Karan may interfere."

"Leave that to me. I'll brief the boss and he'll take care of the political crust. Meet Maulana Rizwan and Colonel Pathania personally and brief them about the training aspects."

Nampoothiri dismissed Bhagat and called in Amrita Bhalla.

In two separate notes he recommended the immediate posting of Pradumnya Karnik to the Moscow FIB station, and the award of a National Medal for meritorious services to Dhiren Bhagat, on the occasion of Independence Day 1965. The officer had done a remarkable job.

Nampoothiri felt relaxed. Closed his eyes. He tried to visualise his favourite longboat race on ***Onam*** (New Year) day, in the backwaters of Cochin. The feeling of smoothsailing, the splashing sounds of oars and lilting folk tunes slackened his eye muscles. He momentarily lapsed into a catnap.

****

Jhun Jhunu, a sleepy town in Rajasthan, boasted of several exquisite marble ***havelis*** (old style houses) and a famous ***Sati*** (woman burnt alive in husband's funeral pyre) temple. The exquisite marble edifice, raised about seventy years back, attracted millions of Hindu devotees. They paid homage to ***Sati Mata***, a fifteen-year-old bride, who was burnt alive in the funeral pyre of her eighty-year-old husband, just two days after her marriage.

This ghoulish religious practice, fertile Brahmin minds ordained, was the ultimate offering to womanhood, whose status in traditional Hindu society oscillated between damnation and deification.

Jhun Jhunu was also advertised in Delhi University campus, as the most important principality in Rajasthan, the lair of its famous lion, Prince Ramendra Kaushal.

His maternal uncle, a Sukhram Chakrapani, well versed in English and Persian language, was appointed ***Dewan*** (minister) in the court of a local king. He owned several ***havelis,*** 500 acres of agricultural land, 1000 cows and few business establishments.

A childless Brahmin, Kaushalya's brother and Dayaram Kaushal's brother-in-law, Sukhram Chakrapani had amassed fabulous wealth. His critics alleged that most of his wealth came from the coffers of an affluent Marwari businessman, Seth Mangeram Chuniram Dhuria.

Dhuria claimed the presence of his ancestors under the same Banyan tree, from where Job Charnok, the English trader and alleged founder of Calcutta, traded jute, silk and other assorted merchandise. Dhuria's fabulous business house was as ancient as the Company Bahadur's (East India Company) empire.

Seth Dhuria, it's alleged, had persuaded Sukhram, to seed his barren wife with his holy sperm. Dhuria wasn't impotent. He suffered from a rare infirmity. His sperms, the specialist said, suffered from genetic deformity. These seeds of life couldn't swim past the ocean of life and fertilise the eggs in his wife's womb.

Taking more than one wife wasn't a social taboo in his part of dusty and rusty India. But he didn't. His ***sethani*** (wife) had brought him a fabulous inheritance, almost all that made him stinking rich. His swanky ***sethani*** fed well on saturated milk fat and ***palangtor*** (a sweetmeat potent enough to endow strength to break a cot during copulation) came from the family of another stinking rich Marwari. And she was the legal heir to her father's business empire spread over to Calcutta in the east and Bombay and Surat in the west. And Dhuria didn't want to be deprived of an additional empire by marrying another woman.

What the hell could he do in the name of Lord Gopal (a variant for legendary Krishna), to avoid landing up in the howling fire of hell! After all, a son saved the soul of a Hindu from visitation to a hell called ***Put***. That's why a son was called ***Putra.*** He must have a son to save his soul and to keep the fabulous wealth of his father-in-law in his line. Failing which, the inheritance was supposed to revert back to his wife's remote male cousin.

And what about his own empire! He couldn't scatter his wealth away among the wolves and jackals, masquerading as his brothers.

The decision to hire Sukhram to seed his wife was taken on the advice of Brahmins from the holy city of Kashi (Benaras). It wasn't a new invention. Didn't the ***Mahabharata*** famed ***Pandu*** resort to the seeding of his wives by males out of wedlock, including one of low origin, to save his lineage and to ensure succession to the throne? Wasn't Hindu mythology replete with instances of seeding of women by hired males? The divine stories depicted series of cosmic drama with countless incidents of chasing women, wife grabbing, swapping and tales of endless debauchery.

On an auspicious full moon night, with the sun in conjunction with ***Ashwini*** (a constellation), Sukhram Chakrapani poured his seeds into the womb of the wife of Seth Mangeram Chuniram Dhuria, making him a proud father of a son.

But poor Chakrapani didn't have a child of his own. Ramendra Kaushal, besides being the son of a deprived and deposed king, was therefore, the natural heir to the properties of his maternal uncle.

Jhun Jhunu, on that balmy morning, was in a festive mood, observing a rare sacred festival after a gap of, may be 70 years.

Seth Mangeram Chuniram Dhuria had expired, three days back in Calcutta. The uncouth obese fellow had died of a heart attack. Relatives, who eyed him for his treasure chest and business empire, however, didn't hesitate to reveal that Dhuria had, in fact, collapsed while trying to mount a bombshell of a beauty. She was imported all the way from Goa; to give a live performance in one of the joints owned by Dhuria. An excited but not aroused Dhuria gulped down a few extra pegs and finally collapsed on her body, even before he could position himself on the hot beauty. He didn't wake up. His heart had ceased beating.

Dhuria's body was flown to Jhun Jhunu in a private Dakota for cremation at the bank of a pond, locally revered as ***Sati Mai Ki Pokhri*** (pond of goddess Sati), named after ***Sati Mata***, who was ritually burnt at the funeral pyre of her husband 70 years ago.

Dhiren Bhagat had chanced to reach Jhun Jhunu on an auspicious day. ***Sati Mata***'s mantle was being thrust on Dhuria's wife. Two brothers of Dhuria had roped in a few Brahmins, who passed an edict that ***Satirani***, wife of late Mangeram Chuniram Dhuria surprisingly matched all the signs of the ***Sati Mata,*** hitherto undiscovered.

And how could they discover these divine signs earlier? An orthodox Hindu woman, the ***sethani*** hardly removed her head cover, called ***pallu***. Even the sun and moon couldn't dare bathe her skin.

Only the divine mendicants from the holy city of Hardwar could envision such sacred signs, through their divine X-ray vision. Their holy vision was activated by payment of a hefty compensation package. The Hindu pantheon was flexible enough to accommodate all such contingencies.

Sukhram Chakrapani opposed the idea, not because ***Satirani,*** Dhuria's wife had once carried his seeds. With her death Dhuria's brothers wouldn't take minutes to boot him out. The fact of his seeding the wife of their brother wasn't a great secret. The midwife, who helped deliver the child, had sold the information to them for one acre of fertile agricultural land.

That knowledge was precious enough to disinherit the minor kid.

Understandably, Sukhram was busy mobilising public opinion against the ***Sati*** ceremony and motivating his nephew and adopted son, Ramendra Kaushal to use his muscle and political clout.

Ramendra Kaushal, seated under the canopy of a gas station was directing his goons to prevent people from participating in the bride burning ceremony. The gas station, next to Pundit Sukhram's house was Ramendra Kaushal's favourite hunting ground.

Another favourite joint of Ramendra was the Shiva temple across the road, named after a former potentate. Shiva, the eternal phallus god, a symbol of fertility worship, was dear to the former king. Legends attributed to him super-human sexual prowess, requiring at least five women every night. His son had established the marble edifice with a view to immortalising his father's fabled masculine attributes that had left behind one legal inheritor and dozens of disinherited bonded serfs.

Ramendra Kaushal wasn't bothered about the bride burning ceremony. He never bothered about sanctity of women. Like the deified potentate, immortalised in the temple across, he had scant respect for them. He was concerned with Sukhram's promise of some extra money, if the job was well done.

Kaushal noticed first with a sense of disbelief. That Commie looking Blue Dart bookseller was standing under the portico of the ***Shiva*** temple. The trademark bag hung from his shoulders. The blighted bookseller had the temerity to follow him here too! What bloody book could he sell here in the desert town of Jhun Jhunu?

Could he be a police informer?

My goodness! Kaushal recoiled inside himself like an injured snake and started scheming for self-defence. The insect must be smothered out, pulverised to dust and thrown to the mercy of the desert scorpions, better still, into the funeral pyre of Dhuria.

"Bhero," Kaushal called out loudly to a midget of a man, with a mismatched big moustache," Go and fetch that bastard."

Bhagat obliged. He walked alongside the dwarf and coolly took a seat next to Kaushal.

"Haven't I seen you in Delhi?" Kaushal asked in a stern voice.

"Correct," Bhagat didn't remove his eyes from those of Kaushal, "We met at Blue Dart Restaurant, behind the Raj Ghat lane and Divine Inn, perhaps."

"Get lost. I don't want to see your face here. This is Jhun Jhunu, not fucking Delhi." Ramendra Kaushal stared menacingly at Bhagat.

Bhagat, a rare smoker, took out a cigarette and offered one to Kaushal.

"I feel like smoking and don't feel like igniting the petrol tanks. Can we take a small walk?"

Bhagat's cool voice unnerved Kaushal. However, the snake inside wasn't yet ready to lower its hood. His eyes narrowed down to mere slits and his voice hissed.

"You're putting your hands in a snake-hole." In a quick move Kaushal slithered his right hand in his trouser pocket and felt the cold steel.

Bhagat followed his manoeuvre and spoke softly.

"Look across the street. Do you see two persons under the portico of the temple? They carry two pistols each and I've one. Between us, we've one hundred rounds to pump into your body. And for your information, we're from the Delhi Police."

He produced a photo identity card, a fabricated one obviously; a deception often practised by FIB officials. Bhagat usually carried on his person half a dozen ID cards of various government departments.

Ramendra Kaushal suddenly shrunk back, like a leech bouncing against a salt pile. Nampoothiri wasn't far from the truth. A bully often turned out to be a coward.

"Let's go out and see the fun."

Bhagat led Kaushal towards ***Sati Mai ki Pokhri***, a big pond, around which the great religious perfidy of human sacrifice was being perpetrated.

The place was now milling with crowd, singing and dancing in praise of Satirani. At a far corner of the pond, next to the temple of ***Sati Mata***, a group of women, seated in circle, sang and swung to the beats of percussion drums and cymbals. One young woman, bejewelled and decked in a costly ***lehanga*** (skirt) swung her body in a circular motion, beating the ground with a green twig. She was supposed to have been possessed by the spirit of the fifteen-year-old girl, who was burnt alive and deified seven decades ago.

A funeral pyre was decked up with sandalwood, pure milk fat and other holy ingredients, about 50 yds north of the temple.

Pundit Sukhram stood at the far edge of the pond, trying to mobilize some of his supporters. Most of the villagers avoided him and jostled with each other to snatch fat portions of the sumptuous food, a rare treat for the desert tribes. They hadn't had a royal treat like this one in their living memory. They were a motley crowd, high on marijuana trip and religious intoxicants

Dhiren Bhagat followed by Kaushal and two other FIB sleuths proceeded towards a cluster of Banyan trees, located on a raised ground that overlooked the pond and the funeral pyre. He lighted a cigarette and offered one to Kaushal.

"Why are you bothering me? What's your problem? How much money do you want?" Kaushal asked while fiddling with the cigarette.

"You can reserve that grease for your God. You know dear, the problem is yours. We know and the law knows, what all you've done. A few murders and a couple of rapes and drug smuggling."

Bhagat flicked the lighter and helped a frozen Kaushal to light his cigarette.

"You've no proof. I've powerful friends in Delhi."

"We know. Ram Karan, you mean?"

"Not Karan sahib alone."

"Well. Mandira isn't in the habit of using a dirty towel twice. They've seen the video and audio evidences of your heinous crimes. And Ram Karan knows when to drop parasites like you." Bhagat hurled a mighty bluff.

"You require proof to arrest me."

Ramendra Kaushal chocked out and spoke in a voice that seemed as if the last ounce of air was escaping his deflated rib cage

"That's not what I intend to do."

Bhagat shifted to a smooth boulder and took out a bunch of photographs from his shoulder bag and handed them over to Kaushal.

Kaushal shuffled through the photographs with an ashen face and a dead fish look. These were black and white witnesses to his acts of crime, the murder of Matang Singh and the rape of Hema's cadaver.

"You can't blackmail me. I've powerful friends in Delhi," Kaushal returned the photographs and tried to put up a brave front, "These are trick jobs. You can't prove anything against me."

"You've only two options," Bhagat put the photographs back in the shoulder bag, and placed his right hand on Kaushal's shoulder," Either you come with me or I arrest you."

"You've no proof." Kaushal made a feeble effort to put Bhagat off.

"We've real video reels of all of your black deeds, and your political friends have already viewed these materials. We don't take false steps." Bhagat spoke firmly.

"What're you going to do with me?"

"We shall talk. Come along."

"Where are you taking me?"

"The first leg of the journey takes us to Delhi."

"Give me half an hour. I've to meet my mother. Please don't mention anything to her."

"Not at all. But my office has an envelope ready for her, if you don't co-operate." Bhagat hurled across a tricky threat.

"Don't give her pain. I'm the man you want, and I'm ready to co-operate." Kaushal finally surrendered.

As they walked down the shaded high ground, Bhagat heard the loud chanting of ***mantras*** (couplets from scriptures), invoking the Fire God and assorted deities.

Amidst thundering applause, Satirani's relations dragged her drugged nimble body to the funeral pyre and forced her to sit on it with the head of her dead husband on her lap. Clad in a bright red sari, profuse red vermilion powder on her forehead and piles of marigold garlands around her neck, Satirani looked like a scared goat, under the butcher's crossbar.

She had reconciled with the inevitable. Amidst frenetic singing, loud drum and cymbal beats and the chanting of ***mantras***, a Brahmin handed over a flaming torch to Mangeram's young son. It was the sacred duty of every Hindu son, to lit the funeral pyre of his parents. He was fortunate, a ***pundit*** commented, to perform the last rites of both the parents; a rare opportunity sought after even by the Saints and Gods.

The puzzled kid looked around, threw away the torch and jumped into the pyre. Satirani clutched her son firmly to her bosom and leaped out.

Some Brahmins snatched the kid away; forced Satirani back on the pyre and lit the fat soaked wooden heap to flames. Yellow flames engulfed the corpse of Dhuria and his drugged wife with a loud bang.

The crowd, estimated at a cool 10,000 went ecstatic in delirious singing and dancing, under the influence of ***bhang,*** a concoction prepared out of green female marijuana leaves and flowers.

Satirani stopped flinging her limbs about and slumped onto the pyre. Some one from the crowd banged the burning bodies with bamboo rods, a ritual observed by the Hindus, for breaking the skull of the dead.

Bhagat looked on in silence and sighed.

There was no use in intervening.

Satirani, in another two hours, would get her place in the honour list of Hindu gods, the second ***Sati Mata*** of dusty Jhun Jhunu. Perhaps another all-white marble temple would come up on her funeral pyre. Village folks would sing in her praise; another goddess added to the innumerable pantheon of Hindu deities, they worshipped.

The ***neem*** (margosa) tree in front of Pundit Sukhram's ***haveli*** acted as a good cover for Bhagat. He whispered into Kaushal's ears to hurry back, as he entered the low ornate gate, leading to the inner courtyard. No dirty tricks, he reminded the caged typhoon, that the officials of Delhi police had surrounded the house and they wouldn't hesitate to force an entry and accost his mother.

"Spare me the humiliation. My mother won't survive the shock." Kaushal pleaded.

"Just remember, no amount of political skulduggery will help." Bhagat warned.

"You're blackmailing me."

"From now on I call the shots." Bhagat answered coolly.

Kaushalya, prevented by her brother, had missed the chance of a lifetime, to witness the holy soul of Satirani rising to the heavens, with the spiralling funeral pyre smoke and dust. She stood near the exquisitely carved window, opening on a small balcony and stretched her neck to catch glimpses of the ascending soul of the just burnt divine woman.

She had dreamt all her life, of immolating herself at the funeral pyre of her husband, bedecked in the finest jewellery and a gold-laced red Banarasi sari. That was the only way for a Hindu woman to die. But back in Jhumra, the court minister, the royal medico and the chief cook had prevailed upon her to escape to India, with her young son. The Niazi tribal raiders, the royal advisors said, had no respect for women and kids. She should live for the inheritor, their son and the only heir to the kingdom.

There was no time left for a ceremonial cremation of her husband. She didn't know if he got a decent one at all. Things were different, they said. Hindus and Muslims had swallowed the bait of communal divide; a blood soaked bitter bait, what they proclaimed as independence. The aged leaders, tired of struggling, especially after the excruciating experiences of the 1942 incarcerations, were disinclined to undertake further, the undefined and uncertain struggle. Power, in any form was welcome to them, even if it came through the surging rivers of human blood and corpses. The tired leaders of 1947 had pushed the people to the brink of a devastating infernal disaster.

"Ma." Ramendra Kaushal meekly stood behind her and spoke in a submissive voice.

"Come Ramu," She climbed down the stairs and from her thoughts, which were meandering over the glens and hillocks of Jhumra.

"Feeling hungry?"

"Yes Ma. But I've to leave for Delhi just now."

Ramendra followed her to the kitchen.

"What's the hurry? You came just two days ago."

She served some sweet made out of grated carrot and condensed milk, fondly called ***gajar ka halua***.

"I've got an excellent job offer, a highly paid one."

Kaushal spoke hesitatingly and with evading looks.

"Where? In Delhi?"

"No Ma. It's in ***vilayat*** (England). I must report to Delhi tomorrow for the interview. I may not be able to meet you frequently. But I'll keep you posted."

He touched her feet in traditional obeisance and locked her in a firm embrace.

"Come home once before you go to ***vilayat***. I must perform a ***yagna*** (ritual sacrifice). Your father had performed one, before he went to see the King Emperor in England, soon after my marriage."

Kaushalya reminisced briefly on the historic sojourn of her late husband, to attend a meeting of the Indian Princes with the King Emperor. That was a memorable journey, accompanied by cooks, valets and Brahmins. He was forced to perform a penance for undertaking a journey across ***kalapani*** (high seas), banned for Hindus, by the sacred Brahminic dictate.

Kaushalya drew Ramendra's head closer, kissed his forehead and blessed him with some dried pieces of flower and green grass; picked from offerings to the family deity.

For the second time, Kaushal's eyes moistened up and tears rolled down his cheeks. The brute gave away to faint but sublime changes. The human in him resurfaced steadily, out of piled up debris of crime and the shattered pieces of his wild life. Ramendra Kaushal wiped away the teardrops and smiled faintly. His punishment and retribution had probably begun.

He shrugged. Okay, fine!

He would face the new life with grit and determination.

The widow of king Dayaram Kaushal raised her folded palms in praise of the Mother Goddess. Her son was sure to restore the family glory. She must convey this to Rama. The poor soul should have the pleasure of knowing that her son had really made it big in life, bagging a job in England, at such a tender age. He was indeed cast in his father's mould.

That night, leaving a mad Jhun Jhunu and his grieving mother behind, Ramendra Kaushal boarded Dhiren Bhagat's car and the wings of an uncertain destiny.

Chapter 8

Triple X, Harfan Bukhari's meteoric arrival in Delhi on the wings of blazing bolts had, for a while, exposed the raw wounds of the National Security India. It sent Balachandran Nampoothiri in a spin over the sudden collapse of India's intelligence edifices inside Pakistan. His exclusive niche that had housed the brightest cluster of long-term resident agents in Pakistan had suddenly exploded. It had left Nampoothiri with the somewhat impossible task of putting back the debris to reasonable coherent collage.

Shocking disclosures by XXX and the subsequent events had left the powers that be in no doubt that agent Double X, Ibadat, was dead correct about the blitzkrieg by Pakistan. His insistence that some whore, dough and Scotch loving guy, a top bureaucrat perhaps, was singing honey in Pakistani ears over India's nuclear secrets, however, kept on foxing India's external intelligence chief. He had no clue to the riddle.

Blanket Mosur and TechInt operations had drawn a complete blank. The NSI telephone monitors had given up hope of homing on to the blue moon, the suspect lines, that could lead to the mysterious elf at the top slot. The target diplomats talked about smell of cordite in the air and dames and drinks, as usual. Nampoothiri was worried to the bone.

"Sir can I come in?" Amrita Bhalla's voice chimed on the intercom.

"Yes dear. Welcome."

Amrita entered with elegant but excited steps, with a headphone in her hand. She plugged the accessory to an embedded socket and placed it on Nampoothiri's ears.

"What's this?"

"Shh! Please listen first. The boys have hit a gold mine." Amrita took a seat and waited for the call to be over.

"Amen, how's the day?" Patrick Goldman, Minister Counsellor in the US embassy, Delhi, whispered on the phone.

"Fine Pat." Replied Amen Gurtoo, Principal Secretary to Prime Minister Mandira, "All work and no fun, no weekend for me. You're damn lucky. What's cooking?"

"You Indians work like slaves and are damn clipped to the empire's gown-frills. Get past it buddy."

"Wish I could. Perhaps you haven't worked in the White House. The flunkies over there too don't have count of time. And my boss is a tough task master, oops... mistress...sorry, or should I say ma'am." Replied Gurtoo with a light voice and followed up with his trademark, shallow, loud laughter.

"I envy you. You can laugh even at a dead corpse."

"As they say chum, laugh it away and fuck it away." Amen transmitted another volley of laughter over the phone.

"Drop in at my Sheryl Street den. Plenty of laughter and pleasure is waiting for you. Recall Maggie? She's just flown in from Islamabad. This one butterfly is still fabs; if she hasn't added more colours from the rainbows and replenished her pod with sylvan nectar."

Goldman sounded extra smooth, like 200-year-old Scotch, just salvaged from the depth of the Pacific, from a sunken pirate vessel.

"Don't entice me pal. What about Joey?"

Amen cautiously enquired about Goldman's wife, a puritan lady from American Midwest.

"She's back home. Her mother's taken another divorce and plans to marry a Texan tycoon. She's there to celebrate, her mom's third nuptial knot." Replied Pat.

"Fine. Expect me around eight." Amen disconnected with a happy chuckle.

"Thank you dear," Nampoothiri sprang back to life, "Let's celebrate."

He pressed the buzzer and ordered Jatadhari to concoct two strong cappuccinos.

"How did you get the lead?"

"It's your top floor boy Zapurello Angami. He chanced to hit the line and I just patched it to your table." Amrita smiled back.

"Thanks dear. I must reward that Naga boy. He deserves it."

Nampoothiri thought he had earned a celebration for himself. The barren spell was perhaps over, he hoped.

Triple X had brought in damning reports about leakage of India's nuclear secrets and secret battle orders in the western theatre. A verbatim report of the CCSA meetings (Cabinet Committee for Security Affairs), if Triple X was to be believed, had found its way to the table of the ISI chief.

A fax intercept of the Pakistan High Commission's dedicated link to Islamabad had exploded another bombshell. The Mission had faxed a copy of an NSI report to the PMO on Pakistani defence preparedness in the eastern sector. Agent Double X had procured the sensitive report, a few days before his death, from a well-placed chameleon in the Chief Martial Law Administrator's office.

Nampoothiri's Mosur, radio bugging and telephone-tapping operations had eliminated almost all the listed suspects, except Amen Gurtoo and secretary of the Atomic Energy Commission. His list of suspects also included Rajinder Singh Dewan, Special Assistant to the PM Mandira. All papers to the PM passed through him.

Telephone taps on the secretary AEC and Dewan had proved sterile.

But the chance detection of the dialogue between Amen and Goldman, Nampoothiri thought should break the embarrassingly dry spell.

He lifted the red RAX communicator and dialled Dewan.

"Good evening friend."

"What good is left of the evening? We've just walked into another war." Dewan replied in his usual jocular voice.

"Some wars are good and inevitable and war is just another form of diplomacy. Don't you fight with your wife when your charms fail you?"

"Well Balu, I'm a bachelor. You should know better."

"Curse me," Nampoothiri regretted his forgetfulness and added, "How is the PM placed?"

"Please hurry. She should leave for the President's Palace in another thirty minutes."

Mandira was busy in her camp office that was transformed into a war-ops room with maps and charts mounted all over the walls. The Director, Military Operations (DMO) was explaining the battle orders of the Armed Forces, punctuated on the grid maps with coloured pins and markers. What worried her most was the deployment of the ragtag Bengali freedom fighters. The motley-armed volunteers were practically leaderless and divided on ideological lines.

"How are you going to integrate these irregular formations with your regulars?" She asked the DMO.

"We've scattered them with our brigades and battalions deployed all along the borders. I think you'd like to see their linkages and assigned roles." The moustachioed Major General unfolded a sheet map and started explaining the nitty-gritty of deployment of the assorted forces of the ***Mukti Bahini*** (freedom fighters).

Dewan peeped in and rattled his throat.

"Ma'am, Nampoothiri is here."

"I'm busy."

"He says it's important."

She looked up with an annoyed look and finally broke into a faint smile.

"Okay. Make him comfortable. I'm coming."

Nampoothiri explained the importance of the telephone intercept and asked her permission to investigate Amen Gurtoo, her Principal Secretary.

"What's special about this? It can be a social commitment." Mandira shrugged and brushed off her external intelligence chief's concern.

"It can be. But ma'am I suspect a classical intelligence sharing protocol between the CIA, ISI and MI6; long standing partners in the strategic security thrust against the USSR, China and the amorphous ghost of Communism around the globe. Our agent Double X had broadly indicated the possible involvement of the CIA station chief in Delhi." Nampoothiri disclosed.

"How do you go about nabbing the US intelligence chief in Delhi? The subtleties of diplomacy shouldn't be ignored. The war situation impedes us from adopting an open hostile stance against the US."

"We can't trust them. They've been tilting towards Pakistan." Nampoothiri commented.

"I don't care about Washington's tilt," Mandira talked in a contemplative mood, "The US is insensitive to the problems of the largest democracy. They're suffering from a cold-war obsession."

"Correct ma'am. The CIA despatches from Delhi are critical of your Pakistan strategy," Nampoothiri continued, "East Pakistan's war of liberation is India's proxy war in East Pakistan, that's what the Secretary of State stated in a recent press conference."

"Don't bother," Mandira was in a contemplative mood, "Neither do I trust the US President and his warmonger Jewish Secretary of State. The US is in the habit of propping up tin-pot dictators. And they're building new bridges with Peking."

"If Washington leans towards Peking, Moscow should tilt towards us." Nampoothiri nodded in agreement.

"You take care Balu. Strengthen your tentacles inside Pakistan. I don't want an intelligence black out there."

"Yes ma'am." Nampoothiri repeated monotonously.

"What about your guests from Pakistan? Have you started debriefing them?" Mandira hinted at Harfan Bukhari and Voodoorume, the South African pilot.

"Your orders are awaited."

"Let me have a precise account of the weapon systems airlifted by the mercenary flights. It's urgent. And let me have an assessment of the damage suffered by your agency in Pakistan."

"The guests are co-operative. The South African pilot has spelt out precise details of some of the flights and I expect Triple X to come out with more sensitive disclosures."

"Fine. Go ahead." Mandira stood up and gestured moving towards her ops room.

"Do I investigate Amen?"

Mandira turned back, collected her thoughts for a few seconds and gave a silent nod of affirmation.

Nampoothiri felt relaxed after the satisfying encounter with the PM. The nod from her had cleared the decks for a thorough interrogation of Triple X. And investigating Amen Gurtoo's links with the diplomatic Mission based intelligence officers should pose no great problem. The CIA station chief was too well recorded a client in the NSI's honour roll.

His gut feel pushed back the arrows of thought to Amen Gurtoo's past.

Amen was no amateur butterfly hunter. His records were impressive. Son of a retired General of the Imperial and Indian army, he was a famous honeybee of his time. A graduate from University College, Amen had hit the bottle very early. Fond of flashy dresses and feminine flesh, he had perfected the art and science of alluring young and not too young women. They invariably cat walked to his bed.

He claimed, he could say for sure, how many hours he would take to floor a woman, after the first encounter. An accomplished artist in late night group orgies, Amen was never tired of advertising his deft manipulation of a newly wed bride, travelling from Dehradun to Delhi. Seated in a crammed train, next to the bride, Amen took advantage of the darkness, kissed her, squeezed her breasts and even tried to reach her private parts. The young bride happened to cast embarrassed looks, in absolute disbelief and amazement at her husband, a schoolteacher, seated on her right flank. The poor fellow was fast asleep, snoring away merrily.

The dumb village belle looked to her left and saw the demonic and vile eyes of Amen. She cried out loudly and fainted.

His intimate circle, Amen boasted, had bought this story as a totem of his masculine excellence. Some interpreted it as the limit of his profligacy.

Amen failed to keep alive the family tradition of making it to the Indian Military Academy. Papa Gurtoo, General Raghavendra, a class fellow of Amritlal at Harrow, secured a position for his son in the Indian Frontier Administrative Service.

Amritlal, keen on following the British policy of grand exclusion and isolation of the tribal areas of the northeast, had hit upon the idea of recruiting young and not so young talents, ready to rough it out in the Wild East, as administrative and development officers. They were designed to clone the British buccaneers.

Amen was consigned to the Northeast Frontier Agency (NEFA). It was a small stepping-stone; the elder Gurtoo had emphasised. Amritlal was there to take care of the rest.

Senior Gurtoo was correct.

In Indian bureaucracy, one wasn't required to be brilliant. Little advantage of age, usefulness to the establishment and proximity to key politicians were some of the glittering steps to the paradise called the Indian Administrative Service (IAS); a worthy successor to the Imperial Civil Service.

Amritlal superseded about a dozen seniors and favoured Amen by inducting him in the national roll of honour, the IAS.

His golf circuit linkages, correct caste connection, wide network of contacts and proximity to Amritlal's family, finally landed him in the Prime Minister's Office; the all powerful hub of the Indian bureaucracy.

To Mandira, Amritlal's daughter, loyalty to her family and her person was more important than the golden norm of efficiency and commitment to the system established by law.

Amen wasn't a wayside urchin or a two-penny informer to be picked up for interrogation, by the NSI agents. His 360-degree linkages inside the cocoon called India, infested with corrupt politicians, barons of industry, top-notch bureaucrats and media sharks had empowered Amen to spin around the entire intelligence bureaucracy. They survived on his mercy.

He could even wish away, by a single scratch of his pen, the Mount Everest from the geological map. Turning the black into white and the white into black were mere wish-games for the top Indian bureaucrats.

Nampoothiri's dilemma didn't end there. His men could mount covert Mosur on Amen and trace his movements to the doors of Patrick Goldman. That wouldn't prove anything. A whale of his stature could swim in any water. Accepting invitations from diplomatic Missions, provided the country wasn't listed unfriendly, was his privilege. An open meeting couldn't be construed as clandestine.

The mere clandestine nature of a meeting could also not be used to nail the coffin of a powerful bureaucrat. It required smoking gun evidence. And that called for the elaborate use of Electronic Intelligence (ElInt), clandestine photo and voice documentation. And these evidences couldn't be produced by any Indian rope trick. It required a well-researched application of technical intelligence tradecraft.

That is what Nampoothiri thought he should go for. The short briefing session in his room was a snappy affair.

"Remember," He finally warned, "I demand the sky. You've to fetch it. But we're dealing with an undercover US diplomat and the Principal Secretary to the PM. I'm keen, but I don't want any messing around. Got it clear?"

"It's a very difficult job sir," Robin Achariya pleaded.

"You don't have to tell me that dear," Snapped Nampoothiri, "We aren't here to suck lollipop. Gambling is a part of the job, and while playing, I make sure that I hold the right cards." He snubbed Achariya.

"We attempt a break in." Suggested Dhiren Bhagat.

"A good approach provided you have the premises empty. I can't assure you that luxury. What do we do?" Nampoothiri called in Jatadhari and ordered coffee.

"Sir, we'll give the matter a genuine try. I can't assure results. I also take your permission to abort the operation, in case of threatened exposure."

Bhagat, now a Senior Operations Officer, spoke with a tone of finality. He didn't leave any option open for the boss.

The guts of this officer as usual, amazed him.

"I appreciate that," Nampoothiri said, "But see that you deliver the goods."

He dismissed the meeting and hit the button for Amrita Bhalla.

"Connect me to Patrick Goldman."

Precise in two minutes Goldman came on the line. Balls, his Golf partner, was an important social circuit contact. To strike an acquaintance with the top man of India's external intelligence was a rare achievement. And Goldman believed that, as the CIA station chief he had made a breakthrough. The golf circuit had always been a gold mine, richer than the diplomatic cocktails and wild social parties.

Nampoothiri was very special.

His unexpected call put Goldman into a spin. This whale was a seasoned professional. He wasn't likely to call in the midst of a busy day, just to exchange data on the size of the breasts of another addition to the honey-club. He wasn't even sure if the Kerala Brahmin appreciated taut breasts.

"Hey Balls." Goldman's cultivated spontaneity effervescently poured out of the earpiece.

"Sorry Pat, I haven't been able to return your earlier call. Thought we could have a bite together."

"Busy, busy all the time. How can you get out of the embrace of your first love, your profession?" Goldman tried to prolong the conversation, "Anything special cooking?"

"Not particularly, but the days are tough," Nampoothiri sighed and threw him a bait, in a bid to measure up Goldman's steam, "You know the tense developments in East Pakistan and the war situation are real tough nuts to crack. Sikkim is another boiling cauldron, you know dear."

"I understand," Goldman tried to put a cork on his steam, " Perhaps we can meet over a quick bite?"

This was a gamble for Goldman, a golden opportunity to pump out information on India's war strategy and Mandira's agenda in Sikkim. The ***Gyalmo*** (queen), Patricia Brooke had flown back to the States and, the ***Chogyal*** (king) was under tremendous pressure to introduce democratic governance, a ruse, the US suspected, for the final take over by India.

The CIA was aware of the not so covert Indian involvement with the pro-democracy leaders. Mandira had almost bottled up the territory, and barring a few journalists and friendly golf-turf friends, there were hardly any sources of information. The only steady source of information was Indermit, a journalist of sort and a creeping climber in the corridors of power.

Kalimpong, the mysterious jewel of international intrigue and the US Consulate in Calcutta couldn't help much. Dacca, in the midst of serious turmoil, was incapable of diverting attention to Gangtok, the capital town of the kingdom of Sikkim.

Silence at the other end irritated Goldman. The blighted shark was flipping its fins around the bait and still hesitating to bite.

"Sorry Pat, you had to hold on. In fact, the PM was on the other line. It's okay with me. Let's meet at Hotel Fort, say at 12.30 sharp."

Nampoothiri replied boisterously, feigning that he had gulped the bait, rod line and sinker. Mention of the PM was an additional counter-lure, added to the bait; he had cast for the local CIA station chief.

"Fine. See you there."

Patrick Goldman triumphantly twirled his impressive whiskers as he entered the hotel lobby. He needed urgent briefing on India's intentions in East Pakistan and military objectives in the western war theatre.

Nampoothiri, occupying a corner table, greeted the US diplomat with an impassioned hug.

"Welcome Pat. It's great to be with you. How're things back home?"

"Absolutely fine. Thanks. But, you know Balls the White House is worried about Indian intentions in East Pakistan. Would you like to create another Bhutan out of it?" Goldman tried to draw out Nampoothiri.

"I appreciate your anxiety Pat. But, my PM is worried too. It's about suspected US involvement in funnelling Chinese and NATO weapons to Dacca, by using CIA sponsored mercenary flights. I hope you've something to say on this." Nampoothiri made a counter move.

"You got it all wrong Balls. We're neutral on this issue. No tilt. Washington on Potomac is no Pisa on the River Arno."

"We've a different perception about Washington on the Potomac, Pat. The tilt towards Pakistan is palpable." Nampoothiri parried.

The dig was expected.

But Patrick Goldman prolonged the brief luncheon meeting and gleefully recorded Nampoothiri's deliberately hesitant disclosures. The NSI chief didn't appear to be hurrying either. He spoke in a measured tone, dragging Goldman from topic to topic. It was an excellent briefing, the CIA station chief thought.

Nampoothiri could talk ceaselessly, without revealing much. He wanted to. He wanted to buy more precious time for Dhiren Bhagat.

Dhiren Bhagat and his assistant, clad in ordinary clothes, carrying two slim imported telephone instruments, wires and tools, appeared in front of the well-secured Sheryl Street residence of Goldman.

"Who're you guys?" Asked the Marine sentry.

"We've been directed to immediately repair the telephones of the ambassador sahib." Bhagat replied.

"Nope. We haven't complained." The Marine scowled.

"Why don't you call the Chancery sahib? He called us."

The caretaker, an all-season domestic from Goa, confirmed that there was indeed a call from the Head of the Chancery to allow Indian staff to repair the lines. These had gone dead since morning.

Bhagat had played the neat trick. He had induced the telephone exchange supervisor to disconnect Goldman's residence lines for at least four hours. His next stop was a public call office. Introducing himself as a member of a breakaway faction of the Bangladesh Government in exile, he called the embassy front desk.

How could he reach Mr. Patrick's residence telephones, which appeared to have gone dead? He had come all the way from Calcutta to meet the ***burra*** (big) sahib. They were, he said, opposed to Sheikh Jainal and wanted a dialogue with Islamabad.

The Chancery officials swallowed the bait and requested speedy restoration of the lines.

The layout inside of the house wasn't familiar. But Bhagat, using common sense, asked the accompanying technical hand, to install a radio microphone inside the drawing room phone. The radio-microphone would keep transmitting signals at a pre-fixed frequency, till detected by anti-bugging operations.

The second radio microphone was planted, with two weeks power supply from tiny cadmium batteries, behind the family portrait, hung over the master bed. A radio television camera, capable of transmitting images to a distant listening post complimented this equipment.

The operation took just about thirty minutes. Bhagat moved around the house with prayers on his lips and ticking mini-explosions inside the neurons. Anything going wrong would mean his dismissal from service and even imprisonment. His prayers were answered. The technical operation was a marvellous copybook success.

The snooping electronic van, with a telephone department sticker, ostensibly on emergency duty, was parked two blocks away behind a junction box. Bhagat and colleagues merrily recorded the audio and video signals from the implanted equipment.

Bhagat was happy. So was Nampoothiri. Quality of the audio and video intercepts was superb. Voices of Amen Gurtoo, Patrick Goldman and their common sex partner Maggie, Margaret Rose in real life, came in booming with shrieks of orgasm. The video images didn't leave anything to the imagination.

Maggie was moulded in the tradition of the fair skin beauties shipped from ***vilayat*** (abroad) for entertaining hungry soldiers of the East India Company, camping in makeshift cantonments, behind the Red Fort ramparts. The only difference being that, Maggie was one of the jet-setting pleasure objects, used for honey traps by the CIA, in stations like India, where fairer skins were worshipped as descendants of the fairies of the court of ***Indra*** (king of the gods).

The recorded dialogues were illuminating.

"Your NSI chief's a bloody gunk. The bastard wasted my day by talking nonsense. He didn't come out clean on Sikkim, the nuclear programme and the war preparations." Pat complained. At the end of the day, he regretted, the crooked Kerala Brahmin, behaved, as if he was debriefing the CIA station chief.

"Keep away from him. He's a bloody sucker. Never trust a Nampoothiri. In Kerala they're called snakes." Amen was more than charitable to the NSI chief.

"Yeah. The bastard is an eel. No bait is good enough to hook him." Pat talked in a frustrating voice.

"Ever tried this fellow Ahooja, Kumar Anand's replacement?" Amen suggested, "He should be useful."

"Well, gimme an intro, call him over for lunch." Pat replied indifferently.

"But Amen, Washington is keen to know what's happening at Pokharan. All the digging can't be for testing land mines. And we're worried about Sikkim as well. How can she annexe the protectorate? We're afraid of the Chinese reaction. And what the hell is your PM aiming for in East Pakistan? Does she want to make it another Bhutan?" Pat sounded desperate.

"But you haven't told me anything definite about my sons. They're rotting in Delhi. You had promised them scholarships at Harvard. My daughter in Boston hasn't yet got her green card, and I'm short of money." Lamented Amen Gurtoo.

"Don't lose your pants. Consider my position. For the last two months Washington has been pestering for a picture of India's nuclear programme. Tell me, how I can convince my people over there! It's after all a game of give and take." Patrick built up pressure on Amen.

He broadly hinted at releasing some photographs.

Amen protested loudly.

"You can't do that. That'll ruin me." He implored.

"I too face peril Amen. Help me! I assure you scholarship for your sons and green card for your daughter, within the next seven days," Pat paused.

"And in another seven days we shall put your dough in your escrow account in the Bahamas. You cooperate, and things will be sugar and honey. I believe you're retiring next July. I won't fail to sound

Washington out to fix up an assignment for you, may be with the World Bank."

The magic words electrified Amen. Employment with the World Bank was the ultimate dream of an Indian bureaucrat. He could do anything, minus fucking his mother, for that plum assignment. A veritable barrage of classified information burst forth from Amen.

For the next half an hour he spoke non-stop, on the time frames of the possible atomic implosion at Pokharan and the blueprint for annexation of Sikkim.

The grand lady was working on a set agenda and very few people had access to her mind. No. She had no agenda to annexe Bangladesh. Her intention was to install Sheikh Jainal in Dacca. In East Pakistan she was busy cooking the goose of General Arif Khan, the Chief Martial Law Administrator and President. She was determined to balkanise Pakistan by creating simultaneous unrest in Sind and Baluchistan.

Maggie's sound track came in superb in the videotape.

"Amen, you've been great," Intoned Maggie's salacious voice, "When shall we meet again?"

"Any time you wish my dear," Amen Gurtoo replied, "When are you back to the States?"

"I take a Pan Am flight in another four hours. Anything I can do for you?"

"I want to send $ 5000 to my daughter. You know the bloody hassles, the Indian Reserve Bank creates. Forget the trouble. There's hardly any time."

"Don't fuss," Pat's voice came in dearly, "The bucks will be delivered and adjusted against your account. Gimme the nuclear documents tomorrow at the golf turf. And don't forget the details of troop and armour deployments along the Pak borders, and the proceedings of last night's meeting of the CCSA. My diplomatic bag takes off tomorrow at 7 p.m."

Nampoothiri was more than pleased. On this rare occasion he didn't insist on the retrieval of the electronic implants from Goldman's diplomatic den. CIA's sweeping operations were sure to detect these gadgets. And the Mission chief was sure to lodge a routine demarche with the Joint Secretary, America Division. He had, in his thirty years with the spooky organisation, mastered the art of deflecting such diplomatic protests with fudgy and incomprehensible notes. He wasn't in a mood to spoil this fine moment of victory and breakthrough.

He called Dewan around ten thirty p.m.

"Has the PM gone to bed yet?"

"Not yet."

"Should I come in now?"

"Is it urgent?"

"Yes. It can't really wait."

"Okay. Than come in right away."

Nampoothiri spent the next four hours with Mandira, playing audiotapes, and explaining the positives of clandestine photographs and other supporting reports. She had declined to view the videotapes, for reasons Nampoothiri understood well.

After two hundred and forty minutes, Mandira leaned back on her chair, cupped her chins between the palms and shot the first question at him.

"Are you sure there's no mistake?"

"I would be the happiest person if these were wrong, but ma'am," Nampoothiri spoke in a straight voice, "These're technical evidences, there's no chance of any fudging."

"What do you suggest?"

"We're convinced that, Gurtoo is the source of leakage. He should be taken out from your secretariat. And my boys are about to locate and identify the suspected Pakistani moles inside our atomic establishments. And you may like to reorient our agenda in Sikkim and East Pakistan."

"The arrows can't be rolled back Nampoothiri. The nemesis is bound to strike Pakistan, may be Dacca first and Karachi and Quetta later. But, tell me what do I do with Amen?" Mandira spoke in a visibly distressed voice.

"I don't recommend any action under the Official Secrets Act. That would compromise your position. But I must share with you that Goldman has a direct line to the ISI station chief in Delhi."

"How come?"

"It cuts both ways. The link can be personal as well as at an agency level. The CIA has a well-oiled intelligence sharing protocol with the ISI."

"So where do we stand? You mean Islamabad will have all the dopes on our nuclear secrets and war preparations?"

"It's a natural conclusion. In fact, my boys have followed up leads given by Triple X and they're on the trail of a major suspected ISI agent. I may soon have more good news for you." Nampoothiri spoke with great relish as he watched the panicky movements of the PM's eyeballs.

"So where do we dump this idiot Gurtoo?"

"Perhaps you may consider giving him a diplomatic assignment, at a station, where he can't interact with his US friends."

"What about Mongolia?"

"That's a nice wilderness."

"I don't want any publicity. You take care of all the nitty gritty."

Mandira pressed the bell and Dewan, ever present by her side, came in.

"Call the Cabinet Secretary, Director FIB, Home Minister, Foreign Minister and the Defence Minister, sharp at seven in the morning."

"Yes ma'am."

"Okay Nampoothiri," the PM wished her NSI chief out and asked Dewan to stay put.

"Talk to Shankar and suggest three names to succeed Amen. I'm posting him out, on a diplomatic assignment."

Mandira ordered her Special Assistant to consult Shankar, her younger son, and a rising sun in India's political firmament. He was in the process of being groomed for higher responsibilities, like she understudied her father, Amritlal.

Chapter 9

"Well boy," Nampoothiri tossed a coconut cookie into his mouth and spoke with a choked voice, " These are really nice."

Ramendra Kaushal refused to take cognisance of the stray dialogue. He knew it was hollow, a mere prop to stretch the conversation. His vacant eyes were riveted at a pair of jet-black finch perched on a dry twig. The male bird was busy soliciting the female companion with flirtatious whistle and body aerobics. The solicitor didn't yet succeed in impressing the female one.

Kaushal wilted his lips and broke out into a mild laughter.

"Are you laughing at the nice cookies, or at me?" Nampoothiri spoke with contrived hurt in his voice.

"No sir," Kaushal turned back from the window, "It's not the cookies or you. I've given you all that I had in store. Can I now go back to Jhun Jhunu with my wife and kid?"

"Not yet dear. We're in the midst of hostility and the ISI won't spare any effort to locate and neutralise you."

"I can take care of them, at least in my own turf."

"You aren't appreciating their reach. They can get at your wife and child. I don't think ISI will spare an Indian agent who has exposed their sinister chemical warfare designs."

"Jhun Jhunu is a small place."

"No place is big enough to hide a twister like you," Nampoothiri stood up and walked down to the window, "The PM herself has congratulated you on the Amen Gurtoo catch. Now tell me something about the ISI plants in our nuclear establishments."

Debriefing Triple X alias Harfan Bukhari alias Ramendra Kaushal wasn't an easy job. But Nampoothiri was sure that the Gurtoo affair wasn't the last of the wonders that could be pulled out by Triple X. Enough juice was still left in his pod.

"Have you checked at Jam Salaya near Jamnagar, Gujarat and Dahisar in Maharashtra? "

"No. What for?"

"The ISI often operate through the sea route for reaching India's nuclear installations in Bombay and Rajasthan."

"Give me the details."

"Sorry. I haven't any. All that I know is about the existence of a veteran ISI resident agent who has penetrated India's nuclear establishments. Double X Ibadat had the details."

"But he's dead." Nampoothiri spoke in exasperation.

"Sorry sir. I can only add that Dahisar is an important point of operation by the ISI. Ibadat had warned me about this several times and I had relayed this in my dispatches," Kaushal shrugged and lighted a cigarette, "What are you doing with Voodoorume?"

He spoke about the mercenary pilot of South African origin, who had diverted the weapon laden Dacca bound Boeing 707 to Delhi and saved India from the catastrophe of chemical warfare by Pakistan.

"Don't worry. He'll be back home safe."

"Can I see him again?"

"No man. It's not done," Nampoothiri lighted his favourite Havana, "Now tell me what should I do with this riddle?"

"Which one?"

"The nuclear installations."

"Merry hell! Try your luck sir." Kaushal glanced at Dhiren Bhagat and winked with a naughty twist.

Nampoothiri threw up his hands. Well! He was, it appeared, a pawn in the hands of dame luck. He picked up his overcoat and collected the Panama hat and said goodbye to Kaushal. The fourth round of debriefing Triple X in an NSI guesthouse, where the agent and his wife and child were housed, proved frustrating.

"Well Bhagat," Nampoothiri shrugged, "Try your luck with the inscrutable fellow. I'm off."

He left Ramendra Kaushal with Dhiren Bhagat for another spell of debriefing, especially on the yet unveiled mysteries of assassination of agent Alamgir and Double X at Bhagatan airbase in Pakistan.

****

Good and bad spell often come in torrents. It was Nampoothiri's turn to be swamped by a tide of favourable events. Ramendra Kaushal had finally rewarded Bhagat by drawing a sketch of the likely location of the Pakistani resident agent at a coastal hamlet in Maharashtra.

But the real break came from a chance observation by an officer hanging on to the tenuous threads of endless time in a non-family station.

Sanchor, a desert station on the Indo-Pak border in Rajasthan was an important strategic border intelligence post with sub-zero temperature in winter and 50 plus Celsius in summer. But the November ground frosts were heated up by war hysteria. Indian and Pakistani troops were holed up in sandy trenches, and were in eyeball-to-eyeball positions.

Abhi Meena, a junior intelligence officer, had tuned his radio to the ***ghazals*** (sub-continental music format) and film tunes broadcast by Radio Pakistan, interspersed with lengthy harangues, calling for ***jihad*** against ***kafir*** India. But Abhi's ears weren't tuned to the ghazals. His mind was floating out of his physical body, busy dreaming of his wife's tender face, left at his village, just after fifteen days of their marriage.

The Pakistani announcer closed down with the usual ***Khuda Hafiz*** and ***Pakistan Paindabad*** greetings. Stratospheric noises kept on crackling and disturbing Meena's dream. As he extended his fingers to switch off the set, a female voice came in from the same frequency.

"Majnu, Majnu, Majnu.... Meet Laila at Oasis.... Meet Laila at Oasis." She repeated the sentence thrice and went off the air.

Abhi Meena, a fresh product from NSI's training institute, brushed aside the lingering mists of his wife's contour and scribbled down the time, frequency and name of the station and the exact wordings of the mysterious broadcast. Next morning he sent a cipher to Delhi.

Meena's cipher gathered dust on Robin Achariya's table. He hurled a few choicest appellatives at the tribal officer at Sanchor and scribbled his valuable comments: hallucination, the officer requires screwing up.

But Abhi Meena wasn't the lone listener to the silvery voice calling for Majnu. In the next three days Achariya received four additional inputs. He finally sat up. Here was something intriguing. The mysterious Laila was still calling for Majnu.

"You have nearly damaged a wonderful lead," Nampoothiri shuffled the pages brought up by Achariya, " It must be the ISI, homing in for a specific agent."

"Why should they use an open radio frequency?"

"That's the easiest way of communication. The fellow must be somewhere in the arch-area of reception of medium-wave signals from Radio Pakistan's Hyderabad station." Nampoothiri pointed his finger on a grid map of the Indo-Pakistan border and broadly indicated the arch of reception.

"So dear, as I was saying, that lady is no Laila calling her lover Majnu. She's conveying a message to an agent, with whom regular communication channel has snapped. This is a time-tested means of clandestine communication. Now get cracking."

"How do we go about it sir?" Achariya finally realised that his indiscretion had created a piquant situation.

Nampoothiri stood up, slowly walked down to the one and only window and lighted a Havana. He opened it and looked down at the buzzing traffic below. A thought suddenly flashed past his mind.

"Cross check with the inputs I've shared with you. Study the hand drawn sketch. These were from a delicate source. Check with the FIB units in the arch area. Check all the listed and suspected counter-intelligence suspects. Order blanket surveillance. If I'm correct some Majnu will try to contact his Laila."

Nampoothiri's flash thought was corroborated by a piece of a puzzle from Jodhpur field unit of the NSI. Security and counter intelligence suspect Mahesh Kumar, fronting a grocery outlet at central road, Jodhpur Air force Cantonment, was mysteriously absent for over ten days.

"When did he first come to Jodhpur?" Achariya asked.

"That's not clear. He's married to the daughter of a cantonment sweeper." The Jodhpur field officer replied.

"Is there a pattern in his prolonged absence? From where has he come? Is it possible to question his wife and discreetly search his belongings and bank account?" Achariya floored his officer with questions.

No one in Jodhpur could put a sure pin on the date of Mahesh's arrival. But his romance with Phulan, a sweeper's daughter was alive in the memory of the scavenger line residents. Mahesh, a Hindu Brahmin, had startled everyone by marrying the scavenger's daughter.

Phulan's reaction to mild questioning from a lady officer was evasive. She was used to Mahesh's periodical business trips.

"How do I know?" His wife replied, " He must've gone to Jaipur on a business errand. He may have gone to his village in Bihar."

"What kind of husband is he? No letter, no trace. Has he run away with another girl?" The psychological dart rattled Phulan. Any damn woman would like to seduce her lover. A handsome Bihari Brahmin won't starve for a female partner.

Yes. He was out on business errands. She mellowed down a bit.

"What bloody business trip does a grocer require to take so frequently?" The lady officer poured more fat on Phulan's fire of suspicion; "Don't you think he's involved with another wretched woman? Take it from me, all men are pigs. Wives at home are just decoration pieces and bed warmers. Haven't you seen him flirting with Sukha sweeper's daughter?"

"That witch? I'll gouge her eyes out." Phulan screamed out.

"We'll sure do that. But let's search his suitcase. There must be some love letters, from Sukha's daughter." The interlocutor succeeded in pushing Phulan down the precipice.

Search of his portmanteau didn't produce any telltale mark of another woman in his life. Nothing suspicious, except a small piece of paper, littered with some numbers and strange characters and copy of some Hindu religious books.

"Don't tell your hubby. Let me talk to my brother first. You know he's in the telephone department. It's easy for him to locate Mahesh even at his village. And we'll sure take care of Sukha sweeper's daughter."

"That witch should be burnt at the stake." Phulan had walked into the trap.

"Sure. We'll burn her with a lot of kerosene." The interlocutor assured her.

The scrap of paper contained some scribbling in Urdu and some digits.

Maulana Rizwan, the official Urdu specialist, deciphered the riddle. It contained the name of one Qamar, Gali Suiwalan, Jama Masjid, Delhi and a Lahore phone number: 912 3089.

Qamar Ahmed had already found his way into the glorious records of the NSI. A visa agent by profession, he was listed as a forged passport and visa peddler and a well-connected linkman of the Bombay and Calcutta underworld dons.

Qamar was befriended by some consular staff of the Pakistan High Commission, who frequented his walled city den ostensibly for offering Friday prayers at the historic Jama Masjid. He operated a mini brothel in his house. Patronised by the Pakistan High Commission based intelligence officials, the shady joint acted as a fertile conduit for priming Indian targets. Qamar was a valuable local recruiting agent and a SAAD, Safe Accommodation Address of the Pakistani intelligence operators in Delhi.

Nampoothiri's Mosurs tracked down Qamar and Bhagat's boys didn't take time to put the heat on.

A Fiat taxi, positioned at the fifth crossroad end of the Pakistan Mission's family exit, observed Qamar peeping out of the High Commission around 8 p.m.

"Brother can I have a word with you?" Dhiren Bhagat accosted Qamar. He was no stranger to the intelligence sleuths. They were either from the FIB or Delhi police. The snooping leeches always sniped at the Indian citizens using the family gate of the Pak High Commission.

"What can I do for you?" Qamar asked.

"I'm Basir from Calcutta. Can you help us with 10 passports? Ashraf Ali of Ripon Street, Calcutta has referred you to me."

The name Ashraf did the magic. He was a known forged visa agent, controlling the entire eastern territory.

"Five thousand bucks each." Qamar replied nonchalantly.

"It's a deal," Bhagat helped Qamar to board the taxi.

Qamar walked into the trap only to be blindfolded and driven to the Madangir village safe house of the NSI. Two night's interrogation with scientific and unscientific tricks broke down his resistance.

Yes. Qamar knew Mahesh alias Safi Indrabi, a Pakistani smuggler, who had entered India through Jam Salaya sea route and was his houseguest for two weeks. He had accommodated Safi on the request of Jamal Khatak, a consular officer in the High Commission. Safi, Qamar revealed, had gone to Bombay to meet a fellow smuggler, Sikander Tandel, a fishing magnate at the sleepy minor port of Chiuchani, next to Tarapur, India's premier nuclear research hub.

At 3 a.m. sharp next morning, Robin Achariya and his team swooped in on the house of Sikander Tandel. Safi Indrabi was taken by surprise in a cosy bed with a naked woman. He didn't get time to draw out the pistol from under his pillow.

Flown to Delhi in a special flight of Kalyani Air Lines Safi Indrabi was dumped in the dreaded interrogation centre.

Safi was trained to absorb pain. He remained lock-jawed for two nights, but scientific application of exotic treatment breached his embankments of training. A clinching trick was used on the third night, by passing a miniature electrode through his anus, releasing a 220-volt charge in minuscule bursts. The frontiers of his training collapsed and he agreed to cooperate.

Given a bath, food and cigarette, Safi talked on the Lahore number: 912 3089.

"Majnu here, I got your message General," Safi talked to his boss in the Inter Services Intelligence, "I was away to target Buland."

It was a reference to Tarapur nuclear facility.

"***Rabba Khair*** (by mercy of Allah)! You bastard really scared me. Are you whoring around? Why were you silent for all these days?" Major General Barqat Khan, in charge of Joint Intelligence Miscellaneous Division, often referred as 'S' Division spoke loud and clear.

"Sorry boss," Safi replied, "I was following up the task at Buland."

"We called you thrice. Note down, next calls will be on Sundays from Multan station, 1430 kHz, at 23.50. What's the programme? When are they performing the marriage?"

"***Sagai pakki*** (engagement ceremony is confirmed). But, the bride's father is yet to give the final nod." Indrabi replied, indicating the uncertain status of Indian preparedness at Pokharan for the impending nuclear experiment.

His contact in the Tarapur plant, a senior engineer, connected with the preparations, had indicated that India's programme had run into some problem. India, he said was ready, but not too subtle pressure from the USA and USSR disagreement stood in the way. Delhi was yet to decide on the timing.

"But you're contradicting our other reports. The Chinese say that Delhi is ready for the big bang," Barqat lost his cool.

"Sorry boss, this is my precise finding. They'll wait for the war to be over. They don't want to provoke Washington on this sensitive front. Listen, I want more money for my Buland contact."

"Are you fucking around? Last month I sent you one grand."

"Boss, things are costly, even fucking has become costlier. And I had to pay my boys in the Punjab and Rajasthan borders."

Indrabi looked up at the pistol in Bhagat's hand.

"My friend here wants a fat amount for the drawings of the Kota nuclear power plant."

"Okay. You contact shop no.106 at Meena Bazar, Jama Masjid. He'll pay whatever you require. The code word is ***ILLAHI***. Call back soon. Listen," Barqat continued, "Activate your Delhi friends and ascertain details about one of our chartered flights, that landed there with important loads."

"There hasn't been much in the Indian media boss."

"Fuck the media. Ask your friends to burrow deep and get the details. We'll like you to get at and extinguish that fellow Harfan Bukhari. Locate that South African pilot too. We need to silence him as well. Hire people to pump a thousand bullets into them. We want them dead. Money's no problem. Understand?" General Barqat sounded vicious on the line.

"Got you sir. Please wait for three days." Indrabi replied from a text scribbled by Bhagat.

"I can't wait indefinitely. You're authorised to spend Rs. five million for the job. Quick, we're already at war with the infidels."

"Yes boss. Can I tap Magnet?" Indrabi referred to a sensitive agent of Pakistan; a North Indian wrestler turned politician, who commanded gangs of goons, drawn from the Bombay underworld and crime holes in eastern Uttar Pradesh.

"No. Keep out Magnet. The loss of Aftab has changed our policy of utilising these assets for one-time jobs: Use hired killers."

"Okay boss. Before, I finish can I congratulate you for your promotion?" Indrabi referred to Brigadier Barqat's elevation to the rank of Major General.

"Thanks buddy. Your promotion is overdue. Complete the mission and you're a Colonel."

"Thanks boss."

Safi Indrabi's curricula vitae sounded impressive. A Signal Corps Major, seconded to the ISI, he was housed in India way back in 1968. His network in Rajasthan, Delhi and Bombay had drilled gaping holes in India's security armours.

Rawalpindi was equally worried about India's strategic planning in the Rajasthan sector. Its war game planners had warned that India wouldn't take minutes to roll down its cavalry once the hostilities jumped the shallow marshy East Pakistan theatres. The Indian strategy of pinning down Pakistan in desert warfare and the simultaneous rapid march to Lahore and Sialkot were obvious.

Nampoothiri's post-operation briefings on Indrabi affair fascinated Prime Minister Mandira.

"It's a puzzling game. You intelligence people are really crooked. And it means that Amen played havoc with our national secrets. We'll require some course correction," Commented Mandira "I'll take care of that. But Pakistan's nuclear quest worries me. Your Triple X had been consistently reporting about the frenetic Pakistani nuclear preparations."

"That's correct ma'am," Nampoothiri added, "The Russian satellite images also support our reports."

"Now that Triple X is out of commission and you've suffered other losses, how do you propose to revitalise the system?" She asked her NSI chief.

"The asset creation process is slow ma'am," Nampoothiri replied, "We'll take at least another five years, if we're lucky, to regain the desired level of penetration."

"I suggest you accelerate your operations in Sind and Baluchistan. How are your friends Sartaj Jamil, Mengel and Mazari responding?"

"Their responses are satisfactory ma'am. But we are yet to achieve the Lotus like penetration."

Nampoothiri elaborated upon his operational mechanism in the provinces of Sind and Baluchistan. Pakistan, he explained, had blunted the Indian efforts of pushing weapons to the Sind rebels through the sea route. The Kabul, Kandahar and Mazar-e-Sharif routes used for pumping weapons to some of the Baluch and NWFP tribal groups had achieved only limited success. Absence of Alamgir, he apprehended, could dry up the USSR-Afghanistan pipeline.

"It's now your headache Balu. All that I want is Islamabad's preoccupation with its internal affairs. Mobilise all your X agents and get going."

It was a tall order indeed.

To Nampoothiri, the exit of Triple X, Harfan Bukhari, from Pakistan, under yet unexplained circumstances, and the mysterious elimination of Alamgir meant irreparable losses. But the tantalising success in neutralising the double forked Pakistani thrust, involving Amen Gurtoo and Major Indrabi had redeemed some lost prestige. This small breather could be used to build up new assets.

A fresh beginning could be attempted only after a thorough post mortem of the colossal collapse. The dramatic ending of Operation Triple X and Alamgir were sure pointers that something had gone wrong with India's top projects.

Nampoothiri delved back into his hidden neuron tissues, like a fond father with hidden weakness for a boisterous son. Tender thoughts overwhelmed his cautious and disciplined emotions. This boy, Harfan Bukhari alias Ramendra Kaushal was indeed a loveable scoundrel. He hadn't experienced another such stormy agent in the 30 years of his intelligence career.

Now that the PM had given the clearance his team would get cracking on interrogating the guests. He expected Triple X to come out clean. He was a patriot, and Nampoothiri hoped he would help the company to reassess and reorient operational modalities inside Pakistan. This one surviving link could help the NSI build anew on the past wreckage.

Perhaps a time had come for him to adopt dynamic new operational philosophy and innovative technique. The fundamentals of operational science and art should be recast. Contradictions inside the Pakistani Establishment could be exploited, like his agency had done with Operation Lotus in East Pakistan. Conceived in the mid-fifties by Rabindra Narayan Dutta, the grand wizard of post-independence Indian intelligence, the project was now paying dividends. Pakistan would not have the same geographical and ideological shape after the Lotus bloomed fully. An independent Bangladesh was a near reality.

What fault lines could he exploit in the post-war scenario? Tap the Sindhis? Incite the Seraikis? Provoke the Pakhtoons? Arm the Baluchis? Well! These initiatives had achieved only marginal results. He should, Nampoothiri thought loudly, have a series of brain storming sessions with his colleagues. Pakistan, he believed, was an aberration of history. It could not be allowed to link up the Muslims of Indian origin with the Arab world. The geo-political map of the Muslim countries to the west of India presented a threatening strategic scenario. Pakistan could not be allowed to coalesce a world Muslim coalition against India. There was no reason for this contrived geopolitical entity to survive beyond the defeat of the two-nation theory in East Pakistan.

Anyway, this fellow Harfan should be a gold mine for reorienting strategic and tactical approaches. He had been deep inside the system and could provide rare insight into the functioning of the ISI. Nampoothiri felt happy that his earlier deactivation order hadn't destroyed this valuable operation. Triple X enjoyed the proverbial nine lives, which a spy of his standing could seldom claim. He was turbulent from day one; Nampoothiri mused, but a likeable rascal at that.

He enjoyed the thrill of recruiting and training this asset. He was often outpaced by his fast and furious penetration inside the Pakistani Establishment. Now he was mystified by his daring escape from the clutches of the Inter Services Intelligence. Harfan Bukhari was indeed a fascinating asset, all the way superbly fascinating.

"Sir," Amrita Bhalla's voice flowed down from the intercom, "You have a meeting with the high-powered delegation of the Government of Bangladesh in Exile at 10.30. You've just two hours left. You'd sure like to have a briefing from the desk officer. Wouldn't you?"

"Come in dear," Nampoothiri invited his secretary with an expansive voice, "Let's have a small private celebration."

"What for sir?"

"I'm happy that I'm again right and wrong. Right, because the Lotus is blooming soon. Wrong, because I've been proved wrong. Have a seat and share my thoughts and pleasure." He ordered Jatadhari to concoct a strong coffee.

Nampoothiri looked back fondly, intermittently chatting with Amrita and reminiscing over the stormy Operation Triple X episode.

This was the time for selecting the right seeds for sowing in the post-war fertile Pakistani soil. He hoped he would be able to exploit the November woes of Pakistan and expected Triple X to lead him through the right furrows.

"You know dear, it has been really a unique experience, recruiting and training that rascal."

"You love him sir."

"I don't know, but he defies most of the tricks of the trade. He's really a freeborn creature. I'm happy he's free again. I'm happy that I've been proved wrong. Some spies do have nine lives."

Nampoothiri allowed himself to pleasantly surfing over the waves of his memory; waves that churned out Harfan Bukhari, Agent Triple X, out of a violent typhoon called Prince Ramendra Kaushal.

Chapter 10

The Second World War vintage DC3, owned and operated by Kalyani Air Lines, a sleek cover for the air-wing of the Federal Intelligence Bureau's Special Aviation Force (SAF), circled over Sirsa airstrip for over 30 minutes, amidst a blinding sand-storm. The fuselage of the old war-horse rattled ominously. The landing approach to the sparsely used dirt-runway had simply vanished from the horizon. Dust haze had narrowed down visibility to a miserly 150 yds.

The pilot finally lowered the elevators, levelled the nose and touched the bird down almost at the end-edges of the strip. He applied the brakes and brought it to stationary position, at the farthest corner of the runway, overlooking some tented accommodation.

The tented tactical HQ of the Second Infantry Division had sprung up a few days ago, in response to the Pakistani incursions in Kachchh. The border skirmishes had flared up into a regular engagement. Pakistani armour and infantry had inflicted heavy casualties on the Indian police formations at Sardar Post, near the ruins of Fort Kanjarkot. Sabre rattling in Kachchh was just about a rehearsal for the events casting dark shadows on the Vale of Kashmir.

Reports of orchestrated Pakistani infiltration in Kashmir had shaken Delhi's lackadaisical defence preparations with rude shocks. The Pakistani irregulars had either overrun or bypassed the penny pockets of Indian paramilitary forces, and had reached the fringes of Srinagar, capital of the contentious State of Jammu & Kashmir. The tribal ***mujahids*** (religious warriors), aided by the regulars of Pakistan Army had inflicted serious losses on the traditional grazers, the Gujjars and Bakkarwals. Their homesteads burnt, their cattle boiled or braised for dinner and their women raped, the mountain and valley populace waited with bated breath for Delhi's intervention.

The DC3, however, wasn't braving the desert storm on any military mission. The Kalyani Air Lines generally flew air reconnaissance sorties deep inside Pakistan and China. It was sparsely used in a support-role for training, deployment and transportation of Special Volunteer Force (SVF), a super secret security adjunct of the FIB, raised after India's China-war debacle.

Essentially a paramilitary commando force, the SVF recruits were trained in guerrilla warfare, for fighting behind the enemy lines. The Force was intended to haunt and harass the enemy behind its lines, in the unlikely event of their advancing deep into Indian territory.

The Dakota wasn't on any SVF operation either. The sturdy bird dared the desert storm to accomplish a special assignment. It carried

Ramendra Kaushal, blindfolded and hands tied at his back, escorted by Dhiren Bhagat and two plainclothes armed men. Their destination was a dilapidated fort, located behind a garland of undulated mounds and remnants of broken stone and mud walls. Locally referred to as the fort of Maharaja Agrasen, the structure was an archaeological fossil.

Agrasen, a ***baniya*** (businessman) by caste, had strangely opted for the sword, contrary to the historical practices of his ilk, which recognised better the wheels of money, rather than the wheels of canons. Fired by rare sparks of nationalism he had quit his moneybag and usual shadowy presence behind the throne, at an uncertain period of Delhi's troubled and tortuous political history. He had carved out a short lived but glorious Hindu interlude.

The British, during the Second World War used the abandoned fort of Maharaja Agrasen as a makeshift rest house for their senior officers. Sirsa, located on the important artery between Delhi and the Indian North West, had witnessed the advances and retreating of many armies, which descended on Hindustan in search of gold and manna, right from the Aryans to the Mughals. The British had, for a change, floated down the blue waters, and to them Sirsa was a firm launching pad for the defences of the vital North West Frontiers, against the Afghan bandits, Tsarist Russia and its Bolshevik successors.

Rabindra Narayan Dutta had simply taken over the property from the Punjab administration, ignoring stiff opposition from the Archaeological Survey of India. To him the perpetuation of the memory of a ***baniya*** king was less important than running a special centre for training his agents in dirty tricks. The School of Black Arts was a feared and dreaded training centre that didn't exist on FIB records.

Located in the midst of desert wilderness, Agrasen's fort wasn't even connected by a tarred road. Two high frequency trans-receivers operating at fixed schedules maintained bare minimum communications with Delhi.

Six underground rooms with modern facilities of civilised living were constructed a few years ago, well below the ramshackle surface and dilapidated façade. The undulating sand dunes, scrubs and bushes provided a natural camouflage to the super-secret edifice.

Karam Chand Pathania, a living legend in the FIB had rooted himself well, in the hostile environment of the desert fort, like succulent cacti. An indestructible life force he could root himself anywhere. A seemingly ageless person, with a head full of white hair and a dyed jet black moustache, Pathania stood six feet three inches on his bare soles. His muscular body defied the laws of ageing in his 68 eventful summers and springs.

Pathania was the master of the place, training FIB's top agents, in the dirty tricks of the intelligence tradecraft.

A retired First World War veteran, Pathania had seen action in the Italian and French fronts and had picked up the coveted Victoria Cross. The Imperial FIB (IFIB) groomed him up as an intelligence operative after the guns fell silent. He had served for years behind the forbidden walls of the Potala Palace; the holy seat of the Dalai Lama, running intelligence network that aimed at the heartland of China. Tibet, in British perception, was a geographical and political cushion between its sprawling empire in India and the Russian Red Bear and the inscrutable Yellow Panda.

Pathania had raised and trained ***FORCE TURAG*** (horse), a formidable Tibetan commando force, following a silent tripartite agreement between London, Delhi and Lhasa. But Dalai Lama's flight to India had cut short the adventures of the Lawrence of Potala, the nickname Pathania had earned for his daredevil forays against Chinese incursions in Tibet.

FORCE TURAG, raised by Pathania, turned out to be another chimera, after India's rout in border wars with China. Pathania, the indomitable buccaneer, was commissioned to lead the FIB contingents and open flag-posts along the McMahon Line and on the unmarked and not too well defined borders with China. Rabindra Narayan Dutta and his Prime Minister, Amritlal were keen to fly the flags. That was, in the absence of any better China policy and war preparations, according to them, the best national policy to stake claim on questionable territories. Pathania's flags were blown to shreds by the winds of Chinese aggression. He was brought down to the plains of Sirsa from the commanding heights of the Himalayas as a concession to his advancing age.

An innovative bulldog, Pathania was moulded into a ruthless trainer by the British SAS and the Airborne US Army Special Forces Group. He specialised in training agents in the classified crafts of stealing information from foreign territories, and carrying out acts of sabotage and subversion. Some of his creations were often endowed with the extra-legal power to kill, in special circumstances, for protecting vital national interests. Pathania had mastered the art and science of silent assassination as a tool for promoting the progress of special agents inside and outside the national borders. Very few officers in the FIB were aware of his acronym: *the butcher*.

Ramendra Kaushal was consigned to Pathania's underground hole for intensive tradecraft training and recasting and remoulding his personality. His psyche required thorough scrubbing and removal of layers of scum and dirt, before he could be tailored for Triple X operations inside Pakistan.

"Where are you taking me? Why don't you free my eyes?" Muttered Kaushal.

"We're on a picnic trip. You'll be free soon."

Bhagat reassured his catch. From a mere talent spotter, he had graduated to being the case officer of Operation Triple X.

"You can't do this to me. My people in Delhi won't spare you. Let me talk to minister Ram Karan Prasad. He'll clarify everything." Ramendra Kaushal pleaded and threatened.

"You'll have your chance to reflect upon Ram Karan. Now get into the jeep." Bhagat sounded sweet but stern.

The dusty road to the fort wasn't visible. It happened in Sirsa and adjacent areas. Drifting sand from adjoining deserts usually buried the road beyond recognition and negotiation.

But, Nafar Singh, the driver was a field bandicoot of the terrain. He sniffed out the route around and guided the jeep immaculately to the foreground of the palace ruin, still guarded by two stone ***Yakshinis*** (female celestial beings), with two massive maces in their hands. High above the ***Yakshinis***, glimpses of a faded fresco of the Sun God driving a chariot, powered by seven multi-coloured horses was still discernible to curious eyes.

Karam Chand Pathania, seated on a cane chair, stood up; body rigid and erect, as Bhagat and team entered the room. The cool airs inside the dilapidated edifice, just after the scorching desert heat outside sent shivers of chill under Kaushal's skin. He still groped in the darkness, his eyes covered with a black scarf.

"Welcome to my nest Mr. Kaushal."

"What's this bloody welcome with my eyes blindfolded?" Kaushal retorted.

Bhagat unfastened the blinds on Kaushal's eyes and unscrewed the handcuffs. The dim pale light pierced Kaushal's painful eyeballs with a thousand needles. He could hardly figure out the contours of the gigantic figure of Karam Chand Pathania, standing imposingly, flanked by two jet-black devil looking Terriers.

Slowly the kaleidoscope of blurred vision cleared up and he saw the imposing frame almost stooping over him. Ramendra Kaushal shuddered inside his bones. A strange cramp gripped his intestines. Though he couldn't co-ordinate his brain signals, Kaushal vaguely figured out that he was being readied for the frying pan.

"Welcome to my palace, Mr. Harfan." Greeted Pathania.

"I'm Prince Ramendranath Kaushal." Replied Kaushal in a curtly formal voice.

"That's the identity of your past life. I'm talking of your present incarnation, Mr. Harfan Bukhari."

"What's this rubbish?" Asked Kaushal, puzzled as he was, looking at Bhagat.

"We shall talk. Mr. Pathania is the boss of this place and you're, now onwards, under his charge."

Dinner was a delicious affair, cooked by Nafar Singh; chicken with plenty of spices and gravy, lentils and fried potato, served with ***chapati*** (flat bread) from a blazing oven. The food tasted like nectar in Kaushal's palate after 18 long hours of near starvation.

But, the damp basement room scared him. A shot of whisky should be able to fortify him against unknown odds.

Bhagat recommended a large dose of patience instead. Better times were ahead, he explained. There could be plenty of whisky, if Pathania endorsed. He was the master here and a legend in the very non-existent underworld of the FIB, of which very few people, even in the organisation, were aware.

"Sleep early," Bhagat sounded a friendly note of caution, "Nafar will serve tea at 5 am. You are expected for the out door activities at 5.30 am sharp. You'll find the morning gear in your room."

"What do you expect of me? Why should I listen? You can't keep me confined here. Inform my people in Delhi. Inform my mother." Kaushal gathered courage after a tasty dinner and two cigarettes.

"If you insist, I can only inform the police and hand you over to them. It'll take only three months for you to walk up to the gallows. I don't mind, if you don't, and I've spare copies of the photographs for your mother."

Kaushal looked at Bhagat with fire-spitting killer eyes, muttered a curse and crushed the third cigarette under his shoes.

"Good night. Don't try to act funny. The place is well guarded. They fire first and talk later. If you're lucky to escape the bullets, Terry and Sparrow, the killer dogs, won't miss your jugular." Bhagat smiled and wished him good night.

Nafar Singh along with Terry and Sparrow on leashes guided Kaushal to his room. He closed the door behind him and unleashed the Terriers, patted them and spoke into their ears. He left Kaushal alone to think over the events of the last twenty-four hours, and snatch a few winks of sleep, if the elusive dame did agree to favour him.

Kaushal's nerves were too raw, as if scratched by spotted leopards. And sleep wasn't the proper incarnation of time to numb his frayed and scared senses.

His eyes itched and ached. He could barely close the swollen lids. Pain and shame and anger and anxiety haunted him. He closed the eyelids hoping to snatch a few moments of rest. But his convoluted psyche was busy churning out the dark thoughts, which he thought he could wish away.

The snowy ashen face of Rajni Krittika Hemaprabha Rao appeared from nowhere, the moment he closed his lids and tried to disengage from the surroundings. Hema stared at him with an impish smile. The ghoulish look scared him. Hema wasn't merely taunting him, her looks conveyed a loud message; in her death she had vanquished the all-muscle campus-macho.

Kaushalya's face suddenly fleeted in from the cosmic vacuum with tonnes of questions in her eyes. Kaushal, since his adolescence, couldn't manage to face those looks and bluff his way out. She would know the truth somehow. Perhaps she had an X-ray vision, hidden somewhere behind her cornea.

Suddenly, a severed head, blood flowing in torrents faded in before his eyes. Was it Matang's head? No, it wasn't. Whose head was it? Kaushal couldn't figure out any sense out of the grotesque apparition. It faded out.

Kaushalya's face faded in again.

He rubbed his eyes and jumped out of the bed. He stomped his feet on the bare floor, wishing to scare away the scornful smile of Hema, the gory head and the heavy eyelids of his mother, pregnant with imponderable questions.

Kaushal stood in front of a wall-mounted mirror and noticed profuse perspiration rolling down his cheeks, mixed with salty tears.

"Ma (mother), excuse me. I'm a sinner." Ramendra cried out and covered his face with trembling palms.

The mirror echoed back his cry.

Nafar Singh tapped open the door.

"Good morning sir. Here's hot tea. The Colonel will expect you in half an hour."

He left the door open. Ramendra Kaushal peeped out. Terry and Sparrow were gone. Thank God!

He sipped the steaming tea and felt better.

In the quiet shadowy cools of the basement, judging the exact time by daylight was difficult. One had to go by the watch. The wall clock in the room chimed 6.15.

Dhiren Bhagat entered silently and stood by his side.

Ramendra Kaushal ignored Bhagat's presence. He kept on squatting on the bed, head buried in the illusory safety of the warm niche of his knees drawn to his chest. He was, in fact, trying to use his fleshy thighs to block his eardrums. The echo from the mirror was still ringing inside him.

"What's happening?" Bhagat placed his hand gently on Kaushal's shoulder, "The Colonel is waiting for you."

"Hang your Colonel, whoever he is," Kaushal retorted, "I must be told, why have I been brought here? What do you expect of me?"

Bhagat drew up a chair, sat next to him and opened up in a low voice.

"I thought, I was doing you a good turn, saving you from the gallows and preparing you for a new life."

"What's this bloody new life? I'm a prisoner here."

"You won't feel so after a few days. You can't get back to the life you left behind. Behind you are the ruins of sin. The light of love and life are ahead of you. It's better that you prepare for the new one. I assure you, it'll be exciting. You'll live to enjoy every moment of it." Bhagat spoke in a seducing tone.

"Enjoy what? What the hell are you talking?" Kaushal straightened his legs and put them down on the floor.

"I'm offering you the exciting career of an intelligence officer, and an opportunity to take revenge on your father's killers, the Pakistani Muslims. You can redeem the prestige of your glorious family. You, a Prince in real life and a patriot, can serve your motherland."

"That doesn't make sense."

"Did you not enlist for the Indian Army in 1962? You did. You wanted to fight the enemies of the nation. You left after your mother objected. Am I correct?" Bhagat sprang him a surprise.

"How do you know that? Tell me more." Kaushal bent down slightly, placing both elbows on his knees, "I hope you aren't selling me stories from 007 fictions."

"Not really. I know more about you than your mother has told you. Listen carefully."

After the storyteller finished his fascinating account of the life story of Prince Ramendranath Kaushal and his father Raja Dayaram Kaushal, king of Jhumra, a tiny but flourishing kingdom off Jhang in Pakistan, the caged tiger stood up. He paced excitedly across the room furiously puffing at a cigarette.

"All these days you've been stalking me just for trapping me as your prospective agent in Pakistan!"

"Well! You're correct. But, you've three points to score, in the bargain."

"What's that trash?"

"You escape the gallows, at least on two counts of murder; you get to take revenge on the killers of your father and finally you pick up a glorious profession, with plenty of opportunity to destroy Pakistan. That's the country and those are the people, who had disinherited you from the Jhumra throne." Bhagat looked up and offered a cigarette to his client.

"Suppose I refuse to buy your story."

"You wanted to fight the Chinese, why not the Pakis?"

"Suppose I don't want to."

"No compulsion dear. You're the loser on all counts. It'll prove that you aren't a worthy son. You're a plain and simple criminal." Bhagat repeated the refrain of his story.

"No. I'm not a criminal." Kaushal shouted back.

"Your definition of crime can be different, but the facts remain where they are." Bhagat replied coolly.

"Are you selling me 007 trash?" Ramendra Kaushal looked up and asked for a cup of tea.

"No. You're lucky to be selected for the honourable task of serving the country, and you've your own scores to square up. I offer you a great opportunity."

"Don't confuse things," Kaushal rebuffed his handler, "I'd have been much better placed as a front line soldier."

"Correct dear," Bhagat continued the bombardment, "Our job, in the realm of espionage, is more adventurous and honourable. You get the real thrill, cutting down your enemy too fine; not by a bayonet, but by intelligent action."

"Shall I be on my own?"

"You'll have the independence of action, subject to tradecraft guidance and control. That's necessary for your safety. We'll take care of your needs and those of your mother. You'll have nothing to fear from the law."

"Do you know the killers of my father? Ma never told me the details."

"You'll get all the dope, in good time. I'm here to prepare you for the journey ahead. It's a tough journey and I'm afraid, you've to rewrite your slate." Bhagat tried to assuage Kaushal's bruised ego.

Bhagat's psychological darts scored the bull's eye. He didn't have to chase Kaushal to wash, have a hearty breakfast and come up to the office room of Karam Chand Pathania.

The old legend, the Terriers removed, was seated on a cushioned chair, behind a formidable table. Quarter inch grid maps of Pakistan occupied most of the walls, strategic locations marked by coloured flags and pins. Behind him, alongside the wall, a bright and polished brass Ashoka emblem buttressed two cross-mounted Tri-colours.

Karam Chand Pathania started with the family history of the Kaushals, tracing the roots to ***Rishi Vishwamitra*** (a mythological Brahmin saint who, against Manu's edict had donned the mantle of a king), the first ever Brahmin king of ***Aryavarta*** (habitat of the Aryans). He had defied the ***Kshatriyas*** (ruling warrior class) and rattled the Gods in their heavenly abode.

Coming from such illustrious lineage, the Kaushal kings had struck up a special relationship with the British; represented by the East India Company and the later day Viceroys in Delhi and layers of political agents and legions, in the Punjab.

Pathania supported his story with the moth eaten pages of history.

The Kaushal kings, like other loyal, pampered and spoiled potentates had collaborated with the white masters, by leading numerous punitive campaigns against the turbulent Frontier Mazari, Bugti, Pathan, Pushtoon, Pakhtoon and Niazi tribal warriors and marauding bands of Muslim ***thuggies*** (band of killer criminals) and ***dacoits*** (robbers).

The Sepoy Mutiny of 1857, as the empire liked to call the first secular Indian revolt against the tactless and mindless rule by the East India Company, had left thousands of Mughal soldiers and other Muslim satraps jobless. The vanquished Muslims were the prime suspects. Hindu collaborators like the Kaushal kings and the English educated Bengali Baboos had become the fulcrum of the empire.

The Kaushals, like other Hindu peers, had become a feared and hated clan. In the heartland of the fierce Mazari, Bugti, Niazi, Pathan and Pakhtoon majority tract, Hindu kingdom of Jhumra was viewed as a festering sore. The advocates of Pakistan, a pure land for the followers of the ***Allah*** had given notice to Dayaram Kaushal in early 1937.

Raja Dayaram Kaushal, the ruler of Jhumra was never rated as a diligent student of history and current affairs. He defied the 1946 communal award and advocated the merger of his territory with India. His links with the Frontier Gandhi and Hindu freedom fighters hadn't gone unnoticed. The departing British and emerging Muslim powers hated him equally.

The British Viceroy and his agent, the Governor General of Punjab, didn't come to his rescue when hordes of fanatic Muslims attacked his palace and killed him in an unfair war.

Ramendra Kaushal, progeny of such a proud Hindu father, Pathania advocated, should dedicate his life to redeeming his family honour. And what's life for, if it wasn't offered to the services of the ancestors and the nation!

Ramendra Kaushal's sensors started responding grudgingly to the psychological particles bombarded by Pathania and Bhagat. Bouncing from junction to junction inside his intricate modules, capillaries and the mysterious wiring system of his neurons, the particles of indoctrination gradually started sinking under the layers of his conscience. New emotions started replacing his carnal desire and bloated ego.

Pathania believed in the perfect synchronisation of neuronal and muscular responses. An agent, planted in enemy territory required razor sharp responses and a flexible body like a Burmese cane, resilient in response and quick in neutralising the adversary. There's no fun killing with a knife or a pistol. He gradually introduced Ramendra to a strong physical regimen of karate, unarmed combat and the use of sharp blades and precision shooting from small and medium combat weapons.

A new instructor arrived, after about a month, to teach fabrication and controlled explosion of improvised explosive devices. This was followed up by field demonstration of planting and disarming anti-personnel and anti-tank mines, use of RDX, PETN and home grown improvised explosives in highly delicate tasks of mass destruction.

Mr. Gonzalves, a tradecraft expert arrived one night, to teach cryptography, encoding and decoding devices. The old wizard of mathematics turned out to be the toughest nut to crack. Kaushal went mad over the use of logarithms, random generation of numerical and alphabet groups.

Gonzalves' load was added to the tricky lessons in Morse operation, use of compact HF wireless for clandestine transmission. The capacity of Kaushal's cranium was pushed to the edge and it refused to receive fresh stimuli.

"To hell with your training. It's better to face the hangman than dying a slow death every day. I'm sick of your damn training." Ramendra revolted.

"Look boy, I'm decent but not weak. I run the show and you've got to stick to my schedule." Pathania, eager to inject every bit of wisdom in one go reasserted his position.

"Hang it, I'm not your slave."

Ramendra didn't blink facing up to the sturdy trainer. He simply shut all his sensory organs out. This was his unique way of striking against the moustached giant. The cold war spilled out of the classrooms over to dinner table and corridors of the dilapidated fort.

Pathania declared the new pupil a persona non-grata.

Dhiren Bhagat appreciated Kaushal's problems. Stuffing the brain with too much of tradecraft and technical data and having no fun on the sidelines were eating into Kaushal's patience. His vacant gaze often engaged the pale white roof that had shut the sky off from him. His mind travelled back in time, to the good times in and outside the University campus. Trickles of saddened joy oozed out from his memory chambers, eroding the neo-elasticity of his mind. It built up a steam of active negation of the regimen prescribed by Pathania.

"Have patience brother," Bhagat commented, "You're almost through with the job."

"To hell with your fucking job. Give me my space back." Kaushal shouted.

"The life of an intelligence officer is as tough as that of an ascetic."

"To hell with your intelligence," Kaushal reacted defiantly, "A dried ginger root life isn't my cup of tea. Give me my sky back."

"Some discipline is necessary in our trade." Bhagat tried to be apologetic.

"Hang it. The Mataharis and Bonds hadn't put chastity belts around their fucking private parts and certainly didn't shun whisky. Your concept of discipline doesn't match mine. Let me be my own self. Take it or leave it." Ramendra Kaushal issued an ultimatum.

Karam Chand Pathania wasn't a guy to bend with times. To him discipline was as inviolable as the chastity of a married Hindu woman. His wasn't the place for philanderers and charlatans, he declared.

Sandwiched between two unyielding granite blocks Bhagat turned to Nampoothiri. He alone could help in breaking the logjam.

"Sir, he's reached a plateau. Can't absorb new inputs." Bhagat submitted.

"Why?"

"I think his brain cells aren't responding to the crammed training process. He requires a break."

"What do you feel?"

"I think a short break is necessary," Bhagat spoke in a frank voice,

"He is responding to motivational inputs. Let's not suspect his sincerity. We can't treat him as a routine cadet officer. He isn't here to earn his bread. Too much cramming would kill his motivation. We should allow him to enjoy a small part of his sky."

Nampoothiri silently looked up at Bhagat. Several questions radiated out of his eyes.

"I've a suggestion," Bhagat added.

"Carry on."

"We can take a break and concentrate on his cover-story. That'll give us some cushion. Rest of the things can be fitted in... if you permit."

Nampoothiri mulled over the suggestion for a few seconds and finally gave a nod.

"I won't say that your job will be on the line, if your "case-colt" bolts his stable. But you know the problems you've to face."

"I understand sir."

Bhagat felt confident that Kaushal wouldn't jump the bond they'd built up on mutual trust. He felt some vague affinity with the target. The guy, a violent rhesus under sedation, was trying to break open the cage once in a while, defying the trainer. Bhagat had noticed a patriot, a motivated nationalist and a nascent fighter in his target. The scoundrel had taken seriously the story of betrayal and the merciless murder of his father by his treacherous Muslim subjects. The revenge motive had sunk into his psyche. It was now up to his trainers to allow the roots to drive deep. These positive developments couldn't be ignored, simply because he felt tired and bored.

"Go ahead. Take care. Build up the cover story with care. I don't want any gaps. And his conversion to Islam is a must."

"I have the arrangements laid down. Maulana Rizwan is ready to accept him. Once the cover story is ingrained into his psyche and he's trained to live with it, we can take him back to the fort, to complete the technical courses and handling of trans-receiver systems and cipher documents."

"I've faith in you, and I hope you understand the time constraint placed on me by the top bosses. This target is to be infiltrated as soon as you finish with the training."

"He's a quick learner sir."

"But he still suffers from an inflated ego. Break it. That's not acceptable, you know it's not in our trade." Nampoothiri advised in a concerned voice.

He dismissed the junior officer with a faint smile on his face. He was happy with the progress. The turbulent typhoon had started learning the tricks of the trade, faster than he had expected him to. Kaushal's motivation, Nampoothiri guessed, had reached the eighth level of satisfaction. He was confident that the target of Operation Triple X should be ready for his tasks ahead, as a fully indoctrinated soldier.

It wasn't bad in tradecraft tricks to allow a deep penetration agent to retain some of his ego and idiosyncrasies. That should allow him easy access to the higher echelons in target areas. Delhi wasn't grooming up a two-penny tom for shallow intelligence gathering. The NSI was aiming real high and Nampoothiri expected Kaushal to hit bang on target.

Chapter 11

"I hope you aren't up to your old trick of catching me on celluloid, fucking another woman." Ramendra Kaushal laughed at Bhagat with a naughty chuckle.

They were seated in a plush hotel room at Ludhiana and cracking jokes.

"Forget that old shit," Bhagat felt embarrassed, "Enjoy yourself. Don't trust the girl. She's a pro, use a condom. I've kept a packet in the drawer. Yes, in the cupboard you'll find a bottle of Old Monk rum. Tomorrow we take on the new job." He closed the door behind softly.

"Don't talk of tomorrow's job tonight." Kaushal lustily walked down to the cupboard and fished out the bottle, kissed and uncorked it.

"Good luck, I'm in the next room. Have fun and be ready for the job ahead."

A professional, Bhagat wasn't known to cave in under emotional stress. His softness for the target wasn't personal. Temporary identification with the emotional vibes of the subject was part of a trade trick. In diplomatic language they called it confidence-building measure. In intelligence vocabulary, it was levelling up with the psychological strata of the target.

Such levelling was often highly rewarding. The facade of mental levelling created an illusion of well being and implicit trust in the case officer. Handling of ideological targets, Bhagat knew, was more tedious and tortuous. They resisted psychological bombardment and deflected all efforts of surreptitious entry through their idiosyncratic diaphragm.

Ramendra Kaushal carried no ideological bug inside his cranium. His psyche was still tangled with raw mammal emotions and reptilian responses. For Bhagat the job was rather difficult, swimming against the known current of the intelligence tradecraft.

He was supposed to inject an ideological motivation into the target and make him respond to new stimuli. Creation of new illusions and making the target respond to those was, in intelligence parlance, an obverse-inverse exercise. It was the toughest exercise, the stuffing of new emotional particles in the inner receptacles of the target's crania lobes.

An intelligence officer, worth his salt, was as remorseless as a saw blade on rotary motion, cutting anything and everything coming its way. In very rare cases, Bhagat's class was allowed to inject genuine emotion into their cutting edges, like the saw blades were often doused with droplets of water and chemicals to keep their teeth moist.

Ramendra Kaushal wasn't sensitive enough to understand the subtle subversion game. His mind was turned on to the blood soaked soil of

Jhumra. He conjured up the facade of the lost kingdom's glory and steadily fastened himself to the dream of avenging his father's assassination.

Bhagat's success in creating an illusion of trust in Kaushal's psyche was another feather in his cap. The foundation of trust grew stronger day by day, as Kaushal developed an emotional dependence on his case officer.

Kaushal allowed a few seconds for Bhagat to settle down in the adjoining room and downed a few shots straight from the bottle. He felt fortified and looked down the hall, at the doll hired by Bhagat. She stood in her bare skins near the sprawling bed.

He walked around the female, in slow unsteady steps, occasionally puffing at a cigarette. His eyes, narrowed into slits, examined intently the intrinsic quality of the product. The doll didn't transmit oscillating waves of desire and emotion. Ramendra looked at her face and suddenly stepped back. Rajni Krittika Hemaprabha Rao was staring at him with the same scornful looks, her lips drawn inside and her eyes sternly rebuking him.

Oh God!

Ramendra shivered for a while and again looked up.

No. The plump woman wasn't Hema. She looked straight at him with an amused invitation.

He gulped another drink and took another round of the smiling doll. Hema again reappeared with her scornful looks.

No he couldn't enjoy sex with this woman, perhaps with any woman, ever.

Ramendra picked up the robes and asked her to dress and quit. Thanks for the trouble, he wished her good night, after pushing a bunch of notes in her clammy palms.

He didn't sleep well. The dumb face of the hired prostitute tormented him. The never-ending celluloid footage of Rajni Krittika Hemaprabha Rao's face and that of his mother kept on flashing past his mind's eye.

He woke up next morning fully drained and exhausted.

"Did you like the girl?" Bhagat asked.

"She was fine, nothing special." Ramendra avoided a direct answer.

"Avoid stray women. That's not good for your profession. Your enemy in Pakistan, the ISI, will use honey traps to neutralise you. Learn the tricks of controlling your responses."

"How do you do that?"

"I've friends in Delhi's G.B. Road red light quarters. I will take you there for a few learning sessions."

"Is this a part of your darn training?"

"You're correct. It's a kind of ***yoga.*** There are more wonders to discover in this wonderful trade."

Bhagat smiled inscrutably and drove his car along the Grand Trunk Road. He branched off to an unpaved rural link road and reached the outskirts of village Faqira, situated below the spurs of the rail track that connected Ludhiana to Amritsar. He parked the vehicle behind a dilapidated mosque and neglected burial mounds and helped Kaushal to alight.

"Why have you brought me here? What am I to do in this darn place?" Kaushal felt intrigued and irritated.

"These are the remains of village Faqira, village of Harfan Bukhari. Seventeen years back, in 1947, he was a seven-year-old lad, studying in the village ***madrasa*** (religious school) and helping his father in his fields and in a ball bearing and minor auto parts factory...

"His father, Maqdoom Bukhari, marketed his products in Amritsar and Lahore.

"On July 5, 1947 the entire Muslim population of the village just vanished, barring a few elderly women. The Hindu and Sikh mob looted and burnt everything and raped every woman they could lay their hands on. Maqdoom Bukhari's entire family was cut to pieces and thrown into a blazing fire. It was a mad time on either side of the border...

"Somewhere," Bhagat pointed his finger to a heap of brick rubble, nature's greenery spreading its soothing cover on the bygone blood and ash. "There was the house of your father Maqdoom Bukhari...

"Only your uncle, Shamim Bukhari, who happened to be at Amritsar, could take a train to Lahore. He didn't return to the village. He's now settled in Karachi, married to a refugee woman and running a factory, producing defence related spare parts."

"Didn't the Muslims deserve the carnage? After all, they did the same to the Hindus and Sikhs! They killed my father."

"It depends from which angle you would like to see the picture. Even the most horrendous criminals in history, say one like Hitler, have their own philosophy of life. Man can justify all his actions. His cerebral capabilities are flexible. Try to rise above the events and you'll see that, all of us are blind and helpless puppets in the hands of the puppeteer called history."

Bhagat tried to explain the queer games played by history in the sub-continent.

"I can't agree with you Bhagat. Your reasoning is good for a Buddha. But we're raw animals, packed with emotions. How can I forget that they killed my father and hounded my mother out, in sackcloth and ash?" Ramendra Kaushal poured out his hatred against the Muslims.

"We're immensely influenced by incidents affecting our lives. At times you're required to rise above the skeletons of events and peep into the soul of philosophy."

"What's your bloody philosophy behind chasing me and turning me into a machine of destruction?"

"You and I are soldiers of a geo-political war. That's different from individual wars. Your and my small wars are controlled by a national strategy. It's a trade, and in our profession we keep the individual buried. The nation gets priority."

Bhagat explained succinctly the role of an individual in intelligence warfare.

"Why should I fight your war? I've my own war to fight inside Pakistan." Kaushal thundered out again.

"Yours is a special case. You've the freedom of pursuing your own agenda... So, as I was telling you," Bhagat continued, " For your cover, our story runs like this: Harfan Bukhari, the seven year old lad managed to escape the slaughter and was restored to his ***phufi*** (paternal aunt). A woman in her fifties, Harfan's aunt and her husband lived in one of the blind lanes of the walled city of Delhi...

"Their nightmare wasn't yet over. Her husband was cut into pieces in the 1950 communal carnage and she just managed to run up the stairs of the Jama Masjid, with you. The old lady had no means to bear the expenses of migration and no neighbour was kind enough to pick her up. In the second exodus too, from either side of the gory border, each one was on his own."

"Didn't she get in touch with her brother in Karachi?" Asked Ramendra.

"She didn't like to desert the memories of her husband... and Shamim's second wife didn't encourage him. Any way, the blackest nightmare came to an end, the blood and flesh were washed clean and the old lady started a new life. She brought up Harfan, educated him and died three years ago. Harfan, a bitter enemy of the Hindus and India, has now decided to go over to Pakistan. His goal is to trace out his uncle and live as an honourable and proud Muslim, in the country of his destiny."

"Why are you telling me this story?"

"This is your basic cover story, the story of Harfan Bukhari. Here are copies of a few letters you had written to your uncle Shamim and his replies. He's now keen to see you and wants you to join him in his business. Here's a pamphlet. This contains all details of the Bukhari family. Mug it up."

"I didn't write any letter."

"We've done the job for you. Read the letters and keep yourself updated, your uncle is expecting you."

"But, I'm a Hindu! How can you forge my birth certificate, school documents and how can you change my physical features?" Kaushal looked up in disbelief.

"You'll be given all the training necessary to make you a good Muslim. We'll take care...Here's another pamphlet. It contains all details about your real father's well wishers back in Jhumra. Some Muslim families are still loyal to him."

"Who are these characters?"

"Find out for yourself."

"Mother never spoke about such people back in Pakistan."

"Don't quiz her if she hasn't. She can't be privy to your new life and assignment."

Back to the car, Ramendra Kaushal lighted a cigarette, inhaled a few puffs and shot back.

"Suppose I decline!"

"Do you have any choice? Why try to slip back to times where you can't go back? For you it's a new life all the way, a new identity. Destiny has provided a path of light for you to walk on."

"You talk differently Bhagat. I wish I knew you before I was trapped by Ram Karan's gang."

"Don't worry. We're humans and we know how to break barriers. You can achieve anything if you so wish. Let's go. We drive straight to Delhi. Maulana Rizwan shall be waiting for you."

Bhagat opened the door and facilitated Kaushal, still puffing away at the cigarette with an audible sound. He understood the game very well by now. In his new incarnation, Harfan Bukhari was supposed to walk past minefields in a new country and live a shadowy existence. One false step and he would be blown into pieces. No quarter was given to anybody in this game.

"Aren't the Pakis going to tear down my cover in no time?" Ramendra asked.

"We'll teach you all the tricks needed to merge yourself in the new milieu. The Pakis can't get at you, if you live by the rules. That's important." Bhagat turned the wheels towards Delhi.

"It's scary."

"A soldier doesn't get scared of shadows. Get ready for the war ahead."

****

Shyam Purohit alias Maulana Rizwan, FIB's cornerstone in Islamic studies and agent moulding for operations inside Pakistan, functioned from a nondescript building located in the wilderness of rural Delhi. The sprawling wooded farmhouse, camouflaged behind cowsheds, chicken coops and a flourishing fruit orchard was the only human oasis in the midst of the sub-tropical Shivalik forest.

The stray shepherds and tribal hunter-gatherers knew Maulana Rizwan as an ardent religious Muslim and a humble owner of the poultry cum dairy farm. He usually dressed as a village ***maulana*** and flaunted a flourishing moustache and beard with a white mosque cap to match. Proficient in Urdu and Persian, Rizwan was an ***alem, maulana*** and ***mufti***, all rolled in one. He took years to perfect the cover.

The ***maulana*** wasn't known as a social creature. But he didn't fail to show up for the Friday prayers at the historic Jama Masjid and ***ijtema*** (religious teaching) congregations organised by the Muslim Jammat and ***Rabita-al-Alam-al-Islami,*** the Saudi based fountainhead of World Muslim League.

Shyam Purohit was both a legend and an icon in the FIB. Recruited way back in 1950, the genesis of his tryst with the intelligence fraternity had actually started way back in 1948.

The FIB was presented with a giant sized problem soon after the transfer of power. The Muslim officers had opted for Pakistan and those who preferred to stay back were shunted out of the prime intelligence edifice. Intelligence in post-partition India, as was with the Empire, was wedded to the ruling clique. The new masters meaninglessly parroted the slogan of secularism but weren't ready to trust the Muslims with state secrets. Communal hatred and distrust still haunted the noblest of souls, both Hindu and Muslim.

The Partition left the FIB almost crippled. The Muslims, a suspect community in the Hindu majority India, had shut all the windows and the Hindus in turn treated them as poisoned cheese balls. The age-old communication links had snapped.

The Pakistan Intelligence Bureau, on the other hand, enjoyed built in advantages over its Indian counterpart. They exploited the susceptibilities and dreams of the Indian Muslims. Some of the talents, recruited by them, believed that their rightful home was in the newly created country, and they were temporary guests, in Hindu India.

The FIB was bereft of penetrating access to the target community that lived in close-knit urban ghettos and rural islands, spinning their lives around ***madrasas*** and ***mosques.*** There was no open sesame magic available to intelligence giants like Rabindra Narayan Dutta.

Behind the facade and slogans of secularism the politicians treated them as a captive vote bank. They were taken out once in five years, like confined ***harem*** beauties, for stamping the ballot papers. The new Indian masters assiduously kept them segregated and insulated, all in the name of secularism. The entire community was pushed behind a massive ***purdah*** (veil). India was imprisoned, in eternity, inside the cursed magic mirror of social and communal stratification, crafted by mutual distrust and religious bigotry.

The politicians harvested sunshine out of the miseries and enforced backwardness of the community, but the FIB faced an endless freezing winter. This was the dark cool side of the moon, never exposed to the national mainstream. The FIB, blind folded in the back alleys of intelligence, bumped around the contours of varied obstacles.

Rabindra Narayan Dutta, an immaculate Englishman in dress, accent and mannerism had something uncommon with his imperial mentors. He shared the post-independence national obsession of distrust for the Muslim minority. He accepted the unwritten national policy of avoiding Muslims, as plague viruses, in sensitive security services. They were, in his eyes, potential Pakistani agents.

Agent recruitment from the Muslim community was equally difficult. Hindu officers simply didn't have access to the ghettos, religious and political organisations. The vitiated and surcharged atmosphere still kept the natural flow artificially constricted.

Dutta and his hierarchy had to circumvent the seemingly hopeless situation. His recipe was simple: train your own officers, give them covers of perfect Muslims and infiltrate them at appropriate levels in the target community. The Dutta doctrine had defined and ordained a new philosophy for the organisation.

Shyam Purohit was one such early talent, trained to don the complete cover of a Muslim. He learnt Urdu, mastered the ***Quran Majid*** and ***Hadis***, all the technicalities of ***Namaz, Kalma*** and intricacies of personal law. He passed the test of all tests by undergoing the process of circumcision.

Dutta doctrine wasn't confined to Muslims alone. The close knit Hindu Sangh, formed well after 19 years the Muslims floated their first monolith communal organisation, was not made of spongy granite blocks. They preached their own kind of patriotism and suffered from the illusions of establishing a theocratic state to the exclusion of the other religious groups. The seeds of hatred sown by the Muslim occupation of India and the British Empire had flourished into a formidable Wailing Wall.

Master sleuth Dutta didn't find it easy to persuade his Hindu officers to don the Muslim mantle. The two streams were destined; it appeared, not to merge in their journey to the ocean of humanity. Centuries of cohabitation didn't change the jaundiced views of the high priests of politics and religion. The singed psyche of both the communities continued to brew the concoctions of hatred.

Shyam Purohit, a committed cadre of the Hindu Sangh had eluded the police and intelligence verification dragnet to gain entry in the FIB. He did need the job, no doubt. But his Sangh trainers and ideologues prodded him relentlessly to infiltrate into the prime intelligence organisation. It was a vital strategic move, aimed at positioning committed cadres inside the veins and capillaries of the system. Purohit's training with the khaki clad Sangh brigade had left at the core of his consciousness, a deep-seated suspicion, if not hatred, for the Muslims.

Once in the Sangh, they said, a Hindu was bound to be an inveterate Muslim hater. They copied the doctrine of hate-laced exclusivism practised by the Muslim Jamaat fanatics. The two hooded creatures were fashioned by history. It was a civilisational conflict, nursed and watered for centuries. Shyam's infiltration was a small but vital step towards capturing the establishment from within.

Shyam Purohit baptised as a hard liner Muslim fundamentalist had infiltrated into several Islamic religious and political bodies. In his new incarnation, bearing the lofty name of Maulana Rizwan, he had accomplished the task of spawning several intelligence hatcheries inside the Muslim Jamaat. He had cloned himself through the process of rigorous training and helped the FIB in achieving deep penetration inside Islamic organisations.

Shyam Purohit fronted the Mumtaj Farm, a novel experiment initiated by Dutta. It floated beyond the realms of reality, marketing poultry, milk and milk products and training officers of the FIB in special tradecraft. The cover was perfect and the trainer was impeccable.

Four trained Alsatian dogs came in with Muhim Khan, an assistant to Purohit. Muhim alias Gautam Rai was earlier infiltrated into the Deoband School of Islamic studies, the alma mater of the ***Wahabi Sunni*** faith. He had mastered all the tricks to become a good ***Sunni,*** but didn't get circumcised. One of the outings to the Bareilly red light area proved disastrous for the neo-convert. The lady he had chosen was a Muslim, and she wasn't amused to see, while having oral sex, that the venerable ***maulana*** (priest) and ***alem*** (scholar) had his foreskin intact. Her profession didn't make her blind to the rituals of her religion.

The story reached the pimps in the red light colony and finally travelled to Deoband. Muhim had to take the first bus out of town to Delhi. That was necessary for literally saving his foreskin and the skin on his back.

Purohit had a surprise meeting with Balachandran Nampoothiri at a deserted park near Qutub Minar, in a southern suburb of Delhi.

"I've a bright but difficult student for you."

"Anything special?"

"Yes, he's special. Make him a perfect Muslim. Teach him the Punjabi dialect spoken in Mianwali area. It is spoken in a peculiar nasal Pushtu accent. Teach him Urdu thoroughly, in short, make him a ***pucca*** Muslim." Nampoothiri spelled out his specific instructions.

"Nothing would be left to chance," Averred Purohit, "But sir, I hope the new student will cooperate."

"I can't assure that. He's not a run of the mill candidate." Nampoothiri explained the background of the new target.

"You've to be patient," he continued, "Break him down into fine mortar and pastel and than shape him up again. I don't want any gap in the process of moulding him. Keep in mind his special cover story and the time frames."

"Leave him at my disposal. Short of scraping out his ingrained character, which at this age can't be changed, I'll turn him into a perfect Muslim."

Maulana Rizwan reassured Nampoothiri.

Chapter 12

Ramendra Kaushal wasn't the first open market talent to enter the hallowed clandestine precincts of Maulana Rizwan. But he was the most turbulent one.

The rickety motor van of Mumtaj Farm was the only means of transportation to Rizwan's secret hole. It honked at the outer gate at six in the morning, with Dhiren Bhagat and Ramendra Kaushal as additional passengers. Other usual passengers and loads included two coops full of broiler chicks, sacks of cattle fodder and rations for human and canine inmates. Muhim Khan opened the gate, allowed the van in and closed it with a bang.

Kaushal jumped out of the van cursing everyone, right from the elusive God above to Dhiren Bhagat, standing next to him. This wasn't the way, he complained, for a gentleman to travel with chattering and foul smelling birds and assorted garbage.

His protestations were drowned in the orchestrated high-pitched howling of the Alsatians, leashed to an iron pole. Kaushal jumped and took cover behind Muhim.

"Do you have to have these killer animals everywhere? And I don't think these animals are in any way a part of your damn training." He grumbled.

"I'm afraid you're correct, they are. But you must appreciate that, for coming to the farmhouse of ***chacha*** (uncle) there's no other transport available." Bhagat smiled feebly.

"You don't travel with your table bird." Kaushal repeated the complaint.

"Welcome to my ***garib khana*** (small place of a modest person). Sorry for the inconveniences." Proclaimed Maulana Rizwan.

"Who're you?" Kaushal blinked his eyes at the unbelievably deceptive figure of Purohit.

"***Banda ko Maulana Rizwan kahte hain*** (the modest person is Maulana Rizwan)."

"Why am I here?"

"Let's talk about that later. Breakfast is ready. Come." Rizwan invited his guests to the dining room.

Breakfast was sumptuous, flat bread fried in ***ghee*** (melted cow milk fat), fried potatoes and roasted chicken nuggets, followed by glasses of buttermilk.

"***Beta*** (son)," Rizwan spoke in a low voice, "I've heard a lot about you. Ordained by ***Allah***, I run this place in my own fashion. In addition to me you have Muhim, a black belt in karate and four Alsatians, all trained to kill intruders, who try breaking through my fences. And for your information, Muhim charges the iron mesh with 230 volts before he retires. I don't like intruders."

Kaushal looked at Bhagat with nervous eyes, for support.

"The van leaves at 8.30 sharp. Get ready." Rizwan spoke to Bhagat; "I don't like guests who overstay their welcome."

"When do I come next?" Bhagat asked.

"After two months, if your friend co-operates," Rizwan replied with an impish look, "That's the schedule for now."

The joint didn't impress Ramendra Kaushal. It wore a ghostly appearance. The brick building, located in the midst of nowhere was surrounded by thick and wild growth of vegetation. The wooded farmhouse, lined with fruit and permanently flowering trees was girdled by a paved jogging track.

Kaushal, 25 years younger to Rizwan, ran slowly behind him followed by the Alsatians and Muhim. This was his morning routine, and he expected the trainees to honour it as well.

"Tired?" Asked Rizwan.

"Out of touch ***ustad*** (captain)."

"Build up your strength and stamina, you'll require a fit body and a super-fit mind." Rizwan advised.

He stopped, took a deep breath and turned to Kaushal.

"Are you religious?" He asked.

"What do you mean by that?"

"How deeply are you attached to your religion?"

"I've no religion. I'm a born Hindu, perhaps a born Brahmin. Why?"

"Just like that. To me, my profession is my religion. It's gratifying to note your status. I have to teach you all the tenets of Islam."

"I hate the Muslims."

"Why?"

"I hate them. They killed my father." Kaushal replied.

"Fine. But to fight a Muslim state you have to be one of them, you must respect and practice their religion."

"I can kill them from outside too."

"That's very difficult. To kill your enemy you must understand him. Practice their religion and ways of life. You win half the war, if you know your enemy well."

Muhim took over after breakfast with lessons in Urdu. The Alsatians snoozed under the mid-summer heat; intermittently sniffing Kaushal's exposed limbs.

"This is the most important part of the job." Muhim pontificated.

"Every bloody step is important. But remove these devils first. They don't help in remembering the queer alphabets."

"Try living with all odds, you'll start loving them."

"Spare me the pontificating. I hate dogs."

"Better give me a check list of things you don't hate. Hope you don't hate yourself!" Muhim retorted.

Kaushal's tangent look almost singed his tutor. Muhim smiled back and started a new lesson on the basic concepts of Islam.

As the afternoon lessons progressed, under an idle cloud covered sun, Maulana Rizwan slithered in silently from a corner. Before Kaushal could move his neck sideways and capture the full profile of the intruder, Rizwan pushed in the needle of a syringe on his left arm.

"What the hell is this?" A shocked Kaushal tried to jerk his arm away.

"You require a little sleep and I'm required to perform a small surgery, ***janab*** (mister) Harfan Bukhari."

Rizwan, assisted by Muhim carried Kaushal's limp body to a dining table, and took out a vapour emitting sterilised steel box. He slipped in latex gloves and shaved the areas around Kaushal's private parts, swabbed it with disinfectant and carefully carried out a microsurgery, removing the foreskin of Kaushal's genital. He bandaged the operated part carefully and administered a shot of antibiotic, a precaution against infection.

Kaushal woke up after about two hours, only to find his hands and legs fettered to the table. His eyes were still groggy but he could hear Maulana Rizwan's booming voice.

"Welcome, Mian Harfan Bukhari. Sorry for the pain."

Kaushal tried to move on to his side and felt a shooting pain in the general area of his crotch, his testicles burning from the effect of the operation.

"What have you done to me? And I'm not Harfan Bukhari." He retorted in a sore voice.

"Don't forget your new name. It's going to stick to you for the rest of your life. Better ingrain it. You have to live the new life of Harfan Bukhari," Rizwan explained, "I've just performed a small surgery and removed a little bit of skin from your genital."

"Why did you have to deceive me into it? Untie my hands and feet."

"You aren't my first student. Only one person before you agreed to undergo the circumcision willingly. I don't like the cries of pain and resistance. Sorry for the pain, but I can assure that, you'll be fit in two days and your sexual prowess will increase. This is an important part of the cover. Circumcision is an integral part of Islam and Judaism."

"You mean all fucking Muslims and Jews are more potent and virile than the Hindus and Sikhs!"

"Mind your language Harfan. All religious communities are equally honourable. These are civilisational practices, which evolved out of the historical and geographical needs of the concerned people." Rizwan chided his student.

"Don't mind me ***ustad***. But look at history of these people. These Muslims are desert locusts, multiplying in millions. They're a demographer's nightmare. Perhaps, people like you have to pray for reducing the virility of this community."

Rizwan didn't reply. It was useless to argue with this conscious ***satan.*** Nampoothiri was correct about the turbulent nature of his student. He carried in a tray of hot coffee and some tempting cakes.

"Son, from now onwards I'll call you Harfan. You have to start living the cover, along with the learning process. Every bit of your personal life should look like that of a Muslim. A keen observer shouldn't be able to detect even a single grain of inconsistency." He spoke in a soft affectionate voice.

"Repeat after me: ***Bismillah-ur-Rehman-e Rahim,*** In the name of Allah, the Beneficent, the Merciful; recite with me, ***La Ilaha Illa Ilah Mumammad-ur-Rasulu'llah*** (there's no God but Allah, and Muhammad is his Prophet). Remember, this is the ***Kalema-e-Tayeb***, the essence of all praises of the Almighty Allah and his Prophet, Muhammad, (PBuH) son of Abdul Muttalib, of the tribe of Qureysh."

He presented a ***Mushaf*** (copy of the Quran) and ***Hadis*** to Kaushal.

"Read these books carefully. These are the Holy Books and foundations of Islam. I'll help you with it. Master the technicalities of the Islamic rituals. These are ***beheshti zevars*** (celestial jewels), like Hindu prescriptions of daily rituals."

"All these buggers are the same. What's so great about these fucking rituals?"

Kaushal tried to provoke Rizwan on several points during the lessons related to ***Namaz, Roza*** (ritual Ramadan fasting) and prescription for studying the ***Quran Majid.***

"Keep your precious views to yourself. Ingrain deep inside what I teach. These are essential for your survival." Rizwan chided his student.

"These are archaic, meant for desert locusts, I mean a people who lived under different social and political dispensations centuries ago. How can these prescriptions rule the lives of modern men? The Manu Smriti is ridiculous and insulting to fellow human beings. The Quran is no better." Harfan tried to compare the lessons in a shallow and immature way.

"That's enough Harfan. It's not a debating class," Purohit snubbed his pupil, "We're here not to write a critique on the Holy Books. ...

"Remember that the Muslims, like the Jews, Christians and Sikhs are people of the Books, Ahl-e-Hadis, unlike the Hindus. Respect other's faith. Don't babble like a baboon."

"It's so difficult."

"I'm here to help. Tolerance is the name of the game. Don't be snappy. Read more. The ***Holy Quran***, the ***Hadis*** and the ***Shariat*** are the pillars of Islamic faith. Read and practice these tenets carefully. Understanding your enemy is the only way to arm yourself efficiently."

"Oh shit!" Kaushal reacted vehemently, " Anyway, I suppose I am to enjoy the raping of my soul."

Rizwan smiled. He knew that behind the foul mouth there was a diligent learner. This one student had sprung a surprise on him outpacing him in the process of learning.

Sixty days flew past.

Maulana Rizwan accompanied by Harfan Bukhari reached the portals of the grand Jama Masjid, built by emperor Shahjahan, to attend the Friday prayers.

He had taught Harfan all the nuances of ***Fajr, Zohar, Asar, Maghrib, Isha*** and ***Jumma Namaz*** rituals, with meticulous stress on the rituals of ***Ruku*** (bending properly) and ***Sijda*** (obeisance in a prostrated position).

Standing next to his pupil Rizwan appreciated the perfect and synchronised performance of the young devil. Behind his apparent foul and sharp tongue he had a receptive razor sharp mind. Harfan passed the test right down to the last details.

He was now a real Muslim, in every sense of it. Even a seasoned ***namazi*** for forty years, with a black spot on his forehead, would not be able to detect any flaw. Harfan was a fast learner, a talented boy.

Bhagat took over from Rizwan soon after Kaushal alias Harfan Bukhari graduated out of the Mumtaj Farm seminary.

"You get just one month to acclimatise yourself in an undiluted Muslim ghetto. Don't forget that you're supposed to have had a ***phufi*** (aunt) living at Gali Qabristan, behind the ***dargah*** (burial place) of Dada Pir Bukhari, ancestor of the Bukhari clan. They were brought to Hindustan by emperor Shahjahan from ancient Bukhara, to lead the faithfuls to prayers under the canopy of the Jama Masjid."

"The history is fine, but what do I do there?"

"Acquaint yourself with the old city. Be a Harfan who grew up in that milieu for the last eighteen years. Learn the finer nuances of living like a Muslim. Live like a true Muslim...

"In Pakistan, where you're assigned to go, you'll be watched by everyone. And you have to pass the vital tests, when you meet your Uncle Shamim Bukhari. The old man must be nursing a lot of memories under his chest. All migrants do."

"I can't get into the roots of a life which aren't mine."

"Come'n Harfan," Bhagat cajoled his agent, "You've done it already. Now just live like one. That's all. We shall be in touch. Remember that my eyes shall all the time follow you. We meet again after a month."

Harfan Bukhari hesitated for a while and turned back.

"Suppose I run away and disappear?"

"I know you won't do that. Raja Dayaram Kaushal's son won't run away without avenging his father's death. Your destiny is waiting there at Jhumra. Anything else? Want more scotch and girls?"

"Thanks, but I don't feel like."

Harfan turned down his case officer's offer politely and boarded a cycle rickshaw and proceeded towards his aunt's place at Gali Qabristan, literally meaning-lane of the burial ground.

He lighted a cigarette and smiled uncertainly at the milling crowd he was passing through. Oh! What a damn tryst it was with witch doctors like Bhagat and Rizwan? He had come to love and respect them. A dedicated trainer, Rizwan had devoted his entire life to the cause of his department, perhaps the nation. He believed in his cause and philosophy, like any orthodox Hindu or Muslim believed in their scriptures and archaic social practices.

Bhagat had, by now, become an inseparable part of his existence. The intimate association and levelling of psychological strata had brought about chemical changes in him. He didn't realise that, his handler had started conditioning his neuronal impulses, by subverting his psychograph.

For next thirty days, Harfan Bukhari lived at 1437/309 Gali Qabristan, off Turkman Gate. The final test was supposed to be very tough, living the life of a Muslim in undiluted surroundings that had warded off civilisational changes for over five centuries. It was a frozen society, where life stood still behind the walls of the great ramparts of the massive mosque.

The nephew of Zubaida Begum, sister of Shamim and Maqdoom Bukhari, settled down in the new surroundings, as a young graduate from Aligarh Muslim University, ostensibly surveying opportunities to start a factory to manufacture ball bearings and auto accessories.

A real estate agent, an under cover FIB officer, chaperoned Harfan around the walled city, explaining the peculiarities of dress, food habits and the minute details of the peculiar accent of spoken Urdu.

"It's a different civilisation," he explained, "Captured in the frozen city of Shahjahanabad, the capital city of emperor Shahjahan. Move around the small lanes; visit the ***havelis*** (old mansions) and markets. Get to know the people."

"In what way are they different?"

"The people here live in the past, both Hindus and Muslims. The later day British and Punjabi invaders haven't been able to change them much. You'll find the same frozen trends in the lanes and markets of old Karachi and

Lahore. A unique rhythm runs through the veins of the people in these traditional settlements. You must discover this world, common to the people, living on either side of the border."

Bhagat's man wasn't far from truth. The walled city, immersed in the past was pleasantly different from the imperial Delhi and the other Delhi built by the Punjabi refugees. It throbbed with life and pulsated with unique rhythm.

Harfan Bukhari patiently peeled off the apparent dirt and modern masks and slowly discovered the lost world of a centuries old culture, preserved by generations of decaying and daring people. They dared the invasive British and Punjabi cultures, which doggedly knocked at there dilapidated ramparts.

Thirty days passed by like wind driven cotton flakes. Harfan didn't know when the jinn of hatred against everything Muslim, subtly yielded to deep channels of love for the people around him. He suddenly discovered that a unified flow of compassion had flooded the deep furrows in his mind. The seeds of life and love, he understood, always triumphed over the debris of death and destruction.

His new birth would have remained incomplete, Harfan felt, had he not lived in this unique world. The experience invigorated him with the life-essence of the people who lived in dark alleys, foxholes, dilapidated ***havelis*** and were enwrapped in the memories of emperors, courtesans, bind-sellers and magicians.

Chapter 13

Rabindra Narayan Dutta and his two deputies were closeted with Prime Minister Jung Bahadur as he burnt the night oil at his Janpath residence.

Tomorrow, 15th August, the Independence Day was a historic event in the life of the nation and his life as well. The previous August had passed through national grief, as India mourned the death of his illustrious predecessor, Amritlal.

Jung Bahadur didn't step into August of 1965 with unmixed blessings. It was mid-monsoon in India, a failed one at that, which had created a gloomy spectre of parched fields and famine and chronic dependence on American dole, with diabolical strings attached.

The war rumblings on the western border compounded the spectre of hunger. Pakistan, the enfant terrible of the sub-continent, had launched a daring attack in the Rann of Kachchh and its trained infiltrators had sneaked into Jammu and Kashmir, to repeat the 1948 encounter, this time in a decisive manner. Jung Bahadur had a lot of explaining to do, to his countrymen.

External forces alone didn't haunt him. A group of cabinet ministers and party men had been calling for his scalp. Not in a very muted voice. Mandira, Amritlal's daughter, spearheaded the encore group.

"Tell me the broad talking points." Jung Bahadur asked his FIB chief, Rabindra Narayan Dutta, seated across the table, accompanied by his deputies, Balachandran Nampoothiri and Kumar Anand Prasad.

"Sir, customarily the PM goes by the text finalised by his office, in consultation with the major ministries."

"I know. I've got one. But the nation wants to hear something new. Our China war was a disaster. Our performance in the Kachchh war has been lacklustre. People are in no mood to hear profane pontificating and moralising talks. Tell me something bold. The country wants a spell of success." Jung Bahadur completed the sentence with extra emphasis on the last three words.

"Sir, Pakistan is ready for another round of war. They call it Operation Gibraltar. Infiltrators have started sneaking in. They have developed strategic bridgeheads with the regular formations of the Pakistan army. It's a better planned military thrust than the 1948 campaign," Dutta explained the internal and external scenario in short staccato sentences, "People will love to hear you come down heavily on Pakistan."

Jung Bahadur nodded in agreement.

Dutta continued explaining that the clouds of communist extremism were building up in the north of West Bengal. They talked of bringing in revolution through the barrels of guns. The Chinese involvement was transparent. In addition to the Naga Hills and Manipur, embers of insurgency had started glowing in Lushai Hills Mizoram as well, with active collaboration of the Chinese and the Pakistanis.

Pakistan, he elaborated, had acquired sophisticated weapons systems from China. And the US had off loaded plenty of Vietnam surpluses at the port city of Karachi in recent months. He suspected a tilt of military balance in favour of Pakistan.

"I understand Dutta," Continued Jung Bahadur, "Pakistan is my headache. But I won't allow it to be my nemesis. I'm afraid; your intelligence inputs are inadequate. I must have a clear forewarning about Pakistan's strategic plans and tactical moves."

"You're correct sir."

"Tell me, what's the status of your penetration? Can we take Pakistan on?"

Dutta maintained a silence.

"Hope there is no problem on that front?"

"No problem as such," Dutta opened up hesitatingly, "Agent Alamgir is doing fine and it's he who has supplied us with the vital inputs on Operation Gibraltar. We're trying to do better than that."

"Better won't do. I want the best," Jung Bahadur looked straight into Dutta's eyes, "I'm mighty worried about the conspiracies brewing up behind my back. My party colleagues are betraying me. What's your feed back?"

Dutta paused for a few seconds. The FIB had adopted a position of neutral activism in matters pertaining to the ruling party. Only the critics and opponents of the PM were subjected to the FIB scrutiny.

"To be frank sir," Dutta continued," Your predecessor didn't authorise us to report on the ruling party."

"I know. I don't enjoy his kind of honeymooning with the nation. I'm facing an internal revolt. Keep me informed." Jung Bahadur spoke in a soft, almost a soliloquise murmur.

He was, no doubt the choice of his predecessor, but the party coterie wielded an iron grip on him. And Amritlal's daughter left no opportunity spreading canards about the dangers faced by the country from a midget of a PM.

"Sir, I can't say there's a revolt, but there are rumblings of disaffection." Dutta spoke in a cryptic manner.

"How much is Mandira involved in all these?"

"Considerably."

"Fine. Keep me informed. She's impatient. That worries me. Take care of this and the Pakistani design in Kashmir. I don't want a repetition of 1948." Jung Bahadur spoke in a steely tone.

The PM stood up and before bidding good-bye turned back.

"What's your report on Ram Karan Prasad? How much is he involved with Pakistani leaders? What're his criminal activities? Does he run a Mafia? I want a quick report on him."

"Any particular angle?" Dutta spoke approvingly, though he wasn't sure of the Prime Minister's depth of knowledge about the fiercest jackal of the Indian politics.

"Nothing special," Jung Bahadur spoke in a whisper, "But it pains me to hear from the Russian ambassador that he has questionable links with the Pakistanis. I should have heard this from you first."

"I'm sorry sir that you carry that impression. I'll dig out the old dossier that I'd shared with your predecessor." Dutta couldn't heave a sigh of relief as yet. The old man wasn't clearly coughing out. Something was brewing under his small oblong skull.

Next morning Jung Bahadur spoke unhesitatingly from the Red Fort ramparts. His warning to external aggressors and internal divisive forces was unequivocal. He warned his countrymen to remain ready for a long walk through dark nights of economic privation and Pakistani aggression.

Nampoothiri rushed up and spoke in his ears as the Prime Minister began to descend the stairs of the ramparts.

Protected from the full view of the diplomatic corps and senior officers by a protruding Mughal time battlement, Jung Bahadur signalled the intelligence deputy to follow.

"Any problem?"

"Pakistan has started amassing troops and armour across the Line of Actual Control in Kashmir. They're expected to roll down the commanding heights any time now. Rawalpindi's Operation Gibraltar has been fully unfolded. It's now Operation Grand Slam."

"How bad is it?"

"Our troop deployment is inadequate. The tank formations are yet to come out in support of the infantry. Concentrated air strikes alone can stop Pakistani forces from occupying the vital Samba-Jammu highway and features between Akhnur and Udhampur."

"Hope your info is on the dot?"

"It's from our top agent Alamgir. He's normally accurate."

The dialogue couldn't proceed further. The national anthem reverberated from the army band and everyone stood up.

The Prime Minister beckoned to his secretary and murmured.

"Call a meeting of the cabinet immediately, inform the Service Chiefs, the Defence, External Affairs and Finance Ministers. Yes, call the FIB chief as well."

Jung Bahadur walked down the stairs to his cavalcade waiting below.

Mandira, a junior cabinet colleague rushed past the milling crowd and confronted the PM.

"Sir, I've returned from Srinagar last night after visiting the forward areas. We must..."

"We're meeting today. The Defence Minister will give you a detailed briefing. Come in a few minutes earlier. I'll like to hear your views on the perfidious Pakistani infiltration."

The move was tactical. He wasn't particularly happy with her tempestuous visit to the forward positions in Kashmir. The national government, as he understood, functioned under certain well-considered rules of business and not on the whims and fancies of any person or family.

But friendly public postures at Amritlal's daughter were a necessary prop. She still carried with her the total support of Amritlal loyalists. They weren't willing to allow an intruder like him to drive down his roots. They were keen to replace the Windsor with the Amritlal dynasty. He couldn't afford to ignore her. The country, he knew, was still beholden to Amritlal's family. Pretty funny eh! The Indians were slavishly mortgaged to the charms of white skins and British-bred aristocracy. Given an option, most of them would prefer to welcome back the House of Windsor.

Jung Bahadur never trusted this stormy petrel of the Amritlal dynasty. She had gathered a bunch of Young Turks around her, who missed no opportunity in demanding his scalp. He understood the game well. In India a successful leader of men is often deified. Amritlal had already acquired a demigod status. And it wouldn't be easy to pitch a battle against his daughter, who was busy preparing herself for deification.

But he would take care of her, once the tiff with Pakistan was over. Rustic India should've the final laugh. They would provide a decent burial to the proxy rule by the distant shores of the Albion.

Perhaps a diplomatic assignment for Mandira, to London, wouldn't be bad!

Well! She had been talking about one, rather loudly, in order to be close to her sons.

****

It wasn't exactly a formal cabinet meeting; it was more of a briefing session. Jung Bahadur played a neat game by exposing his cabinet colleagues to detailed briefings by the COAS and his staff officers. The clever ploy was intended to involve the Amritlal hangers-on, before he formally ordered the Indian troops to mount a counter attack.

"I'd like you to give us a detailed intelligence briefing." The Prime Minister, took out the white Gandhi cap from his head, placed it on the table and asked Rabindra Narayan Dutta.

"Sir," the consummate intelligence chief spoke into the microphone, in a low tone. That was his forte. He never raised his voice.

"As I briefed you earlier, Kachchh was Pakistan's probing mission. Operation Gibraltar, as the Pakistanis would like to call it, is a repeat performance of Operation Gulmarg of 1948. It was conceived way back in 1963, soon after the Chinese invasion and the ***Hazratbaal*** (missing of a holy relic of the Prophet) conspiracy. The Special Services Group and the Inter Services Intelligence, for a surreptitious invasion on Kashmir, have trained selected troops from army regulars and Azad Kashmir units. The main target is the Vale of Srinagar. Rawalpindi had planned to reach Srinagar by August 5, seize the All India Radio station and proclaim an independent government of Kashmir. The military regime has a plan to back up Operation Gibraltar with Operation Grand Slam; a full-fledged attack, all along the western front."

Dutta halted and looked for reaction in the faces of the assembled ministers and military brass.

"Have you got any details of the infiltrating columns?" Asked General Arobindo Mukherjee, the COAS, rather loudly.

Dutta looked up at the PM and continued talking at same pace.

"If the COAS recalls, I had shared a detailed report on August 2, about all the advancing columns. In case the PM has the time I can repeat it."

Jung Bahadur, a small-jawed person, kept on munching something and nodded inscrutably. He was aware of the report but wanted his political colleagues, particularly Mandira to hear out the FIB chief. His government wasn't exactly functioning on the basis of patriotic help from the Kashmiri grazers. His intelligence machinery was well entrenched on Pakistani soil.

"As we understand, 9 main columns have been infiltrated by Pakistan. These have been operationally nom-de-plumed ***Tariq Force, Qasim Force and Salauddin Force*** etc. The total strength should be above 10,000."

"Did you have prior intelligence on Operation Gibraltar?" Mandira asked in a chirping voice.

"Indeed we did have adequate forewarning." Dutta again looked up at the PM. "The PM, Defence Minister and the COAS are aware of this. Pakistan has indeed been planning this since 1963."

"But there are media allegations about our lack of preparations." Shot out Ramachari, the finance minister.

"The government isn't run by the media." Jung Bahadur, in a rare gesture dismissed his finance minister.

Mandira leaned over the table, her eyelids flickering faster. This was a peculiar trait with her. Her eyelids flickered almost involuntarily, like that of a palsy patient, whenever excited.

"***Pradhan Mantriji*** (Prime Minister), I've been to Kashmir, to the forward formations and lived with our ***jawans*** (soldiers). I've been with the patriotic Kashmiri people. They're determined to fight for the integrity of the state. I've seen the Pakistani intruders. Here's my report and suggested line of action." Mandira passed on a thick set of papers to the PM.

"You're welcome dear," Jung Bahadur replied cordially and passed on the paper to his Cabinet Secretary and whispered, "What do I do with this report?"

The Cabinet Secretary placed the report inside a folder and whispered back, "I'll take care of it."

Mandira almost went mad. Her eyelids oscillated faster. Ramachari, a Mandira acolyte, tapped her shoulder and spoke.

"Mr. Prime Minister, Mandiraji has a genuine point. She's the only minister who visited the forward positions and enthused the people and ***jawans***. You'd perhaps like to discuss her report here."

"Mr. Finance Minister, we're here to review the military situation, the deployment of our own forces and that of Pakistan. These important matters can't wait. Mandira is like my daughter. I'll sure read the report before it's discussed in a meeting." Jung Bahadur spoke with an air of finality.

"Well General!" The PM turned towards the COAS, "Let's hear you out."

The flamboyant General, from the Corp of Artillery, wasn't exactly a universally loved person in the Armed Forces. His war game plan was to pile up troops and armour in the Lahore-Sialkot sectors resulting in the Vale of Kashmir being open to the mercy of the infiltrators. Barring one regular battalion at Kupwara and an independent armoured squadron, there was no regular troop deployment in the valley.

In fact, the 68 and 163 Infantry Brigades were flown in impromptu from Ladakh. Other formations were hurriedly inducted to flush out the infiltrators. The people of Kashmir Valley, in a rare display of patriotism, had helped the police and army in hunting down the Pakistani marauders.

"In fact, sir," The COAS spoke in a jerky voice, "The XV Corps has been planning the war games since early August. I'd attended three exercises in Jammu and Pathankot and my troops have already moved across the CFL. The Haji Pir Pass and other surrounding features have been taken. The infiltrators are on the run."

"I want a full capacity mobilisation. You have my cabinet's approval."

The small man had taken a big decision. India's strategic spine and resources couldn't afford another war for more than 10 days. But, this was his only chance to redeem some lost stature, after the black Chinese winter.

"Keep me posted General. You have my full support. And you," He turned towards Dutta and Nampoothiri, sitting at a far corner, "Wait for me."

"Be frank. Tell me the exact ground situation." Jung Bahadur accosted his intelligence chief as soon as the other participants vacated the room.

"Our preparations in Chhamb, Jaurian and Khemkaran sectors are inadequate. Pakistan can break through our defences, at any given moment. Agent Alamgir speaks of the Pakistani intention to cut off the chicken neck, install a puppet government and get it recognised by some friendly countries."

"I'm told that our preparations are adequate."

"We should have a second look at it."

"Leave it to me. Tell me what your boys are doing? Are we comfortable?"

"Intelligence can't be foolproof. But our agents are on the job, and we've set up a special communication channel via Kabul." Replied the FIB chief.

"What about the eastern front?"

"Pak preparations are appallingly inadequate. They're banking on Chinese intervention, once the Indian troops start rolling in."

"Should we?"

"We, in the FIB, feel that our troops shouldn't attack East Pakistan. The Bengalis are feeling fidgety over Pakistani dependence on China. They've received a raw deal from the military regime and Bengali sub-nationalism may soon challenge the might of Islamabad. This is also the view of Lotus, mean our talent in Operation Meghna."

"I appreciate your views. Keep up the dialogue with Lotus. Can't he start condemning Islamabad for neglecting the defence of East Pakistan?"

The PM referred to a top-secret intelligence operation aimed at subverting some East Pakistan leaders.

"The dialogue is on. Lotus is on the job."

"Dutta," Jung Bahadur modulated his voice to a whisper, "I must say that you need to generate new and more incisive resources in Pakistan, I mean West Pakistan."

"What gives you the feeling that we're inadequate on that turf, sir?"

"I was impressed by your deputy's briefing the other day. But I must say that both qualitatively and quantitatively we're way behind the Pakistanis. They've been planning Operation Gibraltar for over two years, but I'm told about this just when the Pakis are rolling in their regulars." Jung Bahadur stiffened his rolling jaw.

"I'm sorry sir. We should be doing better."

"Yes I expect you to adopt a pro-active strategy, rather than reacting to Pakistani machinations."

"Sure sir," Dutta spoke in an apologetic tone, "You'll see immediate improvements from now on."

Rabindra Narayan Dutta stepped out from the PM's room, a worried man. The Prime Minister, a supposed rural bumpkin, had dragged him down to a blind alley and placed his fingers on the raw nerves. The FIB was indeed reacting to Pakistani intelligence and subversion thrusts. There was hardly any pro-active forward thrust. The ***Hazratbal*** incident, with the mysterious disappearance and subsequent retrieval of the holy relic was a national disaster. That was a great intelligence coup by the Inter Services Intelligence. It had left in its wake a series of unanswered questions. The FIB was yet to answer those.

Dutta regretted another blunder. He should've reopened the Operation Gibraltar documentations and briefed Jung Bahadur afresh, soon after he had assumed charge. The PM's secretariat, suffering from the Amritlal hangover, might not have briefed him adequately. It was a major goof-up, a real embarrassment. Jung Bahadur, Dutta knew, wasn't enamoured of him. Being an Amritlal appointee, he was bound to be a natural suspect in the new regime. The boss had a right to choose his intelligence chief.

Well! It was time for him to go. Perhaps he was hanging on to a rotten twig for too many summers. But he must leave some lasting footprint of the FIB on Pakistani soil before that. The stigma of failure shouldn't haunt his soul beyond his death.

The thought of finally retiring under a cloud, after 17 years of glorious innings in the FIB reminded Dutta about another nagging problem. Who would succeed him? Would it be Nampoothiri, a professionally sound person or a politically well connected Kumar Anand Prasad? Well! Dutta stepped into his South Block room with the determination of putting a few kind words to the Prime Minister in support of Nampoothiri. He was, by far, the best choice.

He shrugged off the thought of retirement and picked up the red-stripped top-secret file that contained the latest reports from the war front.

Chapter 14

Rabindra Narayan Dutta felt haggard and harassed even in the cool confine of his air-conditioned den. Last 28 hours had squeezed out whatever juices were left in his old bones. Keeping dame sleep away was a formidable battle that he felt tempted to lose.

Artillery booms, supersonic zooms and rumblings of battle tanks had activated the entire western battlefronts. Pakistani troops had broken through the Indian defences in Kashmir and the Punjab.

But just now he wasn't going to lose any sleep over Chhamb-Jaurian or Khemkaran war theatres. The war in any case wasn't going to be decisive. It was sure to leave both Indian and Pakistani noses bleeding.

But the FIB had just received a damn blow on its nose. Jung Bahadur had called over the Restricted Area Exchange phone to share what he had learnt from the USSR ambassador in Delhi. Transcripts of field telephone dialogues between Pakistani field commanders, picked up by Moscow's spy satellites, had left him in no doubt that GHQ Rawalpindi was in possession of a verbatim report of the proceedings of a CCS meeting (Cabinet Committee on Security) held just eighteen hours ago. Pakistan, the PM had scornfully commented, had caught the FIB with its pants down. What was Dutta going to do about it? Would he have time to look into the gravity of the Russian input?

What worse condemnation could the intelligence chief expect from the chief executive of the country?

"What do you feel?" Dutta lighted a rare cigarette and asked his deputy.

"Absolutely no idea sir," Replied Nampoothiri, "The only Muslim minister in the cabinet is a thoroughbred nationalist. He's clean."

"What about the others?"

"Except Ram Karan Prasad no other minister has any link with Pakistan. You know his links with the Pakistani drug barons. He owns a couple of brothels and pleasure homes all over the country." Nampoothiri revealed.

"Hey Balu," Dutta almost screamed, "This is perhaps the thousandth time you're swearing by that charlatan of a minister. Give me the meat and I know how to cook his goose."

"Well sir," Nampoothiri spoke haltingly, "You may recall that we'd submitted two notes to Amritlal on Ram Karan. These must be lying around somewhere in the PMO."

"Well Balu, I'm sorry for the high pitched shriek. Politicians are creatures of compromise. Ram Karan's caste velocity gets past the boundaries of courage of the Prime Ministers. Anyway, that doesn't prove anything. Prepare a new dossier for Jung Bahadur. Watch Raghu Chawla, Karan's journalist crony. He's frequently seen with the Pak High Commission officials." Dutta affectionately patted Nampoothiri's back.

"He needs a blanket surveillance."

"Wrap him up. Wire up his phones, put the Mosurs on to him and plant moles in his office and home."

"Yes sir. I'll instruct the boys." Nampoothiri replied.

"Do something fast Balu. This old man is a tough customer."

"I'll get on that job straightaway. But sir, the PM's orders to deploy the Special Volunteer Force behind Pakistani lines in Rajasthan sector requires immediate consideration."

The PM had enquired, after a strategy session, about the capability, desirability and feasibility of the Special Volunteer Force carrying out acts of sabotage and subversion behind selected Pakistani positions. He was alarmed by the deployment of the ***Hur Lashkars*** (irregular armed religious bands), commanded by Peer Pagaro, a Pakistani cult leader. Trained by the Special Services Group (SSG), these religious fanatics had penetrated deep behind the Indian lines and threatened vital communication links. Dutta had assured the PM that his SVF auxiliary force would be deployed forthwith to hunt down the ***Lashkars*** and to sabotage the Pakistani lines of communication.

"Withdraw two SVF battalions from Assam and deploy them in the Rajasthan sector." Dutta directed Kumar Anand Prasad.

"They'll require camels and desert guides." Nampoothiri pointed out the basic requirements of the force in a new terrain.

"Don't preach. Take care of the logistics. That's your headache. Requisition a few dozens of camel and desert porters. Now show me on the map the latest position of your X boys." Dutta intervened impatiently.

Nampoothiri walked over to the wall-mounted map, removed the curtains and spoke in cautious measured words.

"***Ghalib*** is at Balakot, about five hours drive from Islamabad. He operates in Pakistan occupied Kashmir. ***Mir Qalandar*** is at Kasur; the third one, ***Nasir*** is at Changa Manga. ***Qurban***, the Double X asset is doing a fantastic job at Jhumra, Mianwali and Sargodha belt. Our other assets are at Qurangi and Hyderabad, in Sind. The brightest one is at Batapu, on the Amritsar-Lahore axis."

"Fine, what're their reports about Pakistani deployments? I want details of armour and artillery." Asked Dutta.

"Collated reports indicate mobilisation of three Azad Kashmir brigades at Bhimbar; one brigade each of 7, 13 and 17 Divisions and an integral armoured regiment opposite Punch."

"Are you in regular communication with them? Can they organise demolition and sabotage tasks?" Dutta interrupted impatiently.

"All the channels are open, but I feel, at this point of time we needn't use them for demolition jobs." Nampoothiri put in his suggestion forcefully.

"Why?"

"These're long term assets. Perhaps we can't use them for shallow tactical operations."

"But I want fireworks inside Pakistan."

"That's the job for *Force 34*. We can arrange the para-dropping of a Company behind the Pakistani lines." Nampoothiri hinted at the deployment of a super-secret commando force, a spin off from ***Operation Turag,*** raised by Col. Pathania for similar operations inside Tibet.

"Fine. I want early action. The Turag boys must hit at some of the Pakistani strategic air bases and radar formations. We must show the PM that our auxiliary forces are capable of delivering spectacular results."

"Roger sir."

And what's your deployment plan for the SVF?" Dutta directed the question at Nampoothiri.

"Sir we've already airlifted three companies to Barmer, Jaisalmer sectors and one company to adjoining Banaskanta, in Gujarat. Excellent local guides have been provided to them. I expect a counter-strike against the ***Hur Lashkars*** in another 12 hours."

"Tackle these fifth column Muslims firmly. Direct the SVF to take on the Hur camps and destroy them."

"Consider that done sir." Nampoothiri replied and hoped that his boss would now relent. He was accustomed to Dutta's occasional hate-Muslim outbursts. He didn't feel like joining in on the issue.

Dutta wasn't in a mood to relax. He opted for another cigarette and started pacing the length and breadth of his spacious room.

"What about the new X talent?"

"The Triple X talent is ready. The handling officers are waiting outside. Better we'd call them tomorrow morning." Nampoothiri replied hoping for an early disengagement.

"Why wait until tomorrow? Call them in at once."

RP alias Ram Krishna Prasanna Banerjee followed by Dhiren Bhagat entered the room, fearfully described as the den by the FIB officials.

"What's your plan?" Asked Dutta.

"Sir, we have to infiltrate the talent to Karachi area. In the first leg of the operation he has to establish contact with his uncle, Shamim Bukhari," Banerjee enunciated the main task ahead.

"When can you execute the operation?"

"There's a problem," Added Bhagat, "Our transborder facilitator Amrik Singh Johal isn't available at his usual rendezvous. We can't execute the operation infiltration till he's located."

"Johal can't simply disappear into thin air," Nampoothiri intervened, "He can't be out of business. Trace him out, I say, at the earliest."

"He has probably gone to the Agra-Mathura area to procure export commodities." Bhagat submitted.

"Is he an exporter? What merchandise does he deal in?" Asked Dutta.

"I'll explain later," Nampoothiri added and winked at Bhagat,

"You get going and seek out Johal."

"Yes sir." Bhagat responded with a flourishing bow.

"Yes sir won't do," Dutta thundered, "I want urgent action."

"Consider it done sir." Bhagat looked up and replied with an anguished expression. He had heard about Dutta's short spell of bad tempers. But to him the top boss appeared to be hanging on a very fragile tenterhook.

****

Amrik Singh's Hotel Capitol office fronted a travel agency, GUNDEV TOURS, a Texan abbreviation for Guru Nanak Dev Tours. He was, in fact, a consultant and export promoter for Ram Karan Prasad, the evergreen cabinet minister. And he was really on a business errand, a business of different kind, exporting novel commodities. Amrik represented the audacious second-generation Punjabi fortune hunters, who believed in making millions from thin air.

His father Devraj Singh Johal, a refugee from Pakistan, had resumed a new life by hawking fruits and vegetables. By 1950, he had saved enough to purchase a shop at Meher Chand market, next to the relics of the Lodi emperors. His dream came true when he revived his traditional family business of operating taxis. He even fondly hung a board up, Lahore Taxi Company, the logo that was owned by his father and grandfather, back at Lahore's Anarkali market.

Amrik wasn't the prototype of a hard working honest Sikh, earning his bread, sweating out the summer and suffering the winter shivers. He hated the ritual of Sunday Gurdwara visits, offering free service at the ***langar*** (common eating area) and partaking of ***Parsad*** (offering to the Almighty). He wasn't an atheist either. He didn't believe in life, he believed in bucks-fast and big bucks.

Old Devraj died early. Amrik celebrated the occasion by entertaining his friends and business associates by throwing a nightlong dance and drinks party. He strayed into the corridors of power and money. Other ingredients of good life followed naturally.

Amrik didn't believe in step-climbing his stairs. He jump-climbed. Once up by a few steps, he didn't bother about the lower ones. He simply believed in climbing up and not down. He didn't care to notice if the steps below were still intact, at least for emergency landing.

Short of leaping into a galactic void, Amrik jumped his way up by corrupting every one, right left and centre. All that he required was enough grease for the palms of the power pinions and good-looking women for the politicians and bureaucrats. Those were the magic ***mantras*** for entering Aladdin's golden cave.

It didn't take time for Amrik Singh Johal to take a few frog-leaps to reach the diamond-studded world of mafia don Mardan Pathan of Bombay and his Delhi associate Salim Langra. They fronted drug, gold and silver smuggling operations and the all important flesh export by Ram Karan Prasad, Jung

Bahadur's precious inheritance from his predecessor, Amritlal. Vidya Sagar Suri had picked up the best talent in that illustrious coterie. The immaculately dressed Sikh looked more like a beach gigolo, much more of a sophisticated operator than the wild buffalo, Ramendra Kaushal.

Amrik was under great pressure from Mardan Pathan and clients across the borders. Starved of fresh supplies for brothels and guesthouses, the connoisseur market in Pakistan and beyond had started breathing fire down his chest. Only the Boss could extricate him from the crisis. That's how Amrik landed at the doors of Ram Karan Prasad with great temerity.

"What's your problem?"

Ram Karan Prasad spoke as he sipped his usual morning tea, brewed with a queer concoction of holy ***tulsi*** (mint) leaves. The concoction tasted bitter and he too was in a bitter mood today.

The crazy PM had called a meeting at 3 in the morning, which concluded at 6. That forced him to miss his customary late nightcap and the engagement to deflower a young beauty, kidnapped from Chamoli, up in the Himalayan heights.

To top his misery, Raghu Chawla, the barnacle of a journalist was seated right in his drawing room, for a report on the cabinet proceedings. He had to, Chwala said, keep a dateline with a Pak High Commission official.

"What bloody business, in the name of your blasted Guru, brings you here?" Ram Karan asked with a pungent grimace.

"Sir, we've run into troubles. This damn war has stopped the flow of East Bengali women in Pakistani markets. They have turned to the Indian market now in a big way. Our Umerkot friend Hassan Rathore has sent an immediate demand for 20 girls. We're late by twenty days."

"What the hell have you been doing till now? What about our agents in Calcutta, Kathmandu and Patna?" Ram Karan scowled.

"Sir, they're scared, because of the war hysteria."

"No but. Have you ever heard of the glamour corps of the Japanese and American armies? They carry planeloads of girls, at gunpoint, to warfronts. Why should the soldiers, be they Indian or Pakistani, fuck only East Bengal women? My supplies shouldn't fall short." Ram Karan gulped the queer ***tulsi*** concoction and grimaced at Johal.

"But sir," Amrik replied in a confused voice, "How do we send our consignment across the border? There are soldiers everywhere."

"Have you got the stock?" Ram Karan was by now impatient.

"No sir."

"You good for nothing fucking asshole. Kalua." Shouted Ram Karan Prasad.

In came a 6 feet tall sack of fat and muscle from Siwan, the hon'ble minister's home village. A rare family heirloom, Kalua, with a pitch-dark complexion and all white hair, looked like a ***jinn*** walking out of the Arabian nights.

Ram Karan had inherited Kalua from his father Kalika Kiran Prasad. Initially used as a passive gay partner by Kalika Kiran, Kalua finally graduated into being the killer arm of Ram Karan, leading his private army. It carried a glamorous name: Surya Sena (Sun Brigade).

Bihar, one of the Indian tracts, lost in a Jurassic jungle, boasted of several such private armies. This private arm of Ram Karan plundered villages, grabbed land, abducted women and eliminated defaulters and dissenters.

On occasions, his Surya Sena fought bloody battles with neighbouring landlords and grabbed land from poor farmers, suffering from the infinite burden of loans that compounded at a galactic rate.

For Kalua life had frozen a long time ago under the moccasin of Ram Karan. He grew up biologically, but the man in him had turned into a robot, a killing machine. He couldn't remember when he was initiated into killing rituals and who his first victim was.

But he remembered the day he was snatched away by Kalika Kiran from his father, in lieu of an alleged outstanding loan of Rs.100, compounded over the years to Rs 10,000. Kalua's grandfather had taken the loan, from Rai Bahadur Durga Kiran Prasad. He failed to repay it and his family was perpetually bonded to the landlord's chattel. Kalua accepted his fate like most of his ilk and started worshipping Ram Karan as his pre-ordained deity.

"Any orders for me sir?" Kalua entered the room, bending his body slightly.

"What's the size of your army at Siwan?"

"There are fifty. But, some may have gone to their villages for paddy transplantation."

"To hell with your paddy," shouted back Ram Karan, "I want thirty young girls and soon. How long will you take?"

Kalua stood silently for a few moments, scratching his baldpate.

"You want all of them young and virgin?"

"Young, yes. But not below 15. Customers are funny these days; they don't like young buds. The buggers don't know the charm of enjoying sweet kid girls. I don't care for their damn virginity."

"Sir, it may take more than just two raids," Kalua submitted apologetically, "The days are difficult. The Patna based journalists are a menace. They created big fuss the last time I raided Mamidpur village."

"You mean Yoganand Shastri, the ***chamar***, who flaunts a Brahminical title?"

"He isn't alone sir," Kalua averred, "Shankar Yadav and your own caste-brother Rohit Mallah were there too."

"Shut up, you stupid son of a whore. You don't have to talk about my caste. My ancestors descended from the ***Yadu*** clan, caste of Lord Shri Krishna."

"As you please sir." Kalua shrank back like a leech, which had hit salt.

Ram Karan dialled Patna and he spoke in a voice akin to death's whisper, as the line came alive.

"Inspector General ***sahib***, I am Ram Karan. Can you recognise me?" He talked to the Inspector General of Police, heading a 20,000 strong force in the state of Bihar.

"Yes sir, ***pranam*** (my obeisance)." The voice at the other end replied shakily.

"Listen, I hope you recall there's an emergency in the country?"

"Yes sir."

"Arrest Yoganand Shastri, Shankar Yadav and Rohit Mallah, under the Defence of India Rules. They're Pakistani agents. We're at war and can't afford to give free movement to the enemies of the country."

"Sir, it'll be difficult to substantiate the charges." The IGP replied.

"Do as I say, or else I'll ask the Chief Minister to transfer you out." Ram Karan hinted that he wanted an officer of his own caste as Inspector General of Police. A Brahmin had no place in his scheme of operations.

"Pardon me sir. ***Pai lagoo*** (I touch your feet). It'll be done."

"That's good. Call me tomorrow to confirm the arrests." Ram Karan banged the phone on its cradle.

"Yes sir, can we proceed now?" Asked Kalua.

"Do whatever you like. Here's Amrik. He'll take a bus for transporting the merchandise. You get them at the earliest. Keep me out of it. This flunky of a PM always keeps on demanding my resignation. He himself moves around with a couple of resignation letters in his pocket."

Ram Karan turned to Amrik Singh Johol.

"And you motherfucker, your problem is solved. Kalua will provide you with the merchandise. Now it's your duty to ship them to the destination. And remember, delivery is strictly against cash, after I get confirmation of an advance remittance from Mardan Pathan. In my business there's no goodwill and no credit."

"Where do I take the bus?" Amrik Singh wanted more precise guidance.

"Follow Kalua and report back after you've delivered the merchandise." Ram Karan Prasad dismissed Amrik. He called aside Kalua and talked to him in a slow and seductive voice.

"Kalua, I want all the girls to be young. No old haggard with sagging breasts. Scout around the low caste villages and impose your own curfew. Lift the girls and put them in Amrik's bus. Fire into the air, if you want to scare the villagers away. Don't kill. Looting of women is a cool business. Handling of body bags is a difficult task. I don't want any complication. And keep Rs 20,000. Pay the ***thanedar*** (police in charge) and others, if necessary."

Kalua left, after being fully briefed by his master. Ram Karan Prasad cursed his stars for being disturbed by Amrik. The disgust turned to a burning thirst for Scotch. The urge to have a stiff dose before he commenced with the strenuous exploration of the Himalayan beauty, still chained to his ornate mahogany bed, propelled his steps towards the bar. He turned back halfway. That pain in the neck, his third vertebrae, bloody Raghu Chawla was waiting in another room.

"***Sala*** (a slang)." Ram Karan uttered a curse. These Hindustanis and Pakistanis have no business sense. What's the use of fighting wars? They should allow business to thrive and that should take care of all the problems.

To him there was no difference between a Hindu and a Muslim woman.

In bed they were equally warm. In fact, given a choice, he preferred Muslim women, middle aged. They were more skilful than the Hindu women.

Ram Karan walked in briskly to the room, where Raghu was biting his nails.

"Hi Raghu, what's the matter?"

"Sir, your obedient servant is waiting for the last two hours."

"What the hell do you want?"

"Friend Mustaq has requested for an urgent meeting."

"Tell him, I am busy." Ram Karan wasn't willing to put off the adventure of exploring the creases, heights and depths of the Chamoli beauty. The thirst of an impatient explorer was violently gurgling inside him. Climb, he must.

"Sir, you'd better make the time, the friends are anxious, they want vital clarification on last night's Cabinet meeting."

Raghu Chawla hinted at the demand of a Pakistani diplomat, who used the budding journalist as a cutout to Ram Karan.

"Shit!" Ram Karan relented, "We can't meet in the open, you understand. We're at war now. Arrange a discreet venue and keep me informed. Any way, wait for a few minutes. Make yourself comfortable. Kalua will take care."

He banged the door and hastily turned towards the chained Chamoli beauty.

Oh Mother Kali! He sighed; life had become so complicated! Business was getting dull and this Jung Bahadur was making life miserable for him by summoning emergency meetings at odd hours.

Ram Karan opened the bedroom door, poured a fat portion of golden liquid in a glass and raised a toast to the wall-mounted portrait of goddess Kali. He touched his forehead to the portrait and offered obeisance to his family deity. He prayed for the quick demise of Jung Bahadur and early accession of Mandira to the prime ministerial throne. She would any day be a better leader of dynamic people like him.

"Kalua" Ram shouted for his father's pederasty partner.

"Yes sir." The jet-black ***jinn*** appeared from nowhere.

"Prepare the girl for me."

"Done sir."

Kalua Mushahari freed open the chain and led the dumb shivering lass to Ram Karan's ornate bed. This was a routine for him.

****

Amrik Singh entered his office room with an exhilarating pace, humming a film tune. He didn't notice Dhiren Bhagat seated behind a huge Bartholomew globe and piles of files and smoking away his favourite brand, Capstan. He hated the guts and tenacity of this intelligence officer.

"Hello Amrik." Bhagat stood up with a stretched palm.

Amrik reciprocated and walked down to his chair.

"Hi Bhagat. What's new?"

"Nothing unusual," Bhagat shifted to a chair opposite Amrik, "Order tea. I have been waiting for two hours for you."

Amrik lamented, as they sipped the thick-brewed tea, about the dull business and a wasteful war. Was it worth fighting foolish wars for nothing? God alone knew when good business sense would dawn upon the Indian and Pakistani warmongers.

"Well brother," Bhagat broached the business proposal, "War doesn't impede your business. Your merchandise appreciates all the time."

"It's very dull brother." Johal lamented again.

"Don't be smart. I know your tricks," Bhagat spoke in a firm voice. "I have a friend to cross over. It's urgent."

"It's very difficult brother." Amrik said with folded hands.

"It can't wait. Tie it up with your counterparts. We prefer the Gujarat sector."

"My contacts have snapped." Amrik gestured his helplessness.

"Don't bullshit. I know you received 100 kilos of gold only 15 days back. We don't keep our eyes closed not for nothing. You've to pay the price." Bhagat sounded a little formal.

"You know the border situation." Amrik tried to parry.

"Who doesn't? And who doesn't know that, on either side of the border your ilk operates usual runs. Your breed thrives on war. You're the same, all over the world, war or no war." Bhagat hammered in his point.

Amrik smiled faintly. There was no way to get past the field rat. He would, no doubt, ruthlessly pursue his goal. Better not irritate a man having his fingers on all the border outposts.

"I'll be out of town for about four days, but your job will be done," Amrik sounded extra sweet, "Do me a favour."

"You want the right of passage?"

"Yes," Amrik hopefully lowered his tone; "I'll prefer Gujarat too. Hassan Rathore will be waiting at Nagar Parkar for the consignment."

"What're you trading this time?"

"The usual consignment of meat. Don't ask for further details. Do me that courtesy and I promise safe conduct for your man."

"Deal. When do I expect a call?"

"Can't say for sure. Complete all the spadework. I can't afford to be caught."

"Don't worry. But I want a firm undertaking."

"Spell it out."

"A safe passage for my man up to Karachi."

"I know Bhagat, one day you'll put the noose around my neck. Anyway I don't mind being hanged for you and the nation. ***Wahe Guru*** is there to help me." Amrik mimicked a patriotic martyr and raised hands in salutation to his Guru.

"Enough Amrik," Bhagat stood up, "Reserve the jokes for your grave. I'll write a touching epitaph, in glowing ***Gurmukhi*** (Punjabi script), extolling the virtues of a fallen front-line warrior, that you are. Believe me."

Bhagat extended his hand. The business partners parted company with a warm handshake, presuming that each had scored a victory over the other.

Crime and intelligence, as the time watchers said, were perfect bed partners. Each one knew the rules of the game. Each one was aware of the sharp edges that he was required to walk on. They managed to smile behind their pains. It didn't come from within. It was another cool business deal as usual.

Chapter 15

Kalua Mushahari (a rat eating low caste), under his bulging muscles and mahogany black skin, possessed all the attributes that nature normally endows to differentiate between a primate and a man. Somewhere beneath his flesh a hidden soul pulsated, though he never betrayed the precious feeling.

He had something extra, the wiring of a robot, controlled by the commands of his bread giver. A bonded labour, in the strictest sense of the term, his childhood memory often disturbed him. Kalika Kiran had subjected him to the ignominy of sexual abuse. Beyond adolescence, when all his instincts were blunted, Kalua Mushahari fully reconciled to his fate.

He never protested. God had ordained thus!

Castrated at an early age, on orders from Rai Bahadur Durga Kiran Prasad, Kalua never ever felt the urge for natural sex. He scrupulously avoided looking at the female human form. Nothing stirred him, and so far nothing had. Beautiful females, fluttering butterflies and dew-laden flowers evoked no emotion in him.

The only object he felt obsessed about was a rupee-sized steel talisman, dangling between his bulging chest muscles. A Hindu occultist had given it, way back, when he was just 18, as a favour from Goddess ***Kali.*** It was a gift of life, not a mere talisman. He was fired upon in a clash over land grabbing. The melted lead ball hit him, straight on the talisman and ricocheted, only to hit the eye of a person standing next to him.

Kalua the robot, since then, worshipped Goddess ***Kali*** surreptitiously. His caste was entitled to worship stones, trees and snakes and of course, a crude form of Lord ***Ganesha***, whose mythological carrier was the divine rat. The Brahmins had barred his caste from worshipping any higher form of divinity.

Kalua's presence at Siwan, a small trading town and administrative centre was sufficient to send shivers through the spines of many. He was regarded as a walking incarnation of ***Yam Deva*** (angel of death). With Kalua around, the long arms of Ram Karan Prasad couldn't be far behind. He appeared unannounced like a violent and moody nor'wester, which usually left trails of death and destruction behind.

Kalua's ritual visit to the ***Kali*** temple normally began with the priest showering him with sacred red hibiscus. This was done after receiving a hefty offering of rupees fifty from Kalua. The priest thereafter violated all the upper caste Hindu norms and allowed the low caste rat eater to enter the sanctum sanctorum and touch the feet of the stone idol.

The upper caste worshippers never dared to protest against Kalua's visit and defilement of the Holy Mother. They performed penance and washed the temple floor with a queer concoction of coconut water, milk, honey and water from the holiest of holy rivers, the Ganges. The chief priest, for self purification and pacification of the offended goddess observed a fast for a day and performed a special ***yagna*** that required the ritual sacrifice of 11 goats and sheep, all jet black from the nose to the tail. The Mother Goddess, he hoped, would understand his compulsions. Who would dare to deny permission to the 'Death' himself?

Kalua's next gracious action, this time, included a meeting with a few leading figures of the town, and making a donation of Rs. 3000 to the town primary school. It was a special act of kindness from Ram Karan Prasad, he announced.

The distinguished crowd assembled there, raised slogans in praise of Ram Karan Prasad, a messiah of the poor, a champion of woman's rights and the protector of the untouchables. Some of them didn't forget Kalua as well, the harbinger of the heavenly manna.

The most important meeting took place late at night, with a discreet call on Kalua Mushahari by the officer-in-charge of Siwan rural police station.

"***Thanedarji*** (station house officer), this time ***sahib*** has given us a big task to accomplish. Arrange the adequate cover."

"What's the matter? Is it land grabbing?"

The Station House Officer couldn't anticipate the seriousness of the business.

"No, no. It's not land." Kalua pushed Rs. 5000 into the police officer's pocket.

"Count it carefully, it adds up to full 5000 right down to the last paisa. Go on a binge and then sleep it off. Take this ***angrezi sharab*** (English whisky), specially sent by the minister. I'll tell you what to do, tomorrow morning. Your police should, under no circumstances, go out; even if frenetic calls are made for help. Take my permission before moving out."

"***Huzoor mai baap*** (master is supreme)." The station house officer saluted smartly and left.

Kalua's next destination was the residence of the market-committee chairman.

"***Pradhanji*** (chief) I'm your house guest."

"You're welcome." The chief touched Kalua's feet.

"I mean I haven't moved out of your house tonight. Understand?" Kalua spoke in an intimidating voice.

"Kaluaji, I swear by my mother. Your order's are divine."

"That's how things should be." Kalua left with a victorious smile on his lips.

Amrik Singh Johal's bus, with a Bihar number plate, reached Siwan market around twelve at night. The station house officer guided the vehicle, as instructed by Kalua, to a far corner of the road leading to Merwa village, located at the end of a three-mile stretch of dirt road.

Merwa, a village inhabited by the untouchables was flanked by two sister hamlets, Bhangipada (hamlet of night-soil carriers) and Chamarpada (hamlet of leather processors and cobblers), which totalled up to about 6000 inhabitants.

The choice of this village cluster was deliberate. Siwan was a friendly turf. The people were as meek as domesticated rabbits. Most of the belles were, by some quirk of genetic engineering, marketable and beautiful.

In Ram Karan's flesh trade, homosapiens, biologically categorised as women, weren't a very marketable commodity per se. Fussy buyers looked for shape, complexion and age as intently as they examined the teeth of a mare and tail of a cow, while bargaining in village fairs.

Ram Karan's Surya Sena descended on Merwa, Bhangipada and Chamarpada around 2 a.m. They corked up all the exits. Two columns, armed with guns and oiled bamboo batons entered the hut-clusters, fired a few shots in the air and ordered the inmates out. The villagers, used to midnight raids, either by dacoits or landlords' goons, hesitated for a while. Kalua, standing behind the gangs, covering himself with a black blanket, ordered a repeat firing in the air.

The trick worked. The inmates were herded into the small square. Kalua's men separated the young belles and lined them up in one corner, barricaded by gun totting men. The young girls, their bodies scantily covered shuddered in fear and shivered in the early morning chill.

Kalua moved around with burning eyes and a powerful flashlight, focusing his expert gaze and the beam on the remaining women. He intermittently picked out a few and threw them at the clutches of his goons. He specially selected a few women in their early thirties, keeping in mind the preferences of some discerning customers for dusky mature women. The seasoned ones gave them a better kick.

The screaming and crying herd, well secured by rope manacles were forcibly taken to Amrik's waiting bus.

Some villagers tried to rush to their women's aid.

Kalua, from beneath his blanket cover, ordered a ***lathi*** (long baton) charge. A few goons jumped on them swinging their batons and broke a few heads and limbs. The wailing and howling villagers were pushed back into their huts. The Surya Sena goons left after shrieking out stern warning of roasting them alive, if they so much as ventured to break out.

The operation, neatly executed by 4 a.m. was a grand success, with no mess and no dead bodies. Kalua boarded his jeep, lighted a cigarette and ordered the driver to proceed to the residence of the village chief.

Amrik Singh Johal's bus was sardine-packed with the wailing village belles. He hurriedly displayed two cloth banners, in the front and back of the carriage, reading: Pilgrimage to 15 holy places, Varanasi, Mathura, Brindavan, Hardwar, Badrinath.... Courtesy His Greatness, Ram Karan Prasdaji, ***masiha*** (messiah) of the poor and great champion of the oppressed and suppressed. Free trip for untouchable women....

A loudspeaker blared out devotional songs, extolling the virtues of the Mother deity and urging Her to rescue the ***Suras*** (Gods) from the clutches of the ***Asuras*** (Demons).

The Station House Officer of Siwan rural police station piloted Johal out of his jurisdiction, after pocketing another gracious amount of Rs. 5000. That was the bottom bargain. Amrik didn't mind it. His net share out of the transaction, if completed, would be Rs. 50,000. Ram Karan should be left with a fat margin of Rs. 1/2 million, if the merchandise was sold at Rs. 30,000 per head

"***Wahe Guru***," (hail the preceptor), Amrik prayed. Good sense should dawn upon both the warring sides and peace should hold for at least one more week. The blind politicians, ***Wahe Guru,*** should be bestowed with more wisdom, like Ram Karan Prasad was.

Johal sighed agonisingly.

That shark Dhiren Bhagat was another peculiar bum, wedded to his profession. He must be waiting for him at Suigam, the final launching pad in Gujarat. He was another hazardous but useful polluting factor in his trade of exporting pleasure items.

Every time Bhagat pushed in one spy from the Indian side, he was forced to provide safe passage to two Pakistani spies. That was the standard deal, an unwritten contract between the winking operatives of the Indian and Pakistani intelligence agencies. Both the countries used Johal's business tunnels for promoting their clandestine war. He didn't mind playing this game. Everybody should be happy, deriving equal peace and prosperity. The ***Gurus*** had passed on this eternal ***vani*** (advice).

"***Saccha Padsha Wahe Guru*** (Guru is the true God).

Amrik cast a glance at the wailing half-naked village women and sighed loudly and closed his eyes for a brief catnap.

****

"It's an important assignment. I want no meddling by the Border Rangers and the Pak Intelligence Bureau. Introduce Mian Mirza Qasim to Hassan Rathore as Ram Karan's partner." Bhagat caught up with Johal at Suigam, a sleepy town in northern Gujarat.

"Who is this fellow Qasim?"

"That's none of your business. He may be a Qasim or a Hashim. Introduce him to Hassan as Ram Karan's man."

"How can I do that?" Lamented Amrik, "Hassan's too clever."

"Don't fool me. The job is important and you'll be responsible if anything goes wrong."

"Got you correct," Amrik replied, "But Rathore may send in two this time."

"What's the delivery point?"

"The Sufi shrine of Khwaja Chisti at Ajmer."

"No problem. Who is the consignee?"

"Amir Khan, a shopkeeper, opposite the Shrine."

"Fine. I'll take care of it."

"Don't embarrass me."

"Have I ever cracked your neck? You're a precious friend. Just take care that you don't sleep with the Pakis without my approval."

"Got you correct boss, I'm like a soft dough, mould me into any shape you like."

Bhagat felt mighty pleased. He was fortunate to have the initial lead. He should get plenty of head-time to exchange pleasantries with Amir Khan and cook a fine curry out of the new Pakistani spies.

But his immediate concern was the successful exfiltration of Harfan Bukhari and housing him in Karachi. His task stretched that far. The second stage of propellant, beyond Karachi, was to be provided by the Indian Mission based FIB operatives.

Suigam, an active theatre of Kachchh skirmishes with Pakistan, continued to be a sleepy hamlet, thriving on cross-border smuggling. Petty border runners smuggled in camel loads of gold, silver and foreign fabrics. They carried back foreign made Indian liquor, ***pan*** (betel) leaves, ***bidi*** (leaf-wrapped indigenous cigarette) and acetic anhydride, which was very much in demand in the heroin refining industries of Afghanistan and Pakistan.

Most of the carriers did a bit of intelligence scouting both for India and Pakistan. They took refuge with their caste-folks and Peer Pagaro devotees. Indian and Pakistani vote-begging politicians wooed the Peer, a religious cult leader, having a large following on either side of the border. Pagaro followers were pay rolled by Sardar Illahi, a drug baron at Pakistan's end of the tunnel, who resembled the likes of Ram Karan on the Indian rim. They controlled the destinies of the border dwellers and trans-border traders. A conventional war were too insignificant a disincentive to deter them from their thriving economic activities.

However, the Suigam field officer of the FIB put a cork on Bhagat's well-oiled tunnel. He illuminated Bhagat on hitherto hazy areas of the operation.

"Is it a shallow run?" Asked the officer.

"May be a deep one, I really don't know, I presume so."

"For infiltrating a deep run, if you don't mind sir, I suggest, you avoid Johal's gang, at least this time."

"Why?"

"Hassan Rathore has links with the Pak Intelligence Bureau and his own brother is a Major with the Sind Border Rangers." The local officer shared his ground knowledge with Bhagat.

"He's a steady friend of Ram Karan Prasad."

"Must be. But the borders are tense. The Pak army is everywhere. We should have an independent channel for exfiltration."

"What's the army deployment like?"

"Some massing of troops has been reported from Diplo. Two squadrons of Patton tanks have been sighted there. Nagar Parker has the presence of two companies of the Baluch Regiment, for rearguard support to the Sind Rangers. Some complements of ***Ansars*** (armed irregulars) and Pagaro's ***Hur Lashkars*** have been deployed in depth."

"What's the state of border vigil?" Bhagat wanted more details.

The energetic field officer pulled out a paper and drew a sketch of the route: Suigam>Kuwala on camel back> bus ride to Nagar Parkar> train journey to Tando Adam and Hala>crossing the Indus by boat and finally a local train journey from Rajri to Karachi Cantonment station.

"Why do you prefer this route over the one controlled by Rathore?" Bhagat asked.

"Rathore's drug cartel is shared by the top Pak army brass. I don't think you'll like the Army and ISI drug traders to share your secrets."

"Are you sure about this?"

"Yes."

"Who'll carry our load?" Bhagat asked.

"***Chacha*** (uncle) Radu Nagar. He's a legend in this route."

"How do you get him over to our side?"

"He should be here tonight with his ***kafila*** (caravan)."

The logic was very transparent. Bhagat wasn't aware of Amrik's precise connections with the important cogs in Pakistan's ruling military clique. Well! Ground realities changed very fast in this fast-track domain of trading in drugs and live flesh.

He thanked the field officer and transmitted a cipher to Nampoothiri seeking a modification in the original plan. Nampoothiri's call came at 2 a.m. Dot, dot, dash, dash—the wireless set hummed for the next twenty minutes. The new route was okayed.

The next task was more delicate. Bhagat had to offload Amrik with a convincing explanation. The smuggler, who lacked a clear conscience, might tip off the Pakistanis, if he was rubbed the wrong way. Finding out Amrik wasn't a big task. He was busy guarding his merchandise in a shabby warehouse, surrounded by high walls. The joint was used for storing red chillies and salt, before the consignments were put on railway wagons. He was singing a lullaby to the Siwan women.

"Look sisters. Back home you owned nothing but poverty, bone-grinding work and indignity. You're treated as bonded labours." Amrik spoke in slow Hindi. The womenfolk stared at him, fear writ large on their faces.

Another agent of Ram Karan spoke fluently in the local Siwan dialect.

"You have nothing to fear. I'm a fellow ***chamar.*** Trust me, I only have your welfare in mind. I'm making arrangements for good jobs that will fetch you all a neat Rs 1000 per month. That's the minimum guarantee, and then there is free housing, running water and electricity too. Imagine, you can send a minimum of Rs 500 to your homes every month." He paused.

"Don't you trust me? Take this," he took out bunches of crisp notes, "I'm giving each one of you Rs 50 as a goodwill advance. It's your money, keep it. Merwa was a nightmare for you with daylong toiling and tolerating heaps of insults. I offer you independence from slavery."

"My sisters," Added Amrik, "Trust me. I swear in the name of Mother ***Kali***. You're absolutely safe. Treat me as your brother."

Some faces lighted up. Many of them hadn't seen a full rupee in their life. They didn't understand what one thousand rupees was made of. It must be a lot. They couldn't imagine what fifty rupees could fetch for them.

"How much are fifty?" Asked a married woman.

The tout took out a bunch of crisp one-rupee notes, counted out loudly up to fifty and handed them over to the woman.

A strange light flashed past her eyes. She clutched at the notes, her fingers quivering. She started counting, using her fingers. She lost count midway, felt confused and suddenly laughed out aloud. She felt happy. The money felt warm, the crisp papers held out many promises.

"How many ***saris*** (apparel used by women) can I purchase with this money?" She asked.

"Ten." Replied the tout.

"Ten? How many ***saris*** makes ten?" Asked another voice.

Amrik took out ten ordinary ***saris*** from a jute bag, and placed them one over the other, in front of the teenaged girl.

She counted them slowly and asked, "How can I send money home, to my blind parents?"

"Don't worry. You can send it by money order. Don't bother your head about the details, your employers will arrange everything." Amrik added.

He smiled. The ice was melting very slowly.

Two women, however, kept crying intermittently. They had left their young suckling babes back home.

"Why do you cry?" Asked the tout.

"Its my child, whose breast will she suckle?"

"Don't cry," He patted her back, "Trust me, I'm a true ***Sikh***. I'll ensure that your child joins you by the next bus."

Dhiren Bhagat witnessed the charade for a while and summoned Amrik out.

"What time do you start?" He asked.

"Tonight. Rathore's guide has crossed over. The police have been tackled. Where's your man?"

"There's a slight change of plans," Bhagat whispered, "My man hasn't turned up. The bastard has escaped."

"I can't wait," Amrik gestured helplessness, "I now have with me a minute to minute programme."

"What do I do if my man doesn't turn up?" Bhagat feigned helplessness.

"What can I say brother! I'm always at your service."

"Can you take me on your return trip?" Bhagat asked.

"Perhaps." Amrik weighed the word alphabet by alphabet. He wasn't in a position to alienate Bhagat. He knew too much.

"Wait for me even if you're delayed by a day. Think of a proper cover for me. And be sure you don't talk to the Pakis about my failed mission. I have my eyes and ears in Pakistan too." Bhagat left, putting Amrik in a quandary.

Hassan Rathore wouldn't like the idea, he knew. The Pakistani guests might protest as well. But, Dhiren Bhagat knew the colours of the marrow of most of the operators in his line, including Ram Karan Prasad's.

Well! Let the moment of truth come, he'd tackle the problem astutely. Amrik resigned himself to the uncertain prospects and muttered ***Wahe***

guru. Why should such nagging problems dog him? ***Wahe Guru***, Amrik sighed out loud.

Bhagat's moment of truth arrived that night itself. Radu Nagar, the key Pakistani carrier had reached village Bharduva with a caravan of five camels.

"Are you sure your man is reliable?" Bhagat asked his field officer.

"You can depend on him. After all, I'm putting my job on the line," he exuded confidence, "I know the ground well."

Only a motorbike could approach Bharduva. There was no defined road. Even if there was one, frozen waves of shifting sand obliterated it. The villagers didn't pester the authorities for one. It was better that way, for their business. A tarred road often offered tempting invitations to the police and revenue officials.

Radu Nagar usually camped at the residence of Jhikhan Malu, a border trader for generations.

"No, this won't do," Radu looked at Mirza Qasim alias Harfan Bukhari, as if he was evaluating a woolly camel, "Your dress is too foreign. You require a proper Sindhi dress. With this kind of ***angreji*** (English) dress you'll get roasted in the Rann sand blast."

Radu directed Harfan to drink a few glasses of water, salt and sugar added. Retention of fluid was necessary during the long trek, particularly in the saline desert tract between Suigam and Kuwala.

"Do you know Sindhi?" Asked Radu.

"I've a working knowledge, rather elementary." Replied Harfan.

"That's fine. Keep your trap shut. Between this place and Karachi no one speaks Urdu and Punjabi. Avoid talking to the locals. It's my job to reach you to Karachi. After that it's your own ass that you have got to cover."

"***Chachaji*** (uncle), take care that my man isn't intercepted by the Rangers. Your boys should safely take him to Karachi." Pleaded Bhagat.

"***Sant*** (saint) Bhit Shah willing we'll cross all the barriers." Radu took out a small dose of cured opium from a plastic vial and put it carefully under his tongue.

"It'll cost you Rupees fifty thousand." He spoke in a whispering tone.

"That's a little unreasonable. Isn't it ***chacha***?" Asked Bhagat.

"It includes incidental expenses enroute. Policemen aren't saints. I have to grease their palms, both the Indians and the Pakis."

"Agreed ***Chachaji***." Bhagat accepted the pure and inevitable logic of Radu Nagar.

"Hang this around your neck." Bhagat fished out a silver chain with a square pendant from his pocket.

"What's this?"

"This is the sacred thread of your trade," Bhagat opened the sealed pendant, took out a charm written in Urdu along with two bluish capsules, "The Urdu charm is real. It's a couplet from the Quran. Devout Muslims carry this for protection from evil forces."

"What's in the tiny capsules?"

"Cyanide powder. Use this only when the pain of torture breaches the limits of your training and physical capabilities."

"You're arming me with death." An eerie laughter throttled out of Harfan's mouth.

"It's an arm of defence. It's part of the trade. You've been taught how to die gracefully and how to kill impeccably."

"It's nice you reminded me."

"It's always nice to die on one's own turf. Bye brother. Bon voyage." Bhagat slipped the necklace around Harfan's neck and turned back.

"See you back in Delhi." Harfan waved.

"Sure." Bhagat waved back.

To utter a few meaningless sweet words at the point of take off had become a ritual with Bhagat. These were dry and futile gestures. Most of them, these resident agents, didn't come back home to a heroes' welcome. They were routinely detected and summarily executed by the Inter Services Intelligence and the Pakistan Intelligence Bureau. He didn't expect Harfan to break the jinx. But somewhere inside he felt a twinge of remorse. He had come to like the jackal.

The caravan left Bharduva well past midnight. It skirted past Suigam and took a detour due southwest. Harfan was gracefully allowed to sit on a spare camel. But not for too long, he was warned, only up to Gidhni Bet, a small green oasis amidst the saline sandy desert. That's where the last border police post was located. It was blessed with a sweet water spring, a scarce commodity, often costlier than gold.

"Whose ***kafila*** (caravan) is this?" Challenged the lone Indian police constable on duty at Gidhni Bet.

"Big father, it's your poor son Radu." The veteran smuggler replied with molten humility.

"What're you carrying?"

"***Huzoor*** (sir) inspector sahib, you know all. Here's your ***salami*** (offering). We shall leave in ten minutes. Can we have some water please?"

Radu passed on a bunch of Indian currency notes, about Rs. 3000. That was the normal rate for small caravans. Another Rs. 3000 would be paid to the Sind Rangers at Junjo Bet post.

The caravan reached the Pakistani out post at Junjo Bet, around five in the morning.

The Rangers' sentry wasn't satisfied with the customary ***salami*** (offering).

"Who's this fellow? He wasn't there when you crossed over last." He pointed a finger at Harfan.

"***Khudaband*** (representative of Allah), he's my nephew Jafferi. Coming to our side in search of a bride. We Christians don't have many eligible grooms in our community. That you know ***malik*** (master), for sure." Radu tried to convince the constable with glib talk.

"You donkey of an ***Ishai*** (Christian)," the Ranger proclaimed, "If you want to marry a Pakistani girl you must pay taxes to us."

Harfan was ready with the cash. He fished out Rs. 3000 and passed it on to the minion of security.

"This is not enough. I want a big party too." The sepoy patronisingly slapped Harfan's back.

"***Huzoor***, leave this to me. You have to come to the ***nikah*** (marriage ceremony). Without you the priest won't perform the rituals."

The Ranger, mighty pleased with the cash and the prospect of an invitation, allowed the caravan to pass. Radu was a known face and a good milking cow. The Border Rangers did not mind these petty ***sawaris*** (passengers) carrying on their trade. His likes kept the economy moving in the absence of a formal trade agreement between India and Pakistan.

Almost at about the same time Amrik Singh Johal's merchandise crossed over to Pakistan, about 5 km below a point chosen by Radu's caravan. Kartik Mallah, a low caste Hindu from Bihar, a caste crony of Ram Karan Prasad, received them. Kartik's job was limited. He was to shepherd the women to the bidding platform across the border.

Rathore's men armed with rifles and assorted weapons joined Kartik, soon after the convoy crossed over to Pakistan. They lined up the Merwa women, hanging between hope and despair, in a sprawling mango grove. Experts carried out detailed examinations of the merchandise and tagged the market value for each.

The rating process depended on physical features, looks and attractiveness. The younger ones were segregated. Each one of them would fetch Rupees one lac. The rest were put in a separate group, meant for the Karachi brothels, each one selling at a lower premium. A few young and attractive ones, who were expected to fetch a fabulous price of half a million each, were earmarked for markets in Afghanistan and Iran. The rest would find their way to the Northwest Frontier Province, Sheikhdoms of the Northern Territory and even to the tents of some desert Bedouins.

The haggard belles from remote Merwa weren't even aware of their market value. They didn't even know that the female species was the prime carrier of genes, all over the globe, in all civilisations. Perhaps two generations later some Uzbek, or some Kazakh would carry the chromosomes and genes of the Merwa women, resulting in the queer mixing of the Central Asian strain with those of the Austro-Negrito stock.

Johal's merchandise was taken in separate tarpaulin covered trucks and driven to the forward destination at Mirpur Khas. The final auction would take place, in a remote village, where Rathore was camping with the prospective buyers from foreign and domestic markets.

The innocent Merwa women joined Kartik Mallah in frivolous jokes and some of them even tried to find out the nature of their prospective jobs. Kartik, an articulate entertainer, had managed to titillate their imagination and expectations. The path ahead, he added, was rosy and money was about to rain down on them, more torrentially than monsoon pouring.

Some of the belles, in their abundant excitement, started humming rhythmic tunes, as if they were ceremonially dancing along to the weekly village market. It was a celebration time, of some sort.

Chapter 16

Dhiren Bhagat too earned a small celebration. A major project had been flawlessly accomplished. The smouldering volcano, Ramendra Kaushal, was tamed and finally placed in the targeted orbit. The bittersweet memories, not so remote, of his association with Kaushal flashed past his mind's eye.

Oh God! What an exciting recruitment and training operation it was?

Bhagat only hoped that the psychological changes etched on the singed psyche of Kaushal would develop roots and that the tradecraft tricks would become his first nature.

Sitting cosily next to Amrik Singh Johal, on the way back to Ajmer, he ruminated over the Triple X case. It was more than just a routine transborder intelligence operation. To tame the loveable jackal was no mean an achievement. The turbulent tornado had been bottled. He hoped the cork of tradecraft training, motivation and his natural dedication would hold well. This one tornado should churn out delightful magic.

Bhagat lighted a cigarette and concentrated on the two Pakistani agents, his co-passengers in Amrik's bus. He activated the memory cells and captured their physical features and behavioural expressions. It shouldn't be difficult tracking them down in Ajmer, Bhagat reasoned.

He managed to strike up a conversation with them, unfolding fascinating stories of the lives, loves, foibles and frustrations in the walled city of Delhi. An itinerant gold smuggler, he often visited the borders; Bhagat tried to explain his presence in the infamous stage-carriage of Amrik.

Would they like to visit the most fabulous women in the walled city? They were not brothel beauties. Some of them were housewives and some of them college students. Bhagat offered an excellent bargain.

"Oh sure!" One of them responded, "that's the first thing I'm going to do after I dispose off the gold biscuits."

"Are they more beautiful than the women on our side?" Asked the younger one.

"Can't say that for sure sir," Bhagat added, "I've not seen the ***huris*** (fairies) on your side. But they're pretty good. I can take you to Shamina, if you so like."

"Who's she?"

"The reigning queen of hearts. Come. It'll be my pleasure to entertain you in my own home turf. Here's my phone number." Bhagat scribbled down a Delhi safe house phone number.

"***Insha Allah.***" The younger one responded effervescently.

"Karim Bhai we've reached your destination." Amrik announced and asked the driver to stop at the outskirts of Ajmer.

They parted company with promises to meet again in Delhi and especially in the warm confines of Shamina's pleasure spot.

Bhagat took another bus ride to Jodhpur and keyed on a crisp cipher to Delhi conveying the completion of the third phase of Operation Triple X. He added two more sentences conveying the urgency of picking up the trail of the new Pak arrivals.

Nampoothiri was thrilled by Bhagat's cipher. A rare success had been achieved by the organisation after a long dry spell. He rushed to Rabindra Narayan Dutta for breaking the news.

Dutta was glued to his phone, responding to a call from the DMI. Full-fledged hostilities had broken out along the western frontiers. Pakistan had launched Operation Grand Slam in the Chhamb-Jaurian sector. It was a well-planned finale to Operation Gibraltar.

India retaliated on September 6, plunging its thrust towards Hudiara. Hudiara to Burki and than to Lahore was a matter of a few turns of the wheel of the Indian cavalry. Pakistan, as anticipated, advanced in the Khemkaran sector with a view to cutting off Amritsar and Harike.

"It's good news. I want Triple X to become operational at the earliest. Hope your line of communication to Alamgir is intact!" Dutta lighted a cigarette. He smoked rarely, but today his nerves were frayed.

"Any special task?"

"Advise him that the new X talent should be helped to reach the target areas pronto. The Prime Minister is keen to see fast results."

"Perhaps, we shouldn't push the new talent too much and too soon. He should have a reasonable amount of time to merge with the background." Nampoothiri reminded Dutta, who was not a kid in the profession.

"Tell Alamgir to take good care of him. With his uncle's background in Karachi, Harfan shouldn't find it difficult to go places. I want speedy results. Come with me." Dutta didn't have time to argue with his deputy.

"The PM has asked for a briefing session, exclusively from the FIB."

"Any particular angle sir?"

Nampoothiri wanted to be sure of his facts before facing the Prime Minister. By now he had sized up the man well, a tough nut below his deceptive rustic appearance. He would ask a few leading questions and expect his intelligence chief to keep on emptying his bag. The man had a penchant for minute details.

As the duo stepped out of the elevator, the COAS, General Arobindo Mukherjee, briskly appeared from the opposite direction, walking with long strides towards the Defence Ministry corridors.

"Hello General," Dutta wished the COAS, "What's new on the western front?"

The COAS, a tall handsome person, turned sideways on his heels and replied, "Hi Dutta! My men are ready to enter Lahore and Sialkot, but the old man is wavering. I don't understand this man. Tell him if you can, that we now have a historic chance to teach the Pakis a lesson."

The COAS didn't wait for the intelligence chief to react. The rhythmic sounds of his hard heels echoed away from the thick South Block walls.

Mandira's presence in the Prime Minister's anteroom surprised Dutta. She was seated on the edges of the sofa, biting her nails. Her right eye flickered faster than the left one.

"Good afternoon ma'am." Wished Dutta.

"I believe the war isn't going well. The Pakis have advanced into the Punjab and our troops have got stuck in the Chhamb-Jaurian and Akhnur sectors."

She talked with a keen piercing look, expecting endorsement from the intelligence chief.

"I don't have the latest facts ma'am. Tides change every hour." Dutta tried to parry with an evasive reply.

"I'd like to go in." Mandira brushed past Dutta, pushed the door and went in.

Dutta and Nampoothiri looked at each other and decided to settle for some small talk with the secretary and ignore the awkward situation. That was a vain effort. Piercing through heavy wood panels and thick walls came out Mandira's angry outbursts.

"You can't do this to the country...I'm told that we're about to enter Lahore and Sialkot."

The PM's reply was inaudible

"You can't agree to a ceasefire at this stage. It'll be a big setback for the nation. We shouldn't accept the Polish sponsored UN resolutions."

The PM's reply could only be gauged from the manners in which she stormed out of the room and banged the outer door behind.

The intercom buzzed and the secretary gestured at Dutta to go in.

"Give me your assessment of the war situation." The PM leaned back on the high-back chair. There was no sign of distress on his face.

Nampoothiri, after obtaining a nod from Dutta, briefly mentioned about the mixed fortunes of the Indian forces; stalemate in Lahore-Sialkot sectors, considerable losses in Punjab and Jammu and some insignificant gains in Rajasthan.

"What have we gained?"

"Sir," Dutta took over, "The country is united behind you; peoples' morale is high. We've proved to the world that Pakistan can't grab Kashmir by deceit and force. The East Pakistan Bengalis have appreciated your decision to not taking the war to their door steps."

"What's the truth behind the reports of mass food poisoning in some forward posts in Punjab. Is it due to substandard tinned food? What about casualties in the higher reaches of Kashmir? Is that because of spurious high altitude clothing?" The PM asked.

"The reports are correct." Dutta admitted, "And sir, one full battalion had deserted their posts in the Punjab sector."

"How come?"

"Because of mass food poisoning."

"Who's responsible for the spurious food and clothing?"

"Initial reports have named a son of Ram Karanji as being the supplier."

"Hmm." The PM's facial muscles contorted for a fraction of a second. He managed to paint a thin smile and reverted back to the war situation.

"I want an immediate report on these two serious incidents. I've asked the army chief to order an enquiry. But you put a senior officer exclusively on the job."

"Yes sir." Dutta replied.

"What're the Chinese up to?"

"They've moved in three Divisions opposite Aksai Chin and Barahoti. Increased movements have been noticed opposite the North East Frontier Agency."

"What'll be the reaction in my Cabinet and the party, if I accept the Polish sponsored Security Council's cease-fire proposal?"

"The Mandira acolytes may revolt."

"What do you mean?"

"Your party coterie thinks they should have a new leader for the Parliamentary Party." Dutta spoke hesitatingly.

"You mean they want me out!" Jung Bahadur spoke in an amused tone. He was aware of the not too muted revolt by Mandira and her allies.

"Sir, I've sent in a blue folder last evening. It'll give you a clear picture. Mandira is working in the direction of forming a new alliance in the party and the Cabinet."

"The acceptance of the cease-fire will be based on ground realities, our national imperatives and international commitment." Jung Bahadur spoke in a soft voice.

"And I've a point to add." Nampoothiri sought the permission of the PM.

The old man nodded in affirmation.

"The media hype aside, the war front isn't very comfortable. Against our gains across the Cease-fire Line, Lahore and Sialkot sectors, Pak troops have penetrated our defences in Punjab and Rajasthan. We're more worried about the ***Hur*** irregulars, followers of Peer Pagaro. He has considerable following on our side of the border."

"You mean, we should agree to the ceasefire proposal because our position on the front isn't comfortable?" The PM spoke in an injured tone.

"It's not a negative approach sir." Nampoothiri could feel the heat in the PM's voice.

"I beg your pardon sir," Nampoothiri tried to extricate himself, "A realistic assessment of the gains and losses should be made before we reject the UN offer. As you know Moscow is also keen that we accept the offer."

"Give me the details of our losses and gains. And I'll like to know what you propose to do with the ***Hurs***. I'd ordered deployment of the Special Volunteer Force, for isolating these fifth columns. What's happened to that?" Jung Bahadur expressed anguish with a painful look on his face.

"The SVF are doing a good job, in tandem with our agents and friends in Sind." Dutta added.

"I expect stringent action against the Indian followers of Pagaro. Don't let the ***Hurs*** have a free run of the border areas."

Jung Bahadur squeezed his jaw, in an indication of deep annoyance.

"One more point, while we're on the ground situation in Rajasthan," the PM spoke slowly, "I'm advised that Pakistan is having a running commentary of our troop and armour deployments over there. Is it because of the ***Hurs*** or the inefficiency of your boys? What're they doing there? Who's in charge? Look into this."

"Any specific feedback sir?"

"Send a senior officer to make a spot assessment. Plug in the weak points. I expect more from you."

It was a scathing censure. The PM, a mild mannered person, had given sufficient proof of his displeasure. It was about time to sit up.

Dutta's face turned red. The PM's opinion must have been biased by the DMI. It couldn't be anything else. They were sure trying to cover up the military failure by blaming the intelligence. That was what the bureaucrats excelled in, passing the buck game.

Dutta returned to his den with a tucked in tail. But the lion in him roared out soon after, and Nampoothiri and Kumar Anand Prasad were at the receiving end.

"No more sweet fiddling. You proceed to Jaipur, first thing tomorrow morning. Either you beef up or scratch the counter intelligence set up there. Haul up the sloppy guys. Dismiss a few, if they don't respond."

He directed Nampoothiri.

"And Prasad," he turned to the other deputy, "I want a detailed report, within a week, on the food poisoning and high altitude death scandals. Keep in touch with the DMI."

"There are reports to suggest that the Pakistanis had poisoned the food stuff." Prasad tried putting across his views.

"Don't start with a closed mind. We can't allow petty contractors to play spooky with our defences. And Balu, you'd better take the PM's observations seriously. Don't return to Delhi till you reach the bottom of the problem."

"Yes sir. I'll do my best."

Nampoothiri understood the finer nuances of the order. It wasn't a motion of no confidence in him. But Counter Intelligence being his baby, he stood in the direct line of firing. Some heads were sure to roll. His head should be spared; Nampoothiri silently uttered a prayer. Lord Ayappa, his family deity should protect him.

****

The Kalyani Air Lines' emergency DC3 flight hovered over Jodhpur air force base for forty minutes before the Station Commander, Air Commodore Gautam Kutum, signalled landing permission. He was ready at hand to explain the delay.

The frontline airport was out of bound for civilian flights and a sortie of Gnat and MIG 21 had just scrambled up on an emergency strafing and bombing mission against Pakistani infantry and armour columns, which had broken through the Indian lines at Munaba and Gadra.

Pakistan's 51 Independent Brigade had disrupted vital supply routes after overrunning the Munaba fortifications and the railhead. The 12 Sikh Light Infantry that defended the Indian lines was taken by surprise, when the

Special Services Group and ***Hur Lashkar*** commandos blew up their ammunition dump. The Pakistani armour simply rolled over the bodies of the Indian soldiers. Another sudden thrust by the 11 Baluch Regiment, ***Hur Lashkars*** and the Sind Rangers had occupied Gotaro Fort and a few important salients in Barmer and Jaisalmer sectors.

The virulent Pakistani offensive had belied Delhi's expectations that Pakistan would respond positively to the Security Council's ceasefire appeal. The enemy was perhaps pushing for more gains as bargaining chips, Gautam Kutum explained. The Indian forces, under severe pressure, had failed to hold on to their initial gains and had conceded fresh grounds.

The warfront situation wasn't as rosy as the Indians were asked to believe by the army handouts and radio broadcasters. The Indian occupation of Pakistani Gadra and few other salients weren't enough to break the enemy's morale. The much-touted third front had turned into a burial ground of Indian tanks.

"There's a serious problem. We suspect the Pakis may have well placed agents around us, who keep on relaying running commentaries on our movements." Air Commodore Kutum wailed.

"What gives you this feeling?" Nampoothiri wanted to probe. Now he knew the PM's source of information.

"There is nothing concrete," Kutum explained, "But there is a nagging suspicion that movements of our armour, infantry and even arrival of aircraft are instantaneously picked up by Pak commanders."

"Did you scan the radio waves to monitor clandestine spy transmissions?"

"Yes. We've even used Direction Finders to home in, but have drawn a blank."

"You suspect air reconnaissance?"

"Nope. The Pakis don't have the capability, and our radars haven't noticed any such flight."

"Possibly the CIA operated U2 high altitude reconnaissance flights are helping out." Nampoothiri explored a very long wide shot.

"No Mr. Nampoothiri," Air Commodore Kutum added, "Our Chief is in touch with the Yankees. They may be tilting towards the Pakis, but they've assured us strict neutrality and the Chinese don't have sophisticated reconnaissance aircrafts."

"What about the ***Hurs***?"

"They are a real pain in the neck. Muslims inhabiting the border villages are the fifth columns. That's your problem, I presume." Kutum rubbed in the point with a tender smile.

Nampoothiri emptied the glass and silently cursed the air force officer. Yes. It was his baby and his job was on the line over that damn stupid mess. The silent war of nerves was hopefully smoothened by a smart JCO, who smartly saluted and announced the serving of dinner, and a candlelight one at that.

Dhiren Bhagat joined Nampoothiri after dinner and in the confines of his bedroom. He narrated the nuts and bolts of Harfan's exfiltration and assured him that the last minute innovation were based on a realistic assessment of the ground situation.

"But sir," Bhagat added, "They've sent in two agents through the smuggling conduit of Hassan Rathore."

"Where have they been housed?"

"All that I know, they're in Ajmer, at the shop of Amir Khan, one of the ***khadims*** (priests) at the ***dargah*** of Khwaja Chisti."

"You should've followed them."

"I've been there and have placed them under surveillance," Bhagat continued, "I suspect there's a Pak resident mole in Jodhpur itself."

"How come?"

"Amrik had dropped a Pak agent at Mahamandir, a little north of the city, about a year back. He should now be operating from a small mosque at Mandor."

"Now you're frog jumping, give me your rationale." Nampoothiri was excited, but projected a poker face.

"Amrik had leaked out this information over drinks. This agent, a communications expert, must have established a communication net work." Bhagat's explanation sounded plausible but tentative.

"Why did you sleep over this information all these days?"

"Sir, this is not my beat. I'm sharing what I've just gathered from Amrik."

"That's a lame excuse. Can you mount surveillance on your Jodhpur suspect and track down the ring?" Nampoothiri scaled down his voice. He was too worked up and excited over the fresh lead.

"We'll try sir."

"I'm camping here. Don't shy away if you require my help." Nampoothiri gave a pat on Bhagat's back.

Mahamandir locality, off Jodhpur town, was just on the verge of taking off as a burgeoning habitat. Shops and business establishment had sprouted over the years, as supporting paraphernalia to the sprawling cantonment and the air force base. Between Jodhpur and Mandor mushrooming shantytowns housed the low-income civilian employees of the armed forces and the inevitable third world slums.

Mandor, a slumbering trading town that flaunted a narrow-gauge railway station, was neither on the tourist map of Rajasthan nor was it a pilgrimage spot. The annual cattle-fair drew large crowds on October 10 every year to the ***dargah*** (shrine) of ***Sufi*** saint Amin Hydari. The pilgrims danced, sang devotional songs and offered sacrifices as tokens of fulfilment of their wishes. Devotees tied red cotton strings to an ancient wish-tree, praying for fertility of barren wombs and success in love and business.

The people's faith in the saint wasn't belied. His miracle flowed down through Baba Sai, the current holy craze at the ***dargah.*** Revered as a reincarnation of Amin Hydari, he appeared at Mandor about a year back. It was preceded by a forecast from a local priest that, the Deliverer had chosen the ***dargah*** for the redemption of his pledge to his devotees.

A shack was set up outside the ***dargah*** and Baba Sai perched himself in front of an ever blazing and smoking fire. The ageless saint, his devotees claimed could cure cancer, tuberculosis and all chronic ailments.

Baba Sai never uttered a single word. Disciples asserted that, he'd been observing a vow of silence for the last 90 years. Baba Sai's presence increased the ***dargah***'s revenue. From an annual affair, the ancient burial place of Amin Hydari turned into a booming business centre. The caretaker had nothing to regret. He kept his flat cut of 5% on the proceeds of all sales and squeezed out an advance of Rs. 1000, before any shopkeeper could erect his shack.

"Is he your suspect?" Commented Nampoothiri.

"Yes sir. I've a fair idea about the linkages between Baba Sai and Amrik's drop at Mahamandir."

"How do you link the two?"

"We'd put a skeleton surveillance on two fresh Pak intruders at Ajmer. One of them traveled all the way to the Mandor ***dargah***."

"Interesting. Next?"

"He'd spent few hours with Baba Sai and disappeared," Bhagat continued the dialogue.

The other one, Bhagat added, was observed sharing meals with a Kabalia tribal couple. The Kabalias thrived on the Cobra cult. They sought out Cobras from semi-desert fields, tamed the reptiles and earned their bread, chilli and salt by performing snake tricks. Bhagat's surveillance team had noticed the Kabalia couple frequenting the residential quarters, off the railway lines leading to Gadra. That was a strange sight. Kabalias didn't normally frequent localities of other castes and tribes, unless they were called in to drag out holed in Cobras. They were followed and finally housed at a village, bang on the Pakistan border, eating luncheon, sitting next to one of Bahgat's fellow travellers.

"Let's go in for the kill. Plan your points of mobile and static surveillance and make suggestions if any technical operation is necessary. We meet at 10, first thing in the morning."

Nampoothiri retired for the night. Sleep eluded him. Perching himself on the sofa, he lighted a Havana and kept on weighing the various options. He could smell the biological odour of the suspect. His experience told him that he was about to stumble upon something big. But how? Miracles didn't happen in intelligence operations. Lady luck wasn't about to smile as yet. The PM's unhappiness, Nampoothiri shuddered to think, could mean a cul de sac for his career. There would be nowhere to go from here and that foul garlic smelling Prasad would be sure to grab the top position.

He tossed and turned on the sofa, when Bhagat tapped on the door and announced his unexpected arrival.

"We've a good news sir." He spoke in an excited tone.

"What's so great about it?"

"We're correct, one of my fellow travellers has been picked up."

"Holy gosh!" Nampoothiri pressed the service button and ordered coffee.

Luck came, Bhagat narrated, in the form of a late night chance observation by a constable of the local FIB detachment. He had ventured out of his shack to empty his bladder, behind a bush, by the railway track. The narrow gauge railway line travelled to Barmer, Gadra Road and Munaba and across the border to Khokropar and beyond in Pakistan.

It was a single man job. He used a rope lever to perch himself on the telephone pole. He spoke in a low voice.

"They've started suspecting us. More people have come from Delhi. Note fast... 11 Brigade moves to Munaba to retake the position... two squadrons of Sherman are likely to proceed to positions beyond our side of Gadra... One additional squadron of Canberra has arrived last night. Five of the birds have been shifted to Jaisalmer. Expect action on our troops and armour with the break of dawn...."

The FIB constable, Paras Ram, a Bhil tribal, sneaked back and assembled two of his neighbours and accosted the operator.

"Come down." Shouted Paras Ram.

The fellow looked down in horror and took a risky leap. Paras Ram's team jumped on him and in matter of seconds overpowered the hefty Punjabi, masquerading as a telephone lineman. They tied him on the back of a bicycle and trudged towards the FIB office.

Paras Ram didn't know much about intelligence work. But, a dare devil Bhil, he ran errands across the borders, working as a conduit to the shallow penetration agents. He was shifted to Jodhpur, from Munaba after Pakistani forces overran the Indian position.

The apprehended agent sang like a trained canary, after he was placed under a pair of scissors, between two wooden planks, followed by an hour-long tango by Paras Ram and half a dozen hefty Bhils.

Their worst fears were confirmed. Pakistani signals units had reenergized the terminated telephone line between Indian Munaba and Pakistan.

The duo, inducted by Amrik Singh Johol were, in real life, senior officers of the Pak DMI, infiltrated to the Indian side for opening up clandestine communication lines. Baba Sai, the master agent, guided the overall operations from his Mandor shelter. The DMI operators were provided with a Siemens High Frequency compact trans-receiver, barely the dimension of a pound sized loaf. However, they preferred to use the line communications. That was the easiest way to communicate with the temporary HQ of Pakistan's 51 Brigade at Jalujo Chaunro.

A diplomat of the Pakistani High Commission in Delhi had hooked Amir Khan of Ajmer, in the course of his numerous ***ziarats*** (pilgrimage) to the holy shrine. Amir acted as a cover accommodation for incoming Pakistani agents. The kingpin, Baba Sai, a senior officer of the Pakistan Intelligence Bureau, operated a wide spread intelligence network in western Rajasthan.

The catch infused fresh oxygen in Nampoothiri's circulatory system.

His DC3 took off from a curfew bound runway, illuminated with improvised goose-lamps. He had earned his return ticket to Delhi.

Next morning, before the sun peeped above the haze covered horizon, Indian armoured columns, instead of rolling down to Godhra, took the Pak troops by surprise at Munaba and the Canberra squadron carried out a carpet incendiary bombing of Pak airbases.

The sweetest revenge, Commodore Gautam Kutum averred, was carpet-bombing of ***Pagaro Lashkar*** camps inside Pakistan. The brave ***Jihadees*** perished in their camps and that was the end of the much-touted Pakistani propaganda that the Indian people themselves had taken up weapons against their oppressive government.

An exclusive meeting with the PM awaited Nampoothiri's return to Delhi, after a good nine days. The Rajasthan leaking channel was plugged, at least temporarily. The inscrutable man gave him a nod. Yes. The job was well done. India had finally recaptured the lost positions and consolidated fresh gains. The lost battle of Munaba had finally turned out to be the graveyard of Pakistan's Patton tanks.

The old man, caught in the vortex of internal and external intrigues had something to celebrate. He ignored a minor Mandira engineered Cabinet revolt and announced the acceptance of the UN brokered Ceasefire. Delhi and Islamabad were caught in the web of another round of protracted diplomatic shenanigan, this time across negotiation tables at Tashkent. The Russian Premier had agreed to preside over as the high priest.

Chapter 17

Radu Nagar and his half brother Mukhtar Masih lived in ***bhangitola,*** a shanty corner of Nagar Parkar, in quarters assigned ages ago by the Hindu kings to the low caste sub-humans; the scavengers, night soil carriers and the rawhide processors. Succeeding Muslim rulers had used their blades for proselytizing the scavenging class to Islam. Worthy Christian missionaries, who saved their souls in the name of Jesus, followed with greater zeal. No one, including Radu and Mukhtar exactly knew if their souls were really saved.

Bhangitola (abode of the scavengers) had assumed a unique character, a rare peaceful confluence of the three major religions, an ancient amalgam of animism and Hinduism, Islam and Christianity. However, the lowest of the low followed their own brand of social and religious customs and continued to process raw animal hides and carry night soil. It made little difference to them, if they carried on their heads, Hindu, Muslim or Christian night soil. Time passed by. They were imprisoned in curses hurled by a million witches; some calling themselves sacred Brahmins, some Pak (pure) ***Mullahs*** and some high sounding Christian priests.

Mukhtar Masih, a practising Christian, was no exception. He had learnt, at a bitter cost that the days had changed. He had climbed a coconut tree about 50 feet away from the house of Ramzan Ali, the sub-registrar, to pluck mature fruits. The Begum behind her veil felt outraged. By Allah! How could a low caste convert Hindu gather the temerity of violating her sanctity, by maliciously and lustily peeping down from a neighbouring treetop!

The sub-registrar pulled down the infidel Mukhtar and awarded him a punishment of 20 lashes, inflicted at the market square. Since then Mukhtar hadn't either plucked his coconuts or tended his pigs, which, though a creation of the ***Allah,*** posed a threat to the sanctity of Islam.

But he had, over time, mastered a few tricks to win over the local police and civil officials. The likes of Mukhtar and Radu knew well the tricks of the illegitimate border trade, and the eternal traders couldn't do without them. Radu and Mukhtar's caste relations in India were too many and too smart in the art and science of illegal border crossing.

They finally succeeded in fusing the tenets of the Shariat, the Bible and the Manu Samhita into a thriving border smuggling syndicate. On this well-oiled ground, all of them co-existed, transcending all taboos, prejudices and sanctions.

Harfan Bukhari, Radu Nagar's guest was consigned to a dark dinghy room, at the far end of Mukhtar's outhouse, next to his abandoned pigsty. Since his arrival he hadn't ventured out, a strict curfew imposed on him by Radu.

Harfan didn't resent the rotten smell and dampness of the room. By now he had learnt to live with all odds. His chemistry didn't explode any more at the slightest provocation. The psychological buffer assiduously created by Maulana Rizwan and Dhiren Bhagat had helped in developing a detached outlook towards the ambience.

Harfan wasn't asleep. His mind flipped over the pages of events during the last six months.

Shit! He laughed out rather loudly. What funny turns his life had taken? What a life it was, that of a freewheeling macho Casanova, murderer and a drug peddler! And what a life he was stepping onto!

Surprise of surprises! His body and soul chemistry had added on new salts. He didn't miss the booze and bumpy female contours. His endocrinal glands triggered off a strange secretion at the very thought of women. He felt a total aversion to them, accompanied by painful flashes of the face of Rajni Krittika Hemaprabha Rao. That was a big foolish girl, too dumb and mighty stupid. The heavens would have not come crashing down if she had shared his bed.

Harfan again felt a ghastly shiver run down his spine, at the thought of raping Hema's cold dead body. He spat out a lump of saliva at a dark corner of the room and coiled up on the cot in a spring action.

Shit! It went his grain to rape a dead body. He wasn't a jackal to feast on rotten meat. The stupid woman had left a deep scar on his psyche; she had defeated him in her death.

Mukhtar Masih slithered into the room like a seeping shadow.

"Qasim Mian, wake up. We've to start at 8 tonight to take the bus for Tando Adam."

"***Ji*** (yes), where is Radu uncle?"

"He's gone to Umerkot to meet Mian Farook." Mukhtar replied.

"Who is he?"

"He's the boss of all of us, the right hand man of Hassan Rathore and his boss Sardar Illahi. In this side of Pakistan he's the law. His men are everywhere, in the police, Sind Rangers, army and civil administration. Rathore's gold, silver and drugs flow freely into India and in many parts of the world. Not the yellow, but white and brown gold." Mukhtar's face lighted up even in the shadowy darkness.

"What's this white and brown gold?" Harfan felt an urge to have a glimpse of the intricate tunnel.

"Opium derivatives, made in the tribal areas by everybody, whoever can dupe and rope the law in, and any one who can keep the army happy. They've their own cartels. In your side the boss is Harubhai Lalwani, a fabulous business tycoon in Bombay. And his big boss in Delhi is said to be a powerful minister."

"Who's that blessed fellow? Ram Karan Prasad?"

"We're too small to know all that."

"It must be him." Harfan muttered under his breath.

"Forget it. These are matters of our bread and salt. You shouldn't be concerned about it. Radu will turn up any moment. He's tying up the loose ends for your safe journey to Karachi. Put on these clothes of a Sufi ballad singer, a follower of Shah Latif of Bhit Shah. That's your cover, till you reach Karachi." Mukhtar explained the props and dialogues for his next act.

"Who's this Shah Latif?"

"A revered Sufi saint in this part of Pakistan. His followers have free access, even in restricted areas."

"Tell me one thing," Harfan offered a cigarette to Mukhtar, "Have you ever heard the name of Ram Karan Prasad?"

"Does uttering his name make you any richer? Hurry and dress up. And don't forget to have your dinner." Mukhtar tried to silence Harfan.

"You didn't answer my question."

"You don't push over death by learning to spell the word. It's inevitable. Get ready." Mukhtar left in a huff.

So, Ram Karan Prasad was the counterpart of Illahi and Rathore! Harfan Bukhari alias Ramendra Kaushal was sure by now. It must be him. Ram Karan's class wasn't concerned with war, Kashmir, Kachchh and any other aspect of the bloodiest relationship between the two adolescent umbilical nations. He used the pivot of power, strength of money and muscle and bled the country white. And people like Vidya Sagar Suri, Ramendra Kaushal and Amrik Johal were sucked into the slick world of easy money, free booze and the occasional woman. That was the eternal Indian motto: everything was done under the veil of a fake philosophy... ***Bahujana Hitaya***; for the good of the greater majority.

Shit! The parasites!

He could now clearly see the obverse side of the canvass. It was painted black, the blackness of space, in which fragments of human skeletons, lumps of frozen blood, sweat and tears floated like remnants of galactic ruins. These were cheap objects of sacrifice at the altars of political greed and bottomless lust. What a cruel peaceful co-existence between the holy politicians and the criminals!

Radu Nagar arrived at about seven, accompanied by a tout, Liaquat Masih, a native of Bohri Bazar, Karachi. A frequent visitor to Delhi, Liaquat was a legend in clandestine border crossing.

"We travel up to Tando Adam by bus and take a train to Hala. We cross the Indus by boat. After I put you on a train at Rajri, you'll be under the care of my friend Liaquat. The train will take you to Karachi City railway station. Don't get down there. Disembark at the Cantonment station."

Radu Nagar described the route on a piece of paper and destroyed it in the flame of a matchstick.

"And keep this." Radu handed over a photo identity card to Harfan with a distinct number, which certified his permanent residency at Umerkot.

"Destroy this as soon as you manage to reach Karachi. Liaquat charges Rs. 5000 as professional fees. Do you have the cash?"

"No."

"Don't bother. We'll raise a credit in India. Get ready. Don't forget to don the costume and carry the Sufi tambourine."

The rail and road journey to Hala was monotonous, except for the occasional police searches. A glib talker, Liaquat kept on entertaining the fellow passengers, mostly army sepoys, with juicy stories about the defeat of Indian forces all along the border. He and Harfan managed to sing a rural Sind tune, in praise of ***Allah,*** beseeching the Lord for a miraculous performance by Pakistan against the heathen Indians.

...Like the Tughluks, Lodis, Khiljis, Ghoris and The Great Mughals, the new nation shall bring the ***kafirs*** under Islamic rule and fly the Crescent Flag on the ramparts of the Red Fort...

Some of the soldiers, high on intoxicants, danced to the catchy tune and dropped coins into the bowl of the followers of Shah Latif of Bhit Shah.

Liaquat and Harfan danced past the Cantonment railway platform and hired a ***tonga*** (horse cart) and made straight for Najma guesthouse at Khajoor Bazar. The first floor dinghy room overlooked shanty shops selling, piles over piles of dried fruits, to the accompaniment of the symphony, orchestrated by the oscillating wings of bees, flies and numerous other winged creatures. The usual crowd milling around was from rural Sind and neighbouring Baluchistan, who forayed into the city seeking the garish women in the red-light areas and good bargains.

"Qasim Bhai, do you know the Sehnaz guesthouse in Delhi's Ballimaran?" Asked Liaquat.

"Yes. How do you know that nice place?" Harfan felt surprised and apprehensive.

"I'm also in your trade, smuggling gold and brown sugar. I've been to Delhi five times, carrying white powder and ***hawala*** (illegal cash transfer) cash. ***Yaar*** (friend), I can't forget Yasmin. She gave me heavenly pleasures."

Liaquat's eyes flashed happiness reminiscing about the good times back in the alleys of old Delhi.

"Yah, some of them are as pretty as fairies. Perhaps I've seen her." Harfan lied.

"Have you seen her? Did you ever sleep with my beauty?"

"No friend. I've my young wife at home and she hovers over me like a mother hen." Harfan lied again.

"Tell her, when you go back, that she is my cherished treasure. I'll be back to Delhi once this bloody war is over and bring her home to Umerkot."

"**Insha Allah**." Repeated Harfan.

****

On his third day in Karachi Harfan moved around the markets and selected a public telephone booth at Bartan Galli post office, next to Bombay Jewellery Mart.

"Is it the Indian Embassy?"

"Yes. It is the office of the Consul General."

"Can I talk to Irfan Cowasjee, your driver?"

"Who's there?"

"I'm Qasim, his cousin from Sialkot."

"Hold on."

"Hello brother Qasim," The voice of Irfan, a Pakistan based driver of the Indian Consulate, boomed on the phone, "When did you arrive?"

"A few minutes back. How do we meet?"

"Where are you calling from?"

"Bartan Galli."

"You ***motherchod*** (motherfucker), is it a question to ask? Take a ***tonga*** and ask him to fly you to my Nishat Road residence, next to Jubilee Market. Reach there by six."

"Six should be fine brother. ***Khuda Hafiz,***" Harfan disconnected.

Irfan Cowasjee, a Parsee by descent, was a vital link in Operation Triple X. A local employee of the Mission for the last 10 years, Irfan was an important asset, an undercover FIB operative, holding a non-diplomatic rank. His prime task was to spot prospective contacts from among the Pakistani visa seekers and arrange their exclusive meeting with the consular officer.

The Jubilee Market residence of Irfan was an elaborate affair. The ancient house, a 6-room ***haveli*** (mansion), a legacy of the colonial past was the ultimate in urban luxury. Irfan's joint family lived in the midst of urban and ancient Karachi, enjoying the rural bounty.

"So Mian Qasim," Irfan initiated the talks, "From now on you're Harfan Bukhari, nephew of Shamim Bukhari."

"How do I get to him?"

"Your uncle lives in a house near Memon Masjid, off Jodia Bazaar and his factory is somewhere at Atmaram Pritam Das road. I haven't seen the factory." Irfan described Shamim Bukhari's residence in graphic detail.

"But how do I get introduced to him? A few tenuous letters are the only link between us. For him, I'm as good as dead."

"Leave this to me. Your main problem may come from his young wife and her two brothers. They're waiting for the old man's final journey to the grave."

"You mean a nephew from nowhere will upset their melon cart!"

"You've got it right. Tackle them carefully. And you won't be in Karachi forever. Consul sahib will brief you. In the meantime, I'll get the necessary papers for you. Give me your Umerkot identity card, which describes you as Qasim and I want 10 copies of your photograph." Irfan spoke in short sentences.

"How much money do I give you?"

"Don't bother, Consul sahib will take care. You require a passport, citizenship card, ration card and it being war time, a movement warrant as well."

Irfan's style of talking worried Harfan Bukhari. In the endless maze of bureaucracy, someone somewhere might raise eyebrows and start burrowing holes like adamant rodents. Could they be pacified by mere offerings of currency notes?

Yes. The rituals were the same, in Pakistan too, assured Irfan.

Irfan's matter of fact approach impressed Harfan. The man exuded confidence and knew his way about the loops and tunnels of the Pakistani bureaucracy. He was as foxy as his counterparts in India.

Irfan broke the news to Shamim Bukhari with a dramatic flourish. He had scouted out the old ***muhajir'***s prayer patterns at ***masjid*** (mosque) Anjuman, a small place tucked away inside the busy market place. Shamim never missed his Friday prayers and giving away alms to the milling beggars.

That Friday too he turned up on the dot at 7 a.m. and bumped into Irfan Cowasjee, who stood next to a melon vendor's stall.

"***Salaam wale kum*** Bukhari sahib," Irfan startled Shamim by the intimate greeting.

"***Wale kum***...I couldn't place you ***janab***."

Shamim's words froze as he looked at the young face standing next to Irfan. It was a replica of yet another faded memory, that of his brother Maqdoom. Is he Harfan, the only surviving member of his brother's family? Or was he dreaming?

He had been receiving letters from the lost nephew for some time; some posted from Delhi, some from Aligarh and a few from Umerkot. He expected him to cross over to Pakistan, but not now, when a war raged on the borders.

"How's the day? Going for prayers?" Irfan fired a volley at the confused and perplexed Shamim.

Shamim couldn't speak. His eyes were glued on Harfan's face.

"***Wale kum asalaam mian,***" He managed to react, " Who's this fellow? And who are you?"

Irfan dragged Shamim behind a movie hoarding and whispered into his ears.

"I'm Khaliq, a border smuggler. That's enough you should know about me. Here's your long lost nephew. Don't mind the small drama. We're at war with Hindustan and I'd to take tremendous risk to smuggle him into Pakistan. Don't advertise his arrival."

"How did he come? Police CID are everywhere."

"The ***sawari*** (border trader) who helped him cross over is my cousin. I thought I'll favour you by arranging a discreet meeting."

"What're your charges?"

"It's a free service to a fellow ***muhajir.***" Irfan turned on his heels towards the mosque with his hands raised in prayer.

"It's all willed by the ***Allah,***" Shamim replied, "His face had scared me. It's a replica of my brother's face. He is my nephew indeed." Old Bukhari embraced Harfan and wept like a child.

The reunion with Harfan sent fresh, delightful but painful streaks of light into the clogged labyrinth of Shamim's memory. Harfan was just a toddler when he had seen him last. His mother, daughter of a former officer with the Patiala State Army, a blue blooded Syed, carried real Arab blood in her veins.

Shamim couldn't remember what had exactly happened to his nephew.

He was presumed dead. Those weren't the times to shed idle tears. He alone had managed to cross over to Pakistan, leaving behind his wife and only child to the mercy of the wild hyenas.

"Don't let your emotions betray your precious nephew, Mian Shamim," Irfan lighted a cigarette and offered one to him, "***Allah Tallah*** has many miracles and wonders in store. He can make a dead alive, and call a living soul back unto Himself. Truth isn't always the truth, though it seems to be true. Dreams often take on real shapes."

"***Subhan Allah*** (praise to Allah)," Chanted Shamim Bukhari, "The wishes of the Almighty shall prevail."

"***Chacha,*** one final word of caution," Counselled Irfan, "Take him home tonight. Don't beat your excited drum. He's crossed over from India without a visa, and a war's going on. Guard him carefully, till I get his papers ready. Pass him off as your nephew from Hyderabad, for the time being."

"Don't you think the police will ask questions?"

"Not really, unless you blabber out something that gives his identity away. He has genuine Umerkot papers with him."

"Why should I? He's my only male inheritor."

"Guard him from your wrestler brothers-in-law. They won't like a strange nephew dropping in on their dinner plate right through the roof."

"I needn't be a burden on you uncle. I'd better stay in a guesthouse and look for a job." Harfan spoke for the first time. He wasn't enamoured with the idea of being confronted by Shamim's brothers-in-law and pretended inheritors.

"Don't be silly son," Shamim hugged him again, "My own blood can't rot in a guesthouse. And you're an educated youth. My friends Jung Sher Khan and Mian Israr Sharief would be too glad to employ you."

"Not so fast Shamim sahib," Irfan intervened, "Let the kid relax for a few days."

"That's fine Irfan ***mian***. But I know they would lap up my nephew. They're the leading military contractors and suppliers."

"As you wish ***chacha***. But take care, I've retrieved your lost diamond." Irfan took leave of them with a discreet wink at Harfan. He had other commitments to attend to.

"***Shukr Allah ki*** (Mercy of Allah). He's a real diamond, the ***Koh-I-Noor*** of my clan." Shamim saluted Irfan and entered the mosque, followed by Harfan, for Friday prayers.

Chapter 18

Karachi's summer air was a continuous bath to Harfan's skin, very different from the dry desert air of Jhun Jhunu. It burnt, itched and oozed out body fluids in a steady stream of sweat.

But Bhagat's brief was a priority assignment, a completion of look-see studies and tourd'horizon of the people and the place in the next fifteen days. He availed of the circular railway and moved around the city, market places, harbours, naval bases, Malir and City cantonments, Qurangi and Mehran industrial areas and the upcoming super-secret missile base at Saudabad.

The memory training imparted by the FIB came in handy. He stored all the information, layer by layer, inside his memory bank and locked the compartments. Only he had the key to these complicated chambers.

Getting to know the people was another important mission. They looked so different, the Punjabis, Sindhis and the Baluchis. Some of the frontier tribals, the people of Pakhtoon and Pushtoon origin were absolutely new to him. In a miniature form, Karachi was an extended part of the same broad-spectrum kaleidoscope he had witnessed in India. Variety was the soul of the people in Karachi too.

On the sixteenth day Irfan sought Harfan out at Bartan Galli market, at a pre-fixed rendezvous.

"The honeymoon is over. The boss wants to meet you."

"Where?"

"Memorise the map, take a bus and reach Makli Hill. It takes about 2 hours." Irfan brushed past Harfan, who was apparently busy in examining a silver trinket.

The meeting took place after three days, under the shadows of the graveyards and ruins at the Little Mecca, the Makli Hill.

"Meet our Consul sahib, Mr. Dagar."

Irfan introduced Harfan to the Consular official, under the walls of the tomb of Isa Khan Tarkhan, a Governor in the Mughal courts.

Makli Hill, the world's largest necropolis with a million graves, mausoleums of the unknown, gave Harfan a scary feeling. A graveyard for the nearby town of Thatta, the ancient capital of lower Sind, Makli Hill had seen dynasties after dynasties getting buried, layer upon layer. The haunted chambers stood as mute witnesses to the glories and foibles of a retreating Alexander the Great, the Tarkhan and Sammah Kings and the other lesser ruling families.

"It's a scary place." Harfan felt an eerie shiver passing through his veins and capillaries.

"Nothing to fear. These people have been dead for centuries," Commented the Consul, "Listen carefully. Leave for Lahore the day after tomorrow. A room has been booked at Azam guesthouse next to Dabbi Bazaar. Memorise the sketch and destroy it. Irfan'll receive you there. He'll give you the onward directions."

"I believe, I'm on my own after that!"

"Not really. This is your last meeting with me. Never try to get in touch with me again. After settling you at Lahore, Irfan'll evaporate. He'll give you some money to set yourself up at Jhumra. Start your business and merge with the background. One Alam will contact you on the 28th of this month, take instructions from him. He takes over from me and hereafter will be your link with Delhi."

"Who is he?"

"He is Delhi's man, that's all I know."

"How do I recognise him?"

"He will recognise you."

"What about my papers?"

"Irfan'll take care. These are as genuine as money can buy. Take care of yourself."

"How do I go back?" Harfan asked Irfan.

"Take a bus back to the city. Your initiation has begun." Irfan cautioned Harfan.

"I presume so. Who's this Alam?"

"Don't ask any questions." Replied Irfan.

"What do you mean by that?"

"You'll learn soon. Listen and obey him. That'll be good for your health." Irfan cautioned the new talent.

****

Shamim didn't like the idea of his nephew moving over to Lahore. The only surviving male member of his dynasty, the Bukharis of Ludhiana, he wished, should settle down in Karachi and take over his business.

"Don't move to the uncertain waters of Lahore. It's not a good place for business. I'll take you to Jung Sher Khan, the biggest military supplier. He has a lot of friends in Lahore. They can fix you up in a steady job. Business isn't the best option in a new place." Shamim suggested.

"I can't be your inheritor. Your wife and her brothers won't agree. I can start a factory, in due course."

"The idea is fine, but Punjab is a choppy sea for the ***muhajirs.*** The Jats hate us. Take up a job and try your luck. Jung sahib is an influential person and Alam sahib will be glad to help you."

"Who's this Alam?" Harfan was confronted with this mysterious name for the third time. Delhi hadn't briefed him about this intermediary.

"He is a big contractor in our line of work, with good links at the top."

"Hope he'll find me useful." Harfan pretended to be sceptical about the idea of seeking a job.

"Leave that to me. Jung sahib is a powerful man. I supply spares to his factory. He can offer you a comfortable placement." Shamim reassured his nephew.

Jung Sher Khan sorted out the minor problem. He fixed up, on recommendations from Shamim Bukhari, the job of a junior executive for Harfan. He was to move to Sangla, in the defence accessory production factory of Israr International. The elder scion of the Sharief empire, an influential army supplier and a burgeoning steel manufacturer, needed a young marketing executive and a liaison manager.

The journey to Lahore city station was monotonous, except for the guttural and intestinal noises produced by soldiers limping back home and marching to the forward trenches on the Indian borders. Some of them groaned under mortal injuries and others whistled dreaming of their homes and the waiting lasses. A few abused Hindu India and a few others wished to consign the mothers of the Pakistani military leaders to the red light abodes in the nearest towns. They were happy and they were bitter too.

The kaleidoscope of emotions charmed Harfan. But the anxiety of alighting in a strange place was taken care of by Irfan, now sporting a Pathan suit, with a colourful headgear to match.

"Hotel? Do you want hotel accommodation brother?"

The voice was familiar, though the body was attired in strange apparel.

"Follow me." Whispered Irfan.

A taxi took them to Azam guesthouse at Dabbi Bazaar. The room was booked in a fake name.

"You get a full fifteen days here, acclimatise yourself with the people and the place." Irfan suggested.

"When do I report to Israr Sharief?"

"Wait for Alam. He's the man to fix your orbit. He'll decide your fate henceforth."

"Is he another ***Paigambar*** (the Prophet-pbuh)? How can he decide my fate?" Harfan fired the sentence forcefully.

"Look brother," Irfan looked straight into Harfan's eyes, "I don't know what ***masalas*** (ingredients) are used in the making of a messiah. But I know for sure that, this man Alam is very important in your present and future laps of the race. Keep this money, Rs 20,000. Get Punjabi clothes stitched. Avoid talking in Hindi, use Urdu and Punjabi. It's the 13th today. Alam will come on 28th. Go by his advice." Irfan delivered quick instructions and prepared to leave.

"How do I get to Alam?"

"Don't bother, he'll search you out."

"Are you so scared of him?" Asked Harfan.

"Yes and no. I've to guard my ass. Take care of yours."

"That means you're scared."

"Find out for yourself. Alam has deep conduits to people like Israr, Jung Sher Khan and the Generals who rule the country. Don't ask too many questions. That's the order from Consul Dagar sahib."

"Why should not I?" Harfan felt a streak of heat irritating him.

"Brother Harfan," Irfan spoke with a touch of finality, "I don't know much about you. But I know for sure that in your kind of job one can't afford to be curious like a naughty cat. It's better if you follow the briefing. ***Shabba khair*** (good night)."

Irfan left in a huff. He was supposed to take a truck ride to Karachi, avoiding the train and long distance bus services. His clandestine visit to Lahore was absolutely unofficial, even without the knowledge of the Head of the Chancery.

****

The Azam guesthouse room, barely 8x10 ft, hung low making Harfan feel claustrophobic. The walls, he felt, were being pushed by a giant hydraulic machine for pulverising him down to a few grams of dust. Lack of space within him and out in the dingy room choked his emotions and breath. Fear of the unknown and the anxiety of facing a mysterious Alam had filled in the space within. Conflicting emotions had begun puncturing his dream bag, the dreams of a perfect launching at the desired orbit and the grand finale of avenging his father's death. The spy-job was a mere platform. His mission was very private and intimately personal.

He opened the window.

A whiff of fresh air disengaged his mind from the claustrophobic gloom inside. The open piece of sky and the cloud formations hanging above the trees suddenly transcended his wildest imagination. A massive tunnel, dark, but momentarily brightened up by pale blue tongues of fire, followed by rumblings of thunder flashed past his screen.

Yes, it was definitely an uncertain tunnel. He had himself burrowed deep dark tunnels underneath the lively pulsating world above, just like a wingless hymenopterans insect. Could he ever fly out into the open skies, to his freedom? Perhaps, he had crawled past one tunnel, wading through blood, rotten flesh, slime and grime of all the misdeeds of his own making. And now he was about to enter another tunnel, colonised by his supposed exterminators. That was a nameless and faceless world of surreptitious activities, a kind of contradictory existence, full of deceit and deception.

Why did he shape his life so wild and walk into the FIB trap? Was it necessary to kill and rape that innocent girl?

The rumblings inside his stomach gurgled loudly.

It was total foolishness. No, he wasn't born out of killer seeds. The tunnels he crossed were nightmares. His will to live and wish to grow new wings of freedom should come real soon. No. He won't accept another phase of tunnel crawling. He must fly free, like the birds, yes those tailorbirds weaving their nests in the trees below Azam guesthouse.

Harfan turned away from the open piece of sky, ordered coffee and lighted a cigarette. His struggle with the conflicting images and emotions, the invitation to the open piece of sky, the birds and nests continued to flutter their rainbow wings around him.

Yes, he'd like to fly on the wings of the rainbow of hope and despair.

The slime, grime and blood were left far behind and another life surely existed beyond the dreaded blue face of Hema. Perhaps, he could put the toxic wastes of his immediate past under a permanent lid and start on a new chapter, a new life in his land of destiny. The darkness of his misadventures had lain open a path of light for him to walk to freedom.

Over a few cigarettes and millions of neuronal explosions Harfan Bukhari finally felt confident of his inner strength to pull down the curtains between the present and the worn out chambers of his past life; all, except one window, the window to the world of his mother, Kaushalya.

Harfan decided to escape the confines of the mossy and messy smelling room and take deliberate and calibrated steps beyond the old curtains. It was time he prepared for the new role; he was supposed to play in the sub-continental drama, scripted by the spymasters in Delhi and orchestrated by his destiny.

Next few days, attired in a Punjabi suit, and a mosque cap to match, Harfan ventured out to breathe in the pulsating spores of Lahore life. He visited the Badshahi, Wazir Khan, and Sunheri Mosques, all in the old city. The intricate woodcarvings and frescoes by craftsmen from Chiniot, the neighbouring district, amazed him.

Wasn't Chiniot a part of his father's kingdom. Yes it was. Kaushlaya had narrated the fascinating stories of the enslaved Chiniot craftsmen, whose exquisite artistry had given shape to the Taj Mahal, the love-dream of emperor Shahjahan. Chinioti folklore still echoed down the valleys and fields with the tragic tales of the finest artists of their millennium. Bewitched by the mausoleum's beauty and obsessed by the desire of perpetuating its uniqueness Emperor Shahjahan had ordered the execution of the Chinioti craftsmen. He didn't want them to recreate a second Taj Mahal for another lover. The white drop of immortal love and dream was brutally sanctified by the blood of a few hundred Chinioti craftsmen. They did not return to the arms and bosoms of their loved ones. They were buried too, not under the canopy of the Taj, but under the mud and slime of the river Yamuna.

Harfan brushed aside the thought. These folk ballads about the distant wailing women pining for their men, executed on the banks of River Yamuna weren't unique to Chiniot. Mountains, valleys and fields all over the world carried the refrains of such pathos throughout the ages. Muscle always brutalised art, but ageless art survived the fragile muscle tissues.

Harfan moved around the throbbing market places and small lanes that were impassable even on foot. The entire space was crammed with all sorts of vehicles, ***tongas,*** hand and ox driven carts and cycle-rickshaws. Harfan enjoyed the pulsating life around him, which exuded a unique vitality. They weren't different from the honeycombed shop cluster of shops in the charmed and vibrant lanes behind Delhi's Jama Masjid.

The same people, the same ecstasies and the same oriental friendliness fascinated Harfan. He didn't find any difference between the rhythm of life in the dingy Lahore markets and those back in the myriad alleys around Jama Masjid.

"Sir, may I borrow your matchbox?" Harfan's charmed introspection was interrupted by a whispering voice.

The slightly built young person standing before him looked quite ordinary, except for his deep-set eyes, which weren't really looking for a matchbox. Harfan's auto-reflex pressed the alarm bell.

A police informer?

An ISI agent?

A Pakistan IB agent?

He offered a cigarette and lighted it for the stranger. The vapour-like shallow person inhaled a lung-full of smoke, exhaling leisurely opened up a small conversation.

"New to Lahore?"

"Not really. I'm from Karachi, hoping to take up a job here."

"A nice place isn't it! Like the walled city of Delhi."

"Can't say. Haven't been to that grand city of the Mughals," Harfan parried, "Lahore is an ***aftab*** (sun) by itself."

"Like to meet ***chandni jaisi*** (moonlight like) girls?" The x-ray eyes of the slightly built person twinkled with a naughty smile.

"Thanks friend, not really looking for one." Harfan was now sure that the stranger was a pimp, looking for hungry wolves, at a fat commission.

"Real beautiful one, a film star."

"Thanks for the offer."

"Don't worry. I'll get her cheap...only for you."

Harfan abruptly disengaged from the strange queer character and briskly walked towards a vendor selling ***sherbet*** (drink).

He looked back. The slightly built pimp was gone.

Thank God! No, he had no appetite for any woman, after the Hema episode. Enough was enough.

The task ahead was stupendous and he was just about to be launched into a strange orbit. This was no time for brooding over a bad dream. The realities yet to be faced, he expected, should be made of sterner stuff.

Harfan hired a cycle-rickshaw, usually driven by East Pakistan Bengalis and left for the Sunheri Masjid to attend ***zohar namaz*** (afternoon prayer).

He went through the motions of bending and prostrating immaculately like a religious Muslim. His mind wasn't in it. He didn't believe in religious rituals, either Hindu or Muslim. But, in Pakistan, as a good Muslim he should be seen more in the prayer gatherings than in the social circuit.

The rituals over, he hired a ***tonga*** and asked the driver to take him to Lahore Fort, another Mughal marvel, built by Akbar the Great in 1560.

Another few hours to kill, he thought, before he returned to the guesthouse for an insipid mid-day meal. Harfan took a cosy seat on a marble platform in front of the ***Shish Mahal*** (palace of mirrors).

"Like me to be your guide sir!" Harfan was awakened out of his thought by a familiar voice. The same pimp stood before him, a slight mocking smile lingering at a remote corner of his face.

"Thanks."

"It's a wonderful place sir," the faint voice persisted, "No charge sir. I'll guide you free of charge."

"Thanks brother," Harfan bridled his galloping temper, "Leave me alone."

He walked past the nagging pimp towards a vendor dispensing small eats and drinks. The rumbling stomach signalled that he was hungry. The intestinal juices were almost eating at the walls, creating a sensation of pain and cramp.

As he turned around to approach the hawker, two ***borka*** (veil) clad women edged past him and ordered cold drinks.

Harfan stepped back to wait his turn, lighted a cigarette and tried to concentrate on a gang of child beggars. His eyes didn't miss the amorphous looking pimp standing under an old canopy.

His roving and suspicious eyes suddenly hit a pair of fabulous liquid blue eyes, which were exploring him. Yes, they were exploring him.

The blue eyes oscillated in quick movements like a pair of summer swallows criss-crossing the skies in search of raindrops.

Harfan's eyes were auto-locked to the pair of bottomless unknown blue eyes. The vapour of suspicion that hovered over the slightly built pimp suddenly gave way to a serene calmness. He was unable to shift his eyes from those of the bewitching blue eyes.

The owner of the fabulous liquid young eyes too didn't shift her gaze. She lifted her veil partially and made a vain motion of sipping the canned drink with indeterminate effort; her lips wide open. Her eyes were in a gridlock with those of the unknown youth with aquiline Greek features.

Oh God! What eyes! Behind the wide ***borka*** slits, the aquamarine eyes, lined by dark black lashes and pink skin invited Harfan to splash in. The miniature seas, tender and apprehensive liquids rippling uncertainly appeared to be a sure invitation to death. Harfan couldn't move. Glued to her gaze, his entire consciousness started burning silently like scented camphor, emitting an imperceptible fragrance.

It wasn't the mammal response; he used to get from the hidden chambers of his cranium. No, his sex organs didn't wake up, pulsating through his veins and sending a tingling sensation to his temples.

The rippling eyes, for a change, were transmitting strange signals. The fluids from the blue eyes were about to transport him to a domain, which was perhaps, called love and caring. His neurons transported him far beyond the ghostly apparition of Rajni Krittika Hemaprabha Rao.

What was it? Was it love? Or was it the old itch? Harfan could not discern clearly as to what was happening inside his chest cavity. He did not like to believe that the old Delhi campus itch had revisited him. It was surely not that fleshy urge.

The alarm bell, which was primed by Bhagat and Rizwan, rang again automatically inside his head.

No. He shouldn't succumb to such frivolities. The allurement of unknown blue eyes could be the harbinger of an intelligence trap.

Harfan struggled with himself to stick to the orbit worked out by the launch directors in Delhi. He was too well burnt a brick in the alleys of desire and lust to fall in love with an unknown pair of eyes. Harfan made educated efforts to remove his looks with a deliberate jerk of his head. But his eyes refused to move. They were still locked with the strange apertures of the scintillating life force standing ahead.

Was he in love, with those ravishing doe eyes? Harfan Bukhari stood frozen under the blazing sun and for the first time felt a faint pain somewhere in the undefined domain of his heart. What was happening to him?

The second lady, perhaps an elderly one, didn't miss the two pairs of eyes lost in each other, fathoming the language of their hearts.

She pushed her younger companion with a slight movement of her elbow and pulled down the eye-strip of her ***borka***. They moved out in hurried elegant strides and advanced towards the main hall, a string of nine rooms with exquisite marble screens. They moved on for a while behind the fine latticed marble curtains.

Harfan moved like a shadow, on the other side of the marble screens, trying not to loose sight of the owner of the fabulous eyes. Fleeting images of the frail and fragrant figure kept on attracting him like a galactic magnet.

The elderly lady escorted the younger one out and hired a ***tonga***. Harfan didn't miss the younger ethereal figure turning her face, perhaps to capture another look at the fair, robust young man, with a fascinating Greek complexion, deep blue eyes and an aquiline nose.

Harfan's effort to board a cycle rickshaw was obstructed by a man standing next to him. He grabbed the cart and threw a benign smile at Harfan.

Holy hell!

It was the same pimp. Was he following him? The fear that the pimp could be a Pakistani intelligence operative rattled his bones again. But the urge to follow the ***borka***-clad beauty prompted him to board another rickshaw and follow the ***tonga.***

The horse cart, after traversing several lanes stopped near Masti Gate, once used as the main gate of the fort and named after the mosque of Maryam Zamani, a Christian wife of the Muslim emperor, Akbar the Great.

The ***borka***-clad figures skirted an octagonal battlement and entered into a narrow footpath. Harfan didn't dare to venture inside the lane, fearing the unknown. For the first time he felt that, to follow a woman, as he was doing now, was an indecent act. It could highly embarrass the owner of the fascinating eyes.

Pursuing a woman, in a blind lane, was against the rules of the game, ingrained in his brain by Bhagat and his Company. Fascinated sure he was, but there was no use jumping into the wild and unknown waters. Fathoming must be done first, like a good sailor.

What about that pimp? The thought came back like an adamant fruit-flea.

Was he an ISI operative? Must be. What for, otherwise, would he follow him doggedly? Perhaps he was no sleuth at all.

The mixed bag of emotions helped Harfan to put his mind on two distinct rails. The pimp, he concluded, wasn't a Pakistani sleuth. The ISI, whenever in doubt, pressed the trigger first. The dreaded Company would have given him a ride to nowhere by this time, if they had the slightest doubt about his identity. That fellow could as well be a genuine pimp, looking for some easy money.

But the other experience filled his mind with a mysterious fragrance. For the first time he felt a strange feeling in the depth of his heart. It wasn't the intestinal juices that stirred up the feeling. The gastronomic fluid had stopped troubling him since he first locked eyes with the fathomless blues of the unknown beauty.

Today he didn't feel the old itch. Biting desire didn't trouble him. The animal in him had elevated itself to a newer plane. His biological chemistry had given way to something new. Harfan couldn't define what it was.

The zephyr left behind by the tender beauty intoxicated him, no doubt, but it also infused a strange strength in him. The frozen, mummified blue face of Rajni Krittika Hemaprabha didn't scare him. She fleetingly appeared like a goblin in his mind's screen. But Harfan catapulted the image away, by using superior mental strength. No, she wouldn't scare him any more.

The sensation was different this balmy afternoon. The strange doe-eyed gaze had penetrated his cornea films and entered the intricate jungle of neurones seated deep below the cortex. Signals from those eyes had scintillated his body cells.

It was love and only love.

He was surely in love, Harfan felt, with the eyes and obviously with the frame and mind behind that ***borka***.

He moved towards an eating joint selling roasted chicken and thin hand made flat bread. The intestinal juices had started functioning normally again. For the first time, after arriving in Pakistan, Harfan enjoyed a hearty meal.

The shopkeeper, a migrant from Nuh, Indian Punjab, was sharp enough to notice Harfan's peculiar Urdu pronunciation.

"A Hindustani Mussalman?"

"Yes," Harfan looked up apprehensively, but retrieved his composure quickly, "Now from Karachi, looking for a job."

"Which part in India?"

"Ludhiana, Punjab."

"Say so. Your Urdu has a distinct Indian flavour. Talk in Punjabi, that's easier."

"Brother I'm looking for a room. I want to start a business. Is there anything available in the lanes around?"

"Brother, the lane in front is known as Masti Galli, historically the homes of the ***mujrawallis*** (danseuses and singers). They've been here since the ***shahi*** (Mughal) days. Interested?"

"Look for one there or near about." Harfan finished the lunch with relish, licking the bowl of lentils.

"The biggest house belongs to Zahoor sahib, a big businessman. One of the ladies you just saw is his daughter."

The shopkeeper gave him a sufficient hint that he had noticed the enchanted gazes of Harfan following the belles in ***borka***.

"I don't understand what you're talking about." Harfan shrugged out the nascent distress signal.

"Mian, it's easier to hide murder in your eyes but not love." The man from Nuh again laughed. His eyes twinkled with naughty sparkles.

"I am not exactly in love," Harfan hedged his emotions, "I'm from Karachi and looking for business opportunities. Accommodation near the main markets would be convenient." He added.

"Welcome, I'll scout for one, for you brother, both a ***makan*** and a ***makanwali***, (A house and the lady who makes it home)." The shopkeeper offered a cigarette and a ***pan*** (betel leaf) free of cost, "Take it Mian, fresh from India."

"How do you get pan now? We're fighting a war with the ***kafirs***?"

"War is government business. We people earn our bread by honest trade. War is a state of mind, isn't it?" The man from Nuh whispered.

"You're correct. ***Khuda Hafiz***." Harfan thanked the Nuh trader and boarded a rickshaw for the Dabbi Bazaar guesthouse.

As the cart started rolling, a middle-aged person jumped in and said, "Can I hitch a lift with you?"

Harfan looked up with pale horror. Perhaps this was the beginning and end of his intelligence career in Pakistan. Perhaps that pimp had returned with the ISI goons.

He darted an oblique glance at the stranger. The fellow was enjoying his predicament. He puffed away at a cigarette loudly and chewed scented tobacco. His multi-coloured beard blew wildly in the soggy late summer breeze.

"What's the time?" The stranger asked.

"It's four p.m."

"What's the date brother?" Harfan looked up at the face of the stranger and again at his own watch.

Oh God! It was the 28th of September.

The date on which he was to meet Alam.

"Drop us at the taxi stand." The stranger ordered the rickshaw puller.

He hailed a taxi and guided the chauffeur to Orient Hotel, McLeod Road.

Harfan followed like a mesmerised lamb.

"The humble person's name is Mian Alam Khan."

The stranger whispered.

Harfan didn't require any further introduction. He knew it by now. His nemesis had arrived.

Chapter 19

Alam's favourite joint in Lahore was room 1003 of the Orient Hotel that provided a bird's eye view of the residential and bustling business districts off Nicholson, Dil Mohammed and Montgomery roads. It overlooked the Bagh-e-Jinnah and the Race Course Park, further to the north. But scenic beauty wasn't his cardinal consideration. The choice was tactical. Located next to the Lahore city railway station and bus terminus, it provided easy access and exit for the Indian intelligence anchor in Pakistan, who masqueraded as a military supplier and international trader.

Mian Alam Khan preferred travelling by road. His Mercedes could make a steady 60 kms in the hill section, and he enjoyed the flexibility of making detours, to suit his extraordinary job assignments.

He avoided air journeys, while on special errands. The Inter Services Intelligence (ISI) and the Pakistan Intelligence Bureau (PIB) religiously scanned the passenger manifests of both domestic and international flights. Their research, as ordained by the military regime, focussed on the travel patterns of political opponents and intelligence suspects. This was one of their precious props, which kept political dissent at bay.

His friends in the intelligence steel-frame, he knew, wouldn't be amused to notice his frequent trotting all over Pakistan and destinations abroad. Some day, some wise guy was sure to ask questions. And an intelligence expert's questions often sank ninety fathoms deep. These creatures had no end to their qualities of the right hemisphere of their brains. Suspicion was a sterling quality among intelligence operatives. Alam knew it well, because he was one of them.

"***Salaam*** Alam sahib." Harfan wished Mian Alam Khan with trepidation as they settled down in the hotel room, "Sorry I couldn't recognise you."

"***Walekum***, Mian Harfan. It's not your fault," Alam clicked a pistol shaped lighter to light a Marlborough, "Mind having a drink? It's time for Scotch."

He poured a stiff one for himself and expectantly looked at Harfan.

"Don't hesitate. People back home may have branded whisky as a vice item," Alam poured one large peg for Harfan too, "Take them seriously, but use your discretion. No harm in drinking a small one in good company. Public drinking is prohibited in Pakistan."

"You appear to be an Indian." Harfan commented as he sipped the drink.

"What makes you think so?"

"Your wonderful Hindi."

"Don't be curious. Curious cats never enjoy nine lives. Never try digging my turf. You'll burn your fingers."

Alam sounded terse. He felt embarrassed, being ticked off, by his understudy, for his indiscreet use of Hindi. This one guy, Alam noted, was one hell of a clever client.

Caution! Alam took a long breath to hide the enormous irritation that welled up within him.

"We should know each other, if we've to work together."

Harfan made a probing comment. He hadn't forgotten the warnings of Irfan Cowasjee about the mysterious and diabolical reputation of Alam Khan.

"Fine, fine. Your grit and guts amaze me. Reserve these qualities, you'll require plenty of these in Pakistan." Alam didn't try to hide the deliberate sarcastic intonation.

"For you, I'm like the Hindu ***Atma*** (soul). I exist and don't exist. I know everything and when you're inside the nutcracker, I'll disown you. Know this much, that I'm your anchor in Pakistan. Don't try to probe beyond this. That way we're safe. Remember, I'm a patriotic Pakistani and you're on the threshold of becoming one." Alam transmitted the message with a razor sharp smile.

"No problems, if you feel so strong about it."

"That's okay."

"Fine with me. Let's talk business."

Harfan changed tracks. He didn't want to annoy the big man, in their very first meeting. Important he sure was, perhaps an undercover officer of the FIB.

But the air of arrogance around Alam didn't escape Harfan's receptacles. His aggressively superior attitude sounded an alarm bell. The initial chemical handshake didn't blend well.

"You seem to have liked the girl. Not bad. But there's no need to turn lovesick. As part of your cover you've to marry a Pakistani girl. Your choice is good. The girl's name is Jamilla. Her mother was a Lucknowi court singer once upon a time. She'd left the profession after marrying Zahoor Choudry, a flourishing businessman." Alam poured another drink for himself.

"Is she from Lucknow?" Harfan wanted to know more.

"Don't panic. She isn't from the red light district. Just know this much that on the eve of partition she happened to give a performance in the court of the king of Jhumra, and couldn't get back. That's a well known story in Pakistan."

Harfan was floored by Alam's depth of knowledge. This man must be a wizard. He must've been observing him for the last few days. Shit! He was too lax to have missed the man shadowing him. Perhaps that pimp was one of Alam's tentacles. Possible, these things were possible in the shady world of intelligence.

Harfan silently enjoyed the quirk of events linking his dream dame with the fateful Jhumra, the cradle of the kingdom, once ruled by his father.

"Worried? How about long I've been trailing you?" Alam offered him a cigarette.

"Not bad for you. Barring a few minor lapses you've fared well. I appreciate your handling of the supposed pimp."

"I could smell rotten fish in him. He was crude."

"He's Ibadat. He'll be your Man Friday at Jhumra. He knows the girl's family. Keep the address of Zahoor. Ask uncle Shamim to send a proposal for your marriage once you're firmly on the saddle. There's no hurry. Go ahead only after I give you the clearance. Let's have dinner. You have a long session ahead. Let's go."

Dinner was sumptuous; saffron treated ***biryani*** with lavish chunks of meat, roasted chicken and beaten curd, laced with shredded cucumber.

With a delicate Benarasi (from the city of Benaras) sweet ***pan*** (betel leaf) in his mouth, Alam eructed unique fragrance of the spices. He appeared full and contented.

"Ah! If there's ***Allah Tallah***, it's in the Benarasi, after a good meal. What do you say Mian?" Alam was in an expansive mood.

"And that should be followed by the warmth of a loving woman. Right? Are you married?" Harfan took another chance with Alam, who by now was in a relaxed mood.

"No, no dear. No personal question. Keep in mind the dictum of restrictive security." Alam snubbed Harfan.

"Now listen carefully. Open up your cranium to store what I have to say. Don't miss anything. Any missing step can lead to disaster."

Alam lighted another Marlborough, but didn't offer one to Harfan. The master in him took over from the friend.

"Hope your vibes with your Karachi uncle is perfect!"

"No problem, I'm his dear nephew."

"Fine. Take care that his end of the cover remains intact." Alam continued, "You'll be located at Jhumra, seat of a former Hindu principality. Look at the map. It's just at the base of a triangle formed by Sangla, Faisalabad and Chiniot. Take a train from Lahore; it'll reach you there in 3 hours. It's before Faisalabad, the west of the territory is locally known as Jhang Maghiana. It was once a strong domain of the Hindu Punjabis, basically Khatris and Aroras (caste classification) and assorted trading castes....

"Take a ***tonga***, avoid a taxi, go past the airstrip, and next to the reserve forest and by the side of a tributary of the River Chenub, you'll find the old palace of Raja Dayaram Kaushal. It's now a hotel, Hotel Royal Palace. Book a room there. Got it so far?"

Harfan's mind suddenly sprouted wings and floated away from the physical surroundings around him. That was his father's palace. He had seen photographs of its facade and interiors and heard so much about its grandeur. Left blind folded, he could probably walk through its corridors.

"Are you listening?" Alam asked.

"Oh yes. I've been trying to store the information."

Harfan didn't like betraying his very private emotions. It was obvious that Alam hadn't read those few pages of the Kaushal dynasty. Perhaps, Delhi didn't tell him everything after all.

"Stay in the hotel as a visitor from Karachi. The following Monday hire a taxi and go towards the Sangla side. After about 15 kilometres you'll find an industrial estate. Ask for Israr Sharief, the managing director, and give him this letter." Alam handed over a sealed cover to Harfan.

"From whom?"

"It's from Jung Sher Khan, an important military contractor of Karachi. Israr supplies defence spare parts for tanks and aircraft through Sher Khan. Sher is also a big importer of defence items."

"Yes, uncle had spoken about him. But how do I justify my intimacy with him?"

"Your Uncle's ball bearing and gasket manufacturing units fill in Sher's pipe line. These're used in the maintenance of tanks, the mainstay of the Pakistani cavalry. Don't bother about these details. I've already briefed Sher Khan and Israr's a trusting type."

"What's the nature of the job with Israr Sharief?"

"Basically he wants a roving marketing manager."

Alam kept on evaluating Harfan with an assessing squint look. He hoped that the new talent would be able to assimilate the complicated brief.

Harfan coolly puffed away his cigarette and smoothly repeated back the instructions quoting Alam verbatim. Alam hadn't expected so much.

"You've been well trained," He charmingly congratulated Harfan.

"Thanks for the compliment," Harfan added, "Any more dope on Israr Sharief?"

"Your job is that of a marketing manager and liaison officer. It'll take you all over Pakistan and you'll have access to cantonments and other defence areas." Alam continued the briefing, mostly in Hindi, his mother tongue.

"Israr enjoys enormous goodwill and his identity card is respected by the military bosses. People like Israr and Sher Khan give hefty cuts to the top Generals, both on domestic products and imported items. The glue of money binds them together."

"Is there no verification process, like we have back in India?"

"Barring the slogan of two nations, we're all the same, on either side of the artificial line," Alam continued, "Israr and Sher Khan are well respected by the Chief Military Law Administration bosses and the President. But avoid his brother Nawab Sharief. He's unscrupulous. Don't ever get trapped by him."

"Any more details?"

"The elder Sharief, Mian Mumtaz had built up a big industrial empire. Israr, the son from his first wife has inherited the major share. The younger son, Nawab, is from his second wife, an Afghan lady. He's a single man demolition squad, who believes more in wrecking than creating."

"A real charlatan!" Commented Harfan.

"Put any sticker you like. He's politically ambitious and is close to Izaz Afroz, the former foreign minister from Sind. He has his own conduits to the armed forces and the intelligence fraternity. In the whole pack, that you're likely to face, Nawab is the most slippery character."

Alam continued briefing Harfan throughout the night. The priority target areas were delineated with meticulous care: coverage of the KANUPP nuclear plant at Karachi, the suspected atomic research facilities coming up near Islamabad and the hush-hush construction activities at Chashma and Kahuta.

The lengthy brief included tasking for the creation of informers at Chak Lala cantonment and airbase, radar formations in Multan, Bahawalnagar and the advance radar system recently installed at Sialkot. The GHQ, Air and Naval Head Quarters required careful penetration, Alam explained.

The most important target, Alam stressed, was the den of the Chief Martial Law Administrator. It was the vital pump house of Pakistan's political and administrative lungs and heart.

"It's a tall order." Harfan demurred.

"You've been designed for these tasks. I'm briefing an important Indian resident agent. Keep this in mind. Delhi wants quick results."

"I'm afraid I'm not a designer creation, Alam sahib." Harfan shot back in rapid fire.

"I'm afraid you are. A trained agent is custom made to the intelligence needs. He's a motivated robot."

"That's funny."

"Well! There are more surprises laid out for you than you can imagine." Alam poured himself another drink.

Harfan noticed that his supposed anchor in Pakistan was really fond of drinks. He had downed six pegs by now.

"The internal political situation in India is very fragile. The bosses would like you to monitor the sensitive aspects of decision making in Pakistan, relevant to internal matters in India and the security threat to very important persons."

"Why? Is there any assassination plot?" Harfan asked.

"In a war situation everything is possible."

"You mean assassination too?"

"War and espionage are extensions of diplomacy. War indicates the bankruptcy of statecraft. Pakistan today, and I think tomorrow and the day after tomorrow as well, will pursue the profane policy of open and proxy wars. Anti-Indianism is the only oxygen that keeps the power elite alive."

"A big deception on the people."

"Hope the people will decide these issues by themselves. Keep this list with you."

"What's this?"

"Brief notes on some important personalities. Memorise and destroy."

Alam doused his cigarette in the whisky, gulped it and advised Harfan to relax and not to worry about getting up early. It had been a long day, a really long one.

They shared a nightcap and said ***Khuda Hafiz***.

Alam started snoring straight away.

Harfan couldn't sleep.

The haze created by Alam's bombarding faded away soon and the liquid salty eyes of Jamilla faded in. Her mellow looks enveloped his conscience. His inner eyes tried to fathom the warmth of her looks, which had bathed him with the honey of love and care.

How mysterious! Fate had linked her with Jhumra! Had he met with his destiny at the Lahore Fort? Did that mysterious force called God or whatever it is design it?

Harfan had a disturbed sleep. Jamilla appeared and disappeared like the patches of rainless autumn cloud. Suddenly the silhouette of the Jhumra palace, the seat of his father's kingdom popped up like a remote galactic blinker, appearing and disappearing with faint pulsating burst of light.

The shadowy montage of his parents hovered over the elegant edifice for a while. His father suddenly appeared on horseback, decked up in full war gear, charging his enemies with an open sword raised above his head.

Harfan cried out in excitement, as his sleep snapped abruptly with unsaturated expectations.

Alam, by now fully dressed and geared up for the day, woke him up with a steaming cup of coffee.

"***Barkhurdar*** (dear son), had a bad dream? I'm ready to hit the roads. You can't reach me. Only in case of real emergency, call Quetta number 76989 and ask for Intikhab. This is the number of Farah Restaurant, at Jinnah Road. In case Intikhab responds, tell him that Alam's nephew would like to talk to him. Don't reveal anything else on the phone. I'll be in touch, if it's possible. I'll reach you once you get your own accommodation at Jhumra. You'll find Ibadat extremely helpful. He can fix a house for you."

Alam took out a fat bunch of Pakistan currency notes.

"I've nothing more to add. Expect you to live up to the brief. Keep this money, rupees 1 lac. It's for your upkeep and professional expenses. Check out, after you've had breakfast. All the bills have been paid for. ***Khuda Hafiz***."

Mian Alam Khan picked up his safari bag and left the room.

****

Harfan slithered out of his bed leisurely and lighted a cigarette. His mind was preoccupied by the mysterious appearance and departure of Alam. The Quetta safe house phone number, Harfan mused, must only be a cover for the master operative. Could he be an officer of the FIB operating in Pakistan under deep cover? That was the most plausible explanation, he concluded. How else could the master Indian spy agency trust another resident spy like him to handle sensitive operations in a hostile foreign country? Well! A jackal on the prowl should know the jackal in the next hole very well. That was essential for his safety and security. Harfan decided to explore the idea at an opportune point of time. He pushed back the curious thought to a back burner and took a leisurely shower, enjoyed a sumptuous breakfast and checked out before eleven.

Back at Azam guesthouse, he closed the door, took out a family photograph snapped way back in 1945, of his parent's in their late youth. Raja Dayaram Kaushal gorgeously dressed in royal regalia stood by a black stallion and Kaushalya bedecked in her finest jewellery looked like a stiff wax doll. The young suckling on her lap, Harfan smiled, had to be the only and one Prince Ramendra Kaushal. He kissed the photo and shoved it back under a pile of clothes.

Yes, his decision to live a shadowy cover life in Pakistan was worth the risk. Destiny had guided him all the way to Jhumra from the torrid campus of Delhi University. The blind dame had set out two challenges before him. He must avenge his father's assassins and must win over Jamilla's hands. The spy, he thought loudly, should have no difficulty in cohabiting with the warrior and the lover.

After an insipid hot and spicy lunch, Harfan Bukhari hailed a rickshaw and asked the puller to proceed to Masti Gate. A mysterious force inexorably drew him towards the blind alley behind Mariyam Zamani mosque. He alighted near the eating joint of the Punjabi from Nuh and ordered a cup of spiced tea.

"Hello Mian ***Ludhianvi*** (from Ludhiana)," The jolly Nuh man offered him a cigarette and continued," Your ***huri*** (fairy) hasn't come out today."

Harfan didn't evince any interest. He supplemented the tea order with a plate of reshmi kebab, garnished with garlic and mint sauce.

"I've news for you, brother ***Ludhianvi***," The shopkeeper continued in an excited tone," She is Jamilla Bano, daughter of Zahoor Chaudry, a man of means and status."

Harfan kept his cool. This was stale news. Moreover, he didn't want to betray his emotions. He wasn't sure how safe it was. The intelligence sleuths, for titbit information, tapped the street corner vendors like the Nuh Punjabi.

"Brother let's have a walk inside the lane. Let's see if we can locate suitable accommodation." Harfan spoke while crushing the kebabs between his tongue and upper palate.

"Sure. But excuse me for being incorrect about Jamilla Bano's mother. She isn't a ***mujrawali*** (courtesan) any more. She gave up the profession 20 years ago, after getting married to Chaudry."

"Don't bother. I'm not hooked to that girl. Show me around. I'm told there are remains of an old Mughal time church in the lane."

"Brother ***Ludhianvi***," The Nuh fellow added jocularly, "Lahore has many surprises. But the church of Begum Mariyam is no more there. The land sharks have eaten up the bricks. Come I'll show you around Zahoor Chaudry's palace."

"Not interested. Just give me a tour."

Zahoor Chaudry's magnificent mansion faced a small park, skirted by the Mariyam Zamani mosque. The main approach to the mansion was from Circular road. The approach from Masti Gate was a shortcut, a remnant from the historic days.

Harfan, with the Nuh friend by his side, sat down on the park greens and kept on looking at the balcony of the house. The house, designed to look like a ship, was reminiscent of Zahoor's ancestry to the ***mohana*** (estuary) tribe of Bhit Island, off the main flow of the Indus.

"Come. Let's go to Anees ***faqir***'s (mendicant) abode." Harfan's companion stood up.

"Who's that?"

"He's a wish healer and can fulfil all your wishes."

"Shh!" Harfan silenced his companion.

His wish, the owner of the enchanted pair of eyes appeared at the edges of the balcony of Zahoor's house.

She was real. There was no mistake about it. Those were the very eyes. From a distance of about 100 yards, Harfan could recognise the azure blue shade, wonderfully long and black lashes and creamy creases around the diamond cut wonders.

Yes. The wise ***faqir*** Anees or not, she was there, his dream had materialised.

Her slim vine like body was draped in a light pink ***salwar-kameez.*** She appeared as fresh as a dewdrop on a pink rose petal, dazzlingly bright, a refreshing breath of air.

She leaned against the wooden railing and looked out, probably at the stratus cloud formations, hanging low over the horizon.

She suddenly sprang back like a tender flowery cane, in an electrifying swinging action.

Yes. It was the same face. Those were the same eyes. His pinkish Greek face, with the lavish growth of black beard looked sad, beaten by many summers. Yet it looked innocent, starving for love and care.

In a final retro-swing action she came near the railing, leaned against it and turned her head, swirling her huge cloud of dark hair and ran back inside.

To Harfan it was an invitation to jump from the parapet and land before his dream maiden.

Electrified, he stood up.

The Nuh friend pulled him down.

"Keep your cool Mian. Love has infinite ways of expression. Reserve your responses for better days. Let's go. It's not safe to loiter in the park."

"Wait for a few more minutes."

"No brother ***Ludhianvi***. The day's tour is over. Sleep with your dream. ***Allah*** willing she'll be yours soon."

He pulled up Harfan, licked by the remote thunder-current that emanated from the swirling cloud like hair of Jamilla. They walked down the lane, the shopkeeper guarding Harfan's rear.

Jamilla, the music of the name kept on bouncing inside Harfan. The space inside his frame was flooded with the sweet fragrance of the belle he had left behind at the enchanted lane.

What was it, love?

Harfan didn't know what love was. He had never cared to know.

In what way was it different from desire?

He managed to get whatever he desired, dead or alive. Could he force Jamilla to love and care for him?

An inexplicable string kept on pouring in a strange tune inside Harfan. His body and soul reeds told him in so many fragrant tunes that he was in love. And love just happened. It could not be earned or looted.

Was Jamilla his destiny? Perhaps. Otherwise, why had he traversed all the way to Pakistan and met her in a lost corner of Lahore?

A conviction that God had especially created her for him started taking root somewhere deep inside him.

The Hindus perceived marriage as a destiny made in heaven. Perhaps the saints were correct. How could he, otherwise, explain the accidental meeting with Jamilla? Some force kept on ticking inside and telling him that this dream belle, in this unknown corner of Lahore, was simply made for him, perhaps by God, perhaps by destiny.

Well! His Nuh friend was correct. Wait he must.

Perhaps Alam's prescription was the best to reach his goal. Jamilla, the new ray of light in his singed and contorted life, must be pursued with patience. To get her he must walk the minefields carefully.

The inner churning slowly settled down and Harfan felt slightly relieved. He had seen a new star. She was sure to guide him to a new destiny, giving him a new lease of real human life. Harfan didn't feel that he was a mere intelligence robot, crafted by Delhi. The human inside had just discovered that for light of love and life had not yet extinguished with the cadaver of Hema.

He packed up and prepared to catch the 7 a.m. train to Jhumra, a small station connected by meter gauge rail, about three hours away from the Lahore Cantonment station.

He spent the rest of the night listlessly, tossing between the shadows of Jamilla and the besieged palace of Raja Dayaram Kaushal. Two passions tormented him. The probability of winning Jamilla's hand appeared to be uncertain and he didn't know what to expect at Jhumra?

Harfan worked his neurons for half the night, yet remained mystified. He didn't get any clear answer. About 3 a.m. his eyelids drooped down as his mind and head filled up with smoke. Harfan dozed off in a dreamless sleep, only to wake up barely 30 minutes before the train steamed out of Lahore.

****

Jhumra railway station wasn't a big affair. Fast trains didn't stop there. But military requirements had changed the strategic importance of the sleepy station. A big supply base had sprung up between Sangla hills and Jhumra that supplemented the forward bases behind Lahore. The Khyber Express, which mostly carried men and materials for the war front slowly rolled into the platform with a cacophony and finally stopped with the engine-exhausts releasing clouds of steam. A few reluctant hawkers leisurely loitered past the platform vending cigarettes, tea and short eats. Harfan brushed past the milling crowd of soldiers and squeezed past the ticket checker.

A baton-swinging policeman, belly protruding beyond his body frame, appeared from nowhere and obstructed his way.

"Haven't I seen you before? Where are you from?"

"Inspector sahib," Harfan replied while lighting a cigarette, "I'm from

Karachi, going to take up a job at Sangla, at the factory of Israr sahib. Can I offer you a cigarette?"

The constable silently extended his hand, pumped out clouds of smoke and signalled at Harfan with his fingers.

"I'm here to check for Indian ***jasus*** (spies). Show me your papers." Harfan brought out his national identity card and movement warrant.

"Come and pick up these tomorrow from the police station." He pocketed the papers.

"***Daroga*** sahib (police chief), I'm new to this place and I've to join my duty, please favour me by returning the papers." Harfan didn't want the law to scratch at him at the very first encounter.

"Five hundred." The constable again extended his hand.

"What about three?"

"Five, that's the tax for taking up a job in my jurisdiction."

Harfan looked around and placed five hundred rupee notes on the big flat palm of the constable, picked up his baggage and walked out of the platform.

Harfan's encounter with the police constable didn't rattle him. This was a routine with the law enforcers, a common feature all over the sub-continent. A little extra earning by the slight swing of the baton, if not by breaking a few bones, was an integral part of the glorious profession. These traits were inherited from the deep past of the feudal society.

"***Janab***, think you require a ride, come to my fairy driven ***tonga***, it simply flies." Announced an old horse buggy driver, as Harfan stepped out of the platform.

Harfan boarded the garishly painted ***tonga,*** drawn by an emaciated and bored horse and said, "How old is your fairy?"

"Not very old ***janab,*** this servant of yours and this beauty used to draw the carriage of the former king, only a couple of years back. But, things have changed now. The king isn't there and the fairies are starving, like your poor servant is." Replied the old carriage pilot.

"What happened to the king?"

"They killed him ***janab***. These mad Niazis and assorted Jats kill in the name of ***Allah,*** at the slightest pretext."

"What happened to the king's family?"

"***Janab***, I was one of the servants of the king seeing the queen off at Hindu Mal Kot. She wept all the way, didn't even get time to perform the last rites."

"Take me to the Royal Palace Hotel." Harfan hardly able to control his tears turned his face against the wind and lighted another cigarette.

"Raja Kaushal's palace?"

"May be. But who's this Raja Kaushal? Appears to be a Hindu name."

"***Ji Janab***," The ***tonga*** pilot opened up his glib tongue," He was a real king, a virile man. He decided to fight and die rather than surrender his kingdom to the newly created Pakistan. The Pakistani government finally imported Niazi and Baluch tribals to attack his small army. He fought valiantly and died."

"Who killed him?"

"Can't say for sure. My father, the master of the royal stable, used to say that the fatal stroke was hurled treacherously by the son of a Niazi chief."

"Very interesting, what's your father's name?" Harfan asked in a placid tone," You know so much. Perhaps you may one day take me on a guided tour of this place."

"***Janab,*** your humble servant's name is Sagir. My father, Tabajju Khan was the chief of the royal stable. He died two years back. Is ***janab*** on a visit?"

"Not exactly. I'm seeking employment in Israr Sharief's factory. Let me settle down. You'll be my guide, to show me around this exotic place."

"You won't be disappointed ***janab***, our Jhumra has many mysteries to reveal."

"Must be. I'm keen to unravel her beauties and tragedies." Harfan muttered to himself.

"Did ***janab*** say something?" The cart driver tried to prolong the dialogue.

"Yes brother. How is this Israr sahib? "

"A fine family. Two brothers. Rather co-brothers. The younger one is from the elder Sharief's second wife, an Afghan lady. He is a very crude person."

"How do you know all that?"

"This sager is an encyclopaedia ***janab***."

" That's very interesting."

"You're welcome ***janab***. Jhumra has many secrets to unfold."

"Yes. And you should be my guide." Harfan replied in a miffed voice. Yes, he was indeed on a discovery mission; discovering himself, Jamilla and the trails of blood of his father and those of his killers.

****

The ***tonga*** cantered past the huge wrought iron gate of the palace of Raja Dayaram Kaushal. The well-manicured garden, lined with bottle palms, acacia, chinar (maple family) and other ornamental trees and bushes looked fabulously elegant. The entrance arch, lined with hazels and dwarf magnolias, was covered with sweet smelling flowery creepers.

The pathway, paved with yellow Jaisalmer stones, meandered through a well-mowed lawn and ended up below the ornamental portico, still decorated with carvings of Hindu gods, nymphs and well sculpted male and female figurines.

An oversized receptionist flaunting a huge moustache and wavy beard looked up with fatigued eyes.

"You want the King's or Queen's rooms? None are available. Already booked for an American group. I can offer you a room originally used by a concubine of the king."

"What's her name?"

"Who cares? ***Janab,*** who cares for dead kings and their concubines! Didn't they maintain a harem full of whores, these kings and nawabs?"

The bored receptionist wasn't interested in continuing the dialogue.

"Any room will do." Harfan put a lid on his emotions. His veins had already started pumping extra blood to his head.

"I'm here only for a few days. Can you give me a room facing the river? That'll definitely be a great favour."

"Done sir, you get room number 16."

"Ibadat!"

He yelled at an employee, who stood at a distance with his eyes glued to the front desk. The face appeared to be familiar. Was it that of the pimp at Lahore? The resemblance was astounding.

"Have I seen you earlier?" Asked Harfan.

"Sir, your servant is a poor employee in this hotel, haven't been out of Jhumra all these years. Your servant is called Ibadat."

"So you're Ibadat?"

"Any problems sir?"

"No. Show me to my room."

Harfan silently analysed the probable relationship between Alam and Ibadat. It was too early to dissect the anatomy of the intelligence operative.

The room facing southwest, with a high ceiling and Greek windows, gave a pleasant view of the river and virgin woods that tapered down along the uneven contours of small hillocks. Whiffs of fresh air filled Harfan's chest. He leaned out of the window to look beyond the woods. He noticed two moderate huts, tucked in a remote corner of the verdant greens. An elderly lady, dressed in a peculiar north Indian ***sari***, was lighting an earthen lamp, in front of a bushy plant.

"Who's that lady?" Harfan asked Ibadat, still waiting with his luggage.

"That's Rama Bai, one of the leftovers of the former royal retinue. She lives in a hut near the riverbank and offers worship to the family deity of the Raj family. What you see now is a daily ritual, lighting of the lamp under the ***tulsi*** (mint plant sacred to the Hindus) bush." The porter replied.

"But, she's a Hindu," Harfan added, "Doesn't anybody object?"

"Sir, she's a lonely heart. Nobody takes her seriously. The ***mullahs*** aren't interested in converting her and the district magistrates have accepted her as part of the ancient vegetation."

"Why?"

"The Hindus were very powerful in this part of India," Ibadat offered by way of an explanation," their spines have been broken and the new power peddlers have replaced them. Rama Bai is too insignificant to disturb their sleep."

"Are you also from the former regime?"

"Yes sir, your humble servant is the son of the former chief chef of the Raja's outer kitchen."

"You must be privy to a lot of inside stories about the king and queen."

"Lower your voice please, there are many strange eyes and ears around here."

"You said your father was the chef of the outer kitchen!"

"The queen, a staunch Hindu, ran her vegetarian kitchen in one corner of the palace, all her cooks were imported from Benaras. The Raja had a separate kitchen for non-vegetarian food, for himself and his guests."

Harfan lapsed back to his memory bank and recaptured the fascinating stories his mother had narrated about the loyal and daring cook. She hadn't mentioned anything about Ibadat, his son. Perhaps he wasn't born before she left Jhumra. Even if he were, a queen wasn't supposed to know of the existence of a cook's son.

"Perhaps you know Mian Alam!" Harfan fired the question all of a sudden.

"Alam? Oh, Mian Alam Khan, the big businessman! Yes. He drops in at the hotel once in a while. His company is engaged in some supply business. Do you know him sir?" Ibadat parried the question.

"How're you related to him?"

"***Janab***, I'm a poor hotel employee. I know him as a business magnet and a customer. And sir, here's the bell. Call, if you require any service."

Ibadat left after enquiring about the dinner preference of Harfan Bukhari.

Back in bed, Harfan looked vacantly at the roof, architectured with an inverted lotus of Persian design, flanked by Greco-Roman figurines. The kings of Jhumra had indeed liberally borrowed from Hindu, Persian and British styles of architecture.

He concentrated on the core of the lotus and ruminated over Delhi's choice of Jhumra, as his launching pad. Something very personal, something very dear and very sacred to him was mingled with the dust and grass in this backyard of Pakistan. These were his own, very own. And the blood of his father, spilled only 18 years ago, must be lying somewhere by the riverbanks.

Cool, cool!

Harfan collected himself. He decided to swallow the blood and fire that blazed inside. It was too early to declare a war. War against whom? The enemy must be sighted first. There was no need to charge like a pine-headed Pinocchio.

He smiled and walked up to the window.

The emaciated face of Sagir, son of the former royal stable keeper fleeted past his mind's screen. His mother, Harfan recalled, had told her many stories about the favourite horses of his father. The emaciated fairy of Sagir, if Kaushalya's memory was correct, was christened ***Bijli*** (lightening). She had drawn his mother's carriage on many a memorable occasions. He must explore Sagir and find out more about Rama Bai. That distant figure, lighting a lamp under the ***tulsi*** bush had intrigued him.

Cool. Cool!

Harfan took a deep breath. He must live his cover well and prepare for the war ahead, the war to destroy the evil Niazis, responsible for his father's assassination.

He recalled Maulana Rizwan's contemptuous description of Muslims as ***Ahl-e-Kitab***, people of the book, blind bigots, ***Ahl-e-Hadis.*** These scourges of human civilisation deserved death and destruction. Harfan swallowed the lump of saliva; the extra juice of anger that had deposited in his oral cavity.

What about this Ibadat? Was he also an agent of Alam? Was he following him back in Lahore too? What could be his motive?

Was Ibadat aware of his real identity? Or was he simply carrying out Alam's orders!

He must figure out the bearings, but patiently.

Harfan walked over to the window. The swift flowing currents of the distant Chenub broke into a rhythmic lullaby, just like Kaushalya's soothing voice, humming the enchanting message of peaceful sleep.

Not very far, across the silhouettes of trees and bushes, faint lights flickered in the rippling breeze. Must be from the hut of the lone-hearted lady, living under the shadows of the palace of her former employer.

He felt tempted to walk down to the source of the light. This lady must be an interesting character, privy to the exciting drama of the last days of his parents at Jhumra.

She must have known the killer of the former king.

Harfan lighted a cigarette and turned towards the door.

"Going out sir?"

Ibadat appeared as if from nowhere.

"Yes. Just for a stroll." Harfan stepped out under the portico.

"Very fine night sir," Ibadat followed," But don't move out in the dark. There are wild animals around."

Harfan felt a sudden surge of irritation. This puny mole of Alam was stalking him all the time. He felt he wasn't a free agent and couldn't make any move without the master resident regent's permission.

"I saw a faint light emanating from the quarters of that old lady, you talked about this evening."

"Oh! That light? She's a lunatic, doesn't sleep, most of the nights."

"Insomniac?" Harfan commented.

"Sir, her life is queer."

"What's it all about?"

"Sir," Ibadat led Harfan back to his room." Most of us are victims of some acts of some drama scripted by the ***Allah***. Who knows whom he casts in what role?"

Ibadat said ***Khuda Hafiz*** and left.

Drama? Yes, he too was a character in the drama scripted by ***Allah***, Goddess ***Kali,*** whoever He or She was.

Well! He was ready to play his role, but not according to Mian Alam Khan's and his stooge Ibadat's script. They sure weren't his designated master puppeteers. A Kaushal was capable of scripting and directing his own act.

There was no need for him to fret and fume. He thought over the scenario coolly and realised the limitations he suffered from. He could free himself from the domineering personality of Alam only when his own channel of communication to Delhi was established. Delhi, he sighed, was too far and too scary.

Chapter 20

The drama back in Delhi wasn't scripted by the unknown entity invariably described as ***Ishwar, Allah*** and God. The dramatis personae were very much mortal. They were busy honing their own axes.

To some, the question of succession to Amritlal was still an unfinished agenda of the transfer of power from the Windsor to the Amritlal dynasty. Jung Bahadur wasn't destined to play the main character, some of them, especially Mandira believed. How could he? God had chosen her, the only child of Amritlal; to walk into his shoes and stretch the dynasty's span beyond the limits of history.

The second Kashmir war had opened up limitless opportunities. Mandira and her acolytes had ganged up against Jung Bahadur to sabotage the UN sponsored ceasefire and the USSR brokered talks scheduled at Tashkent.

Jung Bahadur, busy as he was in harvesting victory out of a stalemate, had pinned down his hopes for diplomatic miracles at the Uzbek capital. But he wasn't blind to the gurgling and rumblings inside his cabinet and party. A high level enquiry ordered by him into the deadly double scandal of mass food poisoning in front-line trenches and high altitude casualties caused by substandard clothing had stirred up the proverbial queen bee's nest.

Mandira, adept as she was in twisting the tiger's tail, had decided to use the proposed Tashkent talks as the immediate spur for positioning her guns against Jung Bahadur. She wasn't alone in this proxy-war. The party overlords, mostly creations of her father, suddenly discovered that the Prime Minister was guillotining Ram Karan Prasad, the cabinet minister, for an imagined offence by his son Ram Charan, a military contractor.

Ram Karan was just an alibi, they firmly believed. Jung Bahadur was really honing his axe for Mandira's neck. And the wily impostor was bound to use the FIB network to hang damning bills on her ally's back. It was time for her to intervene with another creation of her father, Rabindra Narayan Dutta, the FIB chief.

In matters of war and in the art and science of exploiting the loyal lambs Mandira hardly cared for protocols. Her stage wardrobes perfectly suited the dramatic requirements. No one, therefore, was surprised to see a Mandira in an all-white ***sari*** walking down the corridors of South Block towards Rabindra Narayan Dutta's room.

Dutta wasn't a big gun in her eyes. She had seen him growing up under the shadows of her father. He was, in her perception, another fixture in the Amritlal establishment. She didn't surprise Dutta either, when she just knocked and entered the room unannounced.

"Do you think it's correct to accept the ceasefire proposal?"

Mandira drew a chair and settled down with hawkish looks at the FIB chief. Her impatient fingers drummed on the table restlessly.

"Ma'am this was inevitable," Replied Rabindra Narayan Dutta, "The PM's decision is in conformity with the ground realities."

Mandira's fingers stopped drumming. Her oscillating eyelids spoke volumes. She wasn't happy with the reply. She expected the FIB chief, a creation of her late father, to understand the finer nuances of her questions and support her views. Acceptance of the UN brokered ceasefire on September 23 was an act of betrayal of the national trust. The PM should've carried on with the war. The Generals were sure of smothering Pakistan to pieces.

"Don't you think the PM should've allowed the Army to storm Lahore and Sialkot?"

"Ma'am," Dutta felt a hidden heat climbing up his spine, "Between us let's be frank. The war hasn't been going on the way we had wished it would. In short it's a drawn war."

"You're a prophet of doom." Mandira hurled the dig at him hoping it would scratch open the wounds of the China-war faux pas by the FIB chief.

"Ma'am, war isn't fought on the basis of perception. It requires logistics and astute diplomatic manoeuvres. We can't defy the UN."

"You appear to have an apology for each and every action of the PM." Mandira sounded bitingly caustic and sarcastic.

"Ma'am, don't misunderstand me. I'm a professional, I can only speak the truth."

"Well Duttaji," Mandira hurled a sideways glance at the veteran sleuth, "Facts are buried under fiction with you around. I haven't forgotten the Chinese war fiasco and the precious intelligence reports you had manufactured for my trusting father."

"Well ma'am...."

Dutta's resolve to hit back at Mandira was cut short.

Nampoothiri called on the intercom.

"Yes Balu."

"Alamgir was on the High Frequency set. Some interesting messages require your immediate attention."

"Okay. I'm coming down," He stood up and politely begged to be excused from the junior minister, "Sorry for the interruption ma'am. But something important has come up."

"Yah. I think I've to go too. But tell me why you people are trying to hang Ram Karan? Is it because he's close to me?"

"By no stretch of imagination ma'am. The PM has ordered an enquiry against his son, for alleged military supply bungling."

"Spare him. He's my man." Mandira pleaded.

"I can't. Why don't you speak to the PM about it?"

Dutta begged to be excused and took the exclusive elevator to the basement communication room.

Mandira too was in a hurry. The top bosses of the party organisation were cooling their heels at her residence for urgent consultations. She followed Dutta with brisk strides and with a mighty scowl on her face.

Mandira wasn't really concerned with the ceasefire and the scheduled Tashkent talks. Her war game was different. That was confined to oust Jung Bahadur campaign, as a prelude to her anointment as the next PM by an obliging party. And for that matter any weapon was good enough to beat the PM-interregnum. How did she care if that meant a mini cabinet revolt, crisis in the party organisation and international discomfiture?

Wasn't Jung Bahadur's counterpart in Pakistan facing similar problems? Izaz Afroz, the foreign minister under President Akbar Khan had stirred up an orchestrated agitation against the ailing chief. Why couldn't she, the worthy successor to Amritlal, give a pushover to the frail man? In what way was she inferior to Izaz? Both of them carried blue blood under their skins.

She was mighty concerned too, with the welfare of her steadfast political ally and a loyal family retainer, Ram Karan Prasad. How could she allow Jung Bahadur to guillotine him for an unproven crime by his son? The political baron with the widest caste network was too valuable to her at this moment of fluid political ambience.

She summoned Rajinder Singh Dewan, her secretary and directed him to locate Ram Karan and advise him to see her forthwith.

Play it cool! She advised herself. Ram Karan, she knew, wasn't a milk-washed deity. His questionable business links and supposed intimacy with Pakistani smuggler cartels were the talk of the town.

Well! No politician in this free country could be hanged, unless proven guilty. Corruption was a global phenomenon. What's new about the fact that one lot of military supplies had gone sour? Sure, some soldiers died, but where was the proof that they died because of wrong supplies made by Ram Karan's son! And what else could soldiers do in the front but die like heroes, to the accompaniment of tolling bells, drums and cymbals? That's how heroes received martyrdom!

Jung Bahadur was gunning for Ram Karan to weaken her position. Mandira believed she was the main target. She must advise the wily Bihari to hush up the scandal. The fool was as greedy as a marsh jackal! He habitually chewed more than he could swallow.

****

Ram Karan wasn't in Delhi.

He took a flight all the way to Amritsar, the holy city of the Sikhs, critics alleged, soon after newspapers splashed front-page headlines about Ram Charan's involvement in substandard military supplies.

He wanted to be with the soldiers at a forward post near Dera Baba Nanak (DBN), opposite Pakistan's Lahore sector. Formation DBN was the theatre of scandalous desertion of posts by a full battalion of the Indian army, following severe food poisoning. The Commanding Officer, despite contrary efforts by the Quarter Master General, had filed an official despatch to the Chief.

In a public meeting orchestrated by his smuggling cartel collaborators, Ram Karan eulogised the valiant soldiers of India, and promised a personal donation of half a million rupees to the war widows.

A government owned Film Division camera contingent snapped Ram Karan, seated atop a captured Pakistani tank, with tonnes of garlands hanging heavily from his neck. The drummed up propaganda, he believed, would help in whitewashing some of the black deeds his son Ram Charan Prasad, the fourth scion of the illustrious Mallah dynasty.

The damned stupid idiot! Ram Karan uttered a curse. The stupid fellow should've known that business shouldn't be mixed with sensitive issues like war. War was a serious matter and war materials of the day weren't like the supplies he used to ferry to the northeastern borders for the British Indian Regiments. He could take the liberty of supplying rotten stuff to starving brown and black Indian soldiers. But the India of '65 was different. And India's Pakistan war was more patriotic than Britain's Japan war.

Ram Karan's guts told him that his son's blunder was going to catch up with him. He cursed his wife's womb, for the sin of incubating and delivering such a fool. No one in the Mallah dynasty, at least in the last four generations, was caught pants down by the law for committing grievous offence. Acts of crime came naturally to them. No one had attained greatness in human history without plundering properties, wives and daughters of the meek. It was wrong for some seers to assert that the meek would inherit the earth. Might was the right weapon to rule over the teeming millions, who lived like insects in the fringe of history. The Mallahs had played their caste-cards shrewdly and their participation in politics and business were acclaimed as diamond edged chain saws, cutting everything smoothly, sans any pain.

A turbaned policeman, who climbed up the turret of the Pakistani tank and handed over a closed envelope, interrupted Ram Karan's dissection of the historical past of his illustrious family. He could not ignore the bold prints on the cover that announced that the originator of the message was Mandira, the rising daughter of his mentor Amritlal. Mandira's message was too important to ignore. Karan grudgingly boarded a late night flight and rushed back to his mentor's doorsteps.

Mandira maintained a schedule of working late into the night, a habit she had emulated from her father. She preferred to dive deep into the cells of her brain while being seated in the dark confines of her bedroom. Most of her life, so far, she was enveloped by the forces of darkness and she derived the best inspiration by immersing herself in the lightless infinite depth of time. The canvass always remained infinite, encompassing every inch of the sacred territory of India and its people.

That night too, she felt a surge of power bursting out, as she ruminated over the war scenario very intimately. The surge transcended her concern for children, memories of her father and inconvenient pricks of the sad and scornful faces of her mother and husband. The intimate moments flooded her consciousness with the rare realisation of affinity to the people of the country. The fresh elixir of vitality invigorated her resolve.

She was destined to lead the country. Yes. It was her inherent right.

This impostor Jung Bahadur must go. And she badly required the services of loyalists like Ram Karan and the Young Turks. How best could she exploit them?

Her trance was broken by Dewan's whispers.

"Ma'am it's time to go to bed. You've a meeting at 9 am." Dewan informed her.

"And ma'am," Dewan continued to whisper, "Ram Karanji is here, said you wanted to see him tonight itself."

"Send him to the front ante-room. Serve him coffee and I should be there in a minute."

Mandira entered the wash, splashed cold water on her face and wiped it with a soft white tissue towel. She dusted a light cover of face powder, carefully combed her shoulder length hair and proceeded to the anteroom, as if she was starting a new day.

Ram Karan stood up to greet Mandira. He bent forward to touch her feet.

"Don't do that Ram Karanji. You're older to me." Mandira demurred.

"Age isn't the only yardstick of leadership," Ram Karan spoke in liquid buttery voice, "You're our chosen leader. Order me, what can I do for you."

Mandira told Ram Karan in a flat voice what she had learnt about Ram Charan. The FIB had started an enquiry into the sordid episode.

Ram Karan took great pains to explain that, his son was an innocent victim. He had floated tenders for procuring tinned food items and high altitude clothing. A committee of the Ministry of Defence had okayed the samples. How could he be held responsible!

The enemies of Mandira, Ram Karan added, were drumming up charges against him. She was the main target.

"Get in touch with Kumar Anand Prasad, the FIB Joint Director. He's heading the FIB inquiry team. I've spoken to him. His son wants to study in a US University. Help him."

"Yes ma'am."

"Talk to General Raina, head of the Army Supply Corps. I believe he's sympathetic. But, Ram Karanji," Mandira chided the senior minister," You must advise your son to be more careful next time. I don't like tinkering with the defences of the country."

"Be assured ma'am," Ram Karan touched his ear lobes, "The next ten generations of my family won't have anything to do with defence contracts."

"And Karanji," Mandira continued," Because of your son's supply mess, a full battalion had to abandon its posts in the Punjab border. It's a serious charge."

"My son is stupid, ma'am. I'll take care of him. I've already spoken to General Raina. He agrees with me that Ram Charan can't be held responsible for mistakes committed by foreign suppliers. The responsibility for quality control was with the Defence Supply Corps. A Committee of Experts should go into the charges."

"I understand," Mandira talked while putting the sari end around her head, "What're you going to do about these Tashkent talks? We can't remain silent. Mr. Boudhik has resigned from the cabinet. What're you going to do?"

"Don't worry ma'am. I'm in touch with the leaders of the organisation. We'll stir up an agitation against the sell out."

"Yeah. Use the media to highlight the proposed return of the captured territories to Pakistan. We can't allow the sacrifices of our soldiers to go waste." Mandira suggested a potent line of action.

"That's a great idea. Just wait for a day. I'll flood the media market with cash and spirits. I know how to make them sing."

"Fine Karanji. Don't forget to talk to Kumar Anand."

"Sure ma'am." Ram Karan bowed down again and touched Mandira's feet before wishing her good night.

****

Kumar Anand Prasad wasn't at his desk.

"I'm minister Ram Karan. Where the hell has he gone?" Ram Karan rebuked Prasad's secretary.

"He's out on a meeting sir. Your message will be conveyed to him as soon as he's back." The secretary managed to stammer out a polite reply.

"Do that. And tell him it's urgent." Ram Karan banged the handset on its cradle.

Kumar Anand's secretary couldn't communicate to his boss. While Ram Karan was busy working on a strategy to kick out from his court the odd balls thrown by Ram Charan's acts of greed and indiscretion, Rabindra Narayan Dutta was closeted with his deputies, Nampoothiri and Kumar Anand in FIB's Integrated Communication Centre (ICC).

The highly classified basement den was lined with an 18-gauge lead sheet. It was made sound and radiation proof. No signal leakage could take place from the ICC and no hostile agency could snoop in, even on the wings of sophisticated electronic devices.

Dutta and his colleagues were seated inside a bubble shaped cubicle, where two dedicated telephone lines connected the main wireless hub of the FIB.

Alam wanted to speak over the HF radio trans-receiver over 140 MHz frequency. The set, equipped with digital auto-encryption facilities could establish voice communication, denying the pleasure of breaking the code to hostile agencies.

Dutta, a brick and mortar man, didn't approve of the click and browse protocol. A war was on, even though a fragile ceasefire was in force. He couldn't afford any compromises. He had instructed Alam to use the one time personalised cipher pads printed on edible papers.

Alam's auto-deciphered message read like a fascinating piece of fiction.

**DOUBLE QUOTE: Reproduced below is the copy of communication from British High Com in Pakistan **SINGLE QUOTE: Personal from HoM to PM. Sources close to Pak President reveal that a late night meeting between Lee Fang, Chinese Ambassador Plenipotentiary and top Presidential aides took stock of the war situation. Pakistan's gain of territory from India was substantial. Pakistan wouldn't accept any agreement, if India didn't hand back Haji Pir and areas across the ceasefire Line. The Chinese are likely to deploy troops opposite Ladakh, NEFA and Sikkim, with a view to putting psychological pressure on India. The Chinese have agreed to move one Division plus an extra Brigade to Nathu La and Jelep La gaps bordering Sikkim....

"The Pak President has access to top secret medical reports on the precarious health condition of Jung Bahadur. Pakistani doctors have opined that another cardiac attack could be very fatal. The Pak President isn't keen to hold immediate talks with Jung Bahadur. His foreign minister Izaz Afroz is likely to use Kashmir as a spanner in the wheels....

"The Hon'ble PM may discuss this with the US President and prevail upon Pak to honour its international commitment. Learnt from Delhi HC, most Indian leaders aren't happy with the Security Council's cease-fire proposals. The Indian PM is a man of peace, but doesn't lack courage. Pakistani belligerence may force him to succumb to the hawks, headed by minister Mandira. She's expected to take on a tough stance and is close to the COAS. The COAS and the PM aren't on the same wavelength. Learnt from another source that the Indian communists are egging on Mandira. They're not happy with the US and UK roles. Please recheck it independently. SINGLE UNQUOTE** The source is reliable, inside BHC, Islamabad. Triple X has reached destination. Will take another two weeks to settle down. Shall contact him and install the device. Shaping up well. Expect production soon. Material good. DOUBLE QUOTE. EOM. ALAMGIR.**

RN Dutta looked up with loaded questions in his eyes.

"Analyse it word by word," Dutta asked Nampoothiri," I want a complete analysis by eight a.m. The PM must be briefed before he meets the Cabinet Committee on External Affairs."

"And you," He turned to Kumar Anand, "Investigate the leakage of the PM's health report. Identify the mole. I want details in the next five hours, before I meet the PM."

"But sir, its too little a time to tackle such a big problem." Prasad submitted.

"We're talking about leakage of the PM's health reports. The Tashkent talks are at stake. Those who can reach the report can easily reach the man physically and bump him off. I hope this has registered in your mind."

Dutta looked at the wall clock, picked up a red phone and requested the PM's secretary for an urgent meeting.

"Do you think he's being fair?" Fumed Prasad, "Detecting a serious leakage isn't a quick-fix job."

"Try your best. That's all we can do." Nampoothiri replied casually, without lifting his eyes from Alamgir's message.

"Balu, you're being unfair too. This is a needle in a haystack case and you're giving me a sermon." Prasad lamented in an anguished voice.

"Well Kumar, as they say, if you can't resist, enjoy the rape. What choice do you and I have? I've to burn the midnight oil too, it appears. Can I help you?"

"Thanks for the nasty joke." Prasad walked out leaving behind not too mute vibes of hostility.

Nampoothiri smiled and rushed back to his room. He summoned in Jatadhari and instructed Amrita, his secretary, to fetch the master file of Operation Alamgir.

Jatadhari Garo knew well the sequence of the chores he was to follow when the boss was visibly in a bind. He prepared stiff black coffee, served it without sugar and brought out a Havana.

Nampoothiri inhaled the pungent smoke and appreciated the texture of the coffee.

His mind raced against time, trying to piece together the entire spectrum of Indo-Pak relations, British interests and Chinese postures. He was planning to tie and stitch together remotely related patches of intelligence, assessment reports and raw tactical and strategic information, for presenting a logical collage to the PM.

Nampoothiri naturally reposed intrinsic trust in Alamgir. He was involved, from day one, in recruiting, motivating and training the officer.

Nampoothiri had picked up Jiwan Bahutule, an orphaned Marathi Brahmin, from a batch of twelve trainee-officers for the top-secret assignment in Pakistan. He had displayed uncanny aptitude for deep undercover operations from day one.

Way back in 1949, after completion of training, Bahutule was made to resign his post in the FIB. Young Bahutule stunned his acquaintances by kicking his government job and declaring his intention of pursuing Islamic studies in Egypt. He embraced Islam and studied theology for one year at Deoband. He disappeared from India and finally landed in Kabul, travelling all the way through Iran.

From Kabul to Peshawar wasn't a difficult journey. His marriage to the daughter of a Pathan chieftain of Mian Khel sanctified his cover with all the trappings of a genuine Muslim trader, keen to set up his establishment in Pakistan.

Nampoothiri's Operation Alamgir had flourished over the years and the FIB achieved the unprecedented success in creating a number of Double XX category agents inside Pakistan. Alam, as the designated handler of these operations had established himself as the eyes and ears of Delhi in the hostile neighbouring country. He enjoyed the unique status of running almost a subsidiary unit of the FIB inside Pakistan that too without any interference of the High Commission based under cover operatives.

Alamgir's special despatch, on the eve of the Tashkent negotiations, following the second drawn war between India and Pakistan, was a precious input. Nampoothiri wanted to add his best analytical inputs to his agent's gold nugget. The Indian response to Islamabad and the Western capitals would definitely be conditioned by these excellent pieces of gems and diamonds pilfered from the high security vaults of the British High Commission in Pakistan.

Nampoothiri had a personal stake in processing the information to the finest level of perfection.

He was named as a member of the Prime Ministerial delegation to Tashkent. That was the best opportunity to impress Jung Bahadur. The time for naming a successor to Rabindra Narayan Dutta was around the corner.

Chapter 21

Ram Karan Prasad finally tracked down the elusive Kumar Anand Prasad, his Bihari compatriot, around eight in the night. The fish-lord of the Ganges had mastered the art of oaring against the tides and casting his killer nets. He dumped the normal protocols and hooked the elusive intelligence whale at his residence.

"Anandji," Ram Karan declared in lyrical ***Bhojpuri*** (an Indo-Aryan dialect), "You can't ignore a fellow Bihari. Like skunks we emit our own brand of odour and can seek out our compatriots from the deepest of holes."

"Welcome sir. It's an honour for my family." Kumar Anand Prasad smoothened the creases on his face and ushered in the intruding minister.

"No dry welcome will do Kumar. Where's ***bhouji*** (sister-in-law)? I want to moisten my parched throat, and off course have dinner with hot rice and ***hilsa*** curry (a delicate fish) cooked in mustard sauce."

"That's a great privilege sir." Kumar Anand felt flattered and apprehensive.

Ram Karan Prasad, a self-proclaimed freedom fighter and disciple of Mahatma Gandhi and Amritlal was a killer without scruples, master of the flesh trade and the emperor of drug cartels. He figured prominently in the honour roll of the Federal Intelligence Bureau. Amritlal had, at least on two occasions, called for his dossier. But, belying all expectations he continued to pamper the caste baron, instead of sending him to the doghouse.

Amritlal had his compulsions.

A top leader of the Depressed Classes and friend of the Muslim minorities, Ram Karan was an invaluable electoral asset. Amritlal often used him for initiating second track diplomatic dialogues with his counterparts in Pakistan. Ram Karan could walk into the rooms of the top Pakistani leaders, be it in Karachi or Dacca.

An old nestled bird of the FIB, Kumar Anand Prasad had intimate knowledge of Amritlal's tactful use of this wily politician from Bihar.

The worthy heir to the Windsor Empire was eager to checkmate another towering Bihari, the President of India. He could never reconcile with the rustic ***dhoti*** clad ***shudra*** (intermediate caste) scholar, who had grabbed the viceregal palace by defeating his personal choice, another towering Brahmin from the Deep South. Ram Karan stood by his mentor like a granite phalanx and orchestrated the sniping and vilifying campaigns against the other Bihari, entrenched in Lutyens' palace.

Amritlal, like most human greats, preferred to spread himself like a Banyan tree. The mere sight of another towering tree around gave him the creeps. He used Ram Karan's potential as a countervailing ace against another messiah of the Depressed Classes from Maharashtra. That new ***avatar*** (incarnation) had aligned with the Empire for carving out a Hindu sub-nation comprising the social outcastes. Ram Karan didn't disappoint his benefactor. His machinations had assured repeated electoral defeats for the ***avatar.*** And that was the end of his political career, though his name was enshrined in the holy statute book of independent India

Kumar Anand Prasad was naturally rattled by the shadows of evil that inevitably trailed his maniacal visitor. Ram Karan's was a bear hug. It always left broken bones and shattered souls. He couldn't sleep well if he failed in buying up creatures and commodities vital to his survival. Kumar Anand could foresee the shadows of a glistening net in Ram Karan's looks. He was sure out on a massive fishing expedition.

The delicate ***hilsa*** curry with steamed rice, an eastern Indian savoury, temporarily pushed down Ram Karan's anxiety to the lowest strata of his intestine.

The fish was prepared well. The level of satisfaction, tasted through the pores of his palate, was perhaps equal, if not more, to a sweet successful sexual rendezvous. Ram Karan kept on relishing the divine taste, frequently turning his tongue over inside his oral cavity.

"Wonderful," Ram Karan complimented, "After ages have I tasted such well-cooked ***hilsa***. Presume it's from Calcutta!"

"Perhaps," Kumar Anand replied, while putting a betel leaf in his mouth, "We got it from Gole Market. We're happy you liked it."

"Must be Calcutta," Ram Karan helped himself to a betel leaf, "I can say from my long experience."

Kumar Anand didn't reply. Who else could better appreciate fish than the progeny of a ***Mallah*** (fisherman)! Bastard! He cursed the human demon sitting next to him.

The lowly ***Mallah*** had managed, just in three generations, to pick up the 'Prasad' caste title, a speciality of the intermediate caste Hindus. Ram Karan was sure to end up using the 'Singh' caste title, claiming his Rajput (warlord) origin.

"Yes Anandji," Ram Karan helped himself to one more betel leaf, "I believe your younger son is scouting around a scholarship to MIT to study astrophysics. A brilliant boy indeed! I'd have proposed a match, if I had a marriageable daughter."

"Yes sir," Kumar Anand responded, "He's a topper from Calcutta University and wants to do masters in astrophysics. His performance has been commended by Prof. Satyen Bose, you know sir, a colleague of Einstein."

"Einstein the discoverer of ***telephoon*** (telephone)? Great! You should send him abroad. A bright Bihar child should be taller than a ***phoren*** (foreign) ***telephoon*** maker."

"Money is the problem sir. My wife had arranged a matrimonial match. The girl's party, you know them, the Sinhas of Munghyr, were ready to pay Rs. two million in dowry. But, my stupid son is opposed to the dowry system. It is unheard of in Bihar and in our community. How can a Bihari negotiate a match minus the traditional dowry from the bride's home? Now tell me sir, how can I get so much money! Only a scholarship can help him." Kumar Anand bewailed the foolish social attitude of his son.

"See, to what extent we've pushed down our traditions! The younger generation is rotten. They're breaking our age-old traditions, set by the sages," Ram Karan lamented, "Like Islam we should make our social laws inviolable, insulating those from bloody reforms."

"Our matrimonial traditions hinge on the dowry system. How can Bihar survive with such stupid changes? Perhaps, the Bengali communist bugs have infected his soul." Kumar Anand wailed.

"Don't bother. I'm there to help. I've a small job, which requires your help," Ram Karan continued, "You know this military supply mess. My poor son Ram Charan has been falsely implicated."

"It's a bad case. The Prime Minister has demanded an immediate report." Kumar Anand hurled a hesitant and evasive reply.

"My son is not involved. See these documents, He had given contract to reputed British and Swedish firms. The supplies came from Hong Kong and Singapore."

Kumar Anand had seen these papers. All the vouchers were obtained fraudulently. Ram Charan had procured the supplies from a Hong Kong based obscure Muslim trader.

Contaminated tinned food, of Chinese origin, was rendered fresh, with glossy label wrappers. The People's Army had rejected the high altitude clothing, originally manufactured in the USSR. Ram Charan and his Hong Kong partner recycled the gears and supplied to the Indian army, fighting Pakistani troops at the forbidden heights of the Himalayas.

"Look, in such bulk trade some miscalculations are unavoidable," Ram Karan tapped Kumar Anand's hand, "You can't hang my son for this. They'll black list him; the courts may even hang him. He has a brilliant political career ahead."

"165 officers and soldiers have died." Kumar Anand added.

"I don't think it's possible to link all these deaths to my son's supplies and conclusively prove that he is guilty in any court of law."

"There are allegations that Ram Charan's Muslim partner was a Pakistani plant. It was an act of sabotage by Pakistan. Don't you see the China-Pakistan angle?" Kumar Anand added another angle to the tangled dispute.

"The Indian media is irresponsible. No one can prove this in a court of law. The media can't hang my son and you people in the bureaucracy are inclined to see the Chinese ghost everywhere."

Yes. Ram Karan was correct, Kumar Anand reflected. The Indian investigation and legal process would take decades to come to any conclusion. And as long as he wasn't convicted, under the damn system, the law couldn't scratch even his epidermis. In this country of super moral values, drilled in by lofty quotes from the scriptures, the concept of the conflict of interest and constructive moral responsibility were the cheapest offerings to the deity of lust.

Kumar Anand alone couldn't stop Ram Charan from climbing the pinnacle of political power, using his correct caste, moneybag and muscle connections.

Why stand in his way?

Satyameva Jayate (Truth shall be victorious)!

That was the national moral totem.

Kumar Anand quickly surveyed the scenario and reached a conclusion that by submitting a report to the government, he would, at best be truthful to his profession.

But, ***satya*** (truth) itself would be the first casualty, when the politicians strained the truth through their own brand of sieve and picked up their own variety of truth nuggets, to suit their political interests. They, in India, cooked up several types of truths in political cauldrons. Each broth was given a special religious and moral stamp to suit the alchemists.

"Look, Dutta is retiring in February. You're next in seniority. You help me; I'll help you. We Biharis must help each other." Ram Karan pressed Kumar Anand's palms with contrived fervour.

"Nampoothiri is a stronger contender." Kumar Anand sounded uncertain.

"Leave that to me. One Bihari will succeed the other, that's for sure." Karan meant Rabindra Narayan Dutta; a Bengali domiciled in Bihar.

"Help me. The army has already exonerated my son. They've blamed the foreign suppliers. Your support will strengthen the case." Ram Karan intimately hugged Kumar Anand.

"Let me see sir," Kumar Anand murmured, "Our report is almost ready. I've to tie up some loose ends. But I may warn you, Dutta may not agree."

"Leave something to God and me," Ram Karan tightened the embrace, "I'll take care of the rest. Deal?"

"There's another problem which I can't control." Kumar Anand replied hesitatingly.

"What's that? The PM?"

"No sir, the main stumbling block is Savitri Devi."

"Who's She?"

"Wife of Subedar Risal Singh Ahir, from village Jhajjar Khera, near Mathura."

Kumar Anand narrated the stupendous efforts made by Savitri, wife of Risal, who died of food poisoning, after consuming tinned dinner in his war-front trench. The 10 Mahar battalion, reeling under acute food poisoning, had abandoned its posts. The brave commanding officer, Col. Nizam-ul-Haque, made valiant efforts to hold back the advancing enemy, with hardly any support from the regiment stationed at Gurdaspur. The tank borne Pakistan infantry mowed down the remnants of the Mahars. Nizam and his men fought right down to the last man and bullet trying all the while to hold the bridge leading to Chhamb.

The vital bridge link overrun, Chhamb stood precariously exposed to the Pakistani attack. The 9 Northern Frontier Guards whistled past the deserted Indian posts and reached the heart of Chhamb town, wantonly shooting at everything and everyone, including a hundred year old Christian missionary establishment. They won the battle through contaminated tinned food, imported all the way from Hong Kong. Some one down the line had obviously played the Pakistani game.

That's what Savitri Devi was trying to prove. She didn't have any access to the FIB records to allege that the veteran politician had questionable links with Pakistan.

She, however, recovered a piece of paper from the personal belongings of her husband, which gave detailed descriptions of the tainted and poisonous food he was forced to eat in the forward trenches. He'd left a sealed can, which proved beyond doubt that the imported food items were highly contaminated with deadly viruses.

Savitri Devi, Kumar Anand added, had ganged up with the Head Quarters Adjutant General, an officer with impeccable records. He had forced an enquiry, involving the AHQ and the FIB. The contours of a sinister connivance between Ram Charan and a disguised Hong Kong based Pakistani conduit had come out clear.

Even if the AHQ team manufactured favourable reports, Kumar Anand revealed, this adamant and injured lady was sure to go up to the higher authorities. Copies of her petitions were lying with the President and the Prime Minister. They were breathing hot fire on the FIB's shoulder.

"And sir, one more point. There's an effort in the AHQ to blame you for the accident."

"How come?"

"Some people have carried tales to the PM about your alleged links with Pakistani leaders."

"That's trash." Ram Karan laughed heartily, "I'm a veteran freedom fighter. Most Pakistani leaders are my former political colleagues." Ram Karan relaxed the hug and lighted a cigarette.

"That's part of our national history sir." Prasad, a non-smoker, moved a few steps away.

"I'll take care of all this trash. You play your part."

"As you wish sir. I'll try my best. Take care of my son."

"Don't worry, he'll go to MIT. Keep this." Karan handed over a brief case.

"What's in it?"

"A small gift. Keep it. It'll take care of your daughter's marriage. There're not many fools among us Biharis, like your son, not to demand a fat dowry."

Ram Karan left around 1 a.m.

Kumar Anand counted the money till 3 a.m., three million rupees, rounded off. He secured the money in his personal steel cupboard with a combination lock and went to bed.

Sleep eluded him, not because of gastronomic disorder caused by the delicate Calcutta ***hilsa***. Some faint wick inside him kept on burning and reminding of the fact that he was the first FIB officer to succumb to the devil's allurement.

The imperial intelligence was loyal to the white masters and since independence the FIB had blindly identified itself with the ruling clique. But the organisation never allowed criminals like Ram Karan to contaminate its soul.

He tossed in bed, his conscience still unable to shake off the stink left by skunky Ram Karan. These devils and vampires wouldn't take much time to run riot over the system. Perhaps he was the first major outpost to fall to the crawling advances of criminals right up to the core of the nation's power structure.

Finally at 5 a.m. Kumar Anand gulped down two barbiturate tablets and hoped that his conscience and God would develop amnesia and forget to etch the proceedings of the night on His stone tablets.

****

Ram Karan Prasad, the excellent fisherman, did not have to use sonar beams to locate Savitri. His acolyte and partner Raghu Chawla, a new generation journalist, who did not have any qualms in using the honourable trade as a tool of activities that verged on the fringe of criminality, did the job.

Jhajjar Khera, a thriving village, inhabited by the Ahir caste, was just 20 km. south of Vrindaban, the mythological home of the Ahir's kinsman, Lord Krishna. It had a tradition of producing valiant soldiers; from the ages of the Mahabharata wars to the Bengal Lancers of the Company Maharaj

Savitri, wife of Risal Singh Ahir, who died of food poisoning in his frontline trench, gathered the status of an icon of courage by doggedly pushing the case against Ram Charan, the VIP son.

Risal was awarded a Param Vir Chakra, equivalent to the Victoria Cross, in the 1962 Chinese war. His platoon, perched on a frozen gully ahead of Bomdi La had warded off the Chinese advance for three days. The yellow ants overpowered him only after he exhausted his ammunition.

War front bravery, however, carried no meaning for Ram Karan. A soldier was supposed to die and that's the professional hazard he was paid for. Savitri was a minor thorn and Kalua Mushahari was good enough to smother her. She should find a better hanging peg in one of his pleasure abodes.

"Raghuji," Ram Karan called his crony, a journalist of sorts, "There's an urgent job for you."

"Well sir, I'm at your disposal, I will be with you in minutes."

Raghu Chawla, son of a refugee Punjabi scrap dealer, happened to be the resident of a neighbouring village, Dabbu Khera, renamed Lajpat Nagar, after the hallowed memory of the lion of India's freedom struggle.

The master artist, who purchased everyone and everything, had pegged Raghu in his account slot as a sleek operator. A media-savvy juggler, Ram Karan had cultivated and purchased several journalists by the orchestrated distribution of largesse; allotment of government accommodation, residential plots, jobs and scholarships, a steady cash flow and innumerable foreign jaunts.

Raghu Chawla, a college dropout had tried his luck with vending soft drugs in the university campus. An indomitable entrepreneur, he hooked a news editor's drug-addict son and trapped him by supplying a ***banjaran*** (nomadic) woman. In the process he managed to bargain for a position in the vernacular news daily, as a crime reporter.

Within 1825 days Chawla's family shifted from their one room tenement at Lajpat Nagar, to a government accommodation, next to the Imperial War Memorial, renamed India Gate. The spacious bungalow was a minor bargain for helping a cabinet minister in hushing up the rape of a housemaid by his son and the discovery of her husband's dead body from a nearby gutter.

Raghu Chawla was much sought after as a fixer-mixer-media person in India's scandal littered capital.

"Yes Raghuji," Ram Karan welcomed his crony," A thorn is hurting me. It has to be taken out."

"What's the problem sir?"

"Not much. This whore of a woman Savitri of Jhajjar Khera is after Ram Charan's life. Do something." Ram Karan picked up two Belgian glasses, poured Scotch and offered one to Raghu Chawla.

"That's not a major problem. I know the people there."

"Kalua will help you."

"Done sir. Just don't forget your humble servant."

"You'll be compensated adequately. Keep my name out of it."

Raghu Chwala and Kalua descended on Jhajjar Khera early next afternoon. Raghu's emissary, a village teacher had summoned an assembly of the village elders and notables, known by the name of ***Panchayat*** (the elder's council).

While Kalua disembarked with cartons of rum and cooked chicken, Raghu Chawla went about greeting the village elders, assembled at the ***chaupal*** (platform for community congregation).

"I'm here with unique gifts," Chawla started with folded hands, "Before I speak I submit to the ***Panchayat,*** bestowed with divine powers. You all belong to the hallowed Ahir caste, direct descendants of Lord Krishna, who was created by Lord Brahma from his mouth. I bow to you all. You've been petitioning for a secondary school in the village. I've been sent by the hon'ble minister, Ram Karan Prasadji, ***masiha*** (messiah) of the poor, to announce, that he has apportioned funds for a secondary school in your village."

The congregation exploded into ecstatic clapping.

Kalua, in his inimitable way, served Indian made foreign rum in exquisitely cut marble glasses. The stone glasses were considered holy; holy enough to absolve sinning souls from minor vices like drinking rum and chewing on chicken chunks.

"Mandiraji, daughter of our dear leader Amritlal, will come down to lay the foundation stone of the school and hostel buildings." More applause followed the more liberal servings from Kalua.

"Amritlal is next to God Gopal (Hindu deity Krishna). We'll support his daughter. Mandira ***mai ki jai*** (hail mother Mandira)." Declared an aged village elder.

"You also had petitioned the government to raise a memorial in honour of your brave son Risal Singh Ahir," Raghu Chawla continued," Prasadji has got the proposal approved. A grand memorial will be built in honour of your valiant son."

More asymmetric and chaotic applause followed the warm up speech.

"But I regret to say that Risal's shameless wife isn't worthy of her name Savitri, the divine lady synonymous with chastity and single minded devotion to her husband. Your Savitri is a whore. She shares her bed with a Muslim soldier." Announced Chawla in a shame stricken voice.

"How do you say that?" The chief ***Panch*** protested.

"***Tau*** (great uncle),"Raghu Chawla walked down a few paces, took out a bunch of photographs from his folio bag and passed them on to him for examination.

"Why should I tell a lie? Am I not your son from the next village? Don't I regularly contribute an amount every year on ***Janmashtami*** day (birthday of Lord Krishna)? "

Raghu raised his voice to a higher pitch.

"Do I not belong to the ***Kshatriya*** caste (warrior caste), born from the shoulders of Lord Brahma?" Raghu continued," Can a ***Kshatriya*** tell a lie? Haven't I contributed liberally to the construction of the Gobind temple in your village?"

The rest of the ***Panch*** members, swooning and swaying with Raghu's oratory and Kalua's rum admitted, yes, he'd done a lot. The progeny of a pure ***Kshatriya*** could never tell a lie.

The chief ***Panch*** looked at the photographs with wide-eyed disbelief. Yes, it was Savitri all the way clinging to a moustached man. Her naked feminine assets were bursting out from beneath a scanty bikini.

"Oh Gobind!" He cried out loudly and passed on the photographs to other members of the ***Panch.***

The exposed naked photographs titillated the drunken group of elderly and not so elderly men, already sozzled by the liberal flow of rum. How could Savitri, wife of their valiant son Risal Singh Ahir have illicit relations with a Muslim?

"Revered ***Panch***," Chawla raised his voice. "I don't mind a woman placing herself in the red light quarters. What else are women for? But, revered ***Panch***, my head hangs in shame to tell you, that the wife of Risal, who was killed by the infidel Muslims, enemy of the Hindus, has been sleeping with a ***mlechh*** (person of strange religion)."

"She's an honourable lady." One villager intervened." These photos are faked. The minister's son is trying to falsely implicate Savitri. He's the real killer of Risal."

"Revered ***Panch***," Raghu continued with folded hands, "I'm talking in front of the divine ***Panch*** and telling the truth. How can photographs tell lies? A snap of yours can't produce the face of an owl. It's your choice, if you want to live with a sin, in a village sanctified by Lord Gobind. I've no problem. But take care, the surrounding villages may ostracise you."

Chawla spoke the last sentences with conjured up dramatics.

The ***Panch***, seated under the holy Banyan tree, attributed with divine qualities, was silenced to a stupor by the explosive revelations and the liberal servings of rum.

A Muslim fucking one of their Ahir women, a clan connected with the legends of Lord Krishna? What a disgrace!

Couldn't she get any worthy Hindu in the village?

The sizeable crowd, which had gathered around the ***choupal,*** gave a loud verdict.

"Let's punish her, let's kill her."

The village schoolteacher, a Chawla crony, stood up and repeated the verdict in a blurred and inebriated voice.

"The great ***Panch***, you're the embodiment of the divine Lords, ***Brahma, Vishnu*** and ***Maheshwar*** (Hindu Trinity). Your voices reflect the unified wisdom of the Gods and the Cosmos. What you say is sacred. What's your verdict?"

"We're grateful to Raghuji," Shouted another ***Panch***, "We can't sleep over a grave sin like this one. This vermin of a whore must be killed."

"Kill her." Shouted another villager.

"No, let her be punished by our pure Ahir youths fucking her all the way. That way the impure whore's internal organs will get purified. And no Hindu woman, hereafter, shall dare to blemish her blood with Muslim semen." Shouted the teacher.

The ***Panch*** didn't react. The suggestion appeared to be too brutal.

Raghu sensed trouble. The senior ***Panch*** members were perhaps having second thoughts. That's dangerous.

He signalled to the teacher and whispered in his ears to storm Savitri's house.

The teacher climbed the ***chaupal*** platform and opened up a loud harangue, citing from the ***Gita*** (Hindu scripture), that whenever ***Bharat*** (India) faced a moral crisis, Lord Krishna descended on the earth to protect religion, to rescue the good people and to punish the sinners. Why should the villagers now go against the command of Lord Krishna!

A village ***julaha*** (weaver) woman sensed trouble and rushed to Savitri.

"Rush and get out, they're coming to kill you." The lady shouted.

"Why? What's happened?" Savitri was at a loss to understand.

"Argue later." She literally pushed Savitri out.

"Where do I go?" Savitri panicked.

"The Gobind temple is the safest place. Rush and take shelter there."

Savitri ran along with the ***julaha*** woman, clutching her 3-year-old son to her bosom. She rushed towards the nearby temple of Lord Gobind, seeking protection of the deity.

"You can't go in, the Lord and his consort are taking their afternoon nap." The priest blocked her way.

"Allow me in, they'll kill me." The haggard lady pleaded.

"Lord Gobind will wake up only at 5 p.m. Wait near the outer gate."

The priest violently moved his right hand and waved her away.

Savitri, in a desperate move pushed aside the priest, entered the sanctum sanctorum and bolted the door from inside.

"Hai Gobind!" The village priest rushed out in anguish, "The fallen woman has defiled the Lord's sanctum."

How could a non-brahmin lady enter the inner pedestal of the Lord? Only a Brahmin was sanctified by the Gods to go anywhere near Lord Gobind. She should be put to death for this action of sacrilege.

The priest rushed out and addressed the frenzied crowd and shouted that the sinning woman, defiled by a Muslim had forcibly entered the ***garbh griha*** (sanctum sanctorum) and had bolted the door from inside.

"Masters, the heavens are going to curse this village, if you don't remove that witch." He shouted, with his sacred Brahminic threads knotted up in his right thumb, a ritualistic pose for delivering a curse.

"What happened?" Asked the teacher.

"That whore has entered the ***garbh griha***. Oh Lord Gobind! What'll happen to this village! Curse the entire village for disturbing your sleep by a polluted widow."

The frenzied mob rushed up, broke the inner temple door and dragged Savitri out. The baby clinging to her chest was thrown onto the cemented floor and trampled to death.

A few drunken youths disrobed Savitri in seconds. Two of them pinned her down on the floor and four others raped her one by one, to the accompaniment of the chanting of ***jai Gobinda jai Gopala*** (hail Lord Gobind) slogans. The priest tolled the bells, blew the conch shell and sprinkled holy Ganges water with a view to calming down the Lord's wrath.

The hour-long mass rape left Savitri devastated. Her tormented body bounced against the floor twice in painful spasms and turned still. Her cold open eyes vainly implored Lord Gobind for protection.

The villagers left the temple with a rare spirituous and spiritual satisfaction. The cursed widow, contaminated by Muslim semen was delivered of her sins at the very doorstep of Lord Gopal.

The Gods very often expressed their will through human medium. And the Jhajjar Khera villagers had faithfully carried out the Lord's desire, conveyed to them by His true representatives, Raghu Chawla and Kalua Mushahari. Bharat, facing catastrophic deluge from a woman, allegedly contaminated by a Muslim paramour, was finally saved by its patriotic children.

****

The insurance that Kumar Anand Prasad had bargained for his son's scholarship and daughter's dowry had helped him in digesting the inconvenient pricks of conscience and professional itches. His arrows hit the bulls' eye as he paid back Ram Karan's debt.

The final investigation report exonerated Ram Charan and the entire dirt was dumped at the doors of the Defence Supply Corps. The Hong Kong suppliers, suspected Pakistani agents, were blamed for substituting the original samples with spurious items. It was all the way a subversive operation by a rogue Pakistani intelligence apparatus, the Inter Services Intelligence. Raghu Chawla liberally leaked excerpts from the report to the media with a view to passing the buck onto the Pakistani machinations, a part of its much touted Operation Gibraltar and Grand Slam.

The Indian Establishment, except Dutta and Jung Bahadur were happy to put the sticker of guilt on the ISI. They celebrated Ram Charan's exoneration with gallons of Scotch and tonnes of animal flesh, cooked in Mughlai style. Raghu Chawla earned a covetous garden-home in the outskirts of Delhi.

However, Delhi's peace was momentarily disturbed when a communist member of the august house brought up Savitri Devi's gang rape case in the Indian Parliament. It raised a brief storm. The honourable Home Minister made a statement in both Houses of the Parliament, clarifying the incident as an act of wanton crime by some villagers. It was a crime of faith, driven by religious bigotry. He promised to initiate a magisterial enquiry and assured that the law would take its own course. Nobody would be spared.

The hon'ble members listened to the boring litany and wondered what great tectonic slip had occurred by the simple rape and death of a woman! It happened everyday, everywhere on the globe, wherever men could steal the opportunity from the law, society and self-esteem. What else women were for?

As a final coup de grace, the party high command cleared Ram Charan, the 5th scion of the Mallah dynasty, to be sworn in as a cabinet minister in the state of Bihar.

Rabindra Narayan Dutta refused to believe that India's honour was resurrected by Ram Karan's smooth exit through the eye of the needle. Neither did he believe that Kumar Anand had done his best in the enquiry. The Tashkent talks schedule was on the verge of collapse and Kumar Anand's archers failed to hit the bulls' eye in the PM's health report leakage affair.

"What's the hell are you doing Kumar? When are you going to give me the other report?" Normally a soft-spoken person, Dutta raised his voice by a few decibels."

"We're waiting for a vital breakthrough."

"For heaven's sake don't rush through it as you did in the Jhajjar Khera case. I can't face the PM again." Dutta sulked as his eyes sparked out wanton messages of indignation.

"Well sir," Kumar Anand smattered out a reply, "We've narrowed down the search area to the PM secretariat."

"Hum," Dutta picked up a bunch of decoded cipher messages, "That's not great news. You can go now. I want the report latest by tomorrow. I've to brief the PM before he leaves for Tashkent."

Kumar Anand retreated with a sinking feeling. The alarm bells warned him that the noose around him was tightening up.

More alarming were the contents of another coded message from Alamgir.

The Chinese advise to Pakistan to defer negotiations under USSR aegis was topped by Rawalpindi's instructions to its Delhi Mission to activate agent AFTAB and pressurise him for egging on malcontent political leaders to adopt an uncompromising stand. The Tashkent talks should be aborted if Kashmir was not on the agenda. This hard line was sold to President Akbar Khan by his foreign minister Izaz Afroz.

Who could be this AFTAB? Was he a Pakistani agent in India? The FIB had no ready answer. Could he be another senior bureaucrat or a senior politician?

"Do you suspect any hidden conspiracy?" Jung Bahadur asked his intelligence chief.

"I've left a folder on your table, with transcripts of telephonic talks of some of your party leaders and key diplomats. They want the ceasefire deal to flounder and the Russian initiative to crash."

"What's the game plan of my detractors?"

"Only an intelligent guess can be made. They want your scalp."

"My scalp isn't a precious toy Dutta, but I can't surrender to these forces. It's a democracy and they're welcome to capture this chair, but through the democratic process only." Jung Bahadur gave out a rare smile.

"It's better that you tackle the fountainhead of trouble. That should be a fine strategy." Dutta added.

"Mandira?" Jung Bahadur asked.

"That's what I mean."

"Okay. Leave it to me. What's in these papers?" Jung Bahadur took out a blue folder, marked 'for the PM's eyes-only.'

"That's what I was trying to explain sir, the inner thinking of the Pakistani establishment and the leakage of a sensitive report, I presume, from your office." Dutta explained.

"Can you call your officers to give me an in-depth analysis of the communications? I'll like to be briefed about Pakistani troop deployments."

Balachandran Nampoothiri and Kumar Anand Prasad joined their boss and waited till the PM silently stretched his hands, requesting the officers to take their seat.

"What's your assessment of Pak deployments?" The PM asked.

"There is an absence of solid evidence of fresh induction of Pakistani troops." Nampoothiri initiated the briefing.

"Absence of evidence doesn't mean evidence of absence," Jung Bahadur shot back, "Are you backed by appropriate intelligence inputs?"

"We're depending more on reports from the front formations."

"What about your agents inside? Have they gone into hibernation?"

"Not exactly sir." Intervened Rabindra Narayan Dutta.

"Our agents have given details of Pak deployments five miles behind the active fronts. We've shared the nuts and bolts with the Director of Military Operations. All these have been charted and brought under our military ORBAT."

"Fine. Now tell me what's your interpretation of the dope from Alamgir?" The PM asked.

"Taking into account our own inputs, we guess that the contents of the first message appear to be genuine," Averred Nampoothiri, "The British High Commission in Delhi has originated a similar message. We can take the contents as highly precise inputs, if not confirmed ingredients."

The PM kept on listening with rapt attention, as Nampoothiri continued his analysis. The British, he added, had been taking more than a live interest in the present Indo-Pak border war as they did in the last Indo-Pak conflict in Kachchh. Powerful lobbies in the British parliament and government were acting in tandem with the military regime in Pakistan.

"The Pak attempt to internationalise the Kashmir issue is the stumbling block. Do you expect Islamabad to climb down?" Jung Bahadur asked.

"Depends on the Chinese and US attitude. Fresh Chinese deployment across the northern borders speaks volumes of their intentions. The US is pumping in Vietnam surplus through Turkish and Saudi routes." Explained Nampoothiri.

"I feel sir," Dutta added, "The Pakistani President is observing the needle of the scale and weighing all the feathers. Izaz Afroz, the foreign minister, is all set to scuttle the talks, if India refuses to include Kashmir on the agenda."

"We'll have no compromise on Kashmir." The PM said in a straight, matter of fact voice." It's an integral part of India. We're ready for war, if Pakistan wants another round."

Dutta switched over to Alamgir's second report. The PM interjected.

"What's all this carp about my health report? Why should Pakistan be concerned?"

Dutta explained that, all over the world, health reports of the Chief Executives were treated as state secrets.

"Do the Pakistani leaders think that I'm on my deathbed?" Asked the PM.

"Sir, normally such assessments are regularly made in all important world capitals. The Americans snooped on Stalin's health report and the Russians on Truman's," Murmured Nampoothiri, "It's a routine exercise with all intelligence agencies."

"What's the source of the leakage?"

"Sir, the enquiries aren't complete yet. The matter is delicate and we've to proceed with great care." Replied Dutta.

"Should we fuss so much over it?" Asked the PM.

"It's important sir. Most world capitals will calibrate their policy towards India, keeping in view the stability of its top leader."

"Okay. Let me have a detailed report. Send me an analysis of the overall security concerns in the light of Alamgir's despatches."

Dutta had hardly stepped out of the room when the PM called him back.

"I hear that the scandals of tainted food and the sub-standard high altitude clothing have been given a nice burial and Ram Charan is a minister in Bihar." The PM spoke with a sarcastic tone.

"You're correct sir." Dutta replied.

"I'm told, some lady living in the vicinity of Mathura, wife of a Sepoy, who died of food poisoning was killed in a mob fury."

"Yes sir. The villagers lynched her for alleged illicit connections with a Muslim Sepoy."

"Don't you think it may have something to do with the enquiry? Ram Karan can even corrupt the Gods." The PM burrowed his head in a pile of papers. This was his style of screwing in his point emphatically.

Dutta had no reason to disagree.

Ram Karan's drilling bits must have bored through Kumar Anand's soul. Dutta had no illusion about the ways of functioning of Kumar Anand Prasad. The weathercock had started flaunting his plumes in the direction of the Mandira breeze, having made reasonably good deductions about Jung Bahadur's state of health

"You are not far from the truth sir." Dutta managed to add his considered views about the senior cabinet minister.

"Don't mind Dutta," Jung Bahadur continued his low decibel dialogue, "We are politicians. Our ears always remain close to the ground. I have very little doubt about Ram Karan's involvement in criminal and anti-national activities. I want to tackle him after my return from Tashkent."

"As you desire sir."

Rabindra Narayan understood well that he must tighten the screw. Ram Karan could not be allowed to play around with the safety and security of the country. The FIB was a sacred trust, which he had inherited from his predecessors. This one institution should be insulated from the fanged, power hungry jackals. Dutta could hear their growling around the prized kill, the nation as a whole. Their fanged canines were ready to strike.

Not so soon. People like him were still around and he had implicit faith in Prime Minister Jung Bahadur. The small iron man was capable of facing the fanged hungry jackals of Indian politics.

"Now that you are alone, I have another point to make," The PM spoke in almost an inaudible voice, "Your boys in Pakistan must find out the precise points of infiltration by the ISI and Pak IB into our political and administrative edifices. I have a doubt that President Akbar Khan manages to get running commentaries on happenings in the South and North Blocks."

"I assure you sir, I will try my best." Rabindra Narayan Dutta had very little to add to the damning observations made by the PM. He came out of the room after tucking his tail rather disappointingly.

He knew that his assets inside Pakistan were very few and he did not see any immediate chance of bringing about spectacular improvements. But he decided to speak again to Nampoothiri to hasten up the process of infiltrating the most sensitive areas of the Pakistani establishment.

"What about the new asset, you had recently infiltrated into Pakistan?"

Dutta asked Nampoothiri as they approached the corridor that led to the FIB's exclusive wing in the South Block.

"You mean Triple X? He has reached the target area."

"When do you expect to hear from him?"

"It is too early to predict. I can ask Alamgir, if you so wish."

"Come up for a discussion this evening with a review of your existing assets in Pakistan."

"Anything special sir?"

Nampoothiri could sense a faint smell of cordite in the air.

"We must earn our bread at the end of the day Balu. And the chief is our bread giver."

"Very correct sir. I will see you late in the evening."

Nampoothiri was left with no illusion that his boss had a nasty brush with the Prime Minister. The just concluded war with Pakistan in the western theatre and the question of high-grade productivity of Dutta's assets in Pakistan must have figured prominently. He felt the temptation to comment that in high-grade intelligence generation one could never expect miraculous midnight sunrise. It required a long gestation period and hard planning and endeavour. Even a dare devil charlatan like Triple X was not expected to produce sophisticated intelligence overnight. But he resisted the temptation taking into consideration the bruised state of mind of his boss. Discretion was the need of the hour, especially when he was slated to accompany Jung Bahadur to Tashkent and his claim to the top slot hanged precariously at the mercy of the new PM.

Chapter 22

Dutta's new asset in Pakistan was marooned in the confines of Hotel Royal Palace. Incessant early autumn rain and the surging floodwater from the upper catchments had breached the banks of the Chenub and its tributaries. The Jhumra plains and Sangla foothills were heavily inundated. Disruption of rail and road services had put life completely out of gear.

Harfan Bukhari and about a dozen US Air Force technicians working on the construction of underground hangers in nearby Bhagatanwala airbase were bottled up in Hotel Royal Palace. A small Chinese contingent too was housed in an exclusive wing of the hotel. No one knew for sure the purpose of the Chinese presence at Jhumra. Ibadat had hinted that the Chinese were engaged in installation of an array of radars somewhere near Bhagatanwala.

The Americans made good of their forced break by guzzling dozens of beer cans and playing loud music. The Chinese played mah-jong and sipped green and jasmine tea. Harfan was left with the miserable choice of listening to the insipid Pakistan Television broadcast.

For inexplicable reasons Ibadat maintained a cool distance. No hurry, Harfan thought. The ice should melt soon enough. A little more biological and psychological warming should do the magic.

The lobby television was, however, broadcasting plenty of heat. Izaz Afroz, the Foreign Minister, harangued over the idiot box.

"...The Indian dogs, rabid war mongers and enemies of Islam and Pakistan have received a bloody nose for the second time. Our valiant soldiers, one equivalent to ten Hindu cowards, have recorded a resounding victory. They're now talking about peace.... We're likely to meet the Indians at Tashkent. But I want to assure you that Pakistan won't compromise on Kashmir. We'll fight for a thousand years, if necessary...."

The transmission ended abruptly with a sudden power cut. The main powerhouse at Faisalabad was submerged under the floodwaters. The hotel generator provided the barest skeletal emergency lighting.

Harfan looked around.

Burning time wasn't as easy as burning a cigarette. He threw the burnt out stub and looked around for Ibadat. He was apparently sleeping, reclining on a chair, at the far end of the reception area. This should be a good time to have a sneak preview of the palace compound, all by himself.

Harfan walked past the front portico and peeped through the screen of green vegetation. A faint mist, rising out of the flooded Chenub, had enveloped the palace and the surrounding orchards and forests. The soft wet beauty was very inviting. Harfan ventured out, wading in knee-deep floodwaters.

The front lawns of the hotel and the Chenub beds had merged under the floodwater, creating an illusion of a watery vastness. Small islands of lush green trees and bushes swayed in the cross winds, like beautiful maidens swinging their hair, after a leisurely bath.

The earth, trees and grass, soaked in flood and rainwater, oozed out a cocktail of strange sweet fragrances.

Harfan Bukhari, bathed by the naked raw nature, felt a shiver of joy. How did he manage to ignore so much of beauty around him, in Jhun Jhunu and in Delhi? Why did he keep his sensory organs shut all these years?

He took in a few deep breaths. The aromatic air sweeping the palace compound, the vegetation around and the earth enriched by his father's blood injected exciting sensations into Harfan's cortices.

He felt buoyant and sprinkled his hair with a fistful of rainwater.

Harfan concentrated on picking up the ethereal sounds that emanated from the trees, the raindrops and the air that encapsulated him. They were whispering his name; Harfan liked to imagine. He raised both his arms and felt the wet air dancing past him. He felt like dancing, like the rainbow-coloured peacocks, back at Jhun Jhunu.

The magic, floating in the soggy air and the mingled mist dragged Harfan along the trail leading to the orchards, beyond the palace lawns.

The Jhumra kings had planted several spice and medicinal plants, collected from all over the sub-continent. The green cardamom, clove, asafoetida, Ashwagandha, Ashoka, Serpentina Rauwolfia and other medicinal plants supplemented the exotic spice trees.

The distant groves invited Harfan, swinging their twigs and dancing with the rhythm of gusty winds. He lost himself in a charmed trance.

"***Janab***," Ibadat moved closer in silent steps," It's better you don't get drenched."

"Why? What's your problem?"

"No problem sir. But you may not like to fall sick. Early fall rain gives malarial shivers."

"Okay. Let's get back." Harfan didn't like the idea of entering into a debate.

"Look at the eastern skies," Ibadat pointed his finger, "It's time for the sun to paint rainbows in the skies."

Harfan peered out, standing under a Magnolia grove, its pale white flowers swaying in rhythm with the light breeze. The cloud cover was fleeting away under a strong northeasterly wind. The mist had dissipated. The steel-grey clouds hanging low over the western horizon were being painted in bountiful rouge.

Yes, Ibadat was correct. Suddenly the eastern sky started glistening with a scintillating seven-coloured rainbow, buttressed by a shadowy, fainter rainbow, far below the horizon.

"***Janab*** have your coffee." Ibadat kept on stirring the contents intermittently.

"How do you know when the rainbow's going to show up?" Asked Harfan in an amazed tone. He'd never bothered to understand the intricacies of nature all these years. He didn't have the time for these tender things of life.

"***Janab***, this is rustic wisdom," Ibadat opened up again, "We live in a rain fed river basin. My mother used to sing about the sun going to bed, all wrapped in a red quilt, after a spell of rain and coming out next morning with a riot of colours."

Harfan peered out again, stretching his neck. Yes, the sun was a bright crimson now, hanging over the horizon. It was splashing the surrounding clouds with multi-coloured brushes. The sun was perhaps, as Ibadat said, heading for a fine warm night, wrapped up in a red quilt.

Did he hear the same folktale from his mother? Why was it ringing a bell inside! Perhaps this was a common folktale all over rural India.

"Don't mind my foray into the green bushes over there. I feel like it. And I assure I won't fall sick."

Harfan handed back the empty cup, folded up his trouser and ventured out, wading through ripples of floodwater, on the manicured lawns.

Ibadat followed.

Harfan noticed a raised ground on his right, covered with shrubs and plants. Beyond the fruit orchard, behind the clusters of banana groves, he noticed two brick huts. Curiosity dragged him along.

An aged lady emerged out with a silver plate on her left palm as he approached the huts. A bright brass oil lamp burnt at the centre of the plate, some white rice, green grass and vermilion powder were placed around it.

Harfan's steps made splashing sounds in the rainwater.

The lady looked back, her gaze locked on Harfan's face, covered her head and stood motionless, turning her back to the stranger. Harfan couldn't see her flooded eyes, the saline sea inside overflowing the banks of her clogged emotion.

"Excuse me, who's this lady?" Harfan addressed Ibadat in a low voice.

"Rama Bai, the last of the former royal outposts, a companion of the former queen. Let's go to the other side of the palace compound." Ibadat made a feeble attempt at diverting Harfan's attention.

The name wasn't new to him, though his Delhi brief-masters were silent about her existence. Kaushalya had briefly mentioned the name, while explaining the frail figure standing by her side, in one of her wedding photographs.

"***Adab***," Harfan saluted the old lady, "How do you feel?"

The mysterious link with the former regime maintained a stony silence, though the sudden storm in her chest kept on swirling and surging, forcing out tears. She didn't reply. A few moments lapsed before she turned around, trying to control the streams of saline flow. She looked straight into Harfan's eyes, her mouth wide open, in gasping disbelief.

Harfan could see, in the dim fading light, her wide eyes hungrily exploring his face and body contour. Her sad and salty looks, like the reverse arrows of time, probably bent back, trying momentarily to connect herself with the events of yore.

For the first time Rama Bai realised that, her present world was nothing but a chunk of the frozen past. And the young man standing before her was a clone of King Dayaram Kaushal. His live apparition had suddenly materialised, straying from its orbit around another time wrap.

Large drops of tears rolled down her cheeks. Muffled sobs sent spasm of shivers all over her fragile body. Rama Bai paused for a split second, ran into her hut and gently closed the door behind her.

Harfan peeped through a lattice and found the elderly lady seated in front of an image of Goddess ***Kali***, her cheeks moist with flowing tears.

He turned back, questions drilling deep in his mind.

What was she looking for? Was she trying to discover something from her past? What else could be her problem? Did his presence torment the old lady? He must probe this. It won't be prudent to sleep with the shadows of the past, which had the inevitable habit of catching up with the present.

"Why was she weeping?" Asked Harfan.

"She's deranged. You may find her laughing next moment," Ibadat brushed aside the question, "Let's get back. It's getting dark. You sure don't want to be beaten by cobras."

"Cobras?"

"Yes, king and queen cobras. Plenty of them."

Ibadat turned his steps towards the hotel. Harfan followed him silently.

He wasn't sure if Rama Bai was mentally deranged. Her looks were sane and steady. Her eyes didn't betray her spasmodic mind. She was looking for some missing gem. What was it?

He must find out more. The sooner the better, Harfan resolved.

Ibadat's meteorological forecast was dead accurate. The morning dawned bright and glorious. Harfan stared amazingly through the large Gothic window, at the huge red disk hanging and pulsating over the horizon and kissing the endless expanse of floodwaters. Distant sparkles on the water brought back to his mind the liquid looks of Jamilla.

Oh heavens!

Why was the soggy face of Rama Bai appearing in his vision? Harfan buried his face in the pillow and tried to float in that unknown expanse, of the inviting looks of a fairy called Jamilla. He didn't want to see any other face, not now.

Jamilla returned. This time her wavy hair sprayed a whiff of fragrant air on his face. Harfan momentarily travelled back to the cascading hair that had numbed his mind with electrical impulses.

Ibadat's knock pierced the dream diaphragm.

"***Janab***, tea." He entered the room with a tray in hand.

"To hell with you," Harfan looked at Ibadat in mock anger, "You don't even allow your clients to enjoy their dreams in peace."

"Excuse me sir. You've a new dream ahead." Ibadat placed the tray on a bedside table.

"What's that?"

"You've a date at Sangla. Isn't it, sir?"

"***Hai Rabba*** (Allah)! I'd forgotten. How's the flood situation? Can I proceed to Sangla?"

"The Chinese and the Americans have left for their respective work places. You've to take a taxi. The bus and train services haven't resumed yet."

"Can you arrange one?"

"No problem sir. I can drop you if you don't mind."

"Thanks brother. Better you hire a taxi for me, for the whole day."

Israr Sharief dressed in the usual Punjabi suit and routine looks didn't carry the air of an important industrial tycoon. He glanced through the letter from Jung Sher Khan and spoke in chaste Punjabi.

"So, you're the nephew of Shamim Bukhari! Please make yourself comfortable." Israr ordered tea.

"As you know, mine is the prime industry in Pakistan, which produces vital spares for the armed forces. My expertise is in the field of night vision field equipment, batteries for shoulder-pack field communication sets, special alloys used in the manufacture of gun barrels, and high altitude clothing and kitchenware. I scout around for weapons systems in international markets. The war has opened up better business opportunities. Several contracts are pending." Israr added.

"I'm grateful for the briefing sir," Harfan replied politely, "Where do I fit in?"

"Get a feel of the production lines first," Israr advised, "I'll like you to head my marketing division and take care of my international commitments. That's an expanding market and I can't manage it alone. I'll help you get into the grooves of the Army establishment and bureaucracy. They're our main providers."

"You can trust me. I'll put my best." The sincere briefing of his employer impressed Harfan.

"A few more points that you should know about," Israr paused for a while," My half-brother and business rival Nawab is a professional wrecker. I hope you'll understand him better, as you get to know my business affairs."

"Anything in particular?"

"He's ambitious, more than he can manage. And he's unscrupulous."

"Is he a powerful man?"

"He is close to Izaz Afroz, the foreign minister. Has links with several top military brass, intelligence chiefs and the drug mafia. Avoid spilling business secrets to him." Israr spoke in his usual soft voice.

"Any more points to be briefed on?"

"Yes. You'll come in contact with important army officers. They rule the country and they're the biggest bandits and drug barons. Don't antagonise them. I'll tell you how to get past those lusty jackals. Often you've to bribe your way through."

Israr advised Harfan to pick up the tricks of special business management. Grease, he explained, worked better than any other established business stratagem.

"How important is Alam Khan?" Harfan tried to probe about his immediate handler.

"Well! He's important. He has close links with the Principal Staff Officer (PSO) to the Chief Martial Law Administrator (CMLA) and several Corp & Commanders, who control the drug pipelines. He has fabulous connections with international gunrunners and US and British intelligence operators." Israr was liberal in his comments on his business collaborator.

"How important is he to your business?"

"Valid point. We're competitors. But we've to depend on each other. The arms market is a closed circuit operation. My company works in tandem with Alam and Jung Sher Khan."

"Is the competition nasty?"

"Yes and no. We jackals in the arms bazaar do not hesitate to stab from the back, if that's important for promoting business interest."

Israr Sharief explained lucidly his business relationship with two other important suppliers to the Pakistani armed forces.

"Settle your personal affairs fast. Sangla isn't a good place to stay in. You can scout out a fine living quarters at Jhumra. Some elegant old houses are available there. Not much of a distance from here."

"Yes. Jhumra appears to be a nice place."

Harfan agreed with his boss. That was his pre-destined theatre, which he missed out on since the last couple of decades.

****

The job kept Harfan busy; the cover enveloped him comfortably. But he couldn't stop dreaming of the beautiful eyes he had left behind in the rusty Masti Gate of Lahore. But dreams alone were not good enough to get a bride home. A matrimonial proposal would require Alam's approval. The big shark, he presumed, would in turn seek Delhi's nod. A local marriage was a permissible adjunct to his tradecraft requirements, obviously a controlled marriage, minus the hiccups of the heart. Some sort of a sailor's wife! Shit! The idea of taking a sailor's wife bounced violently inside his mind.

To hell with Delhi and Alam. Jamilla was his dream girl. He wouldn't deceive her by inviting her simply to warm his bed, never ever.

Harfan pushed the thought out and hurled it back to the copybook of Dhiren Bhagat, from which he first came to know about some famous and infamous 'station wives'. He didn't require any. Jamilla, if he happened to marry her, would be his life partner, not a 'station wife.'

Seated on the grassy slopes of his backyard that tapered down to the murmuring waters of the Chenub, Harfan kept on throwing small pebbles into the placid waters. He watched the tiny ripples rising up and dissipating on the blue vastness of the fast flowing stream. The blue below his feet transported Harfan to the fathomless blue eyes of Jamilla that invited him inexorably from beyond the clouds, remote verdant hills and the hidden sack of pain, very close to his heart. He felt like singing aloud.

The trained spy in him advised caution. The song was perhaps immature, a figment of his imagination. His lonely dream wasn't good enough to conjure up a palace in the sky.

How could he get into Jamilla's dream?

Should he?

Would that peel off his cover?

No raw nerve should be hurt. Feline curiosity was surely a spy's forte, but he didn't have the proverbial nine lives. His love shouldn't jeopardise his professional security!

Harfan's professional caution was, however, overwhelmed by songs of joy and melancholy. Autumn had silently walked into the fall, lending a riot of colours to the chinar, almond and apricot trees. The greens suddenly yielded to multi-coloured hues. The subtle changes enchanted Harfan. He'd never observed the nature pulsating around him, flourishing in seasonal blooms and changing colours. He was indifferent to the human invasion against nature, grabbing and destroying the essence of life inch by inch.

The nature quietly seeped into his molecules. A strange realisation, that the hands and souls of some unseen artists were busy in frenzied activity, injecting subtle chemical changes in his mind. He could hear strange tunes emanating from somewhere within. His singed and rugged psyche was submerged under cathartic fluids of joy and pain.

Harfan looked up at the cloudless early afternoon blue sky. A few kites and thrush were lazily gliding, perhaps just for the fun and love of singing to the ethereal void. A piece of cloud drifted in from Sangla hill and a red-breasted robin swooped in from nowhere. Her mellow whistle and deep black eyes opened up another tunnel. Jamilla's eyes flew in through the clouds. They were fathomless, placid and deep, deeper than the distant blue of the rippling Chenub, breaking into soft murmurs.

"***Assalam u Alaikum***. Where have you been Mian Mirza Ghalib (a famous Urdu poet)? Dreaming of Jamilla?"

Alam approached Harfan from his right flank.

"***Wale Kum...*** Sorry I didn't notice you. When did you come by?"

Harfan felt intrigued, looking at the grey ***mehndi*** (herbal dye) tinged lush growth of beard on Alam's face. He presumed that Alam had reasons to move incognito.

"Don't be surprised young man. I'm on a mission. But your reflexes are slack. Be an alert cat. Crouch for your kill, but don't ignore the hunter's dart."

Alam headed towards the front room clutching under his arms two bulging brief cases. Once inside the house, he set himself to surveying the accommodation, inch by inch. He softly hammered the walls to feel for the hollows and cavities. There were none.

He examined the wooden floor meticulously. The windows, with opaque glass panes, drew his attention and appreciation.

"A fine home. What's the rent?"

"Only a thousand. It belonged to an official of the former king, different from modern homes." Harfan replied, "The present owner is an absentee landlord from Chiniot."

"Very tastefully done up," Alam settled down over a cup of coffee, took out a pint sized bottle from his brief case and sprinkled the contents on a wooden window panel.

"What're you doing?"

"I'm putting it on fire."

"Why?"

"There has been an electrical short circuit."

"No. You're damaging the nice wood work."

"Visit the stores around the corner. Take this paper, you'll find a shopping list for plugs, connectors, triple insulated wires, and some nails, clips and hinges."

"Jhumra is a small place. Don't you think people may ask questions?" Harfan expressed apprehension.

"What do you do when there is an electrical fire? You replace the wires and do some repair work. Your place is old and a short circuit is but natural." Alam explained that these common electrical items weren't going to trigger off any suspicion.

"What do you need these for?"

"Bring the items first and don't forget to get two Black Labels. Officially booze is banned in Islamic Pakistan. Pay a little extra and you can get it from the Palace Hotel."

Harfan dropped by the hotel and informed Ibadat that his uncle, third removed, had suddenly arrived from Karachi with a marriage proposal. The old crook required at least five stiff pegs before he went to bed. Would he be good enough to deliver two Black Label bottles at his residence!

A trifle of a smile rippled past Ibadat's left eye. He liked Harfan's thin efforts to guard the secrets of Mian Alam Khan. It was a fine effort indeed. He displayed a mask of happiness and offered home delivery of a few plates of ***kebab*** and roasted mutton nuggets. He would take care of dinner as well, Ibadat assured him.

"***Mian***, your ***tangri kebab*** is ***la jawab*** (incomparable)." Alam dressed, as a puritan Muslim, a mosque cap and mehndi-tinted beards and moustache to match, was effusive in his praise of the food.

"Sir, the recipe is a speciality of my late father's." Ibadat proudly declared.

"Must be," Alam spoke through mouthfuls of juicy kebabs, "He must've been a great chef."

"Sir, he was the royal chef, not an ordinary cook."

"I can feel that from the aroma of the spices, uniquely Lucknowvi. Your family may have migrated from there."

"We aren't migrants sir," Ibadat added, "For three generations we were employed in the court of the Jhumra kings."

"That's what gives it the old world flavour." Alam complimented Ibadat.

"You're correct," Ibadat added, "My great-great-great grandpa was a kitchen retinue of the Nawabs of Lucknow, inventor of the delicate ***handi*** (sealed pot) style of cooking. There are some surprise items for dinner as well."

"Must be," Alam continued the juicy dialogue, "Your father must've been an ***alem*** (expert) in culinary art. Mian, these are rare Mughlai delicacies, right from the heart of Central Asia. I intend to enjoy every bit of all that you've inherited from that great artist."

He winked at Ibadat, which meant immediate disengagement.

Ibadat took the hint and left hurriedly.

Dinner over, Alam removed his wig, false beard and moustache and set himself to work.

He sawed off parts of the wooden floor, near the base of the bedroom fireplace. It took the shape of a hidden sunken chamber that was reinforced with leak proof cement and chemical compounds. He dug up the old brick wall, laid an insulated hidden electric connection and completed the circuit for an external aerial, by running a length of thermal coated pipe through the fireplace exhaust.

On the second night of his stay, Alam closed all the doors and windows and opened his brief cases.

"This is your communication set, Barrette 530-D, from the latest NATO inventory. In fact, this is the standard High Frequency trans-receiver for clandestine operations." Alam unwrapped the packing and explained its features.

"It operates on 1.6 to 30 MHz, requires 15w to 125w power input. Basically it operates on SSB system, though there's provision for Amplitude Modulation and CW system. Hope you understand the technical jargon." Alam asked.

"No problem," Harfan asked, "Can I use it for VT (voice transmission)?"

"You can. That's technically possible, but there's a total embargo on VT."

"Now look," Continued Alam, "The system has a twelve memory, scanning facility, a remote control panel. It weighs just 4.1 kilograms. There's a built in error correction facility and you can transmit in continuous as well as burst modes."

"Does it require an external antenna?" Enquired Harfan.

"Yes, that's very important. A unidirectional antenna will do. Don't hang one on the roof. We require a camouflaged device."

Alam opened another small bag and took out a crescent moon crafted out of sensitive alloy that was designed to pick up weak radio signals. He fished out a few miniature minaret shaped ceramic insulators.

"These are materials for the high gain antenna. We'll mount these tomorrow and synchronise with the trans-receiver set."

Alam explained, over a drink, some of the unique feature of the trans-receiver set. Communication wasn't possible till the two ends reached an electronic handshake. This feature minimised the risk of detection. The burst transmission facility, he explained, should guarantee against snooping by Pakistani monitoring stations.

Alam displayed a miniature auto-encryption accessory that could be jacked to the main trans-receiver.

"All that you're required to do is to key on the message and push the auto-encryption button. Push the burst transmission button after the handshaking diode flashes the green light. Your message will reach Delhi in a fraction of a second." Alam explained.

"For reception, switch on the memory button, activate the deciphering key and switch on the printer. The deciphered message will be ready in 2 minutes." Alam kept on narrating the intricacies like a wizard.

"That means I don't use the cipher pads."

"A good question. Something is wrong with me." Alam poured another whisky and lighted a cigarette.

"The auto-encryption ensures low grade encoding, which the enemy can break easily. For all communications to Delhi use the OTP (one time cipher pads). Here's your supply for one year."

On the third night Alam keyed in a trial message.... "Fish in water, swimming well."

That was the pre-determined code for the post-installation communication with Delhi.

Alam explained the schedule protocol.

Harfan should expect calls on 3rd, 13th, 23rd of every month, in 002.007 or 18.009 MHz bands. He should expect calls between 0200 and 0210 hrs. Monitors of Pak Intelligence Bureau, Joint Intelligence Signals of the ISI and the Signals Research Bureau of the Army normally inter-changed their frequencies during this thin margin. That was a part of standard security drill.

For transmission, Alam explained, Harfan should use a random schedule. ***Behest,*** the designated master hub in Delhi, would be on air round the clock.

"Your station nom-de-plume will be ***Huri*** (fairy). In case of emergency, you switch on the station at will and seek protocol with the call sign ***Zam Zam***, over 23.46 MHz." Alam warned Harfan that the ***Zam Zam*** channel was to be tapped only in an emergency, involving his personal security and security of India.

He replaced the wooden floor panels and finally put back the Cashmere carpet on top of it. The camouflage was perfect.

Harfan was introduced to the functioning of an electronic signal scanner that was capable of detecting intrusive snooping devices. Every week, he emphasised, Harfan should carry out electronic scanning of his house, top to bottom; all walls, crevices, behind the wall hangings, undersides of tables, chairs etc, etc.

The enemy was in its home turf; Alam emphasised, and was always steps ahead of an intruder like Harfan. The best way to fox the challenger was to maintain communication ambiguity, sparing use of telephone and never for professional talks. All professional talks, which can't be avoided, should be carried out from lonely and safe PCBs (Public Call Booths), never from the same one. Use of the clandestine radio was strictly prescribed for special communications that required the immediate attention of Delhi.

Harfan was advised to hone up his Drop, Brush, Dead Letter and Live Letter Box drills (DLB and LLB).

"And set up a lab for preparing microdots. Use the FIB prescribed invisible ink. Post your mail to the London cover address, the River Channel, from different towns. Never use the Jhumra post office." Alam refurbished some of the tradecraft lessons earlier imparted by the trainers in Delhi.

"What are my prime and immediate target areas?" Asked Harfan.

"We've discussed this once. Penetrate the CMLA and the GHQ. That's the fountainhead of all information," Alam specified the area of immediate coverage, "And remember Israr is your passport. Develop proximity with Jung Sher Khan. Penetrate the top brass of the armed forces. The Military administration is fragile but they're the jackals of the day."

"What if I fail and commit mistakes?"

"Don't kid. No loony can survive in this game of walking the razor's edge. If exposed, you're either at the mercy of the Pak intelligence or the FIB executioners." Alam replied without blinking his eyelid.

"No protection from the Company?" Harfan asked in a wounded voice.

"Sorry friend, this is a one way plunge into the black hole, if you happen to emerge at the other end, it's ***Allah's*** grace. Don't expect any mercy."

Alam poured another drink and lighted a cigarette.

"The Agency should've some responsibility for its agents."

"Relax. Intelligence is a raw fire walk sans magic insulation and rope tricks. Your innovative skills are the only assets you have to live with."

"Any special dope on the power structure at the top?" Harfan enquired about the lay of land in the Armed Forces' hierarchy.

Alam's comments traversed over a virtual minefield of intrigue and tense power struggle. President Field Marshal Akbar Khan was already sucked into the whirlpool of internal and international conspiracies. A pawn in the hands of USA and China, he was mindlessly playing their geo-political games.

"Is he unpopular?" Harfan asked.

"Yes and no. The drawn war and his acceptance of the UN brokered peace have irked the politically ambitious leaders and Generals."

Izaz Afroz, Alam explained, and a few top Generals were involved in multi-layered conspiracies. They vied with each other to plunder Pakistan and stash away its wealth in their foreign accounts.

The men to watch out for, he said, were Lt. General Sarfaraz, the PSO, General Hyder Bux, the ISI chief and the Corps Commanders of Karachi, Quetta, Chak Lala, Peshawar and Lahore. They controlled, besides their troops, the fabulous drug cartels. It's they and not the system that decided Pakistan's fate. They were the Establishment.

"Any link with Indian drug barons?" Harfan asked.

"Yes. But don't wreck your head over it. It's out of your orbit. Tread cautiously," Alam cautioned his probationer, "It's worse than a minefield, and I won't be there to push your pram around."

"I'm no toddler." Harfan replied.

"So happy to hear that. Bye...." Alam turned back, "Yes. I forgot to tell you about linkages between Nawab Sharief and Izaz Afroz. This slimy character moves in and out of conspiracy plots. His present strategic ally is the Chinese ambassador in Islamabad."

"What about the President? Why does he not intervene?"

"Last of the Pakistani troika, he's a terminally sick person. He has lost the will to fight back...may call in the Chief of Army Staff to step in. Take care."

Alam stepped into his car. Before igniting the engine he summoned Harfan, in the presence of Ibadat.

"I approve of the girl. An excellent choice."

"Thanks uncle."

"Call uncle Shamim. He may like to formally approach Zahoor Chaudry."

Harfan nodded in agreement.

"And don't forget to inform Jung Sher Khan and Israr about the match. Bye." Alam waived and pressed on the accelerator. The car zoomed out bathing Harfan and Ibadat in a thick coat of dust.

"Congratulations." Ibadat extended his palm.

"What for?"

"The dream marriage. Jamilla is a fabulous lady."

"How do you know?" It was Harfan's turn to be surprised.

"I know many people in Lahore and Zahoor sahib is an important industrialist." Ibadat smiled and made his way for the hotel.

Harfan kept on looking at the receding figure of Ibadat and realised that he was finally placed at the designated orbit.

It was a delicate and dangerous orbit, spiked with meteorites. He would have to spin along an impossible booby-trapped apogee and perigee. He recalled the cynic advice of Maulana Rizwan. A spy lived only once and not many of them witnessed a second life.

Chapter 23

Ram Karan Prasad's secret largesse had ensured an MIT scholarship for Kumar Anand's son. A fat dowry had secured a son-in-law, an officer in the Indian Administrative Service, for his daughter. But the goddess of fortune refused to shower manna on him.

The Jhajjar Khera incident of mass rape and murder of Savitri, jumped out of its grave, despite a sterile discussion in the Parliament and crude stonewalling by the treasury bench. It triggered off a new controversy. The opposition benches led by the Hindu Sangh had forced a parliamentary enquiry into the incident. Kumar Anand's misfortune was topped by a stern displeasure conveyed by the stiff-jawed Prime Minister.

Dutta was disillusioned too. Kumar Anand was relieved from the Prime Minister's health-report-leakage enquiry. He was on his way out that's what the FIB rumour mill whispered. However, Delhi's power alley cats weren't unduly exercised over Kumar Anand's future. They had enormous faith in the wizardry of Ram Karan and Mandira. They sure weren't going to watch her favourite officer pushed under the chopping block.

Pompous enquiries in India generally ended up in mutual back scratching exercise between the treasury bench and the opposition. The unique democracy believed in a well-rehearsed bed partnership. Normally such exercises ended up with the ritual sacrifice of some junior bureaucrats. The politicians were too sacrosanct to be enwrapped by the law of the land.

The ***mahayagna*** (the sacrificial ritual) over the PM's health report leakage and Jhajjar Khera mass rape had to have its chosen sacrificial goat. That was the surest way to pacify the gods and bosses. The axe fell on poor Alagar Vellachi Dasa, a Junior Intelligence Officer in the FIB's Unit Wizard, the counter intelligence unit that handled Pakistan. A sticker of inefficiency and dereliction of duty was put on his back and he was directed to report at Aizwal, India's remotest outpost, capital of the insurgency infested headquarters of the Lushai Hills.

Alagar, unceremoniously kicked out from Unit Wizard, was on a rare family outing at the India Gate lawns. Some leisurely bites at the luscious ice cream and the company of his family, he thought, would help in taming the frothy fumes of frustration.

His child, a cute three-year-old girl was, however, more fascinated by the colourful balloons. She kicked off a rhythmic row, demanding the dreams, she thought, were concealed inside the inflated rainbow coloured gossamer rubbers. Alagar's wife, unable to silence the tiny rebel, started walking towards the balloon vendor, across the road.

A Pakistan High Commission vehicle screeched past her at high speed, in the direction of Man Singh Road. For a fleeting moment Alagar could see a figure crouching on the floor of the car. He asked his wife to take a cab back home, kicked off his motorbike, and picked up the trail of the diplomatic vehicle.

The driver, trained in counter-surveillance, didn't miss the dogged biker. He entered lonely stretches of streets with a view to shaking off the bug. Alagar, anticipating his moves had positioned himself, behind a pile of discarded vehicles, just across the rear gate of the targeted Mission. His anticipation was correct. The crafty dodger zoomed past him and entered the Chancery premises at high speed.

Alagar's immediate superior, Dhiren Bhagat, listened carefully and did some hard planning. The Mission intelligence operatives, by set practice, dropped back their picks late in the night. Usually they ventured out before daybreak, around 4 a.m. The Indian intelligence, they knew, were too timid to risk mounting surveillance on deserted stretches of road. No professional agency would risk betraying the identity of their surveillance vehicle and personnel.

Bhagat planned placing mobile surveillance (Mosurs), a mixed bag of two cars and two motorbikes, equipped with digital VHF communication devices and precision video cameras. The team maintained an all night vigil and the reward came early next morning, at ten past four.

The Toyota rolled out stealthily; headlights off, and swung into Shanti Path, taking a sudden turn towards Ashoka Hotel. Kissing the asphalt with a sweet chirping sound, the car surged ahead at high speed.

"Mosur One and Two, move in sandwich formation. Keep the suspect in between. Maintain safe distance." Alagar directed the car borne teams.

"Mobile X and Y follow the sandwich, keep a distance and keep the suspect in view. I'm just behind you. Keep your radio and cameras on." Alagar instructed the Mosur teams.

"He's turning to Jorbagh." In came Mosur One.

"Keep a distance and follow."

"He's taking anti-surveillance measures, taking rounds of Jorbagh market. Send Two to the Aliganj blind end. He may escape through Kotla, direct X and Y to be on guard." Suggested One.

Alagar did some quick thinking. The Indian contact of the Mission could be a resident of Lodi Colony government quarters. That appeared to be the suspect drop zone. His hunch was correct. The Toyota took a few rounds of Lodi Colony, dropped the contact at the corner of D Block, next to Meher Chand Market, opposite a police post. Alagar sighted the middle aged suspect entering quarter No. D/20/X16. The living room light shone momentarily and went out.

The target housed, Alagar noted the landmarks around D/20/X16.

Back in the briefing room, he drew up a sketch of the locale and worked out an elaborate foot-surveillance (Fosur) to pick up the target and house him at his work place.

The Fosur, next morning, tailed the foxtrotting middle-aged person, with profuse sandalwood and vermilion stripes on his forehead, to a ground floor office in South Block that formed a part of the Prime Minister's Office. It was the central registry section of the PMO, which handled movement of general and classified files.

The middle-aged person occupied a table, offered flowers and scented incense sticks before a deity, lighted a cigarette and ordered tea. The FIB Fosur barnacle kept on pressing the button of a clandestine camera, loaded in his shoulder bag. The job over, he briefly enquired about an acquaintance and was advised to look him up in a first floor room.

Crash enquiries established the identity of the suspect, Shreedharan Pillai, a senior section officer in the PMO. Another famous Pillai, a midget of an additional private secretary to Amritlal, the former Prime Minister, had inducted Shreedharan to the PMO's record office, from his home-turf, Cochin.

Moulded in the legacy of Indian baboodom, Shreedharan Pillai had devised novel ways to please the senior cats. He endeavoured to keep everyone pleased, through personalised services, peddling advance tips about promotions, transfers and service-extension cases cleared by the PM. His knowledge of astrology and homeopathic medicine acted as extra props. He claimed to have mastered the cosmic mystery, which opened up access to the inner grains of the stars and planets. The mambo-jumbo magic endowed him with an open general license to the future of men and matters. His forecasts about prospects in love, liaison, promotion and patronage, the gullible bureaucrats believed, were immaculate.

Pillai prescribed the wonder drugs for the gamut of ailments from common cold to impotency and frigidity in middle-aged bureaucrats and their wives. Some senior clients solely depended on Pillai's special aphrodisiac concoctions to keep their wives and mistresses happy.

Obliged as they were to this tiny jack of all trades, the top-cats in the government, showered on Pillai occasional favours, by way of promotions, scholarships to his children and a couple of foreign trips.

A sleek operator, Pillai didn't mind stealing pleasures on the slight. Ostensively a religious person, with layers of sandalwood and vermilion stripes and dashes on his forehead, Pillai had no inhibitions in gulping a few discreet shots of Scotch and enjoying the occasional women. Discretion was the watchword with the Tiger of Cochi, an apt epithet invented by his secret admirers.

A loving husband and father at home, his shadowy personality erupted in torrid emotion and wild ecstasy in hotel rooms; where contractors, suppliers and fortune hunters arranged pretty girls, Scotch and the choicest seafood.

Pillai preferred middle-aged women. They, he believed, were experts in bed, compared to the impatient hotshot youngsters. He enjoyed a delayed orgasm, the key to which was known to mature women only. That came through practice and experience.

Pillai's latest flame Nasreen; a chatterbox beauty from the walled city had lighted up wild flames in his rusted bones. Little did he know that

Safaat Zangi Khel, an undercover functionary of the Pakistan Intelligence Bureau, had planted the chatterbox on him, after months of scouting and research!

Amrik Singh Johol, the celebrated business facilitator of Ram Karan Prasad had introduced the beauty to the diplomat, in return for a major favour. Safaat took just seven days to trap Pillai in Nasreen's silken cobweb. It didn't take more than thirty minutes for her to undress Pillai in the hotel room, electronically treated by Safaat. He recorded all the sexual wonders performed by the Tiger of Cochi, which could put to shame the famous sculptures on the walls of Khajuraho.

One fine late evening Safaat approached Shreedharan, as he alighted from the bus at Lodi Market stand.

"Would you like to see some nice photographs of ***Thirumala Tirupati,*** exclusive shots of Lord ***Venkateshwara*** (famous Hindu deity in south India)?" Safaat whispered in his ears.

For a few moments Shreedharan couldn't correlate the hefty looking Frontier Pathan with Lord ***Venkateshwara*** of Thirumala Hills.

"What photographs?" He turned towards his doors, barely a couple of yards away.

"Better have a look before your wife and boss have access to these fine prints."

Safaat opened an envelope and shuffled the positives of Shreedharan in different poses with Nasreen.

Pillai collapsed.

"What do you expect of me?" The Tiger of Kochi squeaked like a rat.

"Nothing much Pillai sahib. Do me some small favours, from time to time, that's all." Safaat tried to assuage the ruffled feelings of his catch.

"That's impossible. It'll ruin me." He lamented.

"Ruined you're, either way. It's better you cooperate. That way I keep my job intact and you get rewarded for simply helping me keeping my job. And you get Rupees 10,000 per month, your own choice of whisky and cigarettes. Nasreen is anyway all yours, I promise."

Safaat Zangi applied the final squeeze.

Pillai, The Tiger of Cochi slipped down the slippery alley, greased by Safaat Zangi Khel and Nasreen, to the abysmal destination of self-destruction.

Rabindra Narayan Dutta, the FIB chief entered the PM's room in triumphant strides. Nampoothiri waited in the front office.

"Sir, the spy has been located."

Dutta gave a brief presentation of the case, supported by photographs of the Pak diplomat, accepting documents from Shreedharan. Transcripts of telephone interception reports and clandestine snaps of Nasreen entertaining the middle-aged bureaucrat in hotel rooms irrefutably fortified Dutta's case.

"How much damage has been done? Hope the Pakistani rat hasn't compromised all our national secrets!"

Jung Bahadur reacted with a shiver of horror.

"The damage must be massive. We're yet to assess it." Dutta replied.

"Your boys should have been more alert." The old man was visibly unhappy.

"Sir, intelligence is a game of wits. And the PMO is normally out of bounds for my boys. That was the rule of the game laid down by your predecessor."

"It's you, who is responsible for focusing on the contours of security lapses and threats. Hope you won't, hereafter, treat my office as Caesar's wife."

Jung Bahadur mildly reprimanded his intelligence chief.

"Any way, how do you want to proceed on this?" The PM asked.

"I think we should compromise the diplomat and pick them up in live action." Dutta explained the advantages of apprehending the Pak diplomat.

"An intelligence offensive against a diplomat may cloud the skies over Tashkent." Jung Bahadur expressed his reservations.

"Perhaps neutralisation of a spy ring at this stage will put the Pakistanis on the defensive. They'll not crib about your health report any more. You may direct the Foreign Secretary to brief the important missions adequately. They should know that Pakistan was bent upon subverting the talks, by stealing your health secrets." Dutta insisted.

"No. I think we should quietly neutralise Pillai. Consult the Foreign Secretary. The Pak diplomat should be declared PNG, only after I return from Tashkent. I don't want any mess up before that."

"But sir...." Dutta tried to advocate in favour of catching the spies red handed.

"Yes. I accept your position. But these are difficult times. Two spies can stew in their own juices. I don't want any adverse international reactions. And Dutta," The PM looked up straight, "I don't want the entire world to know that my personal office is a virtual rat hole. Spare me the indignity."

"May I suggest a plan?" Dutta whispered.

"Spell it out, quick." Jung Bahadur replied.

"Before your visit to Tashkent I want to plant some misinformation on the Pakistan IB, contradicting the earlier status on your health and on your orders clearing the grounds for bomb-grade nuclear experiment."

"What difference does it make?"

"Pillai has passed on to Pakistan vital information on our nuclear programme. Izaz Afroz, the Pakistani foreign minister is sure to raise the nuclear bogey. And the US won't be far behind in joining the cacophony. I think we should mislead them by using the same channel. If you permit it, we may push in a few doctored reports."

Dutta spelt out his scheme.

"How would you do that?" Asked Jung Bahadur.

"Leave the details to me sir, but I assure you that the trick will surely click. You would find President Akbar more accommodating at Tashkent."

"You know your trade better, I'm as ignorant as a country bumpkin."

"Another point sir."

"Yes."

"Will you like to reconsider Kumar Anand's case? You may like him to stay on." Dutta pleaded on behalf of his deputy.

"You can't live with a disloyal wife and an errant intelligence chief," Jung Bahadur spoke in a firm voice, "No hurry. Let me return from Tashkent."

Jung Bahadur declined to be taken in by Dutta's pleadings. He had better ideas about the intelligence deputy and his mentors, Mandira and Ram Karan Prasad. The threesome had created tonnes of embarrassment for him. And he had serious doubts about Prasad's integrity too. Ram Karan must have had penetrated the chastity belt of the FIB too.

"As you wish sir." Dutta wished the PM and turned on his heels.

"One more point Dutta," The PM walked up to his intelligence chief, "Your man in Pakistan is efficient. Ask him for a report on their likely strategy at the talks. Ask what would be their major bargaining chips and where we can squeeze them most!"

"Thanks sir. It should be ready before you board the flight."

It was a tall order, Dutta knew. But he had implicit faith on Alamgir and he expected Triple X to chip in too.

Chapter 24

Launching Triple X, as a deep penetration resident agent, was a part of the brief assigned to Jiwan Bahutule alias Mian Alam Khan. His job wasn't over with the ignition of the rocket. Bhagat and Maulana Rizwan had accomplished that job. Alam's job involved the firing of micro-retro rockets to place the agent in its desired orbit.

The PIB and the ISI had busted six out of the ten previous launches over a span of 5 years. The remaining four was nestled in peripheral areas and had failed to burrow deep inside the establishment. But Harfan Bukhari, Alam calculated, was made of different stuff. The audacious, moody and daring youth was sure to go places. He didn't seem to be a professional spy, who chipped in mostly for fat moneybags.

Employment with Israr Sharief had provided a snug second layer of cover. That coup had added a certain level of respectability to the high gear resident agent. His marriage to a local girl, coming from the social strata of Zahoor Chaudry should harden the outer shell, argued Alam.

Alam's own linkages with the high profile arms suppliers and manufacturers had flourished into a massive cartel. More than expected dough was piling up in his Swiss account. That was a comfortable rain cheque. His game couldn't indefinitely remain under wraps. Political convulsions and lack of a democratic structure had started rocking Pakistan. The eastern wing was in ferment and the military regime had started lapsing into deeper contradictions.

Ibadat's scouting had helped Alam to zero in on Zahoor Chaudry. Not bad! The shipping and transport tycoon and an industrialist of sort was well connected with the top military brass and his wife Sayeefa enjoyed an intimate relationship with Malika Jahanara, a steady friend of a number of Generals, notably General Arif Khan. He was, if the things didn't sour up for other reasons, sure to be the next COAS of the Pakistan Army.

Harfan's marriage to Zahoor's daughter was sure to cement his own business dealings with Jung Sher Khan, Israr Sharief and the hungry and scheming bosses in the CMLA. That should offer opportunities for gathering golden hay even on cloudy evenings of the present Pakistani polity.

By all accounts, Alam deduced, Harfan and Jamilla were entangled in the sticky cobweb called love.

Alam threw his dice after great calculation and pleaded forcefully in favour of an early nuptial tie for his understudy.

Nampoothiri vacillated. Yes. Marriage sure was a good cover. But marrying Zahoor Chaudry's daughter could generate professional impediments.

Zahoor, he argued, was a high profile businessman and his wife Sayeefa had become a culture-totem in Pakistan. A famous durbar dancer and singer of her days she moved with ease and élan in the highest social strata.

"But he's nose-deep in love with that girl." Alam pleaded.

"I don't approve of it. A XXX agent shouldn't acquire that kind of social prominence. Ask him to settle for a low profile housewife. I know him; all that he wants is a female companion. It should be purely a temporary arrangement." Nampoothiri was firm in his views.

"Boss," Alam pleaded, "I think much water has flown down the Indus since he landed in Pakistan. I find lots of changes in the robot. He has a mind of his own."

"Look Alam," Nampoothiri came up with more information, "Sayeefa is not even a Muslim. Our records say that, she was born to a Hindu mother, but was brought up by a Muslim ***kothewali*** (courtesan), after her mother was kidnapped and killed by a Hindu potentate. It's not good for XXX to get entangled with high profile and controversial personalities."

Nampoothiri finally caved in. Alam's argument that Shamim Bukhari and his associates like Jung Sher Khan and Israr Sharief were keen on the match, forced Nampoothiri to give half a hesitant nod.

Yes. Harfan Bukhari could get married to Jamilla. But Alam should warn the asset to stick to his own rails. His high profile social connections shouldn't throw him in ringside prominence. And Zahoor Chaudry's immaculate reputation in the ruling army clique and assorted politicians should be fully exploited.

A word of final warning, Nampoothiri said, Harfan Bukhari should be advised not to develop any emotional hang-up for the Pakistani girl. It should simply be a marriage of convenience. He required a station-wife and that's all Delhi could concede.

But Shamim Bukhari didn't find the going easy. He encountered unexpected opposition from his young wife. Harfan's match with Jamilla sounded preposterous to her. She wanted the newfound nephew to marry her half-sister. That would be an added insurance to keep the old man's assets under firm control.

Some pedigreed ***muhajir*** families of Karachi too were up in arms against the match. How could a Bukhari marry the daughter of a ***mohana*** (estuary) tribal and a nautch girl of dubious reputation? Sayeefa, a famous ***mujrawali*** (courtesan) of yonder years, still reigned supreme in the memories of her connoisseurs. But, Jamilla's cardinal crime, Bukhari's wife alleged, was her birth in a ***Shia*** family.

The Bukharis of Ludhiana, ***Sunni Hanafis*** and staunch ***Wahabis*** (fundamentalist Islamic sect) traced their common lineage to the Bukharis of Delhi's Jama Masjid. Emperor Shahjahan had imported the first Bukharis all the way from Bukhara. The renowned priestly family managed the imperial mosque, abode of the Almighty, which overlooked the ***Lal Qilla*** (Red Fort), abode of the greatest servant of ***Allah***, the Mughal Emperor of Hindustan. Only pure blue-blooded ***muftis*** and ***alems*** with extraordinary ***ilm*** (education) could lead the folks of ***Allah*** to prayers.

The Mughals, plenty of Mongol blood in their veins, recognised in a subtle way, the inferior status of their clan. Sure were they inferior to the Sayeds and Sheikhs of pure Arab and Turkish stock. Some holy edicts had even pronounced against marriage between the Mughals and the Pathans on the one hand and the Sheikhs and Sayeds on the other. In such matters, a true follower of the Chosen One couldn't make any deviations. The ***Hadis*** had it all laid down.

The Bukharis stood distinctly apart. How could a pious ***Sunni*** think of marrying into the family of a ***Shia*** heretic? An elder of the hallowed clan was expected to follow the religious injunctions. Harfan Bukhari, they ruled should marry the half-sister of Shamim's wife. She was a true descendant of the Khans of Qalat.

Shamim Bukhari, a scared person with failing health, didn't normally defy the charms of his young wife and the muscles of his brothers-in-law. But, the provisions of the ***Shariat*** and ***Hadis,*** social sanctions and the entreaties of his wife and her clan couldn't prevent him from taking a train to Lahore. His business calculations were clear. Jung Sher Khan and Israr Sharief were more important than his wife's tears and the ***Shia-Sunni*** squabble. And he sure didn't want the lone living male member of his clan to be married into his second wife's family. She couldn't bear a child for him. What was the guarantee that her half-sister would come with a more fertile womb? The Bukhari clan couldn't vanish with him. Harfan should keep the roots alive.

Zahoor Chaudry, financially a stronger person, but socially inferior, was flattered by the proposal, initiated by Jung Sher Khan and Israr Sharief. He couldn't imagine that all his money could buy a Bukhari for his daughter, offspring of an estuary tribal and a danseuse.

Sayeefa, a woman of modern values insisted on a pre-marriage meeting between the boy and the girl, a condition unheard of in their social milieu.

Zahoor was a heavenly angel. She had learnt to love and respect him. But, she carried, beneath her bones, her undiluted contempt for the pack of wolves, the human pigs that attended her concerts night in and night out. She hadn't seen any spark of appreciation for her art in their eyes. Their hungry eyes pierced her body contours. Music just helped in fortifying the liquid intoxicants. Some of them bounced fat wads of currency, inviting her to their smelly beds. Sayeefa fended off the pack of wolves, using the crafts she had learnt from her foster-mother.

She wouldn't like to throw her daughter to one more male pig. The boy must be judged well. She wouldn't force Jamilla to walk down to a ritual ***nikah*** (marriage). She didn't want another ***mullah*** (priest) to lead her daughter to a blind nuptial knot that could be nullified by three repeat utterances of the dirty word, ***talaq*** (divorce). Zahoor, like all good husbands, hardly disagreed with his wife. He knew Sayeefa well. She would have her way, in any case.

The glitterati and chatterati of Lahore, Rawalpindi and Islamabad turned up for the grand social evening arranged by friend Jung Sher Khan. Mian Israr Sharief, the ***muhajir*** and the Punjabi elite and the big bosses in uniform led the cheer groups. The nostalgic surroundings of the Faletti's, an old imperial heritage with a majestic structure, arcades and manicured gardens, were decked up elegantly for the occasion.

Nobody talked about the marriage. Pleasant talks, sober drinks, whiffs of French perfume and delectable snacks filled the light hearts.

Sayeefa played a neat trick.

"Here's Harfan. Perhaps you'll like to meet him."

She guided the young hearts to a corner and whispered into Jamilla's ears. She melted into the crowd, leaving Harfan and Jamilla in a storm of silence swirling around them.

Harfan's imagination failed to comprehend that the frame of the owner of the deep blue eyes, now clad in a pink ***salwar-kameez*** and a matching light-rose ***dupatta*** (scarf), could be so unearthly and ethereal.

Her cascading long hair shone like the silken slough of a queen cobra. The colour of her skin was a mysterious mixture of the fully blossomed Bengal ***champaks*** (michelia champaca) and the light pink Bukhara Roses. The heavenly glow, he thought was borrowed from the late evening clouds, hanging low over the horizon. The sun, the master artist, went to sleep after painting the clouds with a tender brush. The colour remained frozen on Jamilla's skin and soul.

The blue eyes, now free from the restraints of the ***borka*** slits, rippled amazingly, with small waves of endless questions piercing Harfan's frozen frame, which was rooted to the marble floor.

Harfan Bukhari was no novice with women. He enjoyed them, never to the lees though. He always felt a strange thirst and depression after every wild orgy. The thirst came, perhaps, from the genes of Raja Dayaram Kaushal and the melancholy was perhaps a gift from his mother.

But the shiver of joy pulsating through his existence transcended the paralysing moments. Harfan felt a benign glow lightening up his senses with a million-volt charge. He didn't feel the thirst and the melancholy was nowhere near. He felt like he was floating on the waves of an unknown sea, a very blue one, reflected in Jamilla's eyes.

The silent waves mesmerised him. Harfan was incapable of opening his lips, the words having lost their way deep inside his neurones. The left hemisphere of his brain was stupefied.

Jamilla recognised the young eyes and now the complete features of the man. Yes. It was he, the lost Bedouin with Greek features. The eyes, light brown, deep-set behind thick brows looked sad; like a captive pool of liquid, struggling to breach its banks. The eyes were asking mute questions, not perfectly co-ordinated with his speech organs.

A strange and mysterious smile momentarily appeared in the left corner of her slightly pouted lips, with a matching vibration in her eye fluids.

"***Allah kasam*** (by God). He's for me." Jamilla silently spoke to herself.

Harfan reciprocated with a silent reply. The vibrations of his eyes matched those of Jamilla and conveyed the magic message.

"By God! You're mine."

Pulsation inside levelled down with the resolution. The eyes disengaged.

Jamilla drew the scarf on her head and flew in the direction of a gathering of young folks.

Back home Sayeefa sounded Jamilla about the young man she had met in the party. Did she like him? Would she like to make him her life partner?

"As you wish."

Jamilla covered her face with a book. Her face, bright pink with delight and glow of love had failed to hide her inner feelings. Sayeefa, the mother, understood the signals and gave the final nod to Zahoor. She liked the boy. Jamilla too had approved the choice. He could now call a ***Qazi*** (magistrate) for the ceremonials and rituals. She was sure the two would make a fine pair. The boy was accomplished and oozed out an aroma of aristocracy.

He wasn't another male pig.

****

The brief honeymoon at Nathia Gali, a scenic and solitary hill resort in the North West Frontier Province was an experience in heavenly bliss for Jamilla and Harfan. The cosy retreats of Pines Hotel, long walks along the grassy Dunga Gali ridges, ecstatic touches and burning flames helped the mingling of their souls, like an ethereal fragrance loosing its identity in the thin galactic void.

Wild exploration of the body and eternal penetration in each other's amorphous consciousness had exploded Jamilla's existence. She was born anew. She reached the pinnacle of a new realisation and resolution. She loved the man. It was beyond physical love. She cared for him.

Harfan felt like a man born-again. A strange faith had burst into a new sunrise. He realised that love wasn't an act of madness! It meant caring and silent emptying and mingling with another soul. By emptying himself in Jamilla's love he felt more enriched. Her spring of love had filled in all the crevices and depressions of his singed psyche. The bliss was more than heavenly, if that state of situation existed anywhere.

Jamilla was only for him. God had specially crafted her and put a wonderful soul in the delicate frame, only for him. Her love transported Harfan beyond his second incarnation, a programmed Indian spy in Pakistan.

He felt a strange transcendental force pushing him through a tunnel, to a third incarnation, a new existence, far removed from that of Ramendra Kaushal and Harfan Bukhari. This was indeed a tunnel to freedom, freedom from fear. She helped him break the glass-cage built around him by Bhagat and Rizwan and reinforced by Alam.

God alone could say wherefore had He gathered all these primordial elements to create this angel of love! It wasn't her outer beauty; something divine in her had mesmerised Harfan.

He briefly remembered the story of materialisation of the Hindu goddess ***Chandi.*** The gods had transferred the best of their molecules to create the finest incarnation of woman, a pinnacle of beauty and power, ever-chronicled in human civilisation. She was the ultimate destroyer of all evils. She had delivered the gods from the evil spells of the demons.

No. Jamilla didn't display the fierce face of ***Chandi***. But Harfan couldn't fish out any better simile from his cultural store. Jamilla was the best woman God had ever created. That's all Harfan could spell out and that was the imagery he could put together. This new goddess had descended on his life to rescue him from the dungeon of hell, the demonic evils he himself had created.

Harfan stood near the window ledge and again looked at the contours of Jamilla's body, wrapped in a silken blanket. The sleeping beauty again reminded him of the unique ***Shakti*** (female power), created by the Elemental Gods.

A couplet from the ***Murti Rahasyam*** (mystery of the image) of the Hindu scripture ***Chandi*** came to his mind..." ***Kanakottama Kantihi Sa Sukanti Kanakambara, Devi Kanakavarnabha Kanakottamabhushana"....*** This Goddess is golden coloured, her apparel is golden and her body is adorned with the finest golden ornaments. She has just stepped out of the dazzling golden morning sun!

Harfan laughed silently for having picked up a couplet from a Hindu scripture to describe his Muslim wife. He felt helpless. Jamilla's beauty could only be described by reciting the classic couplet. No other poet had yet conceived another woman so beautiful, so energised and so resolutely poised against the evils of the universe. This eternal beauty transcended religion. Jamilla's beauty and personality were beyond religion. Harfan regretted that he was by no imagination a poet, to sculpt out Jamilla's beauty in words.

The dream journey to Nathia Gali concluded abruptly. Israr Sharief wanted Harfan back at Sangla urgently. A Pentagon team was flying into Rawalpindi for peddling military hardware. His company was short-listed by the government for attending a meeting with the visiting team.

This was not all. The worst jolt came from Sayeefa.

She poured tea from an ornate hand-painted china pot and spoke in a whispering tone.

"I believe you've hired a heritage home at Jhumra."

"It's a fine place, bang on the Chenub."

"I've been there. Oh! That's a good two decades ago."

Harfan silently sipped the spiced tea. He knew she was there, in his father's ***durbar*** at Jhumra, around the fateful days of partition of India.

"That's a lonely place I believe." Sayeefa looked up at Harfan.

"Yes, splendidly solitary."

"You see my intention isn't to separate you two," Sayeefa spoke in her usual low voice, " Jamilla is just 21. You're most of the time out on business. It's not good for a kid to live alone in that splendidly lonely place."

"But..." Harfan tried lodging a mild protest.

"Jami is a good student. She stood first in her honours and you'll obviously like her to complete the higher course."

Harfan couldn't protest, though the very idea of living without Jamilla tormented him.

"You're new to the job and it's a responsible position," Sayeefa continued, "Your business takes you out very often. She'll feel miserable, all alone at Jhumra. It's not good for a young kid to live alone. You understand the problems."

The argument was irrefutable.

"When does she start her new course?" Harfan managed to ask.

"Next month. You come over and stay with us whenever you're off from Israr's work," Sayeefa poured fresh tea for Harfan, "You're our son, as dear to us as Jamilla is."

The short spell of bliss of being with Jamilla, Harfan realised, was too sublime to be mired by the prolonged interlude of separation. For the first time he discovered the divine meaning of separation. There was pain as well as pleasure in it.

Harfan felt a strong urge to drown his cover identity, cut off the Delhi umbilical and fly away to a remote cuckoos' nest. The third reincarnation was surreal, more authentic than the intelligence cover donned by him.

He shook off the idle thought. That wasn't possible, Harfan knew well.

Alam, whoever this character was, was sure to swoop down like a hawk from his cloud cover, piercing his placid shield and shattering his dreams. The masters back in Delhi and the intelligence hounds in Pakistan wouldn't allow him the pleasure of a romantic escapade.

As a resident intelligence agent, as he was, his destiny ordained walking on the razor's edge all the way. No tilt, no slip. An insignificant miss could blow up his cover and that would spell disaster. A neutralised agent in foreign soil mostly took a one-way journey behind the walls of high security prisons. Never could he expect to crawl back to the love nest. Very few in his class ever did. The jackals growled all around for their pounds of flesh.

He wasn't the knight to tame them, not yet.

Harfan finally okayed Sayeefa's suggestion, but insisted that Jamilla should visit his new home, for a few days at least. The home, without her touch, would just be another wilderness.

Sayeefa understood and agreed.

Harfan's idyllic heritage Jhumra home nestled on the wooded banks of the Chenub, the fall colours and the lush green vegetation around bemused Jamilla. She hated the mere thought of going back to Lahore, leaving her dream man alone. The threads of her life were textured up with those of this strange person only a few days back. It seemed like they had known each other from eternity and had been travelling together on the same arrow of time, never separated from each other.

A new dream had enveloped her

Insha Allah let this be the eternal dream!

"Why don't we spend a night in the royal chamber of the hotel?" The idea first hit Harfan's mind.

"It doesn't make any difference. Wherever you are I'm your queen and you're my prince." Jamilla replied.

Jamilla's reply infected and intoxicated Harfan. A prince he was and Jamilla was his queen of hearts. He couldn't suppress the desire of spending a precious night with her at the royal chamber of his parent's abode, now a heritage tourist hotel. He always felt the amorphous presence of his father, the clanging hoofs of his stallion, and shuffling clothes of his courtiers.

Hotel Royal Palace enchanted Jamilla too. The sheer charm of the place propelled her to take a walk to the edges of the palace compound, beyond the orchards that traversed the undulated ground and disappeared inside the riverbed.

Brought up in the honeycombed clusters in a narrow lane, she felt like spreading herself on the grass and embracing the trees, some of them broadcasting a distinct aroma. She enjoyed the walk.

Walking down with Jamilla Harfan had lost count of their pace and direction. They talked about the river, distant glistens from its blues, the twittering birds and the enchanting fall colours. He suddenly realised that they had reached the edges of Rama Bai's huts.

The frail old lady, seated under the shade of a huge Banyan tree, was busy feeding her pet goats with tender green blades of grass and leaves.

She noticed the couple approaching her hut. There was no mistake, she murmured. He must be Ramu, Ramendra Kaushal, her son, and son of the late king. She had nursed him in her womb for nine and a half long months. This must be her own drop of blood. She hadn't committed any mistake on their first encounter.

Yes, she was sure. She had kissed and loved an exact replica of this very face, decades ago. The pain and pleasure of bearing the child, as a surrogate mother, was rewarding, but at the cost of permanent silence. She was administered the vow of eternal silence, before the goddess ***Kali*** and a raging sacrificial fire, never to claim her own drop of blood.

But her vow of silence couldn't plug the memory lane. The dark magic box of old wounds and pleasures opened up spontaneously. But her thoughts floundered on the rocks of doubt. Perhaps she was dreaming and conjuring up a truth, which she liked to believe to be true. Kaushalya's mail hadn't mentioned anything about their son visiting the lost kingdom. He had taken up a job in ***vilayat***. Why should he be here, in this heartless country, which had mercilessly killed his father?

She was intrigued on the first encounter itself, to see the face of the young Maharaja implanted on the body of the strange visitor. The lower part of the face was a replica of Dayaram's young feature. His lips too were slightly curled at the edges and there was a deep fold at the centre of the upper lip.

She had no doubt about the strange similarity. Harfan's lush growth of beard couldn't deceive her eyes.

They were just a few paces away. Rama Bai noticed through the corner of her eyes, while feeding the goats absentmindedly.

"Here's Rama Bai," Harfan introduced Jamilla, "My wife Jamilla Khatoon."

"A Hindu?" Jamilla whispered.

"Yes, a legacy from the old kingdom. They didn't kill her. She's deranged, I'm told." Harfan stretched the introduction.

Rama Bai stopped feeding her goats, entered her hut and came out with a silver plate on her left palm. White rice grains, green blades of grass and an ivory box full of red vermilion powder flanked an oil lamp at the centre.

She surprised Jamilla by putting a large vermilion mark on her forehead and in the parting of her hair. She showered the young bride with blades of grass and a thimble full of rice grains. Jamilla looked with innocent astonishment. She didn't know how to react. Harfan moved in to protest, but Rama Bai surprised him too by placing some blades of grass and grains of rice on his head. She unfastened the knot of her sari end, took out two gold coins, with the impression of a distinctive Hindu goddess on one side and a strange crowned head on the other.

"What're these? British coins?" Asked Harfan.

"No," Rama Bai spoke for the first time in a slow but firm voice, "These coins were minted by Maharaja Vikramaditya Kaushal, grandfather of the late Maharaja, on the occasion of his accession to the Jhumra throne. Keep this. This'll bring you good luck and happiness."

"You know we're Muslims and our ladies don't put on the Hindu style vermilion marks." Harfan spoke haltingly.

"I know son," Rama Bai continued," I'm a mother and I know only my kind of ritual. Don't mind. You've come for the first time with your wife to a mother's abode. I thought, I must greet the ***bahu*** (bride) in my own way."

"But lady, I've nothing to do with the old regime and your religion. We're Muslims...." Harfan tried a feeble protest, but his words were lost inside his oral cavity.

Rama Bai's looks puzzled him. Her disturbed gaze oscillated alternately between Harfan and Jamilla, drops of tear hanging at the edges.

"I understand son," Rama Bai replied, "Forgive me. Please keep the coins. This'll bring you good luck."

She pressed Jamilla's palms with a message of earnest request.

"Daughter, keep this. The symbol of the Kaushal family will augur well for you. May ***Kali Mataji*** (Hindu goddess) bless you with many children! Let your husband live for a hundred years and may you be loved by him infinitely."

The old lady broke down in tears.

Jamilla, highly embarrassed, wiped her cheeks and promised that she would never part with the lucky gold coins. She didn't bother about the ritual. But something strange about this lady touched her inner chords. She looked like an eternal mother. It didn't matter if she was a Hindu.

Jamilla saluted her in customary Muslim style.

An alarm bell, however, kept on ticking inside Harfan. He was, by now, aware of the strange glimpses in Rama Bai's looks. What was she exploring? Was she trying to discover the image of Dayaram Kaushal in his face?

Her looks, Harfan wondered, weren't merely one's of love. Her eyes and words were trying to convey some hidden message. That would be too close a call, simply disastrous. His delicate cover would be at a tremendous risk. He couldn't afford to be emotional.

Harfan resolved not to venture again to this part of the palace, which harboured a killer umbilical to his past. He whispered into Jamilla's ears and turned back to the hotel.

****

Ibadat served food in the royal chamber's anteroom. Delta prawns fried in garlic sauce, tender smoked chicken nuggets; potato stuffed with minced meat, with thick gravy to match and ***tandoori rotis*** (flat bread baked in a special oven) made the savoury dinner exciting.

"She's very kind and peculiar, isn't she?" Commented Jamilla, still mystified and enchanted by Rama Bai's demeanour.

"***Bhabiji*** (sister-in-law), don't mind her queer ways. She's somewhat deranged." Commented Ibadat.

"Didn't look like one." That's all Jamilla could whisper back. It would be rather impolite for a newly wed bride to enter into an argument with a hotel cook.

"She's taken a fancy to brother Harfan." Ibadat laughed while serving the pudding, a real English one, with brown caramel topping.

"This has been specially baked by my mother, for you ***bhabiji***."

Jamilla appreciated the pudding. She hadn't tasted such a delicacy anywhere in Lahore.

"It's a pity ***bhabiji***, you're leaving tomorrow. My mother still cooks a few special dishes for the hotel. That's how we retain the old quarter of the chief ***khansama*** (cook) at ***mohalla*** (locality) Rajora. Hope you'll like to change your mind. My brother will be the happiest man, if you do reconsider." Ibadat pleaded.

"I'll keep on visiting," Jamilla replied, "I've to complete the course. And Jhumra isn't far from Lahore."

The excellent food did fill Jamilla's stomach. But the ecstasy of body and mind reminded her that the night itself had inclined on the horizon, excitingly chasing its love, the bright rouge coloured dame, daybreak. It was time for her to chase her dream. She decided to keep awake, stretching the dark hours, and keeping Harfan busy, in her own way. She must make him compensate for the impending separation.

The pleasure of the two bodies coming together, in an ecstatic search for the peak of sublime satisfaction, and pangs for not having been able to reach the peak, had warmed up her mind and body. She wanted Harfan alone, all to herself.

She stretched her left hand under the table and pinched Harfan's thigh, with a twinkle in her eyes. The signal was inviting and tempting.

Harfan led his bride to the royal chamber, once used by his father and mother. Jamilla was the angel of love, of his life and he would like her to conceive their first child in this very bed.

The wild Ramendra Kaushal had died the day he chanced to see the blue eyes of Jamilla. The ghost of his past should remain buried back in the dossiers of the FIB.

The kingdom wasn't anyway coming back to him. History created through enormous bloodshed couldn't be undone without much bigger blood baths. He was perhaps not another epochal hero to put the clock back. But he could sure make a new beginning.

Jamilla, winking at him, was history in the making. And he should thank his stars, if he could create a new identity for himself.

No harm in trying. It would be difficult for him, he understood, to break away from his bondage. The puppet Harfan was tied to many strings in the hands of too many puppeteers.

His newest identity, woven around Jamilla, he hoped, wouldn't come into conflict with his profession and his mission in Pakistan. Harfan, the spy, he hoped, could be segregated from the man just sculpted by an artist called Jamilla, with the sublime chisels of her love and imagination. He wouldn't like to endanger this pretty gift of God.

Harfan picked up Jamilla and smilingly walked up to the bed.

Chapter 25

A tiny blue diode flashed intermittently in Harfan's wristwatch.

It was an invitation to switch on his clandestine radio set. A tiny processor in the spy trans-receiver activated the diode whenever ***Behest*** wanted him to be on air for special transmission. There hadn't been many such emergency flashes and special calls from ***Behest*** so far, except for a solitary tasking on the likely Pakistani strategy at Tashkent. It was a low-key task, rather a probing one.

Harfan had browsed the surface, with Israr Sharief as his unconscious browser. The baron of industry, with linkages at the top, had indicated the likely tough bargaining by Izaz Afroz. The Kashmir issue, India's nuclear programme and readjustment of the Line of Actual Control in the Kargil sector could pose a few stumbling blocks. A vengeful person, Izaz wasn't likely to compromise with India, the country that had humiliated his father, a former minister in a princely state. Israr never tired to state that Izaz hated everything Hindu, though he was born from the womb of a low caste Hindu mother from Rajasthan.

The ambitious fortune hunter and the greatest sycophant of Pakistani politics had initiated, on his own, Pakistan's frenzied nuclear quest. The President, sensitive to adverse US reaction was averse to allocating specific budget provision for scouting the world markets by Pakistani scientists. Izaz, Israr added, had made two special trips to Tripoli and Riyadh for soliciting funding for, what he called the IBP, Islamic Bomb Project.

President Akbar Khan had even objected to Izaz's unauthorised energisation of the Inter Services Intelligence for snooping around the world market in the quest of clandestine nuclear components, materials and know-how.

Tashkent, Israr had added, wasn't going to be an easy turf. Pakistanis were promised unfurling of the crescent flag over Delhi's Red Fort. The President, a self-styled Field Marshal and an anathema to democracy had lost the trust of the Armed Forces and the people.

To top his miseries, Izaz Afroz had switched over sides and had overnight turned himself into a pseudo-angel of democracy. Unconfirmed reports, Israr indicated, were in circulation about Izaz Afroz funding some of the frenzied pro-democracy agitations in Punjab, Sind and Baluchistan.

Triple X's initial input was highly appreciated in Delhi. It had corroborated the Mission based reports and inputs from Alamgir. Delhi's calibration of the diplomatic needles at Tashkent was heavily dependant on these reports.

But tonight's diode flashes surprised Harfan. He switched on the set and established electronic protocol.

The recorded printout was crisp.

"30978. GR12. XOUTH 61008.

WPERT KMHCG OUREF SPIQW CZXYY KLHXX QOMPT RMOZZ WOULL BDFRE WNYST BPKTS LONTX UOTRS YWQQO SLRTH. EOM. 00001."

Harfan fished out, from a hidden cavity, a card size one-time pad and deciphered the message, using the key XOUTH 61008.

"Require immediate report on Operation Mardan. Is it a part of OP-Bakhtiar? Pak HQ spoke to Dacca on Mardan."

Harfan secured the set and the accessories, burnt the used cipher card in the washbasin, drained the ashes and settled down in front of the fireplace with a large whisky.

Delhi's first formal request intrigued Harfan. The ISI and the GHQ had scripted Operation Bakhtiar in tandem with the Special Services Group, as a multi-layered corollary to Operation Gibraltar and Operation Grand Slam. It was conceived as a strategic mixture of limited frontal and long-term deep penetration guerrilla warfare in the chicken neck area of Indian Bengal and the eastern Indian States of Assam and Tripura. Removed from the main arch of battle order in the western sector, Assam and Tripura offered strategic advantages to the Pakistan Army. it was a standby contingent plan for swift penetration, in the event of Indian forces knocking at the doors of Lahore and Sialkot.

The UN brokered cease-fire and the Tashkent talks had forced the establishment hawks to stash away Bakhtiar to a temporary chill-tray.

But Operation Mardan appeared to be a red herring. The usual boisterous mess birds normally babbled their hearts out in their drunken stupor and vain brawls. They too didn't react to Harfan's clever probes. His conscious and sub-conscious assets in the CMLA establishment and the GHQ hadn't indicated any fresh military venture against India.

Could it be a super-secret war game planned by the new military junta that had inherited the mantle from President Akbar?

How could Pakistan embark upon another adventure?

The White House had sounded clear signals that the Pak-US honeymoon was virtually over. Pakistan's burgeoning strategic ties with China had generated vapours of suspicion and distrust. Washington had played down President Akbar Khan's state visit with subtle diplomatic noises.

The new junta couldn't risk another war, either of the Gibraltar or Bakhtiar type.

Senior Generals in Chak Lala cantonment and Rawalpindi GHQ didn't talk in terms of another war. They talked, in hushed voices, about augmenting Pakistan's military infrastructure. That's where Israr International and its cartel partners Jung Sher Khan and Alam Khan came into the picture. They solicited the Chinese, the undercover European adventurers and rogue-CIA operators for supplementing the inventory of the starving Armed Forces. Fat slices of drug-money were re-rolled into the arms bazaar. Harfan knew well the thinly papered clandestine conduits. He himself was a major player of the team headed by Israr International.

Pakistan's butchers of democracy needed sophisticated weapons more for scaring and silencing the Pakistanis than fighting the infidel Indians. The new set of dramatis personae weren't in the best of shape for another bout of war with India.

What else could Mardan mean? Could it be a revised concept of low-key proxy war against India, in a new war theatre?

Harfan felt tempted to call Alam's Quetta number to solicit guidance. On second thoughts he aborted the idea.

Demystifying the cobwebs of Operation Mardan was his first major task. Failure would put a question mark on the career of a highly rated agent.

Harfan decided to trek the lonely furrow all by himself. The Kaushals never shied away from challenges. A job was as sacrosanct as his faith and love. He must explore the usual conduits used by Israr Sharief, for reaching the grooves of the top Generals. That alone could unearth the Mardan mystery.

The final resolution made Harfan happy. He poured another stiff drink and lighted a cigarette.

A contradictory stream started flowing upward as the whisky started sinking deep.

Was it necessary to stick his neck out? The pendulum inside oscillated nervously and advised Harfan to look beyond Delhi's brief. Why couldn't he buy a new life? Why couldn't he and Jamilla start a new life in London?

No. That was impossible. Harfan gulped the liquid, squeezed in his facial muscles and moved his head violently. A Kaushal wasn't a finicky colt to bolt the front trenches. His father didn't. Why should he?

He sure loved Jamilla. But she was a part of his cover too. Why should he succumb to the lure and charm of this young woman?

Perhaps the whisky had got into his blood. Harfan jumped out of the chair. Was he thinking of running away from reality? Had he forgotten the pledge of avenging his father's gruesome assassination?

Harfan didn't feel like finishing the drink. He threw the liquid on the dying embers. The flames leaped high for a few seconds. The momentary dance of the fire further melted the neuronal membranes, hurling Harfan into a spin. The earth below, the sky above and everything else started spinning like a churning wheel. Harfan fainted.

Kaushalya appeared first, out of the churning vortex. She stood over a pool of blood; a child clung to her breast, covered with a blood-soaked piece of cloth. An elderly person, whom he didn't recognise, Rama Bai, Ibadat and a white-skinned British guarded her flanks.

One tall young Pathan, with a pockmarked face appeared next. He brandished a sword in his right hand, blood dripping all the way from its sharp edges. He carried a huge round metal plate on his left palm, covered with a blood soaked silk bandanna. Fanged hyena laughter crackled out of his throat. He walked up to Kaushalya and with a jerk removed the bandanna cover.

Harfan could see a severed head, the brown eyeballs starkly staring at Kaushalya with pain, anger and compassion. Whose head was it?

Was it his father's head?

The ghastly scene changed to a grislier one.

Harfan suddenly found himself armed with a curved knife and chasing Rama Bai. She ran across the spice orchard and shouted at the top of her voice.

"Yes, you're Dayaram's mirror image. Who'll pay your blood debt? You're not a Muslim, you're my son."

She disappeared.

A galloping horse faded in, with the beheaded body of Dayaram Kaushal mounted on it. The horse abruptly stopped, splashing warm blood on Harfan's face, mouth and nostril.

The salty taste prompted violent nausea in him.

The headless body passed on an unsheathed sword in his hand, before he could react. King Dayaram's lifeless body suddenly slumped onto his blood soaked lap.

The dream celluloid suddenly snapped. Harfan jumped out of the sofa, switched on the lights and inspected his nightclothes. No. There was no blood anywhere.

He looked at the toilet mirror. No blood.

Yes, his upper lip was swollen, slightly scratched at the edges. He smiled. It was a parting gift from Jamilla.

He moved closer to the mirror.

Was he really a mirror image of his father? Did Rama Bai recognise him?

Harfan abandoned the idea of returning to bed. It was anyway as hot as a sand dune without Jamilla. What about these horrible footages from his past? Did he become a prisoner of history, of his past?

No. He wouldn't allow that to happen. The idea of living in history was good, but he was here, in Pakistan, to create a new history.

He made coffee, lighted a cigarette and mulled over the haunting apparitions. Did he ever think of killing Rama Bai to permanently shut one window to his peril? Did he ever think of eliminating Ibadat, the probable second window?

These thoughts might have crossed his mind as an auto-self defence mechanism. The neurones inside played their strange chess game, even in his dreams, casting an advance shadow of events, still in the womb of the future.

But what about that pockmarked face holding his father's severed head on a platter? Had it really happened? His mother had never mentioned about the grisly event.

And what nonsense was Rama Bai shouting in his dream? The old lady had betrayed her emotions. Some hidden embers must be burning in her blood that had excited her frozen emotions.

What made her greet Jamilla in that peculiar fashion?

The alarm bell kept on ringing inside Harfan's serpent brain, and the wild days peeped out of the gene bag. He must take care of the old lady. A silent liquidation wouldn't be bad!

The fleeting image of passing on the sword flashed past his mind. Yes. He owed a blood-debt to his father. His son couldn't bolt the arena without liquidating the assassins. That black memory would simply not allow him to escape to the cocooned world of Jamilla.

The dreams were real. The mirror of history wouldn't allow him to sleep in peace. The war ahead was more of a personal than a proxy war he was supposed to fight for the FIB. The war this time was on the holy soil of his birth. He must fight it and pay back the debt of blood.

****

Morning dawned and brought with it a headache and a nasty hangover. He must stop these drinking bouts, Harfan reflected. These lapses could land him in immense trouble. And Jamilla utterly detested the stench of stale alcohol and tobacco.

Breakfast wasn't the priority of the day. Harfan didn't feel like having one. The nightmarish dream still haunted him, spinning millions of webs in his clogged loom. He simply couldn't get past the tangled ghastly visions.

He lighted a cigarette and started walking towards the orchards of the Palace Hotel, along the trail to Rama Bai's huts. Some hidden force dragged him to that obscure corner. After the initial struggle he let his steps follow their natural rhythm.

What was happening to him? Why was he drowning himself in the quagmire of his own memory? Was he a prisoner of his dreams? Could he afford to live in the past? At this rate, Harfan reasoned, he was sure to face a crippling crash, if he just kept on looking at the rear view mirror and ignored the events rushing past him. No. He couldn't allow this to happen. The rear-view mirror was necessary, for smooth piloting ahead. But he wasn't surely a creature of fossilised memories.

Harfan's confused rumination and scattered concentration was broken by the sounds of quick footsteps behind him. He turned around.

Ibadat, Harfan noticed, slowed down his pace with a deliberate effort, like a snail drawing its snout in. What was he anxious about? Was he watching his movements, under orders from Alam, or the Pakistani intelligence?

"***Salaam*** Ibadat sahib," Harfan wished him with contrived warmth in his voice, "Taking a stroll, good for digestion!"

"***Walekum janab***," Ibadat replied nervously, "I wanted to catch up with you. Thought you may like to have a detailed conducted tour of the palace compound."

Did Ibadat have a brief to keep him away from Rama Bai? Did the brief come from Delhi, or Alam?

Harfan concealed his anxiety.

"An interesting place, isn't it?" He graciously allowed Ibadat to maintain his tenuous cover. He had no doubt that, this son of the former royal cook, was an integral part of Delhi's networking in Pakistan.

"You're so correct sir," Ibadat continued, "Jhumra and the surrounding areas of the Chenub basin are exquisitely charming."

"So interesting! Must give me company for hiking in the hill tracts and the riverine forests, one of these days."

Harfan suddenly turned his gaze towards the palace ramparts and pointed his fingers at the rear battlements.

"Where's the location of the royal worship room?" He floored Ibadat with an unexpected question.

"It was," Ibadat responded after few moments of poignant silence, "In the inner courtyard of the palace, next to the living quarters of the queen."

"Any photo gallery of the former royal family?"

"No idea. The worship room has become a part of the hotel stores and the deity has been shifted to Rama Bai's shack. The new rulers were kind enough to give this much of a concession to the old lady."

Ibadat, though floored by Harfan's strange question, maintained a straight face. He was given to understand that Alam's new apprentice was an important person. He was under orders to assist and shield him. The son of the former king, his father's benefactor, was back in Pakistan on a special mission. But, why was he asking such questions? He didn't expect Harfan to develop emotional complications over old memories.

Rama Bai was a living minefield, which shouldn't be traversed by Harfan. She could inadvertently rekindle a major fire inside the emotionally charged adventurer.

The old lady, they talked about, was busy sweeping her courtyard amidst a small cloud of dust. She stopped momentarily and sprinkled water around.

"Let's avoid the dust. It's not good for you." Ibadat nudged at Harfan's elbow.

"What's the hurry? The dust will settle down soon."

Harfan walked down to Rama Bai and startled her by asking, "Are you from the old royal days?"

Rama Bai didn't reply. She silently disappeared inside a hut and gently closed the door behind her. Harfan followed and peeped in. He recoiled at the first glance.

Bright daylight, forcing its way through the fine marble lattice had lighted up the smoky room. Rama Bai was seated before a granite statue of the Hindu goddess ***Kali***, with finely carved stone human skulls arranged like a garland around the neck. Her private parts were covered with a girdle of matching human hands, which hung from the waist.

By God! Was this the family deity that his mother used to talk about!

Should he ask about the existence of any old painting of the former king and queen?

"Anything else?" Rama Bai opened the door and spoke for the first time.

"No. Thanks. I'm just curious."

"I know nothing about the royal family." Rama Bai picked up a goat kid on her lap and turned towards the great Banyan tree.

"Listen..."

Harfan couldn't finish what he had intended to say. Ibadat intervened.

"Let's move on. I'll show you the ***Jung Tikri*** (war hillock)."

"What's that?"

"That's where the former king had fought his last hopeless battle with the tribal invaders."

Ibadat led Harfan away from the old lady, who was apparently busy caressing the all white goat-kid.

"Is that so?" Harfan felt the heat of anxiety building up inside of him.

Ibadat led the way, through waist high shrubs and bushes, high above the slopes, towards a raised ground. Few dilapidated stone and baked brick structures were still fighting a losing battle against the advancing nature that covered them up with creepers and tall grass.

"These were the advance battle positions of the king's army, the main defence parameters of the palace. The Kaushal kings had fought many battles from these ramparts, their own battles, and some for the British masters....

"Look down below. Can you see the broken stone and cement walkways, lost in river sands?"

"Yes."

"The river, even ten years back, used to flow below these ramparts and the galleys and boats of the former kings used to berth there."

"Where has the river gone?"

"They've raised a dam upstream. It's now navigable only in monsoon." Ibadat replied and sat on a broad stone covered with dried up moss.

Harfan followed him silently, lighted a cigarette and inhaled a few eager puffs before he spoke.

"Tell me more about the king, his queen and his people."

Ibadat spoke, in a low lingering tone. Harfan failed to keep count of time. But the descending darkness and the sudden wing fluttering of a flock of nesting peacocks and their shrill homecoming calls brought him back to the present surroundings.

"Thanks for the fascinating conducted tour." Harfan stood up and started climbing down the broken track.

"You must tell me more." He added.

"There are more stories, the stories of the last war the king had so valiantly fought." Ibadat followed Harfan.

"Some other day then." Harfan started descending the rough slopes of the hillock.

His mind had flown out of his body cage, following the misty contours of his parents, painted by Ibadat's sedative narration.

No. He couldn't run away from this place. Some rabid Niazi tribal had killed his father, in an unfair battle and a brave cook saved his mother. He himself owed his life, probably to Rama Bai and Ibadat's father. He had lots of people to pay back.

Chance visit to the family battleground, infused new energy in Harfan. Was it purely a chance visit? Was it planned by Delhi, or as they said back in India, ordained by the super-bosses? Whatever it was, the unravelling of some mysteries of the Kaushal kings added a new meaning to his mission in Pakistan. The vague personal stake had taken a concrete shape. He must fight. He wasn't a mere spy. He was an avenger.

The sweetest revenge would perhaps be to work for the destruction of Pakistan, in his own way, with the help and assistance of Delhi. The evil that killed his father must be punished. He must fight valiantly and tactfully, his personal secret wars against Pakistan.

Harfan shelved the idea of deserting his mission. The cover given by Delhi was unique and he thanked his FIB friends, back in Delhi for relocating him at Jhumra.

Jamilla, his dream, could wait. He loved her, was ready to turn the world around to protect her. But he would, under no circumstances, abandon his mission. He must work out a synthesis, between his love and his war.

"Mind coming in for some coffee?" Asked Ibadat, as they approached the hotel.

"I wouldn't mind some."

Harfan perched himself on a couch and Ibadat followed with a pot of coffee.

"Coffee please." He poured the brew, casting a sideways look at Harfan's stiff facial muscles. A brief smile crossed his eyes and face. The visit to the ramparts had worked as a tonic. He could see the taut muscles on Harfan's face and the jaws grinding against his teeth.

Harfan kept on sipping the coffee, but his gaze was lost in a piece of sky, visible through the window. The resolve to fight the secret wars kept on generating steam inside. He lighted another cigarette, thanked Ibadat and slowly walked out. His love and his war were beckoning him. The war had just begun, Harfan told himself loudly. The mute words bounced violently inside his cortices. The stiff climb to his pilgrimage at Jhumra had just started.

Why look back? Ahoy! The enemy was astern.

Chapter 26

The journey to Islamabad, along the historic Grand Trunk Road, built by Sher Shah Suri, the upstart Afghan fortune hunter, who had snatched away, albeit temporarily, dame luck from the Great Mughals, took Harfan about four hours. He himself was on a hunting mission, hunting out a likely target in the Pakistan Army for eliciting vital intelligence on Operation Mardan.

Hotel Khyber, next to the railway station, off Shahrah-e-Islamabad, a posh upcoming neighbourhood was a small joint with moderate charges. Harfan checked in there. It offered two distinct attractions.

Anar Begum, a queen bee in Israr's business operations, who usually warmed the beds of the top-cats in the armed forces, lived just 3 blocks away.

And the Defence Supply Corps office, which was headed by Brigadier Habibullah, could be reached in ten minutes.

Habibullah epitomised the success story of the sub-continental elite. A successful harvester of the Pakistan Army, he had harvested millions in the name of ***Allah*** and ***kafir*** India. ***Allah*** was the ultimate acid that purified the dirtiest of misdeeds and ***kafir*** India was the glue that kept together the building chips of Pakistan.

He boasted of a posh palace at 6th street, Markaz Ramna 7, off Fazlul Haq Road, a Central London apartment, 5000 acres of farmland at Nurpur, off Shahiwal and a couple of millions in green bills in the Swiss vaults. It was rumoured that his numbered Swiss account was no slimmer than $200 million. Besides his paltry salary and a 3% cut in all defence deals, Brigadier Habibullah, earned on the side, what was known as ***shakarkandi***, sugar money; money earned from peddling refined brown sugar.

An integral part of the drug cartel controlled by the five powerful Corps Commanders, Habibullah acted as a conduit to the Lahore and Karachi based dons, who smuggled out consignments of opium and refined heroin, processed in Afghanistan and the Frontier Provinces. India, a porous transit territory, was used by his mafia-cousins on either side of the border, for forward trading with European and American destinations. A major share was diverted to the distant poor cousins in Africa.

Habibullah was an important cog in this mighty machine, controlled by his senior bosses, feudal lords and the powerful underworld mafia. His forward and backward linkages ended with a few dreaded names in the drug cartel. But he wasn't aware of the identities of the hallowed personalities in India, who guided the operations under cover of their exalted political offices.

Habibullah didn't bother about it too. A queer military officer without any political ambition, he had opted for the soft role of a clever facilitator. He greased the tarmacs up and down and plundered the coffers of the fabled forty thieves. A true Aladdin he was.

Only once, way before the 1965 hostilities, he chanced to meet Raghu Chawla, a hyped Indian journalist, at an exclusive dinner. A forward paw of the biggest Indian drug-lord, Raghu was on a sponsored visit to Pakistan to cover the much-touted elections to the basic democratic institutions, a brain wave of Field Marshal Akbar Khan. His visit was approved at the highest level, on a rare recommendation from Pakistan's High Commissioner in Delhi. Ram Karan Prasad, a minister in Amritlal's cabinet had personally spoken to the Chief of the Mission.

Brigadier Habibullah had a minor brush with Ram Karan too, at a diplomatic gathering at Rawalpindi. The Indian minister was in the Pak capital, heading a delegation to the UN sponsored conference on Empowerment of Women. Ram Karan's friends in Pakistan were mighty powerful. They were everywhere, in the armed forces, political structure and the shady underworld. Red carpets were rolled out for him and the cutest socialite, Begum Anar chaperoned him in and out of the conference halls and social evenings. A true friend of Muslims and leader of the oppressed and depressed classes, his visit had triggered off front-page banners in government controlled Pakistani dailies. It was a unique exercise in Confidence Building Measure.

Habibullah didn't care for confidence building or demolishing measures. The big bosses lived above cloud nine and were beyond the reach of warfront bullets. They never faced the stinking cadavers of soldiers. From their vantage position, like high priests around the sacrificial fire, they offered human blood and tissues to the altars of rabid nationalism, fermented in the cauldrons of hatred and religious bigotry. They played political soccer with human skulls. Habibullah and his breed believed in the Hindu dictum: ***Vasudhaiba Kutumbakam***–all creatures inhabiting the planet were friends. Sages anonymous had sung this eternal message thousands of years before the Son of Man preached the message of love and redemption.

Habibullah demanded and grabbed a flat cut of 3% in all major defence purchases. In army conclaves and social circuits he wasn't unnecessarily known as the 'three percentage Habib'. He didn't care for the appellatives. What mattered at the end of the day was the glittering dough. He believed in universal happiness, and shared the extra crumbs strictly according to the ***Hadis*** rules; to each one according to the sharpness of his teeth. The ***Allah*** was no exception. He was liberal in doling out ***zakat*** (charity) to the needy, during Ramadan festival.

Known for his well cushioned catty sense of survival, Habibullah cajoled and humoured people to achieve what he wanted, and what he felt was his rightful claim. The richest creation of the ***Allah,*** according to him, was the circular golden wheel called money, his first love, ***sikka.***

His next preference was ***sharab*** (wine) and ***shabab***, fair looking experienced women. No deal or contract could be finalised without fattening Habibullah's pocket and warming up his bed with a '***hum bister***' (bed partner) of his choice.

Israr Sharief had discovered Begum Anar, a renowned ***ghazal*** (style of music) singer and a bit of film actress, during one of the international conferences of the Pakistan Export Promotion Council. Israr, a devout Muslim, didn't consider the idea of hiring Anar's services as an act of blasphemy. In war and business, such innocuous contamination was permissible. It was nothing but a kind of capital investment. In any case he wasn't warming up his own bed with Begum Anar's biological heat.

Harfan's offer of another liaison job, therefore, didn't surprise Anar. Israr was a respectable client. No problem, she would be available for his services, but for the usual fees. Each successful engagement would cost Rs. 50,000, and for an aborted deal, her compensation package would be Rs. 20,000.

"This job's different," Harfan briefed Begum Anar, who was busy choosing the right eye-shade for her evening engagement," Our business depends a lot on this information."

"What's the big deal?"

The Begum threw the words out casually as she exhaled clouds of smoke. She didn't think any job was unachievable, if it concerned male pigs, born out of a mother's womb. She was fond of boasting scornfully that, so far, no male, born out of nonsensical and imaginary Immaculate Conception dared to ignore her in bed.

"What's your target? For how many nights?" The Begum talked in a straight professional voice.

"You see," Harfan introduced the subject hesitatingly, "Our army has adopted a new war game, Operation Mardan. They'll require plenty of new defence supplies from abroad. Israr wants to bag the contract. Get me the details of Mardan. The Brigadier, I'm told, has full knowledge, as he had visited China recently, as a member of the Mardan planning team."

"It's a very tall order and a risky one." Pouted the Begum, "How much are you offering?"

"The usual fees."

"No dear." The lady spoke with a tone of finality and continued stroking her cheeks with a sable brush.

"The job's risky, will cost you Rs. 100,000 straight."

"It's pretty high." Harfan pleaded helplessness.

"Let's call off the deal," Begum Anar dismissed the meeting, "This Habib bugger is a bull, will do it for a minimum of five times and leave me half dead. And I've other engagements. The younger Sharief, Nawab sahib, has an assignment for me. He's paying one grand."

"Who is the target?"

"Don't bother. These're trade secrets. Each bit of additional information would cost you an amount equivalent to the original contract money."

"Okay, you get the money, but only after completion of the job. We must get the contract of supplying 100,000 pieces of snow boots, and 100,000 pieces of fur-lined parkas, in addition to the Mardan details." Harfan argued.

"Getting the contract is your headache. My job is facilitation. For Mardan you've to cough out extra dough."

"Fine. Contact me in my hotel, after you're through with the Brigadier." Harfan left after paying the customary advance.

That was Anar's style. This was by way of compensation. After all, she was required to take the trouble of using her body, intellect and other skills she had acquired in seducing men, and making them breach the banks of their senses and spill out, what they were oath bound to protect.

After two nights of successful fishing Begum Anar reported back to Harfan.

His company would land the deal, provided Israr transferred Habib's share to his Swiss account, well in advance. This was a fat contract involving 100 million-dollars worth of German small weapons and Swedish snow boots and high altitude clothing.

The Mardan story, Anar declared with an animated pout, had nothing to do with another war. Pakistani armed forces weren't capable of fighting another war so soon. In fact, they would require another five years to match up to India's military inventory. Hectic searches were, therefore, on.

Izaz Afroz and General Arif Khan, during one of their ***shikar*** (hunting campaign) at Larkana had worked out a strategy to bleed India white. The Chief of Army Staff had embarked upon a new war strategy. It was a diabolical game, taking the proxy war inside India's inner belly and bleeding her to a slow death.

He had drummed up support from the Inter Services Intelligence and the Special Services Group (SSG). Habibullah's visit to Peking, Anar disclosed, was partly related to Mardan. China had blessed the new strategy in an exclusive meeting between the Deputy Chief of the PLA and Izaz Afroz. The Special Service Group, besides the Pakistan Intelligence Bureau and the Inter Services Intelligence were working in tandem with the Chinese State Security Bureau. They had set up shops in East Pakistan for training and arming India's tribal insurgents.

Begum Anar had a long story to tell over three hours of debriefing. It was a fascinating story, impugning India's internal security. Operation Mardan, in simple tongue, was a top-secret plan to support, sustain and promote ethnic insurgency in India. India, she hoped would be made to pay for the losses suffered by Pakistan in the last war.

"Thanks Begum," Harfan counted the money, Rs. 1,50,000 in crisp bills and asked, "Would you like to add anything?"

Anar counted the bills and settled for a cigarette.

"Oh yes. I had forgotten a vital point. The ISI has hired the services of some PFLP (People's Front for the Liberation of Palestine) trainers to train a specialised group of commandos for highly sensitive operations inside India."

"Any details?"

"Habib wasn't forthcoming. These PFLP experts specialise in target killing and planned use of explosive devices."

"What kind of target?"

"You're an impossible person Mian Harfan. Target killing could mean an important person or an unsuspecting group of persons."

"Thanks Anar. I may have another assignment for you soon."

"You're welcome."

Harfan Bukhari's blind hunting had produced precious results. He composed a concise cipher and raised the emergency call sign ***Zam Zam***. Operation Mardan, as the ciphers exchanged between Rawalpindi and Dacca, indicated a new strategic thrust against India's Northeast. The smouldering tribal belt, he elaborated, was likely to be on fire. Ethnic insurgency was about to explode with catastrophic bangs. The PFLP factor, he mentioned, would require deeper probes inside Pakistan and in the middle-east stations.

A major task well concluded, he slept well and the next morning took a train to Lahore. Israr allowed him a short break. The just married young executive deserved it.

The deal clinched by Anar Begum and Harfan, however, infuriated Nawab Sharief, Israr's celebrated half-brother. Anar wasn't his private property. But his advance investment of rupees one million in the private account of General Hyder Bux, the Inter Services Intelligence Chief wasn't gift wrapped with Anar. He was slightly late in understanding that Pakistan's war and drug lords were equally hungry for live flesh as they were for cash and golden liquid.

He wasn't pleased to be outsmarted by a puny ***muhajir*** executive. Nawab traced Harfan back to Zahoor Chaudry's cove.

"You've put your hands in the snake pit." Nawab hissed on the phone.

"I don't follow you Nawab sahib." Replied Harfan.

"Anar is my territory, you've to pay dearly for the intrusion."

"Sir," Replied Harfan politely, "A public lady is common property. We're in business. Sometimes you win, sometimes we."

"I never lose. Tell brother Israr. And be ready to pay for it." He banged the phone down.

Israr didn't lose his shirt. Nawab thundered frighteningly but rained miserly, he explained.

"Don't panic. I'll tackle him."

"But he sounded vicious."

"I'll speak to ***abbajan*** (father). And don't forget that we've warmed the pocket of the Principal Staff Officer, Lt. General Sarfaraz. He's a better shield."

"I hope he won't go for my jugular."

"It's better you count your steps. Brother Nawab normally stabs from the back. Anyway, I am there to protect you. Breathe easy and get ready for the trip abroad."

Israr advised Harfan to prepare for the business trip abroad for negotiating with the German and Swedish companies. He could take his bride along. The presence of a charming woman often helped in clinching tricky business deals. Jamilla deserved the treat. The just clinched deal was sure to make Israr International richer by rupees fifty million and Harfan was entitled to 2% of the gross profits.

****

The cipher that Triple X had transmitted after debriefing Begum Anar shook Delhi out of its usual stupor. His first major report, with devastating implications rattled Dutta and Nampoothiri. Operation Mardan was indeed a bombshell.

"Text Begins," The message continued, "Mardan is a multi-layered intelligence and military concept, crafted by Izaz Afroz, the ISI and the GHQ, in tandem with the Chinese State Security Bureau. It has three segments; each to be handled by designated groups....

"Part one: The pro-democracy movement in East Pakistan is rated as an Indian intelligence operation. The GSO-1 (ML-3), which oversees military and intelligence operations, has impeccable proof of Indian linkages with Sheikh Jainal. The junta intends to smother the movement....

"Part two: (1): ISI, SSG and DMI are fully involved in the Lushai Hills insurgency. Camps set up in Chittagong Hill Tracts for training them. The rebel leaders have met the ISI and the Chinese State Security Bureau officials in Dacca...

(2): China is training Naga rebels at Kunming camps. Expect two groups of 500 each leaving this winter. Naga Liaison Office functions at Bara Mugh Bazar, Dacca. Expect a Naga gang of 400 reaching Pakistan in December, for lifting weapons, diverted from CIA's Vietnam inventory....

(3): Four leaders of Garo and Khasi Hills are in Dacca for consultations. Two of them, Provost and Wynndale are planning insurgency there as well....

"Part three: The ISI has hired PFLP experts to train special commando groups for target killing in India. The ISI has floated front organisations: Markaz-ul-Farhan, Inquilabi Mujaheedin, Quami Fidayeen etc. to foment communal carnage in India. The Markaz have plans for assassination of important Indian leaders. EOM."

"What do you make out of this jumbo message?" Asked Rabindra Narayan Dutta.

"There's an avalanche of information. Our Operation Mardan intercept has turned out to be a mine field." Replied Nampoothiri.

"Requires verification. Check with Alam." Remarked Dutta.

"Alam, yes. But I think we should seek corroboration from Northeast stations." Nampoothiri suggested.

"Do we inform the Prime Minister?"

"We should. He should be well armed before the Tashkent conclave. Operation Mardan is a spin off from the just concluded war. Pakistan is about to embark on a different kind of war, more bloody, more painful than Bakhtiar." Nampoothiri favoured immediate consultations with the Prime Minister.

"I agree. But I'm more worried about the Garo-Khasi and Lushai Hills. We must prevent Pakistan from cutting off the Brahmaputra Valley. That'll give tremendous strategic advantage to China and Pakistan. You take care of this contingency."

Dutta left the fine-tuning of the job to Nampoothiri.

"It's a difficult job sir." Nampoothiri submitted, "We can't keep the Northeast by mere fire fighting action. It's high time the nation takes care of its fault lines."

"I agree. But you and I are basically fire fighters for the policy makers. Let's do the job that we're supposed to do well. And ask our stations in Egypt, Lebanon and Syria to confirm the PFLP involvement with the ISI."

Alamgir's follow up cipher, transmitted through Kabul confirmed, in essence, the Triple X reports. A subterranean movement, he added, was indeed gaining ground against the ailing Pakistani President. His future would be decided by the Tashkent outcome. Izaz Afroz was busy maneuvering the derailment of the USSR hosted talks.

A high level Pak delegation, headed by Afroz had indeed recently visited Peking. The delegation included the Deputy Chief of the Misc. (iii) section of the ISI, which worked directly under GSO-1 (ML-4), of the Department of Martial Law Affairs.

Alam's message was silent about the PFLP factor.

Triple X, Alamgir conveyed, was likely to be out of the host country, in connection with his company's business. Someone could debrief him on Mardan and related issues, in London, his transit lap to Germany and Sweden. Triple X would call London River Channel, for confirmation of a safe rendezvous

Alamgir hurled another bombshell. His friends in the Pakistan Intelligence Bureau had indicated presence of a deep-entrenched mole, somewhere at the top of the Indian government. His nom-de-plume, the cipher added, could be ***Aftab.*** The President's secretariat in Rawalpindi was enjoying a running commentary on Delhi's strategic thinking.

The two ciphers, on the eve of Jung Bahadur's Tashkent visit, bolstered up the bag of tricks of the Indian policy makers. Far ends of the spectrum appeared more transparent and the Prime Minister was well briefed about the long-term strategic goals of Pakistan and its allies in Washington and Peking.

The Prime Minister was, however, more concerned over the suspected compromise of ***Operation Meghna,*** India's deep penetration forward intelligence thrust in East Pakistan. The Bengali sub-nationalist movement had started gathering momentum. But arrest of Delhi's Lotus, Sheikh Jainal was a sure indicator of leakage from the top. Someone was singing pretty in Rawalpindi's ears.

"What do we do with ***Meghna*** ?" The PM asked Dutta in an exclusive pre-Tashkent briefing session.

"Sir," The veteran spy master spoke in a conspiratorial tone, "Pakistan is sure in the know of our involvement with the brewing movement of Sheikh Jainal. We suspect leakage by ***Aftab,*** Pakistan's intelligence asset in Delhi."

"Fine. But tell me more about him. Who is he?"

"Sorry sir," Dutta conceded defeat," We're yet to identify the mole. We need more time."

"Your being sorry isn't good enough. You felt equally sorry when a deep-seated mole leaked out my Cabinet meeting proceedings. It's time you get your act together Dutta."

"I'm sorry sir. We'll put our best foot forward, be rest assured."

"I'll like to review your major operations after Tashkent. Tell your Calcutta friends to go slow on ***Meghna,*** till my return from the USSR." Ordered Jung Bahadur.

"What do we do with the pro-Russian Communist groups? They're overlapping our ***Meghna*** initiatives. You may like to brief Moscow."

"I understand the Russian strategy. They want to control the Bengali nationalist movement in East Pakistan. You have to thwart their pincer attack. I don't want another super power to buzz on my back." Replied Jung Bahadur.

"We've another problem. The split in our communist movement has generated pro-Chinese extremist fervour in a small vocal section. They're active on Indo-Pakistan borders, in northern West-Bengal. I suspect Pakistan's involvement." Dutta referred to the simmering communist extremist movement along a thin strip on the Indo-Pakistan border.

"The Chinese can't be far behind the Russians," Jung Bahadur spoke rhetorically, "Nurse ***Meghna*** carefully. The seeds we sow today will bear excellent fruits tomorrow. The Bengalis and the Punjabis can't live together. The history of the last fifteen years bears ample evidence to prove that."

"Yes sir. The leaders in the West are in no mood to accommodate the Bengalis of East Pakistan. "

"That's their Achilles' heel, target these fault lines."

Jung Bahadur yielded another feeble smile and wished his intelligence chief good night. Operation ***Meghna*** was close to his heart. He, as the minister for interior affairs had initiated the process of targeting the nationalist Bengali leaders in East Pakistan. Sheikh Jainal had responded well to the intricate intelligence operations of Delhi. It was a proxy-offensive to keep Pakistan busy in the eastern front as a countervailing measure to Pakistan's involvement with the rebellious ethnic tribals of the northeastern phalanx of India.

Jung Bahadur drummed his fingers on the tabletop and took a mental note of the priority task of accelerating Operation ***Meghna*** after his return from Tashkent.

Chapter 27

Operation Triple X's first major communication alarmed Nampoothiri more than it pleased him. The greenhorn resident agent must have had calibrated a sensitive target at the top and hit the bull's eye. Was it accidental or deliberate?

Rabindra Narayan Dutta had both agreed and differed with his deputy. Hitting the bull's eye wasn't the eighth wonder in the intelligence trade. Even an amateur could hurl an arrow and the law of averages could crown him a victor.

"I'm keen on a firsthand debriefing of Triple X." Dutta told Nampoothiri.

"Alamgir is there. We can trust him."

"No problem with Alam, Balu," The seasoned spymaster continued in his usual soft voice, "I think we've planted XXX as a long-term agent, with an independent agenda. He's not the type to submit to another overbearing intermediary."

"What's bugging you sir?"

"I'm keen to know what tradecraft Triple X has used to achieve such precise penetration. Did he use a short fuse to get to the core? Doesn't his approach smack of recklessness? Such temptations aren't uncommon even in seasoned agents."

"Do you want a direct debriefing by us?"

"Yes Balu. Don't leave him at Alamgir's mercy. I've better ideas for XXX. Alam has been in Pakistan too long. Don't you think he has sprouted innumerable shoots like an ancient Banyan tree? It's but natural. Develop an independent agenda for Harfan."

Nampoothiri silently reflected on the small crisp sentences of Dutta. The old man often displayed a prophetic insight. He couldn't be ignored.

Yes. The chemistry of the message from Triple X contained some salts of conscious revelations by the root source. It wasn't a sub-conscious or unconscious leakage. The chief, he appreciated, reasonably wanted to have clear pictures of forward and backward linkages of the chain established by Harfan Bukhari.

Perhaps the new-babe hadn't taken a one-way jump from the precipice, just to satisfy his bosses in Delhi. The desperate exhibitionist as he was, Harfan could as well have done that. And, as the boss said, it wouldn't be prudent to direct Alamgir to intercede. He shouldn't have direct access to the intricacies of tradecraft adopted by Triple X.

Jiwan Bahutule alias Alamgir was Nampoothiri's personal creation. He had developed the talent all by himself with assistance from Maulana Rizwan.

This unique mole inside Pakistan had developed excellent covers and had penetrated deep inside the Pakistani establishment. Alam was assigned the task of directing the operations of a few Double X talents. As a coordinator of the Triple X talent, Harfan Bukhari, he was supposed to keep a discreet watch on his activities too. That was but natural.

But Dutta, the wizard of Indian intelligence wasn't in the habit of making casual comments on serious business of agent operations in hostile territories. Was he thinking in terms of creating a second Alam out of the Triple X talent?

Nampoothiri partially accommodated the suggestion of his boss and called in Amrita Bhalla to dictate a small note on the probable new guidelines that he would like to share with Harfan during their meeting in London.

London, the River Channel in FIB lingo, was a neutral rendezvous for the cold-war spymasters. Delhi too favoured the jaunt for briefing and debriefing ultra-sensitive agents operating in Pakistan and China. The hotbed of international intrigue was, therefore, the natural choice for establishing direct contact with Operation Triple X.

That's how Dhiren Bhagat landed up in London, as an appendage to Balachandran Nampoothiri. Being the case officer he was considered the best litmus to perceive and record attitudinal changes in the sensitive agent.

Daylong wait in an apartment, off the busy junction of Kensington High Street and Holland Road, however, drilled in pounds of boredom into Bhagat's patience. Rented by the High Commission based FIB station chief, as a safe house, the apartment was ostensively occupied by a non-diplomatic India based employee. For operational reasons Bhagat was alone today, expecting a call from Harfan Bukhari.

The mellow chime of the phone around 6 p.m. interrupted Bhagat's slumber.

"Hello, 473-2207? Is it Cashmere Carpets?" Harfan asked hesitatingly.

"Yes."

"Can you show me some exotic varieties?"

"Oh yes! We hold special Cashmere stock, just flown in from Srinagar." Bhagat shared the pre-set code.

"When can I see it? I require both woollen and silk carpets." Harfan replied.

"We're next to The Mother's Recipe, close to the community housing estate, about three furlongs from the tube station."

"Can you arrange a preview tomorrow this time flat? Is it okay with you?" Harfan asked.

"Sure. See you tomorrow."

Thank god! The bloke had finally called.

Bhagat hailed a cab and enjoyed an escalator ride to Nampoothiri's tenth floor Hotel Wilson Plaza room, a small affair and two blocks due south of the Harrods. His orders were specific, no telephonic contact. Bhagat played by the rules. Nampoothiri had reasons to play cautious.

He was no novice to the complicated love-hate relationship between

India and Great Britain and the paranoiac policy perceptions of the Foreign Office mandarins in London.

India, though not rated Red, was rouge enough to attract attention of the MI6. The monitoring of suspected Indian intelligence officers on British soil was also prompted by the cold war compulsions. Delhi had adopted an orbit, closer to Moscow, rather than London and Washington.

The Indian High Commission was under selective electronic and human surveillance of the MI6, the external intelligence outfit of Her Majesty's Government. The Indo-Pak war and the Soviet initiative to broker the peace talks hadn't pleased the British Foreign Office. The Westminster had earlier brokered fractured peace talks in the Kachhch skirmish, between India and Pakistan and expected Delhi to kowtow their line in Kashmir too.

"What's your impression?" Nampoothiri asked Bhagat.

"He sounded intimate and observed the code-protocol immaculately."

"You think it's safe to see him! Suppose he's trailed by the High Commission based ISI sleuths!"

"I don't think he has come under cloud."

"He is engaged in a highly competitive business of arms supply to the Pak army. His corporate rivals may trail him."

Nampoothiri, the veteran sleuth wanted to play it by the book.

"I see no problem sir. Let's adopt the usual counter surveillance measures. You take a round about route and walk down the last two furlongs."

Bhagat suggested another copybook recipe for shaking off any possible shadow mounted by the ISI and Israr's business competitors.

"Okay. Expect me there in time. Sanitise the room and activate the recording devices. Don't follow me. Take a tube."

Nampoothiri gave a few more security instructions and approved the rendezvous.

Understandably, he took extra precautions in moving to the location of the rendezvous. He rented an old Bentley and drove around a few busy shopping malls before taking the motorway to the Iona Terrace safe house, off Kensington High and Holland. He left the car at a pay parking lot and walked down two blocks.

Bhagat did some shopping at the Mother's Recipe eating joint and idled out the spare time by pretending to watch a cricket match being played at a nearby school ground.

Harfan was sighted after good fifteen minutes. Bhagat refused to recognise the sensitive agent. He surveyed the ambience with great care and was convinced that his contact-man was uncontaminated. He took two rounds of the apartment block to make sure that the safe house wasn't under observation of the unfriendly agencies and entered the designated den after good ten minutes of entry by Harfan Bukhari, the Triple X agent of the FIB.

The debriefing of Harfan, as planned by Nampoothiri, was as detailed as the examination of microbes under an X-ray microscope. It encompassed all the key features of his assignment, starting from the day he crossed over to Nagar Parkar to the tradecraft mechanism that he had adopted to procure the Mardan information.

"What about Irfan? Are you in touch with him?" Nampoothiri asked.

"No. Not in touch since he helped me with the lodging in Azam guesthouse."

"I believe he's left the job and joined a Sufi ***dargah*** as a ***khidmatgar*** (volunteer). Has he embraced Islam?"

"It's possible. His wife is a Muslim. "Harfan didn't understand why Nampoothiri should be worried about Irfan changing his religion and a spiritual life.

"Hope he won't spill the beans!"

"Better ask your men in Karachi. I've no idea."

Nampoothiri made a mental note. Alam should be tasked to permanently silence Irfan. He had over lived his utility as a local talent spotter. He knew too much. Only death could ensure his final silence.

"You should not have jumped into a marriage so soon," Commented Nampoothiri, "What was the hurry?"

"It gives me an excellent cover. Her father is well connected and respected in the military circles. Alam must have had consultations with you."

"You brought tremendous pressure on us. I feel you should've marked your time. There was no reason to rush into this marriage." Nampoothiri explained that he should've allowed room for more acclimatisation.

"You're missing the positive side of the story." Harfan reiterated.

"Hope your vibes with Alamgir are okay?" Nampoothiri changed the topic.

"A fascinating man. Full of himself..."

Harfan avoided debating the issue. He hated Alamgir. Perhaps one of these days they would clash. This intermediate wheel was superfluous. A spy, as he understood, couldn't afford to be polygamous, being handled and fondled by several masters. Alamgir, behind the facade of friendly patronisation, often irritated Harfan. Delhi didn't acquaint him with the training to enjoying the insufferable rape of his conscience.

"Hope you don't keep on hopping from bed to bed." Nampoothiri cautioned the agent.

"What makes you feel that? Don't you believe in evolution?" Harfan shot back, "I love Jamilla. I've powerful relatives having access to important business houses and top military bosses. Zahoor Chaudry's name sells well in the market crowd."

Nampoothiri changed tracks. Harfan's reaction to his opening remarks convinced him that Triple X loved his wife and wasn't callous about his cover. The fellow was dedicated, by all means.

"Is Anar Begum a safe tool of the trade?" Nampoothiri hurled a drilling question while debriefing him on the tradecraft mechanism Triple X had used for collecting materials for his last cipher.

"Well! She's a recognised business facilitator, as honest as a bread earning whore can be," Harfan shrugged wantonly, "Your query was on Operation Mardan and she was the most convenient tool to unscrew Brigadier Habibullah's nuts and bolts." Harfan's witty reply amused Nampoothiri.

"Can't Habibullah be recruited as a steady contact?"

"The only thing steady about him is his bag full of money. His hunger is bottomless. It's better to use dolls like Begum Anar. That way things work out cheaper." Harfan suggested his diagnosis in lucid language.

"Suppose we agree to pay him regularly?"

"I'm not in direct and conscious contact with him. It's too early to make such an attempt. Habibullah aspires to put more stars on his pips, and in Pakistan corruption isn't a stigma. He might not dislike the idea of sleeping with beauties, but I'm sure, he won't welcome any direct contact with an Indian intelligence agent."

"You mean he has no contact with any Indian? Just now you elaborated his contact with the drug Mafia."

"Drug peddling is part of the service ethics of the Pakistani armed forces. It's no crime. As for the Indian end I suggest you better take care of Ram Karan's cartel, I mean my former boss's cartel."

Harfan's clarity impressed Nampoothiri. The agent, a tamed tornado was shaping up well.

"You mean Ram Karan is involved with the Pakistani drug cartel?"

"You should know better. You're the master."

"How sure are you about the ISI front organisations? What's their charter?"

"The information is correct. The PFLP training camp has been located at Isha Khel, in the NWFP. The ISI has started two training centres at Mian Khel and Matti near Peshawar and one at Muridke, near Lahore. The talents, called ***mujahids*** (revolutionaries), are recruited from ***madrasas*** and ***tanzims*** (religious congregations) and trained in the black arts of sabotage and subversion. Several core groups have been infiltrated into India."

"Any possible area of identification?"

"No clue. One possibility, I was told, is the linkages between these trained groups and the upcoming Left Communist extremists." Harfan elucidated.

"What about this assassination story?"

"I really don't know. Appears to be a part of a strategy to whip up communal violence, by killing important Hindu leaders."

"Any big targets?"

"Not that I know." Harfan shrugged.

"Keep your antenna open." Nampoothiri suggested.

"Sure. But you've put me in a big jam."

It was Harfan's turn to put on the heat.

"Why did you put me at Jhumra, my parental home? There're living souls around, who remember my parents and recognise my father's features, not very different from mine."

"Certain things are beyond your comprehension," Nampoothiri sounded mysterious, "Creatures often don't understand the ways of the creator. One thing is sure; you've some souls at Jhumra, still loyal to your family. They may act as your natural shield."

"Who're they?"

"You'll find out in good time."

"You mean Ibadat is aware of my identity?"

"Wait for good time," Nampoothiri comforted Harfan, "Leave that topic. Don't ask too many questions. Listen carefully. Exploit your access for penetrating targets near Izaz Afroz."

"Why give so much of importance to him?"

"He's the minister for Atomic Energy too and the SWO, the Special Working Group created by him is very important. I want all the dope on Izaz's nuclear initiatives."

"These're tall orders."

"Indeed they're. Make graduated efforts. Penetrate the KANUPP reactor facility and the Atomic Energy Department." Nampoothiri continued.

"That's okay. You should be more concerned with the likely political changes in Pakistan. President Akbar, all said and done, is a stable person, not as erratic as Izaz Afroz and General Arif are. I sense cordite in the air." Harfan gave his point of view in clear terms.

"Is it going to be a violent coup?"

"Possibly. Much will depend on how developments shape up at Tashkent and what views are formulated in Washington."

"You've hit the nail. Try to create some sources in the Rawalpindi Missions of the US and China. Go for high-level media contacts. They're the proper barometers for watching Pakistan...

"Keep this list of nuclear scientists and senior officials, who've access to nuclear secrets. Cultivate a few of them" Nampoothiri explained the task to Harfan succinctly.

"It's very risky." Harfan expressed some reservations.

"You've been trained for the job. And one more point, now onwards you're on your own. Alam will be out of your life, except in grave emergencies and special circumstances. For emergency money supply, use this number in Karachi. It's of Adamji Pestonji, a ***hundi*** operator (money launderer). Give us three day's notice, your demand will be home delivered." Nampoothiri stood up to leave.

"Anything else?"

"How bad is the internal bickering in the Pakistan armed forces?" Nampoothiri asked.

"As I just said, precarious. Izaz Afroz and General Arif are plotting the President's ouster. No one is happy with the post war scenario. They were promised victory celebrations at Delhi's Vijay Chowk, but they got Tashkent instead."

"How soon do you expect them to hit?"

"The Armed Forces aren't yet ready to hand over power to a civilian government. Izaz wants power at any cost. There may be an uneasy compromise between him and General Arif." Harfan charmed Nampoothiri with his fine analysis of the internal power crisis in Pakistan.

"Thanks. Develop high-level friends inside the political structure too. And, before we depart, I hope I don't have to remind you about the security drills." Nampoothiri commented casually.

"I understand the stakes." Harfan's reply betrayed a slight tinge of irritation. The big man was in a bossy mood. He would rather prefer to have a heart to heart talk with Bhagat.

"Take care. We don't advertise and reclaim our lost property."

Nampoothiri stood up, walked up to the door and turned back.

"Check, if the ISI front organisations have any plan to assassinate our top political leaders, other than the Hindu protagonists."

"No news as yet, I'll keep the windows open."

"We've some unconfirmed reports about the Markaz boys being trained for intelligence support and assassination jobs in India. Some of them, we're advised by the Mossad, have been trained by PLO ultras and the Special Services Group."

"PLO is supposed to be friendly with India."

"Friendship is a relative term. The armed factions of the PLO are closer to the Islamic fundamentalists, funded by Saudi and Pakistan. And the compulsions of international relations are stranger than fiction. Often we've to sleep with strange bed fellows." Nampoothiri passed on a piece of paper to Harfan.

"Here are some names of Islamic fundamentalist leaders, having close links with the Middle-East terrorist groups. Mug the names up and destroy the paper."

"What do you expect me to do with this list?"

"Just keep an eye on their linkages with international terrorist groups. Assassination and hijacking of aircrafts are their trade specialisations."

Nampoothiri walked out after instructing Dhiren Bhagat on the safe dispersal drill, for shaking off the possible MI6 tail and probable ISI watchdogs. No chance should be taken.

"What did he mean by not reclaiming lost property? Am I a piece of dirt? Don't you have any loyalty to your men?" Harfan accosted Bhagat.

"It's his way of talking, don't take him seriously. You're accountable to us and we're to you. He just reminded you of the security drills. That's all."

Bhagat didn't sound convincing enough. He wasn't too good at imbibing the supreme philosophy of the FIB: discard the compromised assets with no tears and no nice funeral.

"It leaves a bad taste in the mouth. I'm not a garbage carton, that you'll discard at your own sweet will." Harfan complained.

"Don't read too much into his words. That's a cliché."

"How's my mother?" Harfan changed the topic.

"Fine. My boys gave me a first hand briefing before I left."

"Can I write to her?"

"Let me consult the boss." Bhagat reacted cautiously, fearing a sharp reaction from Harfan.

"Fuck him." Harfan betrayed his anger. "Do you take his permission even before you mount your wife? Does he possess your mind?"

"Don't be nasty. I can't take that decision."

"I'm not your bonded serf. Tell me more about my mother."

"Fine brother! We'll meet before you take off for Berlin. Let's move now. It's time we disengage."

Bhagat tried to placate the man, whom he had started liking, simply for his guts and capability of absorbing waves of life and death, as they came his way. Harfan Bukhari was no cheap two-penny intelligence contact. Here was a super-sensitive man who deserved more compassion and careful handling.

****

The high profile briefing had left a flunky stale-beer taste in Harfan's mouth, and a deep scar in his mind. Nampoothiri's 'lost property' dig continued to bounce from neurones to neurones, inside his psyche. A strange chemistry started cooking inside; increasing the gap of emotional attachment with the job he was assigned to. Bhagat's vain patch working didn't help much.

What for was he risking his neck?

For Mother India?

For settling a personal score against an emotional enemy?

Harfan couldn't cull out the correct response from the spiralling cloud of confusion.

Caring was a mutual concept. Even chronic brothel visitors often developed an emotional attachment to their paramours. But the big FIB boss was cruelly callous with his top agent's security problems. He didn't even have the courtesy to wish Jamilla!

Well! Harfan shrugged. He should develop his own philosophy towards the assignment. Should he not?

Committed he sure was to the assignment, but his commitment to his love was no less important. He must cross the dark tunnel, not alone, but with Jamilla by his side. He wouldn't allow Nampoothiri and his henchman Alamgir to treat him as a piece of Delhi's lost baggage.

Nampoothiri's hesitant demeanour over his shadow friends at Jhumra intrigued Harfan. Who could they be?

Ibadat?

Possibly. He had been chaperoning him since the day he had checked in at Azam guesthouse.

Rama Bai?

Harfan felt a queer twist in his intestines. This silent tragic lady gave him the creeps. How much did she know about his real identity? How much did he resemble his father? He didn't get a clear answer to these complicated questions.

He didn't have the time to brood. Another priority overshadowed his real and perceived anxieties. Jamilla, confined to her hotel room, had chalked out her priorities.

They went around London at breakneck speed, to see as much as they could, in the shortest possible time. London, a museum of the Jurassic remains of an extinct empire and a wax gallery of lost glory had a rich collage to offer.

The nostalgic showroom edifices of the pirates and plunderers of a bygone empire fascinated him. And Jamilla was simply swept away by the enchanting pages of history; so well preserved in the glittering monuments and showrooms, cleverly polished and studded with the stolen gold and robbed diamonds. The empire wasn't ashamed of flaunting the riches, it had acquired over centuries of piracy and robbery. A shameless, but brave people indeed!

The tiring hurricane tour didn't dampen Jamilla's appetite for Harfan. The body heat, careful and calibrated touches and the knowledge that the good time together was but short lived, had generated volcanic proportions of passion in her. Her plan to blow off her top and pour out all the churning magma surprised Harfan. She flicked open her lingerie and virtually jumped on her man. Her mad fingers ripped away his nightdress. Her lips showered him with warm kisses. Harfan was swept away by the avalanche of passion. But he wasn't ready for the hurricane.

Jamilla, pulsating in passion, didn't bother to wait for the initial slow responses from her man, lying under her bare body. She was determined to extract her share of pleasure. But Harfan responded very fast, playing the game according to her rules.

And Harfan, after a full hour of stormy gale and warm rain, lay exhausted on the bed. Jamilla, almost unconscious, dozed off, oblivious of her clothes. Harfan struggled out of the bed, washed up and covered her bare fragrant body with a silken rug.

Harfan closed his eyes, seeking comfort in sleep. But his attempts to disengage and slip into the realm of darkness proved futile. Jamilla's fragrance and radiating heat notwithstanding, the dream of his father's severed head placed on the silver platter kept on flashing in his mind's eye.

He couldn't find a common thread to connect the bad dream and the extreme pleasure, just showered on him by the heavenly nymph.

Rama Bai's sad face zoomed in. Her index finger pointed at a lady seated in front of the mint plant, a faint lamp burning before it. Who could it be? Harfan's gaze travelled nearer. Yes it was the face of Kaushalya, his mother.

Oh God!

Harfan jumped out of the bed and went near the window. Condensation had deposited water vapour on the glass. He wiped a foggy portion and looked out at the frozen night, seeking company of the world outside.

The cobbled London streets below sparkled under the bright light. Everything around was frozen, motionless. The city below was dead and Jamilla was almost unconscious under the rug. His seemed to be the only forlorn soul awake, surrounded by the maddening world of intrigue and conspiracy and haunted by apparitions from the past.

Why was he being tormented by the dream, he didn't like to see! Why was he not able to put his two lives on parallel rails? At this rate, his conflicting emotions, Harfan thought, would come to a head on collision.

A flash of light, emanating from some unknown corner of his existence, took Harfan back in time, to Delhi, Jhun Jhunu and his calumnious life of sex, violence and blood.

Only two tender faces, those of Kaushalya and Jamilla, showered him with benign looks. Yes. They were his keys to the ultimate chemical synthesis, between his past and present. He wished that they would spread a beam of light for him to ascend the orbit of his fate-designated trajectory.

The resolve illuminated his screen. The streaks of light bent down and vanished inside him, as suddenly as they had appeared. The impact propelled him to walk down to the writing table.

He switched on the table lamp and picked up a pen and a piece of hotel stationary.

"I touch your holy feet, Mother. My obeisance to you..." Harfan scribbled on a piece of paper.

He read the line and suddenly realised that he was writing a letter to his mother, after a gap of about a year. All these months, he had been preparing for a new life. But he hadn't forgotten his mother, the only blood link with his past. The tormented soul, back at Jhun Jhunu, must have been burning sleepless candles and waiting for her son to return from ***vilayat.***

He must write to inform her that he was alive and well.

Would it violate his tradecraft instructions? Jeopardise his covers?

To hell with it!

Harfan shredded the paper into small pieces. It wasn't safe to write on hotel stationary. He picked up a piece of paper from his folio and started penning down his thoughts to Kaushalya.

"Dear Mother, I touch your revered holy feet. My obeisance to you. I'm alive, well and very near you. I'm busy with my job and sorry for my inability to come to you. I'm a sinner but I'm your son and the son of Raja Dayaram Kaushal. I'm proud of you both...

"I've married a wonderful girl and wish you could meet her. Read and destroy this letter. I'll come to you soon with your lovely daughter-in-law, and God willing your grandson. Mother, I starve for your love and blessings."

Harfan read the letter repeatedly and decided to destroy it. It was perhaps risky to send a letter to India from London. The ISI could trace it back to him.

Harfan lighted a matchstick, but blew off the flame in a split second.

No. He must let Kaushalya know that her son was alive; son of the king of Jhumra was alive. He had embraced a new life, with Jamilla as his partner.

He looked at Jamilla's sleeping figure, wrapped up in the rug.

What a sweet wonder! This small frail frame ignited strange fires in him, the purest fire of the sacrificial pyre, of love and determination to live and die together.

What was the great cauldron of chemistry hidden inside her body and spirit? Harfan didn't find the correct arrow of light to peep into Jamilla's mystery. Perhaps it was a primordial link, textured at the dawn of creation, which had brought them together!

Harfan smiled and put the letter in a white envelope, gummed it and scripted Kaushalya's address. He picked up the phone, dialled Bhagat's room and requested for a meeting at Heathrow next morning at 7 am.

No. He couldn't recant any details on the phone. They would talk one to one. There would be no problems; it was personal, nothing professional about it.

Nampoothiri?

Could Bhagat momentarily shake off the boss's ghost from his shoulder?

That clinched the issue.

Bhagat showed up at Heathrow parking lot sharp at 7 a.m. Harfan quietly walked down to him.

"This letter's for my mother. Don't post it. Your own people may intercept it. Keep this money and deliver it to her."

"How can I?" Bhagat was aghast with the audacious request. This was against the rules of business.

"If you can't do this much for me, I don't work for you. Scrap it."

Harfan replied in a stern voice.

"Here it is. See that it reaches my mother. Don't betray me."

Harfan briskly walked back, teamed up with Jamilla and boarded the escalator to the immigration and customs counters.

Bhagat's looks followed the disappearing figures of Harfan and Jamilla. He smiled and put the letter in his breast pocket and walked towards the tube terminal. The turbulent storm that Harfan was hadn't yet exhausted his power of springing a couple of elemental surprises.

The letter, he thought should be delivered to Kaushalya through a courier, after clearance from Nampoothiri. This important decision, he couldn't take on his own.

The intelligence officer in him took a deliberate decision. He didn't want to wash off his human bondage with Harfan. The man had risked his life and travelled a long way away from himself and his home. The FIB owed him this much grace. The game of espionage wasn't a mere mindless tinkering with robotics. Dealing with humans, the art should have the flexibility of accommodating some earthly fallibility. He would like to bend the rules for Harfan and Jamilla.

Back in Delhi Bhagat made frenetic efforts to see Nampoothiri, but with no success. The big man was busy packing up for Tashkent; attending numerous meetings and preparing briefs for the PM.

Nampoothiri returned to Delhi carrying the coffin of Jung Bahadur Sharma. The poor, brave and courageous man, taller than many around him, and possibly the last of the honest, had passed away at Tashkent, early in the morning of January 11. He hadn't survived a sudden attack of myocardial infraction.

Nampoothiri could finally spare a few minutes in the midst of cataclysmic developments in Delhi after the sudden death of Jung Bahadur. He was aghast with the idea of Triple X communicating with his mother. This was professionally unethical. Humanitarian view? There was no scope for incorporating humanitarian ingredients in cultivating and developing intelligence assets.

"It's purely a professional relationship, don't allow your sentiments to creep in."

"I'm sorry sir. Harfan was adamant and even threatened severance of relationship with us." Bhagat replied.

"And you got carried away by his usual tantrums? You're incorrigible

Bhagat." Nampoothiri finally looked up at Bhagat's small face.

"Fine, don't get involved. Get the letter and money delivered through a conduit. But I don't like the idea of Harfan opening up a line of communication with his mother. That can create immense problems."

Nampoothiri finally relented, not because he was doused with the milk of kindness. He simply didn't have the time for mundane personal affairs of a resident agent. Not at this point of time. He was too deep in distress with his personal affairs. The changed political atmosphere had created cascading uncertainties. Delhi, the eternal rampart of intrigue, best exemplified by the war of the Mahabharata and incarceration of Shahjahan by his son Aurangzeb, was warming up to another gargantuan war; the war of succession to Jung Bahadur's vacant throne.

The air was thick with speculation over a possible war of succession. Bulabhai, the prime ministerial aspirant, ever on the edges, had again thrown in his hat. And Mandira, daughter of Amritlal, was in no mood to accept another interlude. She couldn't afford to miss again the offerings of the wings of destiny.

Nampoothiri wasn't sure where he did figure in the list of priorities of the two main contenders, Bulabhai and Mandira; the former, a dried up coconut, and the later, as amorphous as the mystery of the universe.

Finally, like most Indians did, he went by his astrologer's advice. The ephemeral transition of the stars and planets and their conjunction in the birth constellation of Nampoothiri clearly indicated that Mandira was the rising sun. Described by some as the dumb doll, she was neither dumb nor a doll. She simply pretended to be one. And that histrionic camouflage was her ace card. From her childhood she had acquainted herself well with the art of saying no to what she really wanted the most. Her adversaries in the family had compelled her to sharpen the artistry of feigning to its utmost perfection.

No one from her dynasty could be dumb. At least Nampoothiri hadn't seen one so far. They made their moves like grandmasters, often preferring to act innocent. That was a part of the cosmic drama, they believed the heavens had bestowed on them. The sole right of scripting, acting and directing.

Nampoothiri finally concluded that his fate was intricately tied to Mandira. She was the fatal new star on India's horizon. But he knew well too that the conclusion by itself was not good enough to guide him through the dark tunnel of political and bureaucratic quagmire. Ram Karan Prasad was sure to pitch in for Kumar Anand and Mandira, distrustful as she was towards the 'uncommitted' bureaucrats, was likely to pick up Kumar Anand, the 'committed' and pliable tool as the successor of Rabindra Narayan Dutta.

What should he do now? Nampoothiri mulled over the dilemma and decided that in addition to lobbying with the Mandira loyalists, particularly his friend Rajinder Singh Dewan, her permanent shadow, he should reopen the cupboard that contained plenty of foul smelling skeletons of the misdeeds of Ram Karan Prasad. An indictment of Ram Karan would naturally reflect on the foundations of stability of Kumar Anand.

Chapter 28

"No this isn't sufficient," RN Dutta scowled at Nampoothiri, "Balu, I can't take the risk of implicating a government minister, on the basis of such scanty evidence."

"Sir, Raghu Chawla's telephonic conversation with Brig. Nawajis Ghori, the ISI station chief and his deputy Zainul Akram point the needle of suspicion at Ram Karan. We strongly feel that he's ISI's Operation Aftab."

Robin Achariya, the hop-stop and jumping Pakistan DO (desk officer) flaunted a bunch of transcripts of the telephone conversations between Raghu Chawla and the Pakistani diplomats.

"I agree. He's a charlatan and criminal of the first order. But this is a time of political uncertainty. We can't take a cliff-hanging jump. I must have a pad to land on. You'd better widen the surveillance net and technical coverage. Let's wait for the new PM to take over." Dutta dismissed Achariya and winked at Nampoothiri to stay put.

"We live in a democracy Balu. Mere agency reports and few telephone monitoring transcripts aren't sufficient to hang a government minister."

Dutta shared his considered views with his deputy.

"But sir," Nampoothiri added, "Prasad and Chawla are playing havoc with our national security. It's time we neutralise them."

"Wait. This lady's made of different stuff. She wouldn't like a scandal of this proportion to smear her red-carpeted walkway to the throne. And you know Balu, Kumar Anand is close to her, courtesy Ram Karan." Dutta counselled his deputy to have patience.

"Are you sure sir, about her succession?" Nampoothiri asked.

"The die has been cast. It's Mandira all the way."

Dutta shared his perception of the emerging political scenario with his deputy.

"In fact, Bulabhai had called me yesterday for a briefing session. He still nurses the grievance of being cheated by Amritlal. This time around he's likely to press for voting in the parliamentary party."

"What did you tell him?"

"I told him plain facts, that the party bosses favoured Mandira. We've lost two Prime Ministers in quick succession. Our enemies across aren't likely to live happily ever after with the drawn war of '65. I advised him to seek a solution to his problems in a democratic manner." Dutta, a professional intelligence officer, gave his impersonal views.

"Perhaps he wasn't amused."

"Not at all. He told me not to take out the Pakistani rabbit from my hat every time the country is in a jam. He feels we're responsible for perpetuating discord with Pakistan."

"Funny. How does he come to that conclusion?"

Nampoothiri expressed surprise.

"Forget these political shenanigans Balu," Dutta scaled down his voice, "I'm sorry to say that Kumar Anand has activated all the strings to bypass you and Ram Karan is likely to support him to the hilt."

"I think I'll be supported by some southern stalwarts."

"That's another problem Balu," A faint smile appeared at the edges of his mouth," Mandira won't like the organisational leaders thrusting an intelligence chief on her. She hates being pushed around."

"What can I do sir, if the new PM goes by the words of a suspected Pakistani agent? I've nothing to comment on it."

"Don't despair. She's a good judge of men. And I'll try my best." Dutta consoled his deputy.

Nampoothiri left a dejected and dispirited man.

Delhi's winter ***aftab***, the smog-blurred sun, had failed to warm up his chances to the top slot.

Rabindra Narayan Dutta's primordial wiring sounded a shrill alarm about the changes in the air. The Old World moral and functional orders were about to change. A new star was forcing her way into the political firmament of the country. His days were numbered, he knew well. Kumar Anand had charged up the Ram Karan circuit, canvassing his candidature. Ram Karan, a useful prop in Mandira's fight against Bulabhai and the rightist caucus, had mobilised sixty odd members of Parliament in her support. He had emerged as a key ***durbar*** operator.

He had no illusions about Ram Karan's preferences. He would any time prefer to have a captive FIB tailored to his global business interests. And Mandira's strategic indebtedness to the caste baron was high on her political agenda. She would use him before discarding him as a rotten fly on her piece of pie. That's how she grew up in a family of political climbers.

She turned ruthless and merciless, like a feline empress, when threatened by adversaries. Mandira would brook no compassion for a bureaucrat like him, who still nursed his own view of world order and professional ethics. She preferred everything committed, including her top aids.

Her election as the new leader of the parliamentary party and her anointment as the new Prime Minister were a mere formality. And the induction of Ram Karan Prasad in the new cabinet was a foregone conclusion.

Dutta didn't disagree with his deputies about Ram Karan's questionable links with the Pakistani intelligence operators. All that he lacked was, clinching evidence for unmasking the charlatan. And Mandira, eternally indebted to the caste baron, her prime trouble-shooter, wouldn't, for sure, tolerate an impetuous intelligence chief advising her on political priorities.

It was easy for Dutta to snub Achariya and put off Nampoothiri on the Ram Karan issue. But the battle within wasn't a comfortable cakewalk. Should he not warn Mandira about the risks of accommodating Ram Karan in her cabinet? That bogeyman could play havoc with national security.

Mandira's distaste for advice was well known. She preferred gossip to assessed intelligence. But Dutta's training and upbringing prodded him to play straight poker. His neurones flashed red signals: step down, before you're sacked. The new regime required more pliable bureaucrats, the vain knights of an illusory court.

Dutta took a deliberate decision. It was time for him to lay down the sword.

He leisurely walked into Mandira's room. Rajinder Singh Dewan, mortally scared of the diamond sharp intelligence boss, ushered him in.

"Anything special Duttaji?"

Mandira hated the man and his guts. In fact, she nursed a not so guarded grievance against the man, who, she believed was responsible for misguiding her father before and during the Chinese war. His forward policy had triggered off the Chinese war. That's what she was told by her acolytes in the armed forces and that's what she liked to believe.

Mandira was of the firm view that, the business of intelligence was crucially linked with statecraft, and for external intelligence there should be a separate outfit. Dutta had concentrated too much power in his hands and Indian politicians, novices that they were, deemed him a god; a reincarnation of Chanakya and Bismarck, all rolled into one.

"Ma'am, accept my advance congratulations. You're sure to win the leadership contest." He halted for a while and continued, "I've three requests to make."

Mandira was amazed by the demeanour of the elderly, thin and rigid man. The fool couldn't find any better time to come up with his requests!

"Thanks for the information. What're your requests?" She managed to hide her irritation behind a stony face.

"I'm putting in my papers tomorrow. Don't think that I'm averse to the idea of serving you. I just want to rest." Dutta talked in a surprisingly steely voice.

"Nampoothiri is the senior most Joint Director. Professionally he's the best. I'll recommend him as the next chief. I don't want to prejudice your mind against Kumar Anand, but I'll leave a dossier on him. Even if you appoint him as your FIB chief, you may find this useful."

"What's wrong with him?"

"No comments at this stage ma'am."

"Your third request?"

"I've advised Nampoothiri to brief you about our delicate operations abroad, specially Pakistan and China. Even if he misses the bus, please listen to him. I'll request you to take a personal interest in these matters." Dutta submitted.

"What're these related to? May I know?"

"Ma'am," Dutta submitted in a gentle voice, "I'd like Nampoothiri to brief you. These operations are the fulcrums of our foreign policy in the neighbourhood, concerning Pakistan, developments in East Pakistan and Pakistan's nuclear programme. The US and Chinese interests in Sikkim and several foreign policy thrusts of super-powers are intricately linked to our internal security concerns."

"Why are you taking the trouble to brief me in advance?" Asked Mandira in a terse voice.

"Firstly, I won't be around later. Secondly, your succession is being watched in the world capitals with avid interest," Dutta continued the briefing, "Pakistan, if my assessment is correct, is trying to open up a new strategic axis by bringing US and China closer, tilting the balance of power against us...

"Izaz Afroz, who is highly critical of you, is taking the lead. They expect a political drift in India. I'm just sharing with you my concerns in some of the fragile areas. Perhaps you'll have to face these intractable problems soon after you're sworn in...

"Another matter ma'am," Dutta continued, "Our reports indicate presence of a Pakistani mole in our cabinet."

"Thanks for the advice. But, how accurate is your assessment about the Pakistani mole?"

"Ma'am we have a few valuable assets in Pakistan. They're usually precise."

"Any details you want to share?"

"Ma'am, as I told you, briefing on these matters would be given by Nampoothiri." He paused, "Please keep this envelope."

Dutta passed on a thin packet, sealed with blue lac.

"I know someone will get a place of prominence in your cabinet. Here are some details about him. Not on corruption and crime, but I've mentioned some of his foreign links. If you're interested, Nampoothiri will tell you more."

"What's special about it?"

"I feel, in the coming months and years this person will play a big role in our security related matters."

"You suggest that I shouldn't take him into my cabinet? What're the precise charges against him?"

"We in the FIB are of the considered opinion that Ram Karan is in touch with the Pakistan intelligence."

"I'm aware of his links with some Pakistani leaders. But these are pre-independence links. You can't call him a spy for that."

Mandira reacted in a haughty voice.

Dutta didn't react. He knew that the lady wasn't in a frame of mind to accept his interpretation of Ram Karan's clandestine links with Pakistani spooks. His political utility weighed heavier than the latent threat he posed to the national security. Mandira wouldn't mind a useful skunk burrowing below her feet.

"Thank you ma'am. I've said, what I felt I should share with you. I've enjoyed the indulgence of your father and I'll always pray for your success."

Rabindra Narayan Dutta, a member of the Imperial Police, Director, Federal Intelligence Bureau and a close associate of Amritlal saluted Mandira and quietly left the room. A vital link with the valued past had just snapped.

Mandira felt deflated. This man had punctured her ego and had denied her the pleasure of sacking him, a desire she had been nursing under her chest since 1962.

The fellow had the cheek to advice her on her choice of cabinet ministers! Ram Karan had just manoeuvred the support of 60 members of parliament in support of her candidature. It would be preposterous to deny him a reward. She required, albeit temporarily, Ram Karan's support in the parliamentary party. The Muslim and Depressed Class members of the Parliament were beholden to him. She couldn't overlook the ground realities.

And how could she deprive Kumar Anand of the coveted post of FIB chief? This man had been loyal to her and had kept her abreast of sensitive developments in the government, ever since Jung Bahadur had usurped her rightful position.

Nampoothiri could be the best, but seniority and merit alone weren't the only power-cordite to propel a bureaucrat to the top. Proven loyalty was of paramount importance to her.

To hell with him! Dutta was already on extension and should've retired a long ago. A fossilised bureaucrat couldn't stand in her way. She was above the bureaucracy and the party. She was a part of the nation and one with its people.

Mandira pushed the button and Dewan appeared instantaneously, like the jinn of the bottle.

"Ma'am?"

"Let's call it a day. Don't strain so much." Mandira left for her bedroom.

It was 01.30 a.m. She was supposed to get up at 5 again to attend ***yoga*** lessons. It had been a hectic, but successful day, the morning before the D-day. The developments had been shaping up in her favour, much beyond expectations. Now she was sure of victory.

She decided to write to her children before retiring. They must be anxious to know about the happenings in Delhi.

She wasn't amused with their academic performance. The two brats, busy with extraneous pursuits weren't shaping up well. But, she must share with them her feelings at this moment of ecstasy. 'To be king is within the situation and within me,' she mused, her favourite lines from Robert Frost's poem.

Yes. The power was within her and the same flames must be within her children too. That's what the destiny had willed. This nation must be having a mysterious relationship with her family, generations up and down.

The surge of energy, as she prepared to go to bed, suddenly disappeared from her inner and outer cortices. Mandira knew the magic. Just like discarding a piece of old cloth, she could switch off the active parts of the brain and lapse into the realm of sleep. She really believed that she could bend the course of nature, and at times rise above them. It was a supernatural feeling; she personally believed and liked to live with that magic, the mysterious magic of her feeling of oneness with the country and its people.

****

But, the magic had started waning, soon after her contrived inauguration as the Prime Minister, like a magnet suddenly loosing its natural properties. Mandira's honeymoon with the country seemed to be over and the national elections, due in early 1967, were threateningly knocking at her door.

Misfortune didn't come alone.

Pakistan had intensified its proxy war in the Northeast. The Naga and Mizo hills were on fire. The rabid followers of Chairman Mao had ganged up with the Pakistani left extremists. On either side of the border these ideological paranoids had been infiltrated by the ISI. And the military rulers in Pakistan, the Kremlin had warned her, were pumping in easy drug-money to bolster her political opponents. They wanted to see a vanquished Mandira biting the dust.

The Islamabad junta weren't acting in isolation. Both Peking and Washington didn't like the architecture of Mandira's stiff nose. She had been steering India closer to the Red Bear and Delhi's ***Qutub Minar*** was dangerously leaning towards Moscow, in an orchestrated cacophony over the condemnation of the US misadventure in Vietnam. Her visit to Washington had produced empty promises; sneers behind cuffs and barely a few million sacs of direly needed food grains. The message was clear: Washington was keen to do business with Islamabad and not a three-fourth red Delhi.

It was a time of great worry. It was a time to reflect.

Mandira, seated in her softly lighted office room, was trying to swim past the turbulent memory streams. The events, since she took over the reins, after vanquishing Bulabhai, the veteran challenger, were falling in the slots predicted by Rabindra Narayan Dutta. Perhaps she shouldn't have allowed her prejudice to get the better of her prudence. An astute Dutta by her side could have been extremely useful.

The powerful troika-axis, China, Pakistan and US were clearly poised against her and Indian interests. Her party was on a losing streak and she was precariously hanging on to power with supports from the unpredictable communists, a motley collection of political brokers, who survived on rotten Marxist slogans and Kremlin dole.

She could smell the burning tissues of betrayal, betrayal by her trusted colleagues. Ram Karan Prasad, she suspected, had ganged up with her political adversaries. That wily low caste rat, with the massive depressed and oppressed classes' support base, could pulverise her political ambitions to debris.

Was he acting on advice from his Pakistani masters?

Who could tell her the truth, except her professional intelligence?

But could she rely on Kumar Anand? Perhaps not. He wasn't likely to ditch his mentor. He was a good doormat, but lacked the courage and insight.

She should have listened to Dutta's advice and opted for Nampoothiri.

What should she do to rein in the intelligence apparatus? Change Kumar? Create a separate external intelligence outfit on the lines of the MI6 and the CIA?

Would that help?

A shadow silently entered her room.

It must be Dewan. She could smell the putrid cigarette smoke that had become a part of his biological odour.

"Mr. Prasad, the FIB chief is here."

"What's his problem?"

"Some urgent message from Pakistan, he says." Dewan announced with extreme trepidation.

"Well Dewan," Mandira turned around and looked up squarely at her secretary, "How much can I trust Kumar Anand on sensitive political matters?"

"If I were you ma'am," Dewan spoke with a straight gaze, "I would've gone by the yardstick of loyalty. He's more loyal to Ram Karan. And today's Ram is a wounded tiger."

"Why?"

"He knows that you're denying him the 70 odd parliamentary seats he's bargaining for in the ensuing polls."

"So he's sharpening the knives!"

"I presume so. And Kumar Anand is his creation."

"Fine. Call Kumar in and put on the lights."

Kumar Anand Prasad entered with the gait of a hind-heavy jackal silently approaching its prey. It was a congenital habit, walking on his toes, whenever he approached a dignitary, a habit from his deprived rural childhood.

"Yes Prasad." Mandira wanted to dismiss her FIB chief quickly. Her priority was urgent political consultations over the manoeuvre of that elusive fox, Ram Karan.

"Thought I'll personally give this to you." Prasad handed over a blue folder containing a single page report.

Mandira gave it a cursory glance, but on her second look got glued to it.

Marked top-secret, the top header read: Operation Triple X.

"Reproduced report obtained from CMLA HQ. Possible source ISI station chief in Delhi. Poll prediction: Mandira's party is in trouble. Vote percentage to come down to 40% from 45%...

"Serious erosion in traditional bases, weaker sections and poor. Rout of important leaders expected. Expected to be humbled in northern states. Likely to win about 250 seats. It were the ratings by the US and UK Mission chiefs.... AFTAB activated by the Big bugs here...

"The Great Mughal (President Akbar) keeping indifferent health. Cardiac problem with erratic blood sugar, periodic emotional break down. Imagines he may be violently removed. Suspects Izaz Afroz. Thinks he'd imposed the Kashmir war on him. Worried about development in the East-Pak. Doubts India. Operation Bismil has been put into motion. CMLA HQ Study group, GSO-1 (ML-4), and GSO-1 (CA) controlling operational details in collaboration with ISI....

"Watch out Northeast. Renewed thrust. New approach to Manipur and Assam plains. Rebel N.A.M.M. reps (Nagaland, Assam, Manipur and Mizo Hills) attended Dacca meeting last week. Brigadier M.L.A (Military Law Administrator) Qudrat Khan, an SSG officer is the chief co-ordinator. EOM."

"What's this?" Mandira was visibly annoyed with the poll prediction, "Do you think I'm to be guided by such reports? What's your estimate, what are you there for?"

"Ma'am," Kumar Anand panicked, "I've sent our poll study report. We feel you'll get nothing less than 320. I thought you might like to see the report from one of our top agents in Pakistan. Normally he's accurate."

"Who is he?"

"Operation Triple X."

"Who's this Aftab?"

"I've no clear idea ma'am."

"I thought you people in the intelligence are aware of Pakistani infiltration inside our system," Mandira almost shouted at the FIB chief, "What do I hear about Ram Karan?"

"Is there anything new ma'am?"

"You surprise me Kumar. I'm told that he is trying to sabotage my election efforts."

"I'll immediately have it checked up ma'am."

"Have you seen an item in a Marathi daily that has alleged Ram Karan's suspected links with Pakistani smuggling cartels?"

"No ma'am."

"Well Mr. Director FIB. I must say that you should start looking for new pastures."

Mandira dismissed Kumar Anand and recalled the last warnings from Rabindra Narayan Dutta. Perhaps he was correct about Ram Karan's Pakistan links? Who could tell her the truth?

Nampoothiri should have been her initial choice.

"Dewan." Mandira summoned her secretary on the intercom.

"Call Nampoothiri urgently."

Dewan produced the veteran sleuth just like a rabbit from his hat.

In fact, Nampoothiri was sitting in Dewan's room and unburdening his heart to him. To be superseded by his junior was the worst humiliation a bureaucrat could suffer.

He was both worried and anxious to be summoned by the PM, with whom he was yet to strike a rapport.

"So, what's Prasad been saying about election forecast by the ISI's Delhi station chief? Do you expect a change of guard at Pindi?" Mandira came to the point straight.

It was time for Nampoothiri to be surprised. He was expecting another blow of the chopper and not a complicated professional question.

Normally he was supposed to brief the PM on external intelligence, especially on Pakistan. He momentarily composed his thoughts and took a deep breath.

"A change of guard is highly probable. I'll come to that next. Let's talk about the polls. I feel you may bag 180 to 200 hundred seats."

"I don't care for what you feel. Give me your rationale."

"There has been serious undercutting by the organisational leaders and Ram Karan is sabotaging your interest." Nampoothiri spoke in a steady voice.

"Ram Karan?" Mandira pretended to gasp in disbelief.

"Sorry ma'am. He is now aligned to your opponents. They're plotting your ouster."

"Why Ram? What's his motive?"

"Possibly because you'd denied him 70 parliamentary tickets. And the organisational leaders have promised him the top slot, provided he could help in ousting you. They think he's their best bet for the Prime Ministerial slot." Nampoothiri replied with a straight face.

"Kumar Anand didn't warn me."

Nampoothiri didn't reply. He had done his job; the seed of suspicion had been successfully sown. The lady should understand that a committed bureaucrat wasn't essentially an efficient one. Conspiracy and sycophancy couldn't surpass professionalism. And he didn't regret it. The information was correct. Ram Karan had taken a 360-degree turn, betraying Mandira's trust in him. He had swallowed the prime ministerial bait, hook line and sinker.

Mandira was impressed. This man had the guts to look straight into her eyes and tell the unpleasant truth. Most men trembled and sweated before her. She enjoyed emasculating them.

She spent next thirty minutes discussing internal affairs in Pakistan.

The ouster of the "Great Mughal" and assumption of power by a new junta could only bring more instability in Pakistan. An instable military dictator often developed an insatiable hunger for power. And for a power broker in Pakistan the only elixir to offer to the people was another devastating war with India.

"Who is the next probable strongman over there?" Mandira asked.

"Rationally speaking Lt.General Sarfaraz Lodi, the most accomplished military leader."

"Who's the best running horse?"

"The ailing President," Nampoothiri added, "Would like a pliable trustworthy man. General Arif fits the bill. He's a good soldier, a bad administrator and a lover of the good things of life."

"Talk straight."

Mandira demanded.

"Well, everything that goes into making life easy and pleasant."

"You don't have to hedge. I live in a man's world," Mandira smiled, "Who is this Aftab?"

"Well ma'am," Nampoothiri replied straight, "Dutta told me that he'd already briefed you. Aftab is a deep buried Pakistani agent, located at a fairly high place in the government."

"You mean Ram Karan? Do you have any clinching proof?"

"No smoking gun proof, but we've a very fair idea."

"Bring up your secret sac of evidence. And what's this ***Operation Bismil***? You didn't tell me about this earlier." Mandira spoke in an irritating tone.

"***Bismil*** is Pakistan's counter balancing intelligence thrust, against our ***Operation Meghna*** in East Pakistan. In a way it's a more sophisticated version of ***Operation Mardan.*** You know about it. ***Bismil*** will pin us down in the Northeast by orchestrated insurgency and an escalated level of violence."

"Is ***Meghna*** going to be affected by a change over in Pakistan?" Mandira's anxious queries related to the simmering cauldron of autonomy movement in East Pakistan."

"***Meghna*** is well secured. The struggle for autonomy, headed by our ***Lotus*** is picking up momentum and the junta in Islamabad is too busy fending for its own crumbling edifices. They aren't ready to share power with the Bengalis."

"Correct," Mandira reclined on her chair; "Democracy in Pakistan was buried long back by the entrenched bureaucracy and the Army. I'm not shedding tears for that. Another spell of incoherent military rule will speed up the disintegration of Pakistan. Can we accelerate the ***Meghna*** momentum with the projected change of guard in Pakistan?"

"We've to dissect the emerging anatomy. Let's wait. You'll probably like to be briefed about the nuts and bolts of ***Operation Meghna***," Nampoothiri paused for a while and continued, "Important developments are taking place inside China. Fissures have appeared in the supposed monolith of the Communist Party of China. The US has bogged down in Vietnam. I think this the correct time for Lotus to bloom."

"Do you think that the fault lines in Pakistan are mature to plan a strike?"

"I presume so. But we'll require cool analysis. Perhaps you'd like to wait for the polls."

"That's correct Balu. Keep the powders ready."

Nampoothiri followed up by etching out a clear contour of the autonomy movement in East Pakistan and assured the Prime Minister of the steady linkages between his organisation and Sheikh Jainal.

Mandira was floored.

Yes. ***Meghna*** could boost up her sagging political image. That was the oxyacetylene for welding the diffused nation behind her.

She liked this officer with a straight face and clear vision. She regretted that under compelling circumstances she had to appoint Kumar Anand as her FIB chief.

The rigid and unimaginative policeman didn't have a basic understanding of the sub-continental politics and international intrigues in the Indian Ocean zone and Asia Pacific region. To him the Chinese machinations and US hegemony were as mundane as hawking okra from the corner store.

Dewan came in, Ram Karan Prasad in tow.

"Hello Ramji, what's the news?"

"Shall I talk now?" Ram Karan's eyeballs moved tangentially at Nampoothiri.

"Okay Balu. Thanks for the nice briefing." She stood up and walked up to an open window.

"What's the news?" Mandira asked, her eyes riveted to the bright Venus, twinkling furiously at a far corner of the sky, like her right eyes. It was oscillating furiously too. She was agitated, but didn't want Ram Karan to see her toughened facial muscles.

"I've activated the groups opposed to your rivals. They're sure to be defeated." Ram Karan elaborately briefed the PM about a top-secret operation directed at the electoral defeat of Mandira's political rivals.

"Are you sure of them biting the dust?"

"I've no doubt, you may check with Kumar. But ma'am," Ram Karan interrupted the PM, "Their defeat may weaken the party."

"Take it from me," Mandira shot back, "The people are with me. They'll follow me, they belong to my extended family and I'm one with them. Hope you aren't advocating my adversaries' cause."

Ram Karan protruded his tongue, cut it with his teeth, touched his ear lobes and prostrated before her feet.

"I'm your slave ma'am. How can I advocate their cause?"

Ram Karan sensed danger. She possessed some extra elemental crudities, which helped her in smelling out the faintest stink, immersed under gallons of perfume. She possessed a raw witchy magic.

Mandira threw a tangent smile at Ram Karan, which seasoned observers recognised as the twitching of the facial muscles of a tigress, just before the penultimate leap on her prey.

Ram Karan couldn't shrug off the danger signals. His politics was an essential tool for perpetuating a stranglehold on the system and protecting his vast empire of sin. The thriving empire of flesh trade, drug cartels and chain of brothels required state-protection. It didn't matter who adorned the PM's seat. All that mattered was his continuity in the national cabinet and his control on the power levers. In his India, law didn't apply to the top cats; nobody ever dared to bell their fanged collars.

Ram Karan knew that he was asking for too much. But lady luck usually favoured the brave. He was sure to be crowned as the Prime Minister.

Who in India would dare to oppose his candidature, that of an undisputed leader of the depressed classes?

He must get his 70 followers elected to the parliament; that was the surest ticket to the top chair. And once there, he wouldn't take much time in converting the wealth of the nation to his private fortune and stacking it away in a safe European haven. It wasn't corruption; it was just a simple transfer of head of expenditure, a mere adjustment of accounts.

But, Mandira's cool response and the biting comment triggered the cool cat's alarm bell. Mandira, a super-patriot, suffering from the paranoiac obsession of piloting India to new horizons of economic and social emancipation, wasn't likely to tolerate a potential challenger. The Amritlal clan had never learnt to put up with challenges from their political colleagues.

And this Nampoothiri Brahmin from Kerala, adept in the art of burning his own home simply for driving the rats out, was the most unreliable chef. He could cook up any stinking broth.

Kumar Anand was his best bet. But could he cook the goose of these two clever Brahmins, Kashmiri Mandira and Keralite Nampoothiri?

Ram Karan didn't feel comfortable. Kumar was good at carrying out orders. But in matters of inventing tools of dirty tricks he was a blundering buffoon.

And dirty tricks were the prime elixir in politics.

He bowed out of the tigress' den with trepidation and increased heartbeats.

That night Mandira was in a mood to act fast. She could act like a merciless butcher, when she felt like turning her friends away and emasculating her opponents.

"Dewan." Mandira almost screamed out, as soon as Ram Karan left the room. She didn't like any sermonising, at least not from a scum like him.

Ram Karan's alleged links with Pakistan was a matter of serious concern. What did Dutta say? Aftab? Was that the name of the intelligence nom-de-plume the Pakis had fancifully assigned to Ram?

Well! Well!

She would take a firm decision at the correct point in time. No use throwing muck on her own cabinet at this time of a fragile political situation. She might require Ram's support in forming her own ministry. A little compromise, for a while, even with a scumbag like Ram, shouldn't be an unpatriotic act.

This small deviation should be permissible. Didn't the gods often wink at minor aberrations, while abducting women and fornicating with the heavenly nymphs? The infinitely tolerant Indian system should, she thought, accept such a minor compromise.

She, however, made up her mind to divest Kumar Anand of the foreign intelligence portfolio and position a more reliable person at the helm of the FIB. The prime intelligence and investigation agencies must be made accountable to her. They were too vast and defused right now. Everything that formed a part of the state machinery must be brought under firm control.

The muck thrown up by the scandal of substandard military supplies by Ram Karan's son Ram Charan and the rape and lynching of a soldier's wife had already painted her government's image yellow. She should distance herself from all such episodes. And to start with the removal of Kumar Anand should be a shrill enough message to Ram Karan. He could be axed at leisure, after she formed the new government.

"Yes ma'am." Dewan, Mandira's ever-present jinn, materialised almost from nowhere.

"What's in your engagement pad for tomorrow?"

"At seven forty five the BBC team is coming to interview you on India's stand on Vietnam, followed by the US ambassador's visit at 10."

"Call Nampoothiri at 8.40, the Foreign Secretary at 9.15 and inform the Governors of Assam and the North-eastern states to see me tomorrow at 9 p.m."

Mandira turned back to Dewan and asked, "What's your reading about Ram Karan? Is he trustworthy?"

Dewan wasn't prepared for the question. She hadn't so far asked her doormat about men and matters around her. Her advisers were hand picked and she never trusted any one of them for more than a few weeks. She used people as sounding boards and trouble-shooters, but destroyed the worn-out props mercilessly, with no qualms and no hang over.

She didn't bother about Dewan's existence either. A man from his background was as good or bad as a piece of furniture. She had seen plenty of such people in the lanes and by lanes of Bazaar Sitaram, her maternal grand parent's home. They came aplenty. But, her only yardstick of judging a person was his utility.

"Ma'am he's basically a businessman." Dewan, a good judge of men, had evaluated Ram Karan appropriately.

"What're you driving at?" Mandira was intrigued by the reply.

"Pardon me ma'am. He can't sleep well if he can't purchase everything around him. He has a price tag on everybody's head."

"Anything else?"

"A businessman is nobody's friend. All the finer sentiments are logged in mere digits, in his account books."

Dewan wasn't sure if he had stated too much. The man was close to her and she had been using him for an assortment of dirty jobs.

"Do you think he's mixed up with my detractors?"

"Ma'am, as I told you minutes back, he's close to all the organisation satraps."

"What does it mean?"

"The trader has grown an ambition below his chest. He should be watched."

"Keep your antenna up."

Mandira, in a rare peep out of her cocoon, laughed, rather loudly and doused Dewan's young frame with an affectionate look.

Well! This man was shaping up well, and he had just hit the nail on its head. She removed her eyes from Dewan and re-entered her characteristic mysterious shell. Dewan kept standing before her unearthly stoic silence.

"Okay," Mandira broke her frozen silence, "Call it a day. No phone calls, no visitors. I'll like to retire early. Good night."

****

Nampoothiri turned up right at 8.30 a.m. sharp. He felt uneasy about the early morning unscheduled engagement. A Cancerian, he tried to recall the forecasts made last week by his personal astrologer. His Mercury and Saturn were supposed to enter into an auspicious configuration with Jupiter and Mars, giving a big boost to his career. He was sure to head the organisation, the astrologer had predicted.

Bullshit! How was that possible? That scumbag, Kumar was still sitting pretty.

"How have you been Nampoothiri?" Mandira disarmed him with a broad smile, "What do you make out of this? I forgot to show this to you last night." She showed him the decoded XXX message.

Nampoothiri heaved a sigh of relief.

Thanks ***Ayappa*** (a Hindu god)! The PM had only this much to ask! He silently cursed Kumar for bypassing him and briefing the PM on Pakistan affairs. His knowledge on the subject didn't travel beyond the typed characters.

"Yes ma'am," Nampoothiri continued, "Triple X is a highly placed agent. His reports are mostly authentic, obtained from delicate sources."

"That's not my question," Mandira reacted impatiently, "What's your recipe for counter balancing Pakistan's Operation ***Bismil*** ? We can't silently bleed in the Northeast."

Nampoothiri briefly explained the nuances of developments in Pakistan, the generation of internal political steam, frustration in a section of the armed forces and growing disillusionment in East Pakistan.

The Bengalis were on the verge of asserting, for the first time, their rightful place in Pakistan. And the Punjabi oligarchies were determined to deny this.

Izaz Afroz, the fanatically anti-Hindu Sindhi leader had influenced the President to renege on a number of agreements reached between Amritlal and his Pakistani counterparts. The top bosses in Peking and Washington, he explained, favoured the Mephistopheles incarnate. But the Pentagon and Langley nursed different ideas. They favoured General Arif, a pliable blob, busy with the good things of life.

The armed forces were in no mood to stage a violent coup, though Izaz Afroz and a few Generals weren't averse to the idea. President Akbar Khan, Nampoothiri averred, appeared to have some tacit understanding with his Chief of Army Staff, General Arif. There could be a smooth succession. Pakistan might be under another spell of military rule.

"What is Arif's personal profile?" Mandira asked the next most difficult question.

"As I told you ma'am," Nampoothiri couched his expression in diplomatic language, "He isn't his own master. A powerful coterie of Generals, some of them notorious drug-barons, manipulates his thinking faculties."

"So, the armed forces are divided?"

"Yes. Too many highly decorated chests are aspiring for the top slot."

"How can we manipulate these Generals? What are your sources over there?"

Mandira's sudden question put a break to Nampoothiri's chain of thought. He was caught off guard. The FIB was never called upon to penetrate the higher echelons of the Pak armed forces.

"I won't call it superb. But we're in touch with a few top line Generals."

Nampoothiri replied hesitatingly.

"That's encouraging. I think you need engaging some of them to constructive dialogue. And for that you perhaps require an exclusive foreign intelligence wing."

Mandira spoke in a soliloquy.

It didn't escape Nampoothiri's ears. But he ignored the pregnant comment, and continued sharing his thoughts with the PM.

"We expect upheavals inside Pakistan. Tashkent agreement has left many souls unhappy in the armed forces. They aren't yet ready to restore democracy. A fluid Pakistan can embark upon any misadventure."

"Do you expect another war?"

"Not exactly. That's where ***Bismil*** comes into the picture."

"I agree." Mandira added, "They've been pouring saturated fat in the insurgency situation in the Northeast. Even the predominantly Hindu Imphal valley is being subverted. You're correct. I should be ready to weather seasons of discontent and political instability and severe economic crisis."

Nampoothiri's analysis touched Mandira's chords. The officer was brilliant.

Her moments of reflection intrigued Nampoothiri. He was unable to decide whether to stay put or move out.

Dewan helped the situation.

"Ma'am, you wanted an immediate call to Moscow. Would you like to take the call now?"

She wanted the call, to talk to the Russian Prime Minister. In the event of a hanging election result, she would require support from the pro-Moscow communists. She would like to send an emissary to Moscow carrying her personal letter to the CPSU General Secretary.

"Okay. I'll take the call." She turned to Nampoothiri.

"Balu, I've decided that you should head my exclusive foreign intelligence outfit, a new edifice. Talk to the Foreign Secretary and give me a blueprint in three days time."

She smiled and walked into the next room to take the incoming Moscow call.

Nampoothiri walked out and hugged Dewan intimately.

"I didn't expect it."

"Have a look," Dewan produced a single page noting by the PM, "It's all written here."

Dewan touched his forehead, the inevitable Indian way of complimenting the amorphous deity called destiny.

"I agree." Nampoothiri reciprocated the gesture.

Destiny alone had catapulted him to his cherished domain of external intelligence, the world he had dreamt of all along. He would soon be the master of his own… another CIA? MI6?

Well! Destiny had brought him so far. But it's he who would decide what shape his empire should take!

Chapter 29

Alamgir's priority call from London surprised Nampoothiri.

He wasn't supposed to make a line call, not through the under-sea telephone cable, except in real emergency. Delhi had taken that vital decision after Washington's refusal to deactivate the CIA planted deep-seabed telephone cable bugs off Bombay High. The bugs were installed in 1962, in the wake of the Chinese aggression and as part of a short-lived honeymoon between the FIB and its US counterpart.

Washington's clear tilt towards Pakistan and accelerated bonhomie with Peking had clouded up the bilateral relations. And the State Department hawks sniggered contemptuously at India's ambivalent stand on Vietnam and Korea. The atmosphere of trust had simply disappeared.

Delhi had no illusions about the CIA's competence to monitor all incoming and outgoing line-telephone calls. The cute sealed box-limpets they attached to the cables were capable of transmitting Very Low Frequency (VLF) signals that were monitored by electronic spy vessels.

Delhi had, therefore designated its sensitive agents, especially Alamgir, to communicate either through the Kabul-Delhi diplomatic bag or encrypted high frequency radio message.

The deep cover FIB officer, rooted in Pakistan for the last 16 years, was a top grade asset. Mian Alam Khan was perhaps the longest surviving resident agent run by any agency. Nampoothiri rated the operation as his personal triumph.

"Hearing you after ages, sir. Hope things are fine at your end." Alam came alive on the line.

"Been busy with the changeover here, you know the circumstances. Still fluid." Nampoothiri avoided entering into specifics. "Any special news?"

"Any impact on smaller fries like us?"

"Fortunately not. The new boss is vastly interested in your family affairs. How are things over there?"

"Hope there's no change in policy. I'm always apprehensive of political changes at home."

"Don't wreck your head over such trifle matters. How is your home front?"

"We too expect a change of guard back home."

"How do you rate the likely new bosses?"

"It's a down hill journey all the way. The Indus fox is on the rampage and the new man on the horizon is busy with his newest flame and holy waters from Paisley."

"What. Presley?"

"No sir. I said golden malt from the Scottish city of Paisley."

"Sounds encouraging." Nampoothiri laughed rather loudly, "Who's the newest flame? "

"Jahanara, the famous soprano. Like lady luck, she loves to shower her smiles only on the brave and daring. She bets only on the winning horses." Alam chuckled and continued.

"Can't you explore her?"

"Impossible. She's the personal property of the boss man. Need a meeting. Something startling from Triple X. It's a spin off from your last fishing venture to the River."

"Kabul?"

"No problem shall be there." Alam disconnected. He knew the drill. Nampoothiri would send his itinerary through the diplomatic bag.

Alam had raised Nampoothiri from London after he picked up a coded message from a Quetta Live Letter Box. The surprise crisp message from Triple X said that Alam's consignment of dry fruits had arrived Lahore.

What could have gone wrong with Harfan Bukhari between his visit abroad and the occurrence of fluidity in the Pakistani establishment?

Israr Sharief was enchanted with his new executive and Zahoor Chaudry had just sent a letter inviting him to the first marriage anniversary of his daughter. Things were hunky-dory with Triple X.

Pakistan was shaken up by the post-Tashkent turmoil. There were talks of another coup and power grabbing by Generals anonymous and Izaz Afroz. President Akbar Khan, who liked to be addressed as the second Father of the Nation, was under pressure to hand over the peaceful vacant possession of the ***jagir*** (grant) of Pakistan to his worthy successors, that he himself had usurped over a decade ago. In ***Allah's*** own Pakistan, the uniformed politicians had converted the nation to a mutual benefit fund of the Armed Forces. It didn't matter if a Colonel Hotchpotch replaced another General Abracadabra.

The inveterate fish-curry and rice bowl revolutionaries, the East Pakistan Bengalis were, however, spoiling the army bosses' appetite. Sheikh Jainal, leader of the Peoples' League had cast a magic spell on the Bengali psyche and raised the bet for a better share of the spoils. Izaz Afroz, the irrepressible and insufferable Foreign Minister was busy conjuring up a new political witchery; rebirth of Pakistan under a third Father of the Nation.

But these earth-shaking events had no ostensible bearing on Harfan's routine. For him any goose that laid eggs were good enough, be it Colonel H or General A.

The absence of a plausible correlation between the LLB message and the developing events intrigued Alam Khan. He called Harfan at Israr's Sangla office from a pay phone at Rawalpindi's traditional joint, Hotel Shalimar.

"How's the weather?" He asked a sounding question.

"It's fine here. Little bit cloudy, but no rains. Can we meet for dinner?" Harfan used the pre-set code, giving an all clear signal.

"No problem. Hotel Pilot, Pindi." Alam gave clearance for the meeting, his coast was clear too.

Harfan checked in at Pindi Club and took a taxi to Pilot Hotel, at the other end of the city. The rendezvous was Alam's choice.

"What's the problem?" Alam asked in a patronising tone, "I'm out of bounds as far as you are concerned, you know Delhi's advice."

"It's serious, couldn't inform the details to Delhi without consulting you."

"Cough it out."

"My friend says that Markaz-ul-Farhan and Jammat-e-Mujaheedeen, two important fronts of the ISI, have been working on a project to assassinate the Indian PM. The SSG is co-ordinating the details with Northeast insurgent groups."

"Possible. The ISI had especially hired the PFLP experts to train their assassins."

"That's admitted. But some special inputs point the needle of suspicion at an important political figure."

"Spell it out."

"I'm told that Izaz Afroz is working in tandem with the ISI chief and the chief of the Markaz, Mullah Basir. Some special commandos are being trained in Dacca, for the precise execution of the plan, in collaboration with the Islamic Chhatra (student) Jihad, a Dacca based youth front of the Muslim Jammat."

"You should've informed ***Behest***. The drill is well laid out. Delhi is the point to contact, why summon me!" Alam was visibly annoyed.

"Don't be funny," Harfan retorted, "Friend says that an attempt on the life of the Indian PM is surely on the cards, probably somewhere in the Northeast, during one of her visits. Her execution, they feel, is the shortest route to sniff out the Bengali separatist movement. Hope you understand the seriousness of the information!"

Harfan disclosed his source of information in the Directorate of Military Intelligence, an officer in the Cabinet Division of the GSO-I (CA-I), the all-powerful segment of the Chief Martial Law Administrator's outfit.

This information, Harfan argued, could be a plant. Perhaps test drops, to draw out and compromise him. Planting of such misinformation wasn't uncommon. The information was too good to be true. He wanted Alam's help in fine-tuning the information. This could be done by independent sources. The crude lump of information was too raw to be communicated to Delhi. He didn't want to press the panic button.

"Make it clear," Alam tried to pump out more details, "I'm yet to know how your friend in the DMI came across this startling piece of intelligence. If it is the Markaz boys, the operation should be a babe of the ISI, and not the DMI. They aren't the dirty boys of the trade."

"Fine boss. My friend was travelling in a private plane operated by ISI's Sugar Division, from Isha Khel, the training centre manned by a joint team of the PFLP and the ISI. These flights normally lift refined heroin from isolated factories in the remote tribal areas. Two Markaz boys travelled with the consignment, providing security to the operators."

"Why Markaz boys and not the regulars?"

"I'm told that the big bosses get their dirty jobs done through these non-government operators, for a price of course."

"That makes sense. But that's second hand info."

"That's why I need your help. I don't have access to the Markaz HQ at Muridke."

"What about your SSG friend in Dacca?"

"That comes next. The primer is in Muridke and in the ISI HQ."

"Well! I get the point."

Alam finally softened his tough posture and appreciated Harfan's argument. Yes. His story had all the ingredients of a bubbling potboiler and he did well by not shooting a cipher to Delhi. The input required independent corroboration.

Alam promised help and advised Harfan to explore the possibilities of verifying the information from the office of the Colonel G-II, in the DMI headquarters.

'Section Q' of the Joint Intelligence Miscellaneous (JIM), which exclusively handled the Indian Northeast could as well be in the know of things. Nothing would be planned for that volatile part of India without their clearance.

"It's a tough job, I'm not sure." Harfan expressed reservations. He could perhaps not press his luck too far.

"Try beginner's luck, it works." Alam shared the usual sundown whisky with his apprentice, "Do your bit, let me try as well. But be careful. Don't drag in the name of Pakistani agencies, unless you have definite proof. These aspects have a lasting impact on bilateral relations. The lady in Delhi is very sensitive and suspicious in nature."

"Do you think the agencies can plan such an action without consulting the CMLA?"

"They can. The CIA and the ISI often pursue parallel state policies. The Establishment in Pakistan is different from its people. It has its own mind, independent of the people and even the government of the day."

"But that's not diplomacy."

"Diplomacy is a fig leaf with the ISI. It's a repository of the hate-India forces. And assassination isn't a new tool to them. Innumerable Pakistani stalwarts including a premier had fallen prey to these goons. The CIA has tried this very trick in the Latin American and African banana republics. This is a rogue but tested statecraft ethos."

"Do you think the ISI will stoop down to such an abyss?"

"No harm, if you operate through front organisations. Don't forget Congo, El Salvador, Chile and scores of other theatres of CIA operations. The ISI has only one prime target, the destruction of India and the reassertion of Muslim hegemony in the sub-continent. The use of front-paws like the Markaz is a strategic invention."

"Thanks. Let's be in touch." Harfan prepared to leave.

"Can you try at the Dacca end?" Asked Alam, "That should be the final launching pad."

"Perhaps. Major Anjum Mani, an SSG Company Commander is a dear chum. And there's this PAF officer Khondokar. Israr International had supplied some small weapons for the SSG battalion and spares for the F8 fighters." Harfan replied tentatively.

"That's a good opening. The SSG often operates as the execution arm of the Establishment. Try your luck. But take care. The matter is too sensitive."

****

Alam left Harfan blindfolded in a dark alley. It was a tall and edgy order.

The feasibility of corroborating the information through an independent agent was remote. Talents in such exclusive clubs of killers and hunters were hard to come by. Toughened and baked intelligence operators could take years to penetrate their security diaphragm.

What about starting with a trip to Dacca?

Israr had no problem. The Martial Law Administrator (MLA) over there had floated tenders for a 100 motorboats for coastal and river patrolling. He needed the crafts urgently. Sheikh Jainal had upgraded the language movement to provincial autonomy and restoration of democracy. The Indians, the MLA suspected, had started pumping in weapons and were plotting an armed insurrection.

"Have a nice trip and tap your contacts in the MLA's office. We should bag this contract worth $ 200 million."

"No problem. Can you pursue Begum Anar to fly into Dacca and lodge in Hotel Rangamati?" Harfan asked with a naughty twitch.

"It's your game. Play it as you like, but play cautiously. Some of these Bengalis are funny moralists."

"Don't bother. Most animals respond uniformly to the balls and bed game."

Israr laughed and relented.

But Harfan's Dacca sojourn wasn't a roaring success. Begum Anar harvested titbits from Major Anjum Mani over two night's of sweaty adventures. Existence of some training camps for the Nagas and Mizos were confirmed. The Markaz boys, he averred, were being trained by a special contingent of the 15 Baluch Regiment, at a forward camp beyond Sylhet. Anar also confirmed that a contingent of mixed Naga and Meitei (Manipuri Hindu) gang was also present in the camp.

Harfan confronted him on the third evening after Anar had softened the grounds sufficiently.

"For the contract you approach Commodore Jilani. We're not taken into confidence."

"What's the problem?"

"They don't trust us Bengalis. Things are getting rather tough. Keep in touch. We are heading for a crash." Anjum Mani confided in Harfan.

"Why?"

"The Sheikh is determined to demand the pound of flesh we have been denied for all these years. We support him. A lot many officers of East Pakistan Rifles and the Bengali officers of other regiments support him. We are on the verge of an undeclared war against Pakistan. But you're welcome. I'm ready to help if it weakens the junta rule. Don't supply the boats. Don't supply them with deadly weapons. All these are meant for killing we Bengalis."

"If we don't someone else will do it. You've a friend in me. I can share the secrets with you."

"Fine. Let's remain in touch. You're a brave fellow. Luck would sure favour you." Anjum Mani departed with a hopeful note in his voice.

Dame luck didn't favour the braves alone; she often smiled on the adventurers, pushing some on top of the Everest and some down a thousand leagues below the Pacific. Harfan, by birth a Hindu, believed in luck. In fact, the elusive lady had rescued him out of some intractable screwy jams. He had walked past the minefields of crime and winked at the lady with optimism. She hadn't failed him so far and he expected her to be profusely benign in this new tryst with destiny too.

Alam wasn't wrong. Lady luck or dame misfortune, whichever sticker one liked to stamp on the inevitable femme fatale, virtually knocked at Harfan's door.

Nawab Sharief, Israr's half-brother, and variously sketched as a two-legged viper and a Satan-on-the-rock paid a surprise visit to Jhumra and invited himself to a lunch with Harfan.

"Bukhari sahib, you're a genius. Since you joined Israr, my brother hasn't looked back. His business is flourishing. Why don't you help me? I'll double up your compensation package. Keep this blank cheque." Nawab pleaded over frothy beer and exquisite food at the Hotel Royal Palace.

"Money can't buy everything." Harfan replied in a flat voice.

Nawab digested the dig. He had reasons to.

A ruthless omnibus trader, from military hardware to toilet tissues, Nawab believed that everything in ***Allah's*** creation had a price tag. The expansion of a business-empire and the storming of Punjab's political citadel were the deadly propellants, which powered his wings. And ambition often used the fodder of jealousy, to keep the fire smouldering. His jealousy towards Israr had turned to a scathing hatred for Harfan. How could a puny ***muhajir*** dare spike his march to the top?

Nawab wasn't in the habit of masking his feelings. But today he chose to hang an extra sweet mask on his face. He required the services of Harfan for a queer purpose. This ***muhajir*** had built up enormous contacts with the Indian diaspora in London. And one of his contacts could do a simple job for him, back in India.

He was in the dire need of pleasing Pakistan's most powerful lady. Malika Jahanara, the reigning soprano of millions of Pakistani hearts and the very heartthrob of General Arif Ali Khan, the new ***Sadr-i-Ryasat*** (President) and Chief Martial Law Administrator was in need of some vague medicine for an undefined ailment. And the damn medicine could only be had from ***vaid*** (medico) Dhanwantari of Dehradun, a Himalayan foothill town in India.

The war had snapped the old linkages. No patriotic Pakistani dared to do business with Indians. Who in Pakistan would risk the midnight knocks from the ISI and the scientific torture in its Badr interrogation centre?

But the future of the rupees 8000 million Air Force contract depended on a favourable nod from the mighty lady. Nawab Sharief couldn't afford to miss the bus again.

Nawab surveyed Harfan with a squint spider eye and hoped that a little arm-twisting should help him in wrapping up this prey in his gooey net.

The procurement of medicine for Jahanara and a few more top guns in the CMLA could be entrusted to Harfan. There wouldn't be any adverse publicity. He could deflect all possible flak, directed at him by using Harfan Bukhari and elder brother Israr as expendable shields. That would be sweet revenge against brother Israr. The demolition of Harfan was sure to clip his umbilical tether, tied to Pakistan's commercial fortune.

And a charmed Jahanara, he expected, was sure to shower him with the multimillion-dollar Air force contract.

Harfan didn't miss Nawab's spider-squint. He was mighty worried and intrigued by the sudden surge of love and affection showered by the legendary arachnid. Could it be in preparation for offering his neck to the noose?

A close cohort of the top Generals and intelligence bureaucrats, Nawab boasted of his capability of unleashing packs of establishment hounds after his enemies; police, income tax authorities and of course the omniscient and omnipresent ISI.

Harfan did some quick thinking.

This one was to be a spot decision and a correct one. He couldn't afford to antagonise the merciless double-edged saw blade called Nawab Sharief. His fascination for fellow human beings was no better than the love and affection of a butcher for animals packed in abattoir corridors.

Politically a man of reckoning, Nawab had access to certain delicate quarters in the CMLA's office. His calculation was simple. Pakistan at birth was projected as ***Allah's*** own home turf. But ***He*** (mercy be to Him) sure had abandoned it way back in the mid fifties. Now he alone, the one and only Nawab, backed by the Armed Forces could restore unto ***Allah*** what was ***His*** destined land. The human contents in the blessed country were more at the mercy of ***Allah's*** angels in uniform. The rest of the show, what they called democracy and human rights were chimera, a sort of mirage in the desert.

Harfan made some fast calculations. The jackal across the table had better be kept in good humour. This serpent wouldn't hesitate to snap its fanged hood.

"Anything else?" Harfan asked, breaking the momentary silence of his guest.

"Let's enjoy the drink. What's the hurry?" Nawab smiled and slowly sipped the draught beer. His guts told him that the catch was just about swimming inside his trap.

"Tell me, what can I do for you?" Harfan played it cool.

"I'm not asking for the moon and to act against my brother's interests. He's dear to me." Nawab offered a cigarette and helped lighting it with a pistol shaped lighter.

"I can't do anything without his knowledge. I'm his employee." Harfan tried to probe the intensity of Nawab's reaction.

"Look brother," Nawab picked up a largish drumstick and buried his teeth in the juicy flesh, " Nobody says no to Nawab. My offer will give you the opportunity to go closer to the woman, who sleeps every night with the top man. It's her problem. If you help her she'll help you and me. And no dirty feather will touch brother Israr. The Generals run this country. but this lady makes their phallus pulsate."

"Who's she?"

"Begum Jahanara."

"Whoosh!" Harfan chuckled loudly.

Begum Jahanara, the reigning Aphrodite, was the heartthrob of the nation. The senior army officers, who looked at the country through amber Scotch, served in Belgian cut glasses, compared her with a ***beheshti huri*** (divine fairy). And the CMLA, the mightiest in the land, was her permanent parlour guest.

"It's an easy job. You've better access. Why should I get involved?" Harfan argued.

"Don't act smart," Nawab snapped back, "Don't I know the dirty games you and Israr play by hooking up Anar Begum? Don't ask me to believe that you'd flown that chic to Dacca for a pilgrimage. Don't compel me to go public on your trade secrets, the way you two keep on bagging lucrative army contracts. How does it matter if you hook Anar or Malika?"

"Anar is a market commodity. Malika is not. It's no trade secret. Big money in Pakistan uses easy women for lubricating their business deals. You're in the game too."

"Harfan Mian, don't compel me to go public about your mom-in-law's shameful background. You know well that, before marrying that ***mohana*** fishing tribal, she was a dignified whore." Nawab Sharief spewed fire.

"Don't exceed your limits Nawab sahib. Don't compel me to give you a sound thrashing." Harfan stood up; forgetting that he wasn't having coffee in Delhi's Blue Dirt Restaurant and that Nawab was no Matang Singh.

"Cool down Mian. Nobody in Pakistan dares talking like this to the future Chief Minister of Punjab. Don't kid around. History is the abode of truth and you can't ignore it."

"Why drag in my in-laws? We're talking business and not family matters here. Don't compel me to spill the beans about your mom's background." Harfan retaliated with a forceful voice.

"Harfan Mian," Nawab replied coolly and climbed down, "Lets bury the slandering match. The top lady has some medical problem; at least she feels she has. She wants help."

"How can I attend to her medical problems?"

"You're a ***muhajir,*** and many of you still have contacts with Hindu Indians. Perhaps your Indian contacts in London could tap ***vaid*** Dhanwantari of Dehradun; who is supposed to be a wonder medico. Only he knows the correct medicine. Perhaps you can help in soothing her ruffled psyche." Nawab described the job to Harfan.

"It's a long shot. Why me? You've many friends in London and Colombo."

"I'm not a ***muhajir***, I don't know the ways of these bloody Indian Hindus. You should know them better."

"I don't know any Indian." Harfan reacted sharply.

"I mean Indians settled in Britain. Your last German and Swedish deals were routed through a prominent London based Indian, the Sindhuja. Am I correct?" Nawab shot back.

Harfan held his breath for a while. Thank God! Nawab didn't call him a Hindu Indian. He muttered a silent curse under his breath and managed to hang on his face a faint smile.

"What's wrong with the Sindhujas?"

"Nothing. But many in Pakistan are aware that the senior Sindhuja had negotiated India's submarine deals with the French? Does it not mean a compromise of our national security? The ISI would sure be interested in probing into this queer connection." Nawab spoke menacingly, grinding each word with the roasted chicken flakes.

"You're distorting issues. Sindhuja is a British citizen."

"A Hindu is always a Hindu, it doesn't make any difference if he's a British Singh or a Fijian Patel."

Harfan sipped the beer slowly and tossed the heavy feather around in his mind. It was no good to allow this dirty beaver to dig deeper. His conclusion was quick.

"How do I get to her?" Harfan asked, while he managed to hang on to his face a feeble smile.

"That's good. Leave it to me and don't tell the big brother." Nawab slapped Harfan's back.

"When do I see her?"

"In a day or two. And I won't cheat you. You get a quarter of a million if my job is done. ***Khuda Hafiz***."

Nawab left with a broad smile on his face and a deep curse under his breath. This two-penny ***muhajir*** dared to cross his path and threaten him!

Well! Nawab wouldn't allow this lackey of brother Israr to escape unscathed.

He was happy with the minor encroachment into the microcircuits of his brother's business empire. The point of this needle would one day surely become as deep and wide as the Suez, good enough to drown brother Israr.

Harfan signed the bill and listened to the murmurs of Ibadat, who spoke into his ears.

"It's not a good sign sir. This man is very vicious. He can harm you."

"How does he manage to know my business contacts in London?"

Harfan asked Ibadat, who was busy gathering the plates on a tray.

"Nawab has long arms. He can mobilise the ISI resources to promote his business interests. And individual operatives in the dreaded agency do not mind picking up corporate assignment for high fees."

"That's interesting!"

Harfan restricted his reactions wilfully, but decided to make deeper probes into Nawab's linkages with his London based ISI friends. He wondered if the viper had snooped over his last London meeting with Nampoothiri and Dhiren Bhagat. Hoary hell! He should be more careful in meeting his professional friends, if he was to survive in Pakistan.

****

Begum Jahanara, the mercurial sex kitten did control, not only the libido of the CMLA and President, but also his business interest. All government expenditures required final approval of the top General, who called himself the President of the Islamic Republic of Pakistan. And his signature was a costly affair. It could mean millions, depending on the size of the deal.

Nawab Sharief had waited for months for a few diamond-studded signatures from the boss on vital files related to Air Force contracts. The signing ceremony depended on clearance from the high priestess of pleasure, Begum Jahanara. His social flirting wasn't warm enough to penetrate her exclusive mysterious diaphragm of privacy.

She required, some army birds chirped, an ***ayurvedic*** medicine (Vedic medicine system) from India, for an unknown disease. Nawab had promised the moon to the Aphrodite, on the prompting of General Hyder Bux, the ISI chief. The General, past his menopause, also wanted some nerve tonics from the same medico.

A lot depended on her smile and fattened pockets of the Generals, a lot of his business interests.

Air Vice-Marshal Mohtaj Sarwar, a daily attendant at the ***durbar*** of the dream lady, held the key to the Air Force contract. The Aphrodite used the sucker for collecting 10% cut from all lucrative deals part of which finally travelled to the President's Swiss account.

Nawab didn't mind applying the grease. The multi-million dollar deal would leave a profit of at least one hundred million for him. That dough was enough to make him stand taller than elder brother Israr. But he simply didn't have the correct ladle to spread the cheese.

Israr, when told by Harfan, advised caution. Nawab was unscrupulous and that Jahanara was a class by herself. The man-eater tigress of Islamabad was on the prowl, for man and money. Her gooey net had become a hub for intrigue and conspiracy.

A few powerful Generals were trying to malign the President and the Chief Martial Law Administrator, by spreading juicy stories about his escapades with the soprano. Inspired leakage to the media had fabulously increased the daily circulation of some yellow rags.

There were wheels within the wheel, Israr added. General Nayeem, the Pakistan Intelligence Bureau chief was a real brother of the President. There was a running feud between him and General Hyder Bux, the ISI chief. Lt. General Sarfaraz, the Personal Staff Officer to the CMLA stood somewhere in between. Most of these drug-money rich Generals, carried curved daggers under their sleeves.

The uncanny duo, Israr revealed, Generals Hyder and Sarfaraz had cobbled up one layer of conspiracy. The 'Larkana Shikar (hunting) Club', headed by Izaz Afroz, the unscrupulous sycophant from Sind and a couple of Generals formed another layer of conspiracy. Izaz was mixed up with another gang, the inner coterie of the CMLA, ostensibly for saving the soul of Pakistan. He was busy hurling all and sundry darts in the hope that one of those would hit the bull's eye.

"Where does Nawab fit in?" Harfan asked.

"He's an all-season bird and can nest anywhere. He is very close to Izaz Afroz, who has allured him with the promise of the top political slot in the Punjab. I smell another dirty conspiracy," Israr whispered, "Cooking up in the cauldron of the stinking power structure. Steer clear of these packs of jackals, gnawing their bloody teeth at the raw and exposed wounds of unfortunate Pakistan."

"What about co-operating with Nawab?"

"You're left with no option. Nawab can go to any extent to destroy both of us. He can let the Army and the ISI goblins lose to draw our blood." Israr cautioned his manager.

"So do I do his job?"

"For heaven's sake this should be your last engagement with the viper."

Anything could happen in the military durbar. The highest bidder earned his access to the right ears and wrong orders, from the CMLA directorate. One such order could mean facing the firing squad on charges of treason and sedition. He mildly reminded Harfan of the prolonged incarceration of hundreds of political and tribal Baluch leaders under trumped up charges.

The prospect sent chilled shivers down Harfan's bones. Caught in the forked edges of Pakistan's murky politics he was left with no other choice. He didn't know if he was kissed by lady luck or stung by a whole colony of bees. But he was aware that neither Alam nor Delhi would appreciate his fleeting but dangerous liaison with Nawab Sharief. He remembered his family deity, perhaps for the first time and sent up a silent prayer.

****

Begum Jahanara lived in a sprawling mansion off 57th street, at the crossing of Nazimuddin Road and Ataturk Avenue. The mansion, gossipmongers whispered, was bequeathed to her as a special favour by Brigadier, SIV Division of the CMLA office, in recognition of her cardinal contribution to Pakistan's art and culture. She was carted to the sprawling bungalow from her modest Kashmir Road house in Rawalpindi, ostensibly to run an academy of fine arts.

The Brigadier simply followed the order from the top boss, whose evening courts, sequestered from harsh reality, were enthralled by the beauty queen. Her songs didn't only stir gales in the whisky-moist nights. The nightingale's charms often flattened to dust the stiffest uniformed guardians of the nation. They talked about her in hushed voices and abused her with silent curses.

Harfan wasn't surprised when armed guards stopped his old Nissan at the outer gate. He wasn't a security-vetted visitor. No respectable Pakistani, in his right frame of mind, would choose to turn up at the temple of the Aphrodite, in a self-driven dilapidated car. They came, if they did, in chauffeur-driven Mercedes and assorted made in USA and Japanese cars.

This was expected. Nawab Sharief had briefed him of the possible stonewalls at the front gate. Harfan Bukhari fished out his entry ticket, a letter from Nawab and handed it over to the guard commander.

A smart attendant, a six feet tall ***habshi*** (slave of African stock) in whites, took over from the armed guards and escorted Harfan to the inner sanctum of the mansion.

Jahanara, sporting a bright red headband, which held her heavily coiffured hair, was resting on a divan, imitating her aeons old predecessor, Cleopatra.

Her head, partially resting on her delicate right palm, moved slightly towards the door-curtain, as it rippled under the palms of the castrated ***habshi.*** No hot-blooded male, possessing the gifts of full masculinity, was permitted among the personal staff. Jahanara followed the good old medieval monarchic ***harem*** code.

"Yes?" She crooned in a commanding tone.

"Ma'am, the visitor is here." The ***habshi*** replied from behind the curtain.

"Bring him in."

Jahanara lifted her finely sculpted body, covered with see-through white lingerie; all her feminine assets declaring their presence, rather provocatively. She didn't, as a matter of fact, treat her personal attendants as fully evolved humans and therefore, didn't take the trouble of dressing up adequately.

Didn't her pet dogs and cats often see her in the raw? It didn't make any difference, if her body was seen and appreciated by naives and fools. That should increase the pumping paces of their otherwise morbid and stagnant hearts. Better blood circulation could help in improving the electric currents in their underdeveloped cranium.

Her eyes licked up Harfan with the appreciative look of a tigress sizing up her late afternoon kill. Yes. Here was a fine young and robust body, charming but confused looks.

"Ask Miriam to send in some wine and eats." Jahanara dismissed the ***habshi.***

She stood up. Her imposing frame and dress amused Harfan. He wasn't the type to put on blinkers and ignore a thing of beauty. In his ten years of active sex life, Harfan had derived great pleasure in forcibly undressing feminine bodies and often pinching their bosoms and bottoms, in fits of violent passion.

But this witch appeared to be dressed and undressed to kill.

Harfan took a deep breath, and counted to sixty, a yogic discipline taught by Maulana Rizwan. He gradually released the trapped air and steadied his agitated nerves. He transported his mind back to Lahore, to Jamilla, the fairy that had flooded him with swirling and incandescent love. The sudden surge of blood started levelling down.

The training back in Delhi helped him. Dhiren Bhagat had taken him to Delhi's red light quarters, and made him to hold his breath, in silence and patience, in front of the most attractive beauty in raw skins.

Jamilla had magically transformed Harfan. Her surging and mysterious love, which Harfan failed to understand, had changed his philosophy on sex. Women were not mere sugar dolls to him, not any more.

But Jahanara was just another name of a rare typhoon. Her chiselled bust, inadequately arrested by an undersized red bra, protruded through the see-through lingerie; like mist covered early morning mountain peaks, inviting the initiated climbers.

She didn't believe in sporting a bikini around her waist. The curvature of her body, its static electricity, attracted the fine fabrics of her lingerie to her pink skin. She looked like she had just stepped out of a steaming bath.

Jahanara waived away the lady attendant, who had just entered, pushing in a cart of wine and eats. She left, closing the door behind her.

Jahanara poured vermouth from a Belgian decanter and offered one to Harfan and picked up the other for herself.

"I believe you require some herbal medicine ma'am?" Harfan asked.

"Enjoy the drink first, have some kebabs, the finest in town." She held the stem of the glass between two finely chiselled and manicured fingers.

She placed two pieces of kebab in a fine bone china and sprinkled a few drops of Tabasco. The kebabs prepared with Cashmere saffron and several aphrodisiac ingredients were rare items in Jahanara's parlour; only meant for a few privileged visitors and favourite kills.

She liked such tender moments to be made tenderer by a touch of instrumental music. She tuned on the Akai system, rather loudly. The tape played a ***Sarod*** (a string instrument) recital of ***raga Vasant Bahar*** in a fast beat, depicting joyous reunion of young lovers.

The vermouth, a fortified wine, laced with a fine concoction of cocaine, drained down his gullet to his intestines and warmed up Harfan's young frame. The kebabs, melting under his tongue, travelled faster to the stomach, stirring up a strange sensation. He felt the sleeping jinn rising up again, defeating the shield of love around him.

His eyes could now see only the bulging breasts of Jahanara, the red bra contrasting fabulously against the whites of the lingerie.

Harfan jerked his head away in a voluntary motion to get out of the strange mist. It was perhaps a perfect trap to compromise him. The use of a honey-trap was a common tool of the intelligence trade. He had foolishly walked into it, like an idiot, believing in the trashy story of Nawab Sharief. He regretted the decision to visit Malika, the ultimate temptress.

Jahanara, an expert reader of male demeanour, noticed the sudden change of colour in Harfan's face. The fellow must have been scared to stand so close to the radiating flesh of the virtual first lady of Pakistan. Most war veteran Generals melted down before her biological radiation, in the same predictable manner. And this was a kid of about 30, may be 27. She tried to assess the greenness of the new kill.

"I've a problem," Jahanara turned her back to Harfan and continued, "Darling Nawab told me that some of your clients have good links in India, and you can perhaps get the medicine from ***vaid*** Dhanwantari."

"What's the problem?" Harfan managed to ask and heaved a discreet sigh of relief; it was, after all, not a trap.

"See for yourself." Jahanara, in a magic twist of her body, shed the upper portion of the lingerie, exposing her back and breasts, inadequately caged in a red brassiere.

Harfan could see a few large white patches on her back, around the right shoulder blade, which travelled along the blue capillaries towards the breast.

"Have you seen it?"

"Yes ma'am."

"It's the white patches," She turned around, "I started getting these five years back. Doctors say that my body pigment mechanism is loosing vital melanoma and these patches may spread very fast."

Before Harfan could react to the provocative sight of the protruded pinnacles, Jahanara unhooked the bra and shed it in one swift move.

"Look at my bosom. The cursed patches have started appearing here too."

She, now fully in the raw, held the red and blue capillary lined audacious sacs of membrane for Harfan's inspection.

Yes, a few patches did appear on the breasts and abdomen too. These patches, Harfan thought, looked like blossomed jasmine, on the pink vine of her body.

"I used to get ***ayurvedic*** medicine from this Dehradun medico. But this hellish war has disrupted the treatment. New patches have come up in the last six months."

"Yes Malika, My London clients have connections in India. Perhaps they can help."

Harfan suddenly felt that the inner linings of his oesophagus were cracking up, like wild squirrels scratching at it. He felt a burning thirst and tried to clear his throat by coughing out, what appeared to be a stubborn piece of phlegm.

He must get out, before the enchantress trapped him. Israr's warnings kept on vibrating inside him. Run. Run faster.

"Have a drink." Jahanara poured some more wine.

It didn't help.

He realised that a steady stream of heat, radiating from the naked frame of Jahanara had already enveloped his senses. He felt the tongues of fire singeing his skin; as if he was standing in front of a lump of weapon grade processed plutonium.

No. This wasn't correct. Not fair to Jamilla. She had inundated him with love and this temptress couldn't enchant him by the blatant display of her naked assets. He emptied the glass and tried to make a move towards the door.

"***Khuda Hafiz***, ***mohtarma*** (mademoiselle)." Harfan managed to utter.

"What's the hurry dear? The door's closed and the ***habshi*** is standing guard outside. No use in shouting. No help will come. And dear nobody gets out of my den without partaking of the nectar." Jahanara picked up Harfan's right hand in a sudden move and led him to the bedroom and banged the door behind her.

Harfan thought of shaking her hand off by using a mild karate chop, but resigned from the decision. This lady, desperate for young flesh, could create complications for him. Who would believe him, in Pakistan, which was ruled by men in uniform! They would naturally go by the distressed sob story of the virtual first lady and hang the impetuous young man, who had tried to molest their Aphrodite.

Holy hell! The noose was perfect.

In the next 45 minutes Harfan tossed and twisted in the storm of Jahanara's passion and finally exploded in her in a violent surge. She screamed out and held Harfan to her slithering body, like a primitive Anaconda. Her limbs relaxed after a good ten minutes and Harfan managed to inhale some fresh oxygen.

"You're the most wonderful man I've enjoyed in years." Jahanara, now dressed in more decent attire, helped Harfan put on his clothes.

For the second time, Harfan felt guilty after having sex with a beautiful woman. Jahanara's wasn't a cool dead body. It was made of molten lava. But he didn't enjoy it. The buried feeling of remorse resurfaced. Rajni Krittika Hemaprabha Rao's cold eyes again stared at him with scornful looks. It made him sick to the stomach.

To hell with it!

Harfan tried to down the involuntary guilt with a few sips of wine. He felt steady.

Why not take advantage of the situation? He shouldn't have to suffer the sex kitten for nothing. He had an urgent job to do. He spun the story carefully.

"I've some problems in getting in touch with the Indians." Harfan reverted back to the subject, for which Nawab Sharief had pushed him in the tigress' den.

"What's that?"

"Our relations with the Hindu country have deteriorated. All trade has been suspended. That stupid Mandira is rabidly anti-Muslim. We should do away with her."

He threw a pebble in the steaming pool of Jahanara's still buoyant mind, just out of the stormy and torrid encounter.

"I don't blame our people," Jahanara pulled Harfan gently and made him sit next to her. She pressed a bell and ordered the maid to bring in some coffee.

"This witch has been trying to dismember Pakistan. Haven't you heard of the Indian collusion with the Peoples' League and Sheikh Jainal?" She poured coffee in a transparent hand painted bone china cup.

"No Malika," Harfan sipped the coffee and felt some relief, "I normally don't bother about political news. Simply don't get the time."

"Be a good Pakistani dear. Keep track of what happens in our neighbouring country."

"Any idea what's cooking?" Harfan moved closer to Jahanara.

"Look love," Jahanara nudged in closer, trying to feel the snug heat, "I'm in the thick of happenings in Pakistan. The ***Sadr*** (President) and his Martial Law Administrators won't do anything without consulting me. They rely on my astrological acumen."

Harfan almost blurted out that it wasn't her astrological power but sexual prowess, which dragged people to her parlour. Power, money and glory, besides other outlets, sought out the most prized female, for channelling their hidden and inner frustrations.

Jahanara and her ilk, Harfan thought, were the flaming torches, to which men were inevitably attracted for self-immolation. The poetic perception of such a fatal attraction had not been able to explain the genetic death wish of the human moth for the female flame.

"Really?"

"Give me your hand." Jahanara fondled Harfan's right palm and talked about his troubled childhood, his propensity for violent actions, capability of charming women and success in his career.

"You're great." Harfan titillated Jahanara by shifting closer, "What's your forecast for our great nation? Are we going to give a final drubbing to the Indian dogs? I've no doubt that our ***Sadr*** (President) is capable of giving a bloody nose to that lady."

"You're correct dear, he's the man of our destiny. There'll be a final and decisive war with India, Mandira will fall to the bullets of assassins, the traitors in East Pakistan will be eliminated, Kashmir will be ours and Hindu India will again come under Islam." She spoke as if she were in a trance.

"You mean the Indian PM will fall to the bullets of assassins?"

"Most likely, very soon, not later than October this year."

"That's wonderful."

"Could be in the Northeast of India; people may fire at her, her aircraft could be brought down. This may happen in Delhi itself. She's playing with fire in East-Pakistan and our people aren't nincompoops."

"You mean our leaders?"

"There are people to carry out the assignment, these are the Markaz and Jammat people. You know they're friends of General Hyder Bux, the ISI chief."

Jahanara opened her eyes. She wasn't exactly in a trance. She was enjoying the soft touches of Harfan on the exposed parts of her belly and getting ready for another bout of lovemaking.

"Our people must be working on concrete plans."

"The commandos are ready for the job, the Markaz people, trained by the SSG." Jahanara's hand steadily crawled towards Harfan's private parts.

Harfan disengaged and stood up, intending to make a move.

"I think I should go now," He looked at his wristwatch, "Please tell Nawab that your job is done."

"Don't bother about that pig," Jahanara stood up, drew Harfan closer, kissed him lightly and said, "This is an incomplete visit dear. Come again and again. Keep coming. I need the medicine, don't forget."

She kissed him again, this time driving her tongue deep inside, engaging the root of Harfan's tongue.

"And you're a great medicine yourself, you know that."

Harfan promised to activate his London friends, to get to the Dehradun ***vaid*** and to visit her at the earliest opportunity.

The castrated ***habshi*** took over. Harfan was escorted out in the same fashion and same security ritual.

Jahanara's hungry looks followed Harfan till his figure vanished behind a cluster of dwarf chinars. She turned to the music system and increased the volume of the ***Sarod*** recital, now playing a tune set in ***raga Malkaush***, which reflected a delightful mood. She hummed the tune and prepared to step into the sauna. She should be ready to receive her lover boy, General Arif Khan, the President and the CMLA of Pakistan.

The enchantress was, however, blissfully ignorant that the loud instrumental music had saved the day for her. The noise pollution had obfuscated the sound waves and blunted the electronic receptacles of the radio microphones implanted all over her place.

General Arif Khan was ignorant too of the deep games played by General Hyder Bux, the ISI chief and Lt. General Sarfaraz Lodi, his Personal Staff Officer. They had initiated afresh, another domino game, a conspiracy to topple General Arif Khan, who had deposed his ailing predecessor and imposed himself on Pakistan.

General Sarfaraz, hero of many wars wasn't amused by the silent putsch. Hyder Bux too nursed a multi-tongued fire in his chest. Why couldn't he, a scion of the family that had pioneered the Pakistan movement, put on the crown? He had a more tangible right on the lurching animal called Pakistan, bled white by successive military dictators.

Two tongues of fire that of Hyder Bux and Sarfaraz had mingled at a common burner that sought the ouster of General Arif. The planned infringement of the premises of Malika Jahanara and the bugging of her rooms were part of a super-secret operation.

General Arif spent more of his time in the pleasure abode of the Aphrodite than in his designated office and official residence. His wasn't the platonic thirst for Jahanara's enchanting voice. It was an escaping of a sick mind to his self-designed quagmire of fantasy.

What better joint could the intelligence sleuths seek out for collecting incriminating evidence against the Head of the State?

Harfan too didn't expect bugs in the enchantress' den. Even if he had anticipated it, as he should have by sheer training, he was helpless. One could simply not afford to grimace at a lioness after entering her den, hoping against hope to frighten her away. She was determined to have her late afternoon meal and Harfan was definitely a delicate piece of live meat.

Chapter 30

Harfan didn't raise ***Behest*** to transmit what he considered the most sensitive piece of intelligence. The queen bee herself had sung in his ears and that sweet music confirmed what was initially gathered from acquaintances in the DMI and the SSG.

A radio-wave interception was more feasible than waylaying a well-secured live courier drop and pick up. He opted for the live courier drill and concealment tradecraft device.

Harfan carefully removed, using a fine surgeon's scalpel, about an inch thick chunk from a cake of London Beauty bathing soap. He secured the ciphered text in a waterproof plastic film and tucked it inside the cavity and replaced the top chunk. He obliterated the incision marks by light brush strokes, dipped in a mixture of melted fat and water. The soap was restored to its original shape and factory finish gloss. He examined the cake under a magnifying glass. The job was excellent enough to fox a trained eye!

He placed the soap in an assorted gift pack, marketed by the Harrods of London, and inscribed the name and address of the receiver: Miss. Naina Akhtar, c/o. Dr. Saleem Akhtar, Main Market, Kabul and delivered the packet to a cut-out in the Indian Consulate, Jalalabad.

The Consular officer, an undercover operative of the National Security India, personally carried the gift packet to Hotel Gandhar, where Balachandran Nampoothiri was anxiously waiting for it and for a pre-arranged rendezvous with Alamgir.

His mind leapt out in excitement when Harfan's gift packet was delivered in his hotel room.

Triple X's despatches naturally triggered off Nampoothiri's imagination. An agent of his quality was rare to come by. He was sharper than the veteran Alam, in many ways. And he had surprised this veteran of many intelligence intrigues and encounters one too many times.

Jatadhari opened the packet.

Layers of shredded papers and a foam buffer had protected the lovely gifts of soap, perfume and eu-de-cologne. Must be for the family, Jatadhari presumed.

Nampoothiri directed his shadow to leave the packet and remember to pick it up while returning home. The gifts were from a relation of his wife.

Nampoothiri walked into the anteroom and took out the contents of the gift packet one by one.

No. The perfume spray canister couldn't be used for concealing a message. It must be in the soaps. He placed the soap cakes, one by one, under a magnifying glass and looked for fine incision marks.

It was there, in the sixth soap. The circular incision carried out with a diamond cutter's precision didn't escape his trained eyes. Nampoothiri folded an absorbent tissue paper, soaked it and placed it on the soap with a gentle pressure of his thumb.

Two impatient minutes later the mystery was unravelled.

The circular incision mark surfaced in sharp contrast. He applied lever- pressure with a thin steel knife and removed the upper crust, cut like a diamond that created a minuscule hollow chamber beneath.

It was there, the most important piece of paper, wrapped in a light blue waterproof plastic film.

Nampoothiri carefully lifted it using steel pliers, removed the protective cover and unfolded carefully the message from Triple X.

He pressed the bell, ordered coffee and asked Jatadhari to bring in his car.

"Ambassador sahib," Nampoothiri called the Indian ambassador, "Hope you aren't in bed. I'm coming down to the embassy. Please reach there immediately. Get your strong room keys along."

The ambassador opened the wall-embedded safe and took out the special one time cipher pad. Together they spent 2 hours in deciphering the 130 odd numerical groups with zero error.

The three-page report deluged Nampoothiri with vital details of inner contradictions in the CMLA set up. Devoid of any meaningful co-ordination with the traditional civilian administration, the military brasses were busy in apportioning the Pakistani loaf to their private breadbaskets.

Three top Generals, Triple X revealed, in league with Izaz Afroz, were planning a putsch to depose General Arif, who devoted most of his time to bacchic indulgence and devotion to Malika Jahanara.

Pakistan apprehended, the cipher added, that the Indian PM was bent upon balkanising its territorial integrity. The CMLA claimed to have incontrovertible evidence of the Indian FIB and NSI involvement with the smouldering autonomy campaign in East Pakistan, Sind and Baluchistan.

Sheikh Jainal was suspected to have entered into a spiralling conspiracy to dismember Pakistan. East Pakistan was the tip of the iceberg. The Indian intentions were more diabolical–the total destruction of Pakistan.

The cipher confirmed the existence of a sinister plan, hatched by the Markaz-ul-Farhan, for assassination of the Indian PM. Their links with the ISI and SSG weren't yet confirmed. But the inner capillaries in the CMLA oozed out a vital message; the ISI was on the threshold of delivering a spectacular blow, to a very sensitive Indian target.

The message ominously concluded..." The Special Services Group in Dacca is busy synthesising the Markaz-ul-Farhan and Northeastern insurgent groups. A joint commando group has been formed to carry out ***Operation Janbaaz*** (daredevil), assassination of the Indian Prime Minister. The most likely venue: the northeastern state of Manipur, during a slated visit of PM Mandira....

Action Time frame: September-October 1969....

Source... Impeccable, femme fatale, near the top....

Action... Self-following up. Rest ***chacha*** (Alam) will explain. Shall revert back."

The ambassador, a career diplomat, bubbled up in excitement. He had never handled such hot stuff. The Central Cipher Bureau telegrams he usually handled, contained diplomatic messages, at best the resume of discussions with the head of the state and assessment on strategic issues, obtained from brother diplomats, over drinks or dinner.

This was really hot.

"Like to have coffee sir?"

"Yes." Nampoothiri destroyed the used pads by burning them and washing down the ash and settled for his favourite Havana, "Come to my hotel. We'll have coffee there."

Nampoothiri was hard pressed for time.

Alam was supposed to meet him at 11 a.m. And the meeting place was at a remote corner of the capital city, in a nameless and faceless guesthouse, behind Kabul University.

"Just forget the message." Nampoothiri advised the ambassador, as they drove down to his hotel, "You haven't seen anything, got it?"

The message from Triple X was tantalisingly explosive, too good to be true. The veteran sleuth in Nampoothiri was tempted to churn it with plenty of salt, before coming to an intelligent conclusion.

But Alam's follow up briefing at a Kabul safe house left him in no doubt about the authenticity of the information. Harfan was accurate, almost like an atomic clock. His source was impeccable, the Aphrodite herself, having access to the top players of the Pakistani circus.

"How discreet is she?" Nampoothiri asked.

"Indiscretion isn't one of her problems. But I understand she has become the epicentre of an impending political quake. Izaz Afroz and a few Generals want to use her linkages with the President for scandalising him."

"Is it safe for Triple X to get any closer to her?"

"It's safe as long as she isn't targeted by the ISI. I expect the conspirators to cast nets in her steaming pool too."

"How soon?"

"Depends on how things take shape in East Pak. The President enjoys US and Chinese support. That's what is holding back the sharks."

"Any new input on the VIP security angle?" Nampoothiri asked.

"Yes. It's slated for one of the visits to the eastern region. I understand two experts from the Special Services Group have been selected to co-ordinate the action plan. They're experts in sniper-shooting and the use of explosive devices." Alam revealed his cards.

"Any idea about the Indian collaborators?"

"No specifics. The Markaz boys have been trained for the job. Local collaboration can't be discounted. Harfan is on a brief business trip to Dacca. He should be able to extract more resin out of the poppy pods there." Alam came out clean, in his flowery Urdu.

"Can we take him seriously?" Nampoothiri repeated the latent fear of a seasoned intelligence officer.

"He's accurate," Alam continued, "Daring and dynamic. But sir, I think he should run at a slower pace. In our game a fast runner often doesn't touch the finishing line."

"Some are born to run faster, the spin is almost predestined, buried deep in the genes. Keep your distance and take care of your own security. Harfan's indiscretions shouldn't endanger your cover. Ask him to steer clear of the enchantress."

"Why do you feel so strongly about it?"

"I don't want him getting embroiled in Pakistan's chronic power struggle. If I were the conspirator, I would've targeted her first, before slugging lead into the old man's bones." Nampoothiri closed the discussion.

"One more point. Ask Triple X to disengage from the Israr-Nawab fratricidal fight. Our man in New York has noticed Nawab orbiting around an important official of the CIA." Nampoothiri cautioned Alam in measured and precise words.

"You're correct sir. Nawab is close to the ISI chief and Izaz Afroz. He's angling for the Punjab chief minister's slot."

"That's not important Alam," Nampoothiri added, "Nawab is known to us for fronting the ISI in certain operations across our borders. He's related to an important drug cartel too."

"Aftab?"

"Yes. I'd like some concrete dope on that crook, and very fast."

"Anything urgent?"

Nampoothiri didn't react. His silence spoke volumes. Ram Karan was very high on his agenda. That stinking skunk should be prevented from fouling up the high office of the Indian Premier.

"I'm worried about the PM's security. Do you have any details, other than what Harfan has supplied, on these SSG commando experts? Can you specify their movement pattern? Any profile?"

Nampoothiri preferred to revert back to his current concern.

"Again to quote Triple X, they've been camping with some tribal insurgent leaders in Sylhet, East Pakistan, under cover of an ***Ijtema*** (religious congregation) camp, fronted by ***Islamic Chhatra Jihad*** (students' crusade)." Alam elaborated the information.

"Can you keep tabs on their movement?"

"With pleasure. I shall be in touch. As you know, a few companies of the Special Services Group have been raised in Dacca recently. I've some friends in the Military Law Administrator's set up, but Triple X has better contacts in the force."

"How?"

"His company regularly supplies field hardware to the force."

"Why don't you visit Dacca? It's important."

"I think I should. Leave it to me. You had better hurry sir, your flight should be leaving in an hour and driving to the airport isn't easy." Alam escorted Nampoothiri to the waiting taxi.

"I expect big time assistance from you." Nampoothiri pressed Alam's hand.

"Don't worry. I'll be around. Triple X will remain a stand by."

****

Amrita Bhalla's weary face lit up as the rotating chopper blades generated a dull humming noise above the fourth tower of ***Nakshtra*** Lok. It was time for Nampoothiri to land on the rooftop helipad, at the end of his long journey back from Kabul. Staying on late into the evening wasn't new to her. She had calibrated her vibes with that of her boss. They understood each other well.

Jatadhari stirred the coffee silently and left the steaming mug on Nampoothiri's table.

"Brother," Nampoothiri picked up the hot line to the PM's office and called Rajinder Singh Dewan, "I need an urgent meeting with ma'am."

"Bad, it's a bad evening." Dewan replied.

"Please squeeze in a few minutes, the matter is urgent. It's her personal security, which is at stake."

"Brother, it's never a few minutes with you. You've a long love chat planned out all the time. Hold...." Dewan walked down to Mandira's room and came out immediately.

The PM preferred to give top priority to her intelligence chiefs. Their reports often fascinated her. In this exercise she found a remote echo of her juvenile errand brigade that, she had run for her grand father's political party. She had learnt the tricks more from her mother, a dignified lady, who silently combated a hostile world around her, inside and outside her family.

"You're lucky," Dewan informed the anxious NSI chief, "Come at 10 p.m."

Luck wasn't quick to come, dot at ten.

Mandira was closeted with the Political Officer of India in Gangtok, capital of the mountain top kingdom, Sikkim. Kazi Dhondup, the pro-democracy leader and his European wife, Marie Elizah cooled their heels in Dewan's room.

The lady did the talking and Dhondup, like a painted Buddha of the ***tankha*** (Buddhist scroll painting) listened to all that she was trying to convey to Nampoothiri. Intermittently Dhondup shook his head, it was difficult to assess, if in agreement or disagreement.

Marie Elizah was trying to convince Nampoothiri about the genuineness of the cause of democracy in Sikkim and the heinous conspiracy hatched by that American barmaid; a derisive reference to the commoner background of the American born Queen of Sikkim.

The chatterbox stopped.

Mandira followed the Political Officer to the outer corridor, made a courteous gesture to the Sikkimese couple and advised them to remain in touch with Dewan. Sikkim was very close to her heart and she would strive for improving mutual relations. A fervent effort by the irrepressible chatterbox, Marie Eliza received a snub when Mandira signaled at Nampoothiri to follow her.

Seated in a rocking chair Mandira pointed at a chair and asked her external intelligence chief to relax and talk.

The NSI chief slowly read out the Triple X message.

"Do you act on the basis of a single report?" Mandira asked, her eyes still closed.

"No ma'am. We don't. But this agent is special, and I've personally visited Kabul to seek verification through another top agent."

"How do you do that?"

His professional ethics and discipline advised Nampoothiri not to disclose operational details. But his only and the most important consumer had a right to ask, he knew. He briefly narrated the broad contours of Operation Triple X, and concluded by adding that the agent had developed key sources at vulnerable and sensitive civilian and military edifices in Pakistan. Operation ***Janbaaz*** should be taken seriously, he insisted.

"Give me a detailed report on the contradictions among the dramatis personae in the military regime, along with personal profiles of the junta leaders. Don't miss the provincial governor and Martial Law Administrator of East Pakistan." Mandira spoke in a flat voice.

"Yes ma'am." Nampoothiri noted down the point.

"Visit Gangtok, and give me a firsthand report on the activities of the ***Chogyal*** (king) and study the details of Chinese deployment along the Sikkim borders. Tell the Home Secretary that, I want a proposal banning the visit of all foreigners to Sikkim."

"Yes ma'am."

"Inform the Foreign Secretary and come up for a special discussion on East Pakistan." She paused momentarily and asked.

"Now tell me how serious is this ***Janbaaz*** threat?"

"Our other sources of information corroborate this XXX report. We feel the threat is genuine and serious."

"Look Balu, I've been living under the shadow of death since my childhood. I've seen the British punishing my grandpa and father. They dragged my mother to jail. I'm not afraid of any such threat." Mandira's facial muscles tautened, while she narrated the accounts of martyrdom in her family.

"I understand ma'am." Nampoothiri continued, "But Islamic terrorist groups are spearheading this external threat. Any harm to you at this stage will deluge the country in chaos."

"I appreciate the report, but where are the tactical details?" Mandira startled Nampoothiri by her question.

"Ma'am," Nampoothiri replied with pregnant pauses, "We're working out the details. Agent Triple X and Alamgir are on the job. We expect an early breakthrough."

"I'm not afraid of death. I've been living under its shadow since childhood," Mandira repeated, "But, as you say, for the stability of the country we can't allow Pakistan to have the pleasure of celebrating my funeral. Take care; there should be no leakage of this information. No panic reactions either. I've a plan to visit Manipur and Nagaland in another two weeks."

The Prime Minister removed her eyes and again entered the inexplicable cocoon of silence. She closed her eyes and moved her lips like a meditating nun. Nampoothiri wasn't acquainted with this aspect of Mandira's character. He silently left; presuming that a reply to what she had just said might offend her.

He borrowed a cigarette from Dewan. The smoke, he felt, helped in reducing tension. The lady had an incisive mind; she could hit the nail on its head, without even raising the hammer. He wondered how intricate the inter-connectivity of her brain cells were!

"Happy?" Asked Dewan.
"Can't say. I want your help."
"Always at your service brother."
"Give me her minute to minute programme for Manipur and Nagaland, when finalised."
"Done, dear."

****

The reports from the NSI Imphal station chief alarmed some serious analysts and amused some professional cynics. A comparatively green horn in the NSI, he talked of distinct possibilities of widespread violence and hinted at a possible conspiracy between the hill tribals and valley insurgent elements. The highly charged and instable political and law and order situation might pose a serious threat to Mandira's security.

The Hill Naga rebels ran a parallel government, raising taxes, recruits and dispensing civil administration. The army and para-military forces did some fire fighting exercises, often leading to the massacre of innocent villagers. The villagers, in their remote and inaccessible hilltop abodes lived under the shadow of death, cast both by the insurgents and the security forces.

The Vale of Imphal, an unspoilt jewel of the Indian Far East, was in ferment too. Demand for better political status was the visible fringe of the volatile movement, which rocked the centrally administered former Hindu kingdom. The separatist movement in the Hills had also infected the Valley Hindu Meiteis. They blamed India for all their ills; unemployment, corruption, social and economic injustice.

Precise intelligence from Triple X and Alam synchronised well with the steaming security environment. The ambience of discontent was aggravated by the lackadaisical preparations to secure the Prime Minister. Nampoothiri counselled against the visit.

"I can't be cowed down by such vague threats, that's not in my blood. The programme stands." The PM dismissed the meeting.

"I agree ma'am." Nampoothiri submitted," But my sources are sure that at least two professional assassins have been despatched by Markaz-ul-Farhan. They might have infiltrated the Imphal valley."

"Locate them. It's your job. The Prime Minister of India can't cancel her visit, because two enemy agents have infiltrated the area and my intelligence bosses and state police chiefs can't tackle them." Mandira snubbed Nampoothiri.

Beyond that point, Nampoothiri understood, there was no point arguing with her. This female frame could turn steel-tough and inflexible at the slightest provocation.

Perhaps she was correct. As her intelligence chief, he had on his shoulders the supreme responsibility of developing intelligence inputs right down to its strategic and tactical detail. The real meat was yet to come by.

The attempt to raise Alam, through Kabul proved futile. He was out of Pakistan.

A cipher from Triple X, over special frequency ***Zam Zam***, rattled Nampoothiri, like a fierce twister cutting him into shreds.

Alam was following a trail, provided by XXX, to a remote forest location at Kalakata, in the district of Sylhet, on the India-East Pakistan border. Surrounded by small hillocks and dense forests, Kalakata was used as a launching platform by the SSG, ISI and their front paws. These outfits ran training camps for ethnic Indian insurgents, in secured safe houses, a few kilometres behind the international borders.

Nampoothiri was advised to activate a special VHF frequency, between 88 MHz and 108MHz, for receiving emergency communications from Alam.

He too would be leaving for Dacca with a slight detour in Bangkok, Harfan indicated. His business friends in the East Pakistan capital were expected to help in piercing the shell of the prized intelligence input. He should be around Kalakata in another two days, by September 4.

Zam Zam was asked not to communicate over the usual frequency.

Triple X didn't leave any gaps. His cipher was complete and frightening. Nampoothiri cobbled up a small team and boarded a special Kalyani Air Lines flight for Tulihal airport, Imphal. He had a fiercer twister to face, if Triple X and Alamgir were both correct.

September 23, 1969 dawned with all the glory that bountiful nature had showered on the Vale of Imphal. Light morning mists, which spiralled out of the looms of golden paddy fields and whispering rivers, dissolved fast as a bright sun broke through the cloud cover. A few low white cloud patches, like exotic designer decorations, floated along the contours of the verdant bosom of the distant hills. Siberian cranes and exotic storks and ducks flew in multi-layered garland formations towards Loktok Lake, the vast expanse of open water with floating islands and fishermen's hamlets.

The flying garlands suddenly lost their rhythm and dispersed in various directions at faster oscillation.

Two MI8 helicopter gun ships flew in from the western hills and swooped down on the valley with the shrill sound of the turbo-jets. The steel birds skimmed the sky low, hovered over the adjacent hills, rising high towards Tamenglong and Cachar to the west, and the low undulated features rolling down to the historic town of Moirang and the splendid valleys of Kakching and Chapkikarong.

The vicious machines flew past Andro Hills, stalled over the Loktok Lake and fired a few rockets and flares to scare away hidden insurgents and to deflect heat-seeking missiles. They continued to hang in the air, guarding two flanks of the valley, punctuated by undulated hills and isolated tribal villages that dotted the forested terrain.

The spectacular show of security drill by the MI8s was disturbed by the deafening sounds of a Boeing 707. The bird suddenly lowered its nose over the valley, took few rounds of the runway and landed at Tulihal airport. It quickly moved towards a remote corner of the reserved bay, skirted by high bushes, making way for the second 707.

The real VIP flight landed, escorted by the MI8 gun ships.

Mandira was the second Indian PM to visit the eastern outpost of India in two decades.

She wasn't a welcome visitor. The magic and euphoria of the merger of the princely state with the Indian Union had evaporated. Delhi's colonial style colossal mismanagement had disenchanted the people. Anger pervaded the air, besides the smell of cordite and putrid blood.

The festive airport reception was disturbed by fiery demonstration as the Prime Minister's cavalcade drove past the narrow street to the ***Raj Niwas*** (official residence of the chief administrator), braving stone and wooden missiles and loud abuses.

A rattled Mandira exploded on her security officer and the Chief Administrator. Such a fit of anger wasn't frequent, but this trait, inherited from her father, seized her whenever she developed a feeling of being betrayed, let down and pushed to the wall.

"Let's move to the meeting." Mandira stood up.

"All the approaches are clogged, the crowd is extremely volatile." The Chief Commissioner commented.

"I hope you don't suggest a cancellation of the meeting?" Mandira reacted sharply.

"Ma'am," The police chief offered his advice." The crowd is in a violent mood. They can't be removed without force."

"No threat on earth can cow me down. They tried similar tricks in Orissa and tried to draw on my blood. The blood of my family has sanctified the nation. I must address the public meeting. I must tell the people that Manipur has a special place in my heart."

Mandira draped in a saffron sari and a white blouse looked brilliant and shining like an unsheathed sword, as she climbed the rostrum.

Nampoothiri was in no position to dissuade the iron lady. She always had her way, in private and political life. He silently followed the PM's convoy on foot and concentrated on the surging crowd that had blocked all the approaches to the meeting ground. He felt he had heard two faint beeps from the tiny communication set tucked away in his back pocket. He moved to a lonely patch of wooded land on the banks of the ditch that surrounded the campsite of the Assam Rifles, a paramilitary force, stationed in the heart of the town. He flicked open the set and talked in a low voice.

"Yes Alam, I get you clear and loud. Been waiting for your message. Where are you? Where's TX?"

"Sorry boss. I couldn't reach you sooner. I was on the move."

"Where are you?"

"Hotel Meghdoot, just two hundred yards away from your location."

"You bloody rogue. Why didn't you alert me? I'm in Imphal for the last three days."

"Sorry boss, we're on a short time-fuse. The killers are just ahead of me. TX didn't get any lead-time to pin point the identity of the designated assassins. The killer goons are here, just a few yards away. I want your assistance. Rush up and come armed." Alam whispered.

"Are you sure they're the designated killers?"

"I'm dead sure of the Markaz commando. Been following them for the last three days. There are three local terrorists. I'm covering them, all alone. Hurry up."

"I'm coming in with a force."

"Don't do that. That'd compromise my identity. We'd better do a quiet job. Expect you soon. Keep your set on. Out." Alam's instructions came in sharp and short.

Nampoothiri signalled to the NSI station rep and rushed towards Paona Bazaar shopping arcade, adjacent to the venue of the meeting.

"Where's hotel Meghdoot?" Nampoothiri asked.

"Just across the meeting ground, say a two hundred yards north of the rostrum."

"Has it been sanitised?"

"Suppose so." the NSI rep shrugged.

"Do you carry a weapon?"

"Yes, a Belgian .9mm automatic."

"Lead and cover me. Open fire only on my command."

Nampoothiri and his station officer made their way through the milling angry crowds, who were abundantly armed with projectiles and improvised missiles.

"Yes Alam," Nampoothiri spoke on the VHF set, "I get you fine. Hold them for a while. I'm just paces away. Are you okay?"

"No problem. I'm just 20 feet away from him, behind a thin brick wall. Quick. It's the bank building, third floor." Alam's voice came in distinctly.

"Roger."

"Who's Alam?" Asked the local rep.

"Somebody important. Guide me to the bank location, sharp. Cock your pistol." Nampoothiri dragged the junior officer along.

Mandira climbed the rostrum briskly. Her sari-end now covered her head. Indian folks adored this ritual of feminine modesty. She followed this oriental social gesture consciously to befool the simple countrymen and women. That was a part of her well practiced stagecraft.

In the gorgeous saffron sari she shone like a ***Vedic*** high priestess.

She briefly inspected the screaming crowds, moved closer to the microphone and started her address in a shrill voice.

The crowd at her left flank responded with loud abuses and surged forward in waves. The bamboo barricades collapsed and the teeming angry, hostile and contorted faces hurled stones, eggs and all conceivable missiles at the rostrum. Some called for the blood of the despicable ***mayang*** (foreigner) Indians.

Behind the mad milling crowds, a gang of intoxicated youth torched a police jeep and lynched its driver. The police force wilted and dispersed like wind-driven spring cottonwool, flouting the frenetic and pathetic commands from their officers.

A small posse of policemen, overpowered by the frenzied armed mob, fired at them in panic. The crowd surged forward and lynched two of them, all the way shouting ***Jai Ai Manipur*** (hail Mother Manipur).

Three tribal sharp shooters armed with G15s, Grenade firing rifles and a light machine gun pushed their heads up, from a third floor room of hotel Meghdoot.

Their tense and nervous silence was broken by a terse radio command.

"Poppy, Lily here. What fucking game are you playing? Why, in the name of your fucking mother, aren't you killing her?"

"We're ready commander." Replied Poppy.

"Don't abuse our mothers, you emasculated Muslim sucker pig." Joined another tribal voice.

"Hey you bullshit, don't take the name of the blasphemous animal. You Indian dogs, run up to the roof, fire and finish the fiend. We will talk about your fucking mother later." Lily shouted back.

"I said don't abuse our mothers, you motherfucker Muslim." Poppy shouted back.

"No problem. It's just our way of talking in the Frontiers. Climb up, fire and finish her. There's no police anywhere. Finish the job, leave the weapons and run up to D.M. College. A vehicle is waiting for you there."

The Northwest frontier accent of the commander, with a Pushtu flavour, sounded totally different from the tongues of the people of the northeastern flank of the sub-continent.

"Yes Lily. But where is Nilo, our leader?"

The youth, supposed to be Poppy, responded to Lily, the commander, a SSG trained Markaz commando.

"Asshole." Lily shouted, "It's not my headache. Nilo or no Nilo, you motherfucker, rush up and shoot."

"Come Luikham," shouted Poppy.

"Okay. Alfred," Replied his friend in arms, "Open up the LMG first. I'll launch the grenades."

They rushed up to the rooftop, adopted a prone position and tried to locate their target.

Mandira wasn't on the rostrum. Seconds before the mixed team of rebel tribal youths rushed up to the rooftop she was physically carried away by her security staff.

"Lilly, Poppy here. Mandira isn't on the rostrum. Do we fire on the mob?"

"You shit! What happened to your training? Where's your bloody motherfucking commander, Nilo?" Shouted Lilly in mixed Urdu and English.

The brief radio silence was broken by rapid automatic fire from an adjacent building that housed a bank.

"Lilly, Lilly, what's the matter? Shall we come?" Shouted Poppy.

"You motherfucking Indians, get..." Lilly's angry slang was lost in a hail of bullets.

A tall robust man rushed out from a bank cubicle, a G15 slung on his shoulder and a walkie-talkie in his left hand.

Alam's burst had immobilised the Markaz commando, trained alongside the local terrorists at Kalakata camp. He uttered loud curses in Pushtu and tried to jump down the stairs. His rifle fired aimlessly.

Nampoothiri and his officer pounced on the Markaz commando, and immobilised him, before he could put a cyanide capsule in his mouth.

The Poppy group fired indeterminately, mostly out of panic and in their attempts to make way through the stampeding crowd, killed a few innocent bystanders.

They were overpowered and lynched by the mob, now howling and growling for blood, anybody's blood; the blood of the ***mayang*** Indians or the armed tribal killers on the run.

Alam followed Nampoothiri across a marshy ditch to a neighbouring compound, locally revered as **Kangleipak,** abode of a deity, the Manipuris worshipped before embracing Vaishnavism. They followed a circuitous route and managed to reach the NSI station office, bang on Imphal River.

"You should've warned me ahead." Nampoothiri complained, "Instead of landing here without any notice."

"Sorry boss. I got the final lead from TX in Dacca, and it wasn't safe to communicate from there. I crossed the border following the trails of the commando group. This Pushtu speaking fellow is in fact an Afghan national, recruited by the Markaz. Interrogate him thoroughly, and you'll hit a diamond mine."

"You mean you've been marching for the last two days!" Asked Nampoothiri.

"Exactly three days, partly on foot, partly by jeep."

"Where is Triple X?"

"Can't say, should be out of Dacca by now."

"His Dacca friends have been very precise. Who're they?"

"I don't really know. May be an Air Force officer and a Major of some kind in the SSG."

"Wish you and XXX could have tracked down the killer before we left Delhi."

"Boss," Alam said, "The game of targeted assassination is very complicated. The planners don't leave their trail behind like elephant droppings. Thank Harfan for achieving this timely breakthrough."

Alam demolished Nampoothiri's complaints.

"A damned lucky jackal." Nampoothiri complimented his latest resident agent in Pakistan.

"Well! A jackal he sure is, but I don't know how long his luck will last out."

"Any problems?"

"Oh leave well alone! Some people are born like that." Alam held back his comment

"Sure some are born like that." Nampoothiri repeated after his top agent in Pakistan

"Please arrange for my quiet exit through Dawki (on Indo-Pak border). I'm booked for Karachi from Dacca."

"Thank god, it's been a narrow escape." Nampoothiri settled for a stiff brandy and Alam for his usual whisky.

"Yes boss. Now I know for real that lady luck often favours the brave and daring." Alam complimented the tantalisingly successful venture of Triple X.

"Feeling jealous?" Nampoothiri asked in a teasing tone.

"Not really. I wonder how long his luck will hold out." Alam replied with a sigh of exasperation.

"I hope you don't think Harfan has exceeded his security briefs," Nampoothiri asked a loaded question, "Don't get embroiled in his affairs. Maintain a professional approach. Let me know, when you hear the retreating footsteps of lady luck. She's amorphous and fragile and changes company very fast." Nampoothiri closed his eyes. He wasn't in a mood to discuss the future operational strategies for Harfan Bukhari.

"Fine boss. Yes. Another point. Triple X wants you to activate the River Channel."

"Any special development?"

"Can't say. Just remember to activate the channel after September 28."

"Fine. Let's move for dinner. We deserve it." Nampoothiri led the procession.

"What time do I move tomorrow?" Alam asked as they walked towards the dining space.

"Don't worry. My special helicopter will take us to Shillong and my boys will see you through Dawki border." Nampoothiri reassured Alam.

Alam settled for a regular dinner after a gap of exactly 96 hours and he also looked forward to a sound sleep. He wanted to sleep like a dead log, after three days of dogged surveillance and action packed persistence. He was sure getting old.

The trail was too long, Peshawar to Dacca, to Kalakata and finally Imphal. Thank heavens! It was not a wild goose chase. Pakistan had really started maturing as a terror-exporting nation, a la the copybook prescription of the Palestinian Jihadis. He wondered, as he surrendered to sleep, as to how long his own luck would last. The days were really changing very fast. New challenges were being unfolded every day. His old traditional intelligence tradecrafts were perhaps getting rusted. Perhaps daredevils like Harfan were more suited to the unconventional war of the hungry jackals, which was punctuated more by violence than subtle intelligence manipulation.

Chapter 31

The Imphal saga was a unique experience for Nampoothiri. Indian intelligence and security fraternities were accosted, for the first time, by a foreign inspired assassination plot. The compulsions of dirty geo-politics had borrowed heavily from the mafia games of the Wild West and the violent tools refined and perfected by the Islamic terrorist groups in the Middle East. A new wave of state-sponsored terrorism had hit the sub-continent's shores. The rabid anti-India forces in Pakistan had transformed the democratic values it had inherited from the West Minster to crude weapons of mindless violence.

The ISI, a first cousin of the CIA, Nampoothiri thought, had diligently copied the craft of proxy-war as an extension of foreign policy. Its aspenal of terrorist strikes against important foreign political targets was borrowed heavily from the dirty-tricks department of Langley.

The most precious lesson, he reasoned, was the sudden discovery of gaping holes in the security parameter of the nation. It lacked in the intelligence infrastructure, political awareness and application mechanisms for combating Pakistan's novel war-strategy. It was high time for the NSI to introspect and introduce course correction measures. A new vista of possibilities had been opened up by the aborted assassination attempt at Imphal.

He wasn't, however, sure if Mandira, the super sensitive PM, would give the Imphal incident a silent go by and allow the system to gather more rust. He was mortally afraid of another interference by the parliamentarians, who were adept in demanding fruitless discussions on the floor of the apex law making shrine of democracy and forging another committee to review the intelligence and security machineries of the country. Such committees normally endeavoured to earn more than 900 lives for itself and ultimately produced a couple of volumes, which were hardly perused by the policy makers and their bureaucratic props.

Nampoothiri zeroed in on the decision of formulating a comprehensive report and discussing it personally with Mandira. Sensitisation of her mind was important, because in the Indian system the PM was the final authority to decide the intrinsic inputs that should go in for refurbishing the haggard colonial edifices of the intelligence and security set up of the country.

"Sir, Mr. RS Dewan is on the line. Would you like to talk?"

Amrita Bhalla's voice on the special phone, that provided special connectivity between his and the Prime Minister's office, broke Nampoothiri's indeterminate dalliance with the thoughts of the future contour of the intelligence fraternity in India.

"By all means," Nampoothiri pushed a yellow button that activated the scrambling protocol, "Hello brother, how are you?"

"I'm just earning my bread. Come sharp. Ma'am PM is in a very foul mood."

"Am I on the guillotine?"

"Don't joke. She wants you immediately."

"Who else are coming?"

"I presume the Minister for External Affairs and the Home Minister are slated to reach in another few seconds."

"What's the big deal?"

"Come and see for yourself."

Dewan disconnected the line leaving Nampoothiri with barely 10 minutes to reach the residence of the Prime Minister.

Dinanath Tappoo, Mandira's principal secretary, a man of impeccable integrity and razor sharp intellect, was a welcome departure from Amen Gurtoo, whose wayward ways were terminated by the NSI in a superb intelligence operation. He welcomed the participants and introduced the subject.

"Let me make it clear," Tappoo spoke in his slow bass voice, "What we discuss here is absolutely informal. No record should be kept in any office, except in the office of the NSI. The hon'ble ministers are requested to keep away from the media. The subjects we are going to discuss will also remain out of bounds for the Parliament too, till such time the PM thinks it's necessary to take the august body into confidence."

He looked at Mandira for an approval of what he had just conveyed to the small gathering in the exclusive office of the PM.

"I want you all to listen to me seriously. My last visit to Imphal has exposed the audacious and unorthodox approaches of the military rulers in Pakistan. They have imposed two wars on us. They have patronised our disaffected ethnic groups in the Northeast. Now they have come down to the dirty level of assassination. I was saved by the very timely intelligence catered by Balu's boys."

Mandira spoke rather in an agitated voice.

"Now I want you to apply your mind to what I've to say," Mandira paused momentarily, perhaps to gather her thoughts, "I don't see any reason for Pakistan to survive as a nation. It must be broken into pieces."

The small gathering was stunned by the Prime Minister's pronouncement.

"How do we go about this?" Mandira's minister for interior affairs, virtually a political nonentity, reacted first, "Pakistan is backed by the USA and China."

"I don't care," She turned towards Nampoothiri, "Balu brief us about ***Operation Meghna***. I think we should start from there."

Nampoothiri was not prepared to discuss the top-secret intelligence operation that had received the blessings of two Prime Ministers before Mandira. His work ethics militated against the concept of discussing operational matters with all and sundry government ministers, till that was cleared by the PM.

"I think we can proceed. I hope all of you understood well what was said in the beginning by Tappoo?"

Mandira winked at Nampoothiri, clearing the way for him to make the vital disclosures.

"Meghna is the essence of our diplomatic and intelligence thrust against Pakistan," Nampoothiri continued in a slumberous tone, " Our blueprint incorporate the concepts of providing moral and material assistance to Sheikh Jainal and other leaders of the People's League and convert the disjointed language and autonomy movements to a focussed confrontation between the Bengali dominated East Pakistan and the Punjabi ruled West Pakistan."

Mandira took over from her external intelligence chief. She wanted her minister for external affairs to work on a scheme to pump in clandestine funds to the People's League leaders with a view to strengthen their sinews of the war of attrition.

A few strategic points, she illuminated the meeting, had been selected to train the selected groups of People's League volunteers in guerrilla warfare, at Agartala, Karimganj, Haflong, Tura, Kokrajhar, Siliguri and Bongaon. The Special Volunteer Force (SVF) and the Border Protection Force (BPF) would impart initial training. Some selected army officers would be deputed to help the SVF and the BPF. The combined forces of the People's League volunteers and the SVF and BPF would carry out shallow penetration attack on Pakistani targets. This would soon be converted to a movement to subvert the loyalties of the Bengali dominated East Pakistan Rifles and civilian police forces.

"Would we not incur the displeasure of the US and China?"

Mandira's minister for interior affairs joined his voice, seeking clarification from the NSI chief.

"I presume that the US and China would not endorse our game plan. But we must remember that Pakistani leadership is in disarray. Several Generals and political leaders are involved in multiple conspiracies for grabbing power. Militarily Pakistan cannot match us, though Islamabad is frantically scrounging the arms markets for procuring modern weapons of war. And our ***Operation Meghna*** is a clever admixture of diplomatic, intelligence and military thrust. The Punjabi elite is in no mood to accommodate genuine Bengali aspirations. It is the best time for us to proceed cautiously with the plan unfolded by the PM."

"Please do not enter into a debate. I will request you two to coordinate with the NSI chief and the COAS. I do not want any publicity. I also want astute mobilisation of the world media towards the plights of the Bengali patriots and the excesses committed by the Pakistani establishment. Dinanath will coordinate with the information and broadcasting minister."

Mandira made almost a conclusive statement demanding total support from her ministerial colleagues.

"And Balu," Mandira addressed her NSI chief, "I want the self-rule movements in Sind and Baluchistan to be propped up very carefully. Activate your boys. I will like you to meet the Pakistani Sindhi leaders in London next month."

"My meeting them would not escape the notice of the ISI operatives. I'll like to depute a seasoned officer, if you permit, to interact with them."

Mandira gave silent nod, approving his proposal.

"Any way. I want regular briefing from you on Meghna, Sind and Baluchistan. And convey my thanks to your boys for the Imphal episode. Tell them I expect better results from them."

"Yes ma'am."

Nampoothiri nodded in agreement.

Dinanath Tappoo took over from Mandira and recanted the security drill. This top-secret meeting, he reminded the elite gathering, was informal and off the record. They should take further direction from him and consult Nampoothiri, as and when required.

****

Nampoothiri was flabbergasted by Mandira's audacious and unexpected exposition on ***Operation Meghna***. He personally handled this delicate operation through his Calcutta based representative Vishram Satpore. In fact, he had inherited the operation from Rabindra Narayan Dutta, who had woven the gluey webs for trapping the estranged East Pakistani Bengali intellectuals and politicians.

Personally he did not think that the correct time had come to precipitate another war with Pakistan. Direct interference inside East Pakistan, in collaboration with the volunteers of the People's League, could spill over the porous borders and create another war like situation. He preferred intensifying the tools of subversion and supply of weapons through indirect channels. To implement that scheme he required aggressive intelligence tools and supply of such weapons and explosives those could not be traced back to the Indian armed forces.

Wherefrom should he borrow the novel tricks of the trade and silent supply of sophisticated weapons, which could match the firepower of the Pakistani regulars? Should he turn to the KGB? Or should he break the Indian political taboo of boycotting Israel and take a few lessons from the Mossad?

He ruled out the KGB. The Soviet Union was deeply interested in firming up its presence in the eastern wing of Pakistan. Being a client state of the USA Pakistan had, in all practical purposes, banned the Communist organisations. However, the Bengali intellectuals and trade unionists had kept the red flag fluttering, though precariously. Moscow was trying, Nampoothiri was aware; to infiltrate the People's League and its beleaguered movement. The KGB, inspite of Russian bonhomie with Delhi, would not like India to jump straight into the troubled waters of East Pakistan.

Well! Why not the Mossad? The Jews were discrete business partners and they won't surely run up to Pakistani windowsills to serenade the beauty of its strategic importance. With all its umbilical ties with Washington Tel Aviv was far from being chummy with the Islamic nations. Perhaps he could do some serious business with his under-the-rug friends in Tel Aviv.

Nampoothiri picked up the intercom and summoned Amrita Bhalla.
"Do me two favours dear."
"Order me sir." She stood silently with the calculated knowledge that the boss man was cooking up some broth in the ever-blazing hearth of his mind.
"Recall this fellow Yossi?"
"You mean the Joseph Dayan, the Israeli arms supplier, who fronts an oil exploration outfit?"
"Correct dear. Isn't he a good friend of your late father?"
"Yes sir. They were trained together in UK."
"Yes. I know they were SAS trained buddies. Set up a discreet meeting at hotel Novotel in Bangkok. I will like to reach there by day after tomorrow. Book a room in the name of Mohammad Yasin, a garment importer of Bombay." Nampoothiri ordered.
"He is a former Mossad General. Isn't it?"
"I know dear. That's why you're fixing up the meeting at Bangkok. Use our channel in Rio to contact Yossi."
"I've a point to make."
"You don't want me to go to Bangkok. Am I correct?
"Correct. Bangkok is a deep alligator-pit of international espionage. The American adventures in Korea, Vietnam, Laos and Cambodia have turned the quiet Siamese capital to a cesspool of intrigue and a high profile intelligence watchtower. The CIA and its friends wouldn't miss your arrival."
Amrita Bhalla kept her point of view succinctly.
"Perhaps you're correct. But Yossi is a fussy jackal. He wouldn't like to meet anyone else."
"Why can't you depute Alamgir to meet him?"
"The idea isn't bad. But Alam is a trusted arms supplier to the Pakistani armed forces. And the Mossad wouldn't trust him. You better change our rendezvous to Singapore."
"Hotel Ambrosia I believe?"
"Yes dear."
"And the second favour?"
"You are coming with me."
"Is this a trade craft requirement?"
"Yes dear. No one will suspect if I land up in Tokyo or Singapore with a whiff of fresh breeze by my side. And you know Yossi very well."
"Your are using me sir!"
"No dear," Nampoothiri laughed heartily, "You are helping your boss in a delicate operation. Now call this fellow...what's his name?" Nampoothiri scratched his head.
"Bhagat?"
"Here you are dear. I don't know what I should do without you!"
"Well sir," Amrita shrugged, "I'm here at your service."
Dhiren Bhagat travelled by bus to Kathmandu, the capital of Nepal, as an ordinary Indian tourist and lodged himself at a cheap hotel at Maharajganj market. He called Triple X at a mutually agreed telephone number. Harfan received the call at Pearl Continental hotel, located in a proud corner of Sharah-e-Quaid-e-Azam, a distinct landmark in Lahore.

"Your uncles are happy here," Bhagat talked in an even tone.

"Thanks ***mamuji*** (maternal uncle), we must take our cousin abroad for treatment."

"But they feel you took an unnecessary risk in entering the inner cage of the circus lioness." This was a reference to Harfan's visit to Jahanara's exclusive den.

"I'm a trained lion tamer, ***mamuji***. We shall talk about the circus later. Let's talk about our cousin's treatment." Harfan refused to enter into a lengthy argument.

"Can you travel to the Riverdale Clinic, with our cousin?" Dhiren asked.

"No. The experts are available only in Canada. I'll take him to Ottawa next week. My passage is booked via JFK. Can you make it?" Harfan enquired.

"What's the problem with him?" Bhagat quizzed Harfan about the nature of his assignment in Canada.

"He suffered an accidental exposure to high voltage radiation, for which treatment is available only in Canada."

"Okay. I shall get back to you, same time tomorrow. Anything else?"

"Call tomorrow, positively. Our cousin can't wait indefinitely." Harfan disconnected.

Harfan's use of the radiation code fascinated Nampoothiri. Triple X's visit to Canada was surely linked to Pakistan's nuclear quest. But how come Harfan figured in that top-secret venture too! He was undoubtedly assigned the task of penetrating Pakistan's nuclear edifices. But how did he manage to crack the shell of secrecy and walk into the inner chambers of the reactor!

Nampoothiri couldn't risk taking a decision all by himself, and depute an officer to attend the Ottawa rendezvous. The Department of Atomic Energy was a privileged portfolio with the Prime Minister. And Mandira wasn't in the habit of being presented with surprise intelligence coups. Especially when the super sensitive subject of Pakistan's nuclear programme was concerned.

She listened to Nampoothiri with rapt attention, all the while looking straight and deep into his eyes. She silently pondered over the intelligence input for a few seconds and shot back the first question.

"What's your source of information?"

"It's Triple X ma'am. Our officer had contacted him from our Kathmandu safe house."

"The same fellow, as you said, involved with the Imphal incident?" Mandira asked, this time, with a lilting drag in her voice.

"Yes ma'am."

"Aren't you exposing him too much?"

"I'm helpless. He has to move along with the events around him. I can't deflect his itinerary, if his cover employment requires him to travel to Canada. We've to derive maximum benefit out of his visit, and know what exactly Islamabad is angling for."

Nampoothiri tried to explain the operational compulsions of his agency.

"I get you Balu. But advise the asset not to run a hundred-meter sprint. We require him for a marathon. Any way, depute a seasoned officer, properly briefed by you and the chief scientist of the Atomic Energy Department."

"I will personally brief him ma'am."

"And who is going to meet the Pakistani Sindhi leaders at Baltimore?

"I intend to assign the same officer."

"Do you think he can handle a seasoned leader like Sartaj Jamil?"

"He is a competent officer and he hails from Pakistani Hyderabad. He is fluent in Sindhi."

"That's wonderful. Go ahead."

Mandira concluded the brief meeting with half a smile lingering on in the left corner of her eye. That was indicative of her concern for the burgeoning nuclear programme of Pakistan.

Nampoothiri imbibed the subtle message and in return smiled in recognition of her concern.

****

Dhiren Bhagat travelled to Ottawa, under cover of a special diplomatic courier, carrying a supposed personal message from the Indian PM, to her Canadian counterpart.

The letter was a genuine one, on the Indian interpretation of the grandiose plan of a *'supreme government'* enunciated by Sardar Niyamat, the mercurial leader of Indian held Kashmir. Niyamat had written, many political observers alleged, on Pakistani prompting, to important world leaders, enunciating his perception of the panacea for the troubled state of Kashmir. And sympathetic Canadian voices had staged a couple of rallies before the Parliament building demanding the free world's intervention in the Kashmir imbroglio. The Indian PM explained the ground realities and professed Indian adherence to the UN resolutions. Sardar Niyamat, Mandira added, was trying to complicate the issues by ranting new slogans in favour of Kashmir's independence.

Canada, still a Cinderella in international politics, was an important member of the UN team of observers. Mandira could not afford to antagonise the Canadian leaders, who had openly supported her policies towards the oppressed Bengalis of East Pakistan. Her letter, in fact, had highlighted the abysmal condition of the Bengalis and the flagrant violation of human rights by Islamabad.

Bhagat was lodged at Hotel Chateau Laurier, next to the Parliament building, overlooking the small French-speaking town of Hull and River Ottawa, which was known in aboriginal Indian vocabulary as River Outaouais.

"Hello ***mamuji***," Harfan called over the house phone, "How are you today?"

"Fine. Where are you?"

"Two levels below. Relatives are with me, can't meet here. Let's meet at Tandoor restaurant, next to the K-Mart shopping mall."

"How do I get there?"

"Take a taxi. It's on the Prescott Highway. Avoid an Indian driven one."

Food by candlelight, over strong Miller beer, was slightly hot, hot enough to titillate the palate and warm up the body.

Late October snow flurries had chilled the air down, cool enough to scare the two Pakis; as some Canadians preferred to call the people of East Indian origin.

"What's the big game?" Bhagat asked.

"It's big. But, tell me how is my mother?" Harfan's eyes looked deep into Bhagat's.

"I didn't personally meet her, but one of my boys had delivered your last letter."

"Did he talk to her? How did he find her?"

"Look brother, she's well, but misses you. All these years she has been counting the footsteps of your father. Now, I presume, she's counting yours. She knows you're alive and you'll soon be back." Bhagat's sappy voice didn't amuse Harfan.

"Didn't it occur to you, that you should meet and talk to her personally?" Harfan sounded bitter.

"I'm a government servant. I can't freelance. My man had talked to her. He felt she wasn't surprised. She said, wherever you are, God shall protect you."

"Can I return to her?" Harfan involuntarily touched Bhagat's hand.

"Why not? You'll return to a hero's welcome once your mission is over. The law can't stand in your way." Dhiren poured beer in Harfan's glass.

"Don't bullshit! Suppose I'm caught."

"Don't think negative. Spies get caught and they're periodically exchanged, as security prisoners. This is an eternal game, all over the world. Haven't you heard of periodical exchanges at the Berlin Wall? There's always an element of professional risk. You know all that."

Bhagat reminded him of some of the training stuff.

"What about my wife and kid? "

"***Yar*** (friend), don't imagine things. You're our top man and the PM herself is handling your matter. She acknowledges your contribution in the Manipur case. Trust me, we can spirit your family out to London and from there to India. You should believe me." Bhagat gently tapped Harfan's arm.

"What brings you to Canada? Who's the other fellow with you? Why couldn't we transact this business in London?"

"Patience brother," Harfan replied coolly, "My cover brings me to Ottawa and I couldn't have a tango with you in London. Clear? The other fellow happens to be my boss, Israr Sharief. Our company has bagged a defence contract for supplying anti-tank missiles, amphibious boats and armoured personnel carriers. Four Canadian parties have been short listed."

"You called me all the way to freezing Ottawa just to tell me this!"

"No. There is more. I'm supposed to contact Dr. Carver at McGill University, Montreal and visit Thunder Bay nuclear plant. There I have to contact Dr. Mainul, a nuclear scientist of Pakistani origin, working in a critical area of the reactor."

Bhagat shifted his position and ordered one more dish of ***reshmi*** kebabs. Harfan appeared to have hot stuff beneath his breath.

"Why so many arms and armaments? Is Pakistan itching for another war?"

There was no immediate war itch, Harfan explained. The military regime had carried out ***Operation Baaz*** (falcon), a four-day war game, to test the efficacy of its forces and the adequacy of its war front and ancillary supplies. Pakistani preparations, the Generals had concluded, were inadequate, all along the western sector. Their Eastern Command would be able to hold back a full-scale Indian thrust just for seven days. For the rest of the security needs of the country they would have to depend on ***Allah***, China and US, in that order.

The GHQ, following this conclusion, had raised two new armoured and three infantry divisions. Two independent brigades were formed by a lateral shift from integral armoured regiments of some of the existing infantry divisions. Two squadrons of the Pakistan Air force were integrated with the new task forces.

Pakistan's main concern was in the eastern sector. Besides the ninth, fourteenth and sixteenth Infantry Divisions, one squadron of the Pakistan Air force and a few gunboats, staffed mostly by West Pakistanis, formed the iron frame of the Eastern Command

The CMLA was sure, Harfan commented, that sooner or later, the Peoples' League, under cover of its 6 Point Demand, would demand independence. Sheikh Jainal, they were sure, was acting as a forward paw of India. The ISI had no illusions about it.

Auxiliary forces, like the Bengali dominated East-Pakistan Infantry, National Service Battalion and East Pakistan Rifles weren't trusted by Islamabad. Most of the Bengalis, it felt, had been subverted by the Peoples' League. The Punjabi dominated Eastern Command had little or no hold on them.

The CMLA had definite information of the existence of a joint battle order, between the Indian Army and the ragtag volunteer forces of Sheikh Jainal. He had in his pocket concrete proof, of NSI's involvement with Jainal.

"Keep this. It's a xerox copy of a report of Aftab, stolen from the records of the CMLA office."

"Authentic?"

"Hundred percent."

Some of these crucial inputs, Harfan added, came from a chance interception of enclair and low-grade coded radio traffic of the Indian border police contingents. The ISI had succeeded in stealing the keys to at least two cipher pads developed by India's Joint Cipher Bureau.

"Keep this too. It is a present for papa, with my compliments. These are photocopies of numerical cipher logs with the decoded versions jotted below. The ISI experts have easy access to some of your police and army frequencies. There's a major source of leakage at Pathankot." Harfan passed on a bunch of papers containing coded and enclair versions.

"That's sinister. Is Pakistan preparing for another war? How's it that they're preparing for elections to the National Assembly? How do you reconcile the two?"

"No contradiction brother. The President isn't dying to kiss dame democracy. He and Izaz Afroz won't allow any fishy Bengali to become the Premier of Pakistan... They have had enough of them... Nazimuddin, Bogra etc. Pakistan means Punjab and to a lesser degree Sind. The rest are geographical baggage." Harfan commented in a caustic tone.

"You appear to be biased."

"No personal dig. To the ISI and the military establishment Sheikh Jainal is an Indian agent. Some of them consider Izaz Afroz as a pseudo, a lesser version of your Mandira, and a male version of Jeanne d' Arc, rather a vain Pakistani version of later day Charles Andre Joseph Marie De Gaulle."

Harfan hammered in his point with a flourish.

"Does the President think he can survive after denying power to the elected representatives of the people?"

"The Pakistani gullets are enormously elastic. And the military can push down anything with the barrel of their guns. Since 1958, they're living under military rule. All pretensions of democracy have been thrown to the winds by the successive military regimes."

Harfan elaborated.

"That house-fire should keep Islamabad busy for a pretty while." Bhagat asked more probing questions.

"Don't take that as a placebo. The President may cobble up a rag-tag government of his own. He doesn't trust Jainal, and he hates Izaz Afroz. Peoples' aspirations in Pakistan are likely to end in another act of political puppetry. The Pakistanis are used to this. Democracy brings flu to their political souls. The moment you talk about it, they start sneezing on each other's shirts. And the buttoned up armed forces and the ISI are the best antidotes for such periodical infections."

Harfan laughed, hoping that Bhagat was floored by his ornamental narration.

"You're being unkind to them." Bhagat remarked.

"Take me seriously. Once Delhi allows General Arif to have a go in the East Pakistan, he will launch ***Operation Khyber.***"

"What's that?"

"Keep these papers. I especially called you here to brief on Islamabad's preparations in East Pakistan. You can expect a crack down on the Peoples' League movement over there. The CMLA is in touch with Washington and Peking and his guardian angels have endorsed his tough line."

"Why should Washington and Peking be interested in a full scale Pakistani genocide in Dacca?"

"Tell the boss to take care. China and US don't want Pakistan to go the Bhutan and Sikkim way–becoming just another Indian protectorate."

"Hold your breath," Harfan continued, "The ISI is likely to come up with more dirty tricks with a view to scuttling the scheduled Indian polls. A lot of drug-money is in the pipeline. Ask Delhi to be watchful about Kashmir. The sleuths are working on putting up a spectacular show."

"Be specific." Bhagat demanded.

"That's what ***Khyber*** is all about. They'll export more armed Islamist gangs, like they did in 1948 and '65 and start a large-scale violence. They may go in for hijacking aircrafts, in order to divert attention from the flu of democracy. I've received specific hints about one Aftab, an intelligence asset of the ISI, operating from inside your political structure." Harfan looked at his watch and stood up abruptly.

"Any idea who that Aftab is?"

"Can't say for sure. It may be Ram Karan Prasad. And may be I'm wrong. Keep your eyes and ears open."

"Why Ram Karan?"

"I've been a junior partner in his criminal activities. My guts say it's he and nobody else. Delhi should know better than to trust him."

"Are you serious?"

"You know the meaning of Aftab? It's the dazzling Sun. Remove your opaque bureaucratic glasses and you'll see the truth behind the dazzling disk."

Harfan replied mimicking a couplet from the ***Upanishads*** (classical Sanskrit works) and begged to be excused. Israr Sharief, he said, would be expecting him for a briefing session. Sharief was due to leave for Red Deer, Alberta, next morning and he too had a date to keep in Montreal.

He assured Bhagat that he would brief him again after two days, at the Rideau Lake floating restaurant, over a delicious Manchurian dinner.

****

Sartaj Jamil, the aged Sindhi leader from the lower Sind town of Tando Muhammad Khan, an interior feudal belt, was a man of courage and conviction. A person of Arab descent, he claimed his lineage to the legendary Arab conquerors who had hit the shores of Sind in the 8th century AD One of his ancestors was, according to family tradition, a revenue official in the court of the Abbasid Caliphate. The Jamil family was highly influenced by Lal Shahbaz Qalandar, the famous Sufi saint of Sehwan Sharief, once a dazzling seat of the rulers of the lower Sind. At heart Sartaj was a Sufi too. He believed in human values and cherished the values of sharing and caring. But the spirits of Sufism had also taught him the values of standing up against injustice and oppression.

Educated in Bombay and Karachi Sartaj had left his lucrative job as the Deputy District Collector in the NWFP to join the Khudai Khidmatgar (Servants of God) movement of the Frontier Gandhi. He had aligned himself with the Indian National Congress during the freedom movement. His affinity with the communist leaders from Punjab and Bengal had made him popular to the proletariat masses of Sind, Baluchistan and Punjab. At one point of time Moscow had evinced keen interest in him as a likely spearhead against the British.

Sartaj was one of the microscopic Muslim leaders who stood by Mohandas Karamchand Gandhi and opposed the two-nation theory propounded by the Muslim League and their British mentors. By the age of 40, when he spearheaded the Quit India movement in 1942, in the province of Sind, Sartaj had already spent 11 years in British jails at odd places like Bannu, Dera Ghazi Khan and Peshawar. He was again incarcerated in 1942 and was finally released from the dinghy district jail at Mianwali only in December 1946. By that time the retreating British masters and the tired Muslim and Hindu leaders had decided to tear up India into pieces to create a geographically incongruous Muslim nation called Pakistan and a vaguely secular country called India.

The combined leadership of the bureaucrats and the military had persuaded Sartaj to join the Sind provincial cabinet in 1960. But the diehard Muslim League fanatics and the landed feudals from Punjab soon pushed out the secular and democratic leaders from Sind, Baluchistan and the NWFP. The Urdu speaking migrant leaders from India were branded by the demeaning sobriquet of ***muhajir*** and were pushed out of power too. All pretensions of enshrining the lofty concepts of democracy and secularism were pushed under the soiled pages of religious edicts and military boots. The fond hopes of fabricating a written constitution for the new country were shredded to nullity by the unholy combination of the power hungry politicians, bureaucrats and the Army Generals. By 1962 Sartaj Jamil and a few of his secular friends in the exclusive Muslim nation of Pakistan had reached the end of their journey to disillusionment.

Sartaj's clouds of woes were darkened by the sudden rise of Izaz Afroz in the political firmament of Pakistan. The maverick and self-styled messianic scion of the Afroz feudal family from Larkana had spent most of his time in Britain either as a student or as a playboy. The military-bureaucratic rulers had suddenly discovered that this flamboyant Sindhi was ready to dance to their tune. Though a fully baked Englishman and educated in the practice and spirit of the political philosophies of the West Minster style democracy, Izaz hated everything that militated against his personalised autocratic style of functioning. A pathological sycophant, he danced to the tune of the military rulers and had taken upon himself the task of punishing those leaders of Sind who cherished the dreams of having cordial ties with the Hindu India. He had decided all by himself that leaders like Sartaj had fossilised beyond redemption and required decent burial under the delta sand.

Sartaj had committed the cardinal mistake of openly describing Izaz as a half Muslim. Pureblooded Sindhis never forgot that Izaz was born out of the wedlock of his father to a Hindu woman from Rajasthan, in whose veins royal blue blood didn't flow.

The very next morning Sartaj was picked up by an armoured column of the Frontier Light Infantry and was taken to the Karachi garrison for interrogation. The state controlled media raised a cacophony of trumped up charges that Sartaj was an Indian agent. The PIB and the ISI were made to manufacture a few damning reports implicating Sartaj with the Indian intelligence agencies, which aimed at balkanising Pakistan by encouraging the secessionists like Sartaj.

But Izaz could not keep him behind the bars indefinitely. The influential Pir of Pagaro and the elder brother of President Akbar Khan persuaded the supreme leader to reconcile with the lower Sind leader before he went through the exercises of promulgating a new constitution and holding the elections to the National Assembly. Izaz did not like the idea of sharing power with another Sindhi, but decided to mark time till he took over from the ailing Akbar Khan.

By the end of 1963 Sartaj Jamil had built up a strident movement for better economic and political rights for the province of Sind. His volunteers had started building up resistance groups with minor arms supplies from Baluchistan and the NWFP. His linkages with the Indian leaders had opened up another vista of mutual support for securing better rights for the people of Sind and Baluchistan.

Rabindra Narayan Dutta, the Federal Intelligence Bureau chief did not have much difficulty in persuading and convincing Amritlal, the Prime Minister, to allow him to oar around in the troubled waters of Sind. The events in Kashmir and the Northeast India had convinced him that the subtle wars of sabotage and subversion were to be taken inside the belly of Pakistan. The fault lines of the sick nation could be exploited by his agency.

Operation Meghna had already started taking firm roots in the eastern wing of Pakistan. Dutta targeted Sartaj, Sherdil Khan, and Aliullah Mengel etc in the west.

Sartaj was his prized catch. By 1963 the disillusioned leader firmly believed that the military was in no mood to transfer power to the elected representatives of the people and the sycophants like Izaz were bent upon destroying Pakistan by alienating the majority Bengalis. That fiend of a politician was obsessed with the idea of ruling Pakistan with an iron fist and inviting the deluge after him.

Sartaj had his first meeting with a cabinet colleague of Amritlal, who had shared common political platforms with him during the independence movement. His second meeting was with Amritlal in London. The Indian PM in a subtle move introduced him to Dutta and Nampoothiri. The liaison between the FIB stalwarts and the alienated Sindhi leader flourished steadfastly thereafter. ***Operation Mir Qalandar,*** another heated needle in the troubled flesh of Pakistan, was taken up as the second aggressive clandestine front against the military regime. Dutta's views were clear. He could not allow Pakistan to enjoy undisturbed sleep and export its proxy war to the underbelly of India in Kashmir and the Northeast at the same time.

Mir Qalandar was a favourite baby of Nampoothiri. He had struck a personal rapport with Jamil, Mazari and Mengel and had assisted them with the sinews of often-violent civil unrest through conduits in London, Paris and Frankfurt. India's forward moles like Alamgir were scrupulously kept away from the ***Qalandar*** operation. Briefing and debriefing were conducted either by Nampoothiri himself or through designated embassy based under cover diplomats.

The choice of Dhiren Bhagat, rather a middle level officer, to contact Sartaj Jamil at Boston was deliberate. His sister and her husband had set up their home at a bay front locality. Both of them worked in an insurance company. A small detour from Ottawa to Boston would look natural.

Sartaj Jamil's daughter, married to a Hispanic American, taught astrophysics in the MIT. Jamil's presence in Boston for an urgent medical check up for his heart ailment did not arouse suspicion to the Pakistani and American spooks.

His movements in New York, Washington and high profile cities were meticulously covered by the ISI. The CIA and the FBI too monitored his movements because of his alleged linkages with the Indian and Soviet Communist leaders.

Sartaj's visit to Boston synchronised with the political turmoil in Pakistan. President Akbar Khan had surrounded himself with a band of sycophantic courtiers, whose activities were orchestrated by his son, a retired junior army officer. Izaz Afroz, Sartaj's tormentor and Akbar Khan's hatchet man, had distanced himself from his one time mentor and busied himself with the impossible task of putting together a ragtag opposition. He conveniently donned the garb of socialism too; to satisfy the left oriented democratic forces.

He assiduously cultivated a few top Generals, including General Arif Khan, who was appointed as Chief of Army Staff by a beleaguered President, simply on consideration of his easygoing life style and his weaknesses for wine and women. General Hyder Bux, the ISI chief and the Corps Commanders of Peshawar, Lahore and Karachi and the Air Chief as well were his special targets. They formed a coterie, which had shifted loyalty, like the seasonal sand dunes of the Thar Desert, from Akbar Khan to Arif Khan, after the exact political implications of the Tashkent agreement dawned upon the Pakistani people, especially the Armed Forces.

Only Lt. General Sarfaraz Lodi, the most important commander of the Chak Lala AHQ reserve Corps maintained fearful distance from the Jackal of Larkana, as he preferred to call Izaz Afroz, behind his back. He had no illusion about that jackal. Sarfaraz firmly believed that Izaz had goaded President Akbar Khan to launch the disastrous Kashmir war of 1965. The Pakistan army was not ready for a full-scale war against the superior Indian Army. As the Chief of Staff to the former Army Chief he knew rather too well the weaknesses of the Pak army. Moreover, he nursed a secret ambition to take over the reins of Pakistan at an appropriate moment.

The east also was in ferment. The President had released Sheikh Jainal, an accused in the trumped up conspiracy case with the fond hope of bringing round the malcontent political forces to a round table conference.

Sartaj Jamil and his friends like Sherdil Khan and Aliullah Mengel were disenchanted with Akbar Khan and his coterie. They were also not inclined to trust the highly idiosyncratic and hypocritical Izaz Afroz, who was busy cobbling up a political opposition. Sartaj had his own agenda. He wanted to free Sind from the clutches of the jingoistic Punjabi military rulers and the milling ***muhajirs***, who had encroached into the economic interests of the ethnic Sindhis and Baluchis. Politically volatile, the ***muhajirs*** vacillated in supporting the genuine ethnic Sindhi causes and pretended to fraternise more with the Punjabi satraps, like the hyenas stalking the tails of the killer lions.

Sartaj's game plan was simple. He expected India to pump in more money and weapon for his supporters. The trickling support that he was getting from Delhi was inadequate. His band of followers among the ethnic Sindhis and the Baluchis were fighting pitched battles against the Pakistan army in isolated pockets of resistance. Their antiquated weapons were no match for the ruthless army, which freely used napalm and cluster bombs and air to ground rockets on the defenceless civilian population.

He expected the Boston meeting to be decisive.

But Bhagat's low profile appearance on a chilly evening disappointed him. His expectation that Mr. Balachari (code name for Nampoothiri) would himself come down for discussing the nitty-gritty of the scheme of collaboration was based on assurances given to him by no less a person than the High Commissioner of India in London.

The lake front courtyard of the house of Sartaj's daughter was surrounded by thick vegetation. Sartaj, seated on a camp chair, did not stand up to greet his guest. His straight gaze was fixed on the placid waters of the sprawling lake.

"Sir, I'm Laxman Singh," Bhagat braved the chill reception, "I have a communication for you from Mr. Balachari."

"I expected Balachari to be here. That's what I was given to understand," Sartaj extended his palm hesitatingly, "You Indians are not decisive players. You lack the killing instinct."

"He is busy with the events at home," Bhagat digested the dig and offered an unconvincing excuse, "Lots of things are happening there."

"Yes. I am aware of the developments in Delhi. But that does not deter you people from supporting the Bengalis in East Pakistan. The army fiends in Islamabad are bleeding the Baluchis and Sindhis to death. You don't care even if hundreds of my countrymen are butchered by the Punjabi thugs."

"I am sorry sir that you carry that impression, "Bhagat decided to come straight to the topic, "Mr. Balachari has requested you to consider the following points."

Bhagat spoke with an air of confidence. Delhi, he said, was worried about the fractured nature of the Democratic Alliance of Pakistan (DAP). The rise of Izaz Afroz was also causing concern. The 'Ceylon Tea Party,' Izaz Afroz's secret coterie of some of the power hungry Generals, was in no way friendly to the resistance movements in Sind and Baluchistan. They were working on a different agenda. Much would depend on mass mobilisation, subversion of the police and paramilitary forces in the two provinces and support from the key constituencies like the students, trade unions and the intellectuals. Delhi was unable to decide upon a firm line of action in the absence of significant control of the leaders of the resistance movements on mass psychology.

But Mr. Balachari, Bhagat elaborated, was keen on supporting the movement. Kabul would continue to be the main supply base. Additional routes would be opened up through Gujarat and Sind land borders. A possible new supply route, Bhagat explained, should be the age-old Dhow (mechanised country boat) channel between Indian Jamnagar and Kati Bandar and adjacent minor ports in the estuary of the river Indus. But much would depend on the leaders of the resistance movement. They should be able to mobilise a fleet of trusted Dhow operators to lift supplies of weapon from the high seas in the international waters.

"Mr. Balachari wants to know if you can arrange safe transit through the sea route."

Bhagat finished his exposition with a relish.

It was time for Sartaj Jamil to stand up. He walked up to the waterfront, picked up a few pebbles and threw them on the placid water. The small circular ripples mingled up with his agitated thought process. The daring suggestion of sending arms shipment through the sea route posed several challenges. He knew one person who could help him in mobilising a couple of enterprising Dhow operators. He was Zahoor Chaudry, the famous ***mohana*** tribal, who made it big in shipping industry. But he lived in far off Lahore, a bastion of the Punjabi entrepreneurs. He was a thorough apolitical person. Sartaj was not sure if Zahoor would agree to exercise his clout on the fishing folks of Kati Bandar and the adjacent minor fishing ports.

"Tell Mr. Balachari," Sartaj turned towards his guest, "The Kabul and Gujarat routes should be activated immediately. I will soon revert back to him on the other proposal."

"Fine sir."

Sartaj continued his soliloquy in as placid a voice as the placid water mass before him. He conveyed that Izaz Afroz should be prevented at any cost from capturing the seat of power in Islamabad. He was not capable of toppling the ailing President. The armed forces were not yet ready to hand over power to the civilians, that too to an untrustworthy jackal like Izaz. But there were indications that the new Chief of Army Staff, General Arif would sooner or later depose the old man. Arif was incapable of leading the tottering nation. Izaz had already cast a spell on him and he was sure to lead him up the garden path. Izaz disliked Sheikh Jainal and his hatred of the Bengalis was pathogenic. It was the best time for India to hit back and help the oppressed people of Sind and Baluchistan.

"But sir," Bhagat made a sleek intervention, "Izaz appears to be riding the crest of popular support."

"It's a myth he will like the world to believe Mr. Laxman Singh. He and his band of rabble-rousers are trying to get on to the top with the help of the army Generals. You people in India should know that Izaz is as good a democrat as Hitler was."

Sartaj Jamil poured out in an emotion filled voice.

"Sir, I'll convey your views to Mr. Balachari."

"Do that. And if it is possible request him to convey to Prime Minister Mandira that, Sheikh Jainal is an alter ego of Izaz Afroz. Between them they are bent upon destroying Pakistan. Tell her that I, as a colleague of her late father, want her to intervene in Sind and Baluchistan as passionately as she is helping the East Pakistani leaders. We Sindhis and the Baluchis have better democratic and secularist credentials than the Bengalis. It's they, who had conceived and architectured the Muslim League."

Bhagat understood that he had completed his mission and the old man had nothing else to tell except venting his frustration. He stood up and saluted the veteran freedom fighter in pure Sindhi, the mother tongue he inherited from his parents.

"Are you a Sindhi?"

"Yes sir. My parents, belonging to the untouchable Kahar caste, had migrated from Sind. In India our family had adopted the high caste title of Singh."

"That's a good news Singh. We two Sindhis can do better business. By the way ask Balachari if he is familiar with the name of Zahoor Chaudry of Lahore."

"Anything special sir?"

"Zahoor is a ***mohana*** Sindhi. He owns a flourishing shipping line and some of his Dhows ply between Karachi and the minor ports in Gujarat. He must be having linkages with the Indian Dhow operators."

"Sure sir. I will mention this to Mr. Balachari."

"One more point," Sartaj came out with a tantalising suggestion that surprised Bhagat, " Perhaps Balachari can explore the possibilities of exploiting the business contacts of Ram Karan Prasad. His people freely operate both through the land and sea routes."

"How well do you know Ram Karan, sir?"

"I'm out of touch. But we worked together in the Congress Working Committee and once we were lodged in the same cell at Kathiawar jail. I understand that his business contacts in Sind are very powerful."

"These are valuable suggestions sir. I don't think Mr. Balachari will have any difficulty, if you can firm up the loose ends in Pakistan."

Bhagat left the old soul alone to cook an infinite broth out of his dreams of attaining a better political status for Sind and Baluchistan. His mastery on the political history of Sind and Baluchistan was confined to the textbooks and he did not have any precise idea about the intrinsic depth of India's intelligence operations in these two provinces. The western wing of Pakistan, he understood, was gravitating very fast towards the Islamic nations of the Middle East. Its leaders were very keen to obliterate the past history of the Indian Muslims, and were fabricating a new history to prove that Pakistan was the eastern most vanguard of the cradle of the Islamic civilisation, a civilisation that was reshaped in the image of the Allah by the Prophet (pbuh). Islam had come to India as a ruling force and the followers of the true faith would like to regain that supreme status.

If his feelings were correct, Bhagat ruminated over his exchanges with Sartaj Jamil; Delhi would not go for extending unqualified support to the malcontent political leaders of Sind and Baluchistan. But they could be used for destabilising the political fabrics of Pakistan, which had failed to attain a cohesive texture since the partition.

But the mention of the names of Zahoor Chaudry and Ram Karan triggered off the alarm bell in Bhagat's trained mind. He was well acquainted with both the names. He wondered how Sartaj could hit upon the name of Zahoor? Was it because he was a fellow Sindhi and a person with avowed antipathy towards the foxy feudal from Larkana?

Bhagat had no doubt that Sartaj spoke about Ram Karan out of nostalgic remembrances. Their association in political activities against the British Empire were painted by the individual colour of ideology they carried in their neurons. Sartaj was fired by the ideology of patriotism. Ram Karan had darted into politics fired by the propellants of a favourable combination of his caste configuration and the manipulative practices of the British Home Office. The Congress leaders too had figured out that Ram Karan's support was necessary to wean away the vast lower caste Hindu oppressed classes from the subversive machinations of the Muslim League and the British mandarins.

Sartaj was surely not aware of the true nature of Ram Karan's business links with his Pakistani counterparts. He lived in his past and foolishly believed that with some support from India he could defeat the self-seeking jackals of the new Muslim nation and bring it back on the rails. He was simply not aware that Ram Karan had donned the Congress slough only with a view to facilitating his criminal activities.

Bhagat took a mental note to send a cipher to Nampoothiri immediately after reaching Ottawa. Bhagat framed the sentences of the cipher in his mind and focussed on the formulation that under no circumstances Zahoor Chaudry should be allowed to get involved with ***Operation Mir Qalandar.*** As for Ram Karan, he decided to leave the matter to the discretion of Nampoothiri and the political bosses. A strong willed political shepherd could only tackle a political animal like Ram Karan. They had their own ways and means to use and dump their associates, like they threw away paper cartons after enjoying the crispy chips. Most of them did not suffer from emotional hangover. A shepherd like Mandira surely did not.

****

The 123-mile long Rideau Canal system, developed by the British, mainly against the American invasion, was an engineering marvel. The sprawling lake in the heart of Bytown, modern Ottawa, attracted tourists during summer and fall and in winter the huge frozen bed served as an open-air skating rink. The daunty Canadians enjoyed their snow and sunshine with equal intensity.

Harfan had reserved a waterfront seat in the Chinese restaurant, manned by ethnic looking waiters.

"What's your mission in Montreal and Thunder Bay?" Asked Bhagat impatiently.

"Let's go one step at a time," said Harfan paying back Bhagat in his own coin, "Let's have Manchurian soup first. It's steaming hot and good for fighting cold."

Harfan leisurely poured a few drops of Tabasco to make it pungent and hot.

"In fact, I'm supposed to be working for General Akram, Officer on Special Duty in the Atomic Energy Department of Pakistan. He was recruited by Izaz Afroz." Harfan opened up the magic box.

"You mean you're a double agent?" Bhagat asked anxiously.

"You could say that, if it fits your set definition."

"You should've taken our clearance before accepting assignments from them. Professionally it's incorrect." Bhagat reminded Harfan of his briefing in Delhi.

"Yes, I understand." Harfan retorted, "And for my disobedience you can tip off the ISI and cook my goose. Be practical, Bhagat. My cover is that of a sales executive, in an establishment that specialises in defence supplies. I'm a roving delegate to foreign countries, negotiating the purchase of important defence materials for an equipment starved army."

"Spare me the sarcasm. You could've kept us in picture."

"Look Bhagat, I'm supposed to move in close proximity with the top brass, sleep with one of their heart throbs, and make monkeys of them. I can't take permission each time I visit the loo! Are you lost in Cinderella's charmed wonderland?"

Bhagat wasn't prepared for the outburst, which was very characteristic of the unadulterated Ramendra Kaushal of Delhi University.

Surprise! The snake had probably been injected with warm blood. He noted the change with silent caution and apprehension. The tamed agent had started living beyond his brief, improvising upon the tradecrafts assiduously ingrained in his psyche.

Caution! Caution! Bhagat made a mental note.

Perhaps, this was inevitable, in case of all remote controlled resident agents. They thrived on improvisations, which often generated an inflated sense of self-confidence. Perhaps Harfan had climbed up to that stratum. Wasn't it rather early for him to try to speed past his designated orbit?

"Don't misunderstand. All we want is your safety." Bhagat adopted a studied conciliatory posture.

"Look brother," Harfan still felt agitated, "Don't breath down my neck...you and this mighty Alam. Allow me some elbowroom. It's my neck, which is on the line and I should've the pleasure of escaping the noose, in my own style."

"Fine, fine." Bhagat toned down, "Let's continue with the briefing."

"I'm here to contact Dr. Mainul. He has the original research to his credit, on both the plutonium and uranium routes to nuclear weapons. What you don't know in Delhi is that, the KANUPP has started producing fissile weapons-grade plutonium. My mission is to offer Mainul a lucrative assignment in Pakistan. In fact, I've a carte blanche to offer him, on behalf of General Akram."

Harfan floored Bhagat with his revelation. The Indian government was suspicious about the activities at the KANUPP, because of confusing status of the IAEA safeguards on the reactor.

"Why did Akram select you?"

"I enjoy the confidence of Israr, who supplies machines and spares to Akram's outfit."

"Will Mainul agree to move to Pakistan?"

"No. Every Pakistani is committed to his fatherland, wherever he may be, like the Jews are to their Promised Land of The Book. That's what the religion teaches him. Dr. Mainul recognises his responsibility to the

Islamic nation and duty to the ***Ummah***. That's the peculiar way of life with the ***Ahl-e-Kitab***, people of the Book."

Harfan spoke, while negotiating a rare to medium Shanghai duck, cooked in French wine and fresh oyster sauce, a speciality in this Canadian Chinese restaurant.

Bhagat wasn't prepared for the tonnes of intelligence avalanche in just two short briefing sessions. The sweep was too wide and the depth unfathomable. The crook had really entrenched himself at the right places in Pakistan.

"Understood. But what takes you to McGill?"

"Dr. Carver, the eminent nuclear physicist had helped in installing the KANUPP. He's doing original research on fusion reaction. An acquaintance of our former Foreign Minister, Izaz Afroz, Dr. Carver is likely to visit Karachi next month."

"You mean Afroz is still in the game?"

"Have you read his book The Mythology of Independence?" Harfan asked.

"No."

"Read it. You'll discover the real philosophy of Pakistan's nuclear quest," Harfan continued, "He has an unmitigated hatred for Hindustan and Hindus and he thinks he has been created by the ***Allah*** to destroy the Hindu ***kafirs***."

"That's strange. I believe his mother was a Hindu." Bhagat pricked Harfan with the needle of his knowledge.

"The Afrozs are a vengeful lot and he hasn't forgotten his father's humiliation over Junagarh's merger with India. Now listen," Harfan licked the slightly pungent, season's fresh maple syrup served with pure Canadian pancakes, "Contact ***vaid*** Dhanwantari of Dehradun. I want these medicines to be delivered to my friend in London by next week." He passed on a piece of paper to Bhagat.

"What are these medicines for?"

"Some skin disease caused by the absence of melanin, the pigment which gives colour to our skin. The other is some queer aphrodisiac concoction. The ***vaid*** is supposed to be good. His clients in Pakistan are anxious to avail his services."

"Who requires the sex-stimulants?" Bhagat asked.

"Don't forget that most of the Generals in my host country are past 50 and they're used to extramarital affairs. But don't forget to contact the vaid on behalf of a London based Indian. Your hands should not be seen at all."

Bhagat promised to arrange the delivery of six months supply of medicine at the London contact point. He passed on a leather pouch to Harfan.

"What's in it?"

"A gift from Papa. He's happy with you; especially your wonderful efforts in that Markaz sponsored assassination attempt. There's 10,000 US dollars, for your incidentals. He wants you to visit Dacca once again and furnish a firsthand report on Pak preparations against the Peoples' League. Do you have good friends there? Is any one from the CMLA establishment recently transferred to the Dacca garrison?" Bhagat asked.

Harfan scratched his head, lighted a cigarette and slowly replied," My beat doesn't normally take me to East Pakistan. I've friends in Dacca, but can't give you a commitment without consulting Israr."

"Papa is interested to have authentic information on Pakistani build up in the eastern wing."

"Sure, he should be. Tell him that the Americans have tipped off Pakistan about the recent joint exercises by India's Eastern Naval Command and the Russian Pacific Fleet in the Bay of Bengal. The Amigos feel that the exercise, ***Operation Manthan*** (churning) was aimed at securing total command on all the shipping channels to vital East Pakistani ports."

"Do you think the Americans will intervene?" Bhagat requested for elaboration.

"Washington is uneasy with Delhi's positioning of the INS Vikrant, its aircraft carrier and several frigates, just 200 km below the funnel of the Bay of Bengal. Their satellite images have captured movements of the Russian armada in the Strait of Malacca. Tell Papa to keep a watchful eye on the Chinese and US naval movements. Pakistan has already despatched Ghazi, one of its submarines to the eastern blue waters."

Harfan's briefing amazed Bhagat. The streak of defiance apart, XXX had shaped up beyond their wildest expectation.

"It's been an excellent meeting Ramen," Bhagat added, "I take a morning flight to JFK and thereafter on to Delhi."

"I've to stay put here. Israr is expecting a meeting with the Chinese Trade Minister at Toronto."

"What for?"

"A high level Chinese defence delegation is scheduled to arrive in Islamabad in another four months. We expect to bag a fat contract for picking up Chinese military supplies from a third country base."

"Military hardware?"

"Yes."

"You mean Peking will support the military regime's dirty deeds in East Pak?" Bhagat asked.

"Oh my god!" Harfan searched his jacket and brought out an envelope, "Keep this. It's a classified document from the CMLA secretariat. Tell boss that General Arif and Izaz Afroz are building a secret bridge between Washington and Peking."

"How come?"

"I don't know the details yet. It could be a flank attack against the Red Bear, a strategic cold-war gamble."

"That's a queer cocktail."

"That's real geo-politics for you now. And tell Papa that Aftab requires his immediate attention. I suspect Ram Karan."

"I think you have a Ram Karan fixation."

"You know the Satan well only when you lend your soul to him."

"By the way," Bhagat deliberately stretched the conversation, "Do you think he can be used for some subtle jobs inside Pakistan?"

"He measures everything in terms of money. It depends on your capability of out bidding the Pakistanis. What's cooking up?"

"Just like that," Bhagat dodged the topic and feigned that he was giving a personal touch to the professional meeting, "Hope life with Jamilla is very rosy."

"Yes. I'm happy. I wish this life lasted for ever."

"It's only a part of your cover Ramen. I believe Zahoor sahib is a very influential person in Sind. Do you think he can help us?"

"Look Bhagat," Harfan clicked his cigarette lighter and blew off the blue flame, "Zahoor is a part of my cover too. Don't drag him in your damn intelligence business. I am here under your guillotine chopper. Don't drag them under it."

"There is no need for the rhetoric. I just wanted to know if he takes interest in Pakistani politics."

"No. He is an apolitical businessman, and nothing else. Close this topic."

Harfan fished out a cover from his chest pocket, as they started walking along the gangway and passed it on to Bhagat.

"Please give it to my mom. There's a letter and some Indian currency in it." He begged Bhagat.

"You're taking a huge risk. It's not done in our line." Bhagat reminded Harfan of the security requirements.

"Don't be cruel and I don't bother. You put me in front of a running movie, that links my past and present and ask me to keep my eyes closed and shut up my sensory organs. That's not done. I am made of flesh and blood too," Harfan spoke firmly and added, "And don't betray. I expect you to be true to me."

Bhagat gave a feeble smile and accepting the packet he reassured Harfan by squeezing his palm gently.

Harfan suddenly turned towards Bhagat and asked, "Will you feel sorry for me if I'm killed by the Pakistanis?"

Bhagat struggled for a while for the correct words. He didn't have any. He stood motionless at the wooden gangway, leading to the parking lot. Only the ripples of the lake waters added some sad notes to the silence of darkness.

"Will you take care of my Jamilla and my son Parvez?" Harfan asked again.

"You don't have to ask me Ramen," Bhagat replied, "I stand committed to you and your family. I'll take care of them."

"You've helped me regain my human traits. I trust you. Take care of my Jamilla and Parvez and my mother." Harfan moved closer and hugged Bhagat

"Are you afraid of a compromise, or detection by Pak agents?

Bhagat was intrigued by the sudden change in Harfan's mood.

"Not really. It's just a premonition of a lone walker in a spiked killing field. I'm walking on a fragile rope stretched across a bottomless pit. I don't know when it'll snap. A spy like me, isn't owned by any one and he doesn't have nine lives, you know more than any one else."

"Don't imagine things." Bhagat consoled Harfan.

"You imagine things more when your dear ones are just a few steps away from the chopping block. I'm living desperately with a mirage, expecting a ***jinn*** to materialise my hopes and dreams, just like the palace of Aladdin."

"Don't despair. You're on top of the situation." Bhagat added in a rather hollow voice.

"Yah, I know that. I've to build each stair, brick by brick, before I take the next precarious step." Harfan laughed and lighted a cigarette.

He picked up the bag and walked down to his rented Ford and started the engine without looking back. In his job he could look back with nostalgia, but a revisit was very rare, if not forbidden.

Bhagat felt a streak of pain and anxiety stirring his guts. This pain arose out of the knowledge that the NSI didn't normally reclaim a compromised spy.

The anxiety was generated by Harfan's display of despair. A desperate spy, conscious of his amorphous security status, could literally improvise a new script and direct the drama himself. Some new chemistry was churning inside Harfan. He wasn't the same robot anymore, fabricated by Maulana Rizwan and himself.

He had chanced to meet, in remote Ottawa, a completely transformed Ramendra Kaushal, a man wizened by the bitter knowledge of hanging over a bottomless pit. He could take an uncertain jump any time, and that could spell disaster for the National Security India and the Indian nation. Nampoothiri must be briefed in detail. Bhagat looked forward to an early meeting with the big boss.

But his immediate task was to rush to the High Commissioner's residence and request him for access to the cipher facility of the Mission. He had very important materials to convey to Delhi. Sartaj Jamil was an important shuttle in the clandestine ball game between India and Pakistan. But Harfan's disclosures were more explosive possibly with far reaching implications for the security of the country. Nampoothiri should be able to take a stock of the situation and brief the Prime Minister about the urgency of countering the nuclear quest of Pakistan

****

Izaz Afroz did not nurture very high respect for General Arif Khan, the new Army Chief of Staff and the Chief Martial Law Administrator, who was handpicked by Akbar Khan, the ailing and beleaguered President. The President himself, more of a political conjuror than a war-hardened soldier, had given more weightage to the carnal qualities of his new COAS than his proven battlefield credentials. A fun loving and easygoing person, General Arif was known for his weaknesses for bumpy women and bouncy bottles. Akbar Khan had estimated that the Frontier bumpkin was not likely to develop ambitions for the lucrative throne of Pakistan, which he was cautiously guarding for his worthy son. He did not trust Lt. General Sarfaraz and the most respected Corps commander of Chak Lala, Lt. General Hamidur. The minor fries like General Tarakki and Hyder Bux did not have the capability of conjuring up another coup. They simply did not have the backing of the Corps Commanders and the most respected soldier of the country, Air Chief

Marshal Rahmat Khan and the universally loved Naval Chief, Admiral Shaukat. But President Akbar had under estimated General Arif.

General Arif, like most Pakistani soldiers, harbored some vapor of ambition under his chest and considered Pakistan as the unguarded treasury chest of the people, which could be plundered at will, like his illustrious warlord predecessor Nadir Shah did. But he did not know the tricks of the trade well. All these years he was happy with the booty that came to his share as an important member of the ruling military clique. He had not tried to hone up the techniques of the alchemy that turned a mere soldier to a crowned king.

His first serious lesson in political banditry came from his elder brother, Major General Nayeem, who as an intelligence technocrat and had the opportunity of peeping into the wonder world of power game that was dominated by the witchy combination of the senior bureaucrats and the ambitious soldiers. He finally gathered courage and gave the ultimate push to President Akbar and crowned himself as the new ruler of Pakistan.

However, Izaz Afroz, the Pakistani incarnation of Prince Otto Von Bismarck and Charles Andre Joseph Marie De Gaulle, had other ideas in mind. He had sized up General Arif with the precision of an expert goldsmith and came to the conclusion that the time was not opportune for him, to ascend the throne. There were still a couple of stumbling blocks.

In the eastern wing Sheikh Jainal was the most important challenger. That half-educated son of a farmer was no match for him, who carried pure Arab blue blood in his veins and who had coated himself with the civilisational fineries of the west. He, and not that bumpkin from Dacca were destined to lead Pakistan to greater glories. No doubt Jainal could claim majority support, but majority rule was not the best rule. Islam did not recognize the merit of the masses. It went by the wisdom of the chosen ones of the ***Allah.***

In the event of a poll to the National Assembly his popularity in the Punjab and parts of Sind was bound to give him a sweeping majority in West Pakistan. But he did not know how to oar around in the murky waters of East Pakistan. That was an uncertain turf. He abhorred the idea of sharing power with the stinking fish-eater Bengalis. He could, if circumstances demanded, tolerate for a while that funny nosed Mandira, the Hindu Prime Minister of India. But under no circumstance he could accept the superiority of a half-Hindu Bengali Muslim. Pakistan had enough of the Bongos, the Bogras, and the Nazimuddins. It was high time that a true Pakistani took over the reins of the Nation. Izaz always nursed a dream, that he deserved to be immortalized as the second Quaid-e-Azam of the Muslim nation.

Izaz's precise rationalization boiled down to two priority tasks. President Akbar deserved rest. He had plundered Pakistan for over a decade and a half. General Arif, with the connivance of the 'Ceylon Tea Party', the coterie of Generals, had taken over the reins of the drifting nation of Pakistan. It was important for him, Izaz rationalized, to attach himself to the tail end of the blundering devotee of bacci and his intimate circle of the hungry Generals. They should, in the final count, act as his stepping-stone to the throne of Pakistan. General Akbar had some basic idea about the people of Pakistan. These bunches of Generals were pure and simple bandits. They were in a tearing hurry to loot the nation and Arif had very little time beyond his deadly fascination for Begum Jahanara, who presided over the decision making faculties of the new President. She should also be kept in good humour, till he succeeded in arranging a fine burial for her, in connivance with General Hyder Bux, the ISI chief.

The second task evolved around the idea of teaching historic lessons to the pernicious Bengalis, like Hitler had dispensed loud lessons to the horrendous Zionists. These two races, Izaz rationalized, were irrelevant to the passage of human history. Nothing serious was going to happen if the Bengalis disappeared from the face of the earth and the Jews were buried under the desert sands.

With all such revolutionary ideas in his mind, Izaz Afroz picked up the phone around 11 in the morning, to call up General Arif Khan. The itch to call the new President had been scratching his mind since early morning. But he was helpless. His friend General Hyder Bux, the newly appointed chief of the ISI had tipped him off about the daily routine of the ***Sadr*** (head of the State). He spent most of his evenings at the sprawling residence of Begum Jahanara, the celebrated singer of classical Hindustani music. The grapevine of the power-lobby in Pakistan had painted Jahanara as the illusory lady luck, who favoured only the brave and the bold. She had mastered the uncanny skill of attaching herself to the ruler of the day. And the top echelon in the military ruled Pakistan had an unbridled access to the treasury of the nation. Begum Jahanara was not a petty pickpocket. She knew well the art of robbing the high and mighty of the land by using the finest craft of music and the best gift of the God, her sizzling beauty. The rumour mill was agog with the bounty of charm that Jahanara had showered on the new strong man of Pakistan, General Arif Khan.

General Arif, besides losing himself in the fathomless music and beauty of Jahanara, often remained preoccupied with important matters like jackal shooting in the interiors of Sind and Punjab and walking the golf greens once in a while.

Izaz Afroz therefore selected the appropriate needle of time to call up Pakistan's new man of destiny.

"Izaz this side. May I speak to the President?"

"Sir," A hesitant voice replied, "The President is busy. Can you call later?"

"Listen to me, whosoever you are, a captain or a colonel. I want to see the General immediately." Izaz tried to bamboozle the Aide d' Camp of the President.

"Sir I'm Colonel Munir here," The voice replied politely, "The boss is just getting ready. Hold on. I will connect him."

"Hello Izaz sahib, ***kaisa mizaaj*** (how is the mood)?"

"It's both good and bad General. The good is that you are the rising star and the bad news is that the sick man of Dacca is still haunting the nation. Can I come over?"

"Now?"

"Yes Mr. President. It is urgent."

"Come over. I'm getting ready for the chilled Heineken. Hope you'll like to share the nectar?"

Izaz Afroz lived four blocks away from the official residence of the Chief of Army Staff, who was yet to shift to the official residence of the President of the nation. But he took over half an hour to get past the array of Patton and Sherman tanks, numerous armored personnel carriers, barbed wire fences and armed pickets. The unprecedented security paraphernalia were lined up to meet contingencies arising out of the civil strife against the deposed unpopular President. General Arif was yet to crack down on the mob that had paralyzed the nation. The unique inner democracy, the concept of sharing the spoils of the nation equitably, characterized the veneer of strength of leadership of the Army. General Arif, some cynics in the political parties and the armed forces opined, was waiting for the final nod from the master puppeteers, the powerful Corps Commanders. He was ready with a plan to impose another puppet civilian government with a possible offer to Izaz to head the crucial foreign ministry. Izaz had decided to keep aloof from the present junta. His game was deeper and his aim was the top slot of the nation, either the seat of the President or that of the Prime Minister.

Afroz emerged out of his Ford Classic with a great flourish. Colonel Munir conducted him to the shaded forecourt verandah, where the General was seated amidst a pile of files, a glass of frothy Heineken and a lighted cigarette between his fingers.

General Arif did not bother to rise up to greet the former minister and the architect of the 1965 war against India. He knew this jackal very well. A snob of the first order, he would not have bothered to visit him if he did not have his own axe to grind. He knew rather well that Izaz's machete was merciless. He had used it unscrupulously in the past to promote his political career and he would not hesitate to axe another General if he were offered the slightest chance to ride the tiger of fortune again.

"What brings the brightest star of Pakistan to my modest home?" General Arif offered a seat to Izaz and ordered Munir to pour beer for the honored guest.

"Serious matters of the nation General," Izaz Afroz settled down on the sofa and looked up appreciatively at Munir, who waited with the beer mug, "Have brought me here. I hope you know that President Akbar is plotting a counter coup. And how can he maintain secret links with traitor Jainal? Are we going to be ruled by another illiterate Bengali?"

"Cool down Izaz sahib. Let's not forget that we had chosen to attach ourselves to the Bengali majority at the dawn of our independence. It's they who had championed the Muslim League concept."

"Shit!" Izaz squirmed his lips with disgust, "These Bongos are half Muslims. We can't trust them."

"I understand your sentiment Izaz sahib. Please be sure that I will not allow another Bengali to rule over the nation. We had enough of them. Anything else?"

"Oh yes. I wanted to brief you about my visits to Washington and Peking. There's good news for you. The White House thinks that you've done the right thing by taking over from Akbar Khan."

"What about Peking?" General Arif asked with a squinted look at his maverick visitor.

"They appreciate your dynamic initiative of arranging the ice breaking meeting between the US Secretary of State and the Deputy Premier of the Peoples' Republic of China. It's a momentous diplomatic initiative after the Cold War stalemate."

Izaz spoke with his eyes fixed on the rotund face of General Arif. He knew that this foxy bait was sure to hook the knave General.

"Look Izaz," General Arif spoke in a straight voice, "I'm a soldier. I know best how to solve a situation by pure military means. You're a politician. For you politicians yes means no and no means yes. I cannot indulge in double speaking. I am waiting for this evening's meeting with the senior commanders. I'll take corrective measures after they endorse another brief spell of guided democracy under the Armed Forces. But I'll finally go by the wishes of the people of Pakistan."

"That's what I'm pleading you to do," Izaz spoke ebulliently, "You are the man of destiny. I am here to lend you all the support you require in putting down the Indian inspired civil unrest in East Pakistan."

"Let's speak about this later."

"Fine General," Izaz took the blunt hint rather nonchalantly, "But I have a couple of points to discuss."

"Fire them one by one. You have precise 20 minutes to unburden yourself. But don't deliver another UN type marathon speech."

Izaz Afroz took the blunt hint with a slight squint of his eyes and started with his deep-rooted suspicion about the Indian inspired movement for greater autonomy in Sind and Baluchistan. The unholy forces commanded by Sartaj Jamil, Farooq Jatoi, Sherdil Khan Mazari and Aliullah Mengel, he said, were emulating the pattern of civil unrest in East Pakistan. President Akbar Khan had tried in vain to woo these traitors. Their seditious activities could be contained only by firm military action.

"What proof do you have against them? How can you implicate Delhi?" General Arif wiped off the froth that had nestled in his bushy moustache with a silken handkerchief and asked Munir to help him with a cigarette.

"You can talk to General Hyder Bux and General Nayeem. The ISI and the Pak Intelligence Bureau chiefs should know better. But, as the former foreign minister I can assure you that Prime Minister Mandira has adopted a double pronged strategy to destabilize Pakistan."

"I don't disagree with you," General Arif scaled down his voice, "Tell me how can we get to know the precise working of the mind of that woman?"

"I know a few sure shots. Ask General Nayeem, if you so like, to activate Ram Karan, the Indian minister. He is our man in Delhi. My next trump card is the immediate revamping of ***Operation Mardan.***"

"What's that?"

"This involves accelerated supply of weapons and resources to the tribal insurgents in the Indian Northeast. I have discussed this issue with our friends in Peking. They are willing to invite a few Naga and Mizo groups to the Army managed camps at Kunming. All that you are required to do is to direct our ambassador over there to sort out the nitty-gritty of the Chinese side of the operation."

"Why was ***Mardan*** suspended?"

"Can't say. I presume the ISI needs a little prodding."

"Allah wishing we shall discuss this in a couple of days," General Arif spoke in a condescending tone, "Tell me one thing straight Izaz. Will you agree to serve in a civilian government that I may put together as an interim measure, in preparation to a full fledged election to the National Assembly?"

"Pardon me General. Possibly I can't do that. I'm at the forefront of the Movement for Restoration of Democracy. West Pakistanis have started trusting me. Sheikh Jainal will have the last laugh if I again join an army lead government. Leave me out. It's me, who will act as the final frontier of resistance against the Bengali plague. Can you imagine serving under another half-baked Muslim like Jainal?"

"I get your point."

"I've another important point to discuss, General."

"Shoot out."

"You are the best judge of the present fighting fitness of our armed forces. We can't take on India even for a week long war, if Mandira decides to hit us back at this point of our national crisis."

Izaz lowered his voice as if he was discussing a matter of great conspiracy.

"I agree. But the US and its friends are not yet ready even to replenish the losses we suffered in 1965. They are harping on the conditionality of implementation of the terms of the Tashkent agreement and some European powers have started raising the bogey of violation of human rights in East Pakistan. Do you have an answer to our problems?"

"There is a catch General," Izaz leaned towards the right ear of General Arif and spoke in a hushed tone, "The US is alarmed by the growing entente between Delhi and Moscow. They're worried about the poaching forays by the Soviet fleet in the Pacific Rim and the Indian Ocean region."

"You mean the White House will agree to supply hardware to us?"

"Yes and no. They are agreeable to examine an inventory. And the supplies will have to be airlifted from friendly third country bases. Probably they will like to use some CIA front organizations to do the job."

"That suits me. What about the Chinese?"

"They too are ready to supply against hard cash in green bills. But there is a catch."

"Cough it out clearly."

"They are disinclined to deliver the merchandise at any Pakistani port. You have to tie up with a friendly Gulf government and arrange for airlifting by private cargo carriers."

"Izaz sahib," General Arif stood up, "I'm getting late for a meeting with the leaders of the religious parties. Shall we resume the discussion, say after 3 days?"

"No hurry General. But I want to mention that Nawab Sharief, whom I am projecting as the next Chief Minister of Punjab has excellent business contacts with the Pentagon and the crown prince of Sharjah. Probably you can consider him for the airlifting operations."

"Sure Izaz sahib. Ask him to see Munir one of these days. See you soon."

General Arif extended his hand towards Colonel Munir for support.

"One last point General. What about joining me over a ***shikar*** (hunting) party at Larkana? We have plenty of pheasants, spotted deer and rare quails over there. I am expecting both the American and the Chinese ambassadors."

Izaz threw the last bait with a shrewmouse pout in his mouth.

"Well," General Arif weighed the offer and in a split second came out with a reply, "I don't think I should disappoint the US and the Chinese ambassadors. Hope you are taking care of the entertainment."

"Don't worry General. Nawab is lining up the cream of the female cine stars of Lahore. Perhaps you will like to invite Mohtarma Begum Jahanara Sahiba also."

"Let me see Izaz. I will sure come if the affairs of the state allow me."

General Arif disappeared inside the sprawling bungalow through the main door.

Izaz Afroz lighted a cigarette and displayed a broken smile like a happy hunter, who had just laid a perfect bait for his kill. He should be able to mesmerize the lousy General by his intricate knowledge of international diplomacy and his inside knowledge of the orbital tilt of the US leadership to engage China in strategic parlays. He should be able to walk up to the throne of Pakistan over the rubbles of another military regime, the one headed by General Arif. He only hoped that the fleshy General should not dig in for an indefinite period. ***Insha Allah***, he should be able to tackle this man like he was adept in tackling the political baboons of Pakistan.

His biggest worry was that long and stiff nosed lady in Delhi. Mandira, who had manipulated the political situation to her favour, was pumping in resources to strengthen the malcontent Pakistanis in Sind, Baluchistan and East Bengal. Allah willing he would very much like to prune her stiff nose and put her in a political doghouse. For that historic performance he would require the shoulders of the Pakistani soldiers and the mounds of dead bodies of the Bengalis. He hoped that Washington and Peking would endorse his strategy against Delhi. He required one more final war to unfurl the crescent flag from the ramparts of the Red Fort in Delhi.

****

Mandira's behavioral mercury often jumped unpredictably. This was a family trait, inherited more from her father than her mother, who preferred to suffer silently. She was already in a sulking mood that dark rainy evening. It was not the rain and the slush that made her fume. Her political adversaries had come out with an audacious plan to defeat her in the forthcoming elections to the Parliament. She was ready to take them on. But a stray comment by the visiting Indian High Commissioner to Islamabad had triggered off her torrent of anger.

The fumbling envoy was infinitely intrigued by the sudden silence of the Prime Minister. His bureaucratic mind interpreted it as a sign of unhappiness of the tigress seated before him.

The best antidote that he could surmise was that a personal touch would make the situation lighter. He borrowed on a piece of conversation he had in Islamabad with the Japanese ambassador and mentioned in a lighter tone that Izaz Afroz, the former foreign minister of Pakistan had very unkind words to tell about her.

Mandira looked up with silent piercing eyes

"What I heard ma'am," The envoy continued the embarrassing and unwarranted dialogue with plenty of perspiration under his trouser, "Izaz had mentioned something like 'that lanky ugly girl'."

"Tell him," Mandira had shot back, "I'm here to make him beg before me, his handsome body bent on his knees."

She dismissed the envoy and went back into her shell.

Mandira was not unhappy with Izaz. She knew that character very well. The foolish undiplomatic babbling by the senior envoy irritated her.

She was not disinclined both to confront and demolish the jackal of Larkana. She had had enough of him in a couple of encounters in the United Nations. She would not allow that demagogue to become a pain on her neck. She often witnessed the shadows of her own behavioral airs in Izaz. Two personalities with the same inner propensities could perhaps not rule over the historically inimical countries of India and Pakistan. Perhaps, she often thought, Izaz was more egocentric than the Quaid-e-Azam, the ultimate challenger to her father Amritlal.

She was ready to take on Izaz at a historically opportune moment. Nevertheless, her immediate strategic priority was pegged at the unorthodox idea of keeping the Pakistani Generals busy in their own home turfs, both in the east and the west. They should not find spare space to disturb her already shaky political position. At home the political sharks surrounded her ominously. She did not want a stable hostile neighbor pointing its guns at her and the nation she piloted.

Mandira was not very hopeful of the success of the movements spearheaded by Sartaj Jamil and his colleagues in West Pakistan, though she was assured of steady supply of arms by Nampoothiri's contacts in the KGB. The movement was simply not picking up. The armed forces and the religious parties had also ganged up to maim and murder the activists of the separatist movements in the west.

However, Mandira was happy that Izaz Afroz was facing challenges from a reckonable stalwart like Sartaj Jamil, the Lion of Sind. The Punjabi's, she was sure, would finally discard the charlatan, who would never succeed in identifying himself with the peculiar feudal interests of the landed Jat gentry and the Generals, who nursed deep suspicion about the integrity of the Sindhis.

She naturally pinned more hopes on the movement in East Pakistan. This one weapon, if fired properly, was sure to hit the bull's eye and give her enough breathing time in the troubled Northeast.

She had a feeling that Nampoothiri was dragging his feet and was not keen to involve the Russians in the core aspects of ***Operation Meghna***. He could have his compulsions and she appreciated his allergic response to the Russian helps to the Communist leaders of East Pakistan. But he must explore other alternatives and do that quickly. She was in no mood to give a long lease of life to the military rulers in Islamabad.

"Dewan," Mandira summoned her personal secretary, "Call Nampoothiri."

"He is here ma'am, in my room."

"What is he doing here?"

"He came to personally hand over a special report. Shall I send him in?"

"Yes."

Nampoothiri's unannounced visit to the camp office of the PM was necessitated by his failure to secure an early appointment before his visit to Singapore. The brief report contained only a few paragraphs about his intended meeting with Yossi Dayan, the former General of the Mossad and an expert of the arms bazaar. He sold weapons to everyone, right from the rebel leaders in Congo to the diamond bandits in Rwanda and Burundi. His weapons reached even the drug mafia in Columbia, Peru and Panama. His deadly supplies spurred the civil wars in Peru, Haiti and Guatemala. Yossi was a lone ranger. His corporate entity was a single man show. He did not believe in taking partners in his unique entrepreneurship.

"Did you call me ma'am?"

Nampoothiri walked into Mandira's small office room.

"Yes Balu," She replaced her spectacle and rested her head on the high back chair, "Did your man contact Sartaj?"

Nampoothiri gave a succinct account of Dhiren Bhagat's encounter with the elderly Sindhi leader at a Boston suburb. His request for weapons and other resources were being processed and a team of experts was examining the sea route from Gujarat to minor fishing ports in the estuary of the Indus. He did not think, Nampoothiri informed the PM, that it would be prudent to involve either Ram Karan or Zahoor Chaudry to ferry weapon consignments to the designated estuary islands of the Indus.

Mandira nodded in silent agreement.

The Kabul route was being exclusively used for Baluchistan. That part of ***Operation Mir Qalandar*** had run into trouble. The Pakistan Army had neutralized the conduits selected by Alamgir for activating the underground tunnels to the rugged terrain of Baluchistan. The Yusufzai tribe had betrayed the leaders of the renegade movement.

The National Security India had abandoned the Alamgir route for operational safety. A new Tajikistan based talent had taken up the assignment in collaboration with a Mazar-e-Shariff based warlord.

"No Balu," Mandira shook her head in disapproval, "I'm not happy with the progress with your ***Qalandar*** operation. See this report from Moscow."

Nampoothiri collected the paper from Mandira's extended hand and silently went through the text, an unsigned note, most probably originated by the Soviet ambassador in Delhi.

"Yes ma'am," Nampoothiri looked up straight into the eyes of Mandira, "I don't entirely agree with the report. I've reliable reports both from Alamgir and Triple X about the double game being played by some of the Parcham party (pro-Soviet communist) leaders. Some Pushtoon elements in the Parcham are collaborating with the Pakistan army."

"How come?"

"In that terrain," Nampoothiri continued, "Tribal loyalty is stronger than ideological bondages. The Russians are overrating their followers in Kabul. I know that for sure."

"What do you suggest?"

"Our Tehran based agent has activated some smugglers from Kandhar and Herat, for delivering our supplies deep into the Baluch tribal territories. I expect dramatic escalation in the Baluchistan hills."

"What about your mission in the east?"

"That's a tricky problem ma'am," Nampoothiri spoke in an apologetic voice, "Some of the supplies to ***Meghana*** by our Border Police Force from Indian ordnance factories were intercepted by the Pakistan army. These have been exhibited to the diplomatic corps and foreign media in Dacca."

"That's embarrassing."

"Yes ma'am. I'm shortly leaving for Singapore and here is an unsigned note on my new approach."

Mandira glanced through the brief report and returned it back.

"Is this man Yossi reliable?"

"None of them are. But Yossi has a reputation of delivering the goods at the doorstep of the receivers. He is a time-tested supplier in the international trouble spots."

"What are his linkages with the CIA?"

"None. He is an independent operator and fortunately he is known to our operation Triple X."

"How come? Are you exposing your agents on such errand too?"

"No ma'am. Triple X has had a few brushes with him concerning supply of weapons to the Muslim Rohingya rebels in the Arakan Hills on Pak Burma border."

"Is Pakistan arming the Rohingya's too?"

"Yes ma'am. The CMLA tackles independent operators like Yossi through trusted home based companies. Israr International, the company that employs Triple X had tapped the Israeli General."

"That's a queer world. Explain me your mechanism."

Mandira settled for a brief exposition by Balachandran Nampoothiri. At the end of the fascinating narration she opened her eyes and asked a piercing question.

"Do you think that Jainal's ragtag volunteer force can handle these sophisticated weapons?"

"I am sure they cannot. But the 8th Mountain Division and the Special Volunteer Force experts have set up camps for training Jainal's ***Mukti Bahini*** (freedom fighters)."

"That's okay Balu. However, advise Jainal to subvert the East Pakistan Rifles, the East Pakistan Infantry and the National Service Battalions. He requires a group of trained leaders, who can take on the job of leading the ***Mukti Bahini.*** His ragtag fighters alone can't face up to the Pakistani forces. Ask your officer Vishram Satpore to work in this direction."

"Yes ma'am."

"Engage your trusted men to subvert the key mid-formation Bengali army officers and the top police officers. And take care that your Israeli link is not compromised. I have that damn Muslim problem at home and abroad. My forthcoming visit to Egypt and Iran should not be clouded by your operation."

"That is well understood ma'am.

Mandira gave a silent affirmative nod. Yes. Nampoothiri could go ahead with his plan.

That night Nampoothiri, accompanided by Amrita, boarded a JAL flight to Tokyo. He had ruled out the suggestion of taking a direct flight to the Strait Island. Prying eyes and minds were sure to ask inconvenient questions of the motive behind the NSI chief flying into Singapore tucking his vivacious secretary under his arms. Amrita had never accompanied him on operational errand. Her presence was sure to enliven Delhi's gossip-glitterati, most of whom were regular booze-clients of the foreign missions, Pakistan included.

The deception was well calculated. Colonel Vijay Bhalla, Amrita's father, who had halted the Chinese advance at an outpost near Bomdila till he was bayoneted to death by the frustrated yellow soldiers, was trained at the SAS commando training facility in UK along with Yossi Dayan. The Israeli General was in regular touch with the daughter of the valiant Indian soldier. In fact the request for Amrita's presence had come from Yossi. Nampoothiri had readily agreed to tag her along. It would give, he thought, a natural cover of a holidaying husband-wife duo to his circuitous trip to Singapore.

He had planned to take a third country flight, most probably the Garuda International from Tokyo to Singapore, which was scheduled to land at the Changi airport around four in the morning.

Yossi Dayan, a six feet three inches robust Jew, was seated under a miniature palm grove at Singapore's Grand Capthome Waterfront hotel. He was feigning to watch a group of lively American ladies sunbathing at the poolside. Women did not enthuse him anymore. He had lost his mother at an Austrian concentration camp. He was made to see the rape of his sister by a bunch of drunken Gestapo soldiers, who later consigned her to the gas chamber. Those horrific memories had prevented him from settling down in married life.

He had dedicated his life to the newborn country of the Jews. His bizarre arms bazaar business was not a simple death peddling entrepreneurship. The income generated by the Yossi Marketing Inc was canalized to two Jewish underground outfits, which were committed to fighting the Islamic terrorist forces of the Al Fatah, the PLO and the freelancing terrorist groups headed by Abu Nidhal and other Muslim fundamentalists. Securing Israel against the marauding

Islamic forces had become a passion for him, even long after his retirement from the Israeli army and the Mossad.

Balachandran Nampoothiri's cryptic message delivered to him through the Rio station of the NSI had immensely intrigued Yossi. The Indian rulers had imposed on themselves the funny diplomatic logic of ostracizing the Jewish nation of Israel with a view to pampering the Muslims at home and abroad. They even refused to engage the valiant people of Israel in any meaningful dialogue. What was than the call from the NSI chief for? Was India about to tilt towards Tel Aviv?

Yossi's concentration was broken by the light footsteps of Amrita and Nampoothiri.

"Hello old boy," Nampoothiri greeted the Israeli General with usual gusto, "What are you doing here?"

Yossi looked at the approaching figures and stood up to greet them. He hugged Amrita and planted a kiss on her forehead.

"How have you been dear?"

"Fine uncle. How have you been?"

"Not bad. Trotting all over the globe and selling weapons."

"Aren't you going to rest?"

"Rest? Why not dear? But I've some civilisational serpents to take care of. Any way, I'm happy that you could come."

"Who are these serpents uncle?"

"They are the Islamists. They have been plaguing my nation from day one and it continues to plague all its civilisational ancestors, including your Hinduism."

"Oh no uncle! That's perhaps not correct."

Amrita was aghast at the suggestion of Yossi.

"It's fine child. You are too young to understand the inner meaning of civilisational conflict."

"So General, can I sit down? Hope your family powwows are over?"

"Sorry Balls," Yossi profusely apologized and drew a chair next to Nampoothiri, "I am really intrigued. What brings the Indian intelligence chief to an Israeli outcaste?"

Nampoothiri took out a small radio set from his pocket, set the needle to a music station and actuated the volume at a high pitch. He was not fascinated by the lilting Chinese tune. He required the ambience noise before he opened his mouth. He spoke at a monotonously low voice.

"Can you take up an assignment from me?"

"Me? Why not? But spell out the damn job."

"It's a complicated job. You have to supply a certain quantity of small and medium arms, ammunition and spares and demolition materials."

"Fine. That's how I earn my bread. But tell me more about the target area."

"You have to deliver the supplies at St Martin, Sandeep, Bhola and Bibir Char islands, all located off the coast of East Pakistan. Look at this map. This is a new terrain and the people are new. Do you want to take the risk? There is good money in it."

"So you want to fuel the fire in East Pakistan? No problem with me, if these damn Muslims get another drubbing. But I will deliver the goods only to the people accredited by you. I prefer confidentiality over profit."

"No problem Yossi," Nampoothiri lighted a Havana and spoke through the cloud of smoke, "The whole operation is top secret. I will advance half a million US dollar. Collect the cash from my man at Rio. Start delivering the consignments by the end of September."

"Fine. But tell me if some Vietnam surplus will suit your job?"

"I understand you want to use the Aranya Prathet and Phuket bases of Thailand. Am I correct?"

"Correct. Don't fear the CIA bogey. My suppliers are a few American Generals, who are in the habit of making quick bucks out of the miseries of the people of Vietnam. They have no ideological loyalty to the Pentagon and the White House. They will supply to Pakistan if you refuse to take their stuff on damn moral grounds. Give me your inventory."

"I don't carry one. My Rio man will hand it over to you. Don't disappoint me."

"Cheer up old boy. My record is impeccable, you know that," Yossi lighted a cigarette and spoke in a gusty voice, "Tell your navy boys not to buzz my boats from their Andaman bases. They should maintain radio silence even if they detect my trawlers. The CIA should not get any whiff of the transaction. They are sure to rush in a couple of destroyers and frigates from Diego Garcia and Singapore to thwart your design."

"No problem. I suggest you hire some Thai trawlers and assign some codes for them. Give me the details of your flotilla and their codes. My men at Bangkok will liaise with you."

"Fine Balls. But I will not like to contact him in the Indian embassy."

"No need. Keep this Nana Road address. His name is Parijat Rao, a man who moves at the fringes of flesh trade."

"You keep nice company Balls!"

"In your and my trade the quivers are always full of strange arrows."

"I will like to see you at London before the first consignment is shipped."

"No. London does not suit me. Meet me at Paris. I am supposed to attend the Interpol meeting there in another 15 days," Nampoothiri stood up, his eyes restlessly scanning the visible vicinity, "I will share with you the profile and photographs of the people designated to take delivery of the hardware. Ensure that the correct people contact your men."

"Okay friend. It is a deal. See you dear," Yossi hugged Amrita, "Take care. See you soon."

Nampoothiri, followed by Amrita slowly drifted away from the seafront, "A nice person, isn't he?"

Nampoothiri made a vague comment.

"Sure sir. And a deadly man too."

"Well dear," Nampoothiri gave a lungful puff at his Havana, "Life itself is a deadly game. I have to play it by the rules set up by the Prime Minister. She wants to cook the goose of Pakistan and I am supposed to be her kitchen assistant. That's how the games of strategic diplomacy are played. It's another name for war, indirect and direct war."

"Wait a minute sir," Amrita took out a small receiver set from her unusually largish vanity bag, "There is a call from Delhi."

"Who is calling?"

"It's a message from Robin Achariya. He wants you to talk to him immediately."

Robin, Nampoothiri's Pakistan desk analyst was not supposed to use the emergency channel. That was preserved for his number two, Bhagirath Banerjee and Dewan in the Prime Minister's office.

"Okay dear. Let's rush to the Robinson Road office of the Indian trade representative."

"Would you not like to go to the Grange Road office of the High Commissioner?"

"No dear. The Robinson road fellow is my cover man. I can use his communication facilities. Those are safe. Grange road fellow is a loud mouth drum beater."

Amrita hailed a cab and asked the inscrutable Chinese face to take them to the residence of George Dayal, the Indian trade representative.

"Hello Robin," Nampoothiri locked himself inside the small communication cubicle of George Dayal and spoke to his desk analyst over the secured line, " What's the big problem?"

"Sorry for the intervention sir," Robin Achariya spoke slowly over the secured phone, "There is a special dispatch from Triple X. It talks about a three way secret understanding between General Arif, the Secretary of State and the Chinese Deputy PM."

"Go ahead."

"The Secretary of State is likely to visit Peking soon after his visit to Delhi."

"I get you."

"He wants another live session for consultation."

"Fine. Ask him to hold on and wait for the activation of the Kathmandu channel."

"Okay sir. I will shoot a cipher tonight." Robin disconnected.

Nampoothiri emerged out of the room with a smile painted on his face. He was aware that George Dayal, an old FIB hand and Amrita would not fail to notice even the subtlest change in his facial muscle.

"Okay dear," He smiled at Amrita, "We take a flight to Tokyo tonight. I have an appointment at Geisha Sukimoto's teahouse."

Amrita smiled back. She knew well that her boss was not made of the stuff to spend his leisure at a Geisha teahouse. This small ruse was intended at befooling George Dayal. He was no fool either, Amrita knew. The veteran of counter intelligence was a favouirite of Nampoothiri and understood well the special nature of the mission his boss was on. Amrita was neither new to such crisp jokes from Nampoothiri. That's what kept his old body and young heart going steady at the gravest point of crisis. She concluded from his demeanor that Nampoothiri was anticipating another storm, perhaps a stranger and stronger one.

****

Kathmandu's hotel Pashupati, located at the southern suburb of the dusty capital city, was a nondescript lodge, mostly used by the Indian pilgrims. Named after the Lord Pashupatinath, Nepal's most revered deity, the hotel was shunned by the tourist crowd with bulging pockets. That suited Dhiren Bhagat, who arrived at the lodge in the company of his real life wife. The quiet homemaker was dragged out of her home for providing a convincing cover to the sudden visit of Bhagat to the Nepalese capital. Manjusha, Bhagat's wife too wanted a break. She had never been out of her home, not even for a honeymoon. Bhagat's mother denied that luxury to her. She believed that a woman's right place, was the kitchen and her most important mission was to bear children at reasonable intervals.

Bhagat woke up around midnight, whispered something in Manjusha's ears and walked down to an unmanned all night phone booth operated from a shack next to the Pashupatinath temple. This rare facility was installed by the ***Durbar*** (royal court) for facilitating the believers, who came to cremate their near and dear ones at the bank of Bagmati River, down below the temple.

After a couple of futile attempts he finally accessed the Lahore number of Triple X, at hotel Mughal-e-Azam, a small establishment with a big name.

"***Mamu*** (maternal uncle) here. Am I speaking to my nephew?"

"Yes ***Mamu***," Harfan replied using a pre-fixed code, "My sister's ***nikah*** (marriage) has been fixed. The boy is from Shahiwal. I want some monetary help."

"No problem. But you have to personally pick up the money. I can't get out. Your aunt is unwell. How much would you require?"

There was a short pause.

Bhagat's code was meant for inviting Triple X to the Nepalese capital, and the numerical digit of the amount stood for the days Triple X would take to reach Kathmandu.

"Can't you come to the River?"

"No. As I said your aunt is not well and dad does not like the idea of my leaving her alone."

"Okay ***Mamu***," Harfan replied in a cautious voice, "I will like to have a loan of Rs. 40,000."

"No my dear nephew," Bhagat replied, "I cannot spare that much. Two should be a good figure."

"Three?"

"No. Two. That's final. Call me at 46097."

"Okay."

Harfan Bukhari, the roving executive of Israr International arrived Kathmandu on the second day after his coded conversation with Dhiren Bhagat. The Royal Nepal Air DC 10 flight from Karachi touched down at 19.00 hrs at the Tribhubhan airport and Harfan drove straight away to the cremation ground on the banks of the lean Bagmati river flowing below the Pashupatinath temple.

Bhagat, attired in rustic Nepali dress was seated on the stairs that winded down to the narrow stream below. Funeral pyres burnt all around him, amidst loud recitation of ***mantras*** and occasional outburst of cries from the grieving family members.

Harfan did not take time to locate Dhiren Bhagat. Attired in ordinary shirt and trouser he did not look different from the surrounding crowd. He sat down next to Bhagat and asked if the time and place were propitious enough for lighting a cigarette. Bhagat gave an affirmative nod and extended his fingers for a fag. He too wanted to smoke. The ambience scenario and the smell of burning human flesh made him sick. But he had chosen the safest rendezvous for eluding the prying eyes of the ISI operatives, who had already established safe havens in the Nepalese capital.

"It's a nice meeting place. Isn't it?" Bhagat asked.

"Yes. It's the place of ultimate truth. We all end up here, sooner or later. Aren't you worried that some day some one will burn your body in one of those piles of wood?

"No, not at all. That's the way we have to go," Bhagat tried to size up the expression on the face of Harfan, "What's the big story?"

"Big enough to warrant a meeting in this bizarre crematorium," Harfan spoke in a hushed voice, "I'm scared of this place."

"It's the safest place. Tell me the story. I've to fly back tomorrow."

"It's an interesting story. Listen carefully."

Harfan's story was fascinating indeed. Pakistan, he said had become an unfathomable whirlpool of conspiracies. President Arif Khan was conspiring to consolidate his position in collaboration with Lt. General Hamidur, the Corps Commander of Chak Lala and the garrison chiefs of Peshawar, Lahore and Karachi. They favoured the installation of a puppet civilian government and a sham election to the revived National Assembly. They were hopeful that some fringe political and religious groups could be maneuvered to gain workable majority both in the eastern and the western wings. With a titular PM in position the armed forces could run the show for at least another two decades.

Inside the armed forces two more factions, one headed by Lt. Genenral Sarfaraz Lodi, the Principal Staff Officer (PSO) to the President and the Chief Martial Law Administrator (CMLA) and the other spearheaded by Lt. Gen Hyder Bux, chief of the Inter Services Intelligence, were vying with each other for staging another coup. They waxed and waned in a love and hate relationship. They were not against a limited collaboration, but were highly suspicious of each other.

General Naqibullah Saragarhi, the chief defense advisor to the CMLA headed another nucleus of conspirators. He expected support from a faction of the junior officers, especially from the artillery and cavalry regiments. His efforts to rope in Air Marshal Rahamat and Admiral Shauqat were yet to succeed. The Air chief nursed his own ambitions and he was mostly seen fraternizing with Izaz Afroz and few more politicians from Punjab and the North West Frontier Province.

"Where does Izaz stand?" Bhagat asked.

"He is everywhere," Harfan continued his story, "He thinks he can maneuver the CMLA and obstruct Sheikh Jainal from capturing the prime ministerial slot. The CMLA is not averse to the idea of playing Jainal and Izaz against each other."

"It's a fine ring circus."

"Yes. But Izaz is the most ambitious of all the trapeze artists. He thinks he can jump in the void and land on the laps of both Washington and Peking."

"A nice analysis Harfan. It's all known to our desk officers, I presume so. Where is the meat?"

"So you think that history has no meaning in the evolution of a nation?"

"When did I say that?"

"You are too impatient Bhagat. I am coming to the meat, a lot of it."

Harfan started with the revealing story of secret parlays between General Arif, the US President and the Deputy PM of China. These top-secret contacts were being developed in collaboration with Izaz Afroz in Pakistan and the Secretary of State in Washington.

"That's real big news."

Bhagat pinched another cigarette from Harfan, who too lighted another and continued briefing his handling officer.

"Yes. Here is a copy of a secret note that was smuggled out of the office of the CMLA. Tell Papa that Washington now wants to engage Peking with a view to opening up trade and to explore the feasibility of weakening the flanks of the USSR."

"Where does Pakistan stand in this strategic shift of position by the USA and China?"

"General Arif thinks that USA and China will guarantee his continuity at the helm of affairs in Pakistan and they will resume the supply of much needed military hardware."

"That's a cute arrangement."

"Yes, both cute and ugly. My friends say that Peking has agreed to supply Pakistan with ground to air and air to air missiles to balance the Russian supply of SAM missiles to Delhi."

"That's not cute."

"Yes. And the other ugly story is that Izaz is trying to extract some promise from Washington and Peking, that in the event of a tie between him and Sheikh Jainal they should support him. I believe he has been given some assurance by the US Secretary of State."

"So Pakistan is in for a big fun!" Bhagat leaned back against the pillar of the structure that resembled a sacred bull.

"Yes. But a funny Pakistan may turn out to be highly indigestible to Delhi's stomach," Harfan spoke in his usual flowery language, "Israr International, my company and few other big money grabbers have been sounded out by the CMLA office to submit estimates for airlifting military hardware from the Gulf countries and Saudi."

"Why are they using private operators?"

"Simply because neither Washington nor Peking wants to be caught red handed in this power balancing game. They have resumed playing dirty geo-strategic games in our region. That should worry Delhi."

"Are you sure of grabbing the contract?"

"That depends on a number of factors like humoring the seemingly first lady and greasing a number of key palms. My boss man is an expert in this field."

"Thanks for the briefing Harfan," Bhagat made a move for disengaging the rendezvous, "What is your schedule?"

"I meet the Nepalese defence minister, may be in another two days and submit a tender for supplying 5000 small weapons to the Royal Nepal Army."

"What are the details?"

"Sorry Bhagat. This is a trade secret. I will let you know when we start supplying the toys. Don't force me to compromise on this and ask Delhi not to raise a hue and cry till the supply line is uncorked."

"Well, you understand...."

"I understand Bhagat. Nepal's acquisition of 5000 pieces of small weapons will not endanger India's strategic security. Tell papa that from Kathmandu I will fly to Dacca and return to Karachi via Bangkok."

"Any special significance?"

"Little bit. Israr International has grabbed a contract for shipping half a million metric tons of rice from Thailand to Chittagong. Nothing to do with your trade."

"I am afraid Harfan," Bhagat brought out a piece of paper from his pocket and focused a pencil torch beam on it, "Have a look into it."

Harfan examined the list carefully under the torch light beam and returned it to Bhagat.

"Yes. It's a list of few important Bengali followers of Sheikh Jainal in Pakistan army and air force."

"Hope you know them?"

"I intimately know only two."

"Here is a micro tape. Consume the contents in the confines of your hotel room and destroy it. Give a feed back after your Dacca visit is over."

"Fine. But don't ask me to stretch too much. The People's League leaders are treated as Indian agents. I don't like the idea of getting identified with them. That's not good for Delhi too."

"It's a cut piece job. Give us a response about the feasibility of subverting the Bengali officers of the EPI, EPR and other formations."

"Okay. But this should be my last assignment in East Pakistan."

"Any whiff of danger?"

"Not yet. I think my boss's rising fortune has caused heartburns in high places. Business competition has degenerated into gangsterism over there."

"Another point Harfan," Bhagat brought out another piece of paper from his pocket, "Here is a list of senior Generals of the Pak army. Boss wants an independent assessment on their potential."

"Potential for what? Are you thinking of a counter coup?"

"I really do not know. Deliver the material at our River contact point."

"Okay. But listen carefully. The main tussle is between General Sarfaraz and General Hyder. The joker of the pack, however, is Izaz. He has the capability of giving an uncertain spin to the events in Pakistan"

"Are you in touch with Sarfaraz?"

"No. He is a big shot, the hero of Samba and Khem Karan wars against India. I believe Alam is in touch with him. Watch this General out."

Harfan stood up and fished out a closed envelope from his pocket.

"Reach this money to my mother."

He turned on his heels after a quick glance at his watch. The needles told him that it was past three in the morning. The busy crematorium had also went into a slumber, except few dogs, which were sniffing around for left out unburned human flesh.

"You know Harfan..." Bhagat tried to protest.

"I know Bhagat. Your work ethics does not permit you to reach the money to my mother. You also know that you will do that. Good night...I mean good morning."

Harfan, Delhi's Triple X walked up the stairs and stood before the image of Lord Pashupatinath and briefly prayed for Jamilla, their son Parvez and Kaushalya, his mother.

Bhagat noticed the queer behavior of his trained agent and smiled. The charlatan of Delhi university campus had undergone vast transformation. Ramendra had matured in a big way. But he was not yet sure about the continued placidity of this bottled typhoon.

He waited for a couple of minutes and turned his tired steps towards his sleepy den, hotel Pashupati and hoped that he should find the warm body of Manjusha more inviting and that should help him to overcome the foul stench of burning human flesh and the drudgery of witnessing the last journey of over a dozen of human souls.

Chapter 32

Lt. General Sarfaraz Lodi, Principal Staff Officer to the President and the Chief Martial Law Administrator often suffered bouts of black depression. Joy and melancholy, ambition and despair fleeted past his psyche like the early spring light and shadows. The embers of ambition burnt incessantly, somewhere inside, but lady luck rarely smiled at him.

That bout of despair haunted him again today. His mental focus delved deep inside and told him that frustration and misfortune had cast evil shadows on his life and career, in a cosmic conspiracy. His depression wasn't simply a post-fifty hormonal disorder. Something was wrong with his stellar configurations.

A Cancerian, he should have been at the peak of power by this time; but for this imbecile General Arif Khan, the Peshawari rank impostor.

Hero of the 1942 North African campaign and a shining star of two wars against India, General Sarfaraz suffered from the nagging feeling of being star crossed. It was only five years ago, during the 1965 war, when his cavalry and infantry columns had penetrated deep inside the Indian Territory. Amritsar, his birthplace, was within the reach of his artillery, and a mere three hours march away.

But the command headquarters dithered and allowed the Indians to open new fronts, threatening Lahore and Sialkot. His troops had to beat a hasty retreat. That wasn't his mistake. The Army Chief had developed cold feet. It was a grave tactical error of the GHQ strategists.

The GHQ coterie had put the bad-dog tag on his tail and he had to pay heavily for the fiasco. He was pushed down to the third slot. Dame destiny had betrayed him again.

Otherwise, why should President Akbar Khan have handed over power to the bumbling Chief, General Arif Khan! Why not him? Was it simply because the people of Pakistan had reached the end of their tether? Or was it because the people were offered Tashkent instead of New Delhi's Red Fort? Did the nation waste its men and money only to be saddled with an imbecile like General Arif? The fellow had little time for the affairs of the State. That incompetent bundle of contradictions had frittered his time away by serenading the flaming beauty and soprano, Malika Jahanara.

Pakistan was transformed into a pocket borough of the junior Khan, with indulgent support from few drug-baron Generals and the Sind fox, Izaz Afroz, whose addiction to opportunism out-smarted opportunity itself. The elder Khan, General Nayeem, chief of the Pakistan Intelligence Bureau, provided some skeletal framework of statecraft to the fledgling and bumbling new head of state. General Arif, the younger Khan, failed to notice, that the rotten twig called Pakistan, on which he managed to perch himself was about to collapse any moment.

Trrr...ring... ring...

The intercom buzzed.

"What the hell's happening? Why are you disturbing me?" Sarfaraz shouted back at his secretary as his woolly thoughts snapped suddenly.

"Sir there's a call from General Hyder Bux..." The secretary paused for a while.

"Okay. Put him through."

"Hello sir," Hyder Bux, the ISI chief came alive on the line, "I need your time. Something urgent has come up."

"Come on in." Sarfaraz disconnected.

Sarfaraz again travelled back to his own dark tunnel.

The Peshawari General, Sarfaraz uttered a curse, had managed to win over the support of a few key Corps Commanders and had mastered the art of pitting the power hungry myopic politicians against each other. Their foxy rancour had buoyed up his stranglehold on the nation. He cared less if the Generals and their political hyenas gnashed their teeth at the life and soul of the nation.

Only ***Allah*** knew what the Americans and the Chinese had seen in this man, whose upper limbic portion was devoid of grey material. But for the tacit support of the CIA and the Chinese State Security Bureau, this nincompoop would have been wallowing in the gutter of oblivion.

To hell with it! He should fly at once to London and consult Pundit Uma Shankar. That Hindu astrologer alone could decipher what the stars and planets had in store for him. In this damn country he couldn't openly go to a Hindu pundit. And there were none around. Even if there were one, his devout Muslim colleagues would construe that as a sacrilegious unislamic act.

He was indeed surrounded by the bloody pseudo religious pack of wolves.

Yes. This arms peddler Alam Khan was, perhaps, not wide off the mark, when he advised him to drift closer to the CIA bosses and the leaders of the Pakistani lobby in the US Senate and the Congress. A little wink from Langley, Pentagon and the White House and even a passing nod from 10 Downing Street should be good enough for him to take over from General Arif.

They should understand that, only he could stall the Russian consolidation in the Central Asian Republics and in Afghanistan. The dogma of Communism could only be fought by Islamic resurgence. Only the Islamic forces of Pakistan and the ***Ummah*** (Pan-Islamic fraternity) could tame India, a keystone of the arch of Red influence. And he was the only competent Pakistani, capable of destroying the voussoirs of that satanic arch.

But, sulking alone, without a powerful alliance inside the establishment would lead him nowhere. Real politics was a different ball game, and Pakistan had, in the true sense of the term, become a soccer ground for the Chinese and the American power strikers. To hammer the ball past the net he required borrowing their shooting skills. The local chieftains like Hyder Bux and Izaz Afroz could not be ignored. They had their own rules for kicking Pakistan around.

General Hyder Bux and Lt. General Amanulla, GOC in C of the 3rd Corps were potential allies. But each one of them, Sarfaraz suspected, harboured a sky-skimming ambition below their chests. It was a dog-eat-dog situation.

What about Izaz Afroz? Thank heavens! The wily Sindhi, though rabidly anti-Bengali and anti-Indian, had his own political agenda. The super-sycophant, a suspected US pigeon stool, wouldn't stop at anything to realise his ambition, which was the gilt-edged throne of Pakistan.

Major General Hyder Bux, a puritan Muslim, rather a ***mullah*** in uniform and a thorough professional, besides other compelling commitments, had managed to keep the discreet alleys to the doorsteps of the boss-man well greased. The spymaster didn't, Sarfaraz knew, act in harmonious orchestration with the Intelligence Bureau chief, the elder brother of the CMLA. No General in uniform, nursing even a thin vapour of ambition under his chest, would trust a colleague. Not in Pakistan.

Could he trust Hyder? A colleague could perhaps never be a friend, at least not the ISI chief. Trained by the CIA and British SAS, Hyder had his roots well embedded both in the ISI and the SSG. How could he trust the master of the black arts?

Lt. General Sarfaraz lighted another cigarette and looked up at the front wall. The room was garishly decorated, restricted operational maps occupying three of the four walls. He tried to identify the location of the Corps Headquarters and important cantonments.

Well! General Omar, Chief of the Armed Forces, Sarfaraz knew quiet well, was aligned to the wavelength of the Sind fox. In the event of a putsch against General Arif he would require the support of the key loyal formations. That required, Sarfaraz mused, a contingency plan, to neutralise the Chief within the first few minutes of the coup. Could he count on the support of General Hamidur? He took a mental note to explore that horizon.

Well! He would need the SSG chief's help for securing a remote guesthouse somewhere in the hills for the comfortable incarceration of the Army Chief and a few Generals who were loyal to him.

"Sir," The young Captain, Sarfaraz's aide de camp, saluted smartly and parroted hastily, "The President's military secretary says that he's busy and can't see you today."

"Am I pleased to hear this, young man?"

Sarfaraz interjected jocularly. His frustration stemmed from the hide and seek played by the Head of the State. The sozzled boss preferred to remain enchanted by Begum Jahanara's biological flames. Even pressing affairs of the State couldn't eject him out of the pleasure hole for days together. He knew the reason for his extreme pre-occupation, snoring away his time between the thighs of that Jahanara bitch.

The last four days had been very excruciating. The US ambassador had called twice seeking an urgent appointment with the President. A Saudi delegation was cooling its heels in a five star hotel waiting for strategic discussions. But the CMLA refused to respond.

"And sir," the young Captain reported, synchronising the clicking sound of his boots and voice, "Mr. Izaz Afroz is here. He says it's urgent."

"How urgent? Can't it wait unzipping of the fly?" Sarfaraz threw the innocent joke at his junior, "Okay. Don't blush like a virgin sixteen. Bring him in."

Izaz Afroz, immaculately dressed in an all white three-piece suit and jet black Gucci, entered with a flourish.

"Hi General." Izaz extended his hand, but placed just the fingertips in the warm wide palm of Sarfaraz.

It was just a ritual body contact, not even transmitting the slightest of warmth. He hated these creatures in uniform, half-witted, mostly illiterate and with a bottomless thirst for power and money. He had seen enough of them, starting with Pakistan's first tryst with military rule. But, unfortunately in the Holy Land of ***Allah's*** own Pakistan, a man of his calibre was forced to play an insignificant fiddle to these brats in uniform. Sharing power with these caricatures had not been a satisfying experience. One tenth of his palm was good enough a gesture for greeting these creatures.

"How're you Izaz sahib? Please be seated," Sarfaraz, not a less wily jackal, wiped his palm with a napkin, threw it in a dustbin and asked politely, "What can I offer you?"

"Don't take the trouble." Izaz looked doubtfully at the discarded napkin.

"It's a pleasure. I'm your admirer and fan. The more I hear your speeches in the U.N the more I get convinced that you're the ultimate destiny of this nation."

"Don't joke Sarfaraz. No one can dare to don that mantle as long as you uniformed people are around. Why embarrass me?"

Izaz examined the wall map with a scrutinising look and continued, "What're you doing with that Indian spy, Sheikh Jainal? Why is the President going slow on this matter? Why can't he be hanged?" Izaz Afroz expressed his anguish in impeccable English; few mispronounced Urdu words thrown in.

"What can I do Izaz sahib? The President has no access to professional advice."

"Don't you see, these Bengalis had started this damned movement way back in the sixties? They're half-bred Muslims, mostly converted low caste Hindus. Why don't you advise the President to use force and neutralise that trouble maker Jainal?"

"I appreciate your views Izaz sahib. But the situation is difficult. The professional civil servants have lost their access to the President. He believes that, the martial law administration of his predecessor had failed, because he had reposed too much trust in the civilian sissies. The military took the blame last time, when the civilians goofed up. This time around, he's determined to do everything and take the credit too."

Sarfaraz hoped Izaz would understand the dig. It was he, who, as the Foreign Minister had pushed General Akbar to launch Operation Gibraltar and Grand Slam against India in 1965. He did everything except lead the forces in the front.

"Do you agree with this? Don't you think that the permanent bureaucracy has some virtues? They shouldn't be kept outside the decision making process."

Izaz sipped coffee slowly and posed the questions at Sarfaraz, looking straight at his face, almost in a hypnotic trance.

"I'm not in a position to judge the intrinsic merits of the decisions taken by the CMLA. I'm a technocrat and not a politician like you." Sarfaraz gestured with a feeling of helplessness using his fingers and facial muscles.

"I'm told that the CMLA thinks that my party and that of traitor Jainal aren't likely to secure an absolute majority and he can install a puppet government by cobbling up a rag-tag coalition of the political scums." Izaz exploded in a full-throated condemnation of the election assessment of the CMLA.

"Izaz sahib," Sarfaraz again shrugged, "These assessments are done by the PIB and ISI, you know better."

"Yes. I know General Nayeem, the celebrity elder brother. And Hyder Bux, related to another bed-hopping film starlet, is no better. Do you ask me to buy their sob stories? And anyway, take it from me, there can't be any constitutional solution without me."

"I'm not really aware if the President has received any election assessment as yet. I think it's too early." Sarfaraz tried to avoid the politician, whom he considered unprincipled and unscrupulous.

"Any way Sarfaraz, I'm not here to debate the national elections with you. I know the mood of the people. They want me. Help me by fixing a meeting with the President."

Izaz was too indignant to discuss electoral politics with a General, whose schooling had perhaps ended with a high school degree.

"Izaz sahib," Sarfaraz spoke politely, "I thought you have a free access to the ***Sadr***. As you know, I don't fix his appointment. You've to call his military secretary or better call Col. Munir."

"I've been doing that damn exercise since I returned from Peking." Izaz spoke contemptuously, "There are important messages both from Washington and Peking."

"Must be. Can't we talk over that?"

"Sorry Sarfaraz," Izaz winked at the PSO, "Certain things can't be shared even with the PSO."

"As you wish," Sarfaraz lighted another cigarette and spoke trough half parted lips, "All that I can do is to send a note to the ***Sadr*** stressing the urgency of your message."

"Please do that, and tell him that the US Secretary of State should be in Islamabad next month. And the Chinese Foreign Minister wants to transit through Karachi on his way to Cairo. These are important visits."

"Certainly these are, Izaz sahib!" Sarfaraz tickled the former foreign minister on one of his usual ego trips, "You alone can get the tiger and the cow to lick salt at the same hole. I believe, besides shooting rabbits, you and the top boss had a good meeting at Larkana. Is there any possibility of postponement of the polls?"

"Look General," Izaz spoke patronisingly, "That was a strategic ***shikar*** (hunting) outing. The President had good exchanges with the US and the Chinese ambassadors."

"I understand so. Are there new strategic directions from Washington and Peking?"

"Well Sarfaraz, the East Pakistan has become a playground of that stupid woman Mandira. Both Washington and Peking are highly suspicious about her moves on East Pakistan. We can't trust these Bengali fishmongers any more. I don't know why the CMLA has agreed to a one-man one-vote formula. The fucking Bongos are too many and they would simply inundate us."

"There I agree with you. We in the West are aligned to the Islamic mainstream. The eastern Muslims are fakes. How can we allow them to rule over us?"

"That's what some of you don't understand. Join me and support me. I know how to drown these fishmongers in the Bay of Bengal." Izaz waived his hand vaguely.

"Anytime Izaz sahib. That'll be an immense pleasure." Sarfaraz flavoured his words with a sharp whistling.

"That's a promise?"

"Promise."

"Get your khakis starched. And get your gun oiled. We'll need you soon."

Izaz Afroz extended his palm and held the fingertips of Sarfaraz in a firm squeeze. He left the room, leaving behind tons of airs from his leaking ego-bag and exotic French perfume.

"Fool!" Sarfaraz uttered a curse; "The Bongos are better than this Indus marsh jackal. My foot! I won't even go for a decent guesthouse to detain him in. A small hole in Rawalpindi jail should be good enough for the ego-bag."

****

The young aid de camp entered again with a metallic click of the heel and a smart salute.

"Sir..."

"What's next?"

"General Hyder, sir..."

"Show him in..."

General Hyder Bux entered from a side door, didn't bother to salute and settled on a chair that faced the PSO.

"A stormy perfumed visit indeed..." He alluded to the aroma left behind by Izaz Afroz, who was in the habit of using a costly brand of French perfume.

"Yah... He wants us to join his brigade. Shit! What do you think of him? Can he be trusted?"

"Sir, don't trust him. He's from a Hindu mother's womb and you know that he has a Hindu mistress too."

"Oh Hyder!" Sarfaraz laughed, "You intelligence people are impossible. I'm concerned with his ambition and not his women. He's our competitor. It won't be easy to bypass him."

"Don't worry sir. I'll make him walk the planks before he climbs the throne. Pakistan is ours and we'll share it, between you and me."

"Well said Hyder. Tell me what can I do for you?"

"I have some audio tapes. These are from Jahanara's bedroom and will give you a fair idea of the ***Sadr***'s state of mind."

Hyder Bux fished out two tapes and placed before Sarfaraz.

"Be discreet Hyder. Slight leakage will cost our necks. And we can't afford to have an out of leash tigress roaming the streets of Islamabad. She will eat us raw."

"It's the only shortcut to many of his secrets. That's what had given us definite clues on the boss-man playing the Izaz card to stall the rabid Bong, Jainal. We've to build up a case against him before we dump the President."

"Take care. The elder brother, the PIB chief, is counter-snooping on you and me. And Izaz is a fleeting ghost. His visits are ominous. How far are you from making a demon out of Jainal? Under no circumstances should the boss-man play his game." Sarfaraz whispered into Hyder's ears.

"Don't worry. I'm keeping a tab on General Nayeem too. I've tapped Izaz through a different channel. The Chinese friends will ensure that he sabotages all rapprochement efforts between Jainal and the boss." Hyder whispered back.

"That's fine. Any political settlement, with either Izaz or Jainal on the throne will mean our sacking or imprisonment. Any way, what's special about the tape?"

"I suspect she has picked up a new lover...some Harun, may be Hanif; not sure. The noise pollution was really frustrating."

"That infinite hole can take on anything. But take care. She's all eyes and ears. She guards the ***Sadr*** like a mother eagle and hardly allows him to fly out."

"Another point boss," Hyder whispered, "General Tarakki....you know the doormat ...He's gaining importance. His wings require clipping."

"Don't worry. Keep Tarakki's links with Izaz under watch. These two can give us real headaches. And see that the boss does not make up with General Hamidur. We have to cleverly isolate him from the important commanders"

"O.K. Consider it done. Bye, I've urgent matters to attend to."

"Just one more point Hyder," Sarfaraz brought his lips closer to Hyder's ears, "Keep an eye on General Omar, the Chief of Army Staff. I think he's playing a different symphony."

"Don't worry. He's fully wired up. I've tapped two key Corps Commanders. We can count on the cavalry regiments and the Vice Air Chief will fly with us. Just take care of the timing and keep my interests in view."

"You're the New Chief of Army. That's what ***Allah*** has ordained."

"***Amin*** (so be it). ***Khuda Hafiz***."

General Hyder Bux offered a smart salute and left through a side door.

****

Izaz Afroz wasn't alone in his quest for an urgent meeting with the CMLA. Sarfaraz too was desperate for an exclusive conclave with his boss. The affairs of the State demanded the immediate presence of the ***Sadr*** in the CMLA secretariat. But it was difficult to allure him out of the confines of the temple of pleasure. And if he did he was mostly sozzled.

He was not stupid by any standard. Known for his courage in the battlefield and ready wit General Arif crossed fortune's path at a time when the soul of Pakistan lost its bearings under a protracted junta rule.

But his calculations were based on a different interpretation of Pakistani minds. The East Pakistan Bengalis were on the warpath on the demands for democracy and autonomy. Izaz Afroz thought that he was mandated by the Allah to rule Pakistan with his own version of democracy.

General Arif's hope of legitimising his stillborn junta rule hinged on his implicit faith that the Armed Forces would never agree to allow the politicians to share the loot, in the name of restoring democracy. They hoped that boots and bayonets could still ruthlessly rule over the Pakistanis. The democratic aspirations of the people had thrown up new dimensions that were beyond Arif's comprehension. He didn't have either the courage and the crafts to surmount the wily machinations of the Army hawks, who were backed by the drug money flushed oligarchy. The concepts of contradiction management and conflict resolution were alien to his boorish mind. His thought process ploughed along the beaten grooves that had taught him to use the gun to solve all major problems and allow the issues to die out by sheer negligence.

He often behaved like the proverbial ostrich. He shied away from stark realities and allowed himself to be barricaded by jackals like General Omar, Hyder Bux, Izaz Afroz and the Aphrodite, Malika Jahanara. Sarfaraz Lodi, busy pursuing his own dreams for the crown of Pakistan, simply didn't know how to get the man on the throne to apply his mind.

Hyder Bux proved ineffective too, in tracking the boss' movements. His boys tinkered with Jahanara's phones but the end result proved frustrating. The big man didn't take any call and the dainty witch cooed nonsense and parried all enquiries about her lover boy.

General Sarfaraz determined as he was today, picked up the phone in a desperate attempt and personally dialled the exclusive number of Malika Jahanara.

"***Mohtarma***, Can I see you today?"

"Any urgent business? Can't it wait?"

"It's important and for the sake of ***Allah*** don't say no."

"Why swear by His name dear? He's so burdened with millions of problems. Can I help?"

"Yes," Sarfaraz paused for a moment to curse the bitch under his breath, "Oh yes ma'am. You can help."

"Come along dear, if you so swear by the ***Allah***." Jahanara didn't sound very enthusiastic.

She received Sarfaraz in the outer living room. Furnished austerely with commonplace artefacts and ordinary carpets, the room was meant for fringe visitors only. This wasn't meant for a distinguished visitor like General Sarfaraz, the powerful Personal Staff Officer to the CMLA. Jahanara was helpless. She couldn't receive the star-studded visitor in her main living room. The President was still in her bed, all sozzled and mesmerised. He was drowned in bacchanalia and immersed in the warmth of the bachae.

This, Sarfaraz presumed, was one of those wild bouts when the CMLA surrendered to Jahanara's physical charms and enchanting voice. His relaxed evenings encroached upon the duties of the State. Some nights lingered on, as the alcoholic stupor benumbed his senses. But no one had the authority to disturb him at this sacrosanct altar of love and pleasure.

But Lt. General Sarfaraz was a desperate man today. The President generally ducked the responsibilities of the State and wished that the bad dreams would drift away. He had refused to discuss important matters for the last four days. Complicated developments were shaping up in Kashmir, India and East Pakistan. The ISI, PIB and the DMI chiefs had submitted special reports and were awaiting operational guidance. All these required the President's personal attention.

The only file on which he had scribbled comments pertained to the national elections. The Military Law Administrator in Dacca had recommended postponement of the polls, in view of the aggressive and seditious activities of the Peoples' League. General Arif didn't agree. He was under international pressure to go through the charade of democratic elections. There would not be a dearth of scapegoats to blame and shoot, if the post-election situation went sour. Sheikh Jainal and his fire eating stormy bandwagon, Izaz, the Sindhi fox and Hindu India were the convenient fall guys to blame and shoot. Election and democracy didn't suit the genius of the Islamic people. They preferred to be ruled by the three Ms, the Military, ***Muftis*** and ***Mullahs.***

"What can I do for you General?" Jahanara asked, as she watched the castrated ***habshi*** pouring tea for the star-studded man, figuratively important, next only to the President.

"***Mohtarma***," Sarfaraz cleared his throat, "It's important for the President to attend to affairs of the State. Very disturbing developments are taking place all around."

"Is there a conspiracy to topple him?"

"No ma'am. Which fool would dream of that? The country is facing internal turmoil and external threats."

"That's not new. You're there to take care of these minor things." Jahanara replied with visible contempt.

"I'd like to see him," Sarfaraz asserted, "Affairs of the State are pretty serious."

"General, can't you tell me what's up? Perhaps I can brief him. The poor boy's just relaxing."

"Ma'am that's not possible, certain things are only for the eyes and ears of the ***Sadr***."

Sarfaraz, livid with anger, politely parried the crafty lady, who, in his estimation was good enough for bed, but was poison for the health of the nation.

Jahanara wasn't pleased to hear the brash answer. No one dared to go against her wishes. But there was a steely note in Sarfaraz's voice. He meant business. His ice-cool eyes spurned her coy liquid looks and her authoritative voice that under normal circumstances made the army brasses prostrate before the beauty.

She reluctantly walked down the carpeted corridor and returned in 5 minutes.

"He says you should see him at the ***Aiwan-e-Sadr*** (residence of the Head of the State) at 5 p.m. today."

Jahanara's voice sounded frozen like a glacier, atop the galleries of K2.

Sarfaraz collected his cap and stick and walked out thanking her profusely. He didn't give her the pleasure of the customary smart salute, which she expected as a matter of right, from the high and mighty in Pakistan.

Well! Sarfaraz shrugged as he boarded his car. He could wait for another five hours. But how long was Pakistan supposed to suffer this apolitical adventurer? He wished he could go cracking with the planned coup now, just now. The first salvo, he wished he could fire at the pleasure castle of Jahanara!

A disciplined soldier and a patriot, Lt. General Sarfaraz pushed down the flames of anger arising from his inner cauldron. Wait! He told himself. Wait for a good planetary configuration and opportunity.

Fine! He'd explore at his own leisure ways to teach this bitch a few finer nuances of the art of bitching. Time was yet to freeze at her doorstep.

****

Lt. Genenral Sarfaraz accompanied by two Brigadiers, who handled Martial Law and Civil Affairs in the CMLA's central fort, entered the spacious Cabinet-room of the President, exactly at five.

The ISI and PIB chiefs, as well as three senior secretaries of the departments of Home, Defence and Cabinet Affairs were advised to wait in the anteroom. They would be called in, if the boss so desired.

He greeted the Head of State, seated behind a mahogany table, with a smart salute. The President and the CMLA didn't respond. He feigned being busy reading a fat file.

"Good evening sir." Sarfaraz saluted again.

"What's cooking Sarfaraz?" The President, immaculately dressed in full regimental regalia, finally spoke. He was spruced up with a neat haircut, close shave and a facial massage. Layers of fatty skin hung loose from his face and thick balls of fat dangled below his eyes.

"Sir, I want some of your precious time. Important policy matters require your immediate attention." The PSO submitted ceremoniously.

"Can't it wait for the night? I've some important files to attend." The President didn't appear to be too pleased with Sarfaraz.

"Beg y'r pardon sir," He submitted, "The issues are burning and very important."

"What's the big deal? Hope that lady in Delhi isn't marching her troops tonight itself." The President quipped.

"That too is a matter of grave concern sir. You know the latest despatch from our High Commissioner in Delhi. He feels India is fully geared up to attack Pakistan." Sarfaraz replied.

"Oh that sissy Hanif! He dreams a lot and conjures up most of his reports. I've ordered his withdrawal." General Arif ordered in a triumphant mood.

"But sir," Sarfaraz submitted, "Our friend Aftab has also sent a similar report."

"You mean that minister in the cabinet of that woman! Sarfaraz," General Arif chuckled loud, "Take these reports with sac full of salt. We're prepared to teach India the bitterest lesson to date. That widow won't dare challenging our army."

General Arif waived his hands vigorously, dismissing his PSO's apprehensions.

"***Insha Allah***!" Sarfaraz vigorously nodded his head to appear visibly supportive of the views of the boss.

"Has Aftab been able to pollute her election prospects? Or have we just pumped in a few millions for nothing?"

"I think the ISI and PIB chiefs should be able to brief you better."

"Carry on. Mind some coffee?"

"It's welcome sir." Sarfaraz replied.

He ordered coffee and hoped that the fat ball, seated across, would soon explode in a catastrophic self-combustion. If not, he was there to activate the short fuse.

"So, what were you saying about Dacca?" General Arif sipped the coffee leisurely and asked.

"Sir, there is impeccable proof of Indian involvement with the Peoples' League. Sheikh Jainal is an Indian mole." Sarfaraz concluded the sentence with a tone of lingering continuity.

"That's all?" General Arif pushed the china aside, "I thought you were going to tell me something earth shattering."

The President changed his posture in the heavily cushioned chair and ordered another coffee. An attendant, at his signal, flick-opened a gold cigarette box. General Arif picked up a stick, lighted it and inhaled a lung full of smoke.

"What the hell is that woman up to?" He exhaled the smoke leisurely, "We should teach her a few lessons in statecraft."

The brave dig was directed at the Indian Prime Minister, who was a common hate object in Pakistan.

"Sir, several policy matters are required to be discussed before we embark upon any action against that widow." Sarfaraz played along.

"What's happening with Operation K2? Where is the ISI chief?" The President reacted with a deliberate knee-jerk response, diverting from the current topic. He didn't want to place all his cards on the table.

The Brigadier Martial Law briefly went out and shepherded in Generals Hyder Bux and Nayeem, the PIB chief.

A veteran British SAS trained commando, and an expert SSG guerrilla commander, General Hyder Bux had successfully blended together the rare virtues of professional depth and the Punjabi survival instinct. He used his two arms deftly; the left to touch the feet of the man in power, and the right aimed at his jugular.

This traditional wisdom was essential for survival in Pakistan, ruled in the medieval durbar style, amidst drunken revelry. It was more necessary because the PIB chief, who was the elder brother of the CMLA, was up for grabbing his coveted position. And the ***Amritsaria*** (from Amritsar) PSO had put one of his feet already on the portals of the throne.

The boss-man was a bundle of contradictions; often emitting jumbled up signals. Like all self-proclaimed messiahs, he believed, he was born to save Pakistan and put it back on the rails. He had started well with the experiment but midway through it had lost steam and fuel.

The ISI chief was aware of the influence of Izaz Afroz on this Peshawari old timer. The ambitious Sindhi had used all his charms to bewitch the old toad and had helped in igniting in his psyche the inherent distrust and fear of a Punjabi for fellow Bengali Pakistanis. The logic was simple. The Muslims of West Pakistan were much more superior to the low caste converted Hindus of East Pakistan.

General Hyder, in fact, had prepared a fat dossier on his boss. It helped adjusting his barometer and regulating the ambient temperature.

"Tell me Hyder," The President spoke while fiddling with his thick eye brows, "What're you doing with Operation K2?"

"Sir I want to bring to your notice some related developments." The ISI chief started in a meek squeaky tone.

"Skip the skins, reveal the meat. Tell me about the operation and I want to know what can we do in Kashmir. That's where I want to hit her big with a befitting reply to her machination with the fishy Bengalis." Gen. Arif firmly indicated the parameters of the briefing.

"Shall we talk here?" The ISI chief hesitated to speak in front of the two brigadiers and Col. Munir, his aid de camp. He was reluctant to reveal all the tricks to the President too. This fat-ball relayed everything to Jahanara, who had cast a witchy spell on him.

"No problems. Go ahead." Gen. Arif looked around and winked at Hyder Bux. The ISI chief slowly elaborated the nitty-gritty of Operation K2, named after the highest Himalayan peak in Pakistan.

Fabricated soon after the 1965 drawn war, K2 was aimed at achieving Pakistan's unfinished agenda in Kashmir, through a clever combination of subversion, ethnic insurgency and Islamic ***jihad***. This was a new approach, vastly different from what Pakistan had tried in 1948 and 1965. The experiences of the Islamists in Lebanon and Palestine had proved that war wasn't simply a clash of two armies. An intractable war could also be won by other means, by employing the strategy of Islamising of the political issues. Religious bigotry could win a battle that could not be clinched by weapons.

The Philosophy was straight. The people of Kashmir should be brought into conflict with the Indian system. Distorted ***Sufi*** traditions should be supplanted by ***Sunni Wahabi*** fundamentalism. The calibrated escalation of terrorist violence and fundamentalist indoctrination were sure to subvert the lotus and saffron eater ***Sufis*** of the Vale of Kashmir. Islamisation of the ***Sufi*** Kashmiris was the surest weapon to ingrain in their psyche the umbilical importance of the ***Ummah.*** Islam, the ISI fabricators propounded, was a system of spontaneous revolution, a perpetual ***jihad*** against the ***kafirs;*** the Christians, the Jews and the Hindu ***kafirs.***

"Sir, the Al Fatah and Kashmir Liberation Front boys are ready to stage some spectacular action," Gen. Hyder affirmed, "We've to temper them in the fire of Islamic ***jihad***. It won't be necessary to repeat costly ventures like Operation Gulmarg, Balakot and Gibraltar. We'll overwhelm India through Islamisation of the Kashmiris."

The President, his eyes closed, mechanically lighted another cigarette and twisted his eyebrows. He gestured at the ISI chief to continue. He was ready to listen and wasn't displeased, as yet, with the narration.

"Don't forget Hyder," General Arif spoke in a prophetic voice, "Islam is the biggest weapon we have. Look at the Iranians. Very soon Islam will emerge victorious over there."

"You're correct sir. There are two other layers in the operation.. We've generated enough friends in the Organisation of the Islamic Countries. They're ready to support the Kashmiri Muslims. The Rabita-al-Alam-al-Islami (International Muslim League) has promised financial support. Libya and the Lebanese Fatah leaders have agreed to train some of our special commandos."

"***Shukria*** (thanks). Sounds fine. But what happened to the US promise of training our boys at their School of High Altitude Warfare?"

"The SSG, under supervision of the US School of High Altitude Warfare, has made a beginning at our High Altitude Training Centre at Gilgit. But that would take time."

"What about the Indian Kashmiri leaders? How much have you achieved?" The President sounded impatient.

"Our efforts to penetrate Sardar Niyamat, the chief of Indian held Kashmir are progressing satisfactorily. He now rues Delhi's game of deception." General Hyder added.

"He should, if he's a good Muslim. Tell me if he's ready to play my game. I'm not interested in your operations per say. Tell me what you can do. I'm not going to replay the stupid game of 1965. ***Insha Allah*** I'll take the war to the heart of Delhi. Sahjahanabad will be my capital."

Hyder's open-ended operational incubation could wait, General Arif pointed out. His immediate objectives were the scuttling of the Indian parliamentary polls, generation of communal violence and pushing the Indian PM to the walls. She shouldn't be given a freehand to meddle in the affairs of East Pakistan.

"No, no Hyder, I'm not happy with K2. Don't expect Niyamat to smile like a teenager in love. Don't expect India to buckle down to his blackmailing. Niyamat and Mandira should fight. I want changes in the Kashmiri psyche. They should realise that they're Muslims first and Kashmiri later. Muslims have no other option but to be loyal to the Ummah and Pakistan. We are not a part of the damn east. We are an integral part of the Middle East."

General Arif, in a rare display of cerebral excellence, stunned his officers.

"In fact sir, we've switched over to this strategy. The Muslim Jammat has been funded to induct ***khalis*** (pure) ***alems*** (religious teachers) and seasoned Islamic preachers from Deoband, Lucknow and Bihar Sharif to teach real Deobandi Islam to them. Their so-called ***Kashmiriat*** (Kashmiri culture) is the main psychological barrier."

"Crush their ignorance under your boots," The President talked in a mocking tone, "But do you expect me to wait for five long years just to see the Indians marching on the streets of Dacca and knocking at our doors in Islamabad!"

"Sir, these operations require a long gestation period. We can't help it." Added Hyder Bux.

"Fuck your operations, I want quick result...." General Arif was disturbed in mid sentence, by the strident buzz on the phone.

"Sir, the Governor in Dacca is on the line."

"Oh that imbecile Irfan!" General Arif shouted back, "Tell him that I'm in a meeting. He should try tomorrow."

"He says there's an urgent message from Jainal."

"Tell him to go to bed with Jainal, I don't have time for him."

"It's important sir. Perhaps you'd like to talk."

"Okay, you fucking fool," General Arif picked up the phone and shouted, "Hi Irfan, what's your problem?"

"Sir Jainal wants to meet you. He has a compromise formula and is not keen to push his six point programme."

"Are you sure?"

"I've no reason to doubt sir."

"That's fine Irfan. Keep him on the hold. I'd send Sarfaraz to Dacca. Let him have a talk with Jainal first."

"But sir, he wants to talk only to you."

"Than ask him to go to hell. The President of Pakistan can't dance to his tunes."

General Arif banged the phone down on its cradle and looked up at his ISI chief. He noticed a glitter of a smile in his eyes. Was the bastard going to play a dirty role? Nothing was impossible.

General Arif's fear psychosis, his suspicion of a coup and distrust of his fellow Generals had pushed him to the edge of paranoia. He suspected his aide de camps, secretariat staff and the ceremonial guards. They were chameleons; adept in borrowing colours from every leaf and twig they managed to hide behind. He had chosen a crack company of his personal regiment, the Frontier Guards, for his inner security girdle.

He didn't really trust these men in uniform. Izaz Afroz, minus his ego bag and sac-full of ambition was more manageable. Perhaps he could manipulate him to install a puppet civilian government, after the polls. That should buy him full insurance. He badly required a breather and Sardar Niyamat in Kashmir and Izaz Afroz in Pakistan could provide him the comfortable cushioning that he deserved.

"Yes," The CMLA managed to display a faint smile; "The Jammat strategy is good. But show me some fireworks, pump in more money from your Crescent Account."

The President referred to a special fund raised by the ISI from opium and heroin peddling operations.

The ISI chief smiled. The big hungry man wouldn't even spare the special fund his company had built up over the years! What about his vaults in Switzerland? Must be full by now. Pakistan was up for grabs and why shouldn't the privileged people like General Arif join the plunder!

Most importantly, why should he, Hyder, a pure Jat Punjabi, be left out of the loot!

Hyder reverted back to K2 and explained its intricacies. The key dramatis personae were being unfolded carefully. Niyamat's younger son, a diplomat in Pakistan's Foreign Service was playing a key role. And Mirza Baloch, a First Secretary in the Pakistani Mission in Delhi had developed roots in the K2 edifices.

"In fact sir," Hyder continued, "Our High Commissioner had two intimate meetings with Sardar Niyamat. This operation is progressing well."

"Hyder, please understand that we're hard pressed for time. The Indians should be pinned down in Kashmir. I want a breather in Dacca."

"I follow sir. Wait for a few days. The boys in Kashmir are sure to stage a big show." Hyder assured the Chief Martial Law Administrator.

"I hope you won't let me down. What's your plan for the Indian elections?" Gen. Arif asked.

"Sir, perhaps you may like to hear out the PIB chief." Maj. Gen. Hyder suggested.

He didn't want to face the President alone on this issue, though the ISI was exclusively responsible for operations in India. Under CMLA order 3x/Div S/Misc; the President had vested General Nayeem, the Intelligence Bureau chief, with operational responsibilities in respect of identified political targets. It was a special concession to the celebrity elder brother.

The Pakistan IB (PIB), umbilical twin of the Indian Federal Intelligence Bureau had inherited priceless assets, deep inside the Indian establishment. These weren't transferred to the Inter Services Intelligence, even after it had abrogated to itself the entire foreign intelligence outfit. General Hyder Bux had taken up cudgels, demanding transfer of intellectual assets from the PIB. But Major General Nayeem had stonewalled all his efforts.

"So brother Nayeem, what all have you done so far? Is that woman's popularity on the wane?" General Arif asked in a flamboyant voice.

"I'm afraid sir, she's much too clever to let that happen. In fact, she has emerged stronger than ever." The PIB chief started his briefing with a disappointing note.

"What the hell have you been doing all these days? What in hell's name Aftab is doing?"

The President didn't appear to be happy with what his elder brother had to say.

"Sir, I'm coming to the operational aspects. I thought you might like to have a brief backgrounder." Maj. Gen. Nayeem continued.

"She has consolidated her hold on the communists and has been using them for unleashing cultural intrusion in East Pakistan. Hundreds of books and pamphlets have been distributed free, extolling Bengali nationalism. India is financing rural drama groups, which are spreading the messages of an independent Bangladesh."

"What're you doing to sabotage her electoral prospects?"

"Sir, the boys have been deployed to motivate our friends in the Ummah. They have been funded to tilt the balance in favour of Aftab's candidates. The Lucknowi wrestler is expected to penetrate her armour in important pockets. Some Left-Extremist groups have been motivated to escalate violence in Indian Bengal. Weapons have been pushed in through Nepal." General Nayeem exposed the blue print of his operations.

"What's that bloody Aftab doing?" The President repeated im-patiently.

"Sir, he's providing local talent in some key states. The gangs controlled by him have been deployed for unleashing anti-Hindu violence and random killing."

"But I haven't heard a single bang."

"His latest reports have given us a deep insight into India's strategic plans. He has been successful in rallying Mandira's opponents."

"Fine. Tell him to play our game and he won't find us wanting. Tell him that he's our choice for Delhi's next Prime Ministerial slot. And Washington and its allies would endorse it too. Tell him that on my authority." General Arif spoke expansively and continued.

"Ask him for a detailed report on the Indian involvement with the Peoples' League and that traitor Jainal."

"Yes sir. But...."

"There's no scope for any buts."

"Aftab has of late been showing symptoms of recalcitrance." General Nayeem spoke haltingly.

"Nayeem," the President's voice sounded serious, "If you're incom-petent, tell me. I'll ask Hyder to take over PIB's Indian operations. I don't want a rogue agent to betray us. This wise guy knows too much. Straighten him or finish him off. Do that early, before I decide to divest you of all operational responsibilities in India. Any way, what's bugging him?" The President thundered.

"Perhaps the Indian NSI has tapped him. He dished out three pieces of doctored information. Perhaps he's being used as a misinformation tool."

General Nayeem explained how India had succeeded in planting wrong information about the recent induction of Russian MIG fighters and kilo-class submarines.

"Hyder you take over this operation, forthwith. Aftab knows too much about our linkages in India. I don't want any compromise over Sardar Niyamat's involvement with our boys. Kashmir is my top priority. Dacca can go to hell."

"But that place is burning sir." Lt. Gen. Sarfaraz intervened mildly.

"Look Sarfaraz," The CMLA continued his monologue, "These Bengalis aren't real Muslims. Let them go to hell. Finish them off."

The President lighted another cigarette and exhaled a thick cloud of smoke, perhaps to show his PIB chief the thickness of the smoke he had just referred to looked like.

General Nayeem felt a grating sensation in his oesophagus. He knew only too well that, despite his best efforts, he couldn't halt Mandira's meteoric rise. His boys in Delhi hadn't been sending many encouraging reports. Perhaps, the Indian FIB and NSI had penetrated some of his top assets, including Aftab.

He managed a feeble smile and pulled out, what he thought to be his trump card.

"There's a good news from Aftab," He said, "There have been unusual exchanges between Delhi and Moscow."

"What're the details?" The President opened his eyes, but in an oblique trajectory.

General Nayeem took a deep breath and spoke with a flourish that, Ram Karan Prasad; the Indian cabinet minister had catered draft documents on defence and the friendship treaty exchanged between Delhi and Moscow.

Karan's disillusionment with Mandira, Nayeem revealed, was triggered off by her consistent refusal to concede 70 parliamentary tickets to his candidates. He was offered 7 tickets, that too, after he paid Rs. 8 million to her election fund.

"That's fine. But how does it help in sabotaging her election prospects?"

General Arif Khan, now hanging at the precipice of patience, waved his right hand.

"He's on the job sir."

"Tell Aftab that I don't require the draft documents. Washington has all the details. Moscow can't rescue that woman. And now onwards Hyder handles Aftab. That rogue requires some tough handling."

He dismissed the meeting.

Lt. Gen. Sarfaraz was alarmed to see fresh wrinkles and creases on General Arif's face. He had run out of steam and it was time for his favourite beer. Or was it Scotch time?

"Should we break for a drink sir?"

The President raised his right hand towards the door. His cerebral cortices weren't exactly oriented to absorb the complicated and thorny diplomatic issues. He felt a griping sensation in the gullet. It needed the soothing flow of his favourite Heineken.

General Arif waved both his hands, in synchronisation with his inner thinking. To hell with diplomacy! He was basically a soldier and wouldn't hesitate in pulling the trigger at the correct moment. That was his exclusive prerogative.

As the procession prepared to move to the adjacent living room, Lt. General Sarfaraz moved closer to the President.

"Sir, I've a hunch that Aftab has been compromised."

"What gives you that feeling?"

"It's not an amorphous feeling sir," The PSO explained, "Besides the MIGs, he has misled us on the Indo-French agreement on Mirage fighters."

"I've already given the orders. Smoke him out. Hyder should take care of that rogue."

"One more point sir."

"Go ahead."

"There are sure fire evidences of the blatant Indian support to the Bengali traitors. They've completed the training of several ***Mukti Bahini*** (freedom fighter) formations." Sarfaraz submitted.

"Call a meeting of the CMLA Divisional Heads and the three Chiefs. Inform the US ambassador. I'd like to receive him tonight, over a drink. And summon...."

The President stopped short of completing the sentence. He was hesitant to mention Izaz Afroz's name to his over zealous PSO.

This officer's world didn't exist beyond his profession. Perhaps he didn't even have sex with his wife, not to mention enjoying the occasional extra-marital flings. For him work was more important than the daily ritual ***Namaz***. Perhaps Sarfaraz was getting too ambitious. Too much devotion to duty could inject new ideas below his chest, propelling his steps towards the throne.

Well! He would keep this in mind.

General Arif returned a feeble smile. In his Pakistan, no one should get too ambitious. No. Not this highly decorated officer, regarded as a possible alternative to himself by some doubting Thomases in Washington and twitchy Cheng in Peking.

"Well Sarfaraz, bring this up exclusively. Ask Hyder to be present too. Let's have a drink." He dismissed the PSO.

General Sarfaraz didn't dare to whisper another favourite theme of his, the purging of the traitorous Bengali officers from the armed forces and top slots in the civil services. How could he rule out Indian penetration of the security membranes around the CMLA? The treacherous Bengalis were sure to betray vital secrets.

Sarfaraz always tinkered with the idea of short-listing important Bengali army and civilian officers and neutralising them. They should be done away with before they opened the floodgates to the Indian military machine.

Well! He shrugged. If the top boss was interested in booze and food, who was he to talk shop about the treacherous Bengalis! Whimsical maiden fortune and puppeteers in Washington and Peking had catapulted the brat to the highest slot. The intricacies of politics and diplomacy were beyond him.

Hang him!

Sarfaraz opened the door with an agile move, smiled lavishly and said, "Sir, would you like to have a beer or something else?"

General Arif looked up at the PSO, breathed out a loud silent curse and settled for a chilled beer, as a starter.

"My favorite Heineken, Sarfaraz, mighty chilled, no ice please."

Chapter 33

"Malika." Harfan's voice vacillated like an overcharged needle of an oscillograph.

"Yes, darling Harfan." Jahanara replied in a sweet flat voice.

"Your medicine from the Indian ***vaid*** has been procured. Where should I deliver it?"

"I've a recital commitment in Lahore. I should be there in three days time. Check up with hotel Faletti's." Her voice sounded faint, disturbed by loud instrumental music in the background.

"Perhaps I can't come to Lahore, my job takes me to Karachi."

"Come over, I need you." The soprano crooned in a lilting tone.

Jahanara didn't want the latest acquisition to visit her niche in the capital. Her lover boy, General Arif was in town. He was a possessive and jealous lover. Perhaps, the past-middle age lover felt nervous over the presence of another male-cat in the vicinity of his mistress's den. He won't mind jumping on any suspected competitor, like a male cat on heat, scratching him red and blue.

"Perhaps you would like Nawab sahib to deliver the packet. It's he who really organised it." Harfan suggested.

"No dear. That lousy corpulent fellow is a soggy jelly bag, good for nothing. I expect you in Lahore. Do meet me there." Jahanara insisted.

"Okay ma'am, if you insist." Harfan disconnected.

General Hyder Bux examined carefully the insignificant piece of transcript produced by Brigadier Barqat's boys in the Joint Intelligence Miscellaneous Division.

Operation Red Rose, the grandiose nom-de-plume assigned to the electronic surveillance operation on Malika Jahanara often offered interesting insight into the affairs of the State.

A lady of infinite virtues, she had admirers all over the country. The ***Sadr*** apart, she received kaleidoscopic visitors and conversed with rainbow personalities, who decided or pretended to decide on the fate of Pakistan.

What intrigued Hyder was the use of the direct line by the caller. Very few people reserved the privilege of calling her direct bedroom number. Only the ***Sadr*** had exclusive access to it, a sort of honey laced hotline. Her pet attendant, the trusted and castrated ***habshi***, attended all other calls.

Who could this Harfan be? A new lover boy? An under-carpet pet mole, a new competitor in the presidential hotline! What links could he have with Nawab?

Nawab and medicine...from Vaid Dhanwantari of Dehradun!

Did he say so? Hyder rewinded the tape and listened to the faint male voice. Yes. This bugger, whoever he was, had spoken about the Dehradun medico and medicines.

Hai Rabba!

He had also asked for some energy-boosting medicines from India. Hyder gently massaged his eyes and bushy brows with his left big and middle fingers and concentrated on the transcript.

Who could this Harfan be? Did he ever bump into any Harfan, in a Pakistan Chambers of Commerce annual dinner? Or was it in a meeting with the Consortium of Defence Suppliers? Did he figure in the earlier tape?

How could a petty nobody have access to the big man's hotline? Was Malika entertaining a strange lover? Did it have the potential of a new scandal involving the ***Sadr***? Well! Juicy scandals were welcome. These should help him in driving in the last few nails on the coffin of the usurper, General Arif Khan.

Perhaps the city editor of the *Dawn*, Najibullah could help him. He moved around the defence beat and maintained steady connection with the affluent suppliers and contractors.

"Hello Najib," General Hyder called the *Dawn* representative, a resourceful journalist, "Do you know any Harfan? He is probably a defence supplier."

"Salaam General," Najib was gratified to receive a direct call from the top intelligence boss, "Yes, I know him. He is an employee of Israr Sharief. What's the matter?"

"We are short listing some major suppliers. I could not hit on the name correctly. Come over for coffee. We have a lot of thing to discuss."

"That's great General. Keep a slot free for tomorrow."

Hyder finally plugged in Harfan to his current memory cells. Perhaps he had met a Harfan. Yes. He might have met him at a social gathering in Lahore.

Was he related to that Shia ***mohana*** tribal, Zahoor Chaudry?

Nothing extraordinary. He had just accepted his greetings and had probably said ***Insha Allah*** or ***Khuda Hafiz***. Such creeping climbers among the business executives were a dime a dozen. He had encountered many of them in his long career in uniform.

But?

Hyder Bux wasn't able to quench the raw thirst of a seasoned intelligence officer. The urge to drill deep into the root of the mystery pushed him inexorably. The mystery of a nonentity calling the direct bedroom number of the seductress kept on haunting him.

Hyder pressed his mental drill bits in.

What medicine could this Harfan procure for the presumed first lady? Most of the medical experts in Pakistan, in all branches of the science, would like to prostrate before her and lick the dust of her alley walk.

He had, in his personal custody, the medical records of the President and his lover girl. There wasn't anything extraordinary, except that the nympho suffered from acute backache.

It wasn't an extraordinary ailment. A woman of her post-menopausal age was supposed to suffer from some pain and ache related to osteoporosis.

By ***Allah***! Did he ask that viper, Nawab Sharief to get some aphrodisiac from that Indian medico?

Yes, he did.

Where did this defence supplier fit in? He shouldn't. How could Nawab hook that petty ***muhajir***? That nobody worked for Israr, Nawab's half-brother and sworn enemy. And Nawab wouldn't hesitate to play Cain to brother Israr, his Abel. Did he push Harfan into the tigress's cage to strike any bargain with the ***Sadr***? What could that be? Was the clever fox trying to open a discreet line to Delhi?

No, no. He could not allow this lead to go unexplored. His trained mind told him that some unknown bomb was ticking at his back and this fellow Harfan must be a key player.

Hyder Bux decided to sound out first his business contact and reliable conduit to Izaz Afroz. The Sindhi jackal was grooming that viper as the future Chief Minister of the Punjab. And a seasoned politician of Nawab's stature was not likely to make an uncalculated move.

"Brother Nawab...***salaam,*** Hyder here."

He called the redoubtable sleek operator.

"***Janab...walekum assalam***," Nawab replied, "Any service for your servant?"

"Don't joke. How are things on the political front? Hope your preparations are complete?"

"Politics is an endless wool-ball. You can't get perfection Hyder sahib."

"Any help from me?"

"How can I do without your help brother? Elections require lots of resources."

"Don't worry. I want to see that Punjab is in your safe hands. Fund is not a problem. Let us discuss this separately. By the way, do you know a guy called Harfan?"

"Harfan?" Nawab chewed the alphabets and spoke again, "Yes. I know a Harfan. He is my brother's business executive."

"Is he trustworthy?"

"You can't trust any one these days. Even the Prophet (pbuh) did not trust his own followers. Any special job?"

"It's not that. Anything else can you add?"

"He's a Karachi based ***muhajir.*** Has good connections with London based Indians."

"Find out little more."

"Give me some space...something should come out...wise guys say that the queen has developed ***isq*** (love) for this rag picker."

"Don't tell me Nawab. The big man will tear him up."

"How does it matter?"

"That would harm brother Israr."

"I don't care. Israr is spoiling my business and this ***muhajir*** is playing a big role in pushing down my margins."

"So you're the ring master who threw the kid into the tigress's den?" Hyder spoke in flowery Urdu, "But I'd told you to get some medicines for me too. Hope you wouldn't go to the town with this information."

"You're not alone sir," Nawab replied with a relish, "The mighty PSO is also a client of that Indian medico. Don't worry. I don't open my mouth as long as my interests are not harmed. And you can cook the goose of brother Israr and that ***muhajir***. I don't mind."

General Hyder was intrigued by the suggestion.

Was this Harfan being sacrificed by Nawab to harm his brother? Was he being used as a conduit to some Indian contacts by the CMLA? Was the CMLA up to any new tricks, which he didn't know? Had he opened up a track II dialogue with that Indian widow, Mandira?

Hyder didn't rule out the possibility.

The Sindhi fox, Izaz Afroz was constantly bombarding the neurones of the President with queer political ideas. And the poor old man was more baffled than a circus buffoon was. The ambitious Red Rose was known for running odd political errands for the top man and Afroz.

Was she using the Harfan conduit to Delhi, via the London tunnel?

Which tunnel? The Sindhuja one? Or the one headed by Hirubhai Dasani?

The creepy idea foxed Hyder. Yes, Red Rose could use Harfan to activate her once-upon-a time-lover, the Muslim thespian of the Bombay celluloid world. And the fabled thespian was a political supporter of Mandira.

The boss man too had a couple of crooked tunnels open to Delhi. Yes. His course mate Lt. General Dhillon was still around, leading a command in southern India. The ***Sadr*** could use him too.

That would mean the de-seeding of the war clouds and easing of the military stand off and return to civilian rule. The next natural step would be to invite the politicians to take over the reins of the country. It did not lead him, General Hyder, the claimant to Pakistan's throne, anywhere.

Hyder Bux couldn't imagine that a two-penny whore would scuttle his plans. Surely not. He would fix her and hang that bloody Harfan. No one could stand in his way, not even Sarfaraz. He must immediately sand wall all possible tunnels to Delhi. Only a devastating war could expose the rotten hide of General Arif. The Pakistanis would not hesitate to accept him, a blue blooded Jat, as the next military ruler, if he could conclusively prove Arif's clandestine Indian connections.

But he required valuable evidence against Arif and his ladylove. Advance intelligence was his forte, which wasn't available to his competitor, General Sarfaraz. That ***Amritsaria*** (of Amritsar origin), if he happened to topple Arif, would be a bigger disaster for Pakistan. The country needed, at this critical juncture, a seasoned Lahoria (from Lahore) Jat Punjabi.

He was the one chosen by destiny, to take Pakistan into the next century; a glorious century of ascendance of Islam and the disintegration of Hindu India.

General Hyder pushed the intercom button and summoned his most trusted officer in the super-secret Special Operations Cell (SOC), directly functioning under him.

"Barqat show me the list of calls received by Red Rose in her bedroom hotline."

The officer returned in five minutes. The data was ready. In fact, Barqat updated it religiously.

Yes. She had received ten calls, from friends and admirers, in the last thirty days. Two calls were from Izaz Afroz, the former Foreign Minister. No big surprise. The President often used Malika for intimate dialogues with that possessed politician, with bags full of hatred for the Hindu neighbour and East Pakistan Bengalis.

The PSO called once. Not significant. He just wanted an appointment from the lady. Hyder had received an account of the meeting from the transcript of the audio recorder planted in Jahanara's residence.

One call was from the PIB chief, General Nayeem, requesting her to pass on to the President a top-secret report on Izaz Afroz's latest French mistress.

Well! Well! The top boss wasn't really a buffoon. He was aware of certain prejudicial activities of the ambitious Sindhi leader.

That's a precious input. Izaz should be made aware of Red Rose's special love for him, may be at an opportune moment. Why not? In his quest for power he might require the services of the Sindhi sycophant. He wouldn't be a bad bargain as against the ambitious Sarfaraz.

The only odd call was from this Harfan, a wild dark horse. Unfortunately the contents of the call were polluted by ambient noise, loud instrumental music.

Did this ring a strange bell?

An earlier audio snooping in the nympho's living room had probably thrown up the name of this dark horse. But Hyder's experts weren't sure. That irritating ***Sarod*** recital, with the loud accompaniment of the percussion drum, had polluted the audio quality.

"Barqat," Hyder asked, "Did your boys ever pick up this man's trail?"

"No sir. He's new in our roster of honour."

"Do you think he's a new star in Red Rose's life? These artists are peculiar animals. They often pick up wayside lovers to satisfy their insatiable desire. Loved and admired by all, they often feel lovelorn, deserted and lonely." Added Hyder.

"Perhaps it's not a romantic affair sir." Barqat replied. "If I'm not incorrect, they talked about some medicine and Nawab being the initiator. I can investigate this fellow."

"Look Barqat," General Hyder spoke in a whispering tone, "This lady's very close to the CMLA and I don't want to get axed for any act of indiscretion by your boys. Neither I can trust that jackal Nawab. Anyway I'll like to consult the PSO. There may be a latent security angle to it."

****

General Hyder, the great survivor, never relished the idea of jumping into a black hole, all by himself. He wasn't the type to commit a solitary suicide. Good company was always welcome, which always left the opportunity open to walk up to ***Allah's behest*** (heaven), in company of good friends.

Jahanara was too close to the big boss to be string-fiddled by his sleuths. General Arif was sure to put him in front of the firing squad if acts of indiscretion by his boys leaked out.

Investigation of the affairs of Harfan could lead his boys to the bedroom of the virtual first lady. And it was not unlikely that the soprano would scream out for his blood.

Hyder faced another dilemma. He could not authorise the most sensitive clandestine intelligence operations, involving important personalities, all by himself. The latest secret order of the CMLA had made it mandatory for the ISI and the PIB chiefs to obtain prior sanction from the PSO and the ***Sadr*** before highly sensitive domestic and external intelligence operations were mounted. These precautions were taken to make the intelligence organisations accountable to General Arif, who did not want rogue intelligence chiefs to turn the table on him.

He was peeved by a complaint from the US ambassador about the ISI Mosurs (mobile surveillance) tailing his car, wherever he went. How could Hyder do that? General Arif had ordered a high level enquiry headed by the PSO.

He had seen enough of the funny games of the intelligence community. Flushed with unaccounted secret service fund and drug money they were capable of jumping bed like chaste wayside whores. General Arif did not trust the intelligence community.

General Hyder was aware of this special susceptibility of the ***Sadr***. He did not trust any one around him. As the chief of the ISI he definitely wielded considerable clout in Pakistan's power structure. But Lt. General Sarfaraz was the listed number two, next to the CMLA. He was the designated authority to sanction a specific sensitive intelligence operation. It wouldn't take him more than five minutes to vitiate the ears of the CMLA, in murderous cacophony with the soprano. He would, in all probability, be shunted out to an insignificant diplomatic assignment, if not summarily shot.

Bullets came cheap, often free, from Uncle Sam's inexhaustible caches.

The eerie thought rattled Hyder's bones.

General Hyder Bux picked up the phone.

"Sir, Hyder here. There's something interesting. Can I come?"

"Is it very urgent? I'm expecting the US Deputy Secretary of State at five."

"I'll drop in, just for a few minutes."

Hyder left in a jiffy.

"Let me tell you Hyder," Sarfaraz offered special Kenyan tea to the ISI chief, stirring the brew with a silver spoon, "Don't fiddle with that bitch. She's the top man's property. He won't buy any excuse and won't hesitate in putting your neck under the chopping block. You know what happened last time you snooped on the US ambassador."

"That Yankee was trying to contact Sartaj Jamil, the Sindhi rebel."

"I understand. But America is our provider. You must use discretion."

"Sir," The ISI chief sweated under his crisply pressed three piece angora suit, "We've some delicate feedback about the possible Indian penetration of the security bubbles around the lady. You know her connections with a thespian of the Indian film industry. Her wild Bombay nights are still remembered by the connoisseurs."

"That's an old story. She last visited Bombay three years back."

"But, our source of information is impeccable. Who can prevent the Indian NSI from poisoning the ***Sadr***'s food and drink? That temple of love is vulnerable."

Hyder used one of the hackneyed clichés of the intelligence community, VIP security.

"Your story isn't convincing."

"You don't see the advantage sir," Hyder winked at the PSO, "This is a juicy story. We should develop it as a possible weapon against the ***Sadr***."

Sarfaraz muttered a curse under his breath. The smart bastard was trying to rope him in at the last moment. What for? Was Hyder showing a red herring, for implicating him in a bad jam? India, he knew, was the bedroom ghost; every Pakistani political player would like the common people to be scared of.

"Why do you think this Hanif..er..Harfan is such a mighty ***harfanmaula*** (Jack of all trade)?

"He figured in the first tape that I shared with you. Now this second tape is devastating. He has spelt out your and my name in his conversation with that bitch. Don't you think my lower staff may carry the tale to Izaz or anyone having the ears of the President?

"What do you gain by hanging this minor chap? That may infuriate the lady."

"That's why I want to inject the security angle. Anything can pass through that eye of the needle, even a mountain. That's our holy ghost." Hyder opened up his cards rather frankly.

The seasoned PSO could, however, not ignore the counter-intelligence and VIP security concerns of the ISI chief.

"The developments in East Pakistan have rendered the President almost a nervous wreck. He dreads the goblins and ***jinns*** of democracy, which are chasing his dreams. Don't provoke him beyond a point. A scared infant like him can start shooting wildly. You can get hurt, I can get hurt." Lt. General Sarfaraz spoke rather philosophically.

"His days are numbered. Let's kaput him at the earliest possible opportunity."

"Hyder," Sarfaraz finally said, "In our game we should be patient. We can push him out only after the war that we're sure to face soon. Perhaps I can't authorise such operations all by myself."

"Why not now? He is wrecking the country in tandem with the master demolisher Izaz."

"I'd like to. But Washington and Peking won't be charmed by our actions. They want Arif to bridge the east-west chasm...a new Cold War strategy." Sarfaraz advised caution and reverted back to his pet obsession.

"Don't you think sir that by allowing him time we are helping Izaz? He will take full advantage of the emerging Islamabad-Washington and Peking axis."

"It's not an axis Hyder. The US wants to open a new front against the USSR. I'm worried that fresh arms supply by the US and China will help the old man to consolidate his position. How can we stop this?

"Do you really want to? We need the supplies for East Pakistan. And I don't rule out another round of war with India."

"That's the biggest dilemma. We have to act decisively before the President and Izaz can conjure up new tricks," Sarfaraz spoke with a twitch in his eyes, "Let's heat things up for them in Dacca. We may start with purging the top Bengali army and civilian officers. Give me a list of the traitors, who deserve neutralisation."

"You want them in concentration camps!"

"Jokes apart Hyder," The PSO spoke in a definitive voice, "The movement in Dacca will gather momentum once we start weeding out the Bengali elite. These traitors should be buried alive. Why waste the national wealth by feeding them free?"

"That's not an impossible task." Hyder added, "I get your point. Aggravated skirmishes between Jainal and Izaz will help us. The President, I presume, will get badly caught in the scissors cleaves. I'd like you to consider the mass destruction of the Bengali rats. Jainal has polluted and subverted their loyalty."

"A good point. The boss is considering General Tarakki for the hatchet man's job in Dacca. I wonder since when these fish eaters have started mastering the martial arts! And their so-called fucking love for language is a charade! It's all planned by Delhi. I tell you Hyder, to save Pakistan we require to give them a mass burial."

"That's our common goal. The Bengalis must perish, if we want Islam and Pakistan to survive. I think we should jointly brief Tarakki before he emplanes for Dacca. But allow me to explore this chap Harfan. He could lead us to some strong India connections of the top boss. Why miss on something that could be important?"

"Are you serious? Do you think the ***Sadr*** will open up a secret channel to Mandira?"

"It's not impossible. You've seen Aftab's last report, the one that mentioned that the London fellow Sindhuja was building bridges between the ***Sadr*** and that widow." Hyder twitched his moustache hoping that the weighty input would floor the PSO.

"Fine, if you feel so strongly about that employee of Israr. But keep away from Malika and the President. Any compromise at this front will cost us our necks." Sarfaraz sounded a final warning.

"Thanks."

"Another point to note is that Israr is close to the boss man. Take care that he's not hurt," Sarfaraz paused, "Let's meet in two day's time and finalise the list of the Bengali rats. I like your idea. These buggers have to be eliminated. I can't stand this stupid race."

Sarfaraz concluded the last sentence with wrinkles of contempt that contorted his face.

"Let's wait for details from the Dacca station, keep the date flexible. Don't worry about Malika. My boys'll be very discreet."

Hyder replied and walked out triumphantly. Half the battle was won. The Bengali fixation of Sarfaraz had done the trick.

Back in his office Hyder used the exclusive number to Barqat and summoned him in.

"Trace down this Harfan, I want a run up on this creature. Be very discreet. Put the best boys on the job. No tampering with Red Rose. Explore the possibility of this Harfan brat having a link with Izaz."

"Yes sir."

"Ask Dacca station for two lists, one of the Bengali officers, both civilian and uniformed and the other of the intellectuals. They require a realm of higher wisdom, the wisdom of the grave."

"You mean we give them a quiet burial?"

"Burial yes, quiet or stormy, I don't as yet know. That we'll decide after Tarakki takes over."

"How urgent is this sir?"

"The PSO is serious and I think the boss is keen too. Let's keep the powder dry. Ask your Dacca boys to activate the Mosur and Tesur (technical surveillance) teams on the short listed Bongo suspects."

"Consider it done sir. The University and Dhanmandi areas have been placed under blanket Int. coverage. We've quite a few singing pigeons in our pocket." The Brigadier replied gleefully.

"That's OK. As you said I want a total footage of the Dhanmandi residence of Jainal. You can task Major Khalikuzzaman."

"It will be done sir," Barqat shared additional information with his boss, "We have completed the dossiers on all the important People's League leaders and their Indian contacts. In fact our Calcutta boys have snapped Jainal's meeting with Vishram Satpore, the NSI's Calcutta Bureau chief."

"That's excellent. Let's keep it under the sleeve for a while. Don't even share this with Sarfaraz."

"I'm your officer sir. I'd do as you desire."

"That's superb. I'd keep this in mind during your promotion to the next rank," Hyder affectionately patted Barqat, "Tell me how're you going to cover the Lahore rendezvous?" Asked Hyder.

"A technical operation is the easiest way out."

"Do it with finesse. I want all the dope. Use the best boys you have. I don't want any stinking shit." Hyder dismissed Barqat, his ElInt (Electronic Intelligence) and TechInt (Technical Intelligence) expert.

"We've to treat her hotel room and that of Harfan." Barqat added.

"Go ahead, do it on the quiet. Don't leave dirty droppings behind." Hyder winked and smiled.

Barqat personally dialled Hotel Faletti without routing the call through his secretary.

"Is it 303660?"

"Yes please. Hotel Faletti. May I help you?" The petite receptionist replied in a silvery voice.

"May I talk to your manager?"

"Anything I can do at the front desk sir?"

The young girl didn't like the idea of a customer bypassing her and directly talking to the boss.

"I'm Brigadier Barqat from the ISI, in-charge of President's security. Wire the manager in and do it fast."

Barqat felt irritated. These small time dolls, standing behind the counters, often pretended to dispense favours to their customers.

"Yes sir, Tahir here. What can I do for you?" The manager spoke after offering the ritual apology.

"This is about VIP security. My men, headed by Zamanat Ali, will report to you today. Give them all the help they require." Barkat preferred to be brief.

"Yes sir. Be sure of our sincere co-operation."

"And the name of the game is discretion. No one should get wise about what my boys are doing."

"You can be rest assured sir. We understand your orders."

"That's better." Barqat felt happy after successfully intimidating the hotel manager.

****

The Air Force Fokker F-27 landed at Lahore airport two hours later, with Zamanat Ali and his team of ISI sleuths, who carried a few vinyl portmanteaus stuffed with electronic equipment.

The veteran sleuth coerced the manager to peg room 406 for Jahanara, instead of her standing choice of room number 306. The soprano preferred the third floor room that faced the old Charring Cross and overlooked the Bagh-e-Jinnah. She had developed an infatuation for this room, her detractors surmised, because it's walls were a mute witness to many of her early life escapades.

Jamanat Ali, Barqat's anchor in the Special Operations Cell was a veteran hunter. He wasn't the kind of tiger to raise it paw and fawn upon his prey. Harfan was the target rabbit, but he couldn't be evaluated in a vacuum. Jahanara was the canvass, against which the target was to be probed and evaluated.

Why should that un-Islamic bitch be spared? These clones of the infidel western civilisation were far greater enemies of the country. The ***Quran Majid*** and the ***Hadis*** had never prescribed such frivolous singing and dancing. Jamanat's prejudices and religious inclinations far exceeded his professional brief. For life wasn't worth living if it could not be lived according to the prescriptions of the Holy Books.

Room 406, flanked by rooms 407 and 408 was treated with radio microphones and two micro-video cameras. With radio transmission facility built in; the motorised cameras were capable of sweeping wide spectrum angles.

A few radio microphones were carefully installed in room number 407 too. The room phone was treated with a miniature radio transmitter.

Jamanat's team waited patiently for their kill. The charming lover boy was sure to walk straight into the ISI interrogation centre, Badr, located at the basement hideout of the agency's sprawling building. Very few were born with extra luck to come out of that honeymoon chamber, as they liked to call the dreaded hole.

Jahanara arrived late in the afternoon, accompanied by the inevitable ***habshi,*** her favourite percussionist and a posse of security men. As expected, she raised a storm over the change of her favourite room.

The suave manager politely explained his compulsions. Only two nights back a young Gujranwala couple had committed suicide in the room. He was under police orders not to open the lock, till the investigation process was complete. He begged for Jahanara's understanding and expressed total helplessness. Perhaps she would understand and pardon him. The management wouldn't like to allot the special room to her till it was fully redone.

"Why don't you keep the room permanently booked for me?"

"As you wish ma'am. It'll be done after the renovation work is complete."

"Isn't it foolish?" Jahanara commented with a sexy pout, "It's a pity that, these days foolish lovers prefer to die at the slightest pretext. What's the fun in ending your life, even if society doesn't approve of an affair?"

"You're correct ma'am," Tahir, the young manager tried to synchronise his words with the horizontal movements of his head, "They're pretty foolish."

"Exactly so, dear. Life is for living. Enjoy every moment of it."

Jahanara licked up the strong and charming frame of the manager with the look of a hungry lioness. This man was promising enough for a warm nightcap.

"Thanks young man. You must come up to my room for a drink."

"That should be a privilege ma'am."

The manager escorted the seductress to her room, followed by a retinue of bearers and attendants, herded by the imposing ***habshi.***

Harfan arrived the next morning.

He wanted to make the visit brief and spend rest of the spare time with Jamilla. He was not afraid to face the seductress, but his professional discretion told him to maintain distance from the virtual mine field. The whole affair, as he later coolly analysed, smacked of a tricky plot by Nawab Sharief. That viper, a close associate of Izaz Afroz and Hyder Bux, could blow up his cover any moment.

He alighted from a tourist taxi at a road intersection; about 300 yards off the main gate and walked down to the hotel foyer. That was the normal anti-surveillance protocol he preferred to practice. These lessons were vital for survival.

The receptionist processed his request for a room after several manipulations of the computer. Finally she looked up nervously and whispered in the ears of a male colleague.

"Sir, welcome to the Faletti," The male receptionist replied, "Sorry for the delay. I can give you only room 407. We are, otherwise, fully booked."

"That will do. Harfan brought out his wallet and prepared to complete the formalities. The petite receptionist looked askance at another close-cropped egg-headed male employee, looking more like a cop. He sprinted in the direction of the lift. The bellboy fearfully saluted him and opened the door.

Harfan watched the crude drama, performed by amateurs.

They must be cops, not trained for merging with the posh hotel milieu.

Harfan produced his visiting card with a faint smile in a remote corner of his lips. The ivory white thick card proclaimed his identity as the marketing vice-president of Israr International.

"Any problem with the rooms?" Harfan enquired.

"Pardon me sir," The confused young receptionist spoke, nervously fiddling with a pen," As I said other rooms are already booked. You will like room 407. It's a historical room sir. The Governor of undivided Punjab used to stay there. It was his personal preference. And for an honoured guest like you, we offer a 25% discount."

"Oh great! It's a rare honour. Why not? Bill it to my company. Okay?"

Harfan pretended to be overwhelmed by the gracious offer.

"That should be fine sir." The receptionist summoned the bellboy and asked him to help Harfan with his carry bag.

As he entered the lift, a bellboy, who looked like a cop, followed him carrying his overnight suitcase. He opened the room and courteously ushered in Harfan and even managed to say 'have a good day sir'.

Harfan thanked him profusely and offered a twenty rupees bill as a tip. The untrained hand of the bellboy coiled back in hesitation. Harfan forced the bucks into his clammy palms and casually closed the door behind him.

He was sure that the intelligence rats had laid down a trap. Was the show exclusively for him or was it a part of the security measures for the virtual first lady of Pakistan?

The ISI or the PIB?

Why?

Harfan lighted a cigarette and coolly assessed the situation.

He was definitely expected here, but by which agency?

What could have gone wrong?

Ibadat? Rama Bai?

Nawab Sharief?

Malika Jahanara?

Harfan couldn't hammer the nail on any spatial correlation.

The process of elimination, encompassing all the aspects of his deep-cover glimpsed past his sensory scanner. No. Except Jahanara and Nawab Sharief he couldn't put a marker on any other bull's eye.

It must be the lady, the reigning beautiful bitch.

The intelligence reception team was either a part of her security or a piece out of the ISI's intricate operation, woven around General Arif's Aphrodite. He was just an irritating additional fixture in the frame.

Harfan silently smoked the cigarette and tossed his thought process over and over again. Was he correct in his conclusion? What if the ISI targeted him? Nawab Sharief might have instigated the ISI sleuths. Or was it that his visit to Jahanara's house had generated suspicion in the highest quarters?

Thank heavens! Harfan shuddered to think of the prospect of being cooked in the cauldron of Pakistan's raging power struggle. He wasn't unaware of the darkening clouds over General Arif's rocking boat. It was a matter of time before the hungry Generals could bury him thousand leagues down the Arabian Sea. If they didn't, the events in East Pakistan were sure to rip him and the country apart.

To hell with Jahanara and her lover boy General Arif! To hell with Pakistan!

He wouldn't allow the ISI the pleasure of trapping him. Not any more, like Bhagat & Co had wrapped him up in celluloid at Divine Inn. He decided to play safe and by the rules of the game. If there were no way to escape the net, he would search out its contours and detect flaws in it. He'd tear apart the perfidious dragnet like a killer shark.

Harfan ordered breakfast and meticulously searched all conceivable corners and crevices in the room. He fished out three tiny radio-microphones, made in USA, with 72 hours power supply.

Well! Well! It was an elaborate reception indeed!

He was very much a target of the agency! Not just a mere fixture.

Perhaps he'd picked up the virus from Jahanara's mansion. The Prima Donna must also be under the scanner. The military machine wasn't a monolith. It housed innumerable tiny wheels and pinions within. Many of those rotated in contra-directions.

Which pinion of the military machine could be involved?

The Pakistan Intelligence Bureau, headed by the celebrity elder Khan wouldn't dare bugging the soprano's room. He owed his office to her pleasure and that of the younger Khan.

The DMI wouldn't stray into the minefield of civilian intelligence.

It must be the ISI.

Well! With the Big Brother around he had reasons to worry.

This fanged outfit hardly functioned rationally and rarely used sophisticated tradecraft. It believed more in using canon balls for killing flies, often in the CIA style. The ISI had blindly copied the Wild West characteristics of its American cousin. And in junta ruled Pakistan, nobody expected the butcher's arm of the establishment to play by the rules.

"Act normal," Harfan muttered slowly, "Squeeze yourself, if the nut-cracker closes on you. Make room for the threat before you're threatened beyond limits."

He picked up the phone and called Jamilla.

"Hi darling!" He pumped in, as much sweet juice he could muster, "How're you? I'm here in Lahore chasing an elusive lady."

"Who's that witch?"

"Oh darling! She is the one and only bewitching ***Mohtarma*** Jahanara."

"What're you doing with that whore?" Jamilla screamed on the phone.

"Wait darling. I'm not here by choice. It's Nawab sahib, my boss's younger brother. He wanted me to get some medicine for her and the PSO and the ISI chief from an Indian medico. The consignment has arrived via London, and I'm here to hand over the medicine to her."

"Don't get entangled with her."

"Sure darling. I can't chase a bad dream when the best dream is already in my heart." Harfan whistled lightly over the line and wished Jamilla good night.

He tried to figure out the facial expressions of the wired up ISI operative. Must be furtively logging on and tracing the call.

Well! The call to Jamilla would keep them guessing for a while. The words-PSO and ISI chief- was sure to keep them busy scratching their heads. They should be mighty impressed with the names of the two pillars of the junta figuring in his brief love-talk.

He ate breakfast leisurely and told the front desk not to disturb him. He needed at least two hours sleep.

Harfan pried opened the phone using a screwdriver. Yes. An expert technician had implanted a radio microphone inside the resistance coil, below the dialling mechanism, a cute device with infinite life and having a range of 100 metres.

The transparent scenario rattled Harfan. Both he and Jahanara were under ISI surveillance. The spooks had wired up the entire room. He had unknowingly walked into the minefield of political intrigue that involved the power brokers of Islamabad.

The ISI operation could only be an extension of a conspiracy against the President.

By whom?

It must be another set of hungry Generals, the ISI chief included.

This was good fun!

Harfan lighted a cigarette and refitted the screws with a slow and careful clockwise motion.

He dialled the private number of Israr and informed him about the likely late arrival of the Chinese team. The yellow arms peddlers were expected only in the evening. He could take time, but should be in Lahore by 4 p.m. positively.

It was an important rendezvous. The Chinese side headed by Lin Tao Ping, the Deputy Defence Minister, was to meet his Pakistani counterpart, General Naqibullah, in short Naqi, the Defence Advisor to the President. The Chinese were likely to conclude an agreement to supply tanks, field guns, mortar batteries and MBRLs (multi barrel rocket launchers). All against cash and through the United Arab Emirate based intermediaries. Israr International, Harfan added, could expect to bag contracts for airlifting this military hardware to Sargodha and Karachi.

"But sir," Harfan dragged the dialogue, "Why are we getting the Chinese? We should turn to the Americans."

"There's a problem. The Congress has laid down an embargo on weapons supply to Islamabad after the March 25th crackdown in Dacca."

"That's dangerous for Pakistan."

"Don't worry. We're expecting a US delegation too, in another two weeks. The Turkish, Saudi and Jordanian windows will open up soon. And the Pentagon will foot the bill. Anyway keep General Naqi in good humour. We're basically patriotic Pakistani businessmen. Aren't we?

"Sure sir. What should I offer him for clinching the airlifting contract?"

"Start with 3%. Go up to 7%. That's the upper limit."

"Are you coming?"

"No brother Nawab will be there. I want to avoid him. But raise the butter-bucks if he chips in more commission."

"Will ten percent be fine?"

"No problem, if that's absolutely necessary."

Harfan called Nawab Sharief next.

"***Assalam-u-alaikum*** Nawab sahib, Harfan here," He spoke rather loudly, "Are you coming for the Chinese supply meeting?"

"***Wale kum assalam***," Nawab replied, "No ***yar***, brother Israr has already bagged the contract. I believe he has offered Rupees ten million to the top boss. You should know better, with your access to Begum Jahanara."

"Don't be unfair to me sir. It's you who had sent me to the ***mohtarma*** for helping her to get that medicine from the Indian medico."

"Don't drag my name. So you are getting that Chinese assignment?"

"We're looking for business, not assignments."

"Some business offers aren't worth considering. You've already beaten me to it."

"***Janab***, I'm a small fry. It's all in your family. It's either you or Israr sahib. I want to know," Harfan came to the crucial dialogue," If you'd like to deliver the medicine personally to Malika sahiba. I learn she's staying in this very hotel."

"Why can't you see her and hand over the medicine?"

"Sir, I thought you'd like to do it personally. It's you who had commissioned me to get the medicines. A small rat like me won't dare to enter her room. It's better you give it to her yourself."

"Don't be silly. I'll call her to say that you're representing me. Don't be scared ***yar***, she's a fine lady." Nawab was lavish in his praise for Jahanara.

"And sir," Harfan continued, "The nerve tonics for the respected PSO and the ISI chief, procured from the Indian medico are at my work place. Hope you'll personally deliver it."

"Leave it to me. I'll tackle them. Hope you haven't told brother Israr about this."

"No sir."

Harfan disconnected the line and connected Jahanara's room over the intercom.

As usual the castrated ***habshi*** answered.

"Who is there?"

"***Janab***, Harfan Bukhari here. Can I talk to ***mohtarma***?"

"Does she know you?"

"Not really. I'm speaking on behalf of Nawab Sharief sahib."

"Okay. Hold on."

Jahanara came on the line after a good two minutes.

Begging the indulgence of her exalted highness in the sweetest possible Urdu Harfan requested Jahanara's permission to come down to her room for delivering a packet from Nawab Sharief. He didn't fail to mention that some undelivered packets were meant for Generals Hyder Bux and Sarfaraz.

The dialogue baffled Jahanara. She was looking forward to a warm night, with Harfan's bare body setting fire to her flesh and soul.

What the hell was he talking about?

Harfan's calls had baffled the ISI operatives as well. Jamanat Ali, seated on a sofa, threw the earphone away and uttered a common Punjabi slang, graciously linking Harfan in sexual relationship with his mother. The bastard was either a damn fool or a highly trained agent. He must have gathered the whiffs of his boys and bugs.

Hell with it!

It clearly dawned on Jamanat that his electronic operations were either compromised or he was lead into a serious trap by seemingly wrong judgement of his bosses. This guy Harfan was either a clean fly or he was a highly trained intelligence agent. The trained counter-intelligence salts in him gradually catalysed in favour of the assessment that Harfan was too clever for his boys. He must have detected some of their unusual movements.

The next possible scenario terrified Jamanat Ali. Who could prevent Harfan from leaking out the ISI covert operations against Begum Jahanara? The mercurial lady was capable of getting him skinned for her next pair of sandals. It was possible in General Arif's Pakistan. Simply no one was going to come to his rescue. Not even General Hyder Bux.

Jahanara wasn't trained to hide her irritation.

She dialled Harfan's room.

"What bloody medicine does Hyder require?" She asked contemptuously.

"***Mohtarma***," Harfan drawled his reaction, "I really don't know. Nawab sahib told me that, the General required some tonic. But ma'am I don't have any idea as to what it is." He hastened to add.

"And what's that PSO looking for?"

"***Mohtarma***," Harfan talked with trained hesitation in his voice, "I've no idea at all. I just collected the packets on behalf of Nawab sahib."

"Tonic or aphrodisiac? They should come to me for picking up a few lessons in middle-aged sexual bliss. Any way, you're welcome to come to my room any time." Jahanara banged the phone on its cradle with a vicious sense of delight.

Harfan leisurely walked down the corridor to room 406. The same bearer followed him with a tray full of tea.

The ***habshi*** opened the door and stood guard outside.

Harfan stood behind the curtain, peeped in and looked for Jahanara.

She was seated before a mirror, busy applying her favourite eyeshade, with delicate strokes from a brush, specially made out of the finest antelope hair from the heights of Gilgit.

As she turned towards the door, Harfan placed his right index finger on his mouth and signalled her to be silent. He respectfully walked down to the centre of the room and handed over a packet and a letter, in full view of Jamanat's video cameras.

"***Mohtarma***, the details are in Nawab sahib's letter and the medicine is meant for six months."

He made a move to leave.

Jahanara glanced at the letter with utter disbelief in her eyes.

"Thanks, please convey my best wishes to dear Nawab. I'm so thankful for the medicines. ***Khuda Hafiz***."

Jahanara played along, as desired by Harfan.

The letter wasn't from Nawab Sharief. Harfan had scribbled down a few lines; warning her of possible surveillance and snooping.

Jahanara moved into the toilet signalling the ***habshi*** to follow.

The cameras went blind.

She asked the zombie to chew and gulp down the letter with a glass of water. He obeyed quietly and moved out to the anteroom.

Jahanara perplexed as she was, wondered why General Hyder Bux took such extraordinary pains to bug her room. It must be him.

She was baffled by the turn of events. Was she a suspect in the eyes of the ***Sadr***? Did he authorise the snooping operation?

Or was it Hyder all by himself? Was he building up evidence against her and the President and cooking up excuses to justify a coup? Possible. The ISI boys wouldn't have dared to bug her without his orders. It must be him. Who else could dare violate her privacy? General Nayeem, the elder Khan wouldn't dare.

She smelt the burning cordite of another coup-plot. That was the only possible thing to happen to any military ruler. Arif did it to his mentor. Why should not Hyder plot against Arif?

Bloody heavens! With General Arif's exit these hungry Generals would fuck her to death. She must be on guard and speak to the big man in private.

General Hyder, Nayeem had informed her, had ganged up with Lt. General Sarfaraz and the Sindhi jackal, Izaz Afroz. What had kept her lover boy hanging onto the fragile twigs of power was the Chinese and American support. Minus their support the hungry pack of wolves would've made a hearty meal of his flabby flesh.

Why had they bugged Harfan's room?

Did Hyder bug her bedroom too? Did he have any evidence of Harfan's presence in her bedroom? Oh heavens! That could explode like another Krakatoa!

It couldn't be anything else. She was the barrel, through which Hyder's bullets would reach straight to Arif's heart.

Jahanara thought of calling General Arif's Islamabad number, picked up the handset and hastened to place it back. She recalled Nayeem's warning. Hyder had perhaps hooked up the phones of the President to his trick boxes.

She ordered her ***habshi*** to pour a few ounces of White Horse and settled down after lighting a cigarette.

Well! Well! A coup was nothing new in ***Allah's*** own land, Pakistan. She couldn't probably prevent another General thrusting down the gullets of dear Pakistanis, another stiff dose of patriotic rule in uniform. The Pakistanis were accustomed to these brats in boots, like they were with the annual monsoon and periodical locust visitations.

Jahanara gulped down the whisky, steadied her nerves and shrugged off the foul fear invading her instincts; especially her instincts for survival.

Whether it was a peaceful ouster or a bloody coup, she wouldn't like to go down the drain with General Arif. To be on the right side of the top man was her prerogative. She was basically an entertainer and a courtesan. It shouldn't be difficult to hook Hyder and Sarfaraz. After all, they were born from their mother's wombs, and not from holy dewdrops, impregnated by divine angels.

She ordered another whisky and decided to probe the minds of the two most powerful men in Pakistan, Hyder and Sarfaraz.

Minds of men?

Shit! In her perception it existed in their libido and in a particular organ. She had tasted scores of them. And this Hyder shouldn't be an exception, if he really had the balls between his thighs.

"Hello. Is it the number of Gen. Hyder?" Jahanara dialled the number of the ISI chief.

The young Captain on duty was floored at the mention of her name and immediately connected her to the boss.

"Hello Hyder dear," The soprano spoke in melted-cheese Urdu, "Haven't seen you for ages. ***Bhai*** (brother) ***bhule se hi sahi, kabhi to meri gali me aaya karo*** (stray into my lane, even once by mistake)."

Hyder momentarily lost his bearings, but immediately composed himself and replied in equally charming Urdu, a sweet synthesis of Sanskrit, Persian and Arabic.

"***Wale kum assalaam, mohtarma***. Am I lucky enough to tread the pathway to the most beautiful woman and the reigning soprano of Pakistan? At times I feel that you are greater than that ***malika-e-tarannum*** (queen of melody), Begum Nurjahan!"

"Don't compare me with her Hyder. How can a street singer from Calcutta be my equal? I've pure Arab blood in my veins."

"I entirely agree ***mohtarma***. But I'm so unlucky that I don't find spare time to visit your charmed musical sessions."

"No one's born with luck Hyder. Come and see, if luck is waiting for you, may be between my bosoms." Her whisky-numbed tongue slurred over the words mischievously.

A highly embarrassed Hyder managed to murmur, that he would surely chase dame luck to her doorsteps one of these days. But as ill luck would have it, he didn't get the time even to be with his family.

He assured Jahanara that listening to her audio records usually filled up a good portion of his leisure. ***Insha Allah***! They would surely meet one of these days.

"You know Hyder," Jahanara fired a fatal bullet at him, "I'm told that the Indian medico at Dehradun is very good. Can you get me some medicines from there?"

"***Mohtarma***, our links are totally frozen. Any problem? Can I help?"

"Well Hyder, who else can help me but you? Your presence itself is medicine for my parched soul. Come over, I really miss you dear."

Jahanara disconnected the line and loudly cursed the ISI chief. She cried out to her ***habshi*** and ordered another stiff measure of White Horse.

The bitch! Hyder cursed Jahanara hurling an obscene Punjabi slang, which normally described a woman as a bed-trotting whore.

He was too small a person to receive her attention. What was this openhearted invitation about? She did not sound like inviting him. She used her Urdu like she was fencing with the sharpest sword.

Barqat's Lahore operation must have run into some nasty problem. The bitch must have detected some flaw in Jamanat's EIInt operation. Jahanara was one of the greatest survivors in the high social circuit. Her first success in the power angling had started with a top aid to President Akbar. She later showered her favour on Izaz Afroz. But that thoroughbred Englishman was not interested in settling down with a homegrown beauty. His pasture was far wider and his choice fluttered around the white skin European beauties. Izaz to Arif Khan was not a quantum jump. General Arif, basically a simpleton, liked the easy ways of life. Jahanara was a good outlet for him. He did not look beyond indigenous brands.

Yes. The bitch must be a good survivor. But the instinct for survival did not necessarily endow her with the crafts of detecting a delicate electronic operation. Did the imperial brother, Nayeem the PIB chief, tip her off? Well! Nothing should be taken for granted. This bloody Nayeem could stoop down to the darkest crevices of a melting pot, if that boosted his service prospects.

General Hyder Bux was more worried of the Damocles' sword, precariously hanging over his head. The slimy lady wouldn't hesitate splitting the beans to her lover, with saline-tear and venom-tartar sauces. And the CMLA wasn't known to be a messiah of mercy. He was sure to face the guillotine.

He must get back to General Sarfaraz, and take cover behind his shield. The PSO was correct. He should've avoided pushing his luck too far.

Jahanara was too seasoned a nymph to swim along Hyder's paean of meaningless articulation. She was aware of the ruthless characteristics of this Jat Punjabi. As a commander of the 26th Jat regiment he had wiped out over 15,000 rebellious Baluchis in their mountain hideouts. He simply carpet bombed the villages and rained machine gun fire from helicopter gunship. He was better known as the ***Qasai*** (butcher) of the Pakistan army.

Her temperature still scaled past the boiling point. She wondered if that creature from the realm of shadow did have all the organs at the right places. The s.o.b was too clever and perhaps the only military brass to escape her charms. Perhaps no juice was left in his haggard balls. That's why he cribbed for a supply of aphrodisiac from India. All the herbs of the Himalayas couldn't arouse desire in that frigid toad. Only she could make him jump under his pants. Some men weren't cut out for the finer things of life. They loved carrying the dirty loads of their masters and generally died in harness.

A pug-nosed brat! Jahanara cursed the ISI chief. She would tackle the rogue in her own sweet way. He deserved a sweet death. Gen. Hyder Bux must pay for his audacity. ***Insha Allah***, she would squeeze his balls out, for his audacity of bugging her room and spoiling two wonderfully planned evenings with her new lover boy, Harfan.

What next? Should she check out the other pretender?

"Hello General, how have you been?" Jahanara dialled General Sarfaraz.

"Fine ***mohtarma***, as fine as these bloody Bengalis and Indians allow us to be."

"Let ***Allah*** give you strength. You must come one of these days and taste the best wine and kebabs in the city. I know you require relaxation and darling, you know, that I'm the best for it. You know it." Jahanara's voice sounded inviting and salacious.

"That'll be a privilege."

"Sarfaraz darling, I've a nagging feeling that some one is tapping my phone. I haven't spoken to the **Sadr** as yet. Would you like to look into this? Will you please darling?"

Jahanara threw a probing pebble.

To Sarfaraz, the pebble was reminiscent of devastating volcanic explosion, which rocked him with violent tsunami waves. The bewitching soprano wasn't a nitwit to call him up out of the blue, to tell him this. The bumbling ISI brats must have blundered again.

"Anything special ***mohtarma***?" The seasoned PSO tried to fathom the crest of the killer waves.

"Nothing much darling. I keep on receiving ghost calls and there are silly noises. I was reading a book on the CIA, and I'm told that their sleuths often bug the White House phones too."

"Who would dare do that in Pakistan?" Sarfaraz came out with loud protestations.

"Oh dear," Jahanara sighed sweetly, "In our blessed land no one seems to be safe, not even the highest."

"That's preposterous ma'am. All of us are loyal to the **Sadr**." Sarfaraz replied in the sweetest possible Punjabi.

"Dear, dear!" Jahanara's voice recoiled, paused and fired at a new target," How is dear Ashma?"

A fond reference to Sarfaraz's estranged wife.

"She's fine."

"You know dear, in order to have a child you must consult that Indian **vaid** from Dehradun. I get my medicines from him regularly." Jahanara's blazing meteorite this time hit Sarfaraz straight on the face.

"We're almost at war ma'am. I can't think of contacting Dehradun."

"Dear, dear! What a pity! Come over, I can probably give you a few tips. Life isn't as difficult, as you imagine it to be. There are more hidden treasures beyond the affairs of the State."

Sarfaraz lost his cool.

These ISI gunks must've littered the market with their gooey operations!

This bloody Nawab Sharief! Confiding in a serpent was a mythological mistake, but a lively mistake, which spanned on to creation. But confiding in Nawab Sharief could normally lead only to disastrous consequences. How could that nympho know about his requirement of aphrodisiacs from an Indian **vaid**? Nawab must have carried the tale to her. This double dealer, Sarfaraz muttered a curse, should be smothered at the earliest opportunity.

Well! Most middle-aged men required some props to strengthen their sex prowess. He needed it more for his family peace. Wife Ashma had almost become a psychological wreck, because of his inability to impregnate her. His sperms, doctors had opined, didn't have the capacity to swim the uterine pacific and reach the ovarian isles of his wife.

The lady, daughter of an Imperial Civil Service doyen had given him an ultimatum. He had to improve his technique or else they would have to call it quits.

There was nothing wrong in his seeking out some medicines from India?

India and Pakistan were tied by an unflappable umbilical. They'd fight wars at the slightest pretext and pine for each other's proximity at other levels. That should not bar him from getting medical supplies from that country.

Sarfaraz dipped the pin of his suspicion on General Hyder. He was the real culprit, an African baboon. The stupid had no business to bug her Lahore hotel room. He had forewarned the baboon adequately.

What a massive disappointment!

Jahanara's verbal bullets weren't any less lethal than the fireballs hurtling down from the skies. The bumbling beauty was sure to sing in the ears of the CMLA and he was perhaps hours away from the 'Badr' dungeon of the ISI or the dark chambers of the interrogation centre at Chak Lala cantonment.

Was he getting sucked into a trap laid by the ambitious ISI chief? That crook was capable of fabricating a parallel coup and diverting some anonymous bullets to shatter his skull.

No. He mustn't allow the golden opportunity to slip out of hand, simply because he had obtained a few stimulant pills from India. Didn't anyone have the freedom of getting medicines from abroad, without being bugged by the ISI?

Lt. General Sarfaraz paced up and down the confines of his office room. He must get out of this mess and quickly.

Was it safe to cross the bridge with the unreliable Hyder Bux? He could blow up the planks beneath his feet midway. Thank heavens! Nothing prevented Hyder from telling a sob story to the President about his authorising the telephone tapping operation.

Sarfaraz ***Amritsaria*** must survive. He did survive the partition holocaust. Didn't he? Why not now?

He must throw the blazing meteorite back into Hyder's court, and not allow him to gang up with that Sindhi maniac. That should buy him safe survival insurance.

The resolution kept on gurgling inside Sarfaraz's smouldering psyche. Could he do it alone? No. He must have vital allies. Major players in the junta should side with him.

And what about that fellow Alam Khan, the arms peddler? He had secured well-oiled tunnels to the CIA, MI6 and the Pentagon. This fellow must be tapped. He could influence some key opinion makers in the US Congress and Senate and around the President.

Peking would accept anything, once he assured the yellow Reds about Pakistan's eternal hate-commitment against Hindu India. That elixir alone had kept Pakistan's brittle bones together.

Chapter 34

General Hyder Bux didn't remain idle either. He could ill afford to do that. Who could prevent Sarfaraz from ganging up with Jahanara and Nayeem and ambushing him at the next street corner?

As a commander of a mountain division he had mastered the art of ambushing his enemy at the most unexpected spot. He must, Hyder concluded, activate his own spider web, Izaz Afroz, General Naqi, General Hamidur and the Air Chief. He could even fall back on the Chief, General Omar. Why not? He could blunt the malfeasance of Sarfaraz conclusively.

Why not Nawab Sharief? His might have in store new stories on the bitchy witch and that dark horse business executive. But was that boy Harfan really involved? Or was it that Nawab was using him as a scapegoat to hang his half-brother? That decent boy, married to a distinguished couple's daughter, had never come to the notice of his agency. Israr Sharief was a clever businessman. He was not interested in politics. Why should he give such higher rating to Harfan? Well! Nothing should be left to chance. Pakistan was a tricky quagmire. Any false step could be fatal.

But he must fathom the depth of the muck first, created by Barqat's boys at Lahore.

"Barqat," Hyder thundered at his deputy, "What the hell have you done to Red Rose?"

"No word yet from Jamanat sir. I presume everything's going well."

"Bullshit! I don't think so. Take the Cessna; fly there immediately and check for yourself. I think the operation has misfired."

"***Hai Rabba!*** (Allah) I'd given Jamanat a meticulous blueprint. And he's our best counter-intelligence operator."

"Don't waste time. I think we've hit a hidden rock, more formidable than your planning and Jamanat's expertise."

General Hyder Bux despatched his deputy post-haste and turned to the array of phones. He must call his partners. Sure he wasn't going to offer his neck on a platter. It was now or never. He must make it to the top.

"But sir..." Barqat made a feeble attempt to justify his action.

"Now get lost and repair the damage."

Hyder Bux brushed past Barqat and boarded his car and asked the driver to rush to the office of the PSO, Lt. General Sarfaraz Lodi.

"No, no Hyder, you got it all wrong. Why did you go all the way and bug her room?" Sarfaraz was surprised to receive the visitor at such odd hour and annoyed to hear what he had to say.

"Not at all sir", General Hyder sounded mighty officious and lied all the way, "My boys had plugged in Harfan Bukhari's room. He is the security suspect. I told you so."

"Hyder, let's not pretend that your boys are ***Sufi*** saints. How can you pass him off as a suspect? I'm sure some of your boys have gone beyond the brief and bungled again. It's going to cost you dearly."

"We're supposed to cross the bridge together sir. Let's not walk in different directions"

Hyder sounded an indirect warning to the PSO.

"You can't use that cliché all the time Hyder. We've lots of explaining to do, to the boss. I have gone through the audiotapes. That boy sounded innocent. What was the need for angling him when he was openly parroting our names?"

"I had done that with your foreknowledge. Has she spoken to the CMLA?" Hyder scaled down his voice.

"I hope she hasn't. But she has unfurled the red alert. She has buttonholed you and me. It's a mighty warning. Have your boys found any incriminating evidence?"

"No. Apparently not."

"It is highly embarrassing Hyder. The entire world needn't know that you and I require some nerve tonics," Sarfaraz shared his frustrations, "This lady is definitely going to use her B major for broadcasting our sexual virtues, all over Pakistan."

"Sorry sir. I'll try to control the damage. Leave it to me."

"You'd better do that Hyder, and do that pretty fast, before she sings into the ears of the boss. And one final word of caution, don't try your usual disappearing trick with Harfan. Jahanara won't be amused and he has other influential friends."

"Let's talk about it later, sir," General Hyder stood up, "We're together in the juicer, in our game of toppling the ***Sadr***. You alone can't escape the churning blade."

"You can't blackmail me and I can't support all the misadventures of your boys." Sarfaraz shot back firmly.

"There can be a genuine mistake. I run an agency and I have the mandate to probe reasonably suspicious leads. I can't take chance with the security threat to our VIP, the President and the CMLA."

Hyder smiled with a slight squirm.

"You think you can sell that story!"

"In the intelligence game it's possible. Security is our Holy Ghost. That's our plausible alibi. You can sell any shit to a scared crow. Arif will buy anything if we're not caught red handed. I'll play up this aspect in the print media, highlighting suspected joint Indian and Peoples' League conspiracy to assassinate our President."

"Who would buy that story?"

"Don't forget sir, the Indians had played up the Imphal incident beyond all proportions. We had to do a lot of explaining to Washington and London. Why can't we do the same? The war environs will provide a blue backdrop to our story."

"You've some real hard selling to do."

"Don't worry. I will send across a few fabricated Int. reports. One from Aftab should point the needle of suspicion to Harfan." Hyder smiled as he stood up.

"And you want me to put up those to the boss as genuine reports!"

"That's correct."

"You've a real crooked brain Hyder. But how does it help? Are you not sacrificing an innocent man, this son-in-law of Zahoor"? Sarfaraz laughed with a sense of relief.

"That's what intelligence is made of. It's crooked all the way. And you require a crooked partner, in our common game," A sly smile crossed Hyder's face, "That fellow is not our target. The demolition of Jahanara is a part of our game. Let me play it up."

"I think I should call the media and brief them about unearthing of an Indian NSI plot to kill our ***Sadr***. But who'll be the Indian ghost? Harfan?" Sarfaraz added in a hushed relaxed tone.

"As I said sir, ***Allah*** will guide us through the darkness! Don't bother about details. We can name anyone and shot him. I don't mind if Harfan is the convenient dog."

Hyder smartly saluted the PSO and prepared to leave.

"Well Hyder," Sarfaraz stood up, lighted a cigarette and said, "That should buy us a breather before we administer the final blow to the old toad."

"***Amin.***"

Hyder saluted again and left with the brightest smile on his face. His 28 summers in the army and 3-year stint in the ISI had taught him well the tricks of survival. The top leadership was as clueless as a common man in the street. Any plausible intelligence story could be sold to the ***Sadr***, especially at a moment when he was gripped with panic. It would be too late for him when he discovered the intelligence charade. By then, he would either be shot or incarcerated in a state guesthouse.

****

Howling hell!

Sarfaraz stood near the window and looked with eyes squinted at a funnel of dust and dry leaves that was being sucked up by the strong whirling wind. His mind raced fast. Spiralling contradictory currents thrashed their heads against his chest.

Why shouldn't he take advantage of this mess and roll down the coup ball? Media blitz, as suggested by Hyder, should help in building up a congenial backdrop. A few pot shots at the drunken blabber ball by some paid assassins would fit in snugly with the media hype.

Why not? Delhi had one hundred reasons to bump off the ***Sadr***. Putting a mad dog sticker on a faceless fellow like Harfan and shooting him shouldn't weigh heavily on the Pakistani conscience.

That should be a separate sub-plot, distinct from the one hatched between him and Hyder. He could probably hire some Baluch or Frontier desperadoes. What about a fanatic Hazara? They were good killers. Only they could get past the tough security curtain.

Some quick fence mending would be essential.

But he would like to play a deeper trick.

Sarfaraz dialled Hyder's secured personal number, "Hyder there is an additional point I wanted to mention. Do you have the voice implantation technology?"

"What's your game?"

"Can some people fake Jahanara and Harfan's voice?"

"Technically it's not impossible."

"Erase all traces of reference to our names and add some incriminating dialogue between the two. Can you fake a story of Jahanara's linkages with some Indian leaders?"

"Well sir," Hyder commented with a jackal like broken dry smile, "You are a better intelligence crook than I am. Let me see. I'll get back to you with the finished product."

Sarfaraz felt slightly relieved. That neat trick should be a mighty weapon for public consumption, if he was ever needed to proffer a public statement after the take over. But he must prepare for that historic event.

Yes. The Pentagon and Langley bosses and the White House should be made aware of the blue print of Pakistan's succession riddle. He must strengthen his ties with the real owner of Pakistan, the President on the Potomac.

Perhaps Mian Alam Khan could help. That jackal of an arms peddler knew of numerous subterranean highways to the strategic planners in Washington, London and other European capitals. It was high time he activated that channel.

Hyder, by designation the tallest intelligence executive in Pakistan, rued the self-inflicted hole on his palms. Those holes, he knew, would by no means make him a holy martyr.

He should have not given carte blanche to Barqat and Jamanat Ali, the policeman turned counter intelligence operative.

Holy ***Rabba***! He should save his skin, by any means. The loud sounding tape faking suggestion of the PSO might help. But the immediate cleanup operation was very important.

"What the hell have you done Barqat? Did I tell you to bug her room?" Hyder fumed like a wounded ***cheetah.***

"Sir, it wasn't intended that way. But; I'm not sure how this lady got scent of the bugs, the way she did. It must be that Harfan fellow. Only a trained agent can adopt such counter-surveillance measures. He must have unmasked some of our blundering baboons." Barqat explained.

"Did he tamper with your equipments?"

"I don't think so. There was no sign of any tampering. The clever turn of screws can't be detected."

"I can't put my neck on the line for your blundering baboons. Give me an urgent damage control fact-sheet. Remember, the PIB chief is loyal to the ***Sadr.*** He won't take time to make the old guy wise to all this."

"Copy sir."

"Good. Draw up a few blockbuster reports about the Indian threat to the ***Sadr***. One of those should be from Aftab, pointing a finger at Harfan. I want these in two hours time."

"Yes sir."

"Dig up Harfan's cupboard. I want a few skeletons unearthed, real or dummy, pretty fast."

"He appears to be a clean chap."

"Do what I say. The truth isn't what it appears to be. It's what you make it out to be. That's an intelligence officer's job. Is that clear?"

"Yes sir." Barqat replied meekly.

"Fine. Get going then."

General Hyder dismissed his trusted deputy with a firm warning. No more aimless angling, he had to gather smoking gun evidence.

Jamanat Ali shot down Barqat's assessment.

There must have been a mix up, he agreed. But only a well-trained agent could detect the hair-thin fault lines in his operations.

It was beyond Jahanara to detect the bugs. Harfan Bukhari must have tipped her off. His telephone dialogues sounded like well-researched scripts of a Hollywood movie, full of clever ploys and plenty of misleading drops. The bastard must have had used a scanner to detect the bugs.

Plausible. Barqat agreed.

Or did Nayeem's men play the part of spooky ghosts? Did the ***Sadr*** play up the PIB against the ISI? Did the CMLA suspect the ISI chief for piloting a coup?

It wasn't a new trick. General Arif's predecessor had used the MI Directorate and the ISI against the PIB for its suspected links with those Punjab, Sind and Baluch politicians, who had orchestrated popular agitation against the Tashkent agreement. He had brought in a trusted SSG crony to the highest PIB post. That's how the elder Khan happened to grab the coveted seat.

Holy ***Allah***! Barqat sweated under his suit and switched on the ceiling fan.

Perhaps Jamanat was correct. Everything was possible in Pakistan. It was difficult to fathom the intricate cross currents and measure up the arches of conspiracy against the President. Probably his chief too was mixed up in the odd ball game.

A whole load of shit! But why should he offer his neck to the chopping block?

He didn't want to forego a few more stars on his peeps and a higher slot in the bureaucratic monkey-pole. He should, Barqat decided, steer clear of the conspiracy, but remain in the boss's good books. Few botched up fabricated reports would not necessarily shake the orbit of the earth. The boss and ***Allah*** were the most potent forces to reckon with.

Barqat transferred the **Red Rose** documents to his 'transit morgue'; as he fondly described his personal record room, a concealed locker embedded in his office room wall.

He initiated a file-**Operation Saalamat**-scribbled a detailed note on Harfan Bukhari and flagged in four reports that he had drawn up to spell out the highest degree of physical threat to President General Arif Khan.

He called in Jamanat Ali.

Recruited in the Central Intelligence Bureau in 1935, Jamanat, hailing from the Frontier Province, headed a section in the India-Special Operations Cell. Known better by the endearing sobriquet, 'bulldog', he was respected in the intelligence community as an uncompromising professional.

"Track down the horoscope of this Harfan, from the day his mother had conceived him." Barqat ordered.

"Fine sir," Jamanat clicked his heels, "That would please me most. The bastard had tricked us at Lahore."

"Are you sure? Or was it the PIB spooks?"

"My guts say it's him. He must be a trained agent."

"But your boys had goofed up."

"I regret it sir. But I can smell a counter-intelligence suspect from a mile away. The PIB boys do not have that kind of finesse."

"Fine. But be discreet. It's purely an in-house exercise. Nothing official. I want it to be a steady but low-key probe. And don't put these pig-headed army rejects on the job. Use some of the crack boys."

"Got it sir. Do I use our Karachi resources?"

"Why? Do you suspect him to be an external plant?" Barqat asked.

"I've been getting some whiff of the air around this chap, a distant smell of a rotting rat. This creature Harfan is a fake. Give me time to chisel off his enamel." Jamanat's enormous moustache danced in tune with his beaming smile.

"How come?"

"Nawab Sharief feels that this chap could be an impostor, an Indian agent."

"Isn't he spitting venom to spite his brother?"

"No sir. Nawab's story isn't empty. His friends in London, some MI6 agents, had seen Harfan moving with one of their suspects, a High Commission based intelligence officer." Jamanat produced his trump card.

"When did it happen?"

"About six months back sir. He was on a business trip."

"Have you checked his movements?"

"Yes sir. He was present in Dacca and was noticed meeting his SSG contacts just before the Imphal fiasco."

"That's an important lead. But, aren't these long wild shots? As a supplier he has an alibi to meet the QMG staff." Barqat asked sceptically.

"Here's something." Jamanat fished out a photo positive from his pocket.

"The London based Indian intelligence officer has been identified as Chopra, a first secretary in the Consular section. The other fellow, seen from left profile is Harfan. The frame was shot from a distance of 150 meters on a foggy day. But the contours match."

Barqat closely examined the photograph and handed it back to Jamanat.

"Can't say for sure. It's hazy. Take a few comparison snaps of the suspect, and a few night snaps as well."

The blurred photograph, produced by Nawab Sharief foxed Barqat. It could be a clever plant. And Nawab was no less an expert in fabricating evidence against his half brother. His expertise could put some intelligence fakes to shame.

Nawab's motive wasn't clear. His business rivalry with Israr was well known. And to wreck his brother's fortune he wouldn't hesitate in dragging Harfan to the guillotine.

"Don't take Nawab as the Holy Book. His motives are suspect. And take care, no fiddling with Red Rose." Barqat sounded a strong warning.

"Sir don't panic. In the intelligence game we should be guided by our sixth sense, once in a while." Jamanat replied.

"No friend. I respect your experience, but intelligence is a game of pure mathematics, there's no scope for extra sensory perception here."

Barqat dismissed his junior with another homily on intelligence tradecraft. No. Under no circumstances could he allow Jamanat to run riot with his imagination and half-cooked evidence. He wasn't yet sure what consequences he would have to face for the latest act of indiscretion by Jamanat's boys.

"Okay sir."

"Another point Jamanat. Tie up with the Joint Intelligence Signals boys. Let them hook his phones up to their magic machines."

"That's a fine idea sir. I know the deputy chief of signal operations. He'll be glad to help."

"Sounds fine. ***Khuda Hafiz.***" Barqat dismissed his deputy with a broad grin.

Jamanat twisted his moustache enormously, followed by a gingerly grin and produced a mild metallic sound by clicking shoe heels. The mild sound was a trademark of the Bulldog's unhappy frame of mind. He usually clicked sharply and louder, when in a happy mood.

****

Ibadat did not receive many phone calls at his Hotel Royal Palace desk. The small town, once the seat of power of the former king, received very few tourists. The American technicians working at the nearby Mianwali power plant were the regular customers. The Chinese had started visiting the place only recently, after an agreement between the two countries was signed to install a back up radar station at Jhumra and for up gradation of the near by airbase at Bhagatanwala. The squint-eyed guests did not bother Ibadat. Two cooks accompanied them and most of their cooking materials were flown in from mainland China. The pungent smell from their kitchen, whenever they cooked dried fish, made Ibadat hostile to the very idea of testing Chinese culinary products.

That cloudy evening he was seated at a far corner of the lobby in a pensive mood. In fact, he was delving deep into the incidents that resulted in the assassination of the former king. His father too died at the battle of the Jung Tikri while trying to protect the king. His mind was focused on Harfan Bukhari too. Mian Alam did not spell out that the former king's son had returned to Pakistan with some special mission. Perhaps he was not aware of that fact. But he had no doubt about

Harfan's real identity. There was an uncanny physical and behavioural resemblance between the former king and Harfan. Rama Bai's queer behaviour at the very sighting of Harfan had erased most of his doubts, if he had any. Should he probe her little more?

Ibadat shelved the idea. His mother, presently a cook in the hotel had reassured him about Harfan's linkages with the former king. She could not be wrong. She had made Ibadat to promise that he would protect the prince like his father once tried to protect the king. These human bondages, she had emphasised, transcended the narrow religious and sectarian considerations. Human bondage, she believed, was above divinity.

The sharp rings of the telephone snapped Ibadat's concentration. He picked up the instrument and replied mechanically.

"Hotel Royal Palace here."

"Brother," a voice whispered on the line, "I'm Karamat Suri."

"Hello brother Karamat," Ibadat warmed up to his neighbour's call, "How are things?"

"Fine brother. Please inform my ***ammi*** (mother) that I will be out to Karachi for a few days."

"Are you leaving today?"

"Not today brother. Probably I leave in another two days. A big operation has come up."

"Can we see a movie together before you go? You'll like the classic movie Mughal-e-Azam. Can you come down to Lahore?"

"I was in Lahore only a few days back. That is another fascinating story. ***Allah*** knows what's happening to Pakistan!"

"Come down for a few hours."

"Well brother," Karamat agreed, "Tomorrow is Sunday. Meet me at Sabina restaurant, at the Anarkali bazaar. You know that place behind the bus terminus. Is not it?"

"Yes, I know. I'll be there before lunch. Let's have food together. Don't worry about your ***ammi***. She is fine and I'll visit her tonight and tell that you had called."

"So nice of you brother." Karamat, a native of ***mohalla*** (locality) Rajora of Jhumra town hung up the line.

The former king had exclusively assigned the Rajora habitat to his Muslim employees. Karamat's father, Qalam Suri, served Raja Dayaram Kaushal as a ***subedar*** (junior commissioned officer) and had laid down his life at the battle of Jung Tikri, in the wake of the earth shaking post-independence events. The Suri family title was a distant linkage to Karamat's Afghan ancestors, who had migrated to Jhumra from the old city of Delhi. His family claimed to be the direct descendants from the lineage of Sher Shah Suri, the short Afghan hyphen in the prolonged Mughal rule over India. The Jhumra kings followed the time tested tradition of maintaining a mixed army of Muslims and Hindus. He was especially fond of the Afghan and Pathan fortune hunters. These mercenaries helped him in keeping the turbulent local Muslim subjects under leash.

A Lance Corporal in the 7th Signals Regiment, Karamat was seconded to the ISI and was attached to the Special Operations Cell, headed by

Jamanat Ali. He and Ibadat had developed a special relationship. Their fathers were the loyal employees of the former Hindu king. Both of them had fought valiantly to protect the king and queen. They were also motivated to fight the marauding Niazi, Mazari and other tribesmen with a view to protecting their fertile land, granted to their families by the Kaushal kings. The raiding hoard did not stop after killing almost all the Hindus. They raided the Rajora habitat of the royal employees and plundered their homes and raped their women.

Ibadat did not join Alam's network for the love of money alone. He hated to be treated as a spy. But, he hated the new masters too, who had killed his father, dishonoured his sister and usurped his fertile agricultural land.

Karamat, a childhood friend and a compulsive talker was emotionally dependent on Ibadat. Together they nurtured the secret plan to rout the Niazi usurpers, reclaim their valuable land and take revenge against the killers of their fathers. In the process Ibadat discovered that in Karamat he had a subconscious agent inside a very sensitive area of the Inter Services Intelligence. He did not fail to exploit the opportunity.

Lahore's Anarkali market was a replica of the markets behind Delhi's Jama Masjid. It bustled with life and catered to almost all the needs of the frequenters; right from wet merchandise to bumpy women. A contraption called the cycle rickshaws, which were mostly pedalled by the Bengali Pakistanis, could only negotiate the narrow lanes.

Ibadat hired a garishly decorated rickshaw and asked the driver to take him to Sabina restaurant, situated next to the wet market that exclusively handled fish, meat and vegetables. Left to him Ibadat would have never chosen Sabina for a rendezvous. But Karamat liked the spot. It was situated just at the backside of the inter-state bus terminus and the city railway station was only three furlongs away. It was an important transit station for his journey to Islamabad from Jhumra.

Karamat arrived slightly late. The bus from Islamabad, he said, had suffered a serious breakdown on the way. But he did not brook any delay in opening up his mouth.

Ibadat ordered food, which was spicy and full of saturated fat. He hated the food but relished what Karamat had to say about his interesting missions in Lahore and the forthcoming visit to Karachi.

"Brother Ibadat," Karamat opened up, "There appears to be another military coup in the offing."

"We just had a peaceful one," Ibadat added, "Which one you are talking of?"

Karamat's logic was incontrovertible. How could the ISI mount an elaborate electronic surveillance on Begum Jahanara and her boyfriend Harfan, if the bosses were not sure of a change in the guard? She was the reigning queen of Pakistan. The ISI wouldn't have dared to bug her if his chief was not sure of another change.

Ibadat gasped in disbelief.

"Did you say Harfan? I believe the lady is a personal friend of the President. Who is this Harfan?"

"Did you say a friend of the President?" Karamat continued to talk excitedly, "She is the queen of heart of the top boss. That's what we keep on talking in Islamabad. And to be frank I don't know who this Harfan is."

"Must be a big chap. Otherwise why should your company put him under surveillance?"

Karamat looked around to be sure that no one overheard him and continued his story in a whispering tone. This fellow Harfan, he said, was a clean guy. He had a brief love talk with his wife. His talks with Begum Jahanara and Nawab Sharief had simply mentioned about some medicines he had procured from an Indian ***vaid*** for the big lady and more surprisingly for his own boss and the PSO.

"Why should he go to India for medicines? We are fighting an undeclared war with India." Ibadat provoked his friend.

"Oh no," Karamat made a guttural sound to express his disagreement, "He got it from London on the prodding of Nawab sahib."

"That's a small matter. Why should you be so excited?"

This provocation was too much for Karamat. He alone was not excited; Karamat took a deep breath as he spoke. The entire ISI was in virtual turmoil over the incident. Begum Jahanara, he disclosed, had chanced to discover that her hotel phone was bugged. She did not spare his boss and the PSO and had pulled them up with nasty words.

"Brother," Karamat displayed a victorious smile, "The matter is not so simple. We are now investigating this fellow Harfan in a big way."

"Why? What is his fault?"

"Jahanara has tightened the screw on my boss and he is now trying to screw her and this fellow from Karachi. I am going there as a member of the team headed by Jamanat Ali himself."

"Who is he?"

"My direct boss. He is a fierce person."

"Are you coming home tonight? There is a train at 4 pm. Perhaps you can tell your story in a more relaxed manner.

"I feel tempted. But brother I've to take an early morning flight to Karachi tomorrow."

"It appears you are a big boss now. What's the big deal there in Karachi?"

"That's another story. Jamanat sahib wants to make secret enquiries about Harfan and his uncle Shamim Bukhari."

"Okay. It's fine if you can't come home. But keep me informed about the big coup plot. I hope the next General will be a better one. Who's the likely next hero? Do you have any idea?"

"Very difficult to guess brother. But Jamanat sahib says that ultimately Izaz Afroz will win," Karamat brought his mouth nearer to Ibadat's ears, "But I can tell you for sure brother, it's going to be either my boss or the PSO, General Sarfaraz. He has put the phones of Jahanara and the President on tap. He knows everything."

"Presume you'll have a better time if he wins the race!" Ibadat provoked his friend further.

"Nothing will happen to me. But with the change I want to see that ***randi*** (prostitute) dancing nude in the Anarkali market."

"Do you mean Jahanara? Why? She has not wronged you in any manner."

"I am a poor lance corporal. What can she do to me? She makes every one dance around her. I would like to see her dancing in the nude. You can't stop me expressing my wish."

"I will pray to ***Allah*** to fulfill your wish. Take care and keep me informed about the likely coup. Let's now go for the movie."

"No brother," Karamat declined the offer, "I've to be back to my unit for a briefing session. ***Khuda Hafiz***."

Ibadat said goodbye and rushed to a pay phone booth at the inter-state bus terminal. He dialed a Quetta number and waited for the other side to respond.

"Allahbux here. Who is on the other side?"

The voice at the other end boomed out.

"Is it Allahbux of Masjid Ghorewali?"

"I said so."

"***Janab***, (sir) I am the personal servant of Alam sahib. Will you please tell him that his pet dog is sick? It needs doctor's attention."

"You are a strange person ***mian.*** Here I don't have the time to pray to the ***Rasul*** (Prophet) for human beings and you are worried over a dog!"

"What can I do ***alem*** sahib (the learned one)? I am informing you as the dog is very dear to my master."

"Fine. Rest well. Your message will be delivered."

Ibadat disconnected the line and boarded a bus for Jhumra. He was mighty worried about Harfan Bukhari. He did not expect him to get embroiled in the vortex of power tussel involving the top political players in Pakistan.

He was not sure about the reaction of Alam sahib. That man often behaved in a strange fashion. Should he use the reserved communication channel to Delhi? Ibadat thought over it for a while and decided to wait for Alam's arrival.

Ibadat remembered the innocent face of Jamilla as the bus speeded through the green-forested area between Sangla and Jhumra. The distant waters of the Jhelum River reminded him of another tragic face, the weather beaten face of Rama Bai. The bygone saga of the Kaushal kings, as he heard from his mother, glimpsed past his mind. Well! Ibadat exhaled a deep sigh. Why should Harfan Bukhari, whatever his Hindu name was, should land up at Jhumra and excite new dreams in persons like him, Rama Bai and Jamilla?

Strange were the ways of the ***Allah.***

Chapter 35

Seated at the far end of the banquet hall of Lahore's Hotel Pearl Continental, Harfan allowed his mind to spread wings. He flew over the open canvass of Pakistani power politics and the possible contours of the net that the ISI was likely to cast for him. The collage appeared confusing and no light was visible at the end of the tunnel.

The aborted Lahore rendezvous had rattled Harfan. He thanked his trainers, Col. Pathania, Maulana Rizwan and Dhiren Bhagat. The training rigors, way back in Delhi, were more refined than the crude ISI EIInt techniques. The ISI boys had betrayed their Achilles' heel; the lack of adaptability in a sophisticated social environ. They were simply not equipped to manage a difficult target in a classy hotel like the Falleti.

Superior training in counter-EIInt tradecraft had earned him a reprieve. But the breather must be a transient one. The ISI was definitely not going to sit on their haunches and allow their suspicion to sprout Mexican beans.

The intelligence machinery moved with atomic-clock precision, with single-minded doggedness. They hung on to their prey like the Australian Dingoes. They lingered at every doorstep and advanced with remorseless stealth like the inevitable dark flakes of death.

There was no doubt that Begum Jahanara had given him the flu. But why should the agency pursue him so doggedly? Simply because they wanted to screw up General Arif Khan by releasing evidence of Jahanara's misdemeanour with a two penny business executive?

Was it an accidental contamination? Or was he a logged suspect of the ISI?

Whatever it was, he must deepen his trenches and strengthen his foxholes.

Harfan went back in time and scanned all the events since his clandestine entry into Pakistan.

Had he committed any serious mistake?

Perhaps he had.

His indiscreet visit to Jahanara's mansion must have triggered off panic, in the brittle citadel of the power brokers.

Nawab Sharief could be another source of trouble.

Israr Sharief was correct about the raging struggle inside the Chief Martial Law Administrator's powerhouse. The ambitious Generals were gunning for the President and he, poor Harfan Bukhari, had inadvertently strayed into the minefield, spiked for the top man's favourite girl.

He mustn't stray into that lane again.

The soprano, he surmised, was a clever survivor. She had perfected the art of changing bed partner. For a Sarfaraz to replace an Arif in bed wasn't an earthshaking event for her. She wouldn't hesitate in sacrificing him, a minor business executive, Harfan Bukhari. He was too small a fly to soil her bejewelled swatter.

The invisible ISI line was pretty transparent; he could smell the bait. It would be stupid, Harfan deduced, to presume that the seasoned sleuths would give him another opportunity to measure the floats on their lines.

What about Israr Sharief and Mian Alam Khan? Could he duck behind their coats?

Well! Israr, a thorough gentleman would perhaps agree to walk only to the edges of the minefields. His gentle mask would peel off, as soon as the sleuths accosted him with tangible proof of Harfan's real identity. A Hindu was a hated dog in Muslim Pakistan. That's how the people's psyche was fashioned and conditioned by the power-wizards, in the name of Islam.

Mian Alam Khan was sure to follow Nampoothiri's cliché: the company did never reclaim its exposed and compromised agents.

So? He was there, on his own, in Wild West Pakistan.

Would Jamilla stand by him? Would she like to flee Pakistan with an Indian agent, who wasn't even a genuine Muslim?

Perhaps she would agree to take a walk over the razor's edge. She loved him. Her love had transformed his life. She had infused in him a new desire to live. The buck stopped with Jamilla. Yes, he must live for Jamilla, their son Parvez and for himself, of course. He wouldn't allow the butchers of Delhi and Islamabad to put his neck on the chopping block.

Harfan lighted another cigarette and released thick rings of smoke.

A young Captain, seated across the table, suddenly intruded into Harfan's private dream. He borrowed a cigarette, lighted it and concentrated on his drinks.

Harfan, lost in his dark thoughts didn't notice the young officer. He appeared to be fogged out or lost in the spacious ambience of the banquet hall. The fellow fiddled with the room keys, and looked vacantly at the ornate ceiling, not exactly admiring the marvellous frescos.

Captain Ayoob Suhrawardi, attached to the office of General Naqibullah Saragarhi, the Defence Advisor, was in fact, cursing his immediate superior, Brigadier Chaman of Division L III, in the CMLA's office. That blunt and insensitive idiot had forced him to attend this damn meeting in Lahore.

What for!

Just to take down the minutes and prepare a detailed report for General Naqibullah.

Shit!

A Captain in the Pakistan army wasn't supposed to work as a stenographer! He wished he could hang the imbecile Generals, whose priorities were concentrated in their balls and foreign accounts! That's why the bloody Indians could maul them in consecutive wars.

"To hell with the yellow punks..." Captain Ayoob blurted out.

"Did you say something to me?" Harfan looked up at the seemingly disoriented officer.

"Sorry. It's not you. I'm cursing the Chinese midgets."

"Any problem? Can I help?" Harfan offered another cigarette and helped him light it.

Yes. There were problems galore. Captain Ayoob opened up.

The venue of the important defence liaison meeting was shifted to Lahore from Rawalpindi on the insistence of the Chinese delegation.

Shit! One of these days Pakistan was sure to rue its friendship with these pork-eating yellow ***kafirs***. They were simply using Pakistan for levelling scores with India. They weren't friends of Islam. Didn't they treat their Muslim minorities as desert insects?

The wrap of secrecy was meant for befuddling India. New Delhi had lodged several protests in the UN Security Council, on the suspected induction of Chinese and American weapons to the killing fields of East Pakistan. They had managed to steal minute details of the Army and Air force supply inventories. The DMI and the ISI were still scratching their heads over the security leaks.

"You mean India has positioned agents in our defence forces too!" Harfan asked.

"Oh dear friend!" The young officer stood up almost ceremoniously, "I'm Captain Ayoob Suhrawardi from General Naqi's office."

"Glad to meet you." Harfan poured a drink for Ayoob," Harfan Bukahri here, representing Israr International."

"Did you talk of Indian agents? Why not? They're everywhere. The Hindus are our eternal enemies." Ayoob downed his drink, neat.

"Wish I could meet one." Harfan steadied his gaze on Ayoob's face. No. There was no reaction.

"To hell with this war! To hell with the warmongers." Captain Ayoob blabbered out the curse, through his half hanging lips.

"Don't worry. We have powerful friends in America and China."

"Don't ever be foxed by the Yankees. They aren't anybody's friend, not of Pakistan and nor of Islam. Damn Christians and Jews can't measure up to us Muslims. They promote and create war hysteria in all conceivable corners of the globe to sell weapons and to pump in juice into their economy. All at the cost of human blood, the blood of black, brown, yellow and white people."

"You appear to be upset." Harfan threw an anticipatory pebble.

Yes. He was.

He had reason to be, Ayoob blurted out.

Attached to General Naqi's office, he was literally forced to accompany the Pakistani delegation. The disturbing order was handed over at his leave address, only a day after his marriage to college day fiancée, Reshma. The Brigadier mowed down his entreaties for exemption. His only argument was that Pakistan was on the brink of a war with the ***kafir*** Hindu country and all patriotic Pakistanis were required to come to the Fatherland's rescue.

Did he say that he was yet to consummate his marriage? Fucking a virgin hole could wait for better days. His immediate superior, the Brigadier had dismissed him unceremoniously

"Wasn't it unfair and vulgar?" Ayoob asked.

"Sure it was. The bosses can often be heartless." Harfan played along.

Two junior participants, Ayoob from General Naqi's office and Harfan from Israr International were seated on the same table, at the farthest corner of the banquet hall; almost near the military band, playing a Chinese score, specially composed in honour of the guests.

Harfan didn't take time to size up the young officer, doodling over his drinks. He was either suffering from chronic disease or lost in his soured dreams. And he was a loose talking tree, rather a green sapling.

Ayoob gulped another drink and suddenly turned towards the high table.

Funny creature! The chatterbox corked himself up.

Harfan offered another cigarette and volunteered information about his company having clinched a deal for airlifting defence equipment from Phuket to Dacca, in chartered flights.

The ice melted a little bit.

"It's not chartered flights friend." Captain Ayoob responded in an agitated voice.

"Pardon!"

"You don't fly to Phuket. The fucking Yankees, I mean the CIA is arranging that leg of the operation. In their covert flights."

Well! Harfan rearranged the tools of his trade. The young kid appeared to be a hidden piece of precious diamond bearing rock. He geared up to drill the young Captain more cautiously.

"You mean direct CIA flights! But the US Congress has banned weapons supply to us."

"That's for the matinee show. The late night adult shows start with Phuket and stretches up to Jeddah, Amman and Istanbul." Ayoob flaunted a victorious smile.

"Where do we stand then? Weapons supply by proxy? I thought we've bagged the contract." Harfan spoke in an injured innocent voice.

"Well brother, you may have bagged the Sargodha-Dacca sector. There are more surprises in heaven and earth, than you can imagine, Hora...what did you say your name is! Whatever it is. The Yankees have real long arms. They're the real owners of Pakistan and we are so dependant on three A's."

"What that?"

"America, Army and ***Allah,*** all in that descending order."

Ayoob lifted his empty glass and looked around for another drink.

Harfan summoned a straying waiter and poured a few extra ounces in Ayoob's glass and helped himself to one.

The Captain unfolded his wounded heart as the whisky started sinking in. The Indian dogs deserved exemplary punishment. Weren't these heathens lorded over by Islamic monarchs for hundreds of years? They deserved another spell of purification, under the Islamic rule.

Harfan managed to say that history had the habit of often repeating itself. Another spell of Islamic rule over Hindu India wasn't improbable.

"To hell with them," Ayoob flexed his fist, "Before they try any misadventure, the Kashmiris are hell bent on giving them a bloody shower."

"I couldn't agree less." Harfan lighted a cigarette and helped the Captain with one.

Ayoob's prescription was simple. The bosses in the CMLA suffered from myopia. If India dared fiddle with East Pakistan, it should hit India in its Northeast and Kashmir.

"Yes. We must get Kashmir at any cost."

"Don't worry. Our sleuths are cooking India's broth with fine seasoning. You'll soon see spectacular results. A big bang it would be."

"The Indians must be prepared."

"Shit! These Hindus are capable of reacting, not pro-acting. Haven't we seen Pakistan and China surprising them in the '48, '62 and '65 wars? The Hindu mind is no match for us Muslims."

"Hope we aren't walking into another war?"

War it was, a different kind of war, a slow and steady war, which would bleed India white. The Hindus must be penalised for their involvement in East Pakistan. This dogged and fierce war would be fought in Kashmir and all over India. Each and every Muslim home in India would be converted to a forward citadel of Islam.

Captain Ayoob stopped his monologue as the heads of the delegations stood up to deliver speeches, highlighting bonds of friendship between their ancient countries.

A toast, to the good health of the two Heads of State was raised, followed by speeches.

Captain Ayoob Suhrawardi was in no position to stand up while the toast was being raised. He stared askance at the crowd around and tried to lift his body up. Like a battered scarecrow; cap on the floor, hair dishevelled and limbs numb, Ayoob collapsed. Harfan propped up his body and cautiously dragged him out of the ceremonial dining hall.

Back in the room, Harfan sprinkled water on Ayoob's face, unfastened the uniform buttons and removed his shoes.

"Did they see me in a drunken stupor?" He made anxious enquiries.

"I don't think they did."

"Thanks pal. You know the stress I'm going through." Ayoob explained.

"No thanks required and no excuses, friend," Harfan added, "These bloody Indians are screwing us all. They've ganged up with that traitor Jainal to tear our nation apart."

"To hell with the Indians", Ayoob screamed out, "The Kashmiri boys are planning a big show. They may blow up the residence of the ***Sadr-e-Ryasat*** (Head of the State), hijack and blow up Indian planes and the ***Fatah*** boys may even bomb that hornbill-nosed Indian PM."

"Like to have a black coffee? "

"So kind of you."

"To be precise," Ayoob's drunken rambling continued, "My former colleague in the CMLA, a veteran of the ISI, Col. Akram and his colleague Mirza Baloch, both cover diplomats in the Pak High Commission, Delhi, are in touch with the Kashmiri boys."

"Forget it, have the coffee first. It'll help." Harfan poured the black concoction into two cups.

"The visit of the Chinese delegation isn't an end by itself. The President has already played an ace to ensure US support. Serious talks are on between Washington, Rawalpindi and Peking for making a diplomatic breakthrough." Ayoob sermonised with another victorious smile, "They're highly suspicious of the mysterious shuttles between Delhi and Moscow. Wait for the new axis to emerge. We'll give a bloody nose to the Indians."

"To hell with the Indians. But brother, are we in a position to contain the bloody Indians?" Harfan asked innocently. He was more than delighted to have accidentally hit the jackpot.

"Another cigarette please. I'll tell you how to incinerate the bloody Hindus."

Ayoob felt a writhing motion in his stomach, a violent vomiting sensation. Perhaps the excess fermented malt inside was seeking an escape route. He hadn't eaten solid food since the last working lunch, a good twelve hours ago.

"Don't worry." Harfan lighted a cigarette, placed it between Ayoob's lips and helped him with chocolates and confectionery from the gift tray. He ordered another coffee.

A few crisp biscuits, salted wafers and chocolate pushed back the acrid sensation. Ayoob sobered up.

"As I said, the CMLA and the President, the Chief of Army Staff and their advisors are totally seized of Indian designs in the East." Ayoob continued, "***Operation Kalam*** has been worked out, to blunt the Indian offensive."

"What's that?"

"The operation plans include depopulation of the border villages. The Bengali dogs would be housed in new village groups, guarded by our armed forces. All routes leading to India would be sealed."

"That's a nice strategic move," Harfan quipped, "It's sure going to thwart the evil designs of the Hindus."

"The troops have been directed to detect the Indian thugs and their Bengali collaborators, latest by May 15. The Indian stooges are to be executed. The ISI has prepared a comprehensive list of these Indian agents."

Ayoob felt reassured about his command on the important operational orders issued by the office of the CMLA only 3 days ago.

"Yup." Harfan responded, "Once they kill the rabid intellectuals, it won't be difficult to silence the rest of the ruts; the enemies of our nation."

"Correct. That's why General Tarakki has been posted to Dacca," Ayoob poured out more of his knowledge, "The British had committed a big mistake by exposing the Bengali baboons to liberal education. Take their language away and they'll be as good as dead rats. It has been a mistake all the way, not imposing Urdu and pure Islam on these half Hindus."

"How correct you are!" Prodded Harfan, "These infidels prefer quoting from that Hindu poet Tagore, before saying their prayers."

"There you are," Ayoob jumped on his bed, "We in Pakistan have committed a big mistake by trusting these Bengali ***kafirs***."

The chatterbox continued non-stop, and revealed that the new Governor in Dacca was instructed to prepare a blueprint for disarming the Bengali elements of the Pakistani army and the Police.

"Now sleep," Harfan said, "***Insha Allah***, we'll drown the Indian rats in the Arabian Sea and the Bay of Bengal."

"Let me speak ***ya..ar***." Ayoob continued with his monologue.

"General Sarfaraz and the ISI chief have worked out a plan to narrow down the demographic imbalance. Killing a few million Bengalis won't make any difference. In any case, thousands of them die every year, either from hunger or from the furies of nature. Don't they?"

"Are they going to shift the population?"

"No ***yar***. Who bothers about shifting these Bengali speaking shrimps! Tarakki has the orders to kill them. That's the easiest way to lighten the national burden."

Ayoob continued his loud soliloquy with occasional appellatives hurled at his superiors, Indians and Hindus. The bastards had disturbed his honeymoon and forced him get to Lahore, to spend dull and drab nights, all the way flirting with the flat nosed and slit eyed Chinese.

In drunken delirium he burst into hysterical bouts of sobbing and called out his wife's name.

"Don't weep. You should be back with her in another two days." Harfan comforted the lovelorn young Captain.

"To hell with the bosses. She's in my village and I won't get leave in another 15 days, till my senior returns from his second fucking honeymoon. I'm stuck ***yar***."

"Come on Captain, don't feel small," Harfan screwed in the nut, "A senior always gets preference over a junior. You'll get your turn."

"No friend, the buggers in the operations directorate may push me out to the front by the time I finish with this assignment. And who knows how many of us will trudge back home from the bloody trenches. For me, it may be a one way ticket."

Ayoob picked up a cigarette and walked down to a window, exhaling the smoke with a loud sound.

"Why should you move to the front so early? That's not fair." Harfan tightened the screw a little deeper into Ayoob's psyche.

Ayoob didn't disappoint him.

Pakistan, he blurted out, was on the threshold of another war. The military regime was biding its time to replenish war-field hardware. The build up after the '65 drawn war was appallingly inadequate. The forces were suffering from huge shortages of battle front weapons. The American pipeline was still clogged and the main source of supply was China. That was the mystery behind the red-carpet treatment to the Chinese defence delegation.

Peking had promised big time help. The Chinese team was scheduled to discuss with the Military Law Administrator in Dacca, the quantum of need of the East Pakistan Garrison.

The saddest episode of the drill, Ayoob commented, was his forced deputation with the Chinese delegation.

The grand finale of Ayoob's intellectual oration involved stories of successful interception and deciphering of an Indian Army signal to its front formations. The cipher had advised readiness for an all out war with Pakistan in the third week of November, perhaps the day of the Eid, the auspicious 20th November.

Aftab, Pakistan's deep penetration agent in India had corroborated this piece of SigInt

"You have amazing knowledge." Harfan commented innocently.

"Naqi's office is a big clearing house. He is supposed to be the next President of Pakistan. He gets to know every bit that concerns our national security."

"Who's this Aftab?"

"Some big guy...a minister perhaps."

"Must be right on the top."

Yes. He was at the top. In fact, Aftab had shared with his handlers the typed minutes of the proceedings of the Indian Cabinet Committee on Security. Islamabad had shared the precious input with Washington and Peking. The Indian move was viewed as a proxy expansion strategy of the Russian Red Bear. The new axis, in the process of being welded by Pakistan, was sure to defeat the Russian and Indian thugs.

"Very bad ***yar***," Harfan added, "They don't even have respect for the holy Eid!"

"Why should they? I'll wipe out these scourges of Islam, once I'm at the helm of affairs."

Ayoob banged the table, as if he was only a step away from the throne of Pakistan.

"I've no doubt you would," Harfan comforted the young Captain, "we require some selfless Pakistanis like you, to perpetuate the rising crescent in the entire sub-continent. And I must salute Aftab, our excellent agent."

Ayoob repeated.

"He's a big guy, a minister of sorts..."

"Could be... You'd better get some sleep. We have an early morning flight to Dacca."

Harfan bade ***Khuda Hafiz*** to his milking cow that had delivered more than a bucket-full, in the very first session. He burnt late night candles to encode rather a long message. He did not forget to highlight the new input on Ram Karan Prasad's dispatches to Islamabad. He went a step ahead to suggest that Ram Karan should be kept out of all strategic meetings. The veteran minister was totally sold out to his Pakistani handlers, who were in possession of material evidence of Ram Karan's involvement in flesh and drug trade. Islamabad was in a position to blackmail and hang him.

After securing the DLB drop in a locker of Lahore railway station he called Alam from a pay phone and trudged back to his hotel room. It was time for him to call Israr and share the good news with his employer.

"Morning sir, sorry to disturb you. There's good news. We may have bagged the contract for Sargodha-Dacca sector."

"Congratulations. General Naqi had called. I've finalised his part of the deal. Thank you for the astute negotiations. The airlifting contract would leave fat cuts to our company."

Israr responded in a happy mood, profusely thanking his junior.

"There's a catch. I believe the CIA is loaning two carriers, for the Phuket operation. Perhaps we've to negotiate again with the CMLA's office. And I learn Nawab is putting a spanner."

"Thanks for the tip. I'll talk to General Sarfaraz and the Army and Air chiefs. Wish you a safe journey. Bon voyage."

"Listen sir. Nawab is pushing his claim through the ISI chief."

"I'll take care," Israr assured his executive and added, "I suggest that while in Dacca you meet Sarwar Illahi, the chief of East Pakistan police."

"Anything special sir?"

"He is a good Bengali. I am expecting a large order for small weapons, motorised boats and wireless equipment."

"I have never met him. Please call him up and advise him."

"Don't worry. Agree on a 5% commission if he insists."

"Understood sir."

Harfan hung up and threw himself on the bed, hoping to steal a few moments of sleep. He couldn't.

The shrill crowing of neighbourhood roosters snapped his snoozing sleep. He looked out. The huge bright crimson disk of the sun was just hanging over the tall trees of Bagh-e-Jinnah. It momentarily painted his windowpanes with a fast moving brush.

The innate Hindu in him forced Harfan to fold his palms together, in the direction of the rising sun. He recited a Sanskrit hymn, in praise of the sun god, seeking the safety and well being of his wife and son. They were his final anchors. Nothing existed beyond them. No NSI, no ISI, no Bhagat and no Mian Alam Khan.

The sun, as it always did, reminded him of the stark reality. Another day had come; another piece of bread was to be earned. It was time he got ready, to accompany the merchants of death to Dacca.

****

The Boeing 747 flight to Dacca, with a technical halt at Colombo was boring. Harfan missed the delightful company of Ayoob Suhrawardi. He was made to take a seat next to the Chinese delegation. He and another Chinese knowing Colonel from General Naqi's office made frenetic efforts to humour the inscrutable yellow faces. In between their incessant chattering in Chinese the members of the delegation asked the Colonel once in a while about the strategic Indian presence in the Andaman and Nicobor Islands. Some of them moved their heads both horizontally and vertically and took down notes in their scrapbooks.

Finally the huge bird flew low over the Narayanganj and Tungi industrial areas, plunged deep over the Buri Ganga valley and landed at Kurmitola Air Force base.

Harfan was not a part of the official delegation. He was scrupulously kept out of the discussions between the Military Law Administrator (MLA) and the Governor and the Chinese delegation. Harfan was not unnecessarily worried about the contents of the closed-door discussions. His milking cow, Captain Ayoob was still around to fill in the gaps.

He took out time to seek an interview with Sarwar Illahi, East Pakistan's police chief, and a scion of the former ***Nawab*** family of Dacca. Educated in the USA and married to a lady from an aristocratic Punjabi family of Rawalpindi, Sarwar was a more fanatic Pakistani than his ancestors, who had originally mooted the idea of formation of a separate political party for the Indian Muslims and division of India on religious lines. He was a trusted man of Islamabad, though in certain quarters eyebrows were raised about the impure Bengali blood flowing in his veins.

The meeting with Sarwar was brief too. Israr had done the spadework. Harfan was just required to sign the tender papers on the dotted lines. The police chief waived the formalities of canalising the papers through various departments and pushed up a note to the MLA and the Governor for approval of the proposal on emergency ground. The East Pakistan police immediately required the automatic weapons, communication system and the motorboats. The administration did not have the time to observe the niceties of rules and regulations while the dark clouds of another war hanged over its head. Harfan was not amused by the successful conclusion of the deal. By now he had acclimatised himself to the various concepts of cuts and commissions and the philosophy of keeping everyone happy. That's how the wheel of the nation moved.

Harfan was not invited to the official dinner at the Governor's house in honour of the Chinese delegation. He was holed up in his 7th floor room of hotel Ichhamati and was bored by the distant howls of the jackals from the paddy and jute field marshes on either side of river Buri Ganga. The pungent smell of dried fish that emanated from the nearby fishermen's colony irritated his nostrils. He had switched off the TV and tried to concentrate on a book. This noble effort also was pleasantly disturbed by a lilting Bengali tune that came out from the nearby family quarters. He liked the pathos of the tune, which most probably fluttered its wings in search of a separated lover, but did not understand the language. He tried to train his ears to the craving tune when the unexpected call came in.

"Is Mian Harfan there?"

A whispering voice enquired as Harfan picked up the receiver.

Harfan tried to figure out the identity of the caller. Who could it be? It could be another ISI trap.

"Are you there?"

"Who's there?"

"Mani this side. Come down, keep to your left and walk past the hotel block. You will find a green Suzuki waiting opposite a small mosque. Don't get into the car. Walk into the mosque straightaway."

"Is it safe?"

"You are safer with us than you are in the company of those Chinese louts. Come in on. We have important business to discuss."

Major Anjum Mani of the 3rd battalion SSG hung up.

Harfan gave a brief thought to Major Anjum Mani's invitation. He was already under investigation of the ISI. That unfortunate visit to the pleasure house of Jahanara and his rendezvous with her Lahore had thickened the air of suspicion around him. Should he take another chance?

The ISI, he figured out, could be on his trail in Dacca too. He was not sure if General Naqi's office coordinated its arms procurement agenda with the ISI. Most probably they were not in regular dialogue. In General Arif's Pakistan key departments functioned independent of each other and the office of the CMLA acted as the apex coordination body. The President took pains to keep the key departments under his personal supervision through his Executive Assistant (EA), a post occupied by a very trusted General in his personal office. The EA was not even under the administrative control of the PSO to the CMLA.

Harfan recalled the tasking shared with him by Bhagat at Kathmandu and decided to take a chance and changed over to his jogging suit and track shoes and pulled the head cover on as he walked passed the reception counter. The bored receptionist looked up at the odd time jogger and closed his eyes again. These foreign guests were queer. They were adept in doing the most unexpected thing at the oddest hour.

Harfan looked around and located the faint silhouette of the mosque two blocks on his left. He jogged slowly and caught a glimpse of the green Suzuki as he sneaked past the wicket gate of the mosque.

"Open your shoes before you enter the precincts."

As a sharp beam of pencil torch focused on his face, Harfan looked up and tried to determine if he was in the correct company. Yes. Major Anjum Mani dressed in camouflage fatigue, but bare footed, stood before him.

"How do you know that I am in Dacca?"

"The whole city knows that you have accompanied the Chinese rats. Why are you doing this to us?"

"Am I doing anything wrong? I am here only to finalise a supply contract to East Pakistan Police and Israr International has bagged the contract for airlifting some Chinese supplies to Dacca."

"You are pumping in the weapons of death for the butchers of Pakistan. Stop it."

"Don't be unjust to me brother Mani," Harfan pleaded, "I am a business executive. I do not preside over the fate of Pakistan. Are you alone?"

Harfan asked the question, as he smelt the presence of other people inside the mosque. He could see a group of people seated in a circle in the main prayer hall and discussing something in a low voice.

"No. I am not alone. There are few officers from the East Pakistan Rifles, East Pakistan Infantry and other formations. I want you to do some favours to me and my friends."

"Spell it out."

"Brief my friends about the quantum of arms supply the US and China are planning to pump in."

"I do not have any ready inventory. But I can tell you that the supplies are meant to give the Pakistani armed forces a minimum of 15 day's battle field and support logistics against the Indian invaders."

"Are you going to deliver all the consignments at Dacca?"

"Can't say. Chittagong can be an alternative option."

"Come and meet my friends."

Harfan paused for a while. He recalled his last discussion with Bhagat at Kathmandu. The audiotape given to him had charted out certain tasks. Yes. The tape had instructed him to ascertain the quantum of subversion suffered by the Bengali officers of the Pakistani army and Police forces. It had directed him to identify a few senior officers who could be independently contacted from Agartala, the capital of the Indian state of Tripura and other convenient points. He did not understand as to why the NSI was eager to establish direct links with the Bengali officers.

"Come on in."

Major Mani prodded Harfan.

"I do not think it would be safe. I have briefed you. Now you can share the details with them."

"Don't you believe me? Don't you believe that the butchers of Pakistan have already killed one million people?"

"No one speaks of that in the media. Yes. There may have been excesses, but you are exaggerating too."

"You are a fool like the rest of the Pakistanis. The army and its stooges like the Rajakar, Al Badr and Al Jammat have wiped out innumerable after villages. Our women have been raped and our homes burnt. The Rajakar goons killed my own brother after he was picked up from the Jagannath hostel of the Dacca University. What more proof do you damn Pakistanis want?"

Harfan looked up at the face of Major Mani. He was weeping like a kid in pain.

"Okay. I will meet the others if it helps you."

He walked behind Major Mani and entered the main prayer hall, where about a dozen men in uniform were seated.

"Have you brought him?"

Asked a young officer who donned the rank badges of a Captain of the East Pakistan Rifles.

"Yes Rashid. He is here?"

The Captain stood up and spoke to Harfan brusquely.

"Are you a Punjabi?"

"No."

"A Sindhi?"

"No brother I am a ***muhajir*** from the Indian town of Ludhiana. Why are you worried about my ethnicity? I am a Mussalman like you are and I earn my bread by honestly serving my master and the ***Allah***. Can I help you in anyway?"

"We have heard that Islamabad is going to kill all the serving Bengali officers of the police and armed forces."

"You have the right information," Harfan replied with a steady voice, "And I can share with you another information. They have planned to kill all the Bengali intellectuals."

"And...?"

"And they are about to arrest and whisk away your supreme leader to Islamabad."

"How is it that you are friendly to Mani?"

"Can't two good human souls befriend each other? You could also be a good friend if we had the opportunity to meet earlier."

Suddenly a tall young man with a stubby beard jumped on his feet.

"He must be a Pakistani spy. Finish him here."

"Don't be a stupid Tiger," Major Mani stood like a rock in front of Harfan Bukhari, " He is a good friend. He can help us."

"How?"

"He has promised to keep me and Wing Commander Khondokar informed about all the military supplies airlifted by his company to

Dacca. That is really going to help us to plan our strategy. I hope you all agree?"

There was a murmur of consensus.

"One more point," The Captain took Harfan's hand in his own, "We are determined to fight to the last man and bullet. We have ceased to be Pakistanis. Let us know, if you can, when Islamabad plans to finally crack down on us."

"Wait till Washington and Peking give the final nod. It would not be very long. ***Insha Allah*** we will be in touch. Can I ask you a question now?"

"You are free to ask."

"Why have you picked on me? I am just another Pakistani. Why don't you directly contact the Indians?"

"As you said," Major Mani picked up the thread of the exchanges, "It's me, who wanted to convince my brother officers that we have a reliable friend somewhere in Islamabad. We shall expect you to drop messages at the phone number of this mosque and another number in Dubai, whenever you have useful information to share."

"Hope I too can fall back on you for help?"

Harfan asked the question involuntarily.

"Any time friend. We Bengalis are better friends than the Punjabis are. Just drop in and you are our honoured guest."

"It's time to go. I have to join the team for tomorrow's journey back to Karachi."

Harfan prepared to move out.

"What about the Chinese delegation?"

"They are scheduled to fly to Rangoon in the first leg of their journey back to Peking."

"Wait for a minute. I have one query to make. Why is it that a Hindu Indian minister is advising the low caste Hindus not to cooperate with the freedom fighters?"

"You have asked the wrong person. You should ask this to Delhi."

"It is difficult to reach them."

"Well brother," Harfan shrugged, "I shall help wherever I can. Let's go."

"Wait. Tiger, please go out and see if the coast is clear."

The angry young man in civvies went out briefly and returned in five minutes.

"All clear. You may go now. ***Shabba khair***."

He joined his colleagues to say ***Khuda Hafiz*** to the visitor.

Harfan Bukhari looked back at the congregation of the young officers of the Pakistan army and police and jogged out of the mosque after taking cover of the green Suzuki. He looked back intermittently as he took the short jog to hotel Ichhamati. The Suzuki followed him till he reached the foyer of the hotel. It must be Mani's man, under instruction to ensure his safety. He liked the silent gesture and resolved to honour his commitment to the people who were struggling to free themselves from the bondages of the thugs in West Pakistan.

But the lingering words of Anjum Mani about the Hindu Indian minister continued to intrigue him. That must be his former political boss Ram Karan Prasad, the self-styled messiah of the oppressed and depressed classes of the Indian sub-continent

Chapter 36

Ram Karan Prasad, the legendary fixture in Delhi's political parlour had suffered a real beating under the new Mandira dispensation. She had seen through his crude games of deception. Prasad had bargained with her opponents for the top slot, on the ill-placed calculations that his 70 odd fledglings would waddle buoyantly to the Parliament floor, through the electoral slush. Only 3 injured ducklings came home to roost. His powerful allies had taken a sound beating at the hustings.

Balachandran Nampoothiri had also played his cards well. A defeated and discarded Ram Karan, he had reasoned, would be more vulnerable. Mandira would no more be inhibited by political constraints to sacrifice the powerful messiah of the oppressed and depressed classes. And for him to book Ram Karan under half a dozen laws of the country would be as simple as baking a lemon tart. Mandira's astounding electoral success had changed all equations. The incarceration of, ***Sardar Niyamat***, the Kashmiri satrap, hijacking of an Indian Airlines plane by ***Al Fatah*** terrorists and the sabre rattling over developments in East Pakistan had generated new geopolitical realities.

Her unequivocal support to the popular uprising in East Pakistan had added a new glow to her charisma. Mandira emerged as a new star, out of the debris left behind by her father, and the unfortunate incomplete mission of Jung Bahadur.

Nampoothiri calculated that it was the right moment to hit, especially after the stunning revelations from the latest inputs from Triple X. Left to himself the slimy politician was likely to interfere in the development in East Pakistan, obviously at the behest of Pakistan.

But Nampoothiri's laboratory readings on Ram Karan went haywire. Ram Karan Prasad, a strange organic entity could manage to thrive in the harshest of environs.

Ram Karan consulted his ***guru*** and astrologer and was told that his misfortune was a passing phase, due to a malevolent conjunction of Venus in the tenth house of the fiery planet Saturn. The phase of Jupiter had dawned over his horoscope and he should strike now when the iron was hot. The great survivor, in strange bio-chemical reaction, sprouted new tentacles, in search of a new life force; the ambrosia of political patronage, protection and spoils.

The most important connector, Raghu Chawla, however, had made himself scarce from the operation fields of Ram Karan. Chawla, son of a scrap dealer, had by then categorised his former benefactor and collaborator as a biodegradable political scrap. Raghu, an ardent fortune hunter, was busy casting the anchor of his rocking boat in the power wharf of Shankar, the rising son of Mandira. Like the Hindu divine rodent, carrier of Lord Ganesha, Raghu believed in burrowing holes under the throne of the winners.

Ram Karan, he estimated had metamorphosed into a stinking political corpse. The stigma of his questionable Pakistani connection had added a new stink to the existing fishy and fleshy smell around him. In Delhi, the city of winners, no one touched a political outcaste. The loud whispers in Delhi's power alleys hadn't escaped Raghu's fine tuned antenna: Ram Karan was finished politically. The task of carrying Ram Karan to the crematorium was better left to the stigmatised ***Doms***, the caste-undertakers of unclaimed dead bodies.

But Raghu too had underestimated the strength of Ram Karan's life force, whose voice ominously whispered on the celebrity scribe's exclusive unlisted phone.

"Raghuji, can we meet tonight?"

The 'ji' honorific intrigued Raghu Chawla. He did not expect the former minister to call him with apprehension in his voice. He did not welcome the call and decided to shun the nowhere-man.

"I'm a little tied up with the edit page. Can we talk on the phone?" Raghu replied indifferently.

"Your and my phones are nothing but pig shit," Ram Karan shouted, "It's not a safe vehicle for talking about sensitive matters. This demonic lady has our phones tapped. Her FIB is after my blood. Come and see me at 7 this evening."

"Sir, can we meet at 9 pm?" Raghu bargained.

"Fine, it's your choice. I'm no more a minister and a VIP. I know the ways of you journalists, knockers at the doors of dame fortune. Come at nine."

Son of a bitch, Ram Karan muttered.

Raghu Chawla, the brand new editor-in-chief of *National Expression*, had climbed new heights of journalistic glory, on the recommendation of Shankar, the rising son of Mandira and a budding auto-mechanic.

Shankar had mastered the science of driving the country from the relative comfort of the back seat. And in his quest for power and fortune he partly depended on limpets like Raghu. The creatures of Raghu's ilk scourged the country for connecting the new power-horse to the moneybags. The connectivity was mutual. Power and fortune travelled up and down.

Ram Karan didn't miss out on the new status of his crony. Hence the panicky phone call.

Raghu arrived precisely at 9 pm, in his just imported Toyota Corona. This new chariot was a gift from a Bombay industrialist, a reward for buying a fabulous tax-dodging favour from the rising son of Mandira.

"Come Raghu." Ram Karan greeted his old buddy, "Let me open a real Romanoff in your honour."

"Nothing new has happened to me sir." Raghu was circumspect in his reply, spoken deftly through a well-groomed broom-moustache.

"Why not Raghu?" Ram Karan poured stiff doses for himself and his friend, "I should've congratulated you earlier. It's my fault that I'm late. The world is talking about your new position and your influence on Shankar, the Crown Prince of the holy dynasty."

"Sir, you're being unkind to your friend. I just happen to meet Shankar once in a while. Tell me how can I be useful to you." Raghu talked rather evasively.

"Brother, today I'm out of power, I'm faulted for everything I say. Yesterday people worshipped my morning shit. But don't worry. I'm not the type to be stymied and maimed permanently, not by this lady."

Ram Karan asked his permanent appendix, Kalua to serve fish and chicken ***tikkas*** (nuggets) as starters.

"***Hukum karo Saab*** (order me sir)," Raghu Chawla felt an urgent itch to explore the mind of his former mentor.

"I'm told that the fiend has ordered the Bureau of Investigation to grill me. That's a bad news." Ram Karan started with the fish ***tikka***.

"That's real bad sir, I mean, if it's correct. She has assumed direct control of the FIB, NSI and the Bureau of Investigation. All cloak and dagger business are directed from her office."

"I'm told Shankar, the spoiled brat and third grade motor mechanic, has conjured up charges against me, about my alleged funnelling of Pakistani funds, for sabotaging his mother's election and for stirring up communal riots. Do you believe in that pig shit? Can I, a freedom fighter, do that?" Karan vehemently expressed his wounded feelings.

"That's an abominable allegation. Who told you that?"

"The Home Secretary."

"You're angry tonight Karanji." Raghu added.

"Bastards like your FIB chief, and this bloody Nampoothiri are after my blood. This shit from Kerala says that I am obstructing the PM's initiative in East Pakistan. Can I do that?" Ram Karan, like a wounded Royal Bengal tiger, paced around the room, ready to jump at his tormentors.

"You're too uncharitable to the bureaucrats," Commented Raghu, "All of them aren't suckers."

"Forget the bureaucrats. These suckers are eternal barnacles. Do you know that, Shankar has been abusing fourteen generations of mine, for my alleged opposition to his mother?" Ram Karan continued with his tales of woe.

"Yes sir, I believe you'd asked for 70 tickets for your candidates. That was a wrong strategy. Ma'am Mandira is allergic to any of her colleagues growing big." Chawla replied.

"Isn't it unfair?" Ram Karan's lamentations continued over stiff Romanoff doses," Don't I deserve 70 supporters in the Parliament?"

"Sir, with 70 MPs behind, you can be the Prime Minister. That's what probably frightened her off. You should've known Amritlal's clan better. That dynasty doesn't spare its competitors."

"I think I miscalculated the sharpness of the cleaver, this lady wields," Ram Karan changed tracks, "Raghuji, you aren't new to the game. You've crossed many streams and channels of crisis with me. Now you've to build a new bridge."

Raghu didn't believe in antagonising any one. This old ram might fight back and be a minister again. Any power broker, seeking entry to the portals of power, even the Mandiras and Shankars, couldn't wish him away. His caste vote bank and affiliations were too formidable to ignore. And Ram Karan literally sat on the Everest of black money, earned through flesh trade, drug peddling and government contracts. His money itself was an insurance of his unlimited continuation in power. He could purchase anything and any person.

The Indian political and social jungles were replete with blood sucking leeches. What was the harm, if Ram Karan again drove his snout deep into the bleeding veins of the nation! Plenty of juice was still left in the near anaemic nation and its comatose people.

"Tell me, before I agree, which river do you want to cross." Raghu, after a quick stocktaking, offered his services to Ram Karan.

"Approach Shankar on my behalf and work out a compromise. I was swayed away by the organisational leaders."

"He's a difficult person, you know Karanji."

"I know. But, his appetite for money is legendary."

"There is a lot of stigma attached to you."

"To be frank with you, these Pakistanis had misguided me. I shouldn't have crossed her on the election issue. I know my caste equation can command 70 parliamentary seats, but this isn't the time to fight her. She's the rising sun and Shankar is another sun in the making. These dynastic stars will go on for another fifty years, at least."

Ram Karan displayed his astute and ringside knowledge of the Indian political cosmology.

"But Karanji, this allegation of Pakistani involvement is rather serious."

"I agree Raghu. You've been with me in this game. You can't get away, simply by pushing me to the hungry jackals. I won't sink alone. Talk to Shankar. Tell him that all these allegations are fabricated. You know my contribution to the freedom struggle. I know a few leaders in Pakistan and some of them are my old political colleagues. You know that well."

Ram Karan poured more Romanoff.

"I'm a nationalist. May be I am having some tertiary business interests. But who does not? You can't run away leaving me to the wolves."

"I'm not bothered about your political morality Karanji. And don't express your opinion openly any more. With Shankar and Mandira, disagreement means sedition and disaster. Keep your views to yourself. I'm basically a trader, and you're a trader too. Let's talk business. Keep the Pakistan angle on the back burner. You should know when to stop. Sever all ties with them."

"How can I? They've proof of my involvement with drug cartels and," Ram Karan paused, "You know this business of supplying pleasure commodities."

"Tell your friends to disengage for a while, and don't try to implicate me. My paper has been supporting you. In case I'm implicated, you'll get the front banner. You know what I mean."

Chawla talked in a slow menacing voice.

"Are you blackmailing me? Haven't you been my partner? Your links with the Pakis are well known."

"Don't bull shit," Raghu whispered, "I am a journalist. I can go and meet any diplomat. You can't nail me down. You've minted fortunes out of your Pakistan connections. Don't give any hint to the Pakis, that you're turning your back on them. They can be vicious. They can bump you off."

"You don't have to threaten me. We're in the same boat. Now follow the strategy I am suggesting."

"I'm not threatening you. We may have been in the same boat Karanji, but I've cast new anchors now. I'm no longer your protégé."

Raghu Chawla delivered the dialogue in a slow but piercing voice. He was no longer afraid of Ram Karan, now that he had tied his rope to the fishing wharf of Shankar.

"Take care," He continued, "The ISI often eliminates its sour assets. And I want you to know that, my friend in the High Commission is mighty unhappy with you."

"What's his problem?"

"Your last two despatches about the MIG and Mirage deals had misled them. You had taken a couple of millions from them, for ensuring Mandira's defeat in the parliamentary polls. You know what happened. They suspect you as a contaminated carrier of misinformation. Your proximity to some People's League leaders has confirmed their doubts."

"I have mended my fence on that front. My followers are no more supporting the People's League."

"That's another problem. Disengage from East Pakistan." Chawla winked at the former minister to measure up his reaction.

Ram Karan skirted the issue and guided Raghu back to the main theme. He was aware of the annoyance of the PIB station chief, and had explained the faux pas in an exclusive meeting with him. In fact, the reports in question were passed on to him, by one of his caste cronies, an officer in Nampoothiri's company. The well-calculated misinformation strategy, cooked up in the dirty tricks department of the NSI had achieved two objectives. Ram Karan was exposed and the PIB station chief had cautioned him with unpleasant consequences. Ram Karan, after the PIB station chief tipped him off had taken steps to smoke out the rogue NSI officer. A speeding truck had smashed his skull, while out on an early morning jog. Raghu Chawla wasn't aware of the top-secret operation, conducted through General Kalua Mushahari.

"So it's a deal. You build the new bridge." Ram Karan reiterated his point.

"The Shankar bridge? But you can build that bridge only with money. Normally he doesn't accept anything below ten million."

"That's real big money."

"Not too big for a coat of saintly paint over the Pakistani taint. And what's my cut?" Raghu forked in a slice of broiled mutton in his mouth and continued, "I must be compensated for adequately."

"You're a crook Chawla," Ram Karan laughed, "You won't even spare your mother in bed."

"I won't play the role of Indian Oedipus, Ramji. Certain holes are divine. Even to a crook like me."

He produced delectable sounds from his tongue, in appreciation of the sliced mutton cooked with asparagus and spring onions, with dashes of tender ginger flakes and garlic sauce.

"Have you seen the Marble Arch complex on Duplex Road?" Raghu Chawla continued.

"That costs a fortune. Don't try to blackmail me. I've given you two homes, a farm house and two agencies for your son."

"Karanji, you know I've a big family and one can't stop harvesting as long as shrimps are aplenty. Arrange for an apartment at the Marble Arch."

"Raghu, you're a great explorer. You never tire in your quest for money and fortune."

Raghu now moved over to the dessert, a rare blend of milk pudding with Kabul raisins and Saudi dates.

"Okay. It's a deal, but you've bled me white." Ram Karan wailed out, "Please see that these FIB and NSI goons don't paste the Pakistani sticker on my back."

"They won't dare to. You've purchased a Shankar insurance."

"But the apartment costs a fortune."

"Karanji, the sea doesn't miss the mere theft of a few gallons of its liquid. Arrange for the kitty and tell me when you're ready. I'll meet Shankar tonight."

Raghu Chawla concluded the dinner with a Banarasi ***pan*** (betel leaf from Benaras) and imported cigarette.

It had been a satisfactory hunt, for both the veteran hunters.

****

Shankar, clad in ***kurta-pyjamas***, his personalised sartorial brand, received Ram Karan Prasad in his office, an extension of his mother's residence.

Raghu Chawla did the talking and explained Ram's contribution in the freedom struggle, his political achievements, caste following and his potential as a political ally.

"His offence is serious," Shankar, a man of few words spoke slowly, "Gone are the days of political heavy weights and regional satraps. My mother is the party. She is India. Nothing exists beyond her."

"Shankarji," Ram Karan spoke with folded hands, "I've blundered badly. Allow me to correct my foolish ways, give me another chance. I can't die peacefully, if I'm deprived of the opportunity of serving the daughter of Amritlalji and his worthy grandson. In you I can see the glimpses of your grandfather. Kindly bless me."

Ram Karan touched Shankar's feet.

"Don't bullshit. We have a fair idea of the depth and extent of your empire of sin and act of political betrayal."

Shankar's face became stiff with anger.

"Sir, you're correct. I was misled by the pack of political jokers." Ram Karan prostrated on the ground, in traditional Hindu style and firmly gripped Shankar's feet.

"Okay. Tell me what can I do for you?" Shankar moved his feet away and asked.

"Let me die in harness, in the service of Mandiraji. Let me die as your servant."

"Talk to Raghu." Shankar turned his back to Ram Karan.

"Sir," Ram Karan again touched Shankar's feet, "Spare me from the Bureau of Investigation enquiry. Sir, I can't be branded as a Pakistani agent. I've been the servant of your family, I want to die as one."

"Karanji," Shankar pronounced in a grave voice, "These intelligence people don't normally lie."

"Sir, all these are fabrications by the political enemies of Mandiraji. The CIA is responsible for the misunderstanding. My contacts in Pakistan are known to the Prime Minister."

Shankar removed his feet and said, "We know all about that. Work out the details with Raghu."

Before leaving the room Shankar turned back and asked.

"What portfolio do you want?"

"Sir, what choice do I have? Beggars cannot be choosers."

Ram Karan's lips glued up with sticky froth that escaped from the corners of his mouth. An old problem of chewing too much betel leaves, with queer concoctions of tobacco and other intoxicants.

"Industry?" Shankar asked.

Ram Karan looked in disbelief. His eyes bulged out.

"Raghu will fine tune the details." Shankar left the room with dignified strides.

Ram Karan's old frame started swinging in born-again Christian style. He jumped at Raghu Chawla's neck and danced a short but ecstatic tango.

"The Marble Arch is too cheap for an industry minister Karanji." Raghu whispered.

"Wait, you hungry wolf," Ram Karan again hugged his crony, "Our bumper lottery has been drawn. We'll have many things to do. Let's go. I've to get the money and also visit ***Bhairon*** (Lord Shiva) temple behind Sher Shah's fort and offer two bottles of Scotch to the benign deity. He's great."

"I'll take you to the temple of Lord ***Shani*** (Saturn). By offering 5 kilos of pure mustered oil you can propitiate His adverse juxtaposition in your horoscope." Raghu Chawla offered an additional stellar remedy.

"Yes Raghu. You've reminded me of another great obligation. I'd promised to sacrifice 111 goats and 5 buffaloes to Mother ***Kali***. I must perform the great sacrifice soon, after the swearing in ceremony."

Ram Karan folded his hands in obeisance to the Mother Goddess.

****

Amrita Bhalla floated into the room silently and went straight to the wall- embedded audio-video console. She switched on the official TV channel, Doordarshan.

"Any hot show dear?" Nampoothiri raised his eyes from a pile of files.

"Yes sir. Very hot. Thought you'll enjoy the live show." She drew up a chair and sat at a respectable distance.

The official TV channel was broadcasting live, the swearing in ceremony of two new faces in Mandira's cabinet. The ornate hall of the President's palace was jam packed with Delhi's glitterati.

The President of the republic swore in first a nondescript MP from southern India followed by Ram Karan Prasad. The camera focussed on Ram Karan touching Mandira's feet and drifting to a corner where Shankar was seated, flanked by two senior ministers. Ram Karan stooped down to touch his feet. The camera swung off and zoomed on the radiant face of the Prime Minister, engrossed in animated discussion with the US ambassador.

"Holy hell!" Nampoothiri stood up on his legs and started pacing across the spacious room.

"Hope you enjoyed it." Amrita switched off the set.

"Thanks dear. Send in Jata. I can do with a cup of coffee." He picked up the red restricted area exchange phone.

"Brother Dewan," Nampoothiri dialled the number of the personal secretary to the PM, "What do I see? This Pakistani spy has been inducted into the cabinet again."

"Queer are the ways of politics brother." Dewan sighed.

"Can I come and see her this evening?"

"Come a little late, around 10.30 p.m."

Mandira couldn't be credited, by any stretch of imagination, with the qualities of a patient listener. She believed that she was born to talk to others. An acute sense of inbuilt insecurity pushed her all the time to suspect, even the mildest act of protestation.

"It's not a new allegation. What makes you think that Ram is a suspected spy?"

Mandira accosted her external intelligence chief in a blunt tone.

"Agent reports from Pakistan and surveillance reports amply substantiate our suspicion. I've briefed you earlier too." Nampoothiri pushed forward his argument.

"You haven't convinced me Balu."

"You have the reports on his receiving Pak funds for sabotaging your election."

"That's a political war Balu. Once we cross the hump we resume friendship. No permanent hangover."

Mandira's logic was straight. A veteran freedom fighter, from a distinguished family of servants of the nation, couldn't be purchased by foreign intelligence agencies. Yes, he had tried to sabotage her elections. But nursing a personal ambition was no crime, in politics at least. There were allegations against her father Amritlal and Mohandas Gandhi as well, for their British intelligence connections. Hadn't they spread canards against Amritlal, at one point of time, linking him with the Soviets?

These were CIA misinformation reports, aimed at causing confusion. Some of these were manufactured in the factories of extra-imaginative frustrated political bandicoots, and her enemies.

"Leave the matter to my political judgement. The nation is facing a war situation. I wouldn't like to invite fresh trouble by branding my minister a spy. His face is acceptable to Sheikh Jainal and his Peoples' League colleagues. I require him for mobilisation of a vast segment of East Pakistani Hindus. That's an asset by itself." Mandira finally opened her heart to her external intelligence chief.

"But ma'am there's a long history behind his links with the Pak IB." Nampoothiri protested.

Mandira looked up and gestured to Nampoothiri to sit down and have some coffee. Ram Karan, she reminded him, was close to the last elected PM of Pakistan and Islamabad's incumbent minister for commerce. He, at one point of time, had shown inclination to join hands with the Muslim League and head a government, on the plank of a united independent Bengal. Amritlal's foresight and political wisdom had prevented the queer fishy Bengalis from ganging up on the platform of cultural and linguistic chauvinism.

The caste-lord still wielded considerable influence on the Muslims and lower caste Hindus in the two Bengals. She was, Mandira revealed, thinking in terms of appointing Ram Karan as the co-ordinator of the East-Pakistani refugee camps in West Bengal.

Mandira brushed aside Nampoothiri's next ace, serious corruption charges against Ram Karan.

"Corruption is a global phenomenon Balu. A politician has to oblige people. That's the banality of democracy. It shouldn't be the only yardstick to judge a political leader. His political utility and services to the nation are more valuable than a few extra chips he probably makes on the sly." Mandira added in defence of her minister.

"Ram Karan can be used as a confidence building tool," Mandira whispered, "I'm under pressure from Washington and London. I must go through the motion."

"That's an important aspect. But ma'am...."

"Well Balu, anything that you want to add?"

"I'll suggest attaching a senior intelligence officer with him."

"I appreciate that," Mandira smiled with a terse look from a remote corner of her eye, "I've assured the British PM that, I would be the last person to preside over Pakistan's break up. The world communities aren't likely to support me if Pakistan is dismembered and India is perceived as the villain of the drama. The Ram Karan mission is important for me. He can help in throwing up a smoke screen."

Balachandran Nampoothiri knew that Mandira often turned to cool granite. She refused to allow any opening to her inner thought process. Her perception of the international political drama was impeccable. And the wily Ram Karan must have had oiled his way deep into Mandira's territory, which she often described as politically expedient obligations.

He made a feeble effort to point out that, decision making in Pakistan was the sole privilege of the top military leaders. Ram Karan couldn't be their suigeneris and he wasn't qualified to understand various aspects of suicidology of the pervert junta leaders.

Mandira didn't react. Her stony face and glassy eyes remained glued to a paper, as if the entire universe was pulsating out of those few printed alphabets. The signal was clear. Nampoothiri's presence wasn't welcome any more and she wasn't ready to hear another word on Ram Karan. She had made up her mind.

"If you've any new point to make, discuss it with Shankar."

Mandira advised Nampoothiri before he silently walked out.

He was baffled by the suggestion.

How could this youngster grapple with a national security issue? What training did he have?

"It's unfair, isn't it Dewan?" Nampoothiri walked in, rather annoyed, to Rajinder Singh Dewan's smoke filled room.

"What's the context dear?"

"This Ram Karan and the suggestion that I consult Shankar on a sensitive intelligence riddle." Nampoothiri settled for a cigarette and coffee.

"Well brother! It depends on how you look at the mirror. Ram Karan is a Holy Ghost today. And better stop worrying about Shankar. You pay the same obeisance to the Crown Prince as you do to the Rex."

Dewan's earthly wisdom amused the NSI chief.

"You've been seeing these reports on Ram Karan. Don't you think he's a spy and a security risk?"

"Brother Balu," Dewan spoke through his tightened lips, "I see everything. I may add that your trade and her politics are at variance, for the time being, I mean."

"But it's a national security..."

"I'm not a security expert. All I know you've to spray smoke in her eyes, the smoke of smoking gun evidence. She's a difficult customer."

"Our Triple X and Alamgir reports are precise. We know the identity of Aftab."

"Sure you do Balu. A technocrat's conviction isn't good enough for a politician. It depends at what level you operate. She has to take a wide world view, not get stuck with a tunnel perception."

"God save the country."

"In God and Ma'am I've equal faith." Dewan smiled and lighted another cigarette.

Nampoothiri wasn't contaminated by Dewan's earthy wisdom, but he understood the latent hint. The NSI lacked, what they called, smoking gun evidence. Triple X and Alamgir were precise, but no one had really seen or heard him transacting clandestine business with Pakistani sleuths.

The earthy doormat was correct in his observation that political values vastly differed from professional ethics. Even the mighty MI6 could do little with a Prime Minister having suspected links with the Soviets. They couldn't incarcerate him in the Towers and throw his flesh to the Ravens.

Yes. He required doing some fine homework first.

****

"**S**hyam," Nampoothiri called Shyam Ahooja, Kumar Anand's replacement in the Federal Intelligence Bureau, "Are you free?"

"What's cooking?" Ahooja was surprised to receive the early morning call.

"Am I welcome for a cup of tea?"

"Have you divorced your roasted Brazilian seeds?"

"No dear. I know tea is what you generally prefer. I will be there at ten."

The corner room in North Block looked deceptive like any other cubicle occupied by scores of mandarins of the Ministry of Internal Security.

Ahooja liked it that way, a trait he had inherited from his ***guru*** RN Dutta, who believed in an unostentatious work environment.

Nampoothiri didn't necessarily agree. He liked to deck up his work environment in the mysterious ways of intelligence companies, as narrated in fiction, all cloak and dagger affair, arranged in style. The facade was as important as performance. The stage performer required attractive props. His ***Nakshtra Lok*** wasn't any less mysterious than the profession that his company pursued.

"Let's talk business," Nampoothiri went straight to the point, "We require exchanging notes on Col. Akram and Mirza Baloch of the Pak High Commission."

"Any crisis?" Ahooja alerted himself. The foreign diplomats were his slotted surveillance subjects.

"You know better. These diplomats, according to my reports are ISI cover agents. They've infiltrated deep into the system."

Nampoothiri pretended to open up his heart.

"Balu, you should leave something for me."

"I'm not here to grab your turf. Akram is mixed up with the Kashmir dissenters. He has penetrated deep into our system and is in a position to feed the ISI with running commentaries."

"I agree." Shyam Ahooja opened up, "He's causing tremendous damage. What's bugging you?"

"I assure you again, there is no turf fight. Akram has penetrated a government minister and his journalist crony, besides subverting Sardar Niyamat and other Kashmiri partisans, I suspect..."

Shyam Ahooja shifted his position.

Yes, his turf-rival had something new to tell him. Akram's links with the Kashmiri lion, Sardar Niyamat were well logged and documented. But the government minister was a holy cow of the system, as sacrosanct as millions of gods and goddesses of the Hindu pantheon. He was beyond the FIB's reach.

Nampoothiri narrated the suspected links between Ram Karan, Raghu Chawla and some Pakistani intelligence operatives in India and Nepal. Ghazi Sabbir, he said, a Nepali Muslim criminal turned politician, was Ram Karan's conduit for drug and arms smuggling from the Himalayan Kingdom. He was instrumental in providing political protection to the illegal immigrants for a neighbouring country. The FIB and NSI, he argued, should mount joint operations to workout the clandestine linkages to neutralise the ISI network.

Ahooja, a born conservative, didn't believe in sharing two things-women and intelligence operations. But this special case had its roots in Pakistan. Perhaps Nampoothiri knew more than what he had just coughed out. He appreciated the approach.

"Unlock your cranium, a little more." Ahooja left the initiative to his counterpart.

"Let's share intelligence at our level and review the inputs once in three days. No need to keep the PM in the picture, not at this stage." Nampoothiri suggested.

"Fine with me. Leave the ElInt to my boys. You take charge of the SigInt, coverage of Nepal and Pakistan end. My boys will take care of the surveillance job." Ahooja placed his cards on the table.

"Fine with me," Nampoothiri added, "Your boys have logged evidence implicating Col. Akram and Mirza Baloch with Sardar Niyamat, **Al Fatah**, United Kashmir Liberation Front et all. We require smoking gun evidence of their links with Ram Karan and Raghu Chawla."

"I agree Balu. We can't hang them till we produce hard evidence. I'm told Shankar has rediscovered Ram's virtues. How do you propose to tackle the rising son?"

"Shankar is, all said and done, a staunch nationalist, more Hindu than any Hindu Sangh stalwart. Haven't you noticed his contempt for Muslims? We may not find him wanting, if he's confronted with Ram Karan's links with Pakistan."

"That's reassuring."

Two independent inputs generated a sudden flurry of activities in the joint FIB-NSI operations.

Raghu Chawla made a vital phone call, seeking a luncheon meeting with Col. Akram. He would like, Raghu said, to have the latest inputs on developments in Dacca, for a story he was planning in the special issue of National Expression.

Akram went along and complimented the brave journalist. The Pakistanis were convinced, Akram said, that some Indian quarters were bent upon destroying their country. As a diplomat, he felt, he had a duty to promote harmony between the two nations.

The other past-midnight call was from Ram Karan Prasad.

"Raghu." His voice whispered.

"Yes Karanji."

"A messenger had come, a few minutes back."

"Don't hesitate, this is my unlisted phone and as a minister you're spared by the FIB spooks." Raghu assured Ram Karan.

"I'm not so sure. Who can trust this spooky lady? This fellow is a Saharanpur Muslim, contact of our friend Akram. The message demands an urgent meeting. Tell him that's suicidal right now. Ask his boss, the Brigadier, to contact me at the painting exhibition. That's a natural cover."

"The point is well taken Ramji. Don't worry, I'll manage it."

Ahooja didn't miss the opportunity. Raghu Chawla wasn't the type to talk straight from the heart and plunge into the noble task of promoting people to people harmony. His wagons of greed and plunder moved on the oiled rails of blackmail, dirty liaison work and plain criminal activities.

But what intrigued him most was the call from Ram Karan. That perhaps provided with an inescapable lead.

Ahooja's boys bugged the underside of the hotel table, in consultation with the floor manager. A hand painted Czech flower vase, treated with a powerful radio microphone and decorated with imported tulips, was placed on the table. It matched well with the general table decor of the day.

Col. Akram, before taking a seat, took out a miniature electronic scanner and followed the readings carefully. The needles told a dirty story, indicating the presence of some buried snooping devices near the table. He went down on his knees in one swift move and plucked out a tiny micro radio transmitter, secured with masking tape. Akram deactivated it.

His scanner failed to locate the other one embedded in the cavity of the flower vase.

"Look at the damned hospitality of your FIB." Akram pocketed the device and nonchalantly sipped on chilled beer.

Raghu Chawla realised that he had walked into a minefield, perhaps, because of his closeness to the Pak diplomats and Ram Karan. He surely hadn't bargained for any attention from the intelligence sleuths.

"Any more danger?" He asked.

"Don't think so. The FIB buggers must be sitting somewhere nearby and cursing us. I must put the device back before we leave."

"Why this hospitality?" Asked Raghu.

"Don't bother. They even peep inside our bedrooms." Akram offered a beer to his guest.

"Shall we disengage?"

"No," Replied Akram, "Act natural. That's the way to defeat the spooks at their own game."

Raghu Chawla breathed more easily.

He shared Ram Karan's tentative itinerary to Pakistan. His brief, as the special emissary of the PM was to bridge the widening gulf of distrust and belligerence.

"Islamabad has serious doubts about his integrity."

"I understand. Here too he's come under a cloud."

"Why are they sending him to Islamabad?"

"For confidence building measures, I presume. The lady is hell bent upon another war, I'm sure."

"What's the time frame of Karan's visit?"

"Any day. As soon as South Block gets the green signal from Islamabad."

Chawla disclosed his mentor's tentative programme.

"But brother, the die has been cast. Our President isn't likely to come down and embrace Karan and Mandira." Akram cautioned Chawla.

"Is the war inevitable? Don't you think Karanji should be given a chance?" Chawla asked.

"Can't say. Pakistan isn't going to sit on its ass. You needle us in Dacca we blast you in Kashmir. We can create more problems for you than you can for us. Any way, do me a favour. Find out if Delhi and Moscow are working on the draft of a new treaty."

"What makes you think so?"

"We've been warned by the US. If India opts for Russian help, Pakistan has to think seriously about getting the Chinese and the USA involved in its security umbrella. And the US President has given a personal commitment to General Arif. This time around the war is going to cost you dearly." Akram's voice oscillated viciously.

"Look Akram, I'm not bothered who fights whose war. I'm a trader and I want good compensation. I shall accompany Ram Karan. Arrange for me the full and free hospitality." Raghu made his stand clear.

"Keep this." Akram passed on the latest issue of *The Illustrated Weekly*. Chawla lifted the centre page and noticed a fat bunch of currency notes.

"There are fifty. Keep it. Can you do me another favour?"

"I expected more. Any way, what do you want?"

"A delicate task related to ***Mukti Bahini***."

"No problem. What's your game?"

"Here's a map of the Indo-Pak border in the east. Mark for me the details of the training camps run by the Indian army and the NSI. Mention the units and the names of the camp commanders."

"What's your intention?"

"As a trader you should be content with the compensation package."

"It'll cost you 5 grand."

"That's a whooping half a million."

"The job is risky."

"Fine. You get it."

"Let's disengage."

Akram nodded silently and fitted back the miniature microphone.

Chawla broke off the meeting, cunningly drifting away to another table, occupied by a beauty, with disproportionate fat at the wrong places of her anatomy.

The transcript was tantalisingly rewarding. But Shyam Ahooja had more surprises in store for himself.

Akram's phone, permanently on the FIB hook up, presented solid gold nuggets.

"Raghu, Akram here. We have the list of Indian delegation. Who's this Moti Sagar, Additional Secretary?"

"No such creature in any ministry, as far as I know."

"Can you find out and give me a profile? Oh yes, you'll be a guest of the Press Club of Pakistan and they've fixed you up in hotel Shalimar, off the Mall. It's a fine place."

"Expect a call from me in the evening." Chawla disconnected and dialled the number of the Joint Secretary, Pakistan desk, in the Ministry of External Affairs.

Chapter 37

Captain Ayoob, back to his seat after a short furlough, felt less forlorn. He exuded effervescence, having managed a short and cosy week with his wonder fairy, Reshma.

"Come Harfan," He gestured warmly as the Israr International's executive entered Ayoob's room. By now he had developed a liking for the dashing salesman.

"Just dropped by. The boss had sent some special communication to Gen. Naqi. Thought I should check up if you had a warm holiday."

"***Yar***, She's fabs," Ayoob's happiness exploded in a warm order for coffee and lighting of cigarettes, "These Indians are rotten duds." He followed up with a spatial comment.

"What's new with the enemies of Islam?"

"The fools first send a minister, who's well known to our hooded people, and then tops up the mistake by adding an intelligence officer as his appendage." He politely passed on the coffee to Harfan.

"Funny, who's this blighted gunk?"

"Some bloody Sagar...may be Heera (diamond), may be Moti (pearl). He was specially tagged to keep an eye on the minister."

"Stupid. These Hindu bums are incorrigible." Harfan tickled Ayoob's not too latent hatred for everything Hindu.

"Serves them right. The delegation had plenty of wining and dining and very little meat." Ayoob continued his narration.

"Sad ***yar***. To hell with the bloody Indians! Tell me how was the furlough? Hope you had a swell time. Have you brought her along?"

Harfan initiated a feeble furrow into the fertile and brittle psyche of Ayoob, and expectantly settled down over the coffee.

"No ***yar***. She's back with her parents. Its some funny social custom to be observed there."

"That's cruel! Hope things are okay with your boss man." Harfan pelted an anticipatory pebble. He was not dismayed.

"The boss is fine. Work is fine."

"So when do we start the airlifting operations?"

"Can't say for sure. Washington is loaning us two Boeing 707s, which are owned by a Mexico-based undercover CIA subsidiary. These birds will ferry weapons to Dacca. And watch out, we're going to pin down the Indian Army in its Northeast."

Ayoob continued pouring out his accumulated knowledge of the secrets of the nation. He really felt big, when he unburdened his chest.

"That means Israr International is out!"

"Better check up on that. Naqi should know the details."

"Any sabotage by our rivals?"

"Not sure. He was approached by the ISI chief, on behalf of Nawab Sharief." Ayoob graciously offered the vital information.

"Thanks for the dope ***yar***. Do you think USA will like to take an open plunge?"

"That's the snag. But, we've other options. Don't worry. This time around we're sure going for the ramparts of Delhi's Red Fort."

Ayoob reassured Harfan with an expansive sweep of his hand, as if he was only a furlong away from the fort built by Shahjahan.

Harfan smiled, shared a cigarette and bade him adieu.

"Hi buddy, aren't you from Jhumra?" Ayoob startled Harfan.

"Yea, I happen to stay there, but I'm from Karachi." He replied in an assertive voice.

"That's what I meant ***yar***. I'm flying to Bhagatanwala, accompanying a Military Signals team, from my parent unit. That's not far from your den."

"It's just an hour's drive. Come over for dinner at the fabulous Hotel Royal Palace."

"Can't make it dear. The team is moving in that area with an array of Direction Finders."

"What's that?"

"Oh brother! Direction Finders are used to locate clandestine radio transmission. The Joint Intelligence Signals of the ISI has detected some unauthorised transmission from the general direction of Jhumra. The Military Signals team is moving in to intensify the search." Captain Ayoob explained the working mechanism of the Direction Finders with a flourish.

"How do you fit in?"

"I was trained with the CIA's signal intelligence outfit. I'm an expert DF handler."

"To hell with these brain teasing riddles. I'm happy with my two-penny business. See you later." Harfan said ***Khuda Hafiz.***

"Well brother!" Ayoob continued his dialogue, "There's more. We're locating the 3rd Corp at Chak Jhumra."

"That's next to my den." Harfan wasn't surprised with the information. It must be a part of the war preparations.

"Lt. General Sahbaz will be stationed there."

"Give me an intro to him. I can probably sell a few more boots and belts to his formation." Harfan smiled back.

"Don't joke ***yar.*** I'm happy because it'll give me the opportunity to visit your exotic home."

"Come and spend a few days over there with Reshma."

Harfan extended his arm, pumped Ayoob's palm and said ***Khuda hafiz.***

Back to his nest, Harfan burnt the late night candles and transmitted a short message to ***Zam Zam,*** incorporating some of the strategic disclosures by Ayoob. He emphasised the need for lodging protest with the USA for its reported loaning of aircrafts to Pakistan. The Direction Finder story and the deployment of the 3rd Corp were also highlighted. He conveyed his decision to switch his station off. Alam, he requested, should dismantle and remove his trans-receiver set post-haste.

Ram Karan returned empty handed from Islamabad after two gala dinners and plenty of photo sessions. General Arif was again out of Islamabad to the greener pastures of Larkana, home turf of Izaz Afroz, shooting rabbits and wild fowls. General Sarfaraz and the civilian foreign minister, who smiled profusely for the cameras and finally agreed to meet again, filled in his diplomatic absence.

Mandira didn't expect Ram Karan's visit to bring about dramatic improvement in bilateral relations with Islamabad. Karan wasn't the diamond in her pendant either. It was more of a diplomatic shenanigan; a deliberate deception for buying a breather and to plan an orchestrated international mobilisation. She went through the motion of sending messages of sincere Indian efforts at détente. Karan had taken it physically to Islamabad. And his beaming face splashed on the major Indian print and electronic media and a live interview with one of the celebrity hosts displayed ample proof of the sincere Indian efforts. Ram Karan was even made to say, from a prepared text, that some members of the junta in Pakistan were not in favour of an amicable settlement of the dispute in East Pakistan. The viewers in the Pakistan High Commission in Delhi were not amused to hear him denouncing Pakistan for the flagrant violation of human rights and alleged killing of thousands of innocent Bengalis.

Mandira didn't bother to debrief her minister. It was left to her advisor Dinanath Tapoo and the Foreign Secretary.

She was engrossed reading the reports just sent in by her external intelligence chief, Balachandran Nampoothiri. The latest Triple X report had enormously disturbed her strategic calculations. CIA's involvement with mercenary flights to Dacca was sure to embolden the military regime. And that's what she dreaded the most. The mercenary flights were an indicator that Washington could even go for landing its Marines off the coast of Chittagong and position its Pacific fleet in the blue waters of the Bay of Bengal. That's what she did not want to bargain for.

The proposed visit of the US Secretary of State to Peking was another flaming concern. His visit to Delhi had ended in diplomatic semantics. The bully, an American Jew, had projected himself as a divinely ordained international policeman. He hastened to convey a loud warning: his President, the Leaning Tower on the Potomac, was tilting towards Pakistan.

Mandira wasn't amused. The myopic Yankees often lapsed into a tunnel vision of the world, while selecting their whipping boys. Some days they targeted China and on others it was Vietnam and Cuba and now it was India. This wonderful nation often turned schizophrenic, while hopping diplomatic beds in search of imaginary friends and foes.

She was determined, not to allow the luxury of such perfunctory pleasure to that sly brazen faced of a liar of a US President. He had precious little regard for her personally, and the nation she led. Their mutual apathy was pathological.

Dewan's shuffling feet disturbed Mandira's surfing of the international canvass.

"Yes?"

"Nampoothiri and Ahooja are here."

"Send them in."

"What do you think of the likely US response? What are the chances of their naval fleet intervening?"

Mandira fired the question even before her intelligence chiefs took their respective seats.

"The US Congress and the Senate are divided on this issue. The Democrats are totally opposed to any US involvement." Nampoothiri replied promptly, as if he had anticipated the salvo.

"But the CIA is providing mercenary flights to Islamabad."

"Yes ma'am," Nampoothiri spoke with a chuckle, "The Foreign Secretary has conveyed our concerns to his counterpart in Washington and Friends of India, the New York based Democratic lobby has written to the President."

"That's encouraging. But the US won't hesitate in ordering its Marines to rub shoulders with the Peoples' Army in the killing fields of East Pakistan. They have ignored the genocide perpetrated by General Arif and Tarakki." Mandira opened up with caustic remarks, which was very unusual of her.

"We need balancing support from the USSR and countries of the European and South American continents. The Islamic world should be made wiser about the Pakistani massacre of the unarmed Bengali Muslims." Nampoothiri added, expecting the PM to prolong the topic.

She turned sideways in her chair and talked almost in a soliloquy.

"The Bangladeshi leaders are so divided, even at this hour of colossal crisis. I'm baffled."

"Yes Prime Minister," Ahooja responded, "Some of them are talking in terms of a reconciliation with Pakistan."

"Well, that's the last menu I want on my plate," Mandira responded in a jerky voice.

"Balu," She changed tracks, "I've seen your reports on Ram Karan. You and Ahooja have done a good job. Leave the matter to me. You two should now decide about this diplomat Akram."

"The catch is mature." Ahooja replied, "We've enough material to pick him up and pack him off to Islamabad."

"I don't want any publicity about Sardar Niyamat's linkages with the Pak diplomats. That's the last signal I'd like to send to the Kashmiris and the world at large. Choose any other plausible grounds, if you're so keen to declare him a persona non grata." Mandira's instructions were specific.

"And Nampoothiri," She took a probing sip of the steaming coffee, "I believe the magnetic pole is shifting very fast."

"The world is getting US-centric, despite the Communist block holding on to its apparent monolith." Nampoothiri replied smartly, anticipating the mood of his boss lady.

"I believe the US is trying to divide the Bangla freedom fighters. What're your reports Ahooja?"

"You're correct ma'am. The US consulate officials have had about 7 clandestine meetings with some Bangladeshi leaders. Our monitors feel that the State Department is desperate to arrange a dialogue between them and General Arif." Ahooja responded.

"It won't happen. I won't allow them to catch us napping again. You be prepared to visit Moscow along with the Foreign Minister." Mandira addressed Nampoothiri.

"Give me a brief on Colombo. I believe the US embassy is pressing them for a smooth passage of Pakistani armaments. How much pressure can we put on them?"

"It's pretty difficult to say. The island nation is seething with anti-India hysteria. The US embassy is working overtime to obtain transit facilities for Pakistan. The logic is simple; if Pakistan is truncated today, Ceylon can't be far behind." Nampoothiri summed up the prevailing anxieties in the island nation.

"Dewan." Mandira called for her secretary.

"Connect me to Colombo, I'll like to speak to the Prime Minister," She ordered, but amended it quickly, "Tell the Foreign Secretary to talk to their High Commissioner in Delhi, before you connect me."

Dewan, as instructed by the PM, received the call and advised the personal secretary of the Ceylonese PM to hold on; the Indian Prime Minister would personally take the call.

Mandira took the line first and requested the secretary of her counterpart to connect her to his boss. This calculated diplomatic ploy was meant for pandering the Ceylonese PM's ego.

She sugarcoated her well-rehearsed deliveries. How could she ignore the centuries' old cultural ties between the two nations, Mandira hastened to add! She would like to visit the wonderful sites at Kandi and Anuradhapur at the first available opportunity. Didn't her dad and mom select Ceylon for holidaying, even at the peak of their involvement in India's independence struggle?

Pleasantries over, Mandira cautiously unfolded her heartaches over the ghastly happenings in East Pakistan. Could the Ceylonese PM use her good offices to persuade Pakistan to resolve the issues through mutual discussions? She hoped that Ceylon would facilitate all civilian flights between Islamabad and Dacca and take care that the weapons of death and destruction weren't ferried through its territory.

"Is there going to be a war?" Asked the Ceylonese PM.

No. She was against all wars. She'd be the last person to start any war with Pakistan. How could she, being a true follower of the Mahatma?

Yes. She would definitely remain in touch and exchange notes.

Mandira profusely thanked the Island nation's chief executive and handed the phone over to Dewan.

She turned around and asked him to connect her to the Indian ambassador in Moscow.

The ambassador, probably dragged out from a vodka-induced sleep, couldn't comprehend what Mandira was trying to convey. A shrill shout made the message clear to the diplomat in slumber.

He should immediately seek an appointment with the Soviet Premier, Mandira added. She would like to personally talk to Mr. Anatole Dobrynin and Mr. Wataloo, her. foreign minister would personally carry her message to him and the General Secretary of the CPSU.

The important call over, she turned to Dewan.

"Ask the Foreign Secretary to summon the Soviet ambassador tomorrow. I want to meet him"

"Yes ma'am."

"The FS should be at hand for consultations. And call up the President's office. I'd like to see him tomorrow at ten a.m."

"Yes ma'am."

"Nampoothiri, don't you think we should do something about Ceylon? Why can't you take charge of the more vocal segments among the Tamils? We should prop them up, train them and keep Colombo busy." Mandira suggested opening up of a new front.

"There's a problem ma'am. Most of the Tamil tea labourers are hopelessly divided. Give me a few days time. We're in touch with some friends in the Jaffna area." Replied Nampoothiri.

"Keep the pressure on. Ceylon cannot get away by supporting Islamabad," Mandira added, "Alert your agents in Colombo, I want precise feed back on all Pakistani flights using Ceylonese territory....

"Identify the politicians who are likely to support my pro-Tamil policy in Ceylon, and give me an assessment too, of the likely impact of the growth of a militant Tamil movement in Ceylon, on the common Indian Tamils." She spoke, turning to Shyam Ahooja.

"I don't want them getting fresh ideas. The simmering anti-Hindi movement and anti-Brahmin agitation shouldn't take off at an oblique tangent. Try to divert that against Colombo." Mandira cautioned her domestic intelligence chief.

"We'll come up with a detailed report." Assured Shyam Ahooja.

"And Balu, I'd like your boys in Pakistan to come up with more details of the CIA funded flights from Karachi to Dacca, carrying men and weapons." Mandira's ebullience coincided with the speedy flickering of her left eye. She was bubbling with enthusiasm.

"Tell them, I want photographic evidence too. That will expose the US duplicity in full measure."

"It'll be done ma'am. Our top boys will be deployed for this special task."

"Keep track of other mercenary flights as well."

"Yes ma'am."

"And Ahooja, I want concrete evidence on meetings between the US diplomats and the renegade Bangladeshi leaders. Your reports aren't convincing enough."

"It'll be done ma'am."

"I want to confront the Secretary of State with concrete evidence. And what do I hear about the flesh trade racket in the refugee camps in Calcutta?" Her eagle eyes pierced the FIB chief.

It was a difficult question to answer. Ahooja had in his pocket reports of the flesh business transacted by Ram Karan's stooges, who had infiltrated the camps in the guise of relief volunteers. The Bengali belles were being lured away from the refugee camps by his pimps, promising them dream marriages and a golden career in Bombay's Hollywood.

"We've some reports ma'am. Perhaps you may like to consult Ram Karanji first."

"I wouldn't have tasked you, if I could depend on him." Mandira shouted at her FIB chief.

"Get me the details. And talk to Shankar, he has lots of information on this sordid affair." She vented her utter disgust and walked out of the room. Ahooja didn't get a chance to recant his usual yes ma'am reply.

The order to consult Shankar was part of Mandira's new style of functioning. Top officials of the government were often directed to share matters of the state with her younger son. He apparently had ready solutions for all complicated problems of the country.

"What does it mean?"

Ahooja asked Nampoothiri as they walked out of the PM's room.

"Don't bother. You can brief Shankar on Ram Karan issue. That guy is capable of running berserk and taking the correct decision, what other politicians dither to take."

"The PM should decide."

"I agree. But you cannot expect her to carry the hatchet all by herself. Big leaders often require convenient hatchet men and fall guys. Let's nail down the matter now."

Nampoothiri encouraged his FIB colleague, on the hope that the angry young man would at least agree to take action against the flesh and drug trader, who masqueraded as a patriot.

Chapter 38

Seated alone at his top floor office, Nampoothiri felt a sting of irritation and frustration. The top of the pyramid, secured after years of dreaming and slogging wasn't really strewn with rose petals.

A deft manipulator, Nampoothiri knew the tricks of keeping himself dry even in the worst of monsoon gale. But today his grey cells were totally foxed and smoked out. He failed to analyse Mandira's rationale behind shielding Ram Karan Prasad and sitting pretty on piles of intelligence reports on that scumbag. The wily jackal had caused tremendous damage to the nation, the extent and depth of which could be gauged only after he was subjected to sweet and sour process of interrogation.

Why was she smiling benignly on him?

What could be her compulsions?

She didn't like to expose the ugly chinks in her cabinet at this critical hour!

That had become a rotten cliché.

Ram Karan, a caste baron, could threaten the stability of her ministry!

Yes. The fox had the capability of hitting back, rather ferociously.

Was Shankar protecting the wily master criminal?

What could be his motivation?

Was he angling for finances for his pet obsession, the small car project?

Was Ram in possession of any secret of the PM? Secrets of her personal life?

Possible! The veteran criminal had been in and around Amritlal's family for over a quarter of a century.

Or was it that she wanted to decide on an appropriate time, coinciding with other important events? Her sense of timing had so far worked out well. A woman's mind, as it were, was an uncharted and unfathomable sea. It was even more difficult to have a peep into Mandira's complex psyche.

Nampoothiri felt puzzled. The quiz wasn't clear at all.

Well! He must keep the pressure up and carry Ahooja along. He did not have faith in Ahooja's capability of convincing Shankar. It was better if they worked together and produced the gun, bullets and smoke all in one package. Not the smoking gun alone.

Nampoothiri's intestinal churning was all the more aggravated by the last part of the cipher from Triple X. What compelled him to terminate HF transmission? Who could've deployed the Direction Finders at his location? Who could have peeled off Harfan's cover? Could it be the Inter Services Intelligence?

What else could that mean?

Direction Finders, consisting of sensitive rotating antenna and High Frequency receivers could home in to the approximate location of a suspected radio transmitter. The frequency identification, pattern of Morse and cipher analogue, periodicity and strength of signals could lead the sleuths to the exact location of the source of energy emission.

The ISI wasn't a novice in Signal and Electronic Intelligence, and their arsenal was recently replenished by advanced NATO type monitoring gadgets.

That meant real big danger.

Nampoothiri sat up and asked Jatadhari to brew another cup of coffee.

Something had terribly gone wrong. The clandestine High Frequency radio set of XXX must have come under the scrutiny of the SigInt experts of the ISI. The trained tenacious hounds, as they were, wouldn't easily miss a blazing trail.

Holy heavens! Triple X was in imminent danger. His most productive resident agent in Pakistan was in trouble and the counter-intelligence canines were just about sniffing and licking the droplets of blood. Homing on to the location of the clandestine HF transmission station was just a matter of time, a very thin margin of time.

Did Triple X commit any security breach? Was he careless?

Nampoothiri buzzed the bell for Amrita Bhalla, his glamorous evergreen secretary. He required immediate consultations with his Signal Intelligence experts.

"Yes sir." Amrita dressed in a printed silk sari with a matching blouse and coiffure looked devastating.

The killer look wasn't really for Nampoothiri, she knew him only too well. This seasoned spy was perhaps never interested in sex. If he were, he should have been able to produce at least one child by now. However, Amrita enjoyed his clean appreciative looks. He was a fine connoisseur of beauty sans the ugly x-ray.

"Summon Achariya, Gogoi and what's his name!" Nampoothiri started scratching his head, trying to retrieve the name of the third person, through the follicles of his receding hairline.

"You mean the Joint Intelligence Officer, Dhiren Bhagat?" Amrita correctly anticipated the name.

"There you are! I wonder, why didn't you come to my life 28 years ago, my dear?"

"I couldn't sir." Amrita never felt tired of listening to this compliment, meaninglessly uttered by her boss for countless times. He really didn't mean anything.

"I was born just three years before your desired date of marriage. Too tender, even for a child marriage."

Nampoothiri enjoyed the reply. This vibrant girl always carried a whiff of freshness about her.

They laughed, in a controlled fashion. The old man, Amrita knew, didn't like loud giggling. His scheming grey cells could perhaps not conjure up anything but spies, dirty tricks and the black arts of intelligence.

She wondered what could be the latest crisis!

Dacca? Perhaps not.

Achariya didn't handle the eastern wing of Pakistan. He was responsible for operations in the western wing.

Robin Achariya arrived first. That was a dream corridor for him, but not because of his devotion to Nampoothiri. The rendezvous offered him the rare chances to devour the trim, firm and steely physique of Amrita Bhalla, at least with his moist and hungry eyes. His efforts to escort her to a dinner date met with warm but meaningless giggles. She usually buried his hungry looks in her sweet rippling of laughter.

A leech, Amrita could compare Robin's looks with the probing snout of the eternal elastic blood-sucking creature of the under-growth.

"You may go in." She pressed the button activating the electrically controlled door. She had the licence to do so.

Jatadhari placed cups of aromatic coffee on the table, roasted and ground from special Brazilian seeds, and quietly closed the door behind him.

"Presume, you've seen the last cipher from XXX," Nampoothiri opened up the discussion, "What do you read into it? Why does he suspect the deployment of Direction Finders?"

"The ISI is perhaps trying to locate signals emitted by some unauthorised stations. The triangulation mechanism may have brought them nearer to the station at Jhumra." Replied Gogoi, the technical division chief.

"Can they home in easily on XXX's den? Explain the technical drill." Requested Nampoothiri.

"Modern homing devices can bring the SigInt people as near as one km of the suspected station. The rest is a matter of establishing the pattern of transmission and physical search. The same routine is followed by our SCSB (Signal Communication Security Bureau)." Gogoi replied.

"Hmm." Nampoothiri hummed with a worried expression on his face. "Is there any way to shield the energy leakage?"

"We've provided a thick lead shield in the underground chamber. This can minimise radiation, but can't eliminate it. The main radiation takes place from the antenna. The rotating Direction Finder antenna picks up direct signals and signals reflected back from the stratosphere. That's how the operators measure the general location of a clandestine set. I feel Triple X's set should be dismantled immediately." Gogoi offered a coherent technical explanation.

"Thanks Gogoi. You can go now." Nampoothiri dismissed the technical chief.

He wasn't supposed to share privileged operational secrets with him.

"Sir," Robin Achariya spoke," Contact Qurban has reported the presence of mobile units of the Corps of Signals in Triple X's location. I feel our man has committed grave errors."

"Your conclusion is premature. Gogoi has vouchsafed for Harfan's traffic discipline."

"What are your views?" Nampoothiri turned to Bhagat.

"Can't say sir. Harfan hasn't sent any feedback after my last meeting. I think we should dismantle the station first and debrief him in a face to face meeting."

"Any new inputs from Alam?" Nampoothiri turned to Achariya.

"No sir. He just indicated the likely involvement of XXX in weapons airlifting operations to Dacca." Replied Achariya.

"How do we debrief XXX on this sensitive issue?"

"Kabul is the nearest place." Dhiren Bhagat commented.

"Correct. Leave the details with me. Get ready to visit Kabul," Nampoothiri advised Bhagat.

"I think I should go and debrief XXX." Robin pleaded.

"No." Nampoothiri replied firmly," You've a mission in Dacca. Reach there by tomorrow and activate our friends in ***Mukti Bahini.*** Brief them to monitor the CIA chartered flights to Kurmitola, Chittagong and Rajshahi bases. I want photographic evidence of it. The PM wants to take up the matter with the US Secretary of State and in the UN." He dismissed the meeting.

"But sir, I should tackle the XXX problem first." Robin Achariya tried to maintain his toehold.

"Let me handle this. Your Dacca mission is more important. Sheikh Tajummal, Jainal's deputy, is still hiding in Dacca. Give my message to him. Finish it before Pakistan seals the border and our Mission is withdrawn."

Nampoothiri dismissed his desk chief and boarded the special tubular reinforced plastic elevator to the basement niche that housed the Command Information Centre. It was a top-secret communication hub, hooked to selected diplomatic stations abroad.

Big wall maps exhibited the countries and capitals, connected with the computer controlled multi-modal high frequency digital trans-receiving systems. All in computer generated auto-cipher mode.

"Raise Kabul." Nampoothiri startled the CIC-in-charge by his sudden appearance.

The operator closed the thick soundproof glass door of the cubicle and raised Kabul by manipulating the computer keyboard. The monitor screen displayed presence of Kabul, as light blobs flashed the assigned digits—7910-QMSRI. A blue light blinked, indicating that the station was in receiving mode.

"The station is ready sir, "The operator said, "Any message?"

"Is it safe on auto-scramble?"

"Yes sir."

Nampoothiri scribbled a small message for personal attention of the NSI station chief at Kabul.

"Give me a tinkle when Kabul gets back."

Nampoothiri retrieved the piece of paper and walked out.

****

Alam was startled by Nampoothiri's surprise message. An Attaché of the Indian Mission in Kabul delivered it at his Peshawar residence, which doubled for his business den as well. The cryptic message had directed him to meet Dhiren Bhagat at a Kabul safe house. The personal messenger of the NSI chief was carrying a special communication.

Bhagat was perhaps the second FIB and NSI officer to meet Alam in person. The legendary resident agent, a fabled mystery, always evoked admiration in the informed NSI coterie. Perhaps only two NSI officers, besides Nampoothiri, were aware of his existence.

Bhagat flew all the way to Moscow by an Aeroflot flight and endured another long haul to Dushanbe and on to Kabul, which landed at the ill equipped airport amidst a freak snowstorm, around 9.30 pm. The round about routing was chalked out by the NSI for protecting his identity. There was no emissary from the Indian Mission at hand to receive him at the ungodly hour. He passed through the immigration and ventured out to look for a taxi to take him to Hotel Hasina.

"Do you require a taxi sir?"

An afghan, covered from head to foot with woollen clothes and a balaclava approached him with a whispering voice.

"Yes, I do. Are you a private operator?

"Sir I'm Jaffar and I'm looking for Mr. Bedad Aslam."

"Has the apricot tree flowered?"

Bhagat asked Jaffar to reassure that he was in the correct company.

"Yes sir. There are 900 flowers."

"You've got the correct customer Mr. Jaffar."

"Thank ***Allah,*** " Jaffar Agha, a covert friend of the under cover NSI representative in Kabul spoke slowly, "Mr. Rawat, the First Secretary has deputed me. Please follow. You're not lodging at Hasina. He has arranged a private guest house for you."

"Please to meet you Agha sahib. Please take me to the arranged den."

Bhagat embraced Jaffar in the typical Islamic way and followed him to a waiting Lada, an ugly looking Russian car.

After a quick dinner Bhagat was driven to another corner of the city and dumped in front of an ornate building.

"Aslam sahib," Jaffar spoke out, "You've reached the destination. Go in. Omar, a servant of the household, will receive you. Identify yourself as a trader from Dushanbe and ask to meet the householder."

"Aren't you coming in?"

"I disappear from here. Call this number when you are through."

Omar, a tall but stooping person opened the gate with a squint-eyed welcome.

"Alam here from Dushanbe. Is the householder in?"

"Step in."

He guided Bhagat to a second floor room, where the designated householder was seated on a rocking chair. This was Bhagat's first meeting with the master spy.

"Aslam here sir, ***assalam-u-alaikum***."

"That's fine. Hope you know the rules of the game?"

Alam accosted Bhagat in the confines of the safe house.

"Yes. I've not seen you and haven't met you."

"And you visit Mazar-e-Sharif consulate with a diplomatic bag, before returning to Delhi via Dushanbe and Moscow." Alam added.

"That's how it is, sir."

"Okay. What's the big panic?" Asked Alam.

"The boss is highly concerned over Harfan's security," Replied Bhagat, "The deployment of DF in Jhumra area is an ominous development. The boss feels that the likely exposure of XXX shouldn't lead to your compromise."

"Do I have the authority to neutralise XXX?"

"I can't comment on it. Here's a sealed cover from the boss. I understand you've to take a spot decision."

"I understand, but you, as the case officer should know better. Have you noticed any streak of indiscipline and defiance in him?"

"He's a complex person, aggressive, acerbic and argumentative. But he has a loving nature too." Bhagat added.

"That's what worries me, his love for life and his dear ones. I suspect he's too involved with his wife and child, much beyond the needs of his cover. He's too egocentric a person to survive as a deep cover spy in a hostile country."

Bhagat didn't like to butt in and contradict the top Indian asset. He wasn't on a debating mission.

Alam went through the letter and scribbled a reply and sealed it personally.

"Hand over this letter to the boss. Keep your trap shut."

"Roger sir," Bhagat stood up to leave, "I've been briefed by the boss personally."

"That's fine. Keep it that way. In our profession silence is the golden rule."

Alam dismissed the meeting.

The mysterious Jaffar silently picked him up and asked Bhagat to remain ready for an early morning pick up. His Aeroflot flight to Dushanbe was scheduled to take off at 06.30 hrs.

****

For the second time Alam was surprised in quick succession.

He hadn't expected Jamilla and Parvez at Harfan's Jhumra nest.

Ibadat had given the all-clear signal. The assorted team of Army Signals Corps and the Joint Intelligence Signals of the ISI had finished scanning the general area. They couldn't pinpoint the safe house that sheltered the clandestine wireless station.

The only new thing that happened to Chak Jhumra was the arrival of the 3rd Corp. General Sahbaz was a friend. Alam had traded with him, on usual terms, when he had headed the AHQ Task Force that supervised short listing of the new weapons systems.

The brief meeting with General Shabaz at Hotel Royal Palace confirmed Alam's suspicion that the SigInt sleuths were chasing some unidentified wireless station. The Pakistan army was developing Chak Jhumra as the tactical reserve command post for the Lahore front. The new radar formation was designed to give added capability to the existing radar stations at Sargodha.

"It's tough time Shabaz," Alam spoke with an anguished voice, "It is unfortunate that India is imposing another war on us so soon."

"Well brother," Shabaz spoke in his buoyant military style, "We must fight a final war with Hindustan. Islam must again rule over that ***kafir*** country. And personally I welcome another round of war. We can make more bucks if more wars are fought. You supply the weapons, I get my cut and you get your commission. It's business as usual.'

"It's not like this General. I am concerned about the innocent lives."

"Ha! You make me laugh Alam. It's you who peddle the weapons of death. You should not cry over the body bags. Look this war is going to be decisive. The Bengalis will cease to exist as an ethnic entity."

Shabaz threw up his hand in excitement and summoned a junior officer, who stood guard near the entrance.

"Have the Signals boys arrived Wasim?"

"Not yet sir. I believe they are reaching in another two days."

"Fine. Tell Major Wadood to see me straight away, before he redeploys his DF monitors."

"Copy sir."

The young Captain saluted and affixed himself again near the entrance.

"Are you expecting more troops General?"

"No Alam sahib. These SigInt boys have created a fuss over some clandestine signals, which, they say, were originated from Jhumra."

"Oh shit. It's an additional headache."

"It's nothing. You cannot differentiate one signal from the other. No one affixes trademarks on the carrier waves. It could be from my unit and even from the Bhagantanwala base."

"It's a great pleasure to meet you again General. I was here to finalise some supplies to the Bhagatan base. I should drive back to Lahore tonight."

"When are you crossing the Atlantic again?"

"Very soon, may be in another fortnight. Any service for me?"

"It's a minor matter. My daughter is in Virginia. She requires some cash. Can you pay her the amount?"

"How much?"

"It is about $ 5000. I will return it in Pakistani currency."

"Don't bother General. We will adjust it in another business deal. Let the young kid enjoy herself."

"So nice of you Alam. ***Khuda Hafiz***."

"***Khuda Hafiz***."

Alam said goodbye and brushed past Ibadat, who had approached the table with a decanter of water in his hand.

"I'll see you soon."

"***Ji*** (yes)."

Ibadat saluted the General and politely asked if he would require some more water. General Shabaz tipped him lavishly and signalled at his aid de camp, the young captain, who was still affixed near the entrance.

"Let's make a move boy."

"Yes sir."

The General's convoy zoomed away after raising clouds of smoke.

Harfan had expected the sudden visit of Alam, his uncle from Peshawar. But Jamilla wasn't pleased to have a houseguest. She wanted Harfan all to herself. The pangs of unquenched thirst burnt like fragrant camphor. She missed Harfan's unique love play, which turned her wild and propelled her into an ecstatic journey, transcending her physical limits. Harfan's proximity helped her in sublimating the physical desire to an amorphous pining, which created a void somewhere within. Jamilla simply wanted more and more of Harfan. All the layers of her consciousness were shrouded by the unique love-chemistry.

She was worried too over the rumour mills that had started broadcasting stories about Harfan's links with Malika Jahanara. Pakistan wasn't a big place and Malika Jahanara wasn't the dullest sex kitten around. Harfan's casual contacts with Malika, like all bits of gossip around her, didn't take time to travel down to the lanes behind Lahore's Masti Gate.

Nawab Sharief, beaten by Israr in the arms lifting contract, had taken personal care to drop the gossip in Zahoor Chaudry's intimate circles. He wasn't known unnecessarily as an invisible viper that lurked below the skin. Israr was to be demolished at any cost, and Harfan being both his spearhead and shield, came under his direct line of fire.

Words travelled faster than light to Zahoor's inner courtyard. Jamilla didn't believe in what she had heard, through the remote and distorted transmission by Nawab. But she didn't want to take chances. No, she couldn't. Harfan was too dear and precious to be left alone to the mercy of an enchantress. Her prolonged absence might push her man into the arms of other women. That wasn't an uncommon malaise that affected the male psyche. The ***mullahs*** hadn't framed any rule for male chastity. Only the women were expected to tighten the belts around their groins.

Well! Who wouldn't like to seduce Harfan, the finest flesh and spirit fleeting around! She was his mooring and anchor and she wouldn't allow him to be uprooted by any freak storm, Jahanara or Nawab. Her love, she knew would be an all-compassing mantle of protection for Harfan.

Alam finished with the superficial formalities of greeting Jamilla and Parvez and walked back to Hotel Royal Palace.

"What's the problem with Harfan?" Alam asked Ibadat, his Operation Qurban.

"My friend in the ISI tells me that they picked up his trail from Malika Jahanara's pleasure abode."

"Who is your friend?"

"The information is authentic. The ISI has started a probe."

"That's a disaster. Has he been dancing around her?"

"Not exactly. She's in the eye of the storm, of intrigues and conspiracies."

"How did he walk into her trap?"

"At his level of operation he couldn't avoid it. And Nawab, Israr's brother is after Harfan's blood. He thinks he can destroy his brother by neutralising Harfan." Ibadat argued his case with a straight face.

"What about this Direction Finder problem?"

"They had stationed one mobile scanner a few days ago near his house. Another station has been installed 3 miles down south, towards Mianwali."

"Anything specific?"

"They suspect clandestine transmission."

"How the hell did he get mixed up in all this?"

"Can't say sir. The only important development in between has been a mysterious visit by Nawab Sharief, and his exclusive meeting with Mian Harfan."

"Fucking hell. Why did he get involved with that crook?"

"Can't say for sure. Nawab was heard threatening Mian Harfan with dire consequences over some business deal. Perhaps it has something to do with an airlifting operation and hiring of some German aircraft. I am not sure."

"Didn't you try to find out?"

"I thought I'd better not."

Alam didn't like the terse reply, but decided to digest it.

He was posted with the developments in General Naqi's office. The General and Brigadier Habibullah had awarded the airlifting contract to Israr International after the CIA backed out from loaning two Boeing 707s. The Democrat Congressmen and the Senators had stiffly opposed any open CIA involvement in the East Pakistan imbroglio. Israr had greased Naqi's palm and Harfan Bukhari had warmed up the pockets and bed of Habibullah. Nawab, on the other hand, had depended on Generals Hyder Bux and Amanulla, and had poured money into their thirsty gullets. But Israr finally won the battle, thanks to a mighty wink from Malika Jahanara.

"Why is Jamilla baby here?"

Alam lighted a cigarette and asked.

"They're husband and wife. What's wrong in it?"

"Everything is wrong." Fumed Alam. "This was a marriage of convenience. We didn't want to write a repeat script on a sob love story."

"We're dealing with a human being, not a machine, sir. I think he should be helped to get out of the mess created by Nawab Sharief." Suggested Ibadat in a soft voice.

"Agents are controlled machines. Don't ever try to inject emotion into your work." Alam sounded a warning.

"Keep your antennae open. We can't afford to misfire. The missile has to be shot down if it deviates from its flight path." Alam spoke coolly, but looked at Ibadat with burning eyes.

A rattled Ibadat served coffee silently, spilling some. Alam's last few words; spoken coolly through his teeth almost carried the debris of the aborted missile.

"***Kyon mian*** (what's the matter)?" Alam looked up.

"Sorry, I lost control of the pot."

"I don't want to lose control on Harfan, remember that." Alam sipped the cream topped coffee with relish.

"And watch out for the ISI surveillance teams."

Alam wiped his lips with a hanky, which had AA inscribed in one corner, and prepared to leave for Israr Sharief's factory.

A for Alam was clear to Ibadat, but he couldn't figure out the second A. Did it stand for Almighty? He spoke like one, nonetheless.

"I'm expecting Israr sahib. Receive him courteously and serve the grandest launch you have in your menu."

"Don't worry. I'll take care. Please enjoy the drink meanwhile."

For Israr, the luncheon meeting with Alam was as welcome as the appearance of the Gabriel, from the cosiest niche of ***Allah***'s very private heavenly abode.

They shared frothy beer and spiced Mughlai food and discussed the predicaments of Israr International. His company, Israr revealed, had clinched the contract for airlifting war materials from Sargodha to Dacca, via Colombo.

The CIA chartered cargo aircrafts for ferrying of men and weapons to Dacca were abruptly withdrawn following furores in the US Congress. CIA's Phuket based airlifting operations had also been suspended after stiff protests from the Kremlin. Israr shared with Alam that the Indian intelligence had gathered precise evidence of direct CIA involvement in the East Pakistan imbroglio. New Delhi had circulated a few colour photographs of CIA cover-flights, operated by a fictitious Ohio based aid organisation, apparently flaunting the banner of World Wide Charity, which provided relief to the victims of hunger and plague. The Indians, like elusive cygnets, had done a thorough undercover job, distinctly disturbing the placid White House poodle.

The Secretary of State, according to Israr, had stoutly denied US involvement and blamed the Indians for obstructing humanitarian services in cyclone-ravaged East Pakistan. But the photographic evidence circulated by the Friend's of India, a Delhi funded organisation of the Hindu diaspora, at the United Nations had nailed Washington's lies.

The CIA friends had asked Rawalpindi GHQ to hire private chartered flights. Funds, they said, would flow in from Fort Knox.

Israr had roped in a West-German company to fly the war materials. But the flights were grounded before any one of them could take off. India had tipped off the West-German human rights groups, through their Socialist International conduit.

Brother Nawab, Israr lamented, had played a dirty game too. Beaten in the airlifting bid he had leaked out the information to Izaz Afroz. The maverick politician didn't take minutes to broadcast it in his public speeches.

"Nawab's tricks are understandable, but why Izaz Afroz?" Asked Alam Khan.

"That sly fox plays his own game. He keeps egging General Arif on to crush the Bengalis. But his subterranean strategic moves are directed at denigrating the military ruler. He hopes, I think, to pick up his ***Kohinoor*** from the debris of a devastated Pakistan."

Israr spoke eloquently and succinctly.

"Yes, I understand Afroz's compulsion," Commented Alam, "He's one of the Trinity, bent upon destroying Pakistan. The other two are, I believe, General Arif and Sheikh Jainal."

"Is that his end game?" Asked Israr.

"Haven't you heard of the Larkana Tea party?" Asked Alam, "There's a story that, General Arif and Izaz have reached an understanding to abandon East Pakistan and defeat India in the western front."

"That's too dangerous."

"Who bothers Sharief ***bhai*** ?" Alam lighted a cigarette, "We, in West Pakistan haven't tolerated any Bengali rule over us. P-A-K-I-S-T-A-N, as coined by a Muslim Cambridge scholar doesn't have the alphabet- B-for Bengal. It's a remote colony of the Punjab. Izaz will be the last person to allow Jainal of B to preside over his holy P for Punjab and S for Sind."

"Why?"

"Leave that alone Israr sahib. We Punjabis and Pathans are still haunted by the ghost of Hindu domination. The Bengali Muslims are three fourth Hindus, worse than the Indonesians, where Islam is still shrouded by the Ramayana and Mahabharata."

"But, I've serious problems. Perhaps you can help." Pleaded Israr.

"It's always a pleasure, order me sir."

"Can you arrange a few chartered flights for my operations?"

"Where is my nephew?" Alam asked in his usual booming voice, deviating from Israr's sob story.

"He's a gem of a manager. His untiring efforts have brought us several new contracts and ***Insha Allah***, my company will register rupees 500 million in profits this year." Israr was effusive in his praise of Harfan Bukhari.

"I suggest you get him involved with the airlifting operations." Alam pitched in for his protégé.

"That's precisely what I want to do. But, I need two Boeing 707 cargo planes to carry the merchandise to Dacca. The Germans and the French have reneged at the last moment, as I've already told you."

"You shouldn't go to the West to solve such problems. They have mighty problems with the law and the so called human rights. I've some South African friends, who would be ready to help out at a higher premium, about 10% more. Can you live with that?"

"Excellent! No problem. The bucks, anyway, come from Langley. How long will you take? Why don't call your African friends?"

"The mercenary flights are risky. The carriers have to be given proper cover, a fresh coat of paint, call signs and the registration details. Dacca isn't another Khinzagane, lost somewhere in the African forest. The Indians are present everywhere in East Pakistan. The Hindus are fuelling the Peoples' League movement. You should have a plausible and acceptable cover for these flights."

"You're correct. Can you suggest something?"

"Hope you've consulted General Naqi and Sarfaraz."

Alam lighted another cigarette, scratched the back of his smooth hairless pate and continued.

"Sending international relief items for the cyclone victims should look as the most plausible ruse. That's what the CMLA wants to project. Doesn't he?"

"Great idea. Give it any plausible cover. The GHQ is desperate. They want the immediate augmentation of military hardware in Dacca. Call your South African friends immediately." Israr handed over a cordless phone to Alam.

"Don't use phones in such sensitive matters. The PIB and the ISI might have hooked you up to their love bugs. And there are several Bengalis in our telecom services. Better use a captive wireless set. Have you got any?" Alam asked.

"No. They won't give licence to a private operator." Israr replied.

"Ask your CMLA friends. I can get one from Dara Adam market, if your friends have no objection. That's a wonderful place to make fascinating purchases. Got an operator?"

"General Naqi may possibly agree. The circumstances are favourable. I'll require a trained operator."

"Talk to Naqi and confirm your requirement. I'll take at least a whole day to get the set and another one to install. No questions asked. Tell Naqi that private German and South African operators own the cargo charters. They're mercenaries. They carry men and materials to various troubled destinations. Our bosses shouldn't suffer from soul pricks about apartheid, because of South African involvement. Hope this will have the clearance of the big police boss."

"Who?" Israr asked.

"The White House ***yar.*** They're the supposed conscience keepers of the free world."

"I've to check with General Naqi."

"It's your ball Israr, at the post. Catch it or allow it to go past the net to Nawab's lap."

"It won't be Nawab, in any case. Come to Sangla with me. I'll like to discuss few more details with you." Israr closed the discussion and picked up the phone to make an urgent call to General Naqi, Defence and National Security Advisor to the CMLA.

Chapter 39

Harfan accompanied Alam to his Jhumra residence. He drove silently as Alam grilled him like a veteran criminal lawyer.

"What's the big problem? I hear you got hooked up to this lady Jahanara." Alam remarked in a caustic voice.

"I'm no hookworm and there was no hooking up. But I had sensed the ISI watchers stalking me. I noticed it first, when my stay in Lahore's Faletti coincided with her stay in the same hotel." Harfan explained in simple words. He didn't like to elaborate on his intimate visit to the den of the enchantress.

"What about the Direction Finders?"

"That's what I picked up from my own sources. Ibadat had seen a few antenna fitted vehicles moving in the general direction of Jhumra."

"That's bad. I'm going to decommission the set. Hope you've secured the electronic devices adequately."

"Not yet. But I can give you a location drawing of these gadgets."

"You should have better knowledge of the history and geography of Pakistan. Before you jump into the ring be sure that you know the dramatis personae well."

"What're you gunning at?"

"Before you walked into Jahanara's den you should've known that the Generals are at each other's jugular, and some of them are plotting the ouster of General Arif Khan. Malika is in the eye of the big twister."

"I just met her once, courtesy Nawab Sharief."

Harfan replied in a straight voice.

"Remain miles away from that plague. He isn't happy with you and Israr. You can't afford to take a false step and expect to survive the crash, my dear. This is a merciless game. Delhi is highly alarmed at what has transpired."

"I don't think we've reached that critical stage yet."

"Don't be so optimistic. Ours is a one way journey."

"Don't repeat the doomsday forecast too often. I hope I've some liberty to innovate. That's essential for my own survival." Harfan was tired of hearing the stale warnings once too often and decided to hit back.

"You can't jeopardise the security of the agency." Alam retorted.

"Is that more important than my personal security and that of my family?" Harfan replied with a tone of finality.

"What family? You've no family. It's only a part of your cover. Take it from me dear. Don't develop roots in this country. Yours is a transient existence."

Alam replied curtly. He concentrated on smoking, but displeasure was written all over his face. He was surprised. The mechanised doll, Harfan, the secret agent seated next to him, had started developing a mind of his own!

That was simply an invitation to disaster.

How could he think of a permanent family in Pakistan? The fool should know that in his trade such families were mere props, to be changed at short notice. Jamilla was nothing but a station wife, as good as a hired whore. He must warn Delhi. It was high time to reassess the security grading of Triple X. The devil had started living beyond his brief, accepting the mirage as real. He must be chastised and disciplined before it was too late.

The dinner, served by Ibadat, was excellent. But the ambient was as chilly as the point zero in the North Pole. The taut facial muscles of both Harfan and Alam and the distant vacant looks in their eyes had alarmed Jamilla. She excused herself and retired to the bedroom with Parvez after exchanging a few superficial pleasantries.

Alam and Harfan sat over a drink and reviewed the developments, which had possibly put the ISI on his trail. He snubbed Harfan, in a hushed voice, for walking into Jahanara's trap. Sensational reports could wait and be missed. There had to be no display of bravado and no misadventure. Life of a spy wasn't really like what the fiction authors would like their readers to believe in. Indiscretion could endanger his life and love, his wife and son. Was he ready for that? The ISI wasn't likely to drop the trail of a suspected spy, they never did. The intelligence fraternity scarcely slept over their targeted goals.

"Look Alam sahib," Harfan opened up, "It's but natural for the ISI to target counter-intelligence suspects. I feel there's more to it than what we perceive. It is more than likely that Malika is the target and not I. I suspect a bigger conspiracy around the Head of the State. The powerful Generals and Izaz Afroz want him out. I'm just a part of the side show."

"That's what I told you. It makes the situation more vulnerable. You can't afford to be sucked into the vortex of Pakistani power politics. Pakistan isn't your State and General Arif isn't your Head. You're here on a mission." Alam retorted.

"It's not really possible to completely distance myself from the happenings around. Especially when I'm required to move, eat and sleep with them. You should've selected different target areas, if you're so squeamish about the chastity of your agents." Harfan hit back with equal force.

"It's not chastity I'm talking about, it's your neck. And where's the need for you to get involved."

"I'm not emotionally involved with the crowd around. My business cover takes me to them."

Harfan's diffidence surprised Alam. He hadn't expected the high profile agent to genuflect before him. But he couldn't agree more with Delhi that Triple X's security couldn't be viewed in isolation. He would become, if he hadn't already, a plague-spreading rat, once the ISI succeeded in perforating the thin diaphragm of his cover.

His own security would be in jeopardy.

Alam decided to guard his hide. He had a longer race to run.

"Take it from me Mian Harfan," Alam spoke tersely, "Your bravado comes out of your immaturity. I suggest you take up the airlifting operations to Dacca. Israr will bite the bait."

"Will it help?"

"Yes. Only a patriotic Pakistani will stick his neck out in such risky operations."

"I don't mind." Harfan replied.

"Okay. General Sahbaz also gave me to understand that the SigInt team is likely to return in another two days. Allow me to dismantle the radio set. The ISI should draw a blank on this front, and I've found another use for this machine. Thank God, I did."

Alam suggested a short outing for Harfan and Jamilla. A trip to Murree, at least for two days, should give him enough time to dismantle the set and cleanse the house of all electronic gadgets.

On his return he would receive instructions on alternative communication channels.

And for Jahanara, Alam added, Harfan should continue a low-key contact. A sudden severance could thicken the ISI broth of suspicion. Things should look normal. No feathers should appear to have been ruffled.

"Don't commit mistake, let no emotion or attachment come in your way. In an intelligence mission you're a lone traveller. And remember," Alam lighted a cigarette, "I have the authority to eliminate you, if you become too embarrassing. That's the rule of the game. It's is the same for all agencies, all over the world."

"You treat me as shit? Am I not giving my best, my life, for the country?"

"Don't be a fool," Alam whispered, "In this trade nobody reclaims a loser. You've to earn the right to your tomorrows."

Alam's voice reminded Harfan of the lost property simile used by Nampoothiri.

"What security do my wife and son have? Why should I go by your orders?"

"That's what you've been planted in Pakistan for. You can't plough a different furrow. Your orbit is well defined."

"That's not acceptable. My wife and son are more important to me than your bloody work." Harfan nearly revolted.

"Sorry Mian Harfan. A spy never falls in love at the cost of his trade. They are a part of your cover. Rest is hallucination. Enjoy it, as long as it lasts. Don't believe in it. The moment you do, you violate the cardinal principle of your trade."

"Withdraw me, if you're so panicky." Replied Harfan.

"It all depends on Delhi's final assessment. They're the people to decide your new cover."

"What's new about it?"

"Your cover is like the seasonal slough of a cobra. You shed it periodically for regeneration and survival. Make it a part of your life as long as your profession needs it." Alam gestured towards Harfan conveying a message of finality.

The phone rang sharply as Alam finished with his admonishing.

"Hello Alam," Israr came alive on the line," They agree on both counts, South Africa and the communication set, with one condition."

"What's that? "

"The operator will be theirs."

"It's your problem. What about my share?"

"What share? We're doing it for Pakistan." Israr replied in an injured voice.

"Don't get hurt dear. We're all patriots, but we're businessmen too. The Army bums are bleeding the country white and spitting on ***Quaid-e-Azam***'s ideals. Tell me one good reason, why should you and I, two honest businessmen, not expect our risk money? The Generals don't pay, the bucks flow in smoothly through the Potomac to the Indus."

Alam made his point with a deliberate emphasis on ***risk*** and ***Potomac***. It was no joke to get involved with the South African mercenaries, most of who could as well be hardened war criminals of the Third Reich.

"You've a point. We'll take care of that. What's your expectation?"

"It's reasonable, I'm not expecting the moon, "Alam lowered his pitch to a conciliatory decibel," The HF set will cost rupees 3 million. For the airlift I claim 3% of the total hiring charges."

"That's rather high. If you take three, the CMLA sharks will take another five. Where do I stand?" Israr expressed his helplessness.

"You take another 4% over the usual 3% commission. That's a fat cut. You'll be the largest beneficiary of this military stand off between Hindustan and Pakistan. And that won't make any dent on Fort Knox either." Alam assured Israr about the soundness of his arithmetic.

"It's a drain on the country." Israr still tried to project his patriotic concern.

"Sharief sahib," Alam made a final effort to free Israr's conscience of the patriotism bug, "The Army and the politicians are chewing the country anaemic. We, poor businessmen, should honestly expect what every businessman around the world expects, nothing more, nothing less."

"Tell me when can you finalise the deal." Israr shelved his wounded sense of patriotism.

"Give me a day. I have to get the wireless set from a delicate supplier at Dara Adam. Wait for my next message, your eggs will be in the right basket, at the right time. Tell the bosses."

"That's fine with me and General Naqi." Israr replied.

"Tell the bosses that the pilot, co-pilot and crew may not have impeccable character sheets. They don't have, in this line of philanthropic mission," Mian Alam chuckled, "My friends don't accept crew from the end users, it's their trade speciality. Who'll liase? Don't trust too many barrette tops."

"That's an important point. Harfan suits me."

"I hope Naqi won't have any qualms with a civilian!" Alam asked.

"I don't think so. He wants a chic cover operation. It's hush hush business with them. And I'll get it cleared from Sarfaraz."

"I hope the ghostly shadows of the CMLA office wouldn't raise any objection?"

"Do you mean the ISI? Forget it. Naqi is very secretive about his dear ***Operation Millat***, that's the nom de plume he has assigned to the airlifting exercises."

"I'm happy. Hold on a second, Harfan wants to say something."

Alam advised Harfan to seek permission for a short break to Muree.

Israr welcomed the idea. With Jamilla around he should recharge his batteries and be prepared for a tough job ahead, working out the nitty-gritty of the chartered flights.

Harfan bade ***Khuda Hafiz*** and left Alam to go about his job. In the darkness of the bedroom his mind focussed on a slice of the moon that peeped on Jamilla's face. She was fast asleep, her hand placed on Parvez. This face of Jamilla, saddened by a thick cloud cover, was new to him. The pale moon enhanced the shadows under her eyelids.

What was wrong with her? She hadn't spoken a single word since her sudden arrival a day ago. Her eyes, whenever he tried to engage them, appeared flooded to the brim, ready to breach the banks. Had Nawab Sharief carried the Jahanara tale to her as well?

Oh no! Harfan shuddered to think about the consequences, in case Jamilla had got to know his Jahanara episode. He had experienced her love and ecstasy, but this clouded look was new. He wasn't adept in handling such a situation.

Should he wake her up and tell the real story? Which story? The story of his real identity? His accidental amorous involvement with Jahanara?

No. This wasn't the correct moment to present Jamilla with the harsh truth.

His thought process frog-leapt to Alam's suggestion of getting involved with the airlifting operations. Not a bad idea at all! It might give him a spasmodic breather, till he hit upon a tunnel to bolt from Pakistan with Jamilla and Parvez.

What next? Facing the ISI hatchet men? Not yet. The ISI wouldn't find Triple X a dead frozen rat, before he actually died. And death was the last item in his agenda.

Prospects of trips to Dacca suddenly brought back to his memory the names of two Bengali officers. Major Anjum Mani of the Special Services Group and Wing Commander Ahsan Khondokar, a Bengali officer with the Eastern Command Pakistani Air force. The innumerable business contacts with them had flourished into a friendship. Both were immensely helpful, in their own way, in neutralising the assassination attempt on Mandira. Especially encouraging was the latest assurance offered by Major Mani, during his last visit to Dacca.

Things had been moving very fast and East Pakistan had become South Asia's new killing field. He ruminated over the thought briefly and fished out a peg in a remote corner of his mind to hang the faint hope of escaping to the safety of Dacca. He smiled. He was again gambling with destiny, and the Dacca plan was a long shot gamble, the chance of winning being 1:100.

The moon disappeared. The faint blue of the night lamp added new shades to Jamilla's pink limbs and Parvez, drawn to her bare bosom.

It was a heavenly piece of sculpture.

Harfan didn't have the heart to disturb the placid serenity of the frame. It was a divine image. Perhaps he had forfeited the right to disturb Jamilla emotionally. The moment of truth was knocking at his door. His real identity would surely shatter Jamilla's dream world. He wouldn't blame Jamilla for turning her face away. Would she be scared to see the real colours of his bones?

Perhaps, yes. Maybe, not.

Behind her frail frame and tender mind Jamilla harboured a tensile courage. He had witnessed glimpses of that courage soon after their marriage, when he had tried to persuade her to dump the gold coins presented to her by Rama Bai. She wasn't a Hindu, she said, but she was determined to preserve the coins. This was from a mother to a daughter, from one woman to another woman. What difference did it make if Rama Bai was a Hindu?

But how would he fill in her emotional scars, inflicted by his acts of treachery? Perhaps Jamilla's love for him would evaporate instantaneously. She wouldn't hesitate to wash him out of her existence, like she removed accidental specks of dust from her eyes, by simply splashing cold water on it.

Would she really do that?

Harfan moved near his favourite window that opened out on to the forest greens, tapering down to the murmuring river. The distant rippling sounds and the moon hanging on the remote smoky horizon failed to soothe his ruffled emotions.

Perhaps Alam was correct.

His love for Jamilla had transcended his cover identity, carefully crafted by Delhi. Ramendra Kaushal, the wild son of the wild king of Jhumra had died long ago. His rebirth as Harfan was reshaped by destiny, around Jamilla and Parvez. It wasn't the same Harfan Bukhari chiselled out of the factory of Bhagat and Maulana Rizwan.

No. He could under no circumstances dupe Jamilla. He couldn't plan his life without them, at any cost.

Jamilla turned back on her bed. Harfan could see two silent drops of tears rolling down her cheeks. The wound, whatever it was, had hurt her and it was indeed deep.

Her sphinx like silence tormented Harfan.

No. He wouldn't allow Jamilla to suffer from silent agony. Her silence was cooler than sculpted ice on a frozen mountain spring. The waves were silent but eloquently resonant.

Harfan closed the window and shifted to the drawing room and over another cigarette suddenly remembered Alam's pronouncement of his having a licence to kill. Would he go for Jamilla and Parvez too? No. Not even Alam could arrogate that licence. He must survive the churning clouds of the impending typhoon and survive with his love and the essence of his new existence intact.

He was a better merchant of death and destruction. Harfan released his clasped fists and stretched himself out on the sofa. Alam wasn't correct. He couldn't kill a Kaushal at will, on his own or on Delhi's orders.

A spy reserved the right to live for another day, beyond his tomorrow. He couldn't be executed at the altar of patriotism and putrid animosity, which was rooted back to the middle ages. These fanatics branded humanity by their rotten religion.

No. He would allow neither the ISI, nor the NSI to have the pleasure of liquidating him and his love. Well! If his spy-cover weren't more tangible than a cobra's slough, he would discard it, at the appropriate moment. He knew the story, as they said back at Jhun Jhunu. The cobra's venom turned more potent after every seasonal change of slough. Mian Alam Khan would find this new slough tougher than veritable steel armour. He would rub off the stigma of a spy, if the final crunch demanded it from him.

Harfan switched off the hall lights and stretched his body on the sofa. He required some rest before cruising to Murree first thing in the morning. Mian Alam would have a free run of the house for electronic sanitizing.

He would like to make it a second honeymoon, Harfan mused, in his favourite Pines Hotel at Nathia Gali. At this time of the year, in the blinded rains, they would require light woollens. Harfan made a mental note to remind Jamilla about the need for woollens.

Oh yes! He shouldn't forget to call the Pakistan Tourism Development Corporation to book his favourite honeymoon suite for two nights.

Harfan, lost in his thoughts, failed to co-ordinate the conflicting signals. Alam, ISI, Direction Finders, Nawab Sharief and the moist eyelids of Jamilla—the rush of past events rolled over fast against the canvass of his mind. A sudden black curtain dropped in to cut off his thoughts and Harfan simply dozed off. His brain had peaked to the brim and the circuit automatically switched off.

Chapter 40

Alam carried out 'operation sanitization' in a professional manner. It took him two hours to dismantle the HF wireless system along with the antenna and protective lead cover of the sunken chamber. Ibadat helped with minor masonry and painting jobs to hide the tool marks and other telltale signs. Alam examined the restoration job and suggested textured denting and soiling of vulnerable spots, which were likely to be examined by trained counter intelligence sleuths.

"Smear the underground pit with charcoal dust and kitchen grime," Alam instructed Ibadat, "And soak two leather shoes in warm water and place them below the pile of other shoes and used linen."

"What for?"

"That'll create an antique effect. The grime, charcoal and fungi mixture will make even the toughest investigator nauseous."

Ibadat went about his job meticulously and ended by burning the high-grade OTPs (one time cipher pads) and flushing down the ashes. Alam fished out several electronic spy gadgets from wall crevices and finally left for Hotel Royal Palace with two brief cases stacked with the incriminating evidence.

He slept well and woke up little before lunch to be greeted by Ibadat and a steaming cup of coffee.

"Morning sir, it's time to get ready."

"Morning Ibadat. I'm as hungry as a wolf. Lay down my favourite Peshawari dish. Just allow me time for a nice steam bath."

Alam enjoyed the Peshawari meal, but his mind wasn't on it. He was engrossed, pondering over the daredevil traits of Harfan and the unexpected metamorphosis he had undergone. The valuable agent had started imagining the mirage to be reality. He had donned the Jamilla cover like another layer of skin, which had developed parallel capillaries and vessels. His cover had started breathing in fresh flow of love, care and the dangerous symptoms of a desire to live. Harfan's desire to live beyond his cover could endanger other operations in Pakistan. His own existence, Alam guessed, might face serious jeopardy.

Should Triple X be allowed to breathe freely?

Alam munched over the thought along with pieces of roasted beef. His head gave a decisive jerk. This high profile agent, Triple X, should be snuffed out at an appropriate moment, before the ISI closed in on him.

Should Delhi be taken into confidence?

Not necessarily, Alam concluded.

He would tackle this minor problem all by himself.

Alam smiled under his thick moustache.

He remembered the day he was sent down to Kabul, as an aspiring Muslim trader who made good his escape from Hindu India. His immediate family, as the cover story unfolded, was slain by the Hindu zealots. The FIB had borrowed the name and identity of the supposed son of a Muslim trader in Thane, a burgeoning town in the vicinity of Bombay that had witnessed orgies of killing in the wake of the partition of India.

From Kabul to Peshawar to Islamabad and now right into the eye of the storm, it had been a long walk through the minefields of deception and charade. Starting with a small export-import venture at Khyber Bazar, Jiwan Bahutule alias Mian Alam Khan, Delhi's Alamgir, had emerged as a respectable international trader, vital to Pakistan's defence quests.

His minions, operating in the international sub-ways of illegal arms peddling, procured weapons from pistols to tanks, missiles and jet fighter-bombers to small naval crafts for the Pakistani armed forces. His services were used in the recent past for the clandestine procurement of uranium granules and red-mercury from East-European countries, for Pakistan's infantile nuclear facilities.

The schemers of the Cold War used his services too. He had developed innumerable contacts in the predominantly Central Asian Muslim Republics of the Soviet Union and helped the CENTO allies in opening up subterranean weapon supply channels to the Islamist rebels. The name of this patriotic Pakistani was well known to the key US security and intelligence departments and inside Pakistan he was both respected and feared for his legendary connectivity with the top military and political leaders.

Now he controlled at least five resident agents, planted by the FIB and its inheritor, the NSI. He was India's one and only magnificent spymaster in Pakistan, who enjoyed the authority of affixing and ejecting any talent from his orbit.

But, for how long!

An emotionally raw ram like Harfan could set off an avalanche of disaster.

His second home in Switzerland, where his wife lived with their children, always allured him. Perhaps he too was getting tired with this cloak and dagger game. The onerous responsibility of mastering the art of living with multiple identities had started eating into his personality. Who was he in real life? Was he the same orphan from Maharashtra? Was he a Pakistani or an Indian? Was he a Hindu or a Muslim? He had forgotten his own self, Jiwan Bahutule who had started from a modest background and who simply desired to have a secured job and a nice family. The endless game of deception he played on others had started deceiving him.

Should he call it a day? Should he wind up his tentacles from Pakistan and disappear into the salubrious climes of Switzerland?

No. He couldn't. For him there was no short cut to ***nirvana*** (beatitude). He was destined to live the cover; till he was caught or bumped off by the ISI or until Delhi decommissioned him.
He wondered which one would happen sooner.

"Sir, the ISI agents have taken several rounds of Jhumra in recent weeks. Some of them have made enquiries about Harfan." Ibadat poured another beer and whispered.
Alam didn't reply. Ibadat continued with the motion of pouring beer, while talking.
"Brigadier Barqat, the ISI team leader, was a guest in the hotel. He quizzed me," Ibadat added, "And my friend Karamat Suri and another cruel officer Arman Ali Niazi have been temporarily deputed to locally investigate our friend."
"Has anything special come to your notice?"
"General questions, about Harfan's place of origin, his workplace, in-laws, wife and friends."
"Proceed...."
"The ISI is probing his links with Jahanara. They suspect his amorous links with her. Karamat tells me that the ISI chief wants to stage another coup." Alam looked up at Ibadat and asked through corners of his eyes.
"Is he really involved with Jahanara?"
"Sir, she's a seductress. No virile young man can escape her. Either she takes them to bed or she destroys them. She must have licked Harfan too."
"What gives you that feeling?"
"He loves his wife and child."
"How genuine are his feelings for them?"
"I think it's serious. He may do anything to save her and the child."
"Even sacrifice himself?"
"Possibly sir." Ibadat served Alam some mutton ***biriyani*** (spiced rice)."
"Look Ibadat," Alam negotiated a chunk of bony meat and spoke with a slurry drag, "I must share with you today. There is a possibility that Harfan is related to the former king of Jhumra. It is possible that he may resemble his late father. Have you heard any rumour about that aspect?"
"Sir," Ibadat feigned to open up to his handler, "My mother had once mentioned this to me. I mean this aspect of Harfan's resemblance with the former king."
"You did not mention this to me."
"Sir my mother is an illiterate woman. She is still glued to her past."
"Who else may be aware of his suspected linkages with the former king?"
"If I am correct sir," Ibadat spoke with feigned hesitation, "Rama Bai is the only other person who can recognise him."
"Who is she?"
"A deranged woman from the remnants of the former royal retinue."
"Are you sure?"

"I guess I should be correct."

"Is she safe?"

"No problem. But Karamat tells me that she has preserved some paintings of the late young ***maharajah*** that resemble Harfan."

"Destroy them and if necessary kill the old lady. Don't be sentimental about it. Do you think Karamat has reported this to the ISI?"

"I cannot prevent him sir."

"You should not. Keep this channel open. Why don't you kill the lady before the ISI sleuths reach her? Can she withstand torture?"

"She appears to be a silent granite, doesn't react to anything around her."

"Keep me posted. You may have to eliminate her. Wait for my orders. Don't call the Quetta safe house number. Call Peshawar. Kill Harfan, if the ISI breathes heavily down his neck. Keep this."

Alam passed on a .38 automatic colt, with a sawed off barrel.

"Use the weapon wisely. If it's too hot for you here, escape to Kabul. We'll rescue you from there. Hand over this cover to Harfan, personally. I expect an ISI raid soon. Conceal this carefully. If you can't hand it over, destroy it. Don't dare to open it, you know the cost of curiosity."

"Is it necessary to destroy Harfan?" Ibadat asked.

Alam looked up, wiping the froth of the beer froth with a napkin and buried his teeth on a piece of mutton.

"Any objections? Look Ibadat, in our profession we strictly go by orders. If the decision is to snuff him out, you carry out the order with no question asked."

Alam finished his lunch leisurely, boarded his Toyota and drove off towards Peshawar.

He was in a hurry. A firm date was to be kept up with Israr Sharief. Before that, he should be able to talk to his friend Doug Chris, in Paphos, 150 km from Larnaca, the capital of Cyprus.

Doug Chris, his arms-bazaar friend, headed a chartered airline and flew in and out of the jaws of death, wherever there were wars, conflicts and rancid odour of death. Doug, a one time lieutenant of the elite fighter squadrons of the Third Reich's Luftwaffe administered the show with aid from an able partner, Voodoorume, a South African of Indian origin.

Athena Air Lines, as the merchants of death liked to call their baby, operated in every theatre of proxy and dirty warfare. Often they hawked fiery hard ware for and on behalf of the CIA, Mossad, SAS and the KGB; practically everybody. Doug and Voodoorume worked for all conceivable clients, obviously for fat compensation packages; often touching astronomical figures, all paid into numbered accounts in Switzerland. Their last big assignment, Alam recalled, was in a West African country, where they ferried weapons for CIA surrogates and to Columbia, for the Cuban and the KGB paymasters.

The philosophy of war was ingrained in Chris's soul. Nations would continue to kill each other, with or without any valid reasons. Killing was one of the oldest passions, almost as old as the sexual exploitation of women. People killed each other for scores of reasons—anger, frustration and jealousy and in paranoiac and schizophrenic fits. They killed in the name of God, land and love. Didn't Cain kill Abel, simply because his Lord had preferred the offering of his brother?

So? What was the big deal in killing? His big boss, the Fuhrer had killed millions, for waht... Living space? Racial hatred? Anger? Frustration?

Why bother to figure it out? He might as well have been a compulsive paranoid killer.

The philosophy behind killing people was very clear. Green dollar bills flew in from all directions just because people wanted to kill and get killed. And why not poor Doug and Voodoo could gather some, by practising the honourable trade of facilitating death and destruction.

For Chris, war was another honourable business, the most profitable and most eternal, more eternal than the stupid ideologies of emancipation, ***nirvana*** and ***moksha*** (salvation) put together. The loonies invented this humbugs much later. Killing and war came first and would reign over human society, till Armageddon.

Alam was amazed by Doug's philosophy of life, but didn't violently disagree with it. His life was dedicated to a kind of war, a secret war, fought by nations, in the name of espionage. He was another soldier of fortune, who didn't return home to heroes' welcome and for whom wishes for tomorrow were like loony dreams.

His thought process shifted from Doug to Harfan. He was to attend another urgent call of duty; send a report to Nampoothiri. Harfan was on the edge of jeopardy. It wasn't so serious, but the chances of his bumping against the ISI sleuths were real. What worried him most was Harfan's unconventional attitude towards his cover. The machine had developed a mind of its own.

It would be too risky to allow Harfan to operate in Pakistan. He should be withdrawn or temporarily decommissioned. Changes in operational strategy and a midway course correction were over due.

If these weren't practical, and the ISI really closed in on Triple X, his physical neutralisation would be the most convenient route to safeguarding India's remaining operations in Pakistan. Some vital assets, including himself couldn't be compromised, because of the idiosyncrasies of an unpredictable agent.

The decision had to be cruel. A surgeon couldn't help but amputate a gangrenous limb. Harfan had developed a serious infection. His mind and ideas were infected by the stupid beautiful dol.

A streak of pity travelled intermittently somewhere inside Alam's cortex, sympathy for both Harfan and Jamilla. But he reaffirmed the silent decision to liquidate Triple X. Harfan alone was responsible for peeling off several layers of his cover, by his acts of indiscretion. And he had donned the cover, foolishly believing it to be a part of his body and soul. A spy lived his cover as long as it lasted. Not beyond that.

Walking into Nawab Sharief's trap was Harfan's second act of great foolhardiness. To secure his business interests Nawab had pushed

Harfan into the sex-cage of Jahanara. And that forked-tongued younger Sharief was known for pushing venom into the veins of his benefactors, at the first available opportunity.

His political coalition with Izaz Afroz and a few ambitious Generals meant trouble, tremendous trouble for General Arif Khan and Malika Jahanara. And Harfan's neck was more fragile than were those of the brown rabbits scurrying along the shores of Lake Rawal.

Alam wondered if Nawab could be the invisible informer who had put the ISI onto Harfan's trail. It was possible. General Hyder was his personal friend and business partner. He would do anything to demolish Israr, now on the threshold of bagging a few hundred millions more, out of the airlifting operation. To get at Israr, Nawab was sure to demolish his first shield, Harfan.

The picture presented a confusing collage.

Should he initiate an 'operation neutralisation' of his own? No harm. Delhi was too far away and their reaction time was often painfully stretched out

Alam breathed easy. The decision to neutralise Harfan was his own. Ibadat would fit the role of an executioner well. Till than 'operation airlifting' should be the convenient dust cover. That would provide a breather and take the ISI off Harfan's trail.

The days ahead, Alam felt, were likely to be gory. He smelled cordite and blood, and heard the not too indistinct tentacles of the nemesis catching up with Triple X.

That's when he'd signal Ibadat to pump the bullets in. Time was the essence of strategy.

Alam steadied the wheel and accelerated. The Grand Trunk road started vanishing under his wheels like a celluloid reel, sans the arc lamps.

****

Harfan's Peugeot chugged along the asphalt snugly and whizzed past Lake Rawal. He slowed down as it started climbing the hills towards Murree and on to Nathia Gali. The asphalt below and the rushing air around orchestrated a rhyming sound, keeping pace with Harfan's pulsating heart...blip-blop-blip-blop.

His heart was in agony. It was in great pain.

Agony was because of the hazy uncertain future, and pain for Jamilla's silence, which hung over her face with a pre-cyclonic ember glow. She hadn't talked to him since her unannounced appearance at Jhumra. Neither could he venture a guess, from her injured looks, whether the frozen cyclone was about to unleash itself in torrents of snow and fire.

Young Parvez, fast asleep on his mother's lap, with a lavish black tuft of hair on his head and exquisitely curled up lips, looked simply like a miniature Kaushal; the disinherited potentate of Jhumra.

Harfan smiled. Yes, Parvez was the third generation claimant to the lost kingdom, perhaps a better claimant, being born to a Muslim Pakistani mother.

What a funny quirk of fate!

Harfan played Jamilla's favourite Bade Ghulam Ali ***thumris*** (light classical music) in the car stereo.

She ignored the lure of the music.

Her eyes, not really fixed on any particular object, wore a vacant, remote look. She wasn't looking at Harfan, even from the corners of her eyes. Her elegant long and black eyelashes stood erect, like guards, not allowing the lids to close for even a second. Harfan was amazed to see her gaze, lost somewhere beyond the horizon! She looked like a sculpted image, except for her moist pupils. Accumulated tears were about to escape the brims of her eyes.

What was hurting her? Had she overheard his discussions with Alam?

Good heavens! Harfan shuddered to imagine the portrait of an angry Jamilla. Their moments of togetherness left no space for anger and even feigned aloofness. The intense universe of their love transcended the finite space of physical proximity and an invisible serene glow encapsulated them, in the charged clouds of the monsoon skies.

They pulsated in joy all the way, often lighted up by internal thunder charges, often drenched by the rain of love and care. The chemistry was much more exalting, which brought in a sense of togetherness, somewhat akin to the sky kissing the earth, with tongues of fire.

But today Jamilla looked different. She covered herself with an impenetrably mysterious mesh. Harfan switched off the stereo, slowed the car down and parked it under the portico of a wayside motel.

"Shall we have some breakfast?" He asked, expecting Jamilla to respond.

"If you so wish," She replied without looking at Harfan, her eyes still scanning the horizon, "And Nanha Mian (Parvez) needs feeding." She alighted, collecting the folding pram.

Jamilla moved to a corner of the room to breast-feed Parvez. Harfan lighted a cigarette and ordered Jamilla's favourite dish; minced-meat-stuffed fried flatbread, served with mint and garlic sauce, followed by coffee.

Harfan broke the bread, garnished it with sauce and took his fingers near Jamilla's mouth. Her eyes, an over flowing sea of tears, looked straight into Harfan's, quivered for a fleeting moment and breached the banks in uncontrollable sobs. Her body shook in wild spasm.

"What's my fault? Why are you punishing me?" Harfan took Jamilla gently into his arms and helped her to put Parvez on the pram. She continued sobbing with muffled sounds.

"You can't do this to me." Harfan lightly kissed her lips.

"Am I not beautiful enough? Have I lost my charm?"

"Why do you ask this? You are the essence of my life." Harfan wiped her eyes and cheeks with a handkerchief.

"Tell me, what I hear about that ugly fat Malika is wrong." Jamilla again burst into tears.

So, the story had reached her as well.

Who could it be? The ISI crooks? Nawab?

Well! He'd figure that out later. Jamilla's doubts must be dispelled first.

"Absolute nonsense. The only time I met her was when I delivered some medicines on behalf of Nawab Sharief. You know him, Israr's brother. You shouldn't believe in rumours."

Harfan lied with slick smoothness, as if he was consciously duping a lie detector. He added a little dash of spontaneous emotion to what he had just said.

"***Allah kasam*** (by god)?"

"***Allah kasam.*** You're the highest truth in my life, perhaps higher than the ***Paigambar*** (pbuh)."

"Don't say that", Jamilla put her fingers on Harfan's lips, "***Allah*** is the greatest and his ***Nabi*** (messenger) is above us all. But, why did Nawab call up father to say that he had chosen a wrong man for his daughter?"

"It's because of business rivalry Jami. You know this Sharief tribe is full of vengeance, ready to kill at the slightest provocation. Though they've lived in the Punjab for centuries, they haven't forgotten the wild Chingiside traits."

Harfan enlightened his wife in detail, the deeper implications of the business rivalry between Israr and Nawab; the latest one being the contentious arms lifting operations.

"That means you'll be flying to Dacca, braving Indian fighters all the way!" Jamilla closed in.

"I can't avoid that. Our company's committed. It's a national commitment."

Harfan tightened his grip around Jamilla, whose spontaneous heat accelerated his heartbeats.

Jamilla moved in closer, kissed him with a full thrust and flattened him against the bed. This was one long kiss, Harfan felt, would never end.

"Let's eat. I haven't eaten for the last 24 hours." Jamilla broke the bread, laced it with the hot sauce and put it in Harfan's mouth.

"Let's not waste time driving to Nathia Gali. Can't we go to a more quiet place. Nathia is always crowded."

Jamilla, back to her spirits suggested, as Harfan switched on the ignition for the final lap of the journey.

"Not a bad idea," Said Harfan swerving the steering, "Let's go to Taxila, only 45 km from here, say about an hour's drive. We can stay in the PTDC rest house. Being a Buddhist centre Pakistanis normally don't go there."

Jamilla pushed in the stereo button and her favourite Bade Ghulam Ali's voice filled her senses as nothing else could. Her world was again lost inside the man she loved.

****

After an enduring and satisfying session of love making, nearly after three months, Jamilla covered her bare body with a pink sheet and moved closer to Parvez. It was time to feed him.

Harfan climbed out of bed, stood near the open window and lighted a cigarette. His mind raced on another track.

Should he open up his heart to her? Tell Jamilla all about his real identity, his mission and discuss their future together? He could probably convince her of the compelling circumstances, which had made him succumb to the FIB blackmail. It wouldn't be difficult to convince her to leave Pakistan for a safer haven somewhere in mid-country USA. They could live an anonymous life, comfortably. Why not? It was possible.

Should he unburden his heart completely?

Harfan dithered. No. Probably he couldn't take her back to the wild days of man-eater Ramendra Kaushal, who rampaged the Delhi University campus, peddled drugs, raped women and killed unsuspecting friends. That simply wasn't her world.

Harfan involuntarily shook his head and pushed the idea back, deep into the lowest strata of his medulla. Yes, the serpent should remain buried there, for all time to come.

He moved closer to the bed.

Jamilla was fast asleep. Parvez was busy playing with the locks of her hair and giggling out warm uncertain happiness.

Harfan made a little space for him in the bed. Parvez was still busy throwing his limbs about in the air and making sweet sounds. His eyes recognised Harfan and his face lighted up in a broad smile.

That was an invitation to some heavenly pleasure. Harfan played with Parvez, the very games he had played in his mother's laps. Drops of tear rolled down his cheek. How could the kid Ramen, called Ramu by his mother, transform himself to a criminal? When did he leave his mother's cradle and walk into the world of Ram Karan, Vidyasagar Suri and Matang Singh? Why did he kill that innocent girl? His father was not a criminal. Was it in his blood? Harfan wiped the teardrops and resolved that he would not allow such terrible things to happen to his son. He must live beyond Alam and the ISI to prove that he had performed penance for his mistakes. Only that could, he thought, give some solace and comfort to his mother Kaushalya, who waited back at Jhun Jhunu for her son to return from his foreign assignment.

The resolve helped Harfan to recompose his determination and sleep finally enwrapped both father and son.

It wasn't a deep and dreamless sleep.

Harfan's consciousness hovered around Jamilla and Parvez. It travelled back to Jhun Jhunu, around his mother.

A warm feeling of happiness and anxiety enwrapped him. He wasn't alone any more. He had become many and the seeds of millions were still pulsating in him and inside Jamilla and their son. He couldn't take a decision all by himself. Jamilla was an integral part of his existence. She wasn't just another layer of his secret cover, to be discarded on Delhi's orders.

Harfan slipped out of the bed again.

His mind traversed fast over the endless horizon of life and love. They were fast asleep, and perhaps another part of his life was spending sleepless nights at Jhun Jhunu.

What about his nemesis? His profession?

He had seen the ugly looks in Alam's eyes. He knew that killer look, that look of utter disdain, when the resolve of final rejection flashed out from Alam's corneal mirrors.

There was no friendship in this game. The bastards, who called themselves bosses, were guided by the blind mindset. The most sacrosanct rule, which Bhagat had taught him, was that everyone had a price. Pay the price and close the transaction. That's what a spy's life was all about, worse than a sex-worker's. The NSI wouldn't come to his rescue. They wouldn't for sure. They did not reach out for their lost baggage.

But, Ramendra Kaushal wasn't a two-penny whore, hawked in sleaze market by his former benefactor, Ram Karan Prasad. No. He wouldn't surrender to Alam and Delhi. This son of the Raja of Jhumra, Dayaram Kaushal, who had ruled over the unruly Niazi tribe, wouldn't buckle down under pressure.

His son, Prince Ramendra wasn't on sale. He would fight back the forces of General Hyder Bux. He intended to live the existence of a blazing fire and pass on the flame to Jamilla and Parvez. He wasn't a flashy spark, to disappear into a dark void.

The intelligence bosses should add a new dictum to their dictionary: the buck stopped here, at the door of the Kaushals, the kings of Jhumra. Some creatures weren't for sale at all. The science and art of intelligence should discover a new formula for tackling them. They had none at present.

The resolution calmed down Harfan's mind. He felt like praying, for the first time perhaps in years. He wasn't certain whom to call out in his prayers. The ***Allah***? His ***Paigambar*** (pbuh)? Lord ***Krishna***? Or should he bow down before his family deity, Mother ***Kali***, the supreme source of all eternal energy?

He felt confused.

Finally he bent down on his knees, recited the holy ***Qalma*** followed by the ***Gyatri*** (Hindu hymn for sun worship), he had learnt from his mother, a must for every Hindu. Harfan folded his hands and worshipped Goddess ***Kali***, praying for Jamilla and Parvez's long life and strength for himself.

He perceived a point of light appearing on the front wall and a ray of tranquillity travelling inside of him, from the centre of the mysterious light. He closed his eyes. He felt strong and reassured. He decided to wait for the right time to share his secrets with Jamilla. They'd flee Pakistan to the safety of the USA or perhaps Canada.

He wasn't going to sit around like a pregnant duck and offer the pleasure to Alam and the unknown assailants of the ISI to take pot shots at him. He had negotiated death, like an expert dealer, not too many years ago. Why should he now be afraid of facing the moment of truth?

That truth could come only in the form of executioners, say, in the form of Alam or the ISI spooks. It didn't make any difference to him any more. He wasn't afraid. He had identified the enemies and was ready to strike back.

Sleep and peace suddenly enwrapped tormented Harfan. Like a battle-scarred soldier, he slept well, a soldier's sleep, awaiting and anticipating the next moment's blinding showers of bullet and death. He was, however, determined to defeat both, the NSI and the ISI. He resolved to live beyond the dark nights of war and devastation. To live for and with his love.

Chapter 41

Lt. Gen. Sarfaraz's black mood had partially brightened up after General Tarakki swooped down on the Bengali traitors in Dacca and other major urban centres of East Pakistan. The valiant Punjabis and ***muhajirs***, who had made East Pakistan their homes after the partition, had also joined hands with the Islamist groups headed by the Razakars, Ansars, Al Badr and Jammat activists and fanned out into the riverine rural belts. The treacherous Bengali Hindus and their Muslim collaborators were haunted down and liquidated mercilessly. However, most of the eligible women were taken as war booty and distributed amongst the valiant Islamic warriors. General Tarakki's tanks and armoured vehicles had mowed down thousands of Bengali traitors and Indian collaborators in front of the Dacca University and were given mass burial. Hundreds of dead bodies were thrown into the Buri Ganga and Shitalakshya rivers.

Sarfaraz appreciated the commendable work done by General Hyder in identifying the leading troublemakers and the suspected Indian collaborates. But he was worried about the reports of rebellious activities of the Bengali officers of the East Pakistan Rifles, the East Pakistan Infantry and a few senior police officers.

More disturbing were the reports he received last night from Robert Armstrong, the Deputy Chief of the US embassy in Islamabad. The no-nonsense American diplomat was forthright in his assessment of the situation. the Indians had infiltrated the parochial and separatist movements in Sind and Baluchisatan. He produced apparently convincing reports on two meetings between Sartaj Jamil and an Indian diplomat at a restaurant in New Jersey and a crucial meeting at Kabul between an identified Delhi based agent of the National Security India and Aliullah Mengel and Ashfaq Yusufzai, the rebellious Frontier leaders.

India, the US DCM cautioned Sarfaraz, had finalised plans to flood both Sind and vulnerable tribal pockets in Baluchistan with sophisticated weapons through the land and sea routes. The State Department, he said, had decided to send a friendly demarche to the Indian Mission in Washington after consulting the CIA and the NSA. But the American action could only follow after some tangible ground actions were taken by Islamabad and tangible proof were produced.

The Bangkok station of the CIA, Robert Armstrong revealed, had also reported the visit of an Israeli mercenary, Yossi Dayan to the Thai capital and some remote areas in Aranya Prathet in the north and Phuket in the south. A CIA agent had trailed him to a nondescript Greek restaurant at Nana Road. A vital meeting between a senior

Indian diplomat in Bangkok and Yossi was documented. But the details of the transaction could not be recorded. The CIA's archives had authentic docu-mentation on Yossi's visit to Singapore about thirty days ago and his involvement in supplying weapons and ammunition to various theatres of conflict. A consignment from Yossi to the Armenian terrorists, who fought against Turkey, was confiscated at a Black Sea port. The US, Armstrong had warned Sarfaraz, had reasons to believe that India could have tapped Yossi for supplying weapons to the Bengali separatists through the sea route.

"You can bring pressure both on Tel Aviv and Bangkok to prevent Yossi from succumbing to the Indian allurement."

"The Tel Aviv government might agree. But I must warn you that there are several Jewish secret organizations, which support various anti-Semitic and anti-Islamist groups. The Israeli government has little control on them. These organizations headed by fanatic Rabbis and Hitler's concentration camp survivors are as fanatic as some of your Islamist ***jihadis***."

"What about screwing up the Thai government. They should have no problem in preventing Yossi."

Sarfaraz had argued with the US diplomat.

"I think Sarfaraz you are expecting too much from us. The Thai army is as faction ridden as yours are. A General, who is known for thriving on arms and drug trade, controls the Aranya Prathet tract. My government wanted me to share this information with you and I have done my job. These are unsigned reports. The embassy wouldn't own these up if you happen to leak to the media."

"What do you suggest?"

"Talk to our CIA station chief and ask your own Int. boys to follow up the leads."

"Our President would perhaps like to talk to Washington. These are very serious developments."

"I suggest Sarfaraz you first get into action and sound out Washington for further consultations. I have no other comment to make. Bye."

Robert Armstrong's visit had again thrown the Principal Staff Officer to The President and the CMLA into a spanner. The US DCM would not have visited him if the reports were not vetted and cleared by Washington. It meant real trouble. That bloody lady in Delhi was working on multiple strategies to encircle Pakistan from within. By ***Allah***! His government was still sitting on its haunches on the vital issue of airlifting weapons and men to Dacca. What the hell was happening? What was Hyder doing? Why did his intelligence machinery fail to gather these earth-shaking reports? What was General Naqibullah doing? That holy ghost of an advisor to the CMLA never took him into confidence, as if he ran a parallel government. He should have started off with the airlifting operations by now.

Sarfaraz dialled the number of General Naqi. The Defence and National Security Advisor to the President enjoyed a special relationship with the top man. He was perhaps the first of the new-breed army officers. Recruited in 1949, Naqi had not been exposed to the secular traditions of the British Indian Army. A migrant from the Indian held Poonch in Kashmir, he hated the Indians much more than any other

Pakistani did. He prayed five times a day and observed scrupulous fasting during the ***Ramadan***. He conscientiously followed the prescriptions of the ***Hadis***. He was perhaps one of the few officers who had pioneered the movement for allowing the officers and men of the armed forces to maintain long beard and moustache, as prescribed by the scriptures. Left to him, Sarfaraz shuddered to think, this zealot would one day revert Pakistan to the Sharia rules, no booze, no women and no fun. Naqi's idea of an Islamic Republic was modelled after the strict ***fatwas*** (edicts) from the Al Azhar of Egypt, the fanatic Sunni Wahabi fundamentalists of Saudi Arabia and their nineteenth century Indian protagonists.

President Arif trusted him for reasons other than his religious proclivities. General Naqi was too junior to challenge the power brokers all by himself and being a Kashmiri he lacked the vital networking amongst the Punjabi ***biradari*** (brotherhood). Additionally he was married to the daughter of General Nayeem, the PIB chief and the elder brother of General Arif Khan. Naqi possessed another sterling quality. He and Jahanara were on excellent terms and the duo satisfactorily and somewhat honestly worked as the proxy-snouts of the President, in matters of realizing cuts and commissions from almost all the deals that involved more than Rupees 10 million.

General Naqi dropped in within 10 minutes. He was a man in hurry. That's the impression he liked to throw all around.

"Anything urgent sir?" He asked Sarfaraz even before he took his seat.

"Yes Naqi. I have been informed by usually reliable sources that the Indians have started augmenting arms supply to the Bengalis and to some Sindhi and Baluchi traitors. What are you doing to augment the supplies to our eastern garrisons?"

"Well General, you know the situation very well. The Chinese supplies have piled up at Sargodha. But the CIA and the German approaches have been stonewalled by the dirty Indians," Naqi opened up defensively, "We are now depending on the party hired by Alam. I believe this guy is a Cyprus based German."

"Have you met this guy personally?"

"Yes sir. I had a meeting with this fellow Chris and his partner, a South African of Indian origin at London."

"Is it safe to have an Indian on board?"

"I don't think he is anything beyond a mercenary. His family had migrated three generations back."

"That's okay. When do you start the sorties?"

"My first consignment will leave Sargodha day after tomorrow. The delay has been due to some blockage at Colombo. I believe the old lady over there has finally relented after the US President spoke to her and assured a development grant of $ 500 million."

"Not a bad bargain. I believe Israr has won the contract."

"Correct. This man has wonderful reach to the top. And he has that excellent executive Mian Harfan. He is the main liaison officer."

"Are you not attaching any other officer from the regular forces?"

"Oh yes sir. I have designated two liaison points. Brigadier Mustafa will be at Sargodha and Brigadier Saigol at Dacca. In fact, this fellow Harfan is a dust cover to convince peeping toms in Colombo and

Dacca, that he represents the Red Crescent and is engaged in carrying relief materials."

"How many sorties will you require?"

"About 24 at the present estimate. It may be increased if the American supplies from Turkey arrive in time."

"Go ahead Naqi. Take care that the Indians and the rabid Bengalis do not create any problem with these flights too."

"The cover is water tight sir. And these mercenaries are well adept in this business. Additionally I have talked to the Air Chief to provide some air cover, at least from the funnel of the Bay of Bengal."

"I believe that's a nice additional precautionary step. Good luck Naqi."

"***Insha Allah***, I'll fulfil the target within the stipulated time."

General Naqi saluted the PSO and marched out with his usual air of a man being in absolute hurry.

General Hyder Bux arrived pretty late. Nawab Sharief, who had almost bored him to death over a private luncheon at the Rawalpindi Club, caused the delay. The junior Sharief had a litany of complaints against his elder brother Israr and his 'treacherous' executive, Harfan Bukhari. Why could Hyder not clinch the airlifting deal in his favour? He had paid a fat advance and was ready to pay more.

Hyder wanted to abort the frustrating discussion as politely as he could and rush back to the office of Sarfaraz. He was aware of the mischief potential of Nawab. The viper was sure to rush to Izaz Afroz, his political mentor. Izaz, Hyder knew it well, would pretend to shed a few drops of tears and assure Nawab the top chair in the Punjab after the elections to the national and provincial assemblies were over. And finally both of them would whisper in the ears of some delicate media friends. Hyder was aware of the aborted CIA and the German deals. He was interested in Nawab securing the contract. But Israr clinched the deal after offering 11% commission to General Naqi, who fronted the President in all such deals.

What else could he do?

"Look Nawab, I know you have been hurt. So I am. But certain things are beyond control."

"Don't take cover behind a sterile philosophy sir," Nawab retorted, "Please try once more. I am ready to match the amount paid by Israr."

"Listen carefully," Hyder spoke desperately, "I would surely try. But take care that you do not talk to the media. This is a delicate matter of the state. I can't protect you if I am asked to investigate the source of the leakage."

"Are you threatening me?"

"No. I am just reminding you that the Indians are on the prowl and we do not want this deal to sour."

"You have failed to take action against that Indian agent."

"Who?"

"Harfan. Are you not convinced that he is an Indian spy? I have given you the proof."

"Don't be silly Nawab. Your vengeful spite does not necessarily make him a spy. Rhetoric cannot sway me. I am working on the leads and I'll take action at the correct moment. Hope you wouldn't pester me on this professional matter at least."

Hyder finally left the Rawalpindi Club and directed his driver to take him to the office of the PSO.

"Ah Hyder, finally you are here."

"Sorry sir. It was very difficult to shake off that barnacle."

"Who is the brave soul to hold up the ISI chief?"

"It's that junior Sharief. He still cribs for the airlifting contract. Tell me how can I help? Sharief paid a whooping 11% cut and bagged the loot."

"I know that. The old man's appetite is remarkable."

"Yes. And Naqi and Jahanara have played their usual games."

"Okay Hyder. These things happen," Sarfaraz ordered coffee and fried cheese balls, "While on this topic I want to share with you what I gathered from Naqi. He is using that fellow Harfan as a civilian cover for the Red Crescent. Hope you have no objection."

"Well, I don't want to put a spanner just now. He is being investigated. He can be nabbed at the right time. Brigadier Barqat is on the job."

"Please take care that the bitch is not ruffled."

"Leave the matter to me. He is after all a nonentity. We can hang him anytime it suits us. Now tell me what's cooking up?"

"Too many broths, Hyder, are being cooked by too many cooks. I think I should consult you before we discuss the matters with the ***Sadr***."

"Where is he?"

"At the usual joint. I have asked Munir to drag him out. ***Insha Allah*** we should have a session with him this evening."

Sarfaraz explained, over several cups of coffee and nuggets of fried cheese balls, the details of his discussion with Robert Armstrong earlier in the day. India, he commented, was determined to strike both in the eastern and western theatres. The Indians had even hired a Jewish mercenary to supply weapons to the People's League, from certain safe bases in Thailand. Most vulnerable was the sea route between the Indian Gujarat and the numerous islands in the vast estuary of the Indus and its tributaries. Sarfaraz suspected that the unfriendly regime in Kabul was collaborating with India for pumping in supplies to Baluchistan and that the KGB was playing a vital role from its bases in the neighbouring Tajikistan.

"What are your views Hyder? How should we proceed? Should this be discussed with the Chiefs of the three Services before we go up to the President?"

"I think that's the right course of action. It's better we meet the three Chiefs at the earliest and examine the US input thoroughly. I have outlined some lines of action in my report. You must have seen those. I feel Nayeem should also be consulted."

"Okay."

Sarfaraz called his aid de camp and directed him to convene a meeting of the Crisis Management Committee at 5 pm.

"Can't we request the CIA to identify the mercenary vessels around the shallow waters of the Andaman in the east and the Sir and Kori Creeks in the west?"

"We can make that request. But how do you stop these tiny country vessels?"

"Our helicopter gun ships can strike from the air and our naval patrol boats can chase them all the way."

"It's feasible. But let us consult the Chiefs."

"I think for the Indus estuary area we can request Zahoor to deploy his assets. He controls almost the entire ***mohana*** fishing community. He is the uncrowned king of these low caste Muslims."

"That sounds pretty good. What are your resources in that area?"

"Almost nil. We have paid attention to the land border across the Kachhch, especially after the last conflict. We have very minor resources in the disputed Sir and Kori Creek areas."

"Why don't you straight away tap Zahoor."

"That fellow Harfan is his son-in-law."

"I suggest go slow on that front. Let's attend the burning issues first."

"I think you are correct. Where do we meet at five?"

"Here only. Think over if we can do anything else in the East Pakistan."

Sarfaraz suggested rather casually.

"Well sir," Hyder jumped out of his chair and went over to the wall mounted maps and ran his index finger over a vast area in the estuary of the rivers Padma, Meghna and Brahmaputra, "I suggest we depopulate these islands, say from Bhola and Sandeep to St. Martin. We evacuate the entire Bengali population from the minor ports around Chittagong and Cox's Bazaar. If you agree we can ask Tarakki to evacuate certain coastal villages of the districts of Comilla, Barisal and Noakhali."

"That's a brilliant idea Hyder. Let's call Tarakki right away. This action should brook no delay."

"This is a major strategic decision sir. Shall we wait for the meeting of the CMM?"

"Decision making in Islamabad is not a matter of joke. The Indians would flood East Pakistan with weapons by the time our jokers finish scratching their baldpates."

Sarfaraz personally dialled the Number of General Tarakki and told him that the ISI chief should be in Dacca tomorrow on a special mission. He should implement the orders being carried by General Hyder in person.

****

The meeting of the Crisis Management Committee (CMM) was ultimately converted to a full-fledged meeting of the War Cabinet, which was presided over by General Arif Khan.

He was not spruced up, as he usually was and wasn't even shaven and bathed. A pungent odour of stale beer escaped his mouth whenever he opened the trap to speak through the cloud of cigarette smoke. In fact, Col. Munir had almost physically helped him out of the pleasure den of Jahanara on the insistence of the Chiefs of the three Services. Sarfaraz had to list the assistance of the Chiefs, as the lady had consistently declined to connect him to the President. The Chief of

Army Staff had conveyed a veiled threat that the President should not at all bother to come out from Jahanara's residence if he was not interested in presiding over the War Cabinet meeting. Conveyed verbatim, the message had completely shaken General Arif, who couldn't risk the displeasure of the three pillars of his regime.

Sarfaraz placed the reports he had received from the American DCM and briefed the meeting about his discussions with the envoy. Finally he outlined four scenarios for the War cabinet to consider.

Scenario one: India's success in pumping in sophisticated weapons through the mercenary sources would deteriorate further the balance of logistics between the Pakistani forces and the combined forces of India and the People's League.

Action suggested:

1. To depopulate the likely drop-zones along the coastal area and deployment of some elements of the armed forces and large contingents of the patriotic volunteer forces of East Pakistan.
2. Aerial surveillance of the area, seizure of all civilian boats and increasing the river patrols.
3. Bombing of the depopulated islands by the Pakistani Air Force. General Arif listened to Sarfaraz with rapt attention and looked up to the three Service Chiefs.

"Do you agree?"

"Depopulating the villages will attract international criticism."

Replied the Naval Chief.

"What purpose would be served by bombing the abandoned villages? Moreover, I don't want to expose the only air squadron that is positioned in Dacca. India would hasten to retaliate once our birds take to the skies. I can't risk losing them before the actual engagements start."

Air Chief Marshal Obaidur replied in a forceful voice.

"What are your views Hamid?"

Arif Khan asked his Chief of Army Staff.

"Mr. President," General Hamidur replied rather officiously, "I can't disagree with the views of Sarfaraz. Our troops are very thinly deployed in the coastal areas. Our naval presence is negligible. I will like to go with Sarfaraz minus the bombing part."

"I agree," General Arif spoke firmly, "Direct Tarakki to initiate immediate action."

"If you approve sir," Sarfaraz intervened without waiting for the Service Chiefs to join the issue; "Hyder may fly to Dacca tonight and supervise the operation."

"Approved."

Scenario two: Indian move to pump in weapons to the Sind partisans through the land and sea routes was bound to deteriorate the internal security situation.

Action suggested:

1. The Navy should seize all the mechanised civilian ***dhows*** (trawlers) and deploy those along the shallow waters between the Sir and Kori creeks and the strategic estuary islands and minor ports.

2. The Naval Chief should consider deploying two frigates in the blue waters within the territorial waters of Pakistan bordering the Indian maritime zone.
3. The services of the ***mohana*** tribal leaders like Zahoor Chaudry should be exploited to neutralise attempted Indian infiltration.
4. The Sindhi leaders suspected to have Indian connection should be incarcerated for indefinite period.

The War cabinet agreed with the suggestions but General Hamidur suggested that additional contingents of the Desert and Sind Rangers should be deployed along the land borders between Sind and Gujarat. He also favoured the deployment of the Hurs of the Pir of Pagaro and other volunteer forces.

President Arif, by now half asleep, nodded his head in agreement.

The third scenario: The joint operations by India and the USSR to pump in weapons to Baluchistan in collaboration with the hostile regime in Kabul could pose the most serious challenge to the internal security scenario. The security fault lines in Baluchistan, he added, were numerous and the Baluch tribesmen were more virulent fighters than the plain Sindhis.

Action suggested:

1. The 7th Division at Quetta should increase its vigilance and seal all the routes.
2. Sustained bombing of some selected villages inhabited by the rebellious Hazara, Yusufzai, Mengel and Mazari tribes should be carried out.
3. Washington should be approached to neutralise the hostile attitude of Kabul. A second track diplomatic team should visit the Afghan capital to convey the concerns of Islamabad."

"Agreed," General Arif suddenly raised his head and boomed out his concurrence, "What is your fourth scenario?"

"We augment our supplies to East Pakistan at breakneck speed and request our friends in Washington and Peking to symbolically move their forces towards the Indian borders."

"The Chinese are committed to come to our help," The secretary cabinet affairs, who was maintaining silence all the while opened his mouth, "I think the President may agree to depute Izaz Afroz to Peking for immediate consultations. Increased Chinese presence on the Indian borders will act as an effective deterrence."

"Not a bad idea. Sarfaraz please request the Chinese ambassador to see me tonight. I think there is no need to involve Izaz at this point of time. But how do you really expect the Americans to move in?"

General Arif looked up at the defence secretary.

"Sir," The white haired bureaucrat spoke with a peculiar North Indian accent, which betrayed his origin from the province of Bihar, "I suggest you speak to the US President and explain the emerging scenario. India's design of creating another Bhutan type protectorate out of East Pakistan is very clear. We should offer military bases to the USA in East Pakistan."

"I agree Shafiq," General Arif endorsed the views of the veteran bureaucrat, "We will deny that pleasure to India. But I want immediate US assistance."

"Sir we have to defeat the Indian propaganda that we have killed millions of Bengali Pakistanis. The US should be made to see through the Indian smoke screen and ensure its naval presence in the Bay of Bengal."

"I think it is better you fly to Washington tonight. Take Izaz Afroz with you. They should be made to realise the orchestrated Indo-USSR design against the American and Pakistani interests in the region. Pakistan is a stable ally of Washington. The dismemberment of Pakistan will strengthen the Russian presence in Afghanistan and Iran. That would make the Cold War too warm for Washington."

General Arif stood up indicating that the meeting was over. He turned immediately back and moved to the head of the conference table.

"Gentleman," He addressed the meeting in an impassioned voice, "Our fatherland is under serious Hindu threat. We are not simply facing another war. It is a ***jihad***. Tell me when our logistics in East Pakistan reaches a viable point. I will not hesitate to hit India first. I will like to teach that widow a bitter lesson."

General Arif's impassioned plea was greeted by applauses.

"When are you leaving for Dacca Hyder?"

"I will leave for the Chak Lala airbase straight from here. The flight should take about sixteen hours."

"Wish you the best of luck. Ensure that the Indians don't find any human habitation in any one of the coastal villages to drop their weapons. Kill and dump them into the sea."

"It will be a pleasure sir."

Hyder saluted and left for the airbase. He felt happy that the meeting by and large had approved the lines of action jointly worked out by him and Sarfaraz.

In a tearing hurry to board the special flight to Dacca he forgot to leave instructions with Brigadier Barqat to defer his actions against Harfan Bukhari and to consult Sarfaraz before he contemplated proceeding against Zahoor Chaudry in any manner.

****

Brigadier Barqat's horde, herded by Jamanat Ali, the veteran counter intelligence sniffer, drove down to Jhumra at the wee hours of the same night and sneaked into the residence of Harfan Bukhari. But he was late by a couple of days, for his kill.

Jamilla, inundated and reassured by Harfan's love was back to her Masti Gate niche. Mian Alam Khan had flown out of Pakistan to a European destination for scouting out new supplies of French ground to air missiles for the Pakistani Army. Harfan Bukhari, the all important sales executive of Israr International was already on the wings of the Boeing 707 of Doug Chris's Athena Air Lines, piloted by Voodoorume, Doug's partner and a South African of Indian origin.

Neither Jamanat nor Barqat were at fault for the delayed action. It took Barqat three days to convince the chief, General Hyder Bux, that a physical search of the residence of Harfan Bukhari was absolutely necessary.

The Direction Finders of the Joint Intelligence Signals and the Army Signal Corps had inexorably pointed the needle of suspicion at a cluster of buildings in Liaquat colony. Search of some selected houses didn't make them any wiser.

Jamanat had insisted on searching the house of his prime suspect, Harfan Bukhari. He believed that it was the most proximate source of emission of the clandestine signals. His suspicion was buttressed by other crucial inputs. The SigInt boys had deciphered a pattern of the suspect transmission. The ghost station came to air on specific days and hours that too for brief durations. It's signal patterns were different from the other identified stations in the general arch, which was marked by Jhumra, Sheikhupura, Mianwali and Bhagatanwala.

Hyder Bux had sounded a note of warning that the raid should be like an act of housebreaking and should be precise and incisive. His rationale was simple and pragmatic. Harfan represented an apex company that was associated with sensitive defence activities. He was married in a respectable family. Malika Jahanara treated him as a sacrosanct pet. No indiscretion by Barqat's boys should ruffle her feathers again. There should be no repetition of the Lahore fiasco. At least not till the present boss presided over the destiny of the nation.

Jamanat had checked out the itinerary of the suspect, before he cobbled up his team, for the late night break in. Telephone tapping had confirmed his absence from Jhumra. The monitors gathered vague indications that the suspect was out on some assignment promoted by General Naqi. Brigadier Barqat's attempts at penetrating General Naqi's shield of secrecy received silent rebuff. He failed to get into the depth of Harfan's itinerary.

To top it all Nawab Sharief suddenly turned up as the messiah of deliverance. The younger Sharief had made a last minute bid to scuttle the airlifting contract by playing up the incongruity of hiring a South African owned chartered airliner. It militated against Pakistan's international image, he argued. A Panamanian company was ready to do the job for less. Brother Israr was in actuality trying to fleece the nation.

General Hyder was more convinced by the dollars Nawab had transferred to his Swiss account than the transparency of his information. He had unsuccessfully hurled, as promised at the Rawalpindi Club luncheon meeting, a few spanners at the fast rotating spokes. But events overtook his last minute desperate initiatives. The deal had already received a final nod from the President, only after Malika had put in a word to him, at a most sensitive physical and psychological moment. And who else could influence the lady except General Naqi! The Defence and National Security Advisor had winked in favour of Israr.

Nawab wasn't the kind of cobra to lower his hood before any adversary. Big brother Israr was dear to him, but his business interests were dearer. And that audacious ***muhajir***, Harfan Bukhari should be shown the garbage bin, he deserved that at best.

A prolonged meeting with Brig. Barqat, over luncheon, helped Nawab unburden his agonies of patriotism, woven around the undesirable links between this small time operator Harfan and the supposed first lady of Pakistan. Was it desirable that a punk like him should contaminate the watering hole of the President of the country?

It wasn't. Barqat agreed.

But wasn't Nawab responsible for pushing Harfan into the lioness' den? He argued.

Yes. He was. Nawab admitted.

But, in sequence of time, that event had occurred, before he was made aware of the seamier sides of this character. Could he be an Indian agent? Was he infiltrated at the highest level for wrecking Pakistan from within?

The probability couldn't be ruled out, Nawab hastened to add. After all, he had procured the medicines from the Indian town of Dehradun, through his Indian contacts. And what about the irrefutable evidence of his powwow with the London based Indian intelligence officer, Chopra?

Wasn't Barqat aware of the shift in the power axis? New realities were being churned out of the wombs of time. This President wasn't likely to survive the next war against India. Crunched between crafty Izaz Afroz and rigid Sheikh Jainal, General Arif Khan was caving in to the inevitable chasm of a galactic collapse.

Only Hyder and Sarfaraz could save Pakistan. Why shouldn't Barqat swim along, with the currents of change, warming his own way up?

It made sense. Barqat agreed. But, he shouldn't miss his additional stars, due in the next few months, and the command of a Division.

Sure. Nawab assured. He would personally intercede with the top bosses and Malika. A little donation to her foreign account would do the trick. Moreover, he was destined to decorate the highest chair in the Punjab very soon. He would even consider Barqat for the post of the police chief of the province.

"And Brigadier sahib," Nawab came out with a final offer, "Israr is minting millions out of the national crisis. If you help me, I'll help you."

"What does that mean?"

"Simple. You help me debunk brother Israr and demolish Harfan; I'll enrich your coffers." Nawab placed his proposal across the table with an honest face.

"That's immoral."

"Barqat sahib," Nawab quipped back, "Pakistani morals have been buried long ago with the Quaid-e-Azam. Everyone is on a ***looting*** (plundering) spree. Why should you alone take the contract for performing a national penance?"

"Nawab sahib...." Barqat tried to protest mildly.

"Leave it to me. I'll ask my London bank to transfer rupees two million to your offshore account. Let's be partners in prosperity. There's is plenty of juice left in Pakistan."

Nawab finished the dialogue with a flourish and pointing out that the ***muhajir*** brat was out on a mission to Dacca and suggested that it was an appropriate time to raid his house.

Nawab's suggestion left Barqat bewildered. He briefly pondered over the fortune, just forced upon him by the most notorious trader in

Pakistan. More than Nawab's argument, the size of the offer convinced Barqat that the Jhumra raid should brook no delay.

But vacillation at the top took the air out of Jamanat's wings.

General Hyder Bux ploughed over the bits and pieces of the intelligence inputs and took three precious days to give a hesitant clearance for a limited clandestine raid. The decision came after prolonged deliberations with the DMI and the Joint Intelligence Signals, a top-secret signal-monitoring outfit located at Malir Cantonment, Karachi.

The JIS chief wasn't sure if the intercepted signals were actually originated by a clandestine spy station. The electronic jamming beams operated by the Joint Intelligence North, another division of the ISI also generated similar signals. These beams, oscillated from the ISI's powerful transmitters were aimed at the Indian radar formations along the western front.

General Sarfaraz was noncommittal over the issue of a raid at the Jhumra residence of Harfan at such a delicate point of time. He required the services of both Harfan and his father-in-law Zahoor Chaudry.

But General Hyder had failed to amend his earlier order before he boarded the special flight to Dacca. He was busy sipping fragrant Ceylonese tea at the VIP lounge of the Colombo airport when Jamanat raided the Jhumra residence of his prime suspect. His mind was focussed on the task of depopulating the coastal villages and dumping two million odd Bengali rats into the blue waters of the Bay of Bengal.

****

Jamanat's men entered Harfan's Jhumra house late in the night, drenched like July ravens, after braving a thunderstorm. Some lighted cigarettes and a few of them hoped to discover a bottle or two of liquid fire from the ornate cellar of the business executive that would warm them up.

"Shut up you fools," Jamanat cursed the chattering ravens, "It's not a marriage party. Stop chattering. I don't want the entire colony to wake up."

But Jamanat was shocked to encounter Ibadat, sleeping in the outer living room. He hadn't expected any living soul, except cockroaches and lizards in Harfan's empty Jhumra residence. He had planned a silent break in, looking for the suspected HF transmitter and other telltale signs of a long-term resident agent.

"What the hell are you doing here?" He thundered at Ibadat.

"Who're you? Leave immediately or I'll call the police." Ibadat charged back with shallow bravado. He readily recognised Karamat Suri. It wasn't difficult for him to log another face as an appendage to Brigadier Barqat's entourage. In fact, Karamat had alerted Harfan earlier in the evening about the impending raid. He was prepared for the show.

"We're from the Directorate of Accountability," Jamanat declared and produced an identity card, "We've orders to search the house for the violation of foreign exchange rules. He has several Swiss accounts."

"Show me the warrant."

"I don't require one." Jamanat brought out his pistol.

"Well, in case you represent the trigger end of the law, as you say, go ahead. Would you like to have some tea? It's so soggy and cold in here!"

"Don't mind. Are you the cook here?"

"In a way sir. Please give me five minutes and I'll get you the excellent tea in this town"

Ibadat moved to the kitchen. His perception of Jamanat's real identity was clear. Only the sleuths of the ISI could move in with such daring impunity. They were law unto themselves.

That sounded a sinister ring. Scratches from the ISI paws, as they said in Pakistan, always ended up in gangrene. The company wouldn't take minutes to strip Harfan off his skin and spirit away his remains to eternal oblivion.

Strange! Ibadat pondered as he stirred sugar granules in the teapot. The ISI never operated under a flimsy pretext. They visited like killer desert storms with all the accompanying thunder, lightening and sandblast. This couldn't be a low-key affair, some officer acting on his own. It must be a planned intelligence break-in, in search of incriminating electronic gadgets.

Must be. They must be from the signal intelligence division of the ISI.

"***Janab*** tea is ready." Ibadat served spiced tea, real Lahoria tea garnished with green cardamom and cloves.

"Excellent!" Jamanat relished the concoction and kept on directing his men.

The junior sleuths, short of ripping the house to shreds, searched all possible nooks and corners. They hammered the walls with rubber truncheons and pried open every possible crevice of the wooden floor.

A constable finally hit the sunken chamber. With a disgusting grimace on his face he pulled out used shoes, clothes and assorted soiled domestic items. His palms were blackened by charcoal powder.

"***Janab***," shouted the constable in excitement, "Here's an underground chamber."

Jamanat rushed in and examined the sunken chamber with the intensity of a scientist scanning remote galactic dusts. He brushed his palm against the floor and walls and examined the soiled black dust. His expectations were belied. All that he could sniff out were sweaty, pungent and husky odors. There were traces of charcoal too. Such chambers were essentially an adjunct of a fireplace for storing coal and chopped wood. The bugger was using it as a dirt store.

"Fool!" Cursed Jamanat Ali. Perhaps that was meant for Harfan.

He ordered an electronic scanning of the house, by using an imported Japanese instrument, capable of locating radiation from the tiniest electronic spy gadget.

The signals proved sterile.

A frustrated Jamanat lost his cool, hot cups of tea notwithstanding. He summoned Ibadat and started interrogating him.

"Why the hell are you here?"

"Sir, the matter is very simple. Harfan sahib is our client. I guard his house, for a small fee, whenever he goes out of town. The entire town knows it. Even brother Karamat can testify that." Ibadat answered with a firm gaze in his eyes.

"Do you know him Karamat?"

"Yes sir. We're from the same locality and it's correct that he earns a few extra bucks by guarding the house of the suspect."

"Where has Harfan gone?" Jamanat turned to Harfan.

"How do I know sir?" Ibadat gave an expression of irritation, "You have to find this out from Israr Sharief sahib."

A burly figure with a pockmarked face approached Ibadat, looked intently at him and asked, "Aren't you the son of the traitor ***bawarchi*** (cook) of that ***kafir*** Hindu king?"

"Yes, but he was no traitor."

"How're you related to this fellow Harfan?"

"Who said that to you? I'm a hotel employee. I get some extra money for guarding his house, whenever he's out of town. Hope you don't grudge a poor man earning a few extra bucks."

"Don't act smart. I'll rip open your guts." Shouted the pockmarked guardian of law.

"Is there any law in Pakistan which proclaim that I can't be smart, and what law empowers you to disembowel my guts?"

Ibadat stood up firmly to the bully.

He now remembered the battered face of the middle-aged person. This was Arman Ali Niazi, who, as a kid of sixteen year, had severed the head of King Dayaram with a forceful blow of his scimitar. Arman, son of a dismissed Niazi soldier of the king, had avenged his father's humiliation. This very same killer had stabbed his father to death.

What a surprise! The killer Niazi was now on the rolls of the ISI. How funny and small the world was!

Arman Ali grimaced ferociously, as if his looks were the sharpest scalpel, ready to perform a complicated operation on Ibadat's chest.

"Don't act funny with me," Arman Ali shouted, "Talk straight or I'll fry your brains for breakfast."

Jamanat pushed his lieutenant aside. The last thing he wanted was an ugly brawl and the resulting publicity. He took over the task of grilling Ibadat.

"Have you noticed any suspicious activity of Harfan Bukhari?

"Sir, I'm your humble servant. I guard the house in his absence. How do I know about his activities?"

"Don't try to be clever."

"Sir, I'm a poor man, trying to earn a few extra bucks. Come to the hotel and give me an opportunity to serve you. That's the job I know best."

Ibadat saluted Jamanat with all the humility he could muster.

Karamat Suri intervened in a slick move.

"I know this fellow sir. As I said he lives in my ***mohalla***. He is a mere cook in the hotel and does odd jobs to earn a few extra bucks.

"Fine. But you must work for me and keep me informed about this character." Jamanat directed the words at Ibadat.

"That'll be my privilege sir. Being a Pakistani I feel proud to accept this task. You can depend on me."

Ibadat saluted again, this time almost prostrating on the ground and touching Jamanat's feet.

Next morning, after a lavish breakfast at Hotel Royal Palace, courtesy Ibadat, Jamanat marched to Israr Sharief's Sangla office. This wasn't a part of Brigadier Barqat's brief. But an honest itinerary check up of his suspect was just a part of the job. Jamanat never left his job half finished.

"What!" Israr couldn't believe his ears, "What made you conclude that Harfan was using a clandestine wireless set? I'm operating one, and General Naqi approves that. You are confused."

"No sir, our technical people are sure about it."

"That's a long shot Mr. Jamanat. Your boys must have confused the signals. The radiation, if there's any, is from my set. Could be from any other set in the general area. May be from the new army Division too." Israr offered an inspection of the set installed by Alam.

"That's not possible sir, we're sure. We've a foolproof system."

"I'm sorry Jamanat sahib," Retorted back Israr, "Your system may be foolproof, but it can't fool the big bosses and me. Where is the set? How dare you blame a patriot like Harfan with no evidence at all? I hope you're in your senses!"

"You don't understand sir. Our direction finding mechanism is more or less precise."

"Fine. Where is the radio set you're talking of? You can't accuse a man out of your lurid dreams. You've raided his house, drawn a blank and now you've the cheek of confronting me!"

"I'm doing my duty, Israr sahib."

"You're rushing into dangerous conclusions, Mr. Jamanat. Do you want to say that you are the only sane person in Pakistan and the rest are mad?"

Israr gave forceful vent to his indignation.

"Sir, I've a job to do. We in the ISI don't leave any reasonable suspicion to flow by the Jhelum." Jamanat replied coolly.

"I know you people live and die with your suspicions. But Jamanat sahib, you're off the mark by 25 km. The set is installed in my office."

"No sir, we're talking about a different matter."

"Come on Jamanat sahib! You're impossible."

"You're not getting my point sir."

"Mr. Jamanat, you're behaving atrociously. Who's your boss?

"Brigadier Barqat."

Israr picked up the phone and called Major Gen. Naqi, Defence and National Security Advisor.

"Hello Naqi sahib," Israr could hardly conceal his irritation, "I've a man in front of me, who feels that my chief marketing manager Harfan Bukhari could be an enemy spy."

"Who's he?"

"He's from Hyder's outfit. He strongly feels that Harfan operates a clandestine wireless set from his home. Look, I'm taking a tremendous risk. You know that Bukhari has volunteered to escort the flights only for the love of the country. The Indians can shoot down his plane at will."

"Sorry friend," Naqi replied in a conciliatory voice, "Let me talk to Hyder. Don't worry."

"The chap here says that his boys have picked up wireless signals from a set installed at Harfan's residence. It could have been from my set."

"Don't expose your set. It's top secret. Hyder should not know about this."

Jamanat's cortices suddenly fogged out, having lost neuronal connectivity in the labyrinth of high-sounding names. How could the Joint Intelligence Signals, the top-secret electronic monitoring unit go off the mark!

The veteran intelligence bulldog was mighty confused. He begged to be excused and left. His enquiries about Harfan's family background had reached a cul de saç at Karachi. They had no lead beyond his uncle, Shamim Bukhari. His papers were genuine, and above all, he had impeccable connections, with highly respectable people.

Jamant looked back at the events. It was Nawab Sharief who had insisted on a direct raid. What could his motive be? Destroying his brother's business empire?

Jamant almost fogged out in confusion. Was the clock inside a veteran like him was slowing down? Was he chasing a shadow?

Were Barqat and the top bosses of the company taken for a ride by Nawab? Was the chief following a blind lead, only because of Harfan's suspected access to Malika's bedroom? Was General Hyder conspiring against the President? Were they using the thin Harfan and Malika rope to hang the CMLA and justify a coup? The stink of conspiracy permeated the air in Islamabad. The President was indeed engulfed in the vortex of conspiracies. It was natural with the politicians in uniform.

Jamanat wasn't sure, which chefs were cooking up what kind of broth and in whose kitchen? He was also not aware too of the 'Peking Conspiracy', hatched between Izaz Afroz and the three ambitious Generals, during one of their visits to the Chinese capital. The rules of the new game were simple; pull down General Arif and install Izaz as the new man of destiny. A few more collaborating Generals would find more spicy and sweeter slots, as part of the compensation package.

Jamanat's reach didn't traverse the super orbit of the politicians and the uniformed rulers. He wasn't supposed to know the smoggy games of conspiracy played by the power mongers.

The Jhumra fiasco left many souls bruised and gory. Israr, gentle by nature hadn't found Jamanat's visit amusing. General Naqi's terse phone call sounded an alarm bell in the ISI's neuronal centres. Another blundering failure meant big trouble for those involved in the messy raid. General Sarfaraz, the mighty PSO wasn't going to be amused.

Jamanat too failed to fathom the murky waters he was marooned in. He approached Barqat with great trepidation and anxiety.

"Sir, I've a big problem on hand."

Jamanat clicked his heels producing a faint metallic sound.

"What happened, have you bungled the raid?"

"It looks like. The house wasn't empty and, I think our cover identity didn't work. That fellow Ibadat, who claimed to some kind of a hotel employee, was present in the house. We drew a blank. There was no indication of any clandestine activity."

"How did Israr come into the picture? Why did you accost him?"

"I met him, basically to compare notes on a new wireless station run by him."

"Fool! You've fouled up again. That's a top-secret operation. You're creating complications for all of us." Barqat mildly rebuked his favourite colleague.

"Sorry sir, but the leads must be followed."

"Fine Jamanat sahib. But, we're living in a whirlpool of paradox. I don't know who wants to saw off and take away which part of the nation. The ***thugs*** and bandits are ruling the country and you can't afford to trample over the tails of any of these vipers." Barqat shared his anguish with Jamanat.

"I agree sir, but in our business we can't afford to overlook reasonable leads."

"I don't understand you. What's the new lead?"

"This fellow Harfan has been commissioned by Gen. Naqi for airlifting armaments to Dacca."

"Don't talk too loudly. It's a top-secret operation. There's nothing wrong with that. It has been cleared by our bosses. Our forces are starving for hardware as well as basic needs like boots and vests. The Indians and Russians are playing havoc with our national security. They're training the wretched ***Mukti Bahini*** (freedom fighter) commandos in more than two dozen camps in India."

Barqat shared some national secrets with Jamanat.

"Not many souls in Pakistan are aware of this. By ***Allah*** Jamanat, don't tinker with this operation."

"That spells doom for me, sir. Israr is sure to approach the top and exhibit his wounds, and demand my blood."

"Don't panic, some damage control measures are necessary, follow me."

"Can anything be done sir?"

"It's difficult Jamanat. The boss is in Dacca. Let's see."

Barqat touched a religious charm, which hung around his neck, given by a ***fakir*** (mendicant). It acted as a shield against goblins, ***jinns*** and mortal enemies, and ensured victory over all hostile forces, human and ethereal.

Allah! He prayed, save me from this fool Jamanat.

The operator at Dacca end saluted Barqat and connected General Hyder promptly.

"Sir Barqat here. There has been a minor act of indiscretion by Jamanat in the Jhumra matter."

"What matter? Repeat."

"The Jhumra raid sir."

"By Allah Barqat, did I not tell you to defer the raid?"

"No sir. I had seen you off at Chak Lala. But you did not mention any change in our programme. I followed up your latest instruction."

"You asshole. I was supposed to tell you that the matter should be deferred. That's what Naqi and Sarfaraz had pleaded with me. We could conduct the raid after about a month."

"Well sir," Barqat wailed out on the line, "We have done it and Jamanat has stepped beyond his brief."

"What should I do with you and Jamanat? Anyway, don't panic and don't create more complications for me. I have to carry a diverse team with me. Did Sarfaraz talk to you about visiting Zahoor Chaudry?"

"No sir. Should I ask him?"

"Leave it. I will speak to Sarfaraz. Seal your mouth and ask your boys to plug their leaking cans till I return. I suggest you call on Israr and tell him that there was a mix up and you are sorry for it."

"I will do that right away sir."

Barqat hung up the line, relayed some terse orders to Jamanat and connected the Sangla line of Israr Sharief.

Israr was a man of infinite patience, but the feeling of outrage, caused by the impetuous and ominous visit from Jamanat Ali had breached his emotional embankments. A small cog in the wheel couldn't thwart the entire operation of airlifting direly needed arms and ammunition to East Pakistan. The nation had a big stake in the operation. Hiring of CIA funded mercenary flights, operated by a thug of the Third Reich and a South African pilot of Hindu origin could blow on to the faces of the discredited Junta.

The military regime was left with very little credibility. The only coins it could still cash in on were the US antipathy for the ruling deity in India and its eagerness to build bridges with Peking. Even the White House wouldn't find this scandal a mouth-watering hors d'oeuvre.

Israr wondered if brother Nawab could be the angel of the hell behind the sinister move! It was possible. The man, born with a satanic strain, though from the same seeds as he was, could go to bed with the vilest forces of ***dozakh*** (hell), if that delivered tonnes of money.

Israr was, therefore, not very convinced by Barqat's courtesy call.

"I understand Brigadier sahib that you all are working under great stress. All of us are. The country is passing through the worst crisis. But how could your men brand Harfan as an Indian spy?"

"It's a genuine mistake sir. The clandestine signals had emanated from Jhumra side and the Mian Harfan's home was located within the narrow circle of triangulation. Let's forget the matter."

"I have no problem. But, please ensure that there is no social damage to Harfan sahib. He is married to a fine lady from an elegant family."

"Be assured sir. We have sealed our lips.

But Barqat's brief visit did not assuage Israr's bruised feelings and the sense of insecurity. He surveyed the scenario and concluded that Nawab was not likely to rest on his haunches. He wouldn't hesitate to throw up more dirt. An urgent consultation with Mian Alam Khan was necessary. This buffoon of an ISI officer shouldn't disturb the airlifting operations just garnered by his company.

Israr Sharief picked up the phone and dialled Alam's Peshawar number.

Alam was intrigued by the call. He was more alarmed by another Live Letter Box call from Ibadat, his XX agent Qurban at Jhumra. The call received through one of his Peshawar business numbers had shaken Alam's bones. This one local talent was highly professional. His coverage of activities of the Army and Air Force units at Jhumra, Mianwali, Sheikhupura and Bahgatanwala produced gold nuggets. He wasn't the type to make any frivolous call. That's what worried Alam most, not the panic call from Israr Sharief. He downed his usual evening Scotch and decided to drive down to Jhumra.

Chapter 42

Israr failed to comprehend the paranoid compulsions of General Hyder in entrusting a delicate enquiry to a blundering junior cop! Nothing could prevent the ISI to bring him under their scanner? Hyder could go to any extent to fatten his pocket. Or was he entangled with any latent sabotage plan? Was he aiming at the President's jugular? That would mean a guillotine on his regime.

That was bad business news. He normally didn't agree with the suicidal policies, pursued by the CMLA bosses in East Pakistan. But the prospect of earning a few easy millions were more tempting than few million Bengalis facing extermination at the hands of Islamabad's butchers.

And he wasn't alone in being outraged. Jung Sher Khan, another important member of the cartel was perturbed too. It must be Nawab, they concluded. And Nawab wasn't a lone fighter. He must have roped in General Hyder and Izaz Afroz too. That again was bad business news. Hyder and Nawab were inseparable business partners.

That called for an intervention by General Sarfaraz Lodi, the all-powerful PSO to the CMLA. He was the correct antidote.

General Sarfaraz wasn't amused by the prospect of receiving Israr Sharief and the weighty Pathan ***sirdar*** Jung Sher Khan in his office. He was outraged and scandalised by the telephone tapping incident and the fact that his name figured in it, as an importer of aphrodisiac from India. What could be more damning at this critical juncture of the power struggle? Not even a Pakistani street dog would lick his dead skin, if it were tainted with Indian honey. What a bloody mess!

He wondered as to why Hyder failed to restrain his boys even after they had discussed the issue only a couple of hours before the raid was conducted. Was it a case of deliberate amnesia? Not unlikely. The foxy ISI chief, his partner in conspiracy, should've been sacked for bugging Malika Jahanara's bedroom. But, the fox knew too much of his mind. Their fingers were locked together in the same trigger, aimed against General Arif Khan's scalp. Antagonising him for the sake of a minor business executive wouldn't be a prudent decision. It wasn't a propitious time to be guided by the law books and the true interpretation of propriety.

His recommendation for changing the ISI chief wouldn't register well with the drunken slob, who spent most of his time between the thighs of that dirty woman. The Army chief and the powerful Corps Commanders of Peshawar, Karachi and Lahore, all Punjabi Jats wouldn't agree. Sarfaraz, an Amritsaria was not considered as an authentic Punjabi. How could a Lodi be passed on as a blue blooded Jat?

Sarfaraz felt he was caught in between the sharp edges of a cleaver. This bloody double dealer Hyder, he felt sure, was in cahoots with Izaz Afroz, the desperate demagogue and warmonger, bidding hastily and nastily for the highest chair. Izaz's game was very clear. He wouldn't allow, ***Allah*** willing, a Bengali to be the Prime Minister of Pakistan again. He was pushing the drunken President to the brink of a bottomless pit, in collusion with a few short sighted army officers, like the time he pushed President Akbar to the precipice of a disastrous war in 1965.

The clever intelligence chief, Sarfaraz mused, was playing a double game. How could he agree, in the same breath, to the proposal of mastering the services of Zahoor Chaudry and ordering a raid on Harfan's Jhumra home? How could he face Zahoor after all that happened?

He did not expect Hyder to commit such a silly mistake. It must be an orchestrated game to outsmart him. Was he alone running to the ribbon? Or Izaz Afroz was involved too!

Well! Sarfaraz, the scion of a proud Lodi family from Amritsar should now make a decisive bid for the throne. Why should he allow that pleasure to Izaz and Hyder? That Sindhi meteor should be smoked out of Pakistan's political firmament, permanently. The only way out was a putsch. But that was an uncertain and yet undefined game. The Air and Naval Chiefs weren't likely to support his move, just about, when Pakistan was on the brink of another war with India.

The Yankees and the Chinese wouldn't welcome any change in Pakistan's political landscape. General Arif, they believed, was their diplomatic points man. Washington and Peking, Sarfaraz presumed, would prefer doing business with General Arif, till India's design on East Pakistan was effectively thwarted. The Big daddy wouldn't like to see India emerging stronger and drifting closer to the Red Bear.

This wasn't the time to agitate. This was a time for introspection and fathoming the waters around him. He looked up at his aid de camp, whose smart salute suddenly snapped Sarfaraz's escape to his fantasy world.

"What's the matter?"

"Sir Mr. Israr and ***Sirdar*** Jung Sher Khan are here."

"Please bring them in."

Sarfaraz stood up and opened the door himself. Jung Sher Khan was not only an important leader of the Pathan ***jirga*** (assembly); he was a trusted friend of the President too. His followers in Baluchistan and the NWFP had wholeheartedly supported the military crack down against the Indian inspired rebel forces. The Pathan ***jirga***, headed by Jung Sher had given a call for total cooperation with the military regime.

"Khan sahib," The PSO composed his reply rather cautiously, "Smaller pinions often get stuck. Don't worry. You needn't have come all the way. There appears to be a mistake somewhere. Harfan is rendering valuable services to Pakistan, and we're proud of him."

"General sahib, I'm a true Pakistani and a Pathan. I know Harfan's uncle. I shudder to think what Hyder's people did to the boy. ***Janab,*** suspicion has the potential of multiplying fast. It keeps on stretching beyond the imagination of the originally fertile mind. I don't know how to face Zahoor Chaudry."

"Oh no ***Sirdar*** sahib, Zahoor is a personal friend. I'll call him straightaway and request him to come over for a cup of tea. I need his services."

Sarfaraz asked his aid to connect Zahoor's Lahore number and picked up the handset as soon as he came on the line.

"Zahoor sahib, Sarfaraz this side. Why don't you come down to Islamabad? I have an urgent piece of business with you."

"I am flattered Sarfarazji," Zahoor replied, "But I've received a rather disturbing phone call from Nawab."

"What did he say?"

"It's regarding a raid at Harfan's Jhumra residence. What's the matter? Is Hyder trying to ruin me?"

"I'm sorry Zahoor sahib. There has been a mix up. Some buffoons from Hyder's office have gone berserk. I've pulled them up. Please come over. I've some important matters to discuss with you about the defence of the ***mohana*** area from possible Indian attack."

Sarfaraz sounded highly apologetic.

"That's fine ***janab,***" Zahoor replied with a wounded voice, "Nawab is out to destroy my family. Last time it was a rumour about Harfan's entanglement with ***mohtarma*** Jahanara, now he has engineered a raid on his house. I think I should ask Harfan to change his job. Let Nawab and Israr fight to their heart's content."

"Please listen to me. I promise to pull up Nawab. And Israr sahib is here. Please talk to him"

Israr took the phone and patiently listened to Zahoor for good five minutes.

"I understand your problem Zahoor sahib. Convey our apologies to Jamilla and tell her that her husband is an angel of a man. Harfan is on his way to Dacca on the special mission. Sarfaraz here has promised to take all possible corrective action. I suggest you come and see him."

"I'm reassured Israr sahib. Nawab is seriously hurting my daughter. Tell me how can I face the innocent kid?"

"Tell darling Jamilla that Nawab is a viper. We all have full faith in Harfan and he should be back to her arms in another two days."

Jung Sher Khan pleaded with folded hands after the brief interlude was over. Lt. Gen. Sarfaraz tried to mollify the veteran Pathan chief, rated as one of the most influential persons behind the throne.

"***Insha Allah***," Sarfaraz added, "No harm should reach Zahoor's son-in-law. I'll sort out the misunderstanding as soon as he reaches Islamabad."

The PSO adopted a defensive posture. He did not want to annoy this Pathan stalwart. He might require his help to neutralise Izaz Afroz. He would certainly require support from the Baluch and Pathan ***sirdars.***

Khan and Israr controlled major lifelines of the armed forces. They surreptitiously scrounged the shady weapons markets and supplied precious weapons to Pakistan's starving Army. ***Allah*** willing, he would require the services of Israr in Punjab to neutralise the influences of Nawab and Izaz Afroz. Israr wielded a strong influence on Jat-stock Punjabi civilian bureaucrats and feudal satraps.

General Sarfaraz, the second most important person in Pakistan, escorted the imposing Pathan ***sirdar*** and Israr Sharief to their cars and, as a rare gesture, clicked his heels. The metallic sound was clearly audible to their pleasing ears.

"Leave the matter to me." He reassured the visitors.

Back in his room the first thing Sarfaraz did was to call Salim Raizada, a sub-editor of the *Frontier Post*, a powerful English and Urdu daily.

"Salim sahib, Sarfaraz here. Please come and have a cup of tea with me."

The invitation from the virtual number two was a big temptation.

"What's happening sir?"

"We have been thinking to send a delegation of the mainstream media to Dacca. Would you like to lead it?"

"That's an honour sir. I'll be with you right away."

The tea was sweet and so also the offer of a sponsored visit to Dacca via a stopover at Bangkok, as the leader of the media delegation. Salim Raizada was more than happy.

Sarfaraz too felt happy. Salim had the key to approach the personal valet cum masseur of ***mohtarma*** Jahanara. He readily agreed to plant a very reliable story on the valet, as a personal favour to the PSO.

Sarfaraz couldn't allow a golden opportunity like this to pass by. The ISI chief too should have some share of the dirt on his face. And valet Qader Shams was the most suitable person to whisper intimate gossips into Jahanara's ears, in exchange for a fat consideration. Sarfaraz was sure that the wild lady would run amuck when Qader, while massaging her scantily clad body with imported Italian olive oil, narrated the true story of the blasphemous activities of Hyder Bux and his officers. Salim also agreed to plant a story, quoting sources close to Hyder and Nawab, about the allegations of Jahanara having grabbed 10% commission from the arms lifting operations. Would she allow an unholy axis to develop between Izaz and Hyder? And what about that poor kid Harfan? Wasn't Nawab haunting him out only to destroy his brother Israr? Wasn't Nawab a loyal crony of Izaz? Would the ***mohtarma*** allow the situation to slip out of her hand? Would she allow the ***Sadr*** to be hanged by the power grabbers?

Sarfaraz was convinced that a reasonably motivated Qader Shams was the right person to stir up the simmering cauldron of Jahanara's singed psyche. She was sure to initiate the domino action and he, Sarfaraz Lodi, would wait in the wings, to give a finishing touch to the final act of demolition.

****

Hyder's triumphant return from Dacca was followed by an orchestrated media cacophony about the heroic actions taken by the Pakistan army in shifting the entire population of the coastal islands of East Pakistan in anticipation of another sever cyclone, a fiercer one than the twister that had killed about half a million people last November. This was followed by another outburst of reporting about the vicious Indian bombing and strafing of some of the coastal districts in the Great Estuary area of East Pakistan. The reports exhorted upon the inter-national bodies to prevail upon India to desist from aiding and abetting the terrorists in East Pakistan.

New Delhi lodged a formal protest and presented a horrifying collage before the UN with evidences supplied by the People's League. The People's League and its allies managed to reach the foreign media with photographic evidence that there were no evacuation of population. The entire population of the estuary islands and over two score coastal villages were simply murdered and their bodies were either given mass burial or were thrown into the sea. It was an operation clean up that tried to send a message to the Bengalis that Pakistan meant business and were not averse to accomplishing a total genocide, much more tragic than what Hitler managed to do to the defenceless Jews.

The international watchdog bodies mostly tied to the apron strings of the USA preferred to behave like the three monkeys of Mahatma Gandhi; they preferred not to speak, see and hear any evil.

But the felicitation parties, which tried to convey the message of victory of the Pakistani strategy against the perfidious Indian designs, could not rid Hyder of the nagging feeling that the ground under his feet was slipping away. General Sarfaraz hadn't minced words to convey his displeasure over the Jhumra incident and the likely existence of an unholy collusion between a section of the ISI officers and Nawab Sharief.

Mohtarma Jahanara also did not have very kind words to shower on Hyder. The explosive stories of the misadventure of the ISI at Jhumra were served to her garnished with plenty of pepper and spice. She enjoyed the nimble touches of Qader Shams the masseur, but her intestines burned like they were on paraffin fire. She summoned her ***habshi*** and asked him to connect Hyder Bux.

"How are you dear Hyder?"

"I am fine ***mohtarma***. How have you been?"

"My well-being depends on you and the ***Allah***. How are things in Dacca? I believe you were there to teach the Bengalis a lesson or two."

"The situation is grim. But we are trying our best," Hyder paused for a second and resumed the dialogue, "I believe ma'am there has been a minor indiscretion by my boys."

Jahanara chose not to react. She wanted to hear what the ISI chief had to say.

"It's that Jhumra incident. I presume you want to speak to me about that. There has been a misunderstanding and I want to come and explain the matter to you. When can I come?"

"You are always welcome. I only hope Hyder," Jahanara injected the venom in her final sting, "The intelligence and security of the country have not been mortgaged to people like Nawab Sharief!"

"Things are under control. I'd like to see you this evening if you are free."

"I'm told that you have information about a 10% commission taken by me."

"Don't believe in the yellow press ma'am. They are playing nasty games. They want to destroy the country. I can explain the whole dirty game. When can I come?"

"You are welcome."

Brigadier Barqat was gripped by panic too. He was deflated by the Jhumra faux pas. Jamanat's all muscle and brawn approach had put a dirty blob on his professional reputation. For the first time he felt that he was standing bare-chested before Hyder's barrel.

General Hyder, a veteran of many wars, did not fail to understand the circumstances that had led to the fiasco. He should have put a cork on the Jhumra operation before emplaning for Dacca. Barqat had simply carried out his earlier order that was necessitated by the overwhelming SigInt reports. He decided to face the difficult situation. The crocks in the power-poodle of Pakistan were gunning for his scalp. But he could not bow out of the ring simply because some sensitive feathers have been ruffled. He had let Barqat off with a stern warning. But he hadn't failed to mention that addition of a few more stars on his pips depended on defter handling of operational affairs.

India, Pakistan's enemy number one, deserved a gruelling intelligence combat, not aimless trench firing. Barqat's India Division, Hyder emphasised, should've infiltrated the so-called headquarters of the Government of Bangladesh in exile, operating from Free School Street, Calcutta. The ***Mukti Bahini*** (freedom fighter) training camps, run by India and Russia were yet to be penetrated by his agents. The Dacca station had miserably failed, even though some Indian Left Extremist talents were identified and cultivated as potential collaborators. The ISI, Hyder reminded Barqat, couldn't afford to be fleet-footed with a sensitive target like Harfan. The unofficial first lady deserved more cautious handling. The old man, nursing raw wounds, inflicted by the Bengali separatists, should not be prematurely needled.

Barqat wasn't essentially a political player, like most of his kind was, in the brotherhood in uniform. He understood and accepted as fait accompli, the rape of Pakistan by the military junta. He didn't enjoy it. Son of a noted pre-partition freedom fighter from Kakori, in Indian Uttar Pradesh, Barqat was a silent admirer of the early democrats, who tried to follow the golden ideas and ideals, enunciated by ***Quaid-e-Azam.***

But a lowly ***muhajir*** like him was in no position to challenge the Punjabi muscle and Sindhi deceit. They didn't allow the early democrats, pronouncedly Bengalis, to preside over the new country and pursue the path of constitutional democracy. He didn't expect them to allow another Bengali, this time Sheikh Jainal, to occupy the top chair in Islamabad. He smelt putrid blood in the air. The March massacres in East Pakistan and the latest delta cleaning operations weren't cool enough to quench the thirst of the junta leaders.

Any way, Barqat reflected, he had better follow Hyder's strategic approach and concentrate on developments in Dacca and the Calcutta bases of the rebel Bengali leaders. Jahanara and Harfan could wait. He had no problem if the bosses had none.

All that he could do to assure Hyder that his message was well taken, was to click his boot sharp and say a muted 'yes sir.'

Hyder dismissed his India Counter-Intelligence Division chief with a faint smile. He knew, he too was caught up in the whirlwinds of politics of succession and couldn't force an important establishment ally to abandon Operation Rosewood, the coverage of ***mohtarma*** Jahanara. This sex kitten wielded several keys to the inner chambers of the CMLA.

Barqat, however, couldn't escape Jamanat Ali's gravitational pull. The sword-sharp intelligence operative had something extra built inside of him, a special capability to chase shadow and catch ghosts out of moonless mists. He had successfully netted many counter-intelligence operations by chasing shreds of suspicion, from fragile leads to smoking gun proof. Perhaps, his handling of the Harfan affair was premature, but surely not irrelevant.

The man simply refused to give up. He was not a politician either. A thorough professional, Jamanat was on the verge of superannuating. He did not bother about the pink blushes in the cheeks of the top bosses. His gut feeling told him that he was on the right trail, but he did not yet have the right evidence. His mistake was that he tried to pull off an intelligence coup by applying traditional tools of the ISI. Harfan Bukhari, he finally digested the message, was a key operator and to nab him he would require to apply superior tradecraft.

That's precisely what happened, when Barqat, with Jamanat in tow, appeared before the Security Screening Committee (SSC), appointed by General Sarfaraz, following a subtle hint from the President about the alleged bugging of his girl friend's phone and interference by some unscrupulous business houses in the sensitive matter of airlifting of emergency supplies to Dacca.

This was the inevitable fallout of the Lahore fiasco, followed by the Jhumra bungling. Barqat pressed the talisman hard against his chest and resigned to his fate. But a silent and faceless Jamanat was adamant even while facing the top bosses.

"Sir, I may have gone wrong marginally. But I'm sure the Direction Finders were correct." Jamanat Ali conveyed his assessed views to Gen. Hyder.

"Aren't you imagining too much Jamanat?" The ISI chief made the comment casually.

"Sorry sir," Jamanat replied, still standing at a respectable distance. The subordinates had no right to a chair. It was a protocol passed on from the colonial era, "In my view Harfan can be reasonably suspected as an Indian agent. He has access to our top decision making levels."

"You mean the CMLA's office, the Presidency, the ISI and other vital levels have been contaminated!" Gen. Nayeem, the PIB chief asked.

"I can't put the tag on any particular slot sir," Replied Jamanat, "But, we shouldn't be blind about the possibility of it being so."

"Well Mian Jamanat," Added Gen. Nayeem, "Intelligence is a game of possibilities and probabilities. But in this instance we require more specifics."

General Nayeem, present in one of the very rare inter-agency screening sessions, confronted the veteran ISI sleuth. Jamanat's wasn't a new face to him. Their families hailed from Dera Ghazi Khan and they enjoyed common family ties. But today's meeting was a special one, ordered by the PSO. There was no room for any personal powwow.

The President was furious, he said, to learn that some idiots in the PIB and ISI had tried to embarrass Malika Jahanara, a descendant of the traditional sopranos of the ***Avad durbar*** (former Sultanate in northern India).

"Why are you silent?" Thundered the DMI.

Brigadier Barqat intervened, but was silenced by Gen. Naqi. He asked Jamanat to explain his thesis. HumInt should have buttressed the technical inputs and the hypothetical suspicion of the location of the suspected transmitter.

"Sir, our technical reports were precise, indicating the location of the clandestine station within half a mile of the suspect's residence."

"Was it supported by HumInt?"

"No. We thought of conducting a discreet search, but something went wrong and we couldn't back out." Jamanat explained his point forcefully.

"How do you narrow down your suspicion on this character Harfan? What are his antecedents?" Asked Gen. Nayeem.

"There is no chink in his armour as yet. His papers are genuine. He's from a respectable ***muhajir*** family. But, there are two curious factors. Our Direction Finders have more or less pinpointed the source of transmission to Jhumra, the suspect's house falling within the inner arch of radiation."

"Why don't you arrest and interrogate him?" Asked the DMI.

"We don't have any positive evidence. House search has been futile. He has acquired a martyr's image by volunteering to airlift emergency supplies to Dacca. He has respectable connections and many top people won't be amused, if we detain him. His in-laws enjoy good access to top personalities."

Brigadier Barqat explained the position, with a veiled reference to Malika Jahanara.

"Hasn't the raid been a premature action?" Asked Gen. Naqi.

"There has been a slight miscalculation at our end. My team shouldn't have accosted Israr Sharief; the way they did." Barqat tried to play down Jamanat's mistakes.

"Here I agree," Intervened General Hyder Bux, "Israr has been operating a wireless set, of course with the approval of General Naqi. It was but natural for the boys to check with him. Comparison of the operational frequencies and schedules was necessary. The boys should've taken clearance from the D&NS Advisor. I'll take care of this minor problem."

"I think your SigInt boys have bungled. Signal radiation can be caused by several factors, including solar eruptions and atmospheric interference. Often direction finders go bonkers. Possibly your JIS boys have picked up signals from Israr's set."

Lt. Gen. Sarfaraz made an indirect dig at the ISI chief.

"We know that," Replied Hyder, "There definitely has been a minor operational indiscretion. I can't hang the boys for this. Tell me how do we explain to the President?"

"From what I learn, I feel there's no tangible evidence against this character Harfan." Commented Gen. Naqi, the Defence and National Security Advisor.

"The last thing I want is to convey a message to the President that, some one somewhere has been trying to put a spanner in the arms lifting operation. Let's bury the skeleton here and let's pacify the important lady. And I have taken care of the ruffled feelings of Zahoor sahib." Lt. General Sarfaraz talked in a conciliatory voice.

The PIB chief nodded silently, which meant both agreement and disagreement. He wasn't in a mood to berate Jamanat, his village pal and a former PIB hand. What could a small cog like him do? The ambitious ISI chief was responsible for the sordid affair. He was definitely trying to sully the President's image and that of his anchor, Malika Jahanara.

The meeting dismissed Barqat and Jamanat and reverted to the next agenda.

"To start with," General Naqi initiated the discussion, "I don't think we can pin down any particular business house. Shall we ask the Defence Secretary and the Deputy CMLA, in charge of the Supply Corps, Brigadier Hussain to go into the matter and submit a report?"

"I think that's the correct approach. The second item on the agenda will require some in depth investigation and this meeting can't do that."

General Sarfaraz tried to bail out his senior colleagues. They were all involved with some business house or the other. He did not want to pin down Nawab Sharief on tactical reasons. Such a move would have antagonised Hyder and he did not want to annoy the person who was being projected as the next chief minister of Punjab.

"So we decide that we have no problem with Harfan Bukhari and as Hyder says, there has been no tapping of the phones of Malika Jahanara and we refer the other item to a committee of experts."

Sarfaraz read out the decisions adopted in the meeting.

"Your are correct sir. I can swear by ***Allah*** that there has never been any tapping of the phones of the ***mohtarma*** Jahanara. Our telephone lines depend on badly insulated co-axel cables. Under the circumstances cross connections cannot be avoided. I recommend that we should go for electronic exchanges and optic fibre cables."

"I have noted this. This will be forwarded to the secretary communication for preparing a project report."

"The bastard that he is...." Nayeem muttered under his breath.

"Did you say something?" Asked General Naqi.

"Oh no sir," Nayeem denied with a broad grin, "All that I feel is that the problem hasn't been handled properly."

"It's no time for a fight Nayeem." Naqi whispered.

"You're correct sir." Nayeem widened the circumference of his grin. It was a cosmetic gesture.

General Nayeem wasn't disinclined to offer in charity the intestines of Hyder, to the Himalayan condors. But the existing power equation in Pakistan tilted in favour of the troika of three Generals plus the Sindhi jackal. General Arif, like all tin-pot dictators, was desperately hanging on to the seat that he usurped in the name of restoring democracy. The Punjabi elite, Izaz Afroz and the Bengali separatists had compounded the woes of the younger Khan. The conspirators, inside the armed forces and their political abettors were pushing the country down an uncertain abyss. It was safer to maintain a tactical silence, especially in front of the conspirators.

"We're chasing a shadow." General Nayeem continued, "My counter-intelligence units haven't found anything against this insignificant fellow. The Rangers could have originated the radio impulses in those particular frequencies. They use the same frequencies. The result of spectrum analysis is inconclusive."

"You're digging too many holes Nayeem." Gen. Hyder commented tersely.

"Don't mind me Hyder. I was commissioned in the Corps of Signals. I must add that the Direction Finders aren't precise homing devices; they only give a general indication. I recommend that your JIS and my SIB (Signal Intelligence Bureau) exchange more information, before we come to a definite conclusion. I don't think that the top brass of Pakistan should waste time on a silly errand like this."

Gen. Nayeem spoke forcefully. Signals was his forte and this was his chance to prevent the ISI from grabbing the counter-intelligence turf, an exclusive preserve of the PIB

The ISI chief didn't harbour a profound affection for Gen. Nayeem either. His slit-eyed glance that swept across the table threw a glint of disdain at the PIB chief. He should thank ***Allah*** that he happened to be the elder brother of the boss. Otherwise, Hyder exhaled a deep breath; he would have him incarcerated at the Badr interrogation centre and disembowel his intestines.

The ISI chief recalled how Nayeem had chanced to qualify for Pakistan army in a special recruitment in 1948, soon after the first Kashmir crisis. A crass joker like him wasn't even fit for employment as a batman in the Pakistan Military Academy. But for his younger brother he would've headed a brigade somewhere in the wildernesses of Gilgit or Skardu.

The ISI would never agree to have any joint operations with the PIB, which was a veritable safe house for the acolytes of redundant politicians, civilian sissies and corrupt policemen. But, the wicket was too sticky today. An aggressive outburst wouldn't go hand in hand with today's pungent situation.

Hyder pretended to be pleased to be agreeing with the PIB chief.

His dream fruit, the highest slot in Pakistan was almost mature, hanging like a delicate ripe ***anar*** (pomegranate). He shouldn't allow any stinking jackal to stand between him and his destiny. No. Especially not this foolish junior intelligence officer, Jamanat or a bloody ***muhajir*** like Harfan Bukhari should explode on his face like rotten pumpkin.

"I agree with my distinguished colleague, we'll set up a joint team and pursue the technical leads." Declared Gen. Hyder Bux.

"It's fine with us." Gen. Naqi said conclusively. He was relieved to get past this sticky situation. He couldn't afford to ground the flights to Dacca.

"So," Sarfaraz commented, "The problem has been identified and isolated. We put up a joint front and brief the President. Agreed?"

"I don't say that you move away the needle of suspicion from any particular target." Commented General Nayeem, "But our approach should be based on the accepted principles of counter-intelligence operations. We can't afford to throw the country into a spin, simply because one Nawab Sharief insisted on guillotining his business rival."

"Not exactly..." Gen. Hyder grudgingly demurred.

How the hell did Nayeem get the scent of the base information? Was he running moles inside the ISI cheese balls too?

"Our initial lead came from SigInt." General Hyder managed to throw up a shrivelled smile.

"Fine, let's not go into these details. We have formulated our recommendations to the President. I repeat," Sarfaraz read out the formulation once again "No monitoring of ***mohtarma*** Jahanara's phone was intentionally done. Some foolish telephone linesman had mixed up the junction box wires that connected the Indian High Commission to our juice boxes. And some boys of the company had walked into Harfan's house inadvertently, instead of searching a neighbouring house. It was a genuine mistake. The third agenda has been referred to the committee of experts. Do you all agree?"

The big bosses present in the meeting nodded their heads in agreement. It was indeed a great deliverance.

"Thanks brother officers. I'm seeking a personal audience with the President to explain the accidental breach. Perhaps the ISI chief will like to accompany me."

Hyder looked at the PSO over the shoulder of General Naqi and displayed a smile of concurrence. The meeting ended with practised smiles on the faces of the wary veterans and daggers unsheathed by a few more centimetres. The gentlemen in uniform were simply short of jumping at each other's jugular. Their silent dispersal was louder than the grinding and shearing sounds of sharp edged saws cutting up anything that came its way.

No ground was lost. No ground was won.

Chapter 43

Jamanat wasn't amused to see the veterans gnashing their teeth at each other, instead of allowing the intelligence professionals to pursue their leads.

What was so great about a small mistake like this? When did Pakistan don the mantel of a transparent democracy like the USA? Had the government machineries surrendered their institutional privileges to the idiosyncrasies of a few individuals and their bed warmers?

A personal orderly to N.P.A. Smith, the last British Director of the Central Intelligence Bureau (CIB), Jamanat had emulated one special trait from the outstanding intelligence officer. He'd learnt the qualities of relentless chasing of reasonable intelligence leads. He never tried to digest a reasonable lead with dinner meatballs and forgetfully evacuating it next morning.

A veteran PIB hand, Jamanat was seconded to the ISI's counter-intelligence unit in 1962. His contribution to the staging of a theft of the holy hair relic of the Prophet (Hazrat Baal-pbuh) from a Srinagar shrine had led to a spontaneous revolt in the Vale of Kashmir. What the Indian's later claimed to retrieve was a faked hair. New Delhi paid through its nose to make the ***ulemas*** agree on the genuineness of the retrieved hair. His singularly important services were recognised by a coveted national award.

A counter intelligence expert, he understood the intricacies of tradecraft and deep penetration-defensive and forward-intelligence operations. Most of his colleagues in the ISI were military eggheads, who masqueraded as intelligence sleuths. Jamanat often felt foxed with the ***fauji*** (army) way of handling sensitive intelligence matters. They blindly copied the tantalisingly overt and aggressive traits of their US cousins, the backroom boys of Langley. Strange creatures they were, obsessed with a perverse passion for fireworks, where stealth could win a decisive war of wits by mere application of tradecraft. The masters, both military and political, expected that the gaping holes in their diplomatic initiatives could be papered up by these packs of paranoid punks.

"I'm not going to spare that bastard." Jamanat blew his top, once out of the high-powered committee room.

"Patience Jamanat Ali." Counselled Barqat.

"I hate these fat bellied Generals. What do they know of counter-intelligence?"

"Hope that's not your general attitude to all army officers!" Barqat quipped back.

"Pardon me sir. Their minds are convoluted by the twisting storms of a power struggle." Lamented Jamanat Ali in flowery Urdu.

"Patience Jamanat, the present phase is perilously transient. No one, except ***Allah,*** can now stand between these blind Generals and the balkanisation of Pakistan. We're deep in the quagmire of follies of these Generals, who run the country as their personal ***jagirs*** (grants). But, don't lose heart; every dark night is followed by a bright morning. Let this phase be over. We'll play havoc with the ***jahilyya*** (non-believer) Indians, with whatever we're left with. The peoples' war is spontaneous and continuous. That's what is called ***jihad***."

Barqat spoke in a whisper, as if he was delivering a final commandment. The tinge of pain in his voice didn't escape Jamanat.

"***Saabji*** (sir), I'll retire soon, but I'm with you. Don't hesitate to call me. I won't rest till these Indian ***kafirs*** are finally defeated. The flag of Islam must fly again over the Red Fort. Islam must reoccupy Hindustan, all of it. Our independence has been sullied and soiled by these hungry soldiers."

"Wait Jamanat. We'll live beyond these bosses and see better days. Islam is on the march. No one, not even the USA, can stop it."

Barqat kept on talking in a pensive mood, as they walked along the winding corridors of the ISI headquarters.

"It's strange sir," Jamanat was still unable to escape the churning of the whirlpool of frustration within, "By simply fucking a whore one becomes important in today's Pakistan."

"That's the irony of the moment. You'll have your chance. Take only five trusted officers and continue with the operations. I'll ensure the monitoring of his phones, travel patterns and high level contacts. You take care of his ground level tradecraft, counter-surveillance measures, Live and Dead Letter Boxes and drops and brushes. He should communicate with his people back in India, if he is really a long term planted resident agent."

"That's a tall order sir," Added Jamanat, "Give me three more boys."

"Fine. Select real professionals. If your Harfan's a spy, he'll simply not end up in stealing our secrets. He must've allies inside Pakistan too. If we can't catch him at the far end of his contacts inside Pakistan, we should be able to get good leads from his communications." Barqat reassured his veteran subordinate, respected as a legend in the Pakistani intelligence fraternity.

"You can't keep this operation official now, not after this meeting."

"I know. I'll take it off the unit. Report to me directly. But, Jamanat," Barqat sounded a note of warning, "In the intelligence game, sixth sense is important, but we can't move an inch without solid proof."

"Have you noticed one important development sir?"

"What's that?"

"Those strange transmissions have totally gone off the air. See the connectivity!"

"Well Jamanat, it hadn't struck me."

"Each transmission has its peculiar finger prints. Our boys had picked up the suspect signals weeks ago and Israr's signals came in to the air much later. We're monitoring his waves regularly, though General Naqi is allergic to the idea. Sir, if there's smoke, there must be a fire."

"Keep the lid down. Concentrate on HumInt, till his cover's peeled off. That's the most important asset of any resident agent." Advised Barqat.

"Fine sir. I'm happy that you agree with me. ***Insha Allah***, we'll rip apart his cover, very soon sir. Rest assured."

"***Rab ne chaha to*** (if God desires so)," Barqat nodded in agreement, "I suggest you start with Karachi and I will ask our Delhi station to trace this man's background in India. He must be having a family somewhere over there. I know it's a lengthy process, but the tradecrafts do really work."

Jamanat left, this time without clicking his heels. He normally reserved that protocol of salutation for more buoyant occasions.

****

Another person who refused to digest the suspicion with his ***reshmi kebab*** and olive stones in sherry was Major General Nayeem. He had filibustered his way through the high-powered meeting with a hidden motive. There was the latent fear of this small Harfan affair blowing up into a big scandal, involving his brother General Arif and Jahanara. Nayeem did not really find any wrong with their amorous relationship. Power and wealth inevitably attracted the bold and beautiful women. Human history was replete with such fatal liaison.

He was aware too that the hungry jackals in the ISI and CMLA wouldn't hesitate to don the façade of morality and gnaw their teeth at the President. Malika, he presumed would be raped to death by a couple of these sex hungry Generals. They were jealous of him and some of them were of the view that Pakistan was lying unguarded for the grab.

Nayeem, as he sipped his 7 pm whisky, was sure in his mind that Pakistan was about to enter the vortex of another turmoil. The East Pakistanis were determined to have their Bangladesh and there was no one in Islamabad, including brother Arif, to rise above their petty political interests. He, as a seasoned professional should concentrate on his job, the job of frustrating the evil designs of India. Intelligence was his tool of war and he would use that to the maximum advantage of the country.

His sixth sense told Nayeem that, Jamanat wasn't throwing his darts in the dark. He wasn't the type to walk a fire-strip without the adequate insulation of faith and firm belief to back him up. He was correct with his information, but wrong in tactical application. The ground rat should be tapped on the old Dera Ghazi Khan (DGK) network.

The ISI and the CMLA bosses were probably too busy saving their ass and ignoring the genuine concerns of a counter intelligence expert. The entire matter, Nayeem felt, should've been played down at a lower key, sans the dramatics. He was convinced that Hyder wanted to detonate the Harfan-Jahanara bomb on the eve of another coup. That could be the most convenient rope to hang brother Arif.

General Nayeem picked up the phone after considerable deliberations with himself and made a crucial call.

"Jamanat, Nayeem here. Can you see me right away?"

"That'll be a pleasure, as they say in DGK, ***banda hazir janab*** (your servant is always ready)."

Jamanat turned up pronto at Nayeem's residence in a battered ford that made more noise than a steam locomotive.

"Please sit down." The PIB chief stood up and made the middle-strata ISI officer comfortable.

"What can I do for you sir?" Jamanat didn't feel comfortable with Nayeem's lavish gesture. He, being from the ranks, wasn't accustomed to such generosity from the top bosses.

"Relax. You're from my village at DGK and you surely understand the Indian mindset better than the younger boys in the trade do. Can we talk about some exclusive business matters?" Nayeem ordered whisky for two.

"***Janab***," Jamanat opened up, "What a land it was? How nice was our small village? And what a life we lived! All that appears to be a remote dream."

"Exactly Jamanat. I'm sure to turn up in my grave, if I'm not buried there, near the ***dargah*** (holy burial place) of ***peer*** (saint) Khalil." General Nayeem expansively passed on the glass to Jamanat.

"Wish I had an officer like you in my company," He exhaled a deliberate sigh, synchronising with a vague swing of his hand, "Your deputation to the ISI wasn't the correct decision. I regret the original mistake."

"But you opposed me in the meeting. That's the last thing I expected from you."

"Certain things are done with deeper motives, Jamanat. The high-powered meeting was summoned after a good eight months, to give a nice burial to your effort, if not you. The bosses were too eager to save their ass."

Replied Nayeem.

"***Hai Rabba***. He alone knows what's happening to this dear land of ***Quaid-e-Azam***!" Jamanat lamented, as he sipped the whisky, "I'm your old lad sir. This ISI business is fishy. It's a government within the government. They're busy making and breaking our political and social geography. Counter intelligence is the last menu on their cards."

"Look, My boys are busy in genuine counter intelligence errands. Why can't we exchange informal notes, strictly informal, between you and me, two close DGK friends?"

"Sir, please define the area."

"It's about this Harfan business," Nayeem continued, "Keep off Malika and the President. I know for sure, her contact with Harfan was for a specific purpose. Nawab had played it up with foul intentions in mind. But, the other aspects should be probed deeply."

"Have you talked to Hyder?"

"No, I don't intend to, Jamanat. Let's keep it between ourselves, old DGK conspiracy, like we used to steal apricot from our neighbour's courtyards." General Nayeem spoke in a whispering tone.

"You have a point sir," Jamanat spoke hesitatingly, "India must have penetrated our security shield at fairly high levels. I don't mind the conspiracy, but sir, keep this confidential. Our family is indebted to your ancestors, for generations. It'll be a pleasure to work with you."

"Yes Jamanat," Nayeem continued, "The prime task is to understand if this Harfan is genuine. Let's proceed like intelligence operators, step by step. My boys are trying to dig up shreds from Karachi. We should start investigations in India too. The Pakistani mosaic can be matched at a later stage, after we gather more specifics from Umerkot and Karachi."

"Do you share my concerns sir?"

"I do," Nayeem lowered his voice, "Friend Aftab had indicated the sudden disappearance of one of his key operators in Delhi, which coincided with the neutralisation of our prized network in the Jodhpur area. You know him, perhaps you handled this operation for about four years."

"Yes sir. It's that hungry boatman of an Indian minister, some Mallah. That's interesting."

"Aftab's travel agent had hinted about an important Indian infiltration around the same time, that's about good five years back."

"You didn't tell me this earlier."

"Whom to tell? I was not in the picture then. My predecessor was busy sharing drug money with the Frontier and Sind cartels. He later managed to cultivate Izaz Afroz and ended up becoming an ambassador. I hope you remember that wily Sindhi."

"Oh yes. Now I recall. But how do you remember all that sir?"

"I've been rummaging through some of the old papers related to Indian infiltration into Pakistan. Do you recall that famous story of the Indian infiltration right into the office of the slain Prime Minister Liquat Ali?"

"No sir."

"He had started becoming very friendly with Amritlal, the Indian PM and this Aftab was responsible for softening him up. Liquat was again depending on the blighted Bengalis. That's why, I believe, the army; in collaboration with the Punjabi bureaucrats had got him assassinated. And that's how Sikandar and his successor Akbar could ultimately wrest power."

"Hey Allah!" Jamanat was fascinated by the story, "You are correct sir. Aftab had, for a while, drifted away from our company, I mean the PIB."

"I have been screaming my scalp off Jamanat, since I took over suggesting annual security screening of al the listed security suspects. It was a regular drill with the PIB. Now this ISI has introduced a new work culture. They have thrown the tradecraft rules to the winds."

General Nayeem lamented his woes rather openly.

"Why don't you tell them now?"

"No body is in a mood to listen. The leaders are busy gobbling up Pakistan like hungry jackals. And the ***Sadr*** has now transferred Aftab over to your boss, Hyder."

"Sir we should start from 1965, let's examine the whole trail, right from the usual infiltration routes."

"That's what I want to do and you can help. This Harfan has appeared like a comet, minus any blazing tail. A resident agent must have hidden tracks buried somewhere. That's what we're required to discover, using yours and my intelligence telescopes. It's not a job for the ISI killers and undertakers."

"You're correct sir. But, how do we obtain the vital dope from India? Our boys are under strict surveillance."

"Leave that to me. You activate your old contacts. Examine each speck of lead in Pakistan under the finest microscope. Deploy good professionals on the job. Let's work in absolute silence. We'll explode the crackers in good time."

General Nayeem walked up to Jamanat and spoke after placing his hands on his shoulder.

"Fine with me sir," Jamanat replied, "But protect my skin and soul."

"It's a deal. But, keep your Company bosses out of our old DGK conspiracy. The gunks here won't understand the finer nuances of the operation."

Gen. Nayeem cordially escorted Jamanat out.

"Do we allow Harfan to fly out of Pakistan?" Asked Jamanat.

"Only to return and roost in our nest, I mean in our custody, to face sustained interrogation. But let's not hurry. He can't defect to Dacca. The Bengalis will make delectable ***machher jhol*** (fish curry) out of him. Let's not give the President any provocation. He will sure teach Delhi a good lesson. Let's have faith in him."

General Nayeem walked up to the car of Jamanat Ali as a special gesture. He felt happy that the veteran officer had agreed to collaborate with his outfit. Jamanat should be the correct key to the vital breakthrough.

Pakistan had not netted a big Indian fish since the Tripura conspiracy case. That was a great story, Nayeem silently reflected. The PIB had, on that momentous occasion, neutralised a mammoth Indian intelligence penetration, which had targeted several leaders of the Peoples' League and some important bureaucrats. The unique Indian operation, detected years back by the PIB, was now threatening to break up Pakistan. The military rulers, out of political compulsions had messed up the solid intelligence coup.

Sheikh Jainal wasn't the only snake under the sleeve. More poisonous cobras were lurking under the beds of the top leaders, here, just in the heart of Pakistan's capital. The blighted Bengali officers, still in the services of the Armed Forces and government departments, Nayeem had no doubt, were active Indian collaborators.

And Harfan Bukhari, the comet, which had strayed in from nowhere, was clouding up the Pakistani firmament with poisonous vapours. Aftab, an old reliable friend couldn't be totally off the mark.

Nayeem lapsed into a mysterious silence, as he stood before Jamanat's car.

"One point sir," Jamanat turned around, "You take care of the Malika end too. I'm sorry for the last blunder, I didn't want to hurt her."

"Forget it. I'll explain the finer nuances to her and she'll, in good time, explain it to the President. We're working for Pakistan's security and both of them are better patriots." Nayeem reassured Jamanat Ali.

"Shall I prepare a short summary for the President?"

General Nayeem pondered silently for a few seconds and shook his head in negation.

"Let's get the meat first. Cooking the curry won't take more than a few minutes. You know our old DGK adage. You and me, together we shall cook a fine mincemeat curry out of all the Indian spooks."

"That'll be a great pleasure sir."

Jamanat saluted General Nayeem, in old police training school style, clicking the heels twice, producing a massive metallic sound. That meant he too was happy, at the prospect of cooking up a fine broth out of Harfan Bukhari.

Nayeem reciprocated. He saluted the junior officer in old British style.

He was happy too, in successfully hooking up the veteran counter intelligence termite. It would be a sweet revenge, after a long parched spell, against the rival ISI. The favourites of the green berets had overshadowed him, like the vile Hindu astrological planets, Rahu and Ketu, since Hyder Bux's induction.

He must brief the President about the scheming Generals around him and that Sindhi, Izaz Afroz. They were, Nayeem felt he knew for sure, planning a coup. They could hit out any time, once they were able to rope in the Air and Naval Chiefs.

Nayeem was aware of the emotional problems of Jahanara. She wouldn't simply agree to look at any report against Harfan, till she felt personally threatened. The fear of ***dozakh*** (hell) should be put into her, by bluntly pointing out that, this man Harfan meant a live burial for her, and her lover boy, the President.

That's what he was going to do, Nayeem waved indulgently as Jamanat switched on the ignition of his car. He wouldn't allow the jackals to feed on the carcass of brother Arif and the putrid remains of Pakistan.

Chapter 44

Harfan Bukhari wasn't blind to the gathering clouds and not too distant thunders. His focused eyes and ears ceaselessly monitored the impulses and dissected the anatomy of the threat to his person; his loved ones and his mission. The intelligence sleuths, he was aware, had picked up his scent and he expected them to close in, sooner or later.

The airlifting operation came as a good reprieve, albeit temporarily. That smoke screen, he presumed was quite thin. And that wouldn't deter the ISI sleuths from homing in on their target. The probable scenarios fleeted past his mind's eye as he gravely and vaguely looked at the complicated instrument panels manipulated by the pilot of the mercenary chartered flight, cruelly christened: Lady of the Light.

He was escorting yet another sortie to Dacca.

The Lady of the Light, a Boeing 707 of Athena Air Lines, owned by Doug Chris was painted with a convincing International Red Crescent logo. It flaunted an IATA approved call sign. Flying at 33,000 feet the silvery bird was on auto pilot.

Voodoorume, the pilot, a South African of Indian origin, was busy discussing the peculiarities of the new route and the mission with Harfan Bukhari. His company had never flown in this sector, which was a new theatre of conflict.

Voodoorume, a derivation from the hackneyed eastern ***Uttar Pradesh*** Hindu name, Buddhu Ram, Rama the Fool, had tonnes of dreams stored up at the back of his mind, about his forefather's homeland.

Voodoo's great grand father, Faltu Ram, Rama the Insignificant, a bonded indigo plantation slave, was tied up with a few hundred other indentured labourers by the ***Company Maharaj*** (the British East India Company) and was dumped somewhere near Cape Town, at the tip of the dark continent. Some luck and some genetic and inherent trait of survival of the homosapiens in the most hostile environment, and the process of natural selection had helped him in rearing up a family of slaves.

Faltu Ram had graduated to a cook, from a sugarcane crusher, in the household of a Huguenot Boer family, and had migrated north, after the British occupation of the Cape of Good Hope. Converted to Christianity, Faltu managed to impart good education to his children. Voodoorume's father, Mitha Ram, Rama the Sweet, had climbed up the social ladder further, by qualifying as one of the rare coloured auto-drivers, of Indian descent.

From a slave to a jet pilot was a tortuous and bitter journey for Voodoorume, a quantum jump for any member of the Ram family

Voodoorume belonged to the generation of post-Mohandas Karamchand Gandhi coloured Indians, who gathered courage and voiced their existence as fellow human beings; much, much higher in the ladder of evolution, than the intelligent African ape, the Chimpanzee. The messianic Afrikaners and the self-righteous British had grudgingly accepted their rights to breathe and live, as a slightly higher species than the gutter insects, the aboriginal black Africans.

Voodoorume had managed to go to school and enlist himself in the South African Air Force, at the fag end of the Second World War. He had flown with distinction, as a fighter pilot in the North African campaign. It was a rare break for a coloured sub-human being.

Wars are great levellers. The Second World War was no exception. It ushered in the collapse of many barriers. In a sense its visitation was marked by a new era of liberation and mapping of a new political and social geography.

Voodoo pulled off a miracle of sorts by marrying a white girl, a German Jew, who had managed to survive another perverse human laboratory-Hitler's concentration camp.

His story of drifting into mercenary flights formed an integral part of the shenanigans of the white skins ruling over a land, which they considered as the special gift of the Lord the God in the Dark Continent.

Voodoorume was an unwanted intruder in the last bastion of white supremacy. His biggest crime was his marriage to a white woman and his demand for the rights of his children to study in exclusive white schools. Like another Gandhi he fought a battle for his children's rights. His seditious doggedness had provoked the white masters and ultimately he was court-martialled and sacked.

The story fascinated Harfan.

No. Harfan hastened to add, he had nothing much to say about his life history. He was the only member of his family to survive yet another perverse laboratory experiment of the white masters–the partition of India and the pre-independence communal holocaust.

"Did they kill every one?" Voodoo asked in utter shock.

"Well, not exactly. Even Hitler couldn't exterminate all the Jews he wanted to gas out. But I lost my immediate family."

"That's awful Mr. Bukhari." Voodoorume sympathised with Harfan's personal tragedy.

"Call me Harfan," Harfan replied, "Don't worry. Killing is the most honourable human trait. Thousands have been killed in East Pakistan, where you and I are flying this deadly sortie."

"Do you regret it?"

"Well! All of us have to earn our bread. That's important. And officially we're flying in mercy supplies for the cyclone victims and our sponsors are the International Red Crescent." Harfan parried Voodoorume with a curt but philosophical reply.

Another Greek aviator, Antichopoulas, Voodoo's co-pilot and a Sicilian soldier of fortune walked up the aisle.

"Hi Cap, look to your left. That's India for you. Your blessed land." He drew Voodoo's attention to the tip of the Indian peninsula, as their plane crossed the Palk channel between India and Ceylon.

"Thanks Anto." Voodoorume disengaged from Harfan and peered down the window. It was his land of dreams. He must visit one of these days. But who'd give a visa to a South African national, in this segment of human civilisation? Not India, surely.

Harfan lighted a cigarette and looked at the stacks of reinforced alloy metal pallets, loaded in the cargo bay and fuselage. Red Crescent logos with names of medicines and essential food items were embossed in blue, all over the lethal containers. The crates, if the labels were to be believed, carried precious baby foods and paediatric drugs.

A freak twister ravaged East Pakistan last November that had sent around 50,000 to graves, about equal numbers to no-where destination and more than 100,000 to hospitals. The uniformed masters simply didn't bother, if the wretched Bengalis died in cyclone, starvation and plague and pestilence. The new rulers, with fresh masks in old uniforms, were too busy in consolidating their crumbling power bases, shaken up by the last drawn war with India and the subsequent political upheavals. The masters were clumsily apathetic to the Bengalis, now up in arms for equitable political and economic share.

These bloody Bengalis, the chronic dirty fish eaters, as Izaz Afroz and other made-in-Britain Pakistanis would like to reason with their laboured Oxonian accents, were third grade Muslims, having been converted from the lower caste Hindus. A mere change in religion couldn't place them at par with the Bukharis, Khans, Mirzas, Sayeds etc, all carrying in their holy veins, blue Arab, Afghan, Iranian and Turkish Islamic blood. The Bongos were as bad as the ***jahilyya*** Hindu ***kafirs.***

Who in Islamabad would bother, if these low-caste half Hindus died in thousands or millions? If they died, ***Allah kasam*** (by God), it'd only lessen the burden on the ***Ummah***. These lesser Muslims deserved periodical visitations by the ***Allah's*** divine punitive elements.

Didn't they die every year? Didn't the twisters hit this wretched funnel of monsoon every season of sorrow? What could the politicians do against the acts of ***Allah*** and ***qudrat*** (nature), except praying in studied reluctance?

What a big fun!

Harfan recalled one of Captain Ayoob's masterpieces. These insects didn't even take the name of the ***Allah,*** Ayoob had argued, when hit by calamities. They worshipped, like their perverted Hindu cousins; queer deities called ***Bon Bibi*** (deity of the forest), ***Olai Chandi*** (goddess of cholera) and ***Shitala*** (goddess of small pox).

Pooh! That much for Hinduised Bengali Islam!

Harfan felt extremely sad, sitting next to piles of deadly weapons. Some uneasy bell continued ringing inside of him. It sounded like the endless pensive tolling of funeral bells. He was carrying death and destruction to Dacca.

Harfan recalled his last meeting with Major Mani and his colleagues at the Dacca mosque and took a mental note to update them about the merchandise of death he was carrying to East Pakistan.

Voodoorume didn't feel any guilt pang anywhere in his psyche. Not any more, after the white masters had placed him in the same cage with his not so inferior jungle cousin, the Chimpanzee. For him these mercenary flights were very important to support his kids pursuing their higher studies in Paris on the meagre income of his wife, a pilot with a private aviation company.

"Mr. Bukhari." Voodoorume walked in and took a seat next to Harfan.

"Anything for me Captain?"

"We're approaching Colombo," Voodoo said, "Hope there won't be any hassles there!"

"There were none with the last three flights," Harfan replied, "I expect the Pakistan International Airlines and High Commission officials to be on the tarmac."

"How many people know of this operation down the line?"

"Don't worry captain. The Ceylonese are not in love with India. The two big ladies aren't on the best of terms and the islanders have scores of problems with the Indian Tamils." Harfan comforted a jittery Voodoo.

"I would like to visit India once." Voodoorume lighted a cigarette and offered one to Harfan.

"For sight seeing?"

"Yes. But I'd like to go to Ballia, somewhere in ***Utterprades*** (Uttar Pradesh) to dig out the roots of my family. I'm told my father's cousins are still there."

"Are you of Indian origin?"

"Absolutely correct. I'm the only surviving son of Mitha Ram and the great grandson of Faltu Ram. Funny names? Aren't they?"

"Not really funny Captain," Harfan added, "People, way back there are too deeply immersed in the legends of Lord Rama. For them the world is a mirror of their God."

"You're supposed to be a Muslim. Aren't you?"

"Doesn't matter Cap. We must respect their faith."

"Great! Somewhere deep inside of me there's a Hindu too. They call it genes! Isn't it? I must locate my people back there in Ballia."

"Fine Captain. I'd also like to visit Ludhiana, my native place. Let this war business be over. It'll be a pleasure travelling with you."

"Hope so." Voodoorume shrugged, "Wars never end. I know only too well. I've been supplying fuels to innumerable war theatres. I know, wars can't end, especially when hatred's the main building block of human character. The Hindus, Christians and Muslims, all like wars. We live by killing."

Voodoorume sounded philosophical and bitter. He sounded tired too.

"Perhaps you're correct Captain. We've inherited a fractured legacy. History had initiated the process of assimilation, but the civilisational conflict caught up with us. We're divided within and without."

"What a pity. I hope the madness will subside soon."

"History travels slowly on the arrow of time, Captain. God alone knows, when we'll learn to live together in harmony."

"I beg your pardon, Mr. Bukhari. There's some turbulence ahead. Let me handle the controls." Voodoorume excused himself and concentrated on the landing procedures.

The Ceylonese civil aviation authorities, as usual, facilitated the refuelling of the Lady of the Light, the mercy flight chartered by Pakistan's Red Crescent, on humanitarian mission. The Ceylonese officials, with the Pakistan International Airlines station manager in tow inspected the flight. The manager, an ISI cover agent and his companion, a second secretary of the Pak High Commission, helped the Ceylonese staff with a copy of the inventory and passenger's list. They were finally seen off with plenty of warm smiles and a few crate of Scotch in their boots.

Voodoorume took off with a full thrust of the engine and stabilised at 18,000. Colombo tower asked him to ascend to 33,000 ft and look out for the Indian Air Force fighters, which often buzzed non-scheduled Pakistani flights between Colombo and Dacca. Pakistani flights used the Colombo corridor since India, according to Islamabad, had stage-managed the hijacking of an Indian Air Lines ramshackle F-27 Fokker Friendship, through planted stooges. It was part of an Indian conspiracy to dismember Pakistan; the foreign office mandarins usually proclaimed, in multilateral diplomatic briefings and official communications.

"The Ceylonese officials are a friendly lot." Voodoo commented honestly.

"Indeed they're and they should be." Harfan replied.

"Why? They aren't Muslims."

"Yes Cap, they aren't. It's a long and a short story, a story of legendary love and hatred between the Island people and the mainland Indians..."

Harfan spoke in a languishing tone...The collapse of the empire had generated racial and ethnic tensions between the Ceylonese and Tamil people. India was one day sure to use the Tamil weapon for grabbing the emerald island, the Pakistani and US officials propagated vigorously. Wasn't India, the brute big brother, doing the same to Sikkim, using the Nepalese as their forward paws? The so-called agitation for democracy was a thinly veiled military and political aggression, aimed at annexing that tiny Himalayan kingdom. The propaganda mill egged on the Ceylonese to take a few lessons from the Indian engineered rebellion in East Pakistan. With the Bengalis already swinging to the tunes of unholy Hindu Indian ***Rabindra sangeet*** (songs by Nobel laureate Tagore), the Tamils wouldn't take much time to set their feet in rhythm to the beats of their ***mridangam*** (percussion drum).

The Hindu demon wouldn't spare its small neighbours. A repeat invasion of ***Lanka*** (mythological name for Ceylon), by the new ***avataras*** (incarnations) of ***Rama*** (Indian prince and God incarnate) was just round the corner.

The CIA reinforced the Pakistani propaganda mill. The defeat of the Indian designs in East Pakistan would bring to a halt, at least for some time, the worst imperialist expansionism of the regional shark. Hindu imperialism, they argued, was a part of the recorded history of the Southeast Asia. Didn't Brahminic India wipe out Buddhism from its land of origin by exterminating millions in Nazi style pogroms? What would prevent the demon from hitting at the Buddhists of Ceylon, Burma, Thailand and of countries far beyond?

Most of the Ceylonese, left to them, would love to see the Indian nose cut off. That should be an appropriate retribution, though belated, against the mythological act of crudeness of the Indian prince Laxmana. The fool had rebuffed the love offer of a Ceylonese princess, severed her nose off and finally colonised her country. That was an obvious reference to Ravana and his sister Surpanakha; two demonised legendary non-Aryan villains of the Hindu epic, the Ramayana.

Harfan's story amused Voodoorume. He had a hearty laugh at the interesting broth of history and mythology and thanked Harfan for it. Well! The story was worth listening to. It had spared him the boring blues of the Bay of Bengal down below and the infinite void above.

****

The Lady of the Light, flight AAL-X-356 entered the wild delta funnel of the Indian sub-continent, which drained trillions of cusecs of waters of the Ganges, Brahmaputra, Meghna and scores of other rivers, into the Bay of Bengal.

The sleek bird dropped altitude and followed the contours of Cox's Bazaar and Chittagong. It banked to the left to avoid Indian airspace over Tripura and banked right shortly after; charting a course towards Bhairab Bazaar. Destination Kurmitola airbase was just twenty minutes away.

At 20,000 ft the Boeing 707 was in steady radio contact with Dacca air control, seeking guidance for landing procedure.

Voodoorume saw them first, flying from 3 o'clock, two small sparrow like Gnat fighters. The birds were probably loitering at 20,000 ft, the captain guessed. The Indian Air Force logos on their fuselage shone bright in the blazing mid-day sun.

He asked the Dacca control to advise the intruders to climb over to a safer altitude. They were flying too dangerously close to the International Red Crescent mercy flight. Weren't they violating Pakistani air space?

The Dacca tower crackled into the international civil aviation frequency.

"Intruders, you're too close to a civilian flight. Clear the skies of Pakistan."

The Indian Air Force radar at Shillong, the central hub of the Eastern Air Command, was monitoring progress of the strange flight, flaunting on its fuselage and tails the logo of the International Red Crescent. In a warlike situation, the Geneva central office of the International Red Cross should've normally kept Delhi informed, about one of its flights ferrying supplies to Dacca. It wasn't the first such flight. The previous three flights had evoked Indian suspicion. The IRC was yet to reply to the Indian queries.

And supplies for what? Were these a part of the humanitarian succour for the victims of the violent orgy and genocide by Pakistani armed forces? No international agency had so far sounded the government of India about these flights. The civil aviation mandarins were at a loss to understand the true nature of these flights. No trustworthy intelligence report was coming out from Dacca too.

And that's why the midget sized Gnats were still dogging the flanks of the Boeing 707. They were instructed to harass the flight and escort it to a nearby Indian airport, if possible at Shinger Beel airfield on Sylhet-Tripura border.

"Clear the Pakistani air space. You're violating the Montreal protocol by obstructing a civilian flight."

Dacca tower warned the Indian fighters.

The Indian version of the Folland Gnats, with 4,500 lb. Rolls Royce Orpheus 701-01 turbojet engines, were armed to the teeth; each with two 30 mm Adam Mk 4 canons, two bombs and six rockets.

Like big Amazonian mosquitoes, they criss-crossed the flight path of AAL-X-356, disturbing its intended air speed (IAS), on the descent manoeuvre.

Shillong was in no mood to relent.

"You're endangering an authorised international flight." Voodoorume's voice crackled heavily on the radio, "Move out. This is the Lady of the Light, a mercy mission."

"You're finally warned to vacate Pakistani air space," Dacca tower warned angrily, "You have two minutes, before our missiles zoom in on you."

Delhi's Directorate of Air Intelligence exchanged quick notes with the DMI and NSI. These flights had become regular features. AAL-X-356 couldn't be a holy IRC flight, they agreed. There was no confirmation from any quarter.

Should it be shot down? The AHQ sought clearance from the Prime Minister's office. Balachandran Nampoothiri intervened vigorously. He did not support any precipitating action, which could trigger off a war for which the preparations were yet to be completed.

No... The Prime Minister's office shrieked. No tampering with the IRC flights. The country couldn't afford another international scandal and give Pakistan a propaganda relay-baton.

Shillong, in constant touch with Delhi's Air Force Headquarters, signalled the Gnats to disengage and return to Shingar Beel base, off Agartala, capital of the Indian State of Tripura.

The badgering and vexing Air Force jets had clear instructions not to engage the Pakistani fighters, mostly F8 Sabre jets. These manoeuvres were designed as part of an orchestrated exercise for turf war. With hardly one squadron of airworthy fighters stationed in Dacca, Pakistan was in no position to challenge the Indian birds.

Voodoorume looked out.

The Gnats, now accompanied by two MIG 21s made a rhythmic loop manoeuvre, went past the Boeing 707, about 1000 feet below and levelled up again. The Indian pilots grinned at the worried facial expressions of the International Red Crescent flight commander.

Voodoorume waved back with a matching grin. He was too hardened a veteran of treetop flying, to be cowed down by some intimidating hot-blooded pranksters.

The Lady of the Light took a slight detour to avoid the airspace over Dacca city, which was under virtual control of the paramilitary and civilian police forces loyal to Sheikh Jainal. Some of the freedom fighters, fondly called ***Mukti Bahini*** by the Bengalis, had acquired medium machine guns and light anti-aircraft guns (LAA). These were capable of sniping at low flying aircrafts landing at Kurmitola Air Force base. They had shot down two helicopters in the last thirty days.

The regular armed forces and the East Pakistan Civil Armed Forces (EPCAF) had failed to sanitise the areas around Dacca. The rebels could seep through the high security zones in the capital city with impunity, from their rural and riverine hideouts.

"Hang on, escorts will guide you." ATC Dacca advised AAL-X-356.

Voodoorume hovered over Buri Ganga River. Two helicopter gun ships, armed with rapid-fire machine guns and air-to-air rockets levelled up and fired, rather indeterminately, at some of the near and distant villages. These village clusters, around the suburban town Tungi were strong bastions of the freedom fighters.

The helicopter gun ships peeled off, as the tarmac showed up, enabling flight AAL-X-356 to make a smooth landing.

Chapter 45

The communication protocol for Double X agent Qurban was well laid down by the operation desk Q at the NSI central hub. This agent was designated to work in close liaison with Alamgir. He was operationally architectured to report on the deployment of Army and Air Force units and the radar stations located in the strategic locations of Mianwali, Sheikhupura, Jhang Sadar and Sargodha. Delhi had tasked him to map and photograph the underground hangers at Khusab, an extension of the Sargodha base, which housed three squadrons of F 28 fighter bombers, acquired from the USA and the medium range missiles supplied by China.

Ibadat, a Double X asset, nom de plumed Qurban, was raised by Alamgir way back in 1960. He primarily handled this local agent of intermediate stature. Ibadat was permitted to communicate directly to Delhi only during grave emergency and Alamgir's prolonged absence from Pakistan. His independent channel of communication was well defined. He could, on rare occasions, contact a designated diplomat in the Indian consulate in Jalalabad or pass on his message through a Live Letter Box in Lahore.

His role was slightly modified after Harfan Bukhari, the Triple X agent was housed at Jhumra. Ibadat was tasked to help the new asset to set himself smoothly into the grooves of his deep cover and to keep a watch on his security status.

However, Ibadat did not know when Harfan Bukhari, the Prince of Jhumra, had started driving roots into his mind. A mixed bag of reasons, Ibadat had reasoned, were responsible for driving him closer to Harfan and his wife Jamilla. He often felt that the seeds of old family loyalty had re-germinated. He had started liking the man, whom Alamgir did not consider anything more than another expendable intelligence agent.

That sense of caring resurfaced during Ibadat's next meeting with Karamat Suri at his ***mohalla*** Rajora residence. He was back to Jhumra on a brief furlough, in fact, for attending his own ***sagai*** (engagement) ceremony. He was getting married to a girl from the same village. Karamat called aside his childhood friend Ibadat after several bottles of country liquor, dozens of roasted fowl and bowls of ***biriyani*** (rice fried with chunks of meat) were downed.

"I'm scared."

Karamat lighted a cigarette and offered one to Ibadat.

"What for? Has anything gone wrong at your work place?"

"No brother. I am coming to that later. I am afraid of the girl I am getting married to."

"Why should you be afraid? She is a nice neighbourhood girl."

"I have never been close to any girl."

"Don't be funny. You will get used to her and start liking her. It happens to all."

"Give me a lesson or two. I don't have time. I go back again to Karachi tomorrow."

"What's happening there?"

"Oh dear brother!" Karamat found back his confidence, "My team is going all the way to Umerkot and from there we get back to Karachi for investigating that fellow Harfan. I hope you know that employee of Israr sahib."

"No brother, not very well. To me he is another customer. I'm happy to earn a little extra money from him. As I was telling you should be very kind to your wife..."

Ibadat used the diversion wilfully. He knew that the slightest obstruction infused waves of new surge in Karamat. He was a compulsive talker and that compulsion was always compounded after he downed a few pegs of intoxicants.

"Wait brother. I was talking about that Harfan fellow. The Director General has rebuffed Jamanat sahib for his raid on Harfan's house. There was nothing in it. But Jamanat sahib feels that there is something fishy in that fellow and he had been a petty criminal at Umerkot, before he took up Israr sahib's employment."

"I'm damn confused Karamat."

"Brother Ibadat," Karamat raised his voice slightly, "He was a smuggler sort of criminal with linkages in India."

"Is he a ***jasoos*** (spy)?"

"You can't rule out that possibility. That's why we are going to Umerkot."

"I think that will be another wild goose chase," Ibadat tried to disengage himself, "As I was telling you brother Karamat, a newly married wife is just like a fresh rose bud. Handle her carefully. Don't try to force her to bloom overnight. Patience helps in the germination of love and respect."

"You are talking like a big brother."

"We will talk again. We have too much of food and drink in our stomach. Let's sleep well."

"But I leave for Karachi tomorrow."

"We shall meet on your return."

In the melting darkness of early morning Ibadat surreptitiously left his Rajora residence and boarded the 4 am Peshawar Express for Lahore. He intended to contact Alamgir through his Peshawar Live Letter Box telephone. Karamat's story had reconfirmed what he had earlier gathered from his contact in the office of the CMLA, a telephone operator, who manned the special area exchange. Broken pieces of information from him had vaguely indicated that a high level meeting had discussed a security suspect named Harfan Bukhari. But the contact was not sure of the context. He, however, produced a transcript of the telephonic talk between Brigadier Barqat and Captain Nurul Amin, aid d camp to the PSO. The brief intercept had given a broad indication about the ISI's deep suspicion on Harfan Bukhari. Both the officers had, however, agreed that Harfan should not be disturbed till the completion of the airlifting operations to Dacca and till such time Barqat was not able to dig out culpable evidence.

The Peshawar LLB telephone was attended by a familiar voice, but he informed Ibadat that his master had gone for ***ziarat*** (pilgrimage) to Mecca. He would return home only after a week. The code word ***ziarat*** was used for Alamgir's trips to foreign destinations.

Ibadat did some quick calculations and entered the narrow lanes of the Anarkali market. After an hour-long survey he selected a miniature soap stone replica of the Lahore Fort and settled down for breakfast in an exclusive restaurant, often frequented by the backpack foreign tourists. He curved out a hollow under one of the minarets with the help of a pocket knife and secured a document, along with a small piece of iron nail deep inside the cavity. He covered up the cavity with layers of plaster of Paris. He felt happy with the camouflage and hoped that it would safely reach its destination.

Ibadat boarded a cycle rickshaw after a leisurely breakfast and asked the puller to take him to ***gali kaabarian*** (lane of the scrap dealers), the main trading centre of the solid waste recycling vendors.

Momin Ansari, a veteran ***kaabari*** (scrap dealer) conducted his family business from a small front shop with a sprawling makeshift shed at the backyard. Momin, a weaver by caste, had inherited the business from his father, who owned a flourishing business at ***gali bhishtiwalan*** (lane of the water carriers) at the back of the historical Jama Masjid of Delhi. Part of the extended family had migrated to Lahore on the eve of the partition and had set up business at Anarkali market. Momin's brothers and cousins still operated from the backyards of the walled city of Delhi.

The secret behind Momin's wealth had very little to do with his scrap business. It was a front for another flourishing business that dealt in ***hawala*** (unofficial) transfer of money between India and Pakistan at a high premium. Momin also controlled another shady business, the illegal ***sawari*** (smuggler-passenger) traffic between India and Pakistan. His ***sawaris*** operated on both the sides of the international border and smuggled in and out contraband items. The ***sawari*** business had flourished more in the recent years, following the 1965 war and the present stand off situation.

Momin was a versatile talent. His network operated all over India and the important urban pockets in Pakistan. His genius did not go unnoticed by the intelligence agencies of the two feuding countries. The PIB and the ISI tapped his ***sawaris*** for gathering shallow penetration intelligence from India and the Indian FIB and the NSI too tapped his talents for similar purposes. It was a free for all game and Momin, seated in his ramshackle shop at the backyard of ***gali kaabarian*** controlled his multifaceted financial empire.

"Hello Mian Idris," Momin greeted Ibabat, "I haven't seen you for a long time. ***Sab khairiyat hai*** (hope things are well with you)?"

In and around ***gali kaabariwalan*** Ibadat was known as Idris Ahmed, a smuggler, who once in a while availed of the services of

Momin, for transferring money to Delhi. He normally paid 5% of the total amount as commission.

"***Salam alaikum janab***," Ibadat greet the aged tycoon, "I had been to Dubai for a while. I hope you are doing well too."

"No son. Business is no more attractive. The war clouds have dampened the market."

"How is the ***sawari*** business? I hope you are accepting consignments for India?"

"It's very risky these days. These Indian and Pakistani ***jasoos*** (spy) and police officers are giving me trouble. These days they are asking for 15% commission. How can an honest business be run if you have to dole out 15 to 20% to the spies and the cops?"

"That's correct ***chacha*** (uncle). I have a small gift to be delivered to my ***chacha*** in Delhi. I hope there wouldn't be any problem?"

"There are problems. This time you have to pay 10% commission. Days are very bad."

"That's too high ***chacha***. I can offer only 7%."

"Okay Idris sahib. I am doing the favour only because you are a trusted customer. Give me you uncle's address in Delhi."

"It's Mirza Hafiz Bukhari, Gali Kabristan, Turkman Gate, Delhi."

"Is he your ***dargahwala*** (custodian of a holy shrine) uncle?"

"Yes ***chacha***. It should reach him quickly."

"Don't worry. My ***sawari*** is leaving for Delhi today. Your uncle will receive it tomorrow. Check up with him on phone. Momin Ansari is the most reliable trader in this line."

"I know that ***chacha***. ***Khuda Hafiz***."

Ibadat paid the commission amount and noted down the name of the female ***sawari***, who was supposed to carry the miniature replica of the Lahore Fort to Delhi. It was a trusted channel. He moved over to the Inter State Bus Terminal, made a call to a designated Delhi number and boarded a mid day bus for Jhumra.

****

Israr International's Mercedes picked up Harfan from Lahore airport. His favourite chauffeur, Latiff Masih, a virtual chatterbox, was on the wheels.

"Take me to Zahoor sahib's place." Harfan ordered.

"Sir, it's necessary to meet Israr sahib first." Latiff insisted.

"What's the matter Latiff? What's the big deal?" Harfan asked in a tense voice.

"***Sahib***, you've been busy flying to Dacca. Plenty of water has flown by the Ravi since then. The plague had visited your house at Jhumra." Latiff spoke in his usual flowery and fenugreek flavoured Kasuri dialect.

"What the hell do you mean?"

"They say, I mean some people say, that the ISI cockroaches raided your house for violation of foreign currency regulations. Israr sahib's very upset. He met several military officers. They suspect you.... I believe."

"What else?"

"They searched your house, and people say, unearthed sacs full of US dollars."

"You believe in that shit!"

"No ***sahib***, nobody believes in it. People know that Nawab Sharief is after your life, simply for destroying his brother's business. This arms lifting contract has enraged the viper. What you see outside isn't real. Nawab wants political power and he thinks Israr is his main rival in Punjab."

But, they're brothers."

"Not from the same mother's womb. Their father had three wives. The first one had died soon after marriage, and Israr and Nawab are from the wombs of the later wives."

Latiff kept on narrating the family secrets of the Shariefs. Harfan didn't reply. He lowered the windowpane and lighted a cigarette. He tried to comprehend the scenario that might have taken shape in his absence.

Scenario one: Would Nawab go to that extent, simply because he was beaten in the airlifting bid?

Nawab was mighty inscrutable and unscrupulous. He wouldn't hesitate erasing Harfan's name from the face of the earth, simply to hurt Israr. He was the shining spear and shield of Israr Sharief, the knight of Pakistan's defence production and transportation.

It was probable. Nawab was capable of committing any mischief.

Scenario two: The ISI must have dug up the entire place and stumbled upon some of the electronic devices. These electronic darlings of the intelligence community weren't supposed to be decoration pieces in a business executive's house. He wondered if Alam had removed all the incriminating evidence.

It was possible that he had. Possible that he hadn't

Scenario three: The ghost of his association with Jahanara was still haunting him and the Direction Finders must have zeroed in on his living room fireplace.

It was eminently feasible.

A chilling shiver almost paralysed the pumping muscles of Harfan's heart.

Well! He was as good as a dead scarecrow now. Instead of rotting in the ISI dungeons and being shot through his skull he should make good his escape.

But how was he going to pull off the vanishing trick? Crossing over to India through the land border was impossible. If not the Rangers, the Indian security forces were sure to make fine mince of his meat, bone and tissue.

His visa was still valid for the UK and Canada. Perhaps he could take a chance and disappear from Pakistan.

Without Jamilla and Parvez?

By no means he would do that. Harfan's body chemistry instinctively responded to the absurd thought. He shifted position and lighted another cigarette.

No. Life wasn't worth escaping the ISI dragnet without Jamilla and Parvez.

Could he disappear into East Pakistan, taking help from his friends, Major Anjum Mani of the SSG and Ahsan Khondokar, a wing commander in Pakistan Air Force? They'd helped him in 1969, during the Imphal assassination plot by the ISI-SSG and Markaz combine. Major Mani's latest offer was still valid. The freedom fighters might not find it difficult to push him and Jamilla across the Indian border.

Harfan chewed on the cigarette butt, spat it out and lighted another. Bolting from Lahore and disappearing in Dacca would appear incongruous, even as a figment of imagination. No. He wouldn't bolt the field leaving Jamilla and Parvez at the mercy of the curved beaks and sharp talons of the ISI falcons.

Could he count on Alam? He didn't expect Alam or any one else from the Indian agency to rescue him. His last encounter with Alam, a free and frank one, had helped Harfan to crawl out of the cocoon of false security he had woven around himself. The message was loud and clear; Delhi didn't retrieve its soured agents. In real life, the spymasters hardly despatched rescue planes and choppers, at the wrong end of midnight, to airlift their valuable assets in distress. Alam was correct. An inexpensive bullet was the final reward for a compromised spy.

Harfan smiled silently. The damn fool that he was!

This intelligence fraternity, the NSI and the rest of them were the clearinghouses for falsehood, deceit and clumsy intrigue. They often bluffed their way out with the government of the day. Befouling a novice like him was as easy as a magician pulling out a rabbit from his hat.

Harfan didn't feel angry. Perhaps his foolish romanticism had benumbed his reasoning. Perhaps he was just caught up in the trap of a vague revenge mindset, woven by the FIB psy-war experts. He'd just fallen into their trap. But what would he do about the dream mission of avenging his father's assassination? Had Jamilla's arrival in his life and this latent threat dissolved his resolution?

No. Yes and Perhaps.

No. He could by no means identify Jamilla with Pakistan. His love for her in no way impeded his mission.

Yes. He had sure lost himself in the neo-realities of Jamilla and Parvez. His love for them had transcended the pseudo-reality of his cover, fabricated by the intelligence experts.

Perhaps he was scared of the possibility of walking down to the Badr interrogation centre of the ISI. Perhaps he was afraid of dying the death of a frontline soldier.

Did a frontline soldier fight for patriotism? Or did he kill the advancing enemy simply to preserve his own life? People glorified dead soldiers simply with a view to attracting new fodder for the trenches!

The Delhi spymasters had deceptively and fraudulently bestowed their creation with more than nine lives and had lulled his senses into believing the fables of miraculous resurrection games. No spy had probably lived beyond one life, short or long, to serve his country, in this amorphous and undefined profession.

No one was going to immortalise him in ballads and nursery rhymes. He wasn't another patriotic soldier, falling down to enemy bullets. He was a simple spy, a shadowy creature; no one was ready to own up to. His today was uncertain and his tomorrow might not dawn.

The high priests of jingoistic nationalism usually conjured up magical philosophies for perpetuating the virtues of war and hatred. Very few of these conjurers had ever lived on the razor's edge and faced the booming guns, a few fatal inches away from the enemy trenches. They never limped back home to write edifying accounts of their bravery.

Harfan recalled a poem by Cecil Day Lewis:

There was laughter and loving in the lanes at evening;
Handsome were the boys then, and girls were gay,
But lost in Flanders by medalled commanders
The lads of the village are vanished away.

The poet had sung prophetically. An open or secret war, carried in its wake, death and destruction. No permanent civilisation was ever built by waging wars on innocent people. Some of the ballad singers of holy and golden wars, Harfan reasoned, were victims of the same voodoo rituals, motivated by war hysteria against known and unknown enemies.

Perhaps, men required to invent enemies, like their own shadows, for justifying the ghost of aggression and domination running through their veins, inherited from the dark cave dwelling days, camp fires, primitive tools, gnashing teeth and guttural sounds.

The warmongers, titillated the minds of the innocent gullible people, conditioned by the bombardment of propaganda by the priests, the rulers, the dictators and democrats. They were a class apart. They ruled by extolling the virtues of war. Civilisations had spun their own vainglorious tales around war, and had given them cultural and religious sanction.

Was he trying to formulate a philosophy to support his escape strategy?

The ridiculous thought kept on plaguing Harfan.

To hell with Delhi! Harfan lighted another cigarette.

Why was he weighing the possibility of bolting from Pakistan? Jhumra was his destiny. He would stay put to fight his own war. He wasn't going to bolt Pakistan before he liquidated his father's assassins. This one precious life, bestowed on him, Harfan mused, wasn't going to be submitted under to the scimitars of the NSI and ISI cheerleaders.

Why should he? He wouldn't.

Harfan clenched his fist and banged the back of the driver's seat. The Jhumra war was a personal mission. This was one war, Harfan resolved, that he must fight to the last bullet. Some one must pay with his blood, for spilling his father's blood.

Harfan's eyes suddenly detected the piercing eyes of Latiff intently examining him through the rear view mirror. Was he a suspect in his eyes too? Or did he act abnormally in a fit of shadow boxing?

"We're here sir. Your servant is never late."

The screeching sounds of the car and Latiff's voice brought Harfan out of his woolly thoughts. His car was already inside the factory gates.

Israr Sharief stood at the top of the stairs, flanked by General Naqi and Captain Ayoob.

Thank god! Harfan held his breath and released ounces of captive air slowly, with an audible sound. It was altogether a different reception party!

Was it? How did the canvass change? Latiff wouldn't lie, though he hadn't got the theme correct. The ISI never raided people for foreign exchange violations. They usually dug their teeth in real deep into the flesh of their prey, for a genuine kill.

Harfan's presumption wasn't correct either. Gen. Naqi and Ayoob weren't there to receive him. They were emerging out of a meeting with Israr Sharief, the Managing Director of Israr International.

Naqi was on an urgent visit. A sensitive piece of intelligence from agent Aftab in New Delhi had made the CMLA and the President lose his cool. The Indian forces were in battle readiness, in the eastern front; the probable D-day was November 20-21 night, the day of the holy Eid (Muslim religious festival). CIA's U2 spy photographs and station operators in Delhi and Dacca independently corroborated Aftab's message.

The message from Pentagon was loud and clear. The Indian forces were fox trotting to launch an attack in Chandpura, Belonia salient, Benapole and Hilli, all in the eastern front. It had virtually encircled East Pakistan by deploying 6 Divisions. Artillery brigades, cavalry formations and heavy field guns were observed in Agartala, Tura and Karimganj sectors. Two Para-brigades awaited dropping behind the Pakistani lines in Mymensingh and Tangail sectors.

The sharp and shrill US message had shaken up President Arif Khan. Defending East Pakistan was a greater strategic need for Washington, if not for Islamabad. US interest in South East Asia could not be surrendered to India, a Moscow surrogate. The White House couldn't allow East Pakistan to become an Indian protectorate.

The Chinese ambassador, wantonly sweet and sour, added to Islamabad's worries. Peking, he said, wasn't in a position to roll their forces down the Himalayas. The Russian Bear had been growling menacingly along the Mongolian borders, across the Usuri River. Peking's fighters and bombers were tied up against the renegade, bourgeoisie and reactionary forces of Moscow. The ambassador, however, assured Islamabad that the great Peoples' Republic of China would step up military hardware supplies, of course in lieu of appropriate compensation in hard US currency.

The Chinese volte-face was counterbalanced by the generous under the sleeve offers from Washington. Pakistan wouldn't starve for military hardware, though there was an official embargo on arms supply. The secret tunnels to NATO supplies would be opened up via Riyadh, Amman and Istanbul routes.

Gen. Naqi came calling to explore the possibility of pressing in a few more mercenary chartered flights to augment the airlifting operations at break neck speed. The dough, the visiting Assistant Secretary of State had whispered, would come from Fort Knox. All he expected Islamabad to do was to reinforce the airlifting operations by the CIA approved Athena Air Lines.

"Hello Harfan," Gen. Naqi was mighty pleased to see the daredevil ***muhajir***.

"How was your mission?" Asked Israr.

"Harrowing. The Indian fighters are in total command of our airspace. Two of their Gnats buzzed us for about 5 minutes, before we were allowed to land. It's risky to fly these machines there. And I presume the bloody Bengalis have their eyes and ears open even inside the undergarments of our bosses and men there." Harfan briefly described his latest air adventure to Dacca.

"Interesting. Come up some time. I'd like to get a first hand account of your adventure with the Bongs. I have to rush now. Ayoob will be with you for plugging in the remaining holes."

"But sir, it's risky all the way. I'm afraid whether my boys can live up to your expectations." Israr replied.

"Keep trying and that's all we can do, besides praying."

"Don't you think that the Americans should get directly involved? They can't allow the dismemberment of Pakistan." Israr Sharief asked.

"We've plenty of indications that the rattling sounds from Peking are empty, and they've belied our expectations." Naqi blurted out his bitterness over the alleged Chinese betrayal.

"I'm talking of direct US intervention." Israr added.

"No. They won't. They're afraid of the possible Russian response," Naqi added, "The US President has directed his trouble-shooter to divert military hardware from Jordan and Saudi. You know very well Israr that, our friends are putting pressure on the Security Council to restrain India, and the 7th Fleet is on an emergency sailing order to the Bay of Bengal."

"Hope Washington won't abandon Pakistan." Israr commented, echoing the fervent expectations of fellow Pakistanis.

"That's our only prayer. Only ***Allah*** and America can save our skins now." Naqi asked the driver to accelerate, for the office of the PSO.

"***Allah*** shall not let down his faithful." Israr added. He turned to Harfan and said, "I know it's cruel. But may I request you to spend a little time and get a detailed briefing from Capt. Ayoob, about the latest inventory?"

"I'd like to discuss a few points with you." Harfan tried to convey the urgency of his proposition.

"Let's talk it over dinner. There's no emergency, I hope. Please get going. I've to locate Alam and hire a few extra chartered flights. The situation is getting desperate." Israr left for his executive suite.

Harfan winked at Ayoob to follow him.

"So how have you been?" Asked Ayoob.

"Spare me a minute." Harfan dialled Jamilla's Lahore number.

She picked up the phone.

"You didn't call from Dacca." She complained.

"I couldn't darling. There were problems of communications. How have you been? How's my Parvez." Harfan flooded Jamilla with all the questions he could shoot out in one single breath.

"Talk to your ***farishta (angel)***." Jamilla put the receiver in front of the bubbling and gurgling infant.

For a few moments Harfan lost himself in the world of utter bliss, in the meaningless sounds from Parvez and Jamilla's sweet inviting voice. He must visit Lahore at least for a day. She missed him and she wanted him very much, very warmly and intimately. Harfan could disconnect only after conceding a promise to visit her by the weekend, which was two days away.

Ayoob enjoyed the prolonged telephonic exchange, not less important than the impending war between India and Pakistan.

"Sorry friend," Harfan apologised, "I hope you understand."

"No problem ***dost*** (friend). Such problems are elixirs of life, nobler than carrying weapons to Dacca. Shall we say that this bloody war atmosphere is spoiling our appetite for love and fun? Why can't we bury the hatchet, between our two countries?" Ayoob echoed Harfan's sentiments.

"You appear to have changed your views since we last met!"

"Patriotism is fine ***yar*** (friend), but look at the foolishness we keep on committing on issues not even vital to our survival. Why can't we accept the follies of partition and live in the real world of human values? We didn't bargain for these waves of blood and misery."

"Your lovely lady appears to have brought about changes in your philosophy of life!"

"Look at the folly ***yar***, I'm supposed to take a flight to Dacca and join my unit at Jessore. Is it fair?" Ayoob sounded mighty bitter.

"All's fair in love and war, as they say. Forget it. These politicians and power brokers won't allow us to live in peace. Any way, let's talk business now. What's the new crisis all about?"

Harfan ordered tea and some onion and aubergine fried in batter.

The President was worked up; Ayoob explained, on receipt of a high-level intelligence input about Indian war-plan on the holy day of Eid, November 20-21. A top Pakistani agent in India, Ayoob added, corroborated the Pentagon reports.

"But, how reliable is this highly placed source in Delhi?" Asked Harfan.

"Can't say ***yar***." Ayoob crunched on the delicate snacks and replied, "It's perhaps the same Aftab."

"Do you think it's so easy to access such top secret decisions? Perhaps the ISI doesn't have such deep penetration."

"Don't underestimate them. Aftab, I'm told is a precious asset, and a top politician at that."

"Is this Indian politician a long term asset?"

"I don't really know, but my friend says that the ISI top brass has started developing doubts about his sincerity." Ayoob continued with his sub-conscious leakage.

"Then his days should be numbered." Replied Harfan.

"May be, you don't run a marathon with a leaking oil can. It can spoil your style and gait."

Ayoob, true to his character, revealed more than what Harfan had expected him to.

"Tell me what's the new task at hand." Harfan reverted back to the contents of Israr's briefing.

"Your company has to hire 3 more cargo planes and expedite the airlifting operations. To avoid complications the birds should fly non-stop to Chittagong."

"What about refuelling?"

"Washington has agreed to loan two aircrafts for mid-air refuelling."

"Do these Boeing 707s have aerial refuelling facilities?"

"I don't know. Check with Israr and Alam Khan. Keep this inventory of weapons, the friends have agreed to supply, in addition to earlier endowments."

Ayoob paused for a while and suddenly lowered his voice to a feeble modulation.

"Perhaps this is my last meeting with you."

"Why? Are there any restrictions?" Harfan asked the probing question expecting Ayoob to blurt out additional information on the Direction Finder episode.

"Oh yes!" Ayoob obliged, "Recall that DF story? We'd pinpointed the suspected radio station to Jhumra. Aren't you from there?"

"No. I happen to live there."

"That's it. The ISI had raided few houses and drawn a blank. I believe they visited your house too."

"Don't tell me that, I don't deserve this after all that I'm doing."

"Don't despair. The ISI has queer ways of needling their suspects. General Naqi knows all about it and he has pulled up General Hyder." Ayoob tried to console a visibly upset Harfan.

"So you have to go to the front? What about your lady love?"

"Yes ***yar.*** I'm too junior to be a permanent fixture in the CMLA office. My unit, as I told you, has been shifted to Jessore in East Pakistan. I've received the marching orders."

The young captain stood up, put on his cap and saluted.

Harfan embraced Ayoob, with an overwhelming and surging lump in his throat. The poor fellow, just married, might not return home, to the tolling of welcoming bells. His body might not even be retrieved by the retreating troops. Perhaps he wouldn't even receive a decent burial.

The ISI receded back for a while, and Harfan's mind strayed into the killing fields of East Pakistan: Ayoob trying to defend his bunker and life. Perhaps his imagination would be concentrated on the tender face of his wife, rather than on the advancing steps of death. His bullets perhaps carried the message of love and survival, survival for the sake of his love. It mattered little if the same bullets carried death for his adversaries.

"It's a pity that our wives haven't met." Harfan took out his wallet and carefully fished out a photograph of Jamilla, "Look, here's my soul mate."

Ayoob intently looked at the charming photo of Jamilla and instinctively brought out his wife's photograph.

"Here's Reshma, my wife. She's just twenty. Isn't she beautiful?"

"Heavenly."

A sudden flood of pity and sadness overwhelmed Harfan, for Ayoob, for himself, Jamilla, Parvez and Reshma. Perhaps all of them would be offered at the altar of hatred. There was no escape from the crunch of distorted history, crafted by the wily politicians, on either side of the border.

"See you soon. ***Khuda Hafiz***." Harfan wished the departing Captain.

"***Insha Allah***, if I return alive from the front."

"Most of us live in some kind of front Ayoob. All of us fight some kind of war; mostly for the survival of the vested interests. We sacrifice our today for their tomorrow. But we shall survive." Harfan replied.

"I'm a soldier and I know better when to expect a bullet. I can already sniff the smell of cordite. The fools in Islamabad have sown the seeds of blood and distrust. Pakistan will disintegrate, thanks to the perverted psyche of the Punjabis and this Sindhi demagogue."

"Brother you sound like a bit of politician yourself."

"No politics ***yar***. We ***muhajirs*** created Pakistan, only to be butchered by the Punjabis and Sindhis. We don't want war. The people don't want it. Why can't we live with the Bengalis in peace and sanity?"

"Don't get upset. Time will take care of all the aberrations. History can be corrected by time alone. Convey my ***salaam*** to Reshma." Harfan escorted Ayoob to his vehicle.

Harfan was amazed by Ayoob's brief outburst. He was a bit of a lout. But sometimes he talked sense. There must be somewhere in him some trace genes of a desert troubadour, the irresistible emotional ballad singer.

Caught between in the cleft edges of two religions Harfan hardly said his prayers. But, today he raised his hands and prayed to ***Allah,*** for Ayoob's safe return, to the warm embraces of Reshma.

Chapter 46

The dinner meeting at Hotel Royal Palace started on a tense note.

Harfan spoke in a hushed voice and didn't hide his hurt and apprehensions.

"I'm sorry Harfan. There has been some terrible misunderstanding." Israr responded on a sympathetic note.

"Why should you be sorry? I think I should resign. This has landed me in a heap of social garbage." Harfan spoke with simulated hurt in his voice.

The apparent innocence and bruised feelings were aimed at squeezing out detailed information from Israr. He must know the precise details of the damage control measures taken by his employer. Israr Sharief, his shield, should be used to maximum advantage.

Israr obliged. In a low decibel monologue he narrated his encounters with the PSO and other top brass. They were convinced, Israr added, that a junior officer had bungled all the way. He was probably misguided by some erratic electronic signals. And Harfan's wasn't the only house searched by the ISI. Probably, he hastened to add, Nawab had planted some stories against him.

"That's no insurance against the ISI. Hungry tigers don't simply kiss their supper. They eat it."

"Oh Harfan!" Israr spoke in a flattering voice, "Don't get upset. I'm there to protect you. You'd better get going with the job."

"You know your brother better. I believe he's a partner of General Hyder."

"That's correct. And that's why the ISI is on a demolition operation, against me. You're a mere front. I'm the target. But I've Sarfaraz and Naqi with me. And Jahanara is our good friend."

"That's the problem Israr sahib. She's in the eye of the storm of political conspiracy and I've been sucked into it just for the heck of it." Harfan explained his position.

"I understand. All of us are entangled with one or the other arm of the vicious twister. We'll take care. Please get going with the flights."

"I would like to take a day off."

"Lahore?"

Harfan didn't reply.

"Just take my car after dinner and drive down to Lahore. Latiff will drive you. Return by midday. I'm expecting Alam ***sahib***. He'll help in contracting the additional charters." Israr handed over another fat envelope to Harfan.

"What's this?"

"Keep this. It's a small portion of your share of the profit. The airlifting operations are going to get us millions. This is for your wife and kid."

"But sir," Harfan added, "Money can't repair the damage done by Hyder's people. I don't know how can I show my face to Zahoor sahib."

"Don't worry about that. Sarfaraz has spoken to him. In fact, Zahoor sahib is helping out the government in lower Indus areas."

"What's he doing there?"

"I believe the Indians are trying to pump in weapons to some Sindhi parochial groups through the sea route. He is mobilising a volunteer force in aid of the navy and the border rangers."

"It's a news to me. I did not know that he had that kind of influence over the ***mohana*** people."

"He's the uncrowned king of the ***mohana*** area. Don't wreck your head over that small incident. Zahoor understands the intricacies of the situation. ***Khuda Hafiz.***"

As Israr left with a hopeful note Ibadat closed in with a pot of coffee.

"Spare me a bit of your time."

"Sit down."

"No. Not here. Your mind is in Lahore. Take this cover, read the contents on your way. Follow the disposal instructions. Memorise the contents before destroying it. Meet me before you go on your next errand."

Ibadat took out a cover from inside his hotel livery, handed it over to Harfan and said good night.

The reading light in the Mercedes emitted adequate illumination. Harfan opened the envelope. The letter was from Alam. He had inscribed instructions for disposal on top of the letter.

"These papers are edible and the ink is non-toxic. Chew it and gulp it down with your favourite whisky."

It was one of the standard prescriptions in the intelligence community.

Harfan lighted a cigarette, nudged closer to the reading light and unfolded the pages.

"Read carefully. In your job you won't survive even a slight mistake. This is your last chance, ***Insha Allah***....

"I've dismantled the HF trans-receiver and removed all Ellnt (electronic intelligence) equipment. Be sure, they won't find any trace of it. The raid has been a blind one. The top bosses have closed the chapter, but it's being pursued by a dedicated group of professionals.... I should say that you are yet to be badly scratched.

"Your communication channels have been restructured....

"Lahore has been divided into 6 Dead Letter Boxes (DLBs): Anarkali Bazaar (code: Mughal-e-Azam); Lahore Fort (Almond); Statue of Quaid-e-Azam at Bagh-e-Jinnah (Mazar); The broken wall at the western corner of Shalimar Gardens (Chinar); Underside of the culvert at the junction of Melaram Road and Lower Mall (Jasan); Hollow behind the statue at Mozang Bazaar park (Laila)....

"Twice a month you shall drop your written reports in a pre-selected DLB and disappear. Don't bother about clearance....

"For brush communication: Walk along Egerton Road on the second Sunday between 3 and 3.30 p.m.; attend ***namaz*** on the third Friday at Wazir Khan mosque; the fourth bench on the northern side of Bagh-e-Jinnah should be used on the third Tuesday....

"Only one Live Letter Box (LLB) is suggested: Under the portico of Roshni gate, leading to the tomb of Maharaja Ranjit Singh, look for an old leper beggar, who squats there 365 days a year. Deposit your despatch with him. Code: offer one half of the ten-rupee note enclosed. The other part will be with him. Match the numbers and match the contours and edges before passing on any document to him. Use a new note every time or fix your own code. New LLBs will be developed later...

"Keep up a brave face. Listen to Ibadat. Avoid Rama Bai. Observe all anti-surveillance techniques and all security tradecrafts."

"Latiff, how far are we from Lahore?"

"Another 40 minutes ***janab***."

"Faster friend."

"Don't worry. We'll be there before 11."

Harfan took out a flask, poured a drink and put the papers in it. The rice paper dissolved, leaving a few bubbles on the surface. Harfan sipped the drink and silently thanked Alam for sanitising his house well before the ISI reached there

His thoughts traversed back to Ibadat. The mystery shrouding him was peeling off fast. The sly fox was fast transforming from the amorphous to a solid, a perfect Indian plant at Jhumra. Whatever he was, he used his cover deftly. Was he loyal to the slain king? Did Alam recruit him as an intermediate agent? Ibadat, Harfan reasoned, fitted the description of an intermediate agent, who facilitated the master-agent's multi-directional manoeuvres.

Was Alam a KGB style master spy handler, located in Pakistan? Must be. He surely derived his authority from Delhi. And all that he had said about the termination of a sour agent echoed Nampoothiri's thesis of unclaimed baggage.

What about Rama Bai? Was the agency using her too?

She was guarding, deep in her chest, too many secrets of the former royal family. The ISI wouldn't have any qualms about cracking her bones, if that helped them in reaching an Indian resident agent. She was indeed a weak link in the chain.

What should he do with her? Kill her?

No. It wasn't possible. He wouldn't allow any harm to a friend of his mother.

The car screeched to a halt and Latiff sounded the horn twice.

"Sir it's 11 p.m. and we're here." He declared proudly.

"Thanks a lot ***dost.*** Park the car and rest in the usual room. We start at 9 am sharp."

Jamilla ran. The sound of the car's engine, two familiar honks and the footsteps sent signals of recognition streaming into her cranium. Her pounding heart made her legs wheel faster to the door.

Harfan landed straight into her arms and before he could close the door behind him, she implanted a squirming high voltage kiss on his lips. The invitation to a sleepless night was very warm, warmer than the churning heat in a galactic core.

Zahoor Chaudry and Sayeefa briefly took over from Jamilla and in another 30 minutes Harfan was in Jamilla's arms. The parched soil was really pining for an intense spell of rain. Jamilla reminded Harfan of her expectations for a thundering typhoon and not some miserly pre-monsoon drops.

Harfan slithered out of Jamilla's embrace late in the night, entered the toilet and took out an electronic pocket encoder. He composed a report in convertible numerical code, selecting each group carefully from the generated figures. Delhi would use a mainframe computer to break the code. The FIB and the Joint Cipher Bureau experts had taught him this emergency coding technique.

To say ***al vida*** (adieu) to Jamilla and Parvez wasn't an easy job. The young angel shook his head incessantly and simply refused to release Harfan's collars. His innocuous biological tools to prevent papa from boarding the car seemed to be more powerful than a mighty tow-crane.

Harfan flooded his young angel with kisses and reluctantly asked Latiff Masih to drive straight to Sangla factory, with a small diversion by Roshni Gate.

The old leper was there. His limbs were amply bandaged, with oozing blood marks all over them. Harfan casually walked down to the leper, after directing Latiff to fetch a packet of cigarette.

The beggar examined the finely scissored ten-rupee note, brought out the other half and passed it on to the stranger, with a rather uncertain look in his eyes. Harfan matched the two halves and passed on a neatly secured polyethylene bag. It contained a detailed report on weapons ferried to Dacca and Chittagong and the cipher message encoded last night.

"Some of the papers...." Harfan couldn't finish the sentence.

"Don't talk." The beggar whispered and than started screaming, "***Allah*** is omniscient. He knows your inner wishes and will fulfil your desires."

The LLB noticed Latiff crossing over from the other end of the road and started canting in a wailing voice, "***Allah*** shall give you hundred fold, give ten rupees to the ***kori*** (leper)."

Harfan took out two halves of a ten-rupee currency note, passed on one half to the leper, and put the other half in his purse.

"Sir, you shouldn't go near these ***koris*** (lepers). ***Allah*** alone knows why they allow such dangerous animals to roam free. They should either be shot dead or thrown into the Ravi."

Latiff indignantly emptied his mouth of ***paan*** (betel leaf) juices, directing the liquid spittle hardly a foot away from the leper. That was his social reaction to an ostracised leprosy patient, begging on the roadside.

"Don't be so hard on this unfortunate fellow. It's a curable disease." Harfan tipped the beggar lavishly and followed Latiff to the car. He was satisfied with the LLB arrangement, an excellent cover and a sure-fire conduit. He admired the tradecraft expertise of Alam.

Harfan's mind raced back to his work place. The next few days, he presumed would be tough and his survival would depend on the whims of the Indian fighter jets and the ISI sleuths.

What a choice it was! A nutty Hobson's choice!

Harfan's neurones resumed emitting cross signals as Latiff concentrated on driving and beating the winds. Contradictory waves kept on rocking him.

The most devastating thing had happened to him. The ISI had short-listed him for counter intelligence investigations. Israr was a novice in these matters. In technical terminology of the intelligence fraternity he was earmarked by the ISI as a SIA, suspected intelligence agent. Their sleuths were expected to follow the rules of the trade and investigate him thoroughly. He had very little safety margin left to hedge himself behind Israr. And Israr was too knave a person to understand these complicated matters. What mattered most to him was his business interest.

And what about Nampoothiri? He was sure to scratch him out from his inventory of spooks. By his own admission he never did claim his lost baggage.

So! The situation was far from comfortable.

Neither of the agencies was likely to show any mercy.

He was a lone ranger in this game of foxes. Could he out-fox the master jackals!

The conflicting cross currents started sinking into his brain, like the paralysing toxin of a tarantula, sending signals of numbness through his limbs. Harfan jerked off the sinking feeling with a deliberate motion and stretched his limbs and lighted a cigarette.

To hell with the paralysing feeling and surrendering to fate! That was a trash philosophy taught by the Hindu fatalists. He was the master of his destiny. He was prepared to play the game immaculately, according to his own rules. He would live, Harfan vowed, beyond the copybook regulations of the NSI and the ISI.

But the creeping fear of being bumped off by an assailant's bullets still kept on haunting him. He wondered if the hot lead would come first from the Indian or Pakistani barrels. Bullets carrying death weren't embossed with stamps of religion with marks of the nationality etched on them. He was, Harfan concluded, vulnerable to both, the barrels of the Indians and Pakistanis, sandwiched between the two killer agencies.

Latiff screeched the car to a halt in front of the factory and announced, "Sir, it's twelve and we are at Sangla."

Harfan shrugged off the shadow of death stalking his thoughts. How stupid could he get? Harfan smiled to himself.

"Thanks ***dost***, for the excellent drive."

"Sir, your servant can beat the wind."

"Sure you can."

Harfan climbed the stairs silently.

Yes. He had in him the capability of banishing the dark thoughts that haunted him. The nuclear fission inside was still capable of exploding in deadly eruptions and blinding the forces of death. He could beat the mighty machines of the NSI and the ISI. That power was within him. Why should he be afraid of the lurking shadows? The sun was sure to rise tomorrow and many more tomorrows for him, Jamilla and Parvez. He should better look towards that disc of eternal energy rather than counting the dark footsteps of death.

Harfan remembered and recited slowly but resolutely the couplets from ***Yajurveda*** (one of the ***Vedas***), he had learnt from his mother: O Sun God! Your golden disc hides the face of Truth. Uncover that, O Sun, in order that I, the worshipper of Truth, may see your eternal flame.

Harfan took a deep breath and mustered the courage to kiss the brazen face of truth. He must beat the stalking truth of death and reaffirm his own truth, the truth of love and life.

Chapter 47

It was another bad morning indeed.

Balachandran Nampoothiri was simply caught up in a sticky web of confusion. Two stiff coffees concocted by Jatadhari and the endearing Havana didn't help in dissolving the fog. It still appeared to be seeping inside the crevices of his cranium.

He drew back the curtains and looked down at the traffic zooming past the streets below. From his eleventh floor window they looked like toy buggies. He looked yonder, towards the watery glimpses of the river Yamuna, which was virtually a sewer drain of India's capital. His mind was behaving like that yonder clogged poodle, the dirty Yamuna. It wasn't flowing in any specific direction.

Three top-secret red folders were lying open on his table. Nampoothiri had been leafing through the pages for the last two hours. He couldn't make up his mind.

The thinner red folder with a distinctive marking of the cipher section was on top of the pile. This was yet another message from Triple X, received four days back, through the Kabul diplomatic bag. It contained another bombshell.

His specific information on the Pakistani mole Aftab left no room for doubt. It was Ram Karan Prasad all the way. He was Islamabad's Aftab, Operation Sun, in simple English. Aftab had shared with the ISI the key war-cabinet decision that gave the green signal to the Armed Forces to cross the East Pakistan borders on November 20-21 night. Nampoothiri was present in all the meetings. His inputs on the scanty massing of Chinese troops on the northern slopes of Nathu La, Jelep La and Chumbi Valley features had assured Delhi that the yellow dragon wasn't yet ready to come to Pakistan's help.

China, though it was making symptomatic noises, Nampoothiri had advised, wasn't in a position to roll down the Himalayas, because of internal compulsions. And November wasn't the correct time to negotiate the frozen Himalayan passes.

Washington's anxiety, his report added, over the progress of the Soviet Pacific Fleet towards the Strait of Malacca had prompted the White House to signal a red alert to its Seventh Fleet, stationed at Subic Bay.

His input had emphasised the ominous contacts between the Commander of the East Pakistan Garrison and a prominent pro-Chinese Bengali Marxist-Leninist leader, waging a so-called class struggle, in the tea plantations of Darjeeling Terai. Pakistan, Nampoothiri had concluded, was ready to confront the ***Mukti Bahini*** and the Indian troops in live action, across the borders. Islamabad had ordered surprise raids on guerrilla training camps in Indian Bengal and Assam.

Only eight people were privy to the vital Cabinet decision.

Nampoothiri had examined threadbare all the names, including that of Shankar, the impetuous son of the PM. Mandira wasn't a novice. She had no doubt put Shankar on probation, but he was yet to take over control of the thinking processes of his mother.

The involvement of the Generals was ruled out.

The other ministers known to have access to the information were probed. A tap on their telephones proved sterile.

The President of the Republic, technically the Chief Commander of the Armed Forces was an important recipient of the personal briefing by the Prime Minister. Nampoothiri's telephone spooks had drawn a blank there too.

Nampoothiri was reluctant to take up the Aftab riddle once again with the PM. He was not sure if she would give the nod of consent. He had decided to bide his time till he had some solid evidence to confront her.

He closed the Triple X cipher and pressed the buzzer for Amrita.

"Yes sir." Amrita came on the intercom.

"Call Robin." He opened the other folder that was received from Alam via Kabul station, on the heel of the Triple X message.

The other red cover worried Nampoothiri most. It contained a cipher from Alamgir that analysed astutely the security status of Triple X. The third cover, which contained another interesting report from Double X Qurban, supplemented the cipher from Alam.

Harfan's penetration was unique, Alam's report added, and he possessed the rare qualities of charming his targets with electrifying impulses. But he exhibited the characteristics of a comet, burning brightly no doubt, but leaving blazing trails behind him. A clandestine operative couldn't afford to shine brightly and leave behind smoky trails.

Contradictory psychological traits had made him vulnerable. A thorough nationalist and patriot, Triple X was totally committed to his profession. But his hatred for Pakistan and Muslims had suffered a serious dilution. His marriage to Jamilla had transformed the intelligence robot into a human being. His love had transcended his cover and developed a soft membrane around his soul. He could perhaps die, for his love, but not for the mission.

Alam's analysis charted out three probable courses of action that Harfan could adopt when caught in the ISI net: rot in a Pakistani jail; turn over and serve the ISI as a double agent, with a view to saving his wife and child, and defect to a third country.

The possibility of his neutralisation by the ISI wasn't imminent. The process had just started. Permanent silence of the valuable asset, Alamgir recommended, would spare the agency and India severe embarrassment. His silence would ensure the continuity of at least ten other deeper penetration agents.

Nampoothiri didn't share agent Qurban's message with his desk officer. It had offered more tactical details of the operational mechanism of the ISI. Though officially buried, a dedicated team of counter-intelligence experts was pursuing Operation Salamat, the ISI nom de plume of the investigations against Harfan.

An extraordinary disclosure by Qurban had rattled Nampoothiri. He had noticed, the Double X agent revealed, the existence of growing symptoms of hostility between Alamgir and Harfan. The bridge of trust between the two had collapsed. Alamgir, he suspected, was of the view that, Harfan should be physically neutralised before the ISI caught up with him. This contemplated action, Qurban averred, could vitiate the ambience of confidence that was essential for survival in the hostile environment.

Nampoothiri weighed the arguments proffered by Alamgir and his Joint Secretary, Robin Achariya. These were textbook arguments, taught in espionage schools all over the world.

But he wasn't convinced. There was something in Qurban's message that required very careful evaluation.

Was he in love with his creation? Nampoothiri thought over his possible emotional entanglement with XXX. No. Deep inside the pool of conflicting currents, he couldn't locate an iota of emotional attachment. But the professional spymaster didn't agree with Alamgir. His rational reflected a primeval truth, his urge for self-preservation. That sounded natural enough. But why should he contemplate to take the extraordinary step of liquidating Harfan?

Was Alamgir in love with his own image? Was he trying to preserve his riches or his family, who were secure in Switzerland?

Perhaps he was being too uncharitable to Alamgir. Nampoothiri shrugged off the thought. The NSI, he reasoned, should make an independent evaluation. Objectivity was the key, and he shouldn't be prejudiced by a single report from Qurban. But an ominous signal continued ticking away at the back of his mind. It told him that the correct time hadn't come for ordering physical neutralisation of Triple X.

For a while he weighed the feasibility of a smooth separation process, a final golden handshake with Triple X. The separation process, particularly from an important and sensitive agent was often complicated. Nampoothiri knew this well. Each step required perfect calibration. The quicksand of misfiring had often left dirty debris even for agencies like the CIA and MI6. The KGB and GRU, however, being closet organisations, never publicised their graveyard of follies. They believed in shooting from the hip and giving a frosty Siberian burial to their rogue and soured agents.

Nampoothiri was more intrigued by the arguments of Robin Achariya, who was ushered in by Amrita Bhalla.

"I find that you have recommended the liquidation of Triple X. Why should we?" Nampoothiri asked his desk officer.

"He has outlived his utility," Achariya commented, "He can defect to the enemy camp any time."

"What gives you this impression?"

"He has developed a vested interest in Pakistan. That's amply proved by his involvement with the mercenary flights."

"Don't you think it strengthens his cover?" Nampoothiri tried to draw out his operations chief.

"Triple X knows too much about the organisation. His interception by the ISI will endanger other assets. Why don't we shoot down his next flight over the Bay of Bengal? A heat-seeking missile won't leave any reaction time for the pilot."

"Nonsense! That'd give Washington an excuse to land their Marines at Chittagong."

"We could pass it off as an accident."

"Well Robin," Nampoothiri chided his deputy, "The Yankees may be anything else but dumb fools. Leave the matter to me."

He pushed the file aside and dismissed Robin Achariya.

By late evening Nampoothiri had made up his mind.

Triple X should have a fair chance to explain his position. The NSI should know what had really gone wrong. The disease couldn't be diagnosed by remote control. The ISI was indeed suspicious of Harfan's linkages with certain key personalities in Pakistan. But they had no proof of his being an Indian resident. The clandestine radio was decommissioned well in time and even Alam couldn't pin a sticker on him for any major tradecraft lapse. Harfan, if not seen through the Alam prism and offered to Robin's scimitar, deserved a face-to-face debriefing and rehabilitation. He was still a productive agent and the time hadn't come for giving him a quiet burial.

Balachandran Nampoothiri summoned Jatadhari and asked him to seal and stack away the Alamgir folder in his personal safe, secured by a time lock.

He pressed the intercom button and asked for Dhiren Bhagat.

"How long would you take to activate the River Channel?"

"For Triple X?"

"Yes."

"Isn't it better to go via Kabul or Jalalabad?"

"No. I prefer the River Channel."

"Give me two hours sir."

Dhiren Bhagat returned around 6 pm. He had plenty of news to share.

Triple X was neck-deep in the arms ferrying operations. His employer was in no mood to spare him even for a single day. Moreover, he had hastened to add that certain people might prevent him from boarding a flight to London. The Dacca route was the safest. He could spare a few hours in Colombo, next Friday, three days hence, at hotel Tathagata International, room 1406.

Nampoothiri ruled against Bhagat's meeting with Triple X. It wouldn't be safe. Bhagat, a visible north Indian Hindu would stink like rotten fish. Col. Khaliq, the ISI station chief in Colombo, was a logged subject of the NSI. He could be under orders to place surveillance on Harfan Bukhari.

Maulana Rizwan figured as a natural choice.

He was, as part of his cover, scheduled to visit Colombo to attend a congregation of the ***Alami Tablig Jammat Ijtema*** (worldwide proselytising conference). The meeting, convened by Saudi based ***Rabita-al-Alam-al-Islami*** (World Muslim League), was supposed to voice its concern against the nefarious Indian aggression against East Pakistan. The choice of Colombo was symbolic of the security concern of India's smaller neighbours.

Nampoothiri briefed Maulana Rizwan on all possible aspects of the meeting. The safety of several NSI operations in Pakistan depended on a balanced debriefing of the asset, who was under a cloud. He must get at the roots of the problem.

Having done, what he thought he should do, Nampoothiri felt slightly relaxed.

Alamgir's survival was of paramount importance, but physical elimination of Triple X should be the last option. He felt happy that agent Qurban had opted for reporting to him directly. He also felt relieved that he hadn't opted for disclaiming the doubtful baggage. Nampoothiri had implicit trust in Harfan's personal integrity. The wild prince wasn't made of saleable stuff. The problems of his heart could perhaps be reconciled with his professional imperatives. The situation, he felt, hadn't yet expanded to desperate proportions.

Chapter 48

Raghu Chawla was caught in a knotty jam on that cool morning. The owner of the National Expression, a staunch Hindu protagonist, stormed into the editorial room and thundered at him.

"What do you think you're doing?" The burly aged fighter of many battles against the British Empire threw a bunch of papers on Raghu's table.

"What's the matter ***sethji*** (moneyed boss)?"

"Have you seen today's lead banner?"

"Yes ***sethji***. Hundred people died in a train accident."

"There's something wrong with you Raghu. If that's the banner of the day, may I ask what's happening next door in Dacca? The entire media world is busy selling the exploits of the ***Mukti Bahini*** and the imminent war between India and Pakistan. Don't you find anything better than a rail accident to figure on the front page of my paper?"

"Well ***sethji***, we're giving adequate coverage to the developments in East Pakistan."

"My foot. One requires a magnifying glass to discover those items in the 4th and 5th pages. Who decides the policy of the paper? You or me?"

"It's you sir."

"Have a look."

The elderly ***seth*** produced a computer log of the front-page banners and the edit pages for the last two weeks. The National Expression had failed to bring out a single centre page editorial or article condemning Pakistani perfidies in East Pakistan.

The National Expression, the savant of the Indian print media insisted, should focus on national imperatives. How could Chawla ignore the realities in East Pakistan and keep on fiddling the tune of friendship with the butchers of Islamabad? The agitated septuagenarian virtually sounded a termination notice on Chawla. He should change tracks pronto or quit.

The stormy visit of the ***seth*** left Raghu rattled. He was also shaken over the virtual ultimatum from Shankar, the rising son. The back-seat driver had warned that his paper was publishing junk and shit. The media advisor to the PM had pointed out that the leading national daily was virtually silent on Pakistani perfidies in East Pakistan. At this rate, Shankar threatened, he would be compelled to let lose the youth brigade storm troopers to burn the National Expression building.

No room was left for talks with Pakistan. It was now war till the very end, end to the atrocities of the military regime.

The owner of the National Expression was mighty enough to drive out his editor in sac cloth and ash. That would simply generate a new situation for the most efficient entrepreneur in Delhi. Chawla would not die of starvation. He had amassed enough for his next two generations. But no one could hope to witness the dawning of another morning after incurring Shankar's wrath. Like the Hindu God of apocalypse, after whom he was named, the prince charming was fond of using steamrollers and earth removers for burying people he didn't like.

Holy cow! How could he exit from this jam and catastrophic disaster! The tonnes of fortune he had amassed through Ram Karan and Pakistan's benevolent bounty suddenly appeared to be threatened by the concerted actions of the tax goblins and police jinns. His credibility as an editor was already in jeopardy. But Chawla knew for sure that an angry Shankar could mean broken limbs and skull.

Shit! Raghu lighted a cigarette and cursed Ram Karan and his friend Brig. Iskander for restraining his pen on the Pakistan front. The US embassy and the British High Commission too compensated him adequately for going slow on Pakistan front. It was a grave mistake, no doubt. But to change tracks suddenly, he would require consultations. He was neck deep in the stinking muck of conspiracy against the security of the nation.

Raghu gulped down a glass of water and picked up the phone.

"Karanji," He whispered, "Can we meet?"

"Come for dinner, say at ten."

"Can't it be earlier?"

"Sorry friend, I'm receiving a Nepalese delegation at eight. The guests may linger on."

Ram Karan wasn't really receiving any official delegation from the neighbouring Hindu kingdom. His business partners in the flesh and drug trade had landed in Delhi on an urgent mission; to rescue two of their operators, nabbed with a consignment of Nepalese women from a west Delhi transit shack. Ram Karan had intervened, but the rogue police officer had refused to relent. To add to the minister's worry he brought in some women's rights protagonists to highlight the shameful flesh-trade scam.

Ram Karan was in the midst of giving the final touches to the rescue plan, which involved a hold up of the police van escorting the prisoners to a trial court.

General Kalua, with two professional killers in tow was to execute the operation. But the hired killers were tough bargainers. The prices of potatoes and onions had spiralled and the target was more important than a patch of cabbage. The right price must be paid, they insisted, for harvesting the head of the rogue police officer.

Raghu Chawla, unaware of the gravity of Ram Karan's immediate priority banged the phone on its cradle. He uttered a curse. The jackal had got him entangled in the espionage net. He had survived the Col. Zaved episode by the skin of his teeth.

It was high time he extricated himself from Ram's quagmire. By his own right, Chawla mused; he was now a recognised figure in the tricky world of print media. He should now be out of this game of peddling information for earning a few thousand bucks on the slight. He had earned enough during the last twenty years. Now was the time to don long hair, a goatee and the mantle of an intellectual. The leaking boat,

Ram Karan, could be conveniently jettisoned. That scum had over lived his utility.

He lighted another cigarette and dialled the number of Shankar.

"Morning sir. Are you free?"

"Hi Chawla, your editorial this morning on Bangladesh is superb."

"Sir, we try to reflect the truth and only the truth."

"Don't be silly. I know what kind of truth you sell. Tell me if there's anything special."

"Yes sir," Chawla spoke in a spirited voice, "Some people are keen to organise mass rallies in support of the PM's East Pakistan initiative."

"Spell out the details."

Raghu's scheme was simple. The PM had caught the imagination of the nation and the international community, by boldly supporting the East Pakistan Bengalis. Ram Karan Prasad had come out with a novel idea. He wanted to organise mass rallies all over the country with a view to unify the country behind the PM. A few hundred millions could be raised from these rallies, for national defence.

"That's a grand idea Raghu." Shankar was pleased to hear from his media crony, "Let me consult mom. I'm sure she'll be pleased. Let's go ahead with it."

Shankar thanked Raghu for the brilliant idea.

Chawla's next stop was New Delhi's Tuesday Luncheon Club, an exclusive preserve of the diplomats, to which he was a permanent invitee. The diplomats of the rank of Minister, Counsellor and First Secretary were the institutional members of this exclusive club. It welcomed the new arrivals, bid adieu to the departing friends and provided a placid pool for information hunting and intelligence angling.

"You appear to be jittery." Commented Brig. Iskander, as he drifted in with a beer mug for his friend.

"Yah, with good reason. Ram Karan has been detected." Raghu whispered in Iskander's ear.

"What's fresh? His last tip was rated very highly in Islamabad. It was a real hot piece of information."

"That information was not so secret. Every second person in Delhi knew that Mandira was going to attack Pakistan around twentieth November."

"What's he up to?"

"Perhaps you haven't forgotten the pieces of disinformation catered by him. Those were real cute counter-intelligence operation by the NSI." Raghu whispered.

"What else?"

"He has reneged. He is organising rallies all over the country to kick up an anti-Pakistan hysteria. You know Iskander, he has tremendous influence on the low caste Hindus and Muslims of East Pakistan."

Chawla donned a mask of acute anxiety on his face, as he spoke.

"It doesn't matter. We're on the top."

"It's not so simple Iskander," Chawla tried to hammer in the fear of God into Iskander, "Ram was interrogated by the NSI. And I'm told he has compromised your identity."

"You aren't joking, I hope." Iskander reacted sharply.

"I'm a serious Jhangi (a district in Pakistani Punjab) businessman. And being a fellow Punjabi from Sialkot, you should know that I may poke a woman here and there, but I never joke about a serious matter like this. Ram Karan is surely in the NSI net. I feel you aren't safe. The Indians can pick you up any moment." Raghu Chwala gestured towards a waiter for a refill of his glass.

Brig. Iskander sipped his beer in silence and slowly placed his left hand on Raghu's shoulder, guiding him to a corner.

"Are you sure? I hope it's not a trick."

"Perhaps you say ***Khuda kasam*** (by God) when you swear. We say ***Ma kasam.*** I swear by my mother. You should take care of yourself and also take care of this poor journalist."

"Thanks pal. We shall take care of Karan. My man will see you in your office. It's better that way. Pay my regards to Ram Karan."

"Won't you like to personally brief him?"

"It's not necessary any more. I hope you won't ditch me!" Brig. Iskander uttered the words, as if he was chanting requiem for an old friend.

"I'm a loyal businessman Iskander. Protect my interests."

"Sure you are."

Raghu Chwala, happy over his performance, picked up the whiff of a fair and young first secretary of the USSR embassy, who was passing by and drifted towards the fluttering freyas of the diplomatic corp.

The major part of the day was well spent. He looked forward to a nice and meaningful dinner with Ram Karan.

****

Ram Karan too felt mighty relaxed. The rogue police officer had fallen to the killers' bullets. His Nepal business partners and the rescued pimps had taken a flight to Bangkok. The killers were back to their holes with a handsome bounty. General Kalua, as he usually did after every victorious engagement, had another close shave of his head and went for a brief worship of the carrier of the Lord Ganesha, the divine rodent.

The permanent minister in the Indian cabinet was ready at hand to greet Raghu. Nobody had ever blamed Ram Karan for tardy hospitality. The dinner and drinks were lavish, served by bearers wearing starched livery. As usual, Kalua supervised their discreet movement.

"Kalua." Ram Karan shouted.

"Yes sir, ***hukum karo*** (order me)." The castrated rat-eating tribal bowed in front of his master.

"You bloody low caste idiot." Ram Karan shouted, "How could you forget to serve the fried ***hilsa*** fish (Clupea Alosa) eggs, specially flown in from Calcutta, only for Raghuji?"

"My mistake master."

Kalua bowed out and came back with a plate full of delicate ***hilsa*** eggs, batter fried with garlic and ginger and a dash of green coriander and chilly.

"Heaven's here Raghuji, in these fried eggs." Ram Karan placed the plate in front of Raghu.

"I'm honoured Ramji. But, heaven is like a shifting desert dune. It's here now and moments later it may lie between the thighs of a cute belle. Isn't it?"

"You charlatan!"

Ram Karan complimented his friend for mirroring exactly his own philosophy of life. Heaven, he always felt, didn't exist beyond money, women, wine and good food. He often boasted that God was discovered by deprived people, as an amorphous replica of the powerful and muscled mortal master, who raped their women, looted their belongings and occasionally allowed them to breathe.

"I'm facing tremendous problems from my owner Karanji. On your prompting and that of Iskander, I had toned down my paper's policy on Bangladesh affairs. Because of that I'm facing the axe right now."

"It's always a tight rope walk Raghuji. My words in these matters aren't final. I give you the bare guidelines. And you're as good a friend of Iskander as I am. You're paid for these tasks. Use your discretion."

"Are you disowning me?"

"Come on Raghu," Ram Karan poured another whisky for his friend, "We've been together for all these years. How can I desert you now? I'm suggesting a pragmatic way out. You know the old Hindu saying, ***Sarvanashe Samutpanne Ardhang Tyajati Panditah,*** (threatened by imminent peril the learned readily sacrifices half of his possessions)."

"You're wonderfully correct Karanji. I wonder how you keep your wisdom so well concealed! I must sacrifice my best-half to save my skin."

"Hope you won't sacrifice me in the process."

"Karanji, how can I do that?" Raghu Chawla picked up another morsel of fried ***hilsa*** eggs and hastened to add, "Oh my dear, I forgot to tell you the main story of the day."

"What's so important?"

"It's very important Karanji. Shankarji wants you to organise a series of rallies, all over the country, supporting the PM's initiative on East Pakistan. He expects you to raise funds for national defence."

"Hope you aren't pulling another fast one on me."

"I swear by the ***Gita***" (Hindu Holy Scripture).

"Don't act smart." Ram Karan fumed, "It's the dirtiest book by which the Hindus swear and regale in falsehood."

"Don't berate the divine revelations by Lord Krishna." Raghu mildly protested.

"Ah Raghu, don't provoke me!" Ram Karan blurted out, "I think this Krishna of yours, can be prosecuted under any provision of the penal code for abduction, fornication and debauchery. But you hypocrites swear by him to hang an honest businessman like me."

"Forget all that sir. Shankarji is serious about the proposal. You're his nominee, to lead the campaign. It's a great honour bestowed on you."

"The PM has tasked me to supervise the Bangladeshi refugee camps in West Bengal."

"Shankar's suggestion gives you an opportunity to spread your name and fame all over the country. It'll make you dearer to the PM."

"Raghuji, the goat nearest to the priest is the dearest and the most convenient sacrificial beast. Being close to Mandira can often be dangerous. Any way, if Shankar so desires, I can't probably escape from organising the rallies." Ram Karan enlightened Raghu Chawla with another nugget of his hidden wisdom.

"In fact, I've told Shankar that you've already started preparations for the rallies."

"You're great Raghu. Any compensation for this favour?"

"I'm not that mean Karanji. I'm a patriot too."

"All of us are, but business comes first."

"Business can wait, while we fight the enemy."

"Wrong, you're wrong again. Look at the British. They established empires, while trading, and we Indians will destroy our national independence, because we don't allow honest trading."

Ram Karan, high on whisky, kept on cracking prophetic pronouncements.

"When do we meet Shankar?" He continued.

"At the earliest."

Shankar was thrilled over the idea of organising rallies in support of his mother. He had mastered well that art of street politics. He sincerely believed that the best way to run a democracy was to operate from the streets and from behind the throne. The constitutional edifices and legal structures were meant for the bygone era, the era of innocence and indolence. Violence, he believed, had become an essential tool for enforcing the political will of the people.

He walked into Mandira's room, while tossing the idea of enthralling the country by a series of rallies, over in his mind.

"Mom, there's pressure on me to organise victory rallies in support of your Bangladesh policy."

Mandira, busy in reading despatches from the FIB, NSI and Ministry of External Affairs, about crucial developments in East Pakistan looked up at Shankar and transmitted a dismissive message.

Events weren't proceeding as smoothly as she had expected them to. Her political and diplomatic trigonometry faced serious hurdles from unexpected quarters.

"Do I go ahead with it?"

"Who's going to anchor the massive efforts?"

"Ram Karan has volunteered to do it."

"Do you want him to take it on? I believe you want him to be dropped from the ministry."

"Let's wait till the war's over."

"No problems with me." Mandira smiled indulgently and buried her head in the files.

She was worried over the guerrilla war scenario in East Pakistan. Several armed rebel groups, the pro-Moscow Jangi Bahini, The Army For Liberation of East Bengal, the Communist led Jatiyo Mukti Jot coupled with Qadir Bahini and the NSI regulated Jainal Bahini with a loose-end strength of more than 100,000, were fighting an open war with guerrilla tactics against the Pakistani troops. They were hardly under any unified command. The pro-Chinese leftist elements were collaborating with the pro-Pakistan Jammat-e-Islami, Al Badr, Peace Committees and Razakar volunteers. They were in the vanguard of Pakistan's genocide agenda.

A few exiled Bangladeshi leaders were in direct contact with those US diplomats, who were busy burning extra glucose for early match making between the rebels and the Pakistan government.

She was worried too over some transparent efforts by Moscow for propping up the Communist freedom fighters. Moscow's long-term strategic objective of installing a puppet Red regime in Dacca, next to the Communist ruled Indian States of West Bengal and Tripura was sure to harm the secular democratic values of the country.

The Indian efforts to pump in weapons from Thai sources, through the Israeli mercenary, had achieved only partial success. The Pakistan Army's scorched earth policy in the coastal belt had seriously impeded the arms landing efforts of the NSI. On the other hand some fresh reports from Triple X added to her anxiety. Accelerated pumping of heavy weapons to Dacca and Chittagong rendered her job more difficult. She must not allow Pakistan's Eastern Garrison to dig in for a protracted war.

The Chinese capability of launching an air strike against India from southern and eastern Tibet bases never skipped her strategic calculations. The suspicious manoeuvres of the US Pacific Fleet towards the Bay of Bengal presented another predicament.

She didn't have the time for rallies. She didn't require them. The Indians were beholden to her and expected her to thrash Pakistan conclusively after the drawn bout of 1965. Even her rabid opponents, the ***Hindu Sangh*** had openly hailed her as the Goddess Durga, who had secured victory for the ***Suras*** (gods) over the ***Asuras*** (demons).

But, indulgent as she was to her younger son, Mandira didn't think that a few more straws on her wagon would matter much. Shankar's efforts should be able to generate a mass hysteria, in favour of her surgical operation against Pakistan. It could as well bring unity between the Hindus and the Muslims, who were yet to support her fully. By cutting Pakistan to its rational size she should be able to send a firm message to the Indian Muslims that their ideological homeland had simply lost the ideological mooring to survive as an exclusive Muslim nation. Washington should also realise that its client Pakistan was no match to a resurgent India. India, the strongest bastion of democracy in Asia could alone face up to the emerging political and economic challenges. And she was undoubtedly the rising star of the east. She was the designated leader to frustrate the convoluted Cold War games in Asia.

Next morning Shankar walked down to his office and summoned his Man Friday.

"Bhim Dass," He shouted.

"Yes ***netaji*** (leader)."

"Send Ram Karan and Raghu in."

"They're waiting for the last one hour."

"Send them in."

Ram Karan didn't require a formal summons. Waiting in the wings, Raghu Chawla in tow, Ram Karan shuffled into the room with folded hands.

"Any order for me sir?" The elderly minister, a cabinet colleague of Shankar's mother and grandfather, timidly meowed like a pet country cat.

"Many thanks for initiating the grand rally programme. Can we talk business?"

"Right away sir." Ram Karan tightened his ***dhoti*** (male lower apparel) and touched Shankar's feet.

"Karanji, I'm like your grand son, and feel ashamed to disturb you time and again. But you've set an example by initiating the patriotic rallies. I suggest that the first one should be in Delhi." Shankar fired a sweet shot.

This particular voice frequency modulation was familiar to Ram Karan. Shankar used sweet words only when he wanted to fleece his prey. His talons were aimed for a big catch today. God alone knew for how many millions!

"Don't hesitate Shankarji. I've been serving your family for 35 years. Perhaps you don't know that I had the privilege of carrying the umbrella and slippers of your great grandfather too. I'll carry out your orders with pleasure." Beamed Ram Karan happily, hoping for another warm pat from the master.

"The matter is like this Karanji," Shankar spoke in his usual halting style, measuring each word carefully, "To implement your programme, our youth brigade has decided to organise the first rally in Delhi on 20th October. The PM has nominated you as the star speaker. You're the best person to rebuff Pakistan."

Ram Karan touched Shankar's feet and polished his baldpate with his right palm, in symbolic demonstration of sanctifying himself with the dust of his leader's feet.

"Sir I'm your soldier. I await your orders."

"It's no big deal. Prepare a nice speech and arrange for fifty million rupees, for the rallies of course."

"That's a little too much sir."

"Karanji, I don't have to remind you of the billions you've earned in the last few years. Mom knows about it too. But for me, you would've been in history's dustbin by now. And the railway ministry is an additional bonanza that I granted you."

"Sir, have mercy on me. I've been spending a lot on the refugees from East Pakistan. You know, ma'am PM has given me charge of the special assignment."

"I know everything Karanji. I have an accurate account of every penny you've made out of the miseries of the refugees, and how much you've diverted from the UN assistance, and how many young girls you have spirited away from the camps. I know exactly where have you despatched these haggard girls." Shankar spat fire and fumes.

"Sir, just now I am short of cash." Submitted Ram Karan, again touching Shankar's feet.

"Don't joke. We know where you keep your black money. Want me to ask the income tax people to pump out the juice?"

Shankar splashed a seal of finality on trembling Ram Karan face.

"I'm honoured sir," Ram Karan Prasad stood up trembling, "The Laxmi (money) will reach you tonight. Raghu will bring the stuff in. May I submit a request?"

"Spell it out."

"Do I run special trains to bring in the volunteers?"

Ram Karan anticipated a reply in the affirmative.

"It's your baby Ramji, but I feel you should run 200 special trains."

"It's done sir."

"And disengage your flesh trade touts from the refugee camps. Some foreign correspondents have started flashing news about them."

Shankar scowled at the frightened minister.

"***Ram Ram***." Ram Karan touched his ear lobes, hoping that Lord Rama would rescue him from the cesspool of sin.

"Sir, believe me. I'm a honourable social servant. I'll tighten the security around the camps. In fact sir, some of these Hindu refugees are trying to melt into the milieu. They want to stay back in India."

"Whatever it is, I don't want any complaints from the FIB and NSI." Shankar dismissed the minister and signalled Raghu Chawla to stay put.

"So Raghu! What were you saying about Ram?"

"Have you heard the latest rumour about him?"

"What's new?"

"In the diplomatic circles they call him Pakistan's forked tongue in the Indian milk bowl."

"Are you joking?"

"Sir, how can I dare to? You're my master and Ram's a good friend. But my loyalty to your dynasty is above friendship." Raghu Chawla touched Shankar's feet to reinforce his statement.

"Is it serious?"

"They said so."

"Hum...It's time to take care of the bastard."

Shankar thanked Raghu and disappeared to an adjoining room.

****

The mass rally, in support of the historic handling of the Bangladesh tangle was planned on a grand scale. Never before had Delhi witnessed such a gala rally, not even on the eve of India's Independence or during the mammoth funeral procession of Mohandas Karamchand Gandhi. For the first time Hindu India was on the verge of humiliating a Muslim power, a power that had subjugated and occupied ***Bharatvarsha*** (India) about seven centuries ago. It was a time to rejoice, it was time to reassert the Hindu claim on the timeless mass of land, chronicled in mythology as ***Jambudwip,*** the Jambu island. Some Hindu leaders had described Mandira as the mother goddess ***Durga***, the supreme ***Shakti*** (power) that destroyed the demons and restored the heavens to the Gods.

They came in 200 odd trains and 5000 buses and trucks, from all conceivable directions, dressed in colourful regional apparel, the best they could afford. After all they had been brought to Delhi to see the daughter of Amritlal, granddaughter of Mahatma Gandhi (they believed) and a living incarnation of Mother ***Durga;*** invoked with a thousand names by the devoted Hindus.

The festive crowd, accommodated in huge tented mini-cities, thronged around the wonderful city of the ***Pandavas, Mughals*** and the British and that of ***Mandira Mai*** (mother). They used the sprawling lawns of India Gate as open-air lavatories and kitchenettes, with the green canopies serving as a natural cover.

October 20th dawned with a surge of human waves thronging the ramparts of the Red Fort. Mandira arrived precisely at 09.45, dressed in a white sari with a golden border, a golden blouse and a coiffeur in traditional Indian style. She exuded the looks of a Mother Goddess. She surveyed the crowd of 1.5 million from atop the rostrum and spoke briefly on the threat from Pakistan and other foreign forces.

"I've precise information that the military demon in Pakistan is preparing for an all out war against India. They've got weapons from China, America and other sources." Mandira tried to touch the raw chords of the crowd.

"But, your daughter, whom you've given a strong mandate, shall not betray your expectations. You're members of my extended family and the people of Bengal, now being killed in millions, are your brothers and sisters. I shall protect you all with the last drop of my blood. Our armed forces are much stronger now. We shall emerge victorious."

Spontaneous claps and roaring greetings reverberated with thundering echoes from the walls of the historic Red Fort.

"Evil forces inside and outside the country are bent upon assassinating me. I'm not afraid of such threats. I vow to fight the enemies of the nation to the last drop of my blood. They tried to kill me in Manipur and Orissa, but your affection and prayers have saved me...

"Even at this venue enemy agents are on the prowl with deadly weapons. Ram Karanji, our veteran freedom fighter, who was a colleague of two former Prime Ministers and a worthy representative of the toiling masses, will be with you, to recount the harrowing tales of genocide by Pakistan."

Mandira, followed by son Shankar and members of her entourage left the rostrum, amidst thunderous applause and slogans.

Ram Karan Prasad, in a rare realisation of self-fulfilment, started addressing the gathering. He invoked the names of Mahatma Gandhi and other leaders, who had guided the destiny of the nation from darkness to light. He was a small spark from those galactic events, Ram Karan added. He assured the roaring crowd that, his small spark would surely add up to the blazing torch of freedom, democracy and secularism, carried by Mandira on her shoulders. Goddess **Durga,** nemesis of all evil would be victorious, he had no doubt about that.

"***Bolo Mandira Mai ki jai***... (Hail mother Mandira)....

Ram Karan Prasad's words instead of being blared out through the loud speakers were suddenly shattered down to inaudible low decibel sound fragments.

A sudden flash and fire, followed by a big bang threw the rostrum high up into the air. Ram Karan Prasad, the veteran freedom fighter and a permanent fixture in the union cabinet was hit directly by an explosive charge, hidden below the specially built podium.

Ram Karan wasn't alone in death.

The media described the gory and pathetic death of 50 others including a few security personnel. A devastating fire triggered off a menacing stampede, leading to the death of another sixty villagers, who were huddled into Delhi to have a glimpse of the city of the ***Mahabharata,*** Maharani Victoria and ***Mandira Mai.***

Mandira loudly attributed the incident to the evil designs of foreign hands. She reminded the media of her speech, just before the explosion, which had shredded Ram Karan to bits and pieces.

Raghu Chwala, in a front-page obituary described Ram Karan as the first Indian soldier martyred in the struggle for freedom of Bangladesh. His was a poetic sentimental tribute from an old associate.

Brigadier Iskander didn't wait for a formal farewell from the Tuesday Club. He stealthily boarded a Cathy Pacific flight to Singapore. His last assignment in Delhi was a roaring success.

Chapter 49

Mapping the precise contours of the depth of the psychological and situational quagmire, in which Triple X was just about to sink, was a specialised task. Nampoothiri had no better choice other than Maulana Rizwan. He was known for his superb navigational acumen.

Rizwan's Mumtaz Farm facility, besides training the FIB and the NSI officers and agents in the Islamic way of life, often functioned as an encyclopaedic reservoir on Pakistan. He was, in his own right, an accomplished Islamic scholar. He was the root-bulb of the Hindu crusade against Muslim Pakistan. He helped in the flowering of the Hindu lotuses, which were offered to the services of the motherland. Rizwan alias Shyam Purohit often derived a silent pleasure from the fact that his infiltration into the FIB at the instance of the Sangh Chalak (the Chief Executive) of the Hindu Sangh had partially achieved the prime objective. He had succeeded in cloning a number of Rizwans, who were now dedicated to the cause of the Hindu nation. These cloned Muslims were well poised to map the Indian and Pakistani Muslim nation and destroy them from within. The Sangh, Rizwan knew, was excellent in ideological demagogy and poor in actualisation and realisation. The daydreamers were still wedded to the mythological past. They had failed to realise that the concept of Islam had undergone vast changes. It had rearmed itself with the original fanaticism that had distinguished the early crusaders, who had led gallant charges against the ***Dar-ul-Harb***, the nations of the non-believers. The services of his clones were more important than the stick-wielding Sanghi zombies in fighting the menace of the advancing Islam. As an ace operator of the FIB and NSI he had had the satisfaction of serving the Hindu India better than the most of his brethren in saffron.

In the absence of an institutional arrangement, Rizwan acted as the undeclared but official psychiatrist of the NSI. Officers and top agents entangled in a psychological labyrinth were first referred to him. His job was to interact with them and patiently unwind the complicated knots that troubled their psyche. His considered diagnosis and prognosis were highly valued in the organisation. It helped the top boss in making decisive evaluations: to retain or to eliminate. There was no undefined territory in between, in the highly charged domain of intelligence generation and dissemination.

Rizwan was ironically described in the NSI as ***Yamdev*** (angel of death). Very few emerged unscathed from his laboratory. But he himself was of the view that the prime intelligence organisations should have in house psychiatrists to sieve the troubled officers and agents from time to time.

Nampoothiri's decision to depute Rizwan to Colombo was, therefore, described in the informed NSI circle as a decisive step. The back room boys were convinced that the boss was giving a final chance to Triple X.

It wasn't customary for Nampoothiri to visit a nondescript hotel to meet a deep-cover agent. The top boss didn't customarily involve himself in minor operational tasks. But this was an unusual case. The usual NSI premises were out of bounds for Maulana Rizwan. And Nampoothiri didn't want his desk officers to debrief the Maulana, on the completion of his Colombo mission.

Rizwan, by pre-arrangement, had checked into a little known inn. The seedy establishment, fronted by a charming lady, an off the roster secret service funded employee of the NSI, was very sparingly used for delicate agent meetings.

Jatadhari Garo chauffeured the car and Nampoothiri, donning a beard and a mosque cap to match, visited the inn at the wrong side of midnight. He tapped the door using Morse language, read correctly by a discerning Rizwan: as BOSS.

"Welcome sir."

"Well Purohit, I need coffee first and tell me what's your report."

Rizwan's briefing enthralled Nampoothiri.

Triple X was candid and open, the ace trainer disclosed. His cover was still intact. But a single act of indiscretion, though not a voluntary one, had put the ISI sleuths on his trail. The ISI hunters had no doubt started at the Jahanara end of the thread. But the signal intelligence boys were more skewed up by the mysterious emissions from his clandestine radio station. Rizwan commented that usual security parameters were probably not observed while installing the trans-receiver. Harfan had no control over it. The later developments, like the induction of an Infantry Division to Jhumra and the presence of the Chinese radio transmission facility at the Bhagatanwala airbase had also narrowed down the signal security parameters for Harfan.

He was sure, Rizwan added, Triple X's accidental foray into the political minefield of Pakistan had created an explosive situation. He was entangled in the cross-conspiracies of the ambitious Generals. They were more anxious to give a dirty burial to General Arif than in fighting a war with India.

"Any other special developments?"

"There are two. His employer's brother Nawab Sharief is after his blood and he could not vibe well with Alamgir from day one."

"Triple X didn't give me any hint of it." Nampoothiri was happy to receive a confirmation of the report of Qurban from his most trusted officer. "The moral of the story is," Rizwan tersely commented, "We simply can't afford to have an intermediate master in important remote operations."

"But we have a system of controlling such operations through our Mission based operators."

"That's fine sir. But the clash of idiosyncrasies is a personalised matter. Their entire chemistry misfired."

Nampoothiri digested the dig silently. Rizwan was too much veteran of an intelligence artist and scientist to be ticked off. He made a mental note of the observation. This nugget of advice received from Rizwan required microscopic examination.

"Is his cover still intact?"

"Yes and no. The ISI hasn't been able to crack his cover. But sir, you know the intelligence professionals. They won't take years to penetrate Harfan's cover."

Rizwan spoke in his usual flowery style.

"Well said Purohit. Have all the equipment been removed?"

"No problem. Alam has taken care of it, but..." Rizwan abruptly stopped.

"What's the problem?"

"Arms ferrying is a transient cover for Harfan. I think they've chosen him out of compulsion."

"You mean he's a disposable tissue!"

"I suspect so."

"What's your suggestion?"

"There's one more point."

"Don't hesitate in putting it forth."

"I feel Triple X and Alam have developed, not merely temperamental, but functional incompatibility. Harfan has perceived whiffs of nascent hostility.... perhaps, professional jealousy, from Alam's behaviour."

Rizwan explained the most delicate part of the briefing. He was aware of the special relationship between Nampoothiri and Alam.

Nampoothiri didn't respond. He lighted a Havana and asked for another coffee.

"Would you suggest neutralisation? What're the chances of his defecting to the other side? Can he betray us?" He made anxious enquiries.

"How did you get that impression? I've trained him. I know he won't do that."

Rizwan asserted.

"Don't be emotional Rizwan," Nampoothiri mildly chided his expert, "Things have changed since you last trained him. He has a Pakistani wife and a child. He loves them. Our strategy to place him at Jhumra was intended to arouse the fire of hatred and revenge in him. Any spark of that fire left in him?"

"Pardon sir," Rizwan came out frankly, "A spark flies to extinction. I feel Harfan is guarding the fire under his chest. No doubt he has changed. The beast in him is dead. He's now a loving husband and a caring father. The wild days appear to have been buried."

"That's the problem. I wouldn't like his wife to become a part of his life. She's a cover, nothing more, nothing less."

"I get you sir. I suggest you deactivate the operation for the time being. Let him temporarily hibernate in a new station. In the mean-time he should be advised to observe anti-surveillance measures, protect his cover and use communication channels sparingly."

"Any other psychological change in him?"

"He's suffering from anxiety. Didn't open up on his future plans. He maintains a sullen silence whenever Alam's name is mentioned."

"Has he developed hostility towards him?"

"Better say, distrust."

Nampoothiri gave an imperceptible nod. Yes, he could see the debris of the bridge of trust.

"Thanks Shyam," Nampoothiri stood up, "You're excellent, as usual. Let me think over the inputs."

"One final request." Rizwan followed the boss to the door.

"Be frank."

"Handle the situation yourself. Don't allow Alam to decide Triple X's fate. And do it as soon as possible sir."

Nampoothiri nodded approvingly. He understood the gravity and sensitivity of the situation. The Triple X affair had suddenly thrown up important issues, threatening a total operation collapse in Pakistan. No more gambling was possible. He would have to take a fine chiselled decision.

Under no circumstances, should a war, open or mute, between Harfan and Alamgir be encouraged. The agency had important stakes in Harfan. But Alamgir was in virtual command of several operations in Pakistan, and some selected stations in the Central Asian Soviet Republics. His compromise would mean total intelligence blackout.

Perhaps Triple X could be relocated, albeit temporarily, in a safer station. He deserved neutralisation, not physical, but a rational deactivation, a planned withdrawal from Pakistan. He should be located somewhere in Europe, generating intelligence on Pakistan's shopping spree in the European Arms Bazaars.

Back to his hole, Nampoothiri closed the door and asked Jatadhari and Amrita Bhalla not to disturb him, unless calls were from the Prime Minister and stations Zebra and Cobra; the head quarters of the Provisional Government of Bangladesh in Calcutta and Dacca respectively.

Nampoothiri opened the electronically controlled safety vault, took out a numerical cipher pad, specially designed for important individual agents abroad.

The message was simple. ***Operation Retrieval*** was set in motion: Triple X should shift to London immediately and await fresh instructions. His family could join him later. The NSI would make arrangements for spiriting him away from Colombo by a clandestine sea route controlled by the northern Tamils of Jaffna.

Nampoothiri sealed the communication in a tamper-proof hollow capsule, resembling a piece of broken edged brick. He buzzed the intercom.

"Yes sir!" Amrita entered promptly.

"There's a small job dear. Send this to Kabul by the A Category diplomatic bag."

"Anything else sir?"

"Yes dear. Originate a cipher and ask Kabul station chief to personally hand over the packet to Alamgir."

"Done sir."

Amrita walked out gracefully with the packet.

The drill devised by Nampoothiri was ingenious. Alamgir would place the drop at a pre-determined Dead Letter Box. He would direct

Triple X to pick up the drop and adjust his needle, in accordance with the new instructions, direct from ***Behest.*** This, he would understand, was the final signal for him to vanish into thin air, another piece of Indian rope trick.

****

Vanishing into the thin air wasn't exactly what was churning inside Harfan. His world had changed, in its entire connotation, since Voodoorume's flight landed at Bhagatanwala, a subsidiary air base of Sargodha. Israr Sharief's soothing nonsense notwithstanding, he could hear the alarm bell ticking away, somewhere deep inside. The animal in him whispered loudly that, its primordial radar had picked up signals of a rumbling quake.

Harfan, seated in a corner of Imperial Plaza, a special dining room in Hotel Royal Palace maintained a cultivated brave face. Dinner served by Ibadat was superb, ***shahi khazana***, a tantalizing combination of giant delta prawn ***biriyani***, chicken ***tangri kebab***, fried cow brain served with curd-chilli sauce, with lots of green grated cucumber thrown in.

Last night's food at Dacca was abominably insipid. The Cantonment, under a virtual siege, depended even for the staples and greens on Pakistan International Airways flights. The Bengali freedom fighters had cordoned off the cantonment. All supplies to the Pakistani troops were embargoed. The armed ***Mukti Bahini*** Volunteers hounded the local suppliers, mostly Bihari Muslims and Bengali collaborators.

The rank and file subsisted on flatbread, rare servings of tinned meat and thin lentil soup. Officers somehow managed the occasional supply of greens and live table birds, frozen Australian beef and lamb, butchered in accordance with the Islamic ritual, to make the slain animals fit for consumption by the faithful of the ***Allah***.

"How do you like the food sir?" Ibadat's question snapped his chain of thought.

"Excellent, straight from heaven. How have you been?" Harfan applied delicate pressure on a chunk of prawn and enquired.

"Fine. How's Jamilla ***bhabi*** and Parvez?"

"They should be fine. Haven't met them for two weeks. This bloody job is killing me."

"I've something special to talk about." Ibadat whispered while pouring water.

"Let's take a stroll, the rooms may not be safe."

"There's a problem. Place order for home delivery of your dinner at the front counter. Expect me at 8 p.m. Draw the heavy curtains in your living room and keep the TV on, no harm if you play a music cassette. ***Khuda Hafiz***."

Ibadat collected the plates and moved away behind the pantry curtain. And Harfan ignited his car engine for the next thirty minutes' journey to Sangla. His thoughts hovered over a scattered spectrum... Jamilla...Parvez...the ISI dragnet...Alam and his latest encounter with Maulana Rizwan.

He was convinced that the end of the road was just around the corner and that the time had come for taking a firm decision, a joint decision with Jamilla, for a life beyond the ISI and the NSI. A spy was bonded to the ethics of his profession, if there were any; but he surely had a right to his life and liberty.

Harfan's broken collage of thoughts was snapped by a queer spectacle. Two Toyotas were piloting and escorting him, in a sandwich mobile surveillance format. The Mosur (mobile surveillance) teams maintained a studied distance of about 50 yards, at either end. This was a known surveillance pattern, caging the suspect in between the sandwich.

Yes. Ibadat wasn't behaving funnily. He was living up to his tradecraft training. His hints simply reflected the truth: that the noose around his neck was tightening up.

Who could they be? The ISI nemesis!

Thank God! Harfan felt a shiver travelling through his spine. Chain reactions burnt spontaneously in the psyche of some intelligence professionals. They hardly slept. Some people in the dreaded agency didn't sleep at all.

Israr's assurances were playroom palliatives. The poor good soul! The false assurances from General Sarfaraz swayed him. General Hyder and the ISI weren't likely to miss their kill, simply because an expendable ***muhajir*** was helping them out in the arms lifting operations. Somewhere, some determined sleuths were keeping the pendulum swinging, silently but inevitably.

That was bad news indeed.

Harfan didn't make any effort to dodge the surveillance vehicles. He maintained a steady 60 km. and drove straight to Israr's factory. The Mosur officials baffled by the total lack of concern of their target, peeled off, half a kilometre short of the factory gate. The Toyota on Harfan's tail took a right turn, exposing full profile of the surveillance officer. It was an evil looking, pockmarked face, with a deep furrow on the forehead; resembling a carpet-bombed battle terrain. The eyes looked cool and fierce, ready to pump out liquid lead. Harfan couldn't focus his gaze straight on that killer face.

Yes. The nemesis was closing in. Counter intelligence was a game of endless reflecting mirrors. Its vista stretched the captured image to infinity, till the eternal crunch finally smashed the suspect to ionised particles.

Harfan didn't take long to perceive the ultimate peril enveloping him. He was captured inside the dark mirrored chamber. There was no doubt about it. But, why the killer looks?

Harfan tucked the idea deep inside his mind as he walked into Israr's office.

Israr wasn't alone. Alam, seated on the right end of the table was sipping coffee and General Naqi, with a Brigadier in tow, was busy discussing some papers.

"You needn't send a chit in," Israr fondly admonished Harfan, "Even when I'm not alone. You know all, I presume."

"I'm Harfan Bukhari." He extended his palm in greeting palm to the Brigadier.

"I'm Zia, Zia-ul-Mansoori, from 9 Azad Kashmir Regiment. Glad to meet you. I'm an upgraded version of your old friend Captain Ayoob. You're a legend by now. Doing extremely well, I hear."

The Brigadier heaped praises on Harfan, while speaking through his protruding incisors. His deep sunken eyes, almost lost below bushy brows emitted different signals. Harfan noticed the lack of harmony between his words and looks.

Well! He must watch out for this Punjabi Jat, a veritable climber with daggers hidden behind the charming leaves and flowers of his visage.

Atmospheric and static noises of a radio trans-receiver disturbed the monotony of the meeting. The sounds came from a cubicle next to Israr's toilet. Alam's station was busy, Harfan presumed. Business as usual, eh!

"We've worked out the broadsheet of supplies delivered so far. Ten sorties are over, eight more to be completed before November tenth." Israr tossed the papers at Harfan.

"There are problems." Alam intervened, "My contacts in Cyprus are fidgety over the dangerous buzzing by Indian fighters. Capt. Voodoorume has serious reservations about flying there again. Other pilots are unwilling to fly too. The sorties aren't safe any more."

"What do you say Harfan?" General Naqi asked.

"Alam sahib is correct. You can even see the Indian pilots grinning at us. I wish I could pump few bullets into their birds," Harfan replied, "Without protective air cover it's a touch and go affair."

"You'll know the problem best. We can't expose our few Air Force birds to the Indians, not at this stage." General Naqi added.

"***Bandish*** (code for Doug Chris) has jacked up his rates by an additional 9%." Alam commented stoically.

"Bastard," Swore Brig. Zia menacingly, while pushing up his thick drooping moustache, "The dogs are demanding more than they can chew. Do we have to pay all that much?"

"It's our national compulsion." Alam walked towards the anteroom and closed the door behind him. He emerged out in 5 minutes, with a paper in hand.

"What's new?" Asked Israr.

"Station ***Bandish*** is negative. We have to cough up an additional 9%, if we want to get the extra charters. Else we can fuck off. That's a clear message."

"That's not my cup of tea." General Naqi, the Defence Advisor threw up his hands, "Only the top man can decide on our further course of action. Let's go Zia. We'll be in touch. The materials have piled up at Sargodha and Karachi. We're getting perilously late. We must act fast, if we want to keep East Pakistan with us." He left, a disappointed man.

"Are you home tonight?" Alam asked Harfan.

"I presume not. May go to Lahore. Any urgent business?" Harfan sounded dry and formal.

"Nothing special." Alam stood up and gestured to Harfan to follow him in the transmission room.

"I feel the noose is tightening around you." Alam whispered.

"Thanks for the information." Harfan smiled back, rather nonchalantly.

"It's time for you to wind up, if you want to avoid the bullets."

"Whose bullet Alam sahib? For your information I refuse to be frightened. Tell me something new."

"Aren't you afraid?" Alam looked at Harfan, standing before him like a defiant rock.

"No more of it Alam sahib, you can't frighten me any more. Tell me if you can help. Remember, if I'm pushed to the gallows, you're sure to follow suit."

"You can't betray the country."

"That's the last thing I'll do, be rest assured. But, the country can't write me off either. I'm not a bad debt."

"It's better you pull up your guard, and take my advise seriously. The ISI is ruthless, when it comes to firing at Indian targets." Alam's naughty wink pained Harfan.

"Thanks for the tip." Harfan replied mechanically.

"Bravado won't pay Harfan. In our job we take, very well considered decisions. Wait for fresh instructions." Alam shifted his gaze, uncomfortable with Harfan's opaque looks.

"***Amen***." Replied Harfan coolly.

Alam's departing dead-fish looks scared Harfan. He looked like a frustrated hangman moving down the planks, with knotted ropes tucked behind, his mission unfulfilled.

Alam gave an effusive jerk as he shook Israr's hand. He didn't look back at Harfan.

"Don't disappoint me Alam sahib." Israr pleaded.

"The disappointment will be mutual brother Israr. It'll be a national disappointment, if that fellow Doug reneges."

"Try your best to get him on our terms."

"Oh sure, I will. And my friend Harfan will take care of the rest." He threw a dry smile and left.

Harfan was momentarily lost in his dark thoughts.

Was Alam planning a nasty trick, his own very brand of Russian roulette? Or was there a rat race between the NSI and the ISI for reaching his jugular? The perceived super agent felt like he was hanging precariously above a bottomless pit. His facial muscles tightened, reflecting his resolve to dare the hooded vipers and cobras hissing menacingly below.

"Where are you? In Lahore? Bloody lucky guy that you're," Israr's words brought Harfan's thoughts back to the present, "You two are unique love birds. Let's finish the job quick and you can zoom down to your ***mehbooba*** (lover), tonight itself."

"How're things in the east?" Israr added without waiting for Harfan's reaction to his innocent joke.

"Hopeless. The Bengalis feel cheated and they are not ready to co-habit with us. Bangladesh appears to be a reality." Harfan replied.

"Is it safe for the sorties?"

"No, not really. Our forces are living in isolated islands; surrounded by hostile Bengali rebels and the superior Indian forces, breathing down their necks. The officers and men haven't lost the will to fight and are ready to die for Pakistan. But they're simply starving and not a day goes by when they chew their bare ***chapattis*** (flat breads) without abusing the ass holes of the President and his concubine." Harfan exaggerated the feigned degree of bitterness.

"What's keeping up their morale?"

"The false expectation of Chinese and US intervention. Everyday there are messages from the COAS to the Eastern Command chief, assuring him a massive Chinese push against India." Harfan commented in a bitter tone.

"Do you think the Americans can afford to betray their only ally in this region?"

"Pardon me sir," Harfan continued, "Our President keeps on dreaming a lot. That witch has atomised his power of reasoning and the Sindhi superman is leading him up the grave yard."

"Sssh!" Hissed Israr, "We're in business. Let's not talk politics."

"Sure sir, but you asked for it."

Getting down to business talk Harfan explained that, if Alam's party was asking for 9% more, Israr should as well demand an added 3%. The risk factor was enormous and, he wouldn't like to fly to Dacca any more only for the same amount. Israr should consider some extra allowances for him, all paid in dollars to his offshore account.

"In this business your share is well above Rupees five million. You can take it any time." Israr made a generous offer.

"Please transfer the money to my off-shore account. I don't like the tax people troubling me again."

"That's fine with me. In the meantime sort out the pending inventory of weapons. I would be out at Karachi."

"How much are you paying Alam?" Asked Harfan.

"I don't pay him. Probably he has an arrangement with Doug. Perhaps Naqi takes care of it. Why ask?"

"Don't you think Doug's additional 9% is pretty high?"

"What can we do? Any way, the money flows up, I mean subterranean, the Indus from the Potomac. If Alam makes a few extra bucks in the bargain, I don't have any qualms about it." Israr disengaged and left Harfan to complete the paper work.

Harfan energised the computer and after about half an hour concluded that, Alam, the super patriot, was cornering a cute cut of about Rupees 20 million out of the arms transaction. Where was he stacking his fortune? Not in Pakistan obviously. The airlifting operations were laying golden eggs for every body's breakfast plate, excepting the people of Pakistan and perhaps, the hapless Bengalis!

Fine! It was fine with him, if it was fine with the Pakistanis, who were opiated by the hate-India elixir. It's a pity that a naive Washington had put blinkers on its conscience, all in the name of Cold War tap-dancing. Well! The self-styled cop of the free world couldn't really boast of prudently investing its citizen's money, in the worldwide theatres of conflict. They hadn't shown real flare of wisdom in Korea, Vietnam and countless other theatres of conflict.

Why bother about the spoilt brat, a Richie Rich of sorts, presiding over the White House! He was there temporarily. The intrinsic integrity of the people of America was stronger than the vaults of Fort Knox, Harfan believed. They would wake up one day and ask their self-righteous leaders to reformat the nation's conscience.

With Latiff behind the wheel Harfan concentrated on the surveillance tails. He didn't have to look back. A small pocket mirror helped him keep track of the tails cruising in a pair formation. One of them was falling back, once in a while, giving a chance to his colleagues to go ahead. They played a funny game, like young monkeys trying to climb up a greased pole, under the cover of assumed trees and bushes, where there were none.

The fools!

Harfan asked Latiff to speed up and to take care of the fleet of trucks whizzing past in the opposite direction. The ISI Mosurs didn't expect the sudden surge of the Mercedes, already cruising well above 100 km. Their mothballed cars faded away in Harfan's mirror and he was well within the sight of his Jhumra home a few minutes later.

He anxiously waited for dinner. Not so much for the food, but for Ibadat. The old loyal had whispered to him in the morning about a special message. Ibadat's special talks often turned out to be prophetic.

Harfan was not worried about the Mosurs anymore. He wasn't even anxious about the Tesurs (technical surveillance). He had seen their faces, understood their intentions and expected them either to fire from their stunted barrel. 38 colts or spirit him away to one of their torture chambers.

He wasn't ready to oblige the ISI hunters yet.

To Harfan it didn't matter any more, if the lunatics in Delhi and Islamabad preferred to lock their horns together in another mutual suicide pact. The fools were capable of doing that.

He had seen the mad politicians and their bureaucratic minions on either side of the border. They were made up of the same rubbish staff, more or less. They stoked the fires of hatred just for stuffing their private treasure-chests. Periodically they pushed the common people to the war front as cannon fodder to prove that war was the best demonstration of patriotism.

Shit! There was no fun in serving these zombies, the hay and clay stuffed politicians and bureaucrats, any more. He had had enough of patriotism!

Fine! The underlying philosophy had crystallised. But should he forget his father's assassins? That was his personal agenda. But destruction of Pakistan was no more a feasible proposition. It never was. Harfan laughed, while he lit another cigarette. He was a fool to believe that one-man Harfan mission alone could fight the mighty establishment of Pakistan and its people.

And what for?

Revenge? The people of Pakistan weren't responsible for his father's death. The jaundiced system and the fanatics had killed him.

Those fanatics didn't exist in Pakistan alone. They were busy on either side of the border. In India too they killed in the name of ***Rama***,

Krishna, ***Kali*** while their counterparts in Pakistan killed in the name of ***Allah***. Some others preferred to kill in the name of the Son of Virgin Mary. They were the same, all over the world. The human hunger for power, Harfan realised, simply used Gods and messiahs for enforcing their physical and contorted psychological muscle on weaker fellow-beings.

That was fine too.

The debate continued to shred Harfan into pieces.

That didn't mean that he should spare his father's executioners. He must square up with them, one to one at least. No. He wouldn't abandon that agenda. The fire of revenge continued to churn inside. He must pay back the blood debt. This was a small but all-important private war.

Harfan sat facing the fireplace after a quick shower, with his favourite choice of whisky. He dialled the Lahore number and reached Jamilla. She was, Harfan mused, the most proximate and important person in his life, whom he could face frankly and boldly at any moment of truth. That moment was almost around the corner. He could discern the footsteps of destiny catching up with him. Jamilla should know the truth, from his mouth and not from the rumour mills.

Ibadat's footsteps broke the serpentine rhythm of his thoughts. Harfan declutched and looked out. A lone foot-watcher was still lurking at the entrance alley of his home, taking cover behind a cluster of dwarf spruce pines.

Ibadat didn't look at the burly Multani with a rustic ambience and a massive moustache on his bloated face. He was almost a permanent fixture, standing there from 2 pm till 12 pm to the dot. His bulging loin betrayed the presence of a pistol and a VHF communication set.

Fools! Ibadat mused. They should have the common sense of changing the faces at random. What was the fun in ritually positioning that fat blob in front of Harfan's gate?

"Have you noticed that guy?" Ibadat asked.

"Yah. I've smelt him, more than I've seen him."

"How come?"

"He uses the spruce bush as his urinal. The whole place stinks." Harfan laughed.

"You haven't drawn the curtains and the TV is off." Ibadat wasn't happy to see Harfan in a contemplative and depressed mood.

"What difference does it make?"

"Lots." Ibadat arranged the curtains, increased the television volume and continued.

"You should take care of voice activated vibration recording devices, which pick up and transmit wave modulations. A specially designed oscillograph decodes the audio waves and brings out the noise eliminated room conversations."

"How do you know that? Who are you?"

Ibadat didn't reply. He silently went about his chores.

"Food is ready." Ibadat announced.

"Go to hell, you and your food." Harfan stood up in an aggressive mood, "You haven't replied to my questions."

He emptied his glass into the faint fireplace embers. The tongues of flame momentarily jumped up licking the stale air. Harfan's gaze, fixed on the fire, reflected his inner turmoil.

Ibadat looked squarely into Harfan's eyes and displayed a cross sign with his index and middle fingers.

Harfan stepped back in surprised recognition of the code taught by Dhiren Bhagat. It meant that Ibadat was something special. They were on the same side of the fence. Ibadat wasn't a small time agent of Alam. A Double X agent of the NSI he had direct links with Delhi, most probably through Station Kabul, with an independent communication channel.

"Perhaps you'd like to wash." Ibadat silently led Harfan to a toilet and closed the door behind.

"You're required to keep a date at point Chinar, at the battered west wall of ***Shalimar*** Gardens on October 24th, and pick up an important drop."

Ibadat whispered.

"Is this room safe?"

"Yes. See that blue lamp? It's an infra ray vibrator, oscillating at 240 cycles and creating a sub-sonic noise, not audible to human ears. It's capable of driving all electronic listening devices crazy. To ordinary eyes it's nothing but an insect repeller."

"What're the timings?"

"Read this. Don't ask questions aloud. The enemies are on the prowl. Act according to new instructions. My instructions are to de-clutch from you. Henceforth, we'll meet only in the hotel. Don't visit Rama Bai."

"Why?"

"She's on the ISI hit list. She knows your real identity and may buckle down under pressure. Don't fiddle with her."

"Why should she figure in their hit list?"

"She knows who you are. Yours is a carbon copy of your father's face. She has some old paintings of his younger days."

"Can't she be spirited away to India?"

"Not now. Let the storm-clouds blow over. We shall try."

"What're the chances?"

"It's still fifty-fifty in your favour. They're professionals and won't give up easily."

They emerged out of the toilet and ate dinner amidst small talks about Parvez, Jamilla and Harfan's risky job of ferrying weapons to East Pakistan.

Ibadat tuned on the television and started talking in a low voice.

"Listen carefully. I'm not a great guy, but I've my ears to the ground. Your mission is almost over."

"Is the old lady safe?" Harfan abruptly asked.

"Think of yourself and your mission. Leave the rest to us." Ibadat almost admonished Harfan.

"Tell me the identity of my father's killers."– Harfan wrote down on a piece of paper.

"Why?"– Ibadat too scribbled.

" Do me this favour."— Again a silent scribble.

"The pockmarked battered-moon face, the one on your tail. He's Armán Ali Niazi, an employee of the ISI. He's the killer. Take care. He shoots, before asking questions."— Ibadat scribbled back.

"Thanks for the good dinner, brother Ibadat."

"Another question. What are your orders? To kill me?"

"No comments. Be sure that your father's salt still runs in my veins. I won't fire the first shot." Ibadat scribbled back and stood up.

Harfan opened the door for him and said ***Khuda Hafiz***. He turned back at the fireplace, threw the paper pellets on the dying tongues of fire, which were still emitting the mellow fragrance of pine resin.

Chapter 50

Mian Alam Khan's dark-alley diplomacy, Israr Sharief's treasure chest and favourable winks from Malika Jahanara finally clinched the issue of hiring additional chartered flights from the CIA short-listed Athena Air Lines. General Sarfaraz, Major General Naqi and the Chief of Army Staff too had pitched in. The American ambassador and the CIA station chief in Islamabad had facilitated their task. Their boys had crosschecked with Doug Chris and vetted the genuineness of the enhanced *'risk factor cost.'*

Washington, Alam boasted, had gladly signed on the dotted line, approving an additional expenditure of $ 500 million. Islamabad couldn't have any reservations, if Washington had none. The hardware was sure to reach Dacca before the mid-November deadline and the coffers of whoever mattered in Pakistan were sure to get filled to the brim.

It was indeed a time to celebrate.

But Nawab Sharief had very little to celebrate. He had failed yet again to reach the source of the supply bonanza. His coterie of Generals and politicians, no less illustrious than the Sarfaraz-Naqi faction, had failed to have their way with the Americans, and of course with the CMLA. The top boss and his lady love developed neuronal flu whenever the name of Nawab figured in talks with Hyder Bux and other Generals. That evil fungus, Jahanara openly blurted out in one of the meetings, was poisonous.

General Hyder Bux, a profound admirer of Nawab Sharief's business acumen and political penetration finally threw up his hands. He got a clear message that General Arif wouldn't touch Nawab with a bargepole. Washington wasn't willing to change its horse midway. The same Cyprus based company, an established CIA surrogate, had bagged the contract. That meant an addition of more than rupees 100 million to Israr's coffer.

To hell with it!

Nawab stormed into his Volvo and shouted at the chauffeur to drive straight to General Hyder's residence.

Merry hell! Hyder wasn't there. Of all places, Hyder's batman informed him that, his boss had gone to the ***jama masjid*** at Ramna-6 for offering ***eshan*** prayers (last prayer of the day).

Nawab's car screeched to a halt in front of the ***jama masjid.*** He removed his shoes, performed the ritual oblations and walked up to the prayer hall.

General Hyder, standing in the last row of the gathering of the faithful, with a mosque cap on his head looked entirely lost in his prayers. Nawab crawled up and joined the ***namazis*** (people offering namaz) and positioned himself next to the General.

"Sir..." He tried to open up a dialogue. "Shh..." Hyder bent down with the rest of the faithful, his eyes still closed.

"There's a big problem..."

"Not here..." Hyder concentrated on his prayers.

"Your prayers can wait. My problem cannot."

"Shh! Follow the rituals." Hyder whispered back.

The prayer assembly dispersed after about twenty agonising minutes. Nawab finally cornered General Hyder near the foyer of the ***hujra*** (room of the chief ***mullah***)

"It's a blatant betrayal General. I've been let down."

"Can't get you Nawab." Replied General Hyder Bux."

"I'm talking about the airlifting contract. I paid a million in advance, yet the fresh contract has been awarded to brother Israr."

"Sorry Nawab. I'd pitched in with Naqi and the COAS," Hyder shrugged, "But you know that I'm not the final authority in Pakistan."

"Why don't you remove that imbecile Arif and rape his girl friend? Pitch in with Izaz and I assure you a top slot in the new dispensation."

"Have patience Nawab. We shall have our day.

"What about my money?"

"You can take back my share of it, but I can't stand guarantee for the rest." Hyder started walking towards his car.

"You mean that whore will decide our fate and that bloody Harfan will keep on fucking her! What're you doing about that lousy Indian agent?" Nawab gave vent to his frustrations in a rather loud voice.

"Shh." Hyder advised caution, "Not so loud."

"Why can't you hang him?"

"Nawab sahib, have patience," General Hyder started walking down the steps, "We're on the job."

"Should I tell the Director Military Intelligence? You're taking the matter very lightly. Are you afraid of that whore?"

"Nawab sahib," Hyder replied in a grim voice, "Don't mix up your business rivalry with matters of the state. I'm the spymaster. I know who fucks whom in Pakistan. I know when to cast the net and when to haul the catch."

"You're wrong Hyder sahib," Nawab protested, "It's not my business I'm referring to. I'm talking about Pakistan's security."

"Leave that to us, we're the professionals. Don't interfere with what Harfan is doing now. And don't stretch the elastic beyond a point. Paying advance goodwill money doesn't guarantee any contract. You know the system."

Hyder asked his driver to accelerate to the office of the Chief Martial Law Administrator. He was supposed to be present in an inter-services briefing to the President.

Nawab sulked for a while under the arch of the mosque, and hurled abuses at General Hyder, for milking him of rupees one million.

Once inside his Volvo, Nawab picked up his car phone and dialled the number of General Nayeem, the PIB chief.

"Hi General, how's life? Can I drop in? There's something hot that's come up and it's related to our national security."

"Come on if you're so keen." General Nayeem didn't like to offend the most poisonous viper in Pakistan. Hanging on precariously to his position at the mercy of brother Arif and Jahanara, he had discovered to his charm, that patience paid. These politicians were strange animals and democracy was a curse to the humanity. Tomorrow this bloody Nawab could dump him in the garbage bin. And even vipers like Nawab kissed sweetly once in a blue moon, if it served their business and political interests.

Nawab switched on the engine and added his anger to the fuel. The Volvo kicked up a cloud of dust and raced towards General Nayeem's residence. He had made up his mind to share with the PIB chief some sensitive secrets concerning Israr and Harfan. The celebrity brother must also be made aware of the conspiracy hatched by General Hyder and Sarfaraz. He had in his pocket a few transcripts of the telephone conversations between the ISI chief and the PSO. That should give clinching proof of their evil designs. Brother Israr and Harfan were intrinsically entangled with that conspiracy. And he had enough colour in store to paint Harfan as an Indian spy.

Nawab lighted a cigarette, spat out a curse directing Israr and Harfan to the abyss of roaring hell. He must bag this contract at any cost.

****

Harfan Bukhari was out on his own errands.

The new contract and the additional flights sounded good. But he wasn't sure of the ground below him. The smiling faces and the bulging pockets couldn't lull the scratched psyche of the injured jackal. How could he fathom the depth of the trouble scaring him?

The thought of fathoming the waves of the swirling tsunami about to hit his coastline struck him as he was driving leisurely along Lahore's busy market place. Tailed by the Mosur he swung the Toyota Corolla into the highway. The surveillance vehicle was determined to shadow Harfan bumper-to-bumper, afraid of losing his tail.

Harfan sighted the pockmarked face and muttered a silent curse. He deserved some tail twisting. The beast must pay for his crime.

But Harfan's priority was to shake off the leech, as quickly as possible. He required some free space and time to himself, to be with Jamilla and Parvez. The time had arrived to face the moment of truth, to bare his heart out to Jamilla. She must know his real identity now, yes now. The ISI might not give him enough time to dance around the bush. Dacca could wait. He wasn't keen to invite a stamp of martyrdom. He wasn't keen on allowing Alam or the NSI or the ISI to decide his fate. Ramendra Kaushal would script his own act, in his own inimitable style.

The decision to dodge the ISI tail dawned on him suddenly. Harfan swung his car again, and guided the wheels towards General Naqi's office. He'd like to buy some time, share his thoughts with Jamilla and work out a strategy. And he couldn't allow the Mosur to trail him up to his bedroom at Zahoor Chaudry's place. He must protect Jamilla from that prying pockmarked battered-moon face.

He suddenly remembered that Brigadier Zia-ul-Mansoori, the jackal with rodent teeth and sunken eyes, had replaced Ayoob. What excuse could he proffer for visiting the ubiquitous General?

Why not discuss the met-report! Voodoorume had called in from Karachi to say that the US satellite reports had detected a swirling cyclone hanging over the funnel of the Bay of Bengal. It wouldn't be safe to fly for another two days, unless the wild swirling demon took an unexpected turn towards the Indian coast.

Harfan sped up along Circular Road and entered Anarkali market. He cut through a lane across Nasir Road and emerged at Montgomery. The Mosur car, cruising along the narrow lane, lost control, hit a few handcarts vending vegetables. An angry mob instantly surrounded the occupants. The pockmarked face took out a pistol and fired in the air. The mob pounced on him and the frenzy left Arman Ali Niazi seriously battered.

Harfan looked back and accelerated for the Cantonment area. Poor chap! Harfan felt sorry for the battered face with a drooping moustache. He had become accustomed to the rotund and overfed killer, who often liked his lips, like a hungry hyena on the prowl.

Harfan's visit, an unannounced one, surprised Brigadier Zia, the camp officer-in-charge. His drooping moustache moved up and down, and his thick eyebrows twisted in all conceivable directions conveying surprise and displeasure. Zia sucked his sunken cheeks in, displayed his rodent teeth and made a grunting sound. It was suppose to be a smile of a kind.

Harfan had no plausible excuse to be there.

His next flight to Dacca was scheduled for 23 October, and Harfan's brief was to join Capt. Voodoorume at Sargodha. He wasn't supposed to visit this office. Not many were welcome to his hole. The entire operation was graded top-secret, and many in Pakistan weren't even aware of the clandestine airlifting of Chinese and NATO weapons to Dacca and Chittagong, using the services of internationally infamous mercenaries.

Harfan was no doubt an integral part of the operation. But he wasn't a part of the decision-making hierarchy. Efficient he was, but very expendable. There'd be no tears, no epitaph and no requiem, if his flight disappeared from the East Pakistan skies. He was just another mercenary, a means to an end.

Gen. Naqi had accepted Harfan as just another bit of front line fodder, for which any unmarked bullet was good enough, Indian or Pakistani. Names of victims weren't inscribed on the bullets. They simply carried death, like any other carrier. A mosquito! A cobra! A binary poison! It didn't matter.

Why should he show up his asshole here?

"What brings you here?" Zia didn't try to suppress his anxiety, if not annoyance.

"Well Brigadier sahib!" Harfan drew a chair and thrust himself on the puzzled officer. He enjoyed Zia's not too opaque discomfiture.

"I've a message from Capt. Ram."

"Who's this bloody Ram? We don't know anybody by that damned Hindu name."

"I mean Voodoorume. You know he is a Hindu of Indian origin." Harfan enjoyed the dancing of the eyebrows of the Brigadier.

"He doesn't exist for me. He's your baby."

"That's not the point. The pilot says that the depression hanging over the Andaman is likely to travel northeast and hit the East Pakistan coast any time. He requests for clearance from the US weathermen, before he agrees to fly his bird."

"Have you informed the General?"

"I'm on two day's furlough. Perhaps you'll like to attend to such a grave official matter. I'm here to help you. You're the boss man."

"Have coffee."

"Thanks boss. I must move on. I wish to see a movie. The Delight hall is screening an old Raj Kapoor starred movie."

"How can they show an Indian movie?"

"Sir, I'm an ordinary man. I'm not concerned over such complicated matters."

Harfan winked at the distorted furrows on Zia's face and threw him a twinkling smile, as he left the room.

He didn't completely bluff the seasoned Punjabi ***Jat***. He had just exaggerated the preliminary report received from Voodoorume. October-November was the usual time for cyclones and typhoons in the delta funnel of the Ganges, Meghna and Brahmaputra, which often penetrated deep inland, carrying apocalypse in their trails.

The Bengalis, living on either side of the vast delta, dreaded, hated and worshipped these churning weather demons and gods. They worshipped the storm deities with more fervour than they observed the Islamic rituals, to the serious consternation of the better Islamised West-Pakistanis. The hardened ***mullahs*** couldn't follow the psyche of these low castes, half-Muslims, still deeply rooted in Hindu traditions.

Needling Brigadier Zia was a pleasure. Harfan didn't take a liking to his drooping moustache and slit-python eyes. His rodent smile betrayed that Zia was another military ruler in the making.

Harfan didn't like to take a chance with the cheeky Brigadier either. He was cock-sure about Zia calling up Gen. Naqi and apprising him of the sudden dislocation. The Defence Advisor, Harfan was sure, wouldn't take seconds to cross check with Alam. The chain dialogue was sure to travel up to the desk of Doug Chris, finally bouncing back to the Karachi camp of Voodoorume. It was better to keep Voodoo in the picture.

Doug Chris, the chartered operator was in facsimile contact with the US agencies offering professional satellite meteorological services via the INMARSAT. And Voodoo was a stickler for the rules of the skies and safety of his bird.

He decided to get back to Voodoo and give him an account of his encounter with Naqi's deputy.

"Hello Captain," Harfan called up Voodoorume, "Have you anything on the latest met report?"

"Twisters over the Bay?"

"Yea. We call it a cyclone, which is often more deadly."

"Yea, the US WSAT (weather satellite) predicts that the cyclone is likely to hover over the delta for another two days and hit the East Pakistan coast with a speed of 200 miles per hour. Fine with me. I don't like the idea of getting sucked into the eye of the cyclone. Relax, and my best wishes to your queen and crown prince." Voodoo replied.

"I need the wings of your prayers to be there with them. Thanks pal." Harfan disconnected.

****

Jamilla, dressed in rose-pink silk lingerie, had covered her body with a fine embroidered tribal Baluchi rug. Harfan had purchased this precious piece from Karachi's Zainab market, Pakistan's best address for carpets and rugs. Parvez was fast asleep in his cradle.

Harfan walked over to the window, opened a panel and lighted a cigarette. The silhouettes of the minarets of the Mosque of Maryam Zamani looked eerie in the shallow opaque darkness. The grey sky, still studded with a few departing stars, provided an infinite and uncertain panoramic canvass.

A pale reddish hue momentarily gleamed on the white makrana marble dome of the mosque. A slice of moon, still hanging reluctantly behind the tallest minaret of the house of God, reminded Harfan that the sun was about to make its inevitable appearance; as it had been doing for the last four billion years or so.

The ***muezzin*** (mosque-crier) was about to remind the faithful, over his loudspeaker, of the greatness of the God- ***Allah-o-Akbar***. It was time for the believer to say ***fajr namaz*** (morning prayer).

"Come to bed." Jamilla whispered.

Harfan extinguished the cigarette and turned back.

"I want to say something."

"Come closer."

Harfan didn't move. His bare upper body glistened with sweat, not because of the volcanic convulsions of the conjugal encounter that had lasted two hours. This was usual with Jamilla. She extracted the last drop of Harfan's energy and still yearned for more.

This early morning sweat was due to nervousness and anxiety. Harfan faced the silhouette of the mosque and said a silent prayer, ***Bismillah-ar-Rehman-er-Rahim.***

"I want to say something." He advanced towards the bed.

Jamilla covered her body with the rug and sat up.

"What's bugging you dear? Any problem at the work place?"

"No. Pardon me for betraying your holy trust."

"I never said anything about that witch."

"It's not that. Let me have my say. This is the best time to face the truth. This is the time for saying the prayers and facing ***Allah***."

Harfan continued.

"I'm not a Pakistani and not a born Muslim, though I was in a way converted, in a fake way. I'm in Pakistan to spy for India." Harfan spoke fast; the words overlapped and produced a whispering effect, as if his lung was emptied of oxygen.

"You're a spy! Of all things you're a spy!" Jamilla moved away from Harfan.

"Let me tell you my story. Listen carefully. You've the right to do whatever you like after you hear me out. But be sure, I'm true to you and Parvez. I love you both. Without you my life has no meaning."

Harfan spoke haltingly, narrating the essentials of his story and the threat he was now facing from the Inter Services Intelligence and the National Security India's station boss, Mian Alam Khan. They were bound to catch up with him, sooner or later.

"Harfan, you married me only because you wanted a shield, a believable cover?"

Jamilla tightened the rug around her body.

"No. It wasn't in any way a part of the scheme. I lost myself in your eyes, at our first meeting at the Lahore Fort. It wasn't your body, your beauty that had mesmerised me. It was the blue eyes, where I lost myself. My love has nothing to do with my profession. Yes, I'm a spy. A real spy doesn't care for emotion and love. I could've disappeared, leaving you two behind and gone back to India. I love you."

"And you're the Prince of Jhumra! You came to take revenge on your father's killers and destroy Pakistan in the bargain!"

"A Prince I could have been. Thank ***Allah***, I'm not one. Yes, I want to square up with the killers of my father. I'm not an enemy of the people. The Armed Forces and the foolish politicians are better at that job."

"How can you love us Harfan, me and Parvez, when you're propelled by hatred?"

"I was, when I was launched, as a tool of destruction. My love is my life now. I've lost the keys to my steaming storehouse of hatred in your love. All of us have been victims of deceit, prejudice and perverse political manoeuvres. I've been through the cruel mill, which had ingrained hatred in my psyche. You've transformed me. You've gifted me the desire for life, life with you and Parvez and my mother. I want to live on."

Harfan gently put his hand on the covered shoulder of Jamilla and applied a slight squeeze.

Jamilla tightened the rug, and momentarily disappeared to the toilet. Harfan gently tapped on the door and begged her to come out.

"Listen. I'm confessing my faults, if loving and marrying you can be labelled as faults. Do whatever you like, but come out. I've very little time left. Listen to what I have to say."

Jamilla, now fully dressed, opened the door.

The ***muezzin's*** distant voice recited—'Praise be to ***Allah***, unto Whom belongeth whatsoever is in the heavens and whatsoever is in the earth.'

She walked straightaway to the cradle, stirred the milk for Parvez and started feeding him.

"I suspect my cover is about to be blown up. The ISI is closing in on me."

"Harfan, I feel cheated, not because you're a spy. You're a pawn in the power game between our two stupid countries, a prop in the hands of the professional killers. I've nothing to do with your politics and espionage." Jamilla's facial muscles relaxed. Tears cascaded down her cheeks.

"You should understand how they killed my father and forced my mother live in penury. I came to take revenge."

"On whom? All Pakistanis? I'm a Pakistani too. Why this drama of love? Why don't you kill this Pakistani first! Killing doesn't solve problems." Jamilla spoke in a choked voice.

"Jami, the truth can be seen only when the debris of turmoil settles down. Truth is a layered onion, you keep on peeling it and finally you get lost. Now I understand, my love is my truth. I'm a soldier of real politics, and I've done my duty. Now, as a loving husband and father I have to stand by you and Parvez. That's my truth." Harfan spelt out everything he truly felt and believed in.

"What do you expect of me?" Jamilla asked.

"Your options are open. If you like call the ISI and hand me over."

"You don't have to be brave and say that to me. I'm not your enemy, in the bunker ahead. You have no business to doubt my love." Jamilla replied, this time with a calm and composed voice.

"I've only three options before me." Harfan moved over to Parvez's cradle.

Jamilla didn't react.

"I escape from Pakistan alone or with you and Parvez; I get caught in the ISI net or Alam's bullets get me. Finally, I've the option of swallowing the capsule."

Jamilla looked up in silence.

"What's that?"

Harfan brought out two blue cyanide capsules gifted by Dhiran Bhagat, from a tiny steel container tucked in his purse and placed them on his palm.

Jamilla looked at the capsules and asked.

"Poison?"

"Yes, cyanide. Death is instantaneous."

Jamilla looked up. Tears rolled down in torrents.

In a sudden move she snatched the capsules away from Harfan's open palm and rushed into the toilet.

"Jami, ***Allah kasam*** (by god), don't swallow the capsules. Don't leave me and Parvez alone." Harfan kept on lightly banging on the toilet door, crying in miffed voice.

There was no response from Jamilla.

"If you don't come out I'll pump bullets into my head. I'll count up to five." Harfan started counting loudly.

Jamilla opened the door.

"Now you've only two options left. Choose any one you like. Don't talk of death, talk of life. I can't die, leaving you and Parvez all alone." Jamilla spoke in a soft steely voice, still sobbing.

Harfan, benumbed and frozen by Jamilla's sudden action, involuntarily dropped the loaded pistol on the carpeted floor. A big sigh escaped his chest, with an audible sound.

"Where are the capsules?"

"Don't bother, I've taken care of it. If they're capable of killing, by this time millions of insects and microbes down the gutter must have perished."

She concentrated on feeding Parvez.

Harfan heaved a sigh of relief. Thank God! She hadn't swallowed the capsules. Obviously she hadn't. His heart had almost stopped beating and the legs were glued to the floor. Slightly relaxed, he attempted lighting another cigarette.

"Don't smoke, Parvez can't stand it." For the first time she objected to his smoking.

"What's your decision?"

Jamilla asked, looking straight into Harfan's eyes.

"I've told you everything. I'll go by your decision. If you like, hand me over to the ISI. They're only a phone call away." He put his shirt on and sat on the edge of the bed.

"Harfan," Jamilla spoke in a straight and steady voice, "I'm neither a Muslim nor a Hindu. I believe in God, I believe in man and love. I've never believed in what the power hungry and corrupt politicians on either side of the border, called Hindustan and Pakistan, try to do in the name of religion. Mummy has taught me the intrinsic values of life and nature. I'm your woman, take me wherever you can, ensure that our son remains unharmed."

Jamilla's words, spoken in soft syllables, penetrated deep into Harfan's heart. He seemed to have lost his power of speech. He burst into tears and sobbed loudly. He had always enjoyed tormenting his victims and had loved it when people begged for mercy with folded hands; most of them prey to his lust and criminal past. As a messenger of death he looked upon his victims as mere insects, waiting to be smothered under his feet.

This morning Jamilla's compassion and love engulfed Harfan in the fragrant juices of love and life. Her intrinsic strength transmitted in him a strong desire to fight back, like his father did, in the face of insurmountable odds. Fight he must, against the ruthless machines of India and Pakistan.

Unsuspectingly he recited, perhaps for the first time, consciously—'***La Illaha illa'llah Muhammad-ur-Rasulu'llah***.'

Jamilla was surprised too, to hear Harfan reciting the holy verse. She had never bothered about religion and rituals. Like her mother she had grown up as a free soul. It didn't bother her if Harfan said his prayers five times a day and kept the Ramadan fast. She never observed it anyway.

She gathered Harfan's head in her hands kissed his cheeks and wiped tears away.

"Destiny is an inescapable force. But I won't be tricked by that cruel time machine. I'm your woman, you decide. This isn't the time to cry. We must live on."

Jamilla's warmth transmitted a sudden surge of excitement in Harfan. A fresh life force ignited the molecules in his brain, and new chemical droplets started creeping under his skin, giving him goose pimples. The new ***mantra*** warmed up his soul. Harfan raised his head, walked down to the window, looked at the new sun. It looked like a giant red hibiscus. The new sun, he knew, as they said in the ***Upanishads***, washed away all past sins. He folded his palms and saluted the maker of the new day.

"We'll escape, we'll escape from these vicious vipers. We'll escape to live in the future."

"Where and how?"

"Be ready. Something is germinating in my mind. I won't be able to give you enough notice. Don't bother about money, I have plenty. Let me tie up the loose ends. Do you drive?"

"Yes. Why?"

"Keep a car ready, no driver," Harfan kissed Jamilla and Parvez and said, "The spy in me is dead. To me India and Pakistan don't exist any more. Let them fight and exterminate each other. I've only one more job to accomplish and I've more stories to tell. Please make coffee and tell Parvez that we'll go for a picnic to Shalimar Gardens today. You will drive me there."

Harfan ducked his head under a pillow and felt he was walking above the clouds amidst the exploding galaxies. He was ready for his third birth. They said in India that, a Brahmin was a ***dwija*** (twice born), once from his mother's womb and again when he underwent the thread ceremony.

Harfan felt that he was transcending into the third dimension of his life, totally submerged in Jamilla and Parvez's love. This new life was holier than the life of the twice born Hindu Brahmin, Ramendra Kaushal, son of Dayaram Kaushal, Raja of Jhumra and a spy in jeopardy. He felt like he was being sucked into the core of a delightfully bright and swirling fiery cloud. Suddenly a silken tunnel opened up; Jamilla stood at the far end, with hands outstretched, waiting to embrace him.

Harfan realised before he lapsed into sleep, that he had just stepped into a new phase of life, a crucial third birth. The bond of love had engulfed him. He felt safe and secure after a long time. The scared Harfan was dead. There was no place for Bhagat, Nampoothiri and Alam in this new galactic tunnel.

No Pakistan, no Hindustan. No war, no espionage.

It was his own small world, with his Jamilla and his Parvez.

He must protect that world, at any cost, the world of love and caring.

Chapter 51

With Jamilla at the steering, Zahoor Chaudry's brand new Toyota Corolla chugged along the Grand Trunk Road with a monotonous rhythmic sound. Harfan, ostensibly engrossed with Parvez, diligently monitored the single Mosur vehicle, a Nissan, which was piloted by the battered-faced ISI operative.

Harfan advised Jamilla to drive straight, at a steady speed of 60. That was the ideal speed to drive at in the maddening traffic of trucks, military vehicles and assorted kaleidoscope of camel, bullock and horse carts.

Driving was really frustrating, especially for the ISI tail.

The pockmarked face, Arman Ali Niazi, was foxed to see a lady driving the car and his subject blissfully playing with a child, without betraying any anxiety.

He was told, in the ISI briefing room, about the extremely sensitive nature of his target. Conscious about tails he usually adopted anti-surveillance measures, often jumping red lights and going round and round the roundabouts in busy intersections. Only the other day he happened to taste the vagaries of tailing the conscious fidgety target in a narrow lane off Lahore's Anarkali market.

The lady driver too displayed studied unconcern. She should've noticed the persisting Nissan and made some evasive manoeuvres. She didn't. That's what foxed the trained Mosur team.

"Cee Aarr (Control Room), this is ***musafir*** (traveller)," Arman Ali spoke on his car radio, "The target is going to the Shalimar Bagh, probably with his wife and child."

"Cee Aarr to ***musafir***. Follow him at any cost. Don't miss him like you did the other day."

"No sir, it won't happen again. I'm just behind him. He can't play with me any more."

Arman Ali was disappointed. The unexpected move came suddenly.

Jamilla avoided the main entrance to Shalimar Bagh and swung the car left, and hit a dirt road, which wound through the congested localities of Bhagbanpura.

Arman Ali faced a major technical problem. Mosur teams were instructed not to mother their subjects, chaperoning the fledging under their wings. He decided to flout the copybooks. He was determined not to lose his target. His Nissan surged forward and almost rear ended Jamilla's Toyota.

"Take care. He's aggressive. Don't be nervous."

"Don't worry. I'll take care."

Jamilla didn't betray any nervousness. She followed Harfan's instructions and piloted the Toyota to an opening, along the rear western wall of the garden. She parked the car under a ***chinar*** (maple) tree and helped Harfan unload the picnic materials, a foldable mattress, eats, playthings and Parvez's special basket. They leisurely walked past a few dwarf bushes and entered the garden through a breach and selected an isolated spot, next to a dilapidated Mughal period wall. It faced an open lawn, well manicured and studded with flowerbeds and ornamental bushes.

The Mosur tail encountered a series of problems. His instructions had cautioned him not to park next to the suspect car.

Fine. Arman Ali followed the rulebook and parked his car at a distance of about 50 meters. He lighted a cigarette and set the car stereo to a loud pitch, hoping to generate congenial ambience noise.

What next? Join the picnic party?

Arman Ali and his partner negotiated the breach and hurriedly walked into the garden, and parked themselves behind a Chinese bamboo bush. Harfan's picnic party was clearly visible through a maze of yellow bamboo leaves and stocks.

Harfan and Jamilla ate their lunch leisurely and stretched out on the garden greens. Parvez wasn't in any mood to make small talks. He toddled on the grass with a broken, uneven and uncertain rhythm.

It was a sure invitation to an exciting afternoon. Harfan gently pushed a multi-coloured plastic ball towards the broken wall. Parvez followed it. Jamilla walked along guiding and guarding him.

Point Chinar was just another five feet away.

Harfan pushed the ball gently and invited Parvez to take it, by gesturing with his hands and making encouraging sounds. Jamilla helped the toddler by gently holding his fingers.

Hai Rabba!

The Mosur team felt enormously befuddled.

A troupe of giggling, prancing and singing lasses, dressed like unislamic fluttering butterflies suddenly descended near the bamboo bush. Arman Ali grimaced furiously. These fluid pretty creatures, though good in bed, had no respect for the law and established order. Weren't they responsible for all the apocalyptic catastrophes in human civilisation? For all the wars men had fought? For all the thrones they had lost or grabbed? Hadn't the ***sharia*** excluded them from all such frivolous activities? The best place for such volatile characters, Arman Ali thought, was the secured corners of homes and behind the veils. They should derive all heavenly pleasures, as prescribed by the ***alems*** (learned teachers), from cooking dinners and delivering children at regular intervals.

Arman Ali, the Mosur captain, uttered a loud curse and spat out at the belles. He lighted another cigarette and asked his mate to crawl closer to Harfan's location.

By the time the Mosur team could place themselves behind another transparent bush, Harfan's plastic ball had reached ***Point Chinar.*** Parvez and Jamilla followed suit. Harfan picked up a small briquette, placed in a hollow of the old Mughal wall and put it in his trouser pocket.

Parvez, toddling like a lump of sugar, reached the ball and kicked it to a considerable distance, towards the bamboo bush. One of the giggling lasses picked up the ball, brought it back to Parvez and hugged him fondly.

Jamilla thanked the girl, picked up Parvez, and flooded him with kisses.

The Mosur moved in closer, as Harfan approached the car to pick up a cane basket that contained a coffee-flask and Parvez's feeding bottle. It was time for his drink and early afternoon nap.

Jamilla followed a pre-set drill. She occupied the front- passenger seat and started breast-feeding Parvez. Harfan concealed the briquette in a cavity, behind one of the speakers of the music system. Arman Ali peeped in and spontaneously stepped back. His cultural education told him that it was not in good taste to pry on a mother breast-feeding her child.

The sly spy, immensely happy with the copybook pick up, lighted a cigarette and whistled a popular film tune. He signalled to Jamilla and jumped into the Toyota. The car accelerated to 100 km, even before the Mosur could react.

Arman Ali jumped out of the bush, dashed past the screaming college girls and scrambled into the Nissan. He picked up the radio handset.

"Cee Aarr, this is ***musafir***, target on way to Lahore."

"What has he been doing all these hours?"

"Family picnic sir."

"Shit! Follow him and don't miss him again."

Harfan drove leisurely keeping a steady vigil on the rearview mirror and allowing the Mosur to pick up his trail. He slowed down behind a truck and captured the gushing eyeballs of Arman Ali. They spewed out anger, hatred and murder at him.

Here were the eyes of his father's killer. God willing, he shouldn't miss the opportunity to empty a full magazine on his chest.

Harfan swerved right and surged ahead of the truck and pressed on the accelerator. Arman Ali again missed him.

****

Back to Lahore, Harfan prised open the plastic capsule, shaped like a piece of broken brick. The coded message was short. Harfan decoded it with the help of a pocket computer, generating groups of numerical keys, buried deep in its memory.

Jamilla tiptoed behind Harfan and placed her hands around his neck.

"What's my spy doing so attentively?"

Harfan placed the decoded message in front of Jamilla.

"Behest. November 10. In the absence of the usual communication link Sparrow has chosen this DLB mechanism. Read carefully and comply....

"YOUR COVER BLOWN. WITHDRAW AND PROCEED TO RIVER. GOOD LUCK."

"What does it mean? What're these calculations?" Jamilla was really intrigued with the calculations littered on a piece of paper.

"Don't mind my smoking a cigarette?" Harfan walked down to the window.

"This is my withdrawal warrant, from my bosses in India. They want me to escape to London and wish me good luck."

"London is a good idea."

"No doubt. But the ISI surveillance is total. I'm allowed to fly to Dacca, because it suits them. I'm the convenient fall guy. Delhi has dumped me and Islamabad is about to shoot me. A very fine situation indeed! No Jami, General Hyder's men won't allow me to fly out of Pakistan, by PIA or any other foreign carrier."

"How do you escape otherwise?"

"It's a no-win situation Jami. Delhi Is gracious. But I doubt if Alam would spare my life."

"Don't feel down and out. ***Allah*** is with us. Have you planned anything for escaping from the ISI noose?" Jamilla tightened her hands around Harfan's shoulder.

"Don't worry. We shall overcome, we shall be victorious. We shall live for Parvez and for ourselves, not for India and not for Pakistan. Do you recall Edmund Burke's famous line: 'to make us love our country, our country ought to be lovely?' I can't say our countries are lovely enough, beyond what nature has gifted them with."

Harfan collected the scraps of paper, burnt them and flushed down the ashes. He carefully wiped out the pocket computer's memory and stacked it away under a pile of used clothes, in Jamilla's personal closet.

"Why can't these two countries live in peace? What eats into their grey matter? Are they mad?" Jamilla tried to console Harfan.

"Forget it Jami, We're victims of history's cruel pranks. But our problem is immediate. Remain ready, don't talk to anyone, not even your mother."

"Why is Delhi so insensitive to your welfare?"

"They call it professional risk, a soldier's right to die, because he has no better option to earn his bread." Harfan encircled Jamilla's waist with his hand.

"You mean they're not responsible for your safety!"

"I should thank my stars that they've given me a final disengagement message. It means they're worried, not about my safety, but about other assets in Pakistan. I know too much."

"Have they disowned you?"

"Yes. And the message is very clear, if I don't clear out quickly enough, they'll silence me permanently."

"Will they kill you?"

"Yes. If they fail, the ISI will carry out the sacrificial ritual."

"***Allah*** !" Jamilla pressed closer to Harfan.

"Poor ***Allah*** has nothing to do with these mundane things. Men spin circumstances and the fabric of time wraps them up. The ***kafan*** (shroud) is now ready for me. They think I should don it now." Harfan lifted up Jamilla and took her to bed.

"Come. Let's drink the nectar while it's still there. They can't be wiser jackals. The two of you'll live to see me foxing both the Indian and Pakistani killers. I'm a jackal of the Chenub marsh, more cunning than the NSI and the ISI professionals put together. I'm the knight of all these jackals."

"That's a grand knighthood. I like it. But what's your game plan?" Jamilla fastened her grip around Harfan.

"Perhaps, we'll fly out of this mess. May be we'll fly to Dacca."

"That's one hell of a place to go to." Jamilla whispered.

"That's a new horizon Jami, a nation in birth pangs, and all births are painful. Our mothers understand that truth better, you know it all. But let's enjoy these few precious moments, in our infinite love together. Destiny may or may not give us another chance."

Jamilla smiled and yielded.

Chapter 52

Some breeds of intelligence jackals never sleep. Their neurones keep on ticking and clicking, like the inevitable galactic clock; till the needle of suspicion punctures the membranes of doubts and reaches the core of the truth.

Jamanat Ali, the veteran counter-intelligence sleuth, one such irrepressible jackal, entered Barqat's room with a flourish. His inner ecstasy made his mighty moustache twitch involuntarily.

"So Jamanat, where are we?"

Brigadier Barqat asked his intelligence bulldog, who just entered his room with a mighty clicking of heels; a trade mark of his very happy frame of mind.

"Sir we've almost made it. I've narrowed down the circle of suspicion. I'm just waiting for a few more verifications on his background in India."

Jamanat bubbled out his frothy disclosures.

"Wait Jamant. Allow me to digest your frothy recipe." Barqat offered coffee to his junior colleague.

"As I was telling you sir, my men are going crash on the job. I've no doubt that this man Harfan is a real ***harfan maula***, a jack-of-all-trades. There are important leads in Jhumra. I want your permission to lift a few suspects for interrogation. With no police meddling."

"There's no hurry friend. Let's chop this piece of meat with finesse. Give me the names of your suspects and allow me a day or two. We've to be extra cautious. The bugger is well connected and I don't want the Indian NSI becoming any wiser."

"He might escape our net sir."

"He can't. The borders are sealed. He can't board any foreign flight."

"What about the flights to Dacca?"

"He won't dare defect to the Bongs. They'll eat him up."

Barqat smiled with satisfaction.

"But sir, we should hurry up. He's a sly fox."

"The name of the game is hush-sh-sh, till we get at the jugular of that bastard. One fish isn't good enough Jamanat; we have to haul up the entire Indian network in Pakistan. As of now we don't know the extent and depth of the Indian penetration. A hasty move may spoil the entire game."

"Sir I've no personal axe to grind. I only seek the truth."

"Fine Jamanat, I understand. We've some constraints and I don't see any reason to go crash driving. Would you not like to haul up the entire Indian network? He can't escape our net. Give the names of the suspects you want to lift."

Jamanat scribbled the names of Ibadat and Rama Bai on a piece of paper and handed it over to Barqat.

"Don't you want to interrogate Shamim Bukhari and Zahoor Choudry?"

"Not yet sir. They're important in their own way. If I touch them the other leads may dry up."

"What do you expect from that old Bai?"

"Sir," Jamanat puffed in a few quick breaths, like a fish starved of air, "You know our Mosur chap, Arman Ali?"

"Perhaps. That battered moon-surface face?"

"Yes sir. His father was in the employment of the former Raja of Jhumra. He had personally beheaded that ***kafir*** despot. He knows the secrets of Rama Bai. She had given birth to a son of the king. And this man Harfan, if Arman's to be believed, resembles the former king."

"Aren't you stretching it too far?"

"It sounds odd. But sir, there was a Hindu king and this lady was a concubine of that sacrilegious ***kafir***. Please allow me to get to the bottom of the well, the juice is down there." Jamanat pleaded.

"Okay," Barqat shrugged. "I'm doubtful though. But don't worry, I'll swim along old boy as long as you don't commit another faux pas."

"And sir..." Jamanat stopped midway.

"Don't hesitate. There's no shortage of secret service funds. Take as much as you require."

"It's not money sir. Our man Karamat Suri has been able to dig up a few fresh skeletons."

"Please Jamant, spare me the chaste Urdu. Who is this Karamat?"

"Sir he is our junior officer from Jhumra. I'd sent him to Umerkot and Karachi with a crack tem. His stool pigeons inside the flesh and drug trade rings have given valuable leads. Perhaps Harfan's Umerkot records are forged. I know a man, who used to chauffeur the Indian embassy cars in Karachi. Let me locate him. He can be useful. He knows a lot about these bloody Indians."

"Do you mean to say that your target was infiltrated more than half a decade ago?"

"Please have faith in me sir," Jamanat pleaded with folded hands, "I've the experience of busting a ten year old Indian ring in Lahore-Sialkot area. I have thirty three years of experience of working with the legendary CIB and PIB bosses."

"I don't doubt your professional integrity Jamanat. Please don't get me wrong."

"A few pieces of my information have been corroborated by Nawab Sharief too. He has a vast network in Sind, courtesy his closeness to Izaz sahib."

"Best of luck Jamanat. But lick Nawab's salt with dashes of honey."

Barqat sounded a note of caution about Nawab's conflict of interest status.

Jamanat didn't receive the affirmative nod even after a week.

Hyder Bux could reach General Arif Khan only after a delicate intervention by Malika Jahanara.

She was not surprised by the news. General Nayeem had already briefed her, but at the same time had cautioned that Harfan could only be the tip of the iceberg. And he, the chief of the PIB and the brother of the President should have the privilege of concluding that operation.

The unholy combination of General Sarfaraz and Hyder was more interested in implicating the Malika with the ulterior motive of slinging mud on the President. She should, Nayeem had pleaded, try to delay the process by at least two weeks. That would give him sufficient time to complete the emerging intelligence collage.

"I agree Hyder," Jahanara started on a conciliatory note, "This fellow could be an undesirable character. But how do you say that he's a spy? Where's the proof? Do you want to hang a devoted son of Pakistan only because some intelligence officers don't like his face and a certain Nawab Sharief demands his blood?" Malika Jahanara winked at the President.

"Mr. President sir," Hyder Bux argued. "We should be allowed to pick up some of the suspects for interrogation. That's a part of our investigation process."

"Do you want to pick up Harfan now?"

Jahanara intervened.

"Well Hyder," The President finally spoke, "This business of arms ferrying is complicated. Our Chinese and US friends apart, some delicate friends in the Islamic fraternity are keen on keeping their names under wraps. A South African mercenary and a Third Reich thug aren't the most beautiful tunes to hit their ears."

"Perhaps you may like to entrust Nawab Sharief with this task." Hyder added. The undissolved salts of the younger Sharief were still rubbing against his bruised conscience.

"No Nawab business." Roared out Jahanara.

"You keep out of it dear," The President waved his hands at her, "I can't change horses at the last lap Hyder. The irredentists Bengalis are the biggest blow-horns in the world. They talk and talk incessantly, like monsoon rains. I don't want any turmoil. Come back with concrete evidence and I'll be the first to lynch this small time employee of Israr."

The President made his intentions clear.

"Can I add a small point sir?" Hyder demurred peevishly.

General Arif moved his thick eyebrows to give a signal of affirmation.

"Nawab has the support of few important Generals. Perhaps we can't ignore him."

"Well put Hyder," Gen. Arif burst into a rare loud laughter, "They too want to join the looting, eh?"

"Not exactly sir...."

"Tell them that with the lion around the jackals don't have any right to the kill. The CIA, so also the Athena Air Lines, has cleared Israr. I can't undo this without consulting them." Gen. Arif waved his hand and signalled for Jahanara to light a cigarette for him

Hyder measured up the President's mood and quickly changed track.

"You're correct sir. There are too many fragile linkages," Commented General Hyder Bux, "Izaz Afroz will be the first to embarrass your Excellency. And you know sir, the PSO is in cahoots with him."

Hyder pelted the stone into the disturbed pool of Arif with great care. This was a propitious opportunity to generate waves of doubt in the bubbling psyche of the instable man. Barqat and Jamanat and their case against Harfan could wait for a while. The ***Sadr*** of the country wasn't in a hurry.

"Are they plotting against me?"

"Excellency, I'll like to brief you on the details. They're too ambitious. And sir, General Sarfaraz and Izaz have roped in the Air Chief too."

"How dare these scums do this?" Jahanara pitched in with a shrill voice.

"Quiet darling," General Arif mildly admonished his pleasure queen and continued, "Is that son of a low caste Hindu woman, I mean Izaz, really involved?"

"My reports are fairly accurate sir."

"What's their time frame?"

"Any time sir."

"You didn't warn me earlier. How can I believe you?"

"Please consult the American ambassador. The CIA is aware of the conspiracy." Hyder Bux pumped in more adrenaline into the President.

"Do you suggest that I arrest and intern them?" General Arif lighted a cigarette and asked for a whisky.

"I think we should watch out for a few more days. In the meantime," Hyder continued, "I suggest your Excellency may like to mobilise the loyal elements in the Armed Forces. Perhaps you may call all the Corps Commanders for consultations and assess the situation yourself."

"I can't disturb the battle order deployment at this stage. The Armed Forces have started the reverse counting after the last input from Aftab. All the formations are set for action before November 20th."

"In that case sir," Hyder came out with a novel suggestion, "You may like to encourage Izaz to visit Dacca. He is a red rug to the Bengali bulls. You may also think of latching Sarfaraz with him. Their absence from the capital will give you a breather to interact with the other Corps Commanders."

"I really don't know, whom I can count on." General Arif shrugged, as he nervously sipped whisky.

"Your humble servant is e'r present Excellency. I'm ready to die for you and the country." Hyder made a deliberate effort to touch the most sensitive chord in General Arif Khan.

"Thanks Hyder. Remain in touch. You should be my Chief of Staff. Wait for my return from Dacca and keep all the material ready. Any way, is this fellow Harfan in a position to escape?"

"Not really," Hyder hastened to add with a broad smile thrown at Jahanara, "He won't be allowed to board any international flight. The land borders are sealed. And I don't think he'll find the prospect of defecting to the Bengalis very charming."

"Let that fellow continue with the airlifting. It's a small matter. You can always share your thoughts with Malika sahiba. I'm with you. I've assured Washington that we'll square up with Indian build up in another ten days. I must teach that adamant widow a bitter lesson." General Arif dismissed the briefing engagement with a warm handshake.

General Hyder Bux saluted smart, bowed wantonly at the virtual first lady and left with a glint of a smile in his eyes. Holy hell! Was he going to learn a lesson or two on intelligence from that whore? Never. He would squeeze the balls of that small time ***muhajir*** at his own pleasure.

Hyder felt happy that he had finally squeezed in enough venom into the boss' veins. He hoped that Begum Jahanara would stop fuming and fretting, for a while at least. That much of precious time, he hoped, would be good enough to arrange a nice burial for her and her lover boy. The standoff with India could wait. Sheikh Jainal could rot for a few more months at Muree guesthouse. Harfan and Jamanat could wait till Hyder Bux's coronation was complete.

His destiny, Hyder calculated, as he stepped out of ***Aiwan-e-Sadr*** (President's palace), was beckoning to him with the stars and insignia of the Chief of Staff of the Pakistan Army. He would require only a few more paces from that slot to reach the throne of Pakistan.

What was his name? Harfan Bukhari? Any way, he was a useful slave. What was the harm if he was allowed to breathe fresh air for another couple of days! The ISI could wait till the airlifting operations were complete. The needs of national war efforts were more important than hounding out an insignificant man. Especially when there was no way that he could jump-clear the ISI's dragnet. In the meantime Barqat should widen the investigation and haul up the entire Indian network, if any such evil machine was being piloted by that ***muhajir.***

Important of all was his personal agenda; incarcerating Sarfaraz and Izaz to a convenient dungeon and arranging a fine burial for Arif Khan. The joint visit to Dacca by Izaz and Sarfaraz should expedite that process. It shouldn't be difficult for him to persuade General Tarakki to stage a blood bath on the streets of Dacca to coincide with their visit. That should be the precise time for him to march along with his supporters to the throne room of the ***Aiwan-e Sadr.***

The holy land of Pakistan rightfully belonged to him. Yes, it was within his reach.

****

Brigadier Barqat felt happy to see General Hyder alighting from his car blowing a gutsy whistle from a popular film song. Hyder's cathartic mood, Barqat knew, could arise from two sublime factors: a satisfactory encounter with his latest ***hum-bister*** (bed partner) or a happy meeting with the CMLA. Five in the evening wasn't his usual time for a romantic trip to his latest obsession—a Cambridge educated wife of a national level politician. It must be the President and the CMLA.

Barqat was right and wrong. Right about reading the situation and wrong in assessing Hyder's frame of mind.

"Hey Barqat," The chief greeted his junior with a jovial tone, "What's the latest from Dacca?"

Barqat fumbled with his words.

" Sir, did you expect any special report from Dacca?"

"Oh Barqat, don't be stupid. Dacca is the most important point on earth for we Pakistanis. Mobilise your media contacts and plant stories about demands made by the People's League leaders for direct dialogue with Izaz Afroz and Lt. General Sarfaraz Lodi."

"Any other coordinate sir?"

"I want to see them on the streets of Dacca at the earliest possible. And ask our EP Division to produce a couple of reliable reports about the need for direct talks between Izaz and the leaders of the People's league. You're authorised to spend half a million rupees for creating a media symphony and for generating the reliable agent reports."

"Fine with me sir." Barqat again struggled for the correct words. He couldn't decipher the strategic meaning of the strange instructions. Was the boss aiming at an immediate coup?

"See you soon. Get going with the task."

"I need a clarification sir. Should we proceed with the lifting and interrogation of the suspects in Operation Salamat?"

"Oh no Barqat. You haven't understood my priority. Get going with the Dacca stuff. Don't be disappointed over Salamat," Advised Gen. Hyder Bux." The boss man wants that salesman Harfan to continue with the operations for another two weeks at least."

"We should listen to Jamanat, sir. He has a solid case." Barqat pleaded.

"The case may be solid. What about the evidence? Come up with smoking gun evidence boy, that's what the situation demands. Jamanat's impatience can kill the operation. You can arrest, interrogate, torture and liquidate the suspects without deriving any lead as to the depth and spread of the Indian network. I can't ignore these ramifications."

Hyder's smokescreen didn't convince Barqat.

"I agree sir," Barqat argued, "But we have to depend a lot on the background information from our station in Delhi. Vital clues are buried in his past, I presume."

"Presumption cannot be the guiding light of an intelligence operation Barqat. What about your journalist friend in Delhi?" Hyder referred to Pakistan's important asset in India, Raghu Chawla.

"He's lying low, after Aftab's death in that blast."

"It was time for Aftab to go. The blighter was button-holed by the NSI."

"How come sir?"

"No details please. It's over. Any way, ask Delhi station chief to energise Chawla. Offer him as much as you want and gather relevant feedback." Hyder dismissed the meeting and hoped that he had sufficiently obfuscated his subordinate.

"Nawab has a feeling that Harfan's Umerkot papers are rigged." Barqat pressed in his point.

"Don't go by that snake's inputs alone. He isn't reliable. Check it up for yourself." General Hyder looked up, with a final twinkle of disengagement in his eyes.

Barqat felt mighty disenchanted. What the hell was happening to the top guns of Pakistan? Were they bent upon committing suicide? Well! He wasn't the messiah to save them from the calamitous events.

But he wasn't born to lose. His inner passion always propelled him to reach the marker at any cost.

And Jamanat wasn't a closet spook either.

They interpreted Hyder's acts of obfuscation as another smoke-signal of an intense power struggle. Hyder was one of the foremost bidders for the highest seat in Pakistan.

"Pakistan is in for worse days sir." Jamanat lamented with a prophetic gesture.

"I can't agree less Jamanat. But we can't help it. Hope our people will take care of these power hungry jackals. I hope it happens sooner than later." Brigadier Barqat added philosophically.

"What do I do with that ***harfan maula,*** I mean that blighter Harfan?"

"Don't disturb him, that's what the boss wants. Investigate the characters on the side," Barqat advised Jamanat, "Drag the net in quietly. Avoid headlines. The political and war situations are fragile. You know too well that no one is going to throw the line to rescue you and me, if the deluge hits us."

"That means I can chop the lamb." Jamanat wasn't too happy with the decision.

"Cut it very fine and no blood please. I've alerted Delhi for more background information." Barqat added.

"My agents back there have started sending in bits and pieces of the mosaic. But there are complicated gaps. I'm sure, his skeletons are buried shallow, back there, somewhere in Delhi." Jamanat tried to cheer up his boss.

"I can't agree more Jamanat. Twist the tails of some of the minor characters. Let's see what ***ghazals*** (form of music) they sing."

Jamanat nodded in silent agreement.

He didn't disclose his trump card, the secret exchange of information with the Intelligence Bureau chief. Most of the feedback from Umerkot, Hyderabad, Karachi and India was steadily pouring in through that channel. Barqat was a fine officer, but the ISI ***jinn*** (elf) were strongly perched on his shoulders. He wouldn't have the courage to stand up to Hyder's pressure, and the Chief was busy angling for a different whale.

"Why not start with Rama Bai?" Jamanat suggested.

Barqat looked up and acquiesced. There was no harm if Jamanat had a quiet go at that friendless lonely soul. The hungry hound had been straining at the leash for too long.

"Don't involve the Badr interrogation centre, at least not yet. Keep things informal." Barqat gave him a final okay.

"Don't worry sir. I'll depute a crack team to pick her up for interrogation in one of our innocuous safe houses."

"It's better that way."

Jamanat left with a mighty click of his heels and a smart salute. He was happy with the orders. Rama Bai, he was sure, would sing pretty when put under the nutcracker.

Chapter 53

Jamanat's men arrived almost ceremonially, three of them, dressed up in Pathan suits, chewing beetle leaves mixed with tobacco, smuggled from the hated Hindu country, India. As they entered the front portico of Hotel Royal Palace their Vietnam vintage jeep fretted and fumed enormously.

"Hey you, park our jeep." One of the sleuths shouted at Ibadat.

"Yes sir." Ibadat could read their faces and placed them in their correct slots in the company; junior commissioned army officers, seconded to the ISI.

"We want rooms, and where's your manager?"

"Sir, he's off duty today. Anything I can do for you?" Ibadat asked politely.

"Here's my card, we're from the ISI. Hope you give a concession to our company?"

"Sir for you the rooms are free, and there's a 20% discount on food and beverages."

Ibadat led his guests to the front office and helped the desk clerk to note down their names and designations.

"What would you prefer for dinner sir?" Ibadat asked while scanning the high sounding names of the ISI agents, headed by a middle-aged subaltern, Qutub-ud-Din.

"We want room service, in the Kaptan's (Captain) room." Said one of them, glancing respectfully at the team leader.

Ibadat served a five-course meal, typical Punjabi fare, ***sarson da saag*** (mulled green mustard leaves fried in butter), ***makki di roti*** (baked maize flour bread), beef tenderloin, chicken kebab and fish fried in Amritsari style.

"Excellent!" Qutub-ud-Din was effusive in his praise for the food, "How did you know that we're from Punjab?"

"Sir," Ibadat submitted with a trained stammer, "I'm from Mianwali. A Punjabi should know his clan. And sir, this bottle of Royal Salute is with the compliments of the manager, on the house."

"Oh that's great." Whistled the Kaptan, "Sit down. I've a few questions to ask you."

Ibadat had anticipated the moment, but felt relieved that he wasn't their target. Their visit might have something to do with Harfan. He took a seat next to the subaltern.

"What do you know about this Rama Bai? What's this lone Hindu lady doing here? Why was her life spared by the ***Ghazis*** (living martyrs) of Islam?"

"Sir I don't have answers to all your questions. She's believed to be a companion of the former queen. Our ***Ghazis*** killed her husband, during the partition turmoil. She didn't migrate to India thereafter."

"Who all live with her?"

"She lives alone, with a goat, a cat and a dog. She doesn't socialise. She performs Hindu rituals and worships the family deity of the former royal family."

"What are her connections with this character Harfan?" The captain asked in a hushed tone.

"Can't say sir. This Harfan fellow works at the Sangla factory of Israr sahib. I often carry food to his house."

"Why shouldn't we treat you as his accomplice?"

"Sir, you're the master. I'm at your mercy. But sir, this servant of yours is a true Pakistani and I'm a friend of Karamat Suri. Very often he calls upon me to help him in his professional matters."

"He's in the clear Kaptan." One of the officers came to his rescue.

"Okay. I take it that you're helping our company. But, have you noticed anything fishy lately?"

"No ***janab***. This old lady is treated as a part of the vegetation." Ibadat carried the team along with his studied innocence.

"Is Rama Bai contacted by outsiders? Any mail from India?"

"Not that I know of sir. She lives in her own fantasy world. And appears to be imbalanced."

"Ha! Once she faces our interrogation she'll forget her god and dreams." Qutub-ud-Din and his colleagues loudly licked at and cracked the chicken drumsticks and reached for the bottle.

"Fine. You guide us to her place tomorrow morning, say at about 9." Said one of the officers.

"I'll be here at nine sharp. But sir," Ibadat bowed in Japanese style and continued the dialogue with a seducing hiss, "Your humble servant suggests that you have a comfortable breakfast before moving out. We specialise in ***keema paranthas*** (fried flat bread stuffed with minced meat). Any other service sir? More whisky?"

"Get another bottle. And I hope it's on the house." The subaltern gestured with drooping eyes and slurred voice.

"It's our pleasure sir."

Ibadat returned in minutes with another bottle of Royal Salute and wished ***Khuda Hafiz***.

The Scotch malt had numbed Qutub-ud-Din and his fellow ISI operatives to a dreamless stupor. That was what Ibadat waited for. He slipped out and ran fast towards Rama Bai's hut, finding his way through the frozen darkness. His mind raced before his steps. She must be insulated and isolated from the ISI sleuths. The silent safety-vault of many secrets of the royal family wouldn't survive the dirty tricks of the ISI interrogators. Their tradecraft ranged from the absurd to the gory often involving the application of burning cigarette butts in private parts to hanging upside down for hours on end. She wouldn't withstand the brutal torture. And if she opened her mouth it would spell danger for Harfan Bukhari.

Ibadat was surprised to see Rama Bai in her worship room. He wasn't aware that she suffered from insomnia. The goddess of sleep had deserted her, since the horrible night, when Dayaram Kaushal was decapitated and her own husband was cut into pieces. Their only daughter Durga was kidnapped by one of the Niazi ***sirdars*** (chief).

Rama Bai was seated in front of the deity, a unique idol of Goddess ***Kali***, her nine hands wielding weapons and assorted totems. She was busy reciting ***sutras*** (stanzas) from the Hindu scripture ***Chandi.***

The ***Kali*** idol, royal traditions said, was brought from somewhere in Bengal, the land of mother worshippers. One more image of its kind was installed somewhere in the pink city of Jaipur by Raja Man Singh, a General in the army of the Mughal emperor Akbar.

The Jhumra idol, sculpted out of black granite, about 2 ft high, glistened in the dim light. The red hibiscus garland around the neck added a grotesque sheen to its galactic blackness.

Ibadat looked at his watch and removed his shoes to enter the room. He did not think it prudent to wait for her rituals to be over. He wanted to pre-empt the ISI nemesis.

His steps froze, as Rama Bai pricked her finger with a sharp needle and smeared a few drops of blood on the protruding tongue of the deity, simultaneously reciting some Sanskrit verses.

"Wait, don't come in," Rama Bai woke up from her trance, as if she had smelt Ibadat's silent breath, "I'd a premonition that you would come with the inevitable bad news. The Mother had told me in a dream that you, son of the chief cook will save my son."

She spoke in a hushed voice, "Is the Prince safe?"

"Can't say for sure, but the police are investigating him. They suspect he's an Indian spy. Shall we go in?"

Ibadat tried to prod her to the adjoining hut, near the palace compound, silhouetted by heavy vegetation.

"I wanted to tell him all the while that, the time wasn't right for him to come here. Why did you people get him here?"

"That's a different story. I've bad news. The police suspect your involvement with the Prince and believe that you have evidence of his being an Indian spy. The police goons are here, to investigate and interrogate you."

Ibadat squatted on the steps of the room.

"Are you frightening me?"

"No. To tell you the truth, you're only six hours away from probable death. They will not only interrogate you, but will inflict severe torture as well, to extract a confession out. You won't be able to survive that."

"That means they'll search my room."

"Anything is possible."

"Wait." Rama Bai went inside and came out with a bulky photo album and two oil paintings.

"Take these away. Destroy these, if you can't secure. The Prince has a striking resemblance to his father. The police won't take time to get to his roots."

"And keep these," Rama Bai took out a thick bunch of letters, "These are from the ***maharani*** (queen). She's been in touch, ever since we parted company. In one of the envelopes you'll find some photographs of the Prince."

This was bad news indeed, explosive enough to blow up Harfan's cover. Lousy! He thought. The entire operation was damn lousy.

Ibadat's silence puzzled Rama Bai.

"And will you do me a favour?"

"Just say the word." Ibadat replied in whispering tone.

"Keep this jewel box. There are diamonds and gold ornaments in it. Can you reach it to my daughter Durga?"

"How do I get to her?"

"You can reach her at Pannu, at the house of Sardar Allahbux Niazi. She has been renamed Ayesha Begum."

"You got her married to a Muslim!"

"No. She was kidnapped the night the king, my husband and your father were killed by the Niazi chiefs."

"I am sorry to here that."

"Don't feel sad. She is alive and well and is the mother of four kids. Promise that you will give the jewels to her?"

"Sure, you have the promise from a true Mussalman."

"How real is the danger to my son?" She asked.

"Did you say your son?"

"I mean the Prince."

"Very real. The police are on his trail." Ibadat's frankness sounded fearsome.

"That's bad. I must protect him."

The old lady, on the verge of a violent death stood like a gleaming sword before Ibadat. Her looks didn't implore for mercy. Ibadat couldn't meet her eyes. A sense of guilt gripped his conscience. He was here tonight as a cruel messenger of death. She must die, before the ISI caught up with her. He wasn't left with any other choice.

"The police are coming for you in a few hours," Ibadat continued, "It's better you don't face them."

"I've the courage." She stood firm with her lips drawn in.

"We can't take that chance. Your arrest will expose the Prince. You're a vital link to the prince."

Ibadat felt the cool steel of the pistol in his pocket. A single bullet through her head would be good enough. He withdrew the hand on second thoughts. The bullet would kill this frail old lady. But the sound waves from the .38 colt were sure to betray his presence.

"Do you suggest that I escape?" Rama Bai asked.

"You don't have time for that."

"You mean I've to die and you, our cook's son, want to kill me!" Rama Bai's gaze looked moist, even in the thick darkness of the room.

"***Khuda kasam*** (by God)," Ibadat brought out a tiny steel snuffbox from his pocket, took out a capsule and held it on his palm, "I've no intention of killing you. But the road ends here and now."

"What's this?" She glanced with a detached look at the death pill on Ibadat's palm.

"Poison. Take it and you'll die peacefully. Hope you aren't afraid of death."

"Ibadat," Rama Bai spoke in an icy voice, "I've had a long journey. I'm waiting for my time to run out. Your father knew that I've been living with death, ever since I stepped into Jhumra. I consider death to be the ultimate cure for a disease called life."

"What do you mean by that?"

"Read these letters. Protect my son. Your father was loyal to the king. He knew all my secrets, my happiness and my shame. Hope you won't betray the king's son, my son?"

Rama Bai opened a tin suitcase and brought out a faded black and white photograph and a silver box.

"What's this?"

"Give it to our son, the Prince of Jhumra. The photograph is for him and the box is for his wife. The blue diamond in it used to adore the neck of the former queen, my ***saheli*** Kaushalya. You're here to dispense death; I give you the essence of life, a life you were never aware of. Your father was. Give me the tablet of death."

Rama Bai extended her palm.

"Pardon me mother. It's the only way to minimise the Prince's risk. If they close in on me, I've the pills for my own death as well. Our family shall never betray the king."

Ibadat handed over two capsules to Rama Bai and picked up the jewel box, the album, letters and the paintings.

"Take care. ***Allah*** shall be with you in your final journey."

Ibadat suddenly bent down and in an un-Islamic way touched Rama Bai's feet.

****

He turned back on her frozen figure and walked away in doubles, in the direction of the Chenub waters. He must destroy the incriminating evidences by burning them. The forest slopes meandering down the riverbanks should be the ideal place to do it.

Ibadat settled down under the flowering hazel and lilac groves, and carefully read the letters, under the faint beam of his pencil torch.

Allah! His bones rattled.

Harfan, whatever his Hindu name might have been, was born from the womb of Rama Bai, the queen's companion. That's what had prompted the moving stone to remain rooted to the relics of the bygone kingdom! That's what motivated her to receive Harfan and Jamilla in that queer Hindu fashion!

He examined the faded photo positive. Rama Bai, with a suckling child in her arms, flanked the king, seated on an ornate chair. This was perhaps the only evidence of her legal status as Harfan's blood-mother. The legal mother indeed she was, in a queer way, as prescribed by the Hindu scriptures.

Damn Harfan! The jackal on the special espionage mission should know the truth before something drastic happened to his real mother. No. He couldn't be the harbinger of death to this noble soul. ***Allah*** wouldn't pardon him for this abominable crime. No. He wouldn't play by the rules of the other sinister jackal, the wily Alam Khan.

Ibadat climbed the slopes and started running along the tracks to Rama Bai's hut. She hadn't exaggerated; he realised, when she had talked of living with death and the dark shadows of death being the ultimate medicine of her life. Her life had hung, all these years, on a frail twig of hope, the hope of embracing her son, at least once in her lifetime.

Rama Bai, after her fatal encounter with Ibadat, wasn't left with any illusions. She coolly entered the worship room and changed into her decades old clothes, a red gold-threaded Benaras sari. She was made to wear that gorgeous apparel on the eventful night of her first and last co-habitation with the king, in a secret chamber of the palace. A ***mantra***-chanting priest had escorted her, for the eventful ritual.

Rama Bai stood in front of a broken mirror, in the dim candlelight, and put on a few pieces of heritage jewellery and the ***mangal sutra*** (a symbol of a married Hindu woman). She squatted on the ground, in ***padmasana*** (a yogic posture), lit the oil-lamp and a few incense sticks and started reciting ***slokas*** (stanzas) from the Hindu scripture ***Chandi***. She ended by appealing to the mother goddess to protect her son.

Rama Bai closed her eyes and travelled back to the days when she had arrived from Benaras as the companion of the queen. Was she persuaded or forced to? Perhaps she herself had felt thrilled, to substitute the queen, bear the seeds of the king and ultimately give birth to the heir apparent. But the cost had been tremendous. The world outside rejoiced and celebrated the birth of the Prince, the only successor to the throne. But she was banished to the outskirts of the palace; her mouth and emotions sewed up for ever. She was administered an oath before the image of Goddess ***Kali*** for securing her silence. The son born from her womb would never call her mother.

What a cruel joke!

Why should her drop of blood turn up after two decades and shake up her failing emotions and frail frame? Perhaps she should have gathered the courage and told him the truth, the secret of his birth. But the sacred vow, taken in front of the holy sacrificial fire, stood as an insurmountable barrier between herself and her son.

What cruel game was fate playing again?

Who was responsible for this cruel joke? Why should her son be in Pakistan, married to a Muslim and living a shadowy life?

Why should the police be after his blood?

Rama Bai didn't find answers to her questions. Her goddess watched in mute silence. Perhaps there was no god, no goddess and no eternal linkage between them and mankind. Had she been wasting her life worshipping a stone, carved into a queer shape, after the crooked contours of imagination of an eccentric artist?

Rama Bai, in a synchronised shiver of her body and soul brushed off the blasphemous idea.

What was happening to her? She would prefer to die a believer. It wasn't in the domain of mankind to dissect the anatomy of gods. They existed in faith and belief. Perhaps the Mother had designed her son's life in a special texture, which was beyond her comprehension. Perhaps her death was the final wish of the Mother, a mechanism to shield her son. Some deaths, she believed, helped in the recycling of the matter and soul. Her death was sure to create a shield of safety around her son. Her spirit would prevent anything that threatened his life.

Rama Bai etched the fairy like face of Jamilla, her son's bride, in her inner canvass, and uttered a blessing- ***Aum***. The Mother is perfect; this tiny girl is perfect. She has been born from the perfect Mother. ***Aum shantih, shantih, shantih*** (peace, peace, peace).

In a final act of obeisance she prostrated before the image, now glistening faintly against the feeble oil-lamp and re-positioned herself in the ***yogic*** posture. She controlled her breathing, by alternately closing and opening her nasal orifices and tried to achieve equilibrium within herself. She felt an ethereal aromatic air entering her inner crevices, in an even and sustained flow.

Her supra-conscious mind was now aligned with the rays reflected from the benign eyes of the Mother. There was a sure invitation, for the eternal journey, to her lap.

Rama Bai looked straight into the fiery and kind eyes of the deity and swallowed the capsules. Her frail body slumped on the oil-lamp. The old ornate dress caught fire, that spread fast with roaring and crackling sounds. Rama Bai's body received a holy cremation at the feet of her deity, the granite statue being a mute witness to the spectacle.

Ibadat ran as fast as he could in the frozen darkness, but arrived a little too late. Rama Bai's hut was reduced to a few kilograms of ashes.

A lump of emotion and guilt stuck in his throat and the silent tears came streaming out. He was responsible for her death. It was unfair to Harfan.

The lump dissolved soon. The distant horizon was becoming lighter with the promise of another day. Ibadat checked his wristwatch. It was about time that he returned to his quarters.

No. He shouldn't allow his emotions to run riot! Rama Bai's death was the safest insurance for Harfan. She was born to suffer. Death had delivered her from the disease, often-called life.

Ibadat secured the jewel box, placed the letters, saving four of them, the album and the paintings on the dying embers of the fire. This was perhaps a thirty-year-old fire, preserved in the wicks of the oil-lamp. Death, her ultimate cure, came soaring on the fiery wings of the same fire. Perhaps she had always wanted to embrace death that way.

Ibadat silently saluted the remains of Rama Bai and hurried back to his Rajora residence.

****

After a steaming hot water bath, groomed and dressed in crisp hotel livery, Ibadat knocked at the door of Qutub-ud-Din's room.

"It's nine sir, I'm ready sir."

"Your food and whisky were excellent."

"My pleasure sir. I shall feel obliged if your honour gives more such opportunities to serve you." He bowed in Japanese style.

The walk from the hotel lobby to the far end of the palace compound took about fifteen minutes. The ISI contingent reached the ashes of what used to be Rama Bai's hut after wading through a small crowd of curious onlookers.

She was gone, forever, leaving behind a few grams of ash, bones and charred tissue. One of the onlookers, on order from the officers, scrounged the debris and took out, what appeared to be the remains of the umbilical sinews, a few pieces of bones and lumps of gold.

"***Reham karo Khuda*** (oh God be merciful)." A former subject of the Kaushal king covered the scrawny remains with a piece of cloth and stepped back.

"She was a pious lady." Commented another.

"How the hell did she die?" Thundered Qutub-ud-Din, "We were here to arrest her."

"***Janab,*** you can't travel to the land she has transcended to. Let ***Allah*** give peace to her." The villager raised his hands in prayers.

The ISI officials pushed back the small crowd and ordered another search of the rubble, hoping to decipher Rama Bai's secrets.

"The fucking old whore. She couldn't have died at a worse time." Muttered one officer.

"Bullshit!" Cursed another officer, "What do we say to our bosses? There appears to be a conspiracy, an attempt to hide the trail."

"Nope." Qutub-ud-Din uttered a final judgment; "It must have been an accidental fire."

"Perhaps her worship room caught fire. She was in the habit of worshipping late into the night." Commented a villager.

The officer nodded in agreement.

"Perhaps you'd like to go back to the hotel sir, and enjoy our ***keema*** (minced meat) stuffed ***parantha*** (flat bread)."

Ibadat invited the ISI team with a trained bow.

"Sure. Hope you've some of the English stuff left." The leader winked expectantly.

"Sure sir. It's a pleasure." Ibadat led the way, praying and hoping that the Jhumra trail was convincingly buried with the ashes of Rama Bai.

That should give Harfan a breather.

He tried to guess the likely next movement of the ISI.

"Sir, can you send Karamat down to me?" He spoke the team leader in a conspiring tone.

"Why?"

"I believe her daughter is married to a Niazi ***sirdar*** at Pannu. Perhaps she can throw some light."

"No brother Ibadat. That's not what we propose to do. This bugger's uncle lives at Karachi. And there are other leads. Let's consult the boss."

Qutub-ud-Din thanked Ibadat and occupied the front seat of the jeep.

"One more point," He said, directing his fingers at Ibadat, "I am enrolling you as an agent of my company. I expect regular feed back on Harfan, our main suspect."

"It will be an honour sir to serve you and the company." Ibadat bowed again as the jeep kick started with a plenty of noise and acrid smoke.

Chapter 54

General Nayeem, a rugged Peshawari wasn't known for his love for music. But today he was in a rare ecstatic mood. He softly whistled a ***ghazal*** (light music) tune by Begum Noorjehan, the empress of classical melody. He felt good and buoyant. There was real good news to celebrate. His company, the Pakistan Intelligence Bureau, had made a significant breakthrough and had unearthed valuable clues on Harfan Bukhari.

His meeting with Lt.General Sarfaraz, a few hours ago, attended by GSO-1 (CA-1)- a colonel representing the Ministry of Foreign Affairs and the GSO-1 (ML-3)- a Brigadier handling intelligence affairs in the office of the Chief Martial Law Administrator had gone off very well. Short of spilling the rare beans Nayeem had given broad indications that the PIB was on the threshold of busting an important Indian spy ring.

He played with the precious time fuse, just to beat big brother Hyder in the cat and mouse game. They'd sneered at him, all these months, simply because he happened to be the brother of the President and had entered the portals of the Armed forces through the Emergency Commission, in the wake of the first Kashmir war. But he was commissioned nonetheless! His guts told him, from day one, that there was meat in Jamanat Ali's story. The long term Indian resident agent, with a credible deep cover, was moving with impunity. Harfan Bukhari was squatting all the while like a pregnant duck. It was time for the kill.

Nayeem flipped over a two-page decoded telegram at Jamanat Ali, seated across the table.

"See, what a wonderful job's been done by my boys," The General beamed a brief but wide smile, "My boys in Delhi have traced out the roots of the Bukhari family. Harfan, son of Maqdoom Bukhari and Shamina Begum of village Faqira, Ludhiana and nephew of Jubaida Khatoon of the walled city of Delhi did exist. Agent enquiries in remote Ludhiana villages, markets and lanes of Amritsar and Delhi have established that. But Harfan, Maqdoom's minor son had perished in the communal riots. He was roasted alive way back in 1947."

"***Mubarak*** (congratulations) sir," Jamanat clicked his heels, "It's the best gift ***Khuda*** could bestow on us before the Eid."

"The Indian Intelligence Bureau had used that grain of fact and built upon it the entire cover for their long term resident agent in Pakistan. It was indeed a very clever ploy." Nayeem blurted out his thesis.

"A wonderful copybook operation sir." Jamanat added.

"***Masha Allah***, Jamanat. We have to take a conscious and cautious decision on this character. The network is big, and we should haul up all the eels and pikes, buried deep under the mud." General Nayeem's effervescence spilt over his usual cautious approach.

"Let's talk it over with my chief. He can't put off a decision this time. Hope the ***Sadr*** and Malika won't stand in the way." Jamanat's ebullience matched that of Nayeem.

"I've cast-iron proof now. It won't take much time to convince the ***Sadr***, and it's my job now to convince the big sister." The PIB chief warmed up to Jamanat's bubbling effusion.

"But Jamanat," Nayeem applied the break, "Wait for a few days. We require untying all the knots; the real Gordian knots this time. I wouldn't like Hyder to have the pleasure of cutting it."

"But sir..." Jamanat stopped in mid sentence.

"Don't worry," Nayeem assured him, waving his hand, "I've discussed this with the PSO. Harfan should be busy with the airlifting operations for another week. We've plenty of time to fill in the Umerkot and Karachi mosaic."

"These enquiries are almost over sir. I'm yet to confirm his links with the Indian Consulate in Karachi," Jamanat added and confronted Nayeem with an embarrassing question, "Would you please make it clear as to why the top bosses are dithering so much on a minor counter-intelligence issue?"

"The matter isn't minor Jamanat. The suspect is well connected and his mother-in-law is a friend of sister Jahanara. Many big heads Jamanat, Israr, Jung Sher and a couple of others would come tumbling down. Let's be clear that I do not want to trigger off a violent cascading effect that can threaten the present regime. Surely you don't want an illustrious son of DGK to go down the drain."

"That's not my intention sir. But, I am sure that the Indian FIB had infiltrated him through the Nagar Parkar route. Mian Rathore, the drug baron of yesteryears and now an important leader of Izaz Afroz's party had collaborated with the Indian side."

"That's good news. Now try to explore the links between Harfan and the Indian Consulate at Karachi. There must be a fifth column somewhere, who had betrayed Pakistan."

"I believe that at that point of time one Irfan Cowasji, a Pakistani national used to chauffer the car of the Consul General. He can probably throw some light."

"Locate him first and then go for Shamim Bukhari. Let's guard these nuggets carefully. And give me a few days time to brief the ***Sadr***, when you are ready with all the details."

Nayeem wrapped up the small private meeting with great élan, by offering a full bottle of Scotch to Jamanat. It was celebration time, he said and his old bones deserved some relaxation.

General Hyder had very little to celebrate.

Izaz Afroz had visited Dacca and faced the belligerent People's League leaders, who reiterated that a national government could only be formed with Sheikh Jainal as the Prime Minister. Izaz Afroz's party, in consistence with the democratic principles could occupy the opposition benches.

Izaz, before emplaning for Karachi had advised General Tarakki that General Noor, the chief of the Eastern Command should be directed to decimate the incorrigible Bengalis. He wouldn't be a party to handing over the nation on a platter to Sheikh Jainal, an Indian agent.

General Sarfaraz too returned home with a good harvest. On the second night of his stay in Dacca a few elite cavalry and infantry contingents had raided the known bastions of the rebellious Bengalis. They returned to their barracks after harvesting the bodies of over a thousand 'Indian agents.'

Brigadier Barqat's secret coffer had influenced some of the leading newspapers to highlight the developments in Dacca and to blame Izaz for the political impasse. Some oblique mentions were also made about Sarfaraz's suspected involvement in the latest act of genocide.

But General Arif, even after two exclusive briefings by Hyder refused to believe that the duo of Izaz and Sarfaraz had acted against the interest of Pakistan. The country, General Arif had pointed out, was ready for another decisive war with India.

Hyder's discreet parley with the Corps Commanders of Sialkot and Multan was equally frustrating. They were not ready to accept him as the leader of a new junta. With another war ahead they could not risk embarking on an uncertain adventure. They advised Hyder to mind his own job, the job of generating intelligence about the war plans of the Indian forces.

Hyder did not like to be pushed to the walls. But normally he didn't react violently against his opponents. He was trained to store all his frustrations in an exclusive pouch of his mind and recycle these unpleasant ingredients into powerful explosive devices. He preferred to demolish his competitors mercilessly, in his own inimitable way, by focusing his total energy against them. He sincerely believed that he was the rightful owner of Pakistan and Izaz and Sarfaraz were the stumbling blockades. Should he use the ultimate weapon of secret assassination to get rid of his opponents? The blame could easily be passed on to the Bengali renegades and the Indian agents.

That was what he was planning for Sarfaraz and Izaz, when General Nayeem walked in for an informal discussion. Hyder was piqued, if not embarrassed, by the bombshell thrown by General Nayeem. He claimed to have solved the major riddles concerning Harfan Bukhari. How did this imbecile bumblebee develop a sting and steal a march over his boys?

"How authentic are your boys?" Hyder asked rather casually, "How can our Mission in Delhi venture out to the interior villages and make such detailed enquiries in the rural areas of Punjab? They're supposed to be almost under house arrest."

"No Hyder, nobody is required to move out of Delhi," Nayeem explained the operational mechanism, "Our boys win over Indian Muslim visa seekers and entrust them with bits of enquiries. These reports are pieced together and over a period a coherent collage emerges. It's time consuming, but the trick works."

"Why should they oblige?"

"Leave that aside. The trick has worked and that's it." General Nayeem rubbed in the point forcefully.

"But I've a right to know."

Hyder felt humiliated to receive a homily on intelligence operations from General Nayeem. His company, the ISI, should have the final say in all matters pertaining to India.

Hyder couldn't instantaneously clear up the foggy mirror. His efforts to place Nayeem in an appropriate slot eluded a solution. Was this upstart of an intelligence novice trying to foul up his high voltage game, the game of planning and staging a coup. Was Nayeem trying to hijack Operation Salamat with a view to protecting Jahanara and his brother? He obviously wouldn't like a major spy scandal to rock the nation's boat, especially the boat of the CMLA and his concubine. A dead Harfan was sure to divert media attention and give the opportunity to the CMLA's acolytes to lionise their sinking hero. But that scenario would deprive him of a valuable tool, the tool of using the Harfan affair to defame both Jahanara and General Arif.

Did Jamanat, a former PIB hand and a bonded labour of the DGK landlord foul up the broth? These border dwelling Khans were queer characters. Their tribe loyalty transcended all other considerations.

"Now that reasonable suspicion has been raised about the scoundrel, we should pick him up for interrogation." General Nayeem boomed in a confident assertion.

"Perhaps a week or two more Nayeem," General Hyder echoed the views of the Sadr, "My boys have identified the major players of the Indian network. We should haul the net up carefully. They're real big fish, all his collaborators."

"What else do you want?" Major General Nayeem asked.

"I would like to lift Shamim Bukhari for interrogation, followed by the questioning of Jung Sher Khan, Alam, the Sharief brothers and Zahoor Choudry. It's a big and pregnant list Nayeem. We have to consult the ***Sadr*** and the National Security Advisor."

Hyder replied, but what he refrained from telling was that Jahanara was a prime suspect too. He wasn't inclined to lay his cards on the table. He should, under no circumstance, concede the prime pleasure of breaking the sensational news to the President and the CMLA to this nitwit. The joker shouldn't walk away with the cake at the end of the day.

"Interrogation of Harfan Bukhari alone can clear up these messy knots. The big guns can be lifted at leisure." Nayeem made a counter move.

"You see Nayeem, we can't interrogate them without clearance from the top." Hyder parried. "All of them are involved, some way or the other, in our war preparations. The nation can't afford a mega-scandal now. Why don't you apprise General Sarfaraz of the latest developments? He should be helpful."

"It's fine with me, if you so insist. But it appears that no one is ready to take a decision." Replied the PIB chief.

"Decision making is a tough process Nayeem. As I said, Alam is close to the PSO. He should be able to persuade him to talk straight. Alam had introduced Harfan to Israr Sharief, I'm dead sure of that."

"Not a bad idea."

Gen. Nayeem commented in a cracked voice. He sensed hostility oozing out from Hyder's demeanour. The wily jackal was definitely stonewalling his efforts.

What was he bargaining for? Jealousy? Could be.

Or was it a part of the coup d'etat planned by Hyder's coterie of Generals and the Sindhi marsh jackal, Izaz Afroz?

Not impossible.

Why should they, otherwise, sit pretty on the explosive spy scandal? Why should they allow an Indian agent a freehand in ferrying weapons to Dacca? New Delhi must be having a running commentary on Pakistan's war preparations in the eastern theatre.

Nayeem thought of reshuffling his cards. Why could he not replace Hyder, as the new ISI chief? That Jat landlord didn't have any extra cerebral quality to cling to his position for an undefined tenure. Why not pitch in with Sarfaraz, Pakistan's Cassandra? Any one, right from the President to the Chiefs of the Armed Forces did not take his predictions of doom seriously. The seasoned officer, Nayeem knew, had a balanced head on his shoulder and lots of grey matter inside. He didn't suffer from an alcoholic stupor. He didn't surround himself with imbecile booty-hunters.

But his love-hate partnership with Hyder had become the talk of the town. Each one of them harboured a not too secret desire of hijacking the nation's thorny crown.

Nayeem's snoopers and shadowy goblins had gathered enough dope on Sarfaraz. The able, ambitious and frustrated General was trying to get a direct connection to Langley. His efforts to cultivate the White House and the National Security Agency hadn't gone unnoticed. The Yankees, Nayeem figured out, wouldn't hesitate in accepting Sarfaraz as a substitute to General Arif.

Was Izaz Afroz still having an edge over Sarfaraz? The Chinese backed him and the Air Chief and a few other Generals were on his side. The Secretary of State and the Pentagon fancied him as a sure shot. Important of all, Izaz had garnered support of the masses. They had started idolising him as the deliverer. They were exhausted with the stinking military rule.

It was one hell of a puzzle! Nayeem decided not to approach Sarfaraz. It was better to go straight to brother Arif and Malika Jahanara. He should apprise the boss man of the wheels of conspiracy and the importance of the immediate grounding of Harfan Bukhari, the Indian spy. A concise executive summary on the coup plots should nail Hyder down. And the top ISI slot should fall on his lap like a sun-ripened mango.

Chapter 55

Sarfaraz's modest and cool bearings could hardly conceal the bushfire burning inside his chest, fanned by accumulated frustration. The needles of his intentions and decisive action were not coinciding at the final take off point.

Was it his cowardice? Or was it his spiked stars?

Sarfaraz could not buttonhole the precise cause and effect relativity.

Field Marshal Akbar, the former President had baby-walked General Arif to the presidential palace with the fond hope of quelling down the post-Tashkent political turmoil and conducting the state-symphony from behind the screens. But the Peshawari Chief of Army Staff had grabbed the crown in yet another bloodless coup. Once in power he had insulated himself from the affairs of the state. The chronic bacchanal as he was, General Arif had abandoned Pakistan like a rudderless ship and all conceivable state powers were being wielded by the reigning Army Chief. The President was usually inaccessible.

The crown of Pakistan was, in fact, lying there just for grabs. Any one, with support from the majority of the Generals and the USA could pick it up.

Why should he, the Principal Staff Officer to the Chief Martial Law Administrator, not pick up the crown? The fire inside had been pushing him inexorably to the throne of the CMLA and the President. He had secured the support of three top Generals and at least two important Corps Commanders. The elite Special Services Group could be mustered for a determined assault on the presidential palace. General Mukhtiar Ghori, the SSG chief was beholden to him for an out of turn promotion.

The Naval chief, a misfit in General Arif's court, could be bullied to submission.

He could take care of the Chiefs of the Army and Air Force.

The people who gave him creeps were the wily and ambitious Izaz Afroz and General Hyder. General Tarakki, an Izaz crony was sure to lend support to his Sindhi foster father.

Izaz had, Sarfaraz reasoned, pushed the CMLA to the brink of another war with India, by manipulating the post-election impasse. He deftly exploited the susceptibilities of the Punjabi army brass and foreclosed all possibilities of assumption of the reins of Pakistan, by Sheikh Jainal, leader of the majority party.

The President, more immersed in sundown frivolities didn't know how to get past Izaz Afroz, the inveterate sycophant and a cruel manipulator and the landed Punjabi feudals and bureaucrats. He was caught in the cobwebs of indecision, hesitation and prevarication.

Intellectual venality, generated by chemical interaction of his brain cells with alcohol had incapacitated his rational thinking process.

And that buffoon General Hyder, Director General of the Inter Services Intelligence was a real thorn in his flesh. His coterie of Generals had secured the support of the Military Governors of the Punjab and Baluchistan. These delicate balancing factors, Sarfaraz thought, would need deft handling, before he launched a decisive putsch against General Arif.

As a veteran military strategist, Sarfaraz didn't think much of the war efforts of Pakistan. The East was virtually lost, even before Pakistan crossed swords with India. And he wasn't sure if the West could be defended. He was, General Sarfaraz concluded, the ***Allah***'s chosen person to pick up the shattered pieces of Pakistan and lead it to greater heights.

The clicking of heels and the swish of a smart salute disrupted Sarfaraz's journey through the wild maze of his neurones.

"Sir, General Hyder Bux is here." Announced his aid d'camp.

"Oh yes." Sarfaraz sported a weary smile, "Send him in please."

General Hyder Bux's visit, one of his infrequent ones, was specific to Operation Salamat-neutralisation of the suspected Indian agent, Harfan Bukhari. He couldn't sit tight any more, especially after the unsavoury encounter with the PIB chief.

Hyder Bux came straight to the point. He requested permission for immediate interrogation of Mian Alam Khan.

General Sarfaraz didn't disagree. Intelligence was Hyder's business and he was best suited to brand any suspect as an Indian virus. But he politely reminded Hyder of the importance of being Alam Khan. He enjoyed the confidence of several heads of West Asian Islamic countries. Pakistan's most illustrious hunter in the arms bazaar had access to the corridors of the White House, State Department and Langley. He was a vital link to the mercenary operators, who airlifted direly needed men and weapons to East Pakistan. His good offices had helped in securing additional flights and crucial aerial refuelling facilities from Diego Garcia base.

General Hyder Bux, apparently apologetic, pointed out that it shouldn't be the usual dark-chamber interrogation. It should be done, if feasible, at the level of the PSO.

"We can't sit over the issue any longer. Nayeem has come up with claims of breaking Harfan's cover. He may upstage us by influencing his brother, and you know the consequences we may face, if he manages to replace me." Hyder argued.

"That's a valid point. Why don't you arrange an accident for him?" Sarfaraz sounded out Hyder on the possibility of a discreet liquidation.

"That's not easy," Hyder replied, "Izaz and the ***Sadr*** use Jahanara and Nayeem for some of their secret political manoeuvres. That's what explains his closeness to them."

"It means they don't trust you!"

"Sir, I'm, like you, a suspect in their eyes."

"It's better we sniff out the air from time to time. That's essential for ensuring our good health and will prevent our detractors from pumping in poison in our oesophagus."

Sarfaraz replied evasively. He didn't want to stonewall the suggestion of his bete noire. His dirty outfit, he reasoned, had deep penetration in the armed forces. Hyder wouldn't hesitate to stage a counter-coup, sending Sarfaraz behind barbed wire camps.

"I agree", Hyder added, "You had better call the big man Alam and talk to him informally. We should sort out this minor pinprick. Nawab Sharief has blown up the spy scandal beyond proportions. The real problem isn't this spy. It's a deliberate sabotaging of our establishment by the CMLA and some imbecile and ambitious Generals around him."

The calibrated release of little bit emotion eased up Sarfaraz. It was a deliberate effusion for sounding out Hyder's reaction.

"You're correct sir. And the Sindhi fox is even ready to preside over a truncated Pakistan. Let's move fast and frustrate his evil designs. A Sindhi can't be trusted with the fate of the nation." Suggested Hyder.

"I agree Hyder. How can we Punjabis trust the son of a low caste Hindu woman? Don't you think Izaz pretends to be a better Muslim than he really is? We can't push Pakistan into the laps of a philanderer."

"Correct sir. I don't think we should give him the pleasure of donning the mantle of the second father of our nation. But we must secure the support of Washington. They appear to have plenty of confidence in this buffoon." Hyder added.

"He's no buffoon Hyder. He's a ruthless manipulator."

Sarfaraz suggested caution. The people wouldn't accept an aborted coup at this critical juncture. And Izaz would burst his jugular shouting for and demanding their scalps. He pleaded for time. Perhaps the post war situation would bring favourable tidings for them. The people would appreciate a lightening push, once Pakistan was defeated in the East. The two of them, Sarfaraz spoke with a luscious smile, could hang General Arif and Izaz Afroz leisurely, at least ensure a quasi-judicial hanging, if not orchestrate their assassination in a midnight shooting spree.

Sarfaraz's exposition convinced Hyder that his supposed collaborator was a dreamer and not a performer. Brave heart leader of the fighting forces could only stage a successful coup. He was the one to lead the nation to another level of change and not Sarfaraz. He made a move to disengage from the sterile discussion.

"Are you in a hurry?"

Sarfaraz commented with a bland look at his apparently bored partner.

"Not exactly."

"I find you're too eager to conclude your Operation Salamat. I have a suggestion."

"You are welcome sir."

"Why don't we shoot down his next sortie somewhere over the Bay of Bengal? We can kill several birds in one stone."

"Please clarify, sir."

"You get rid of Harfan and we are relieved of the contradictory directions from the CMLA and his girl friend. This should be done just before the President's scheduled visit to Dacca, for the final round of talks with the Bongs. Cook up a few reports highlighting the possibilities of such dastardly attacks by the Indians on Pakistani flights carrying important personalities. We can pass on the blame to Delhi and request the USA for an early intervention."

"Are you sure that the White House will purchase this story?"

"The Yankees are more gullible than you can imagine."

"That's okay. But, where would you get the missiles to bring down the giant jet? You can't trust the Air chief."

"We have a couple of ground to air missile batteries at Cox's Bazaar and Feni. Tarakki can take care of the logistics."

"Are you sure that he will cooperate?"

"He's a taxi. You can hire him any time for the correct fare plus a decent tip. In our new dispensation we can offer him a plum posting."

"I think sir," Hyder finally stood up, "We have to think over the suggestion seriously. At the end of the day General Arif and Izaz shouldn't get away with our heads and play soccer with them. Let's keep our options open."

He saluted the PSO and left with grave thoughts etched all over his face. The two conspirators parted company with trained smiles on their faces, daggers hidden under their respective sleeves. General Hyder was happy that the PSO had accepted his agenda of informally interrogating Mian Alam Khan. Sarfaraz, on his own account, was keen for an informal chat with Pakistan's best-known wheeler-dealer. He had his own agenda to pursue too.

****

Mian Alam Khan had anticipated the move. He had his own telescope trained on the gathering clouds around Triple X. He nursed no illusion that sooner or later the ISI would like to tap him for a few gentle questions, initially, followed by the big crunch. They were, he estimated, about to drag the net in for the big counter-intelligence catch.

At least he knew what they were up to. The realisation gave him peace and anxiety. The peace came from the resolution to liquidate Triple X on his own initiative.

The burrowing anxiety emanated from the shaken foundations below his feet. This meteor of Delhi was about to vaporise his own existence by a sudden thunderous impact.

Sacrificing one Harfan wouldn't bleed his conscience. He should be able to protect the intelligence network, which he had helped in building up over the last two decades. It was all the more important to save his skin and soul. How could he neglect the illusory business empire he had built up and the fortune he had stashed away in Switzerland?

Mian Alam Picked up the phone and replied in a submissive voice.

"I'm honoured sir. It's a privilege to have coffee with you."

He readily accepted the invitation to coffee from General Sarfaraz, the second most important pinion in the Pakistani establishment.

"I know you're a busy person Alam sahib. Spare at least an hour for me." Sarfaraz sounded extra sweet on the phone.

Alam took a deep breath and allowed his mind to sweep the surface and the crevices of the panorama of events that could have prompted the PSO to invite him for a long parley. He shuffled his strategic arguments that he thought he could deftly use to befuddle the seasoned General and boarded his sterling silver coloured Mercedes.

"We've no chance of winning this war, without the direct support from America and China." Sarfaraz initiated the discussions and offered a cup of coffee to Alam.

"The Yankees are fooling us. Their arms-pushing exercises from Phuket ended in a fiasco. And I think, all these talks about their Seventh Fleet coming to our rescue are too vague."

Alam very gingerly warmed up to the dialogue. He was still circumspect about the invitation to coffee. He continued the dialogue in an exploratory manner.

"I'm told the CMLA has a direct line to Washington and that the White House is committed to preserving Pakistan's unity."

Alam intended guiding the dialogue to Sarfaraz's Achilles' heel - the grim security situation and his burning ambition.

"What do you think of the power sharing scenario, if we get a beating in the war?"

Sarfaraz directed a probing question to gauge Alam's depth of knowledge of the strategic thinking in Washington. It's the White House, Pentagon and the Langley, who would decide the contours of fresh political alignment in post-war Pakistan.

"***Janab***," Alam harvested the hint and titillated Sarfaraz's dream theme, "I think you're the man of destiny for the nation. Why wait for a routing in Dacca? Strike now. But sir, take care of the ISI and PIB chiefs. They aren't your well-wishers."

"Thanks Alam, careful, not so loud," Sarfaraz cautioned his visitor, "The defeat in Dacca is bound to take its toll and I depend on the good wishes of friends like you. You know how the old man is wasting himself away!"

"***Janab***, I've a submission to make," Alam scaled down his tone, "Plug on to the White House, Pentagon and the CIA. They should know you're the man of destiny. They should deal with you and not that flunky Sindhi orator; whose words carry more air than substance."

"I require your help. Activate your conduits in the State Office and the CIA. Hyder gives me the creeps. He has direct linkages with the CIA."

"Any time General. The Deputy Assistant Secretary of State and the Under Secretary for Defence are my good friends. I suggest you have a free and frank dialogue with the Secretary of State." Alam assured the worried PSO.

"That Jew isn't dependable."

"I know. A Jew can't be a friend of Islam. They'd even betrayed our Prophet (pbuh). But in today's US he matters. And he's rabidly anti-Indian and nurses hatred against PM Mandira."

"Once our forces are routed in Dacca, like I'm sure they would be, it won't be difficult to make a mild push over. What do you think about the likely war scenario? Do we have any chance?" The PSO tried to carry Alam along the desired line.

"One to one, the Pakistani soldiers are superior to the Indian monkey brigade," Alam spoke with an assumed tinge of scorn, "But General, we don't have worthy battle field leaders, like you, to lead them. I wish you were there at the helm of affairs."

"***Insha Allah***! But who cares in Pakistan? The President doesn't meet his officials for weeks together. The Cabinet Committee on War hasn't met for the last one month. That's a bad situation."

"Why don't you push the old man out?"

"I can't. That bitch guards him like a mother eagle, and there's that small time actress Ruksana, Hyder's mole in the CMLA's closet." Sarfaraz expressed his indignation in forceful words.

"Don't tell me that he is hooked to that young actress too!"

"It's real bad Alam sahib. I wish I had a serving colleague like you," Sarfaraz echoed Alam's words and added, "There's a small point Alam. This blighter Hyder isn't able to get out of his paranoid fixation, about Harfan. Hyder has been unduly influenced by that unscrupulous fellow, Nawab."

"He's doing a fine job in the airlifting operations. Anything wrong?" Alam asked in an innocent tone.

"Nothing serious. Some one in Hyder's company wants to verify a few points about him and wants to talk to you too. Hope you don't mind."

"Why should I? I'm ready, if it helps Pakistan." Alam finished the coffee without raising his eyes.

"Has he any suspected Indian link?" Sarfaraz asked.

"Not that I know of. Jung Sher Khan, a business associate of Harfan's uncle, referred him to me. I don't mind Hyder probing the frequent flyer, if there's anything wrong with him." Alam paused, "The coffee is excellent. Can I have one more?"

"My pleasure." The PSO pushed the buzzer and ordered another round of coffee.

"I'll be out to Paris and London for a few days. The unofficial NATO supplies of multi-barrel rocket launcher batteries are to be air lifted, from bases in Turkey. These are special supplies for our western front. You can tell Hyder to get in touch with me, say in another four days time."

"That should be fine. Give him a call. Don't forget to talk to your friends in Washington. Perhaps you may like to cross the Atlantic from London and meet your friends. Don't bother about the funds," Sarfaraz pleaded, "And don't forget to tell Washington that Izaz, during his Peking visit, had charted out a coup plan, of his own. Keep these papers for briefing them"

"***Hai Rabba***!" Alam wailed, "That would mean a virtual Chinese take over."

"Yah. Also tell them that the yellow insects will inundate Pakistan with Izaz at the helm of affairs; it will become the North Korea of this part of Asia. It will topple the apple cart of America's geo-political interest."

"Be rest assured General," Alam replied, "I'll activate the correct circuits. You'd better activate the US ambassador here. His views will carry weight. And you know this fellow, Hansen Lindsey, the CIA station chief? It is all the better if you carry him along."

"What about the British?"

"It's good that you have raised the point. The High Commissioner is a personal friend of Izaz Afroz. They served together in the UN. Better not activate him. My friends in MI6 can be of better use to us."

"Know any one in that company?"

"Yeah. Michael Brandon, the deputy chief, is a personal friend."

Alam paused a little to finish the coffee.

"Anyway Sarfaraz, thanks for the coffee and I'll be in touch with the US and Brit friends. You take care of Izaz Afroz and Hyder. Let ***Allah*** light up your skies."

"***Amin.***" Repeated Lt. General Sarfaraz.

Chapter 56

Alam turned the car towards Jhumra Valley.

Sarfaraz was sweet. But it was foolish to expect him to come to his rescue when Hyder's scimitar slit his jugular. And why should he risk his neck for a two-penny Triple X agent? No. He wouldn't. It was about time that he eliminated that major irritant. He should direct Qurban to liquidate Triple X before he boarded the next flight. That was the easiest way to get out of the jam. A dead Harfan wasn't going to speak to Hyder's spooks. That would stonewall the pathway of the twister.

There was no need to consult Delhi. Who would keep track of a small road accident?

For the first time Alam felt that he was facing the wall of doom—the firing squad, ready with fingers on their triggers. It was now a personal war. Sacrificing Harfan was the best way out. Alam gulped a dash of whisky, straight from the silver canteen and lighted a cigarette.

The hurried road journey from Islamabad to Jhumra exhausted Alam. Millions of insects of anxiety and suspicion had started scratching at his intestines. But his resolution was clear and transparent. Harfan's liquidation was the only solution; a seeming automobile accident should look natural enough. He couldn't be allowed to face the ISI interrogation.

Ibadat hadn't expected Alam. This must be a crucial visit. He entered Alam's hotel room with a tray of tea and took a seat.

Alam didn't disappoint him.

"So, one soft point has been taken care of," Alam referred to Rama Bai's death, "A good job done. Now it's time you eliminate the main threat."

"Who's that?" Ibadat asked.

"Mian Harfan Bukhari. He should die, before the ISI closes in on him."

"Why should he die? We can spirit him out." Ibadat spoke as he poured tea.

"Nope, Mian Ibadat-ud-Daula. His death is important, for our lives, for our entire network."

"We can push him back to India."

"Leave aside your emotional secretions. I'm here on an urgent mission. When does Harfan return?" Alam sipped his cup of tea with relish.

"Perhaps tonight," Ibadat replied, "This is his eighth consecutive sortie."

"The ISI sleuths are closing in on him fast. Harfan has to be eliminated."

"You told me. Is there no other way out?"

"I'm here to convey the orders from Delhi."

Alam took out a piece of paper and sketched a route map between Jhumra and Sangla. His pen stopped at a major crossing, a north south highway intersecting the Grand Trunk road.

"The truck should naturally speed up from this road. Nothing should be left to chance. It should be a hit and run case. Pay the driver heavily. And ensure that he vanishes."

Alam spoke coolly, like a hardened butcher, for whom killing was a part of his daily bread.

"Is that the only way? Can't we push him to Kabul?" Ibadat asked.

"***Mian***," Alam spoke through his teeth, "Why don't you understand? In our business we carry out orders and don't ask too many questions."

"What's wrong with discretion? Our objective is to protect the system. That'll be met with even if he quietly disappears."

Alam stood up with an impatient gesture, walked up to the window and whipped out a .25 Spanish automatic Astra, which snuggled nicely in the curvature of his palm.

"I always carry this in my pocket." He pointed the pistol at an unspecified corner of the ornate colonial ceiling.

"My own life is just micro millimetres away, between this barrel and skins on my temple. My trade is more important than my life. And remember I'm not alone in this game. If you ever try to betray me, you won't even know when the hot bullets kiss you. My people are everywhere."

Ibadat shuddered in his bones. The chill of death brushed past his soul. He hadn't seen Alam in this frame earlier. The suave, sweet and charming businessman had just disappeared behind the burning silhouette of a professional killer. He again looked at the pistol, barely visible, behind Alam's thick fleshy palm. Its greyish blue tinge looked like a cobra's forked tongue.

Perhaps most spies ended up like this, quietly, often violently, kissing the lips of death.

No, not spies alone? Rama Bai wasn't one.

Mercy, love, affection and tender bonding had no place in this trade. It was more of a merciless game, than fighting trench wars and facing the flaming bayonets of adversaries, in hand-to-hand combat. He had to kill, simply to avoid getting killed. In the shady game of espionage, Ibadat thought, betrayal and backstabbing were the penultimate fruits, ruefully harvested by the sacrificial lambs, in the name of profession and patriotism!

So that was it! To ensure his own oxygen supply he would have to arrange Harfan's assassination, or face the bullets from Alam or his butchers!

"Where are you lost?" Alam placed the Astra back in his pocket.

"I have an idea!" Ibadat threw a deliberate spanner to misguide Alam, "I know of some army drivers who operate between Jhumra and Lahore. Perhaps one of them can be hired. The ISI tails too would take the event as a genuine accident."

"A bright idea indeed!" Alam placed a briefcase on the table.

"Keep this. There're two grands in it. Spend wisely. I don't bother if he's trampled under the wheels of an army seven tonner or a rotten leather laden butcher's truck. His death should be sure and certain. We're safer that way."

As Ibadat bent down to pick up the brief case, Alam tapped his shoulder and gave him a gentle squeeze.

"Don't mind the tough talk. It's all part of the game. In our profession our dearest consort is death. We accept it when it comes, like one goes to bed with a faker femme. We dwell uncertainly between life and death. Pardon me, I didn't want to hurt you."

"What do we do with his wife and kid?"

"Nothing!" Alam shrugged wantonly, "She can take another husband under the Islamic law. And Zahoor has enough money to support them."

Ibadat returned a feeble smile, not knowing what would exactly please Alam.

"Don't bother about small things. What happens to my wife if I die today? She will cry a bit and than get going with her life. That's the law of nature."

"That's correct sir."

"Don't delay. We don't have time to squander, and I feel the ISI is just a couple of steps ahead of us. I'll be out for a few days and I must rush to catch the early morning flight."

Alam reinforced his pleading by gently squeezing Ibadat's shoulder and asking him to place his car under the porch.

****

Ibadat left Hotel Royal Palace, soon after Alam turned his back, and boarded a Lahore bound train. He followed a gang of ***coolies*** (porters), sharing their loads to avoid the hawk eyed police and intelligence personnel. Out in the dung-littered parking lot, he hired a rickety horse cart and asked the driver to proceed to Masti Gate.

The driver, a resident of the walled fort settlement, offered free commentary on the various landmarks of the historical city. The ***padisah*** (sovereign) of the streets of Lahore concluded by asserting that, the Mughal emperors were real fools to deny Lahore the status of their permanent capital. Lahore and not Delhi was the chosen city of the ***Allah.*** Ibadat silently suffered the friendly but unsolicited comments and dismounted about a kilometre away from Masti Gate. He followed a service lane to reach Zahoor Chaudry's house.

Jamilla wasn't expecting Harfan at this time of the night. His special flight was supposed to land either at Jhang Maghiana or Bhagatanwala airbase late next evening.

Jamilla paused before the door.

Who could it be? The Police, the ISI sleuths?

Were they here to pick up Harfan?

She partly opened the security latch and peeped out.

She was surprised to see Ibadat, the hotel attendant. She liked him no doubt, but never expected him to visit them.

"***Walai-kum-assalam***," She returned Ibadat's greetings, covered her head with the scarf and enquired, "Hope things are fine at Jhumra."

"Fine, absolutely fine. I'd been to Lahore on business and thought of looking you up and enquiring about brother Harfan and dear nephew Parvez."

Ibadat's feeble efforts to justify his visit didn't convince Jamilla.

"Please be seated." She disappeared behind the fine muslin curtains and returned with Parvez, followed by Begum Sayeefa.

Ibadat wasn't ignorant of the name and fame of the living legend of music and a former courtesan. Neither was she a stranger to Jhumra palace. Ibadat had heard of her life-story from his father; the story of her destiny dragging her from far away Lucknow to the court of Raja Dayaram Kaushal and her marriage to Zahoor Chaudry, the affluent estuary tribal.

"Welcome to our ***garib khana*** (modest person's abode). Thanks for giving us an opportunity to receive you." Sayeefa's Lucknovi humility was at its best.

She turned to Jamilla, instructed her to serve hot ***jelebis*** (a kind of sweet) and reshmi kebab and excused herself.

"Any news from brother Harfan?" Ibadat asked.

"No idea," Jamilla wasn't in a mood to talk. She had promised not to betray any hint of their escape plans, not even to her parents. It was their decision, between man and woman, between two hearts.

"Any message for him?" Jamilla tried to fathom Ibadat's intention.

"Nothing ***bhabiji*** (sister-in-law). Just thought I'd look you up since you haven't been to Jhumra for months together."

"So kind of you. A little more tea?"

"Thanks, I don't mind having some more," Ibadat had one more serving of ***jelebis***; "There has been a terrific accident at Jhumra." He tried to drag the dialogue on.

"So sorry to hear about it."

She poured tea and pretended to be unconcerned.

"Hope there hasn't been much damage to the fine hotel."

"It's not the hotel. Remember the old Hindu lady? She died in an accidental fire in her worship room. Poor soul, there was nobody around to save her from the fire."

For a moment Jamilla's eyes twitched involuntarily, her gaze diverted to a patch of starry sky visible from the drawing room. She tried to recall Harfan's suspicions; the old lady had perhaps recognised him, as the son of the former king. Yes. Soon after her marriage, the old lady had greeted her according to Hindu rituals. How could she forget the coins, minted by one of the kings of Jhumra! These were still with her, kept as talisman, a totem of good luck.

Was Ibadat trying to convey an indirect message to her? Were the nets around Harfan closing in on him? Did the Pakistani police kill her? Or was it a mere accident?

"Let ***Allah*** give peace to her soul."

Jamilla lowered her eyes to avoid Ibadat's prying looks. The fellow was trying to analyse her looks and reactions. He wasn't behaving normally.

"***Allah-hu-Akbar***," repeated Ibadat, "Please tell brother Harfan to see me urgently, in case he happens to visit you first."

"Anything wrong?" The words escaped Jamilla's mouth involuntarily, betraying her anxious looks.

Ibadat walked up to the window, looked around for the possible presence of static surveillance. The ISI would be foolish enough not to watch Harfan's in-law's home and not to tap their phones. No, the smart spooks weren't there. Perhaps, the watchers were specific to Harfan only. Jamilla was still not a target of the agency.

"Has he told you anything?"

"About what? Anything specific?"

"About the ISI stalking him." Ibadat made a direct comment and waited for Jamilla to react.

"Has it got anything to do with Bai's death?" Her eyes twitched again with an expression of anxiety.

"Possible. Tell him that very little time's left and he must do whatever he can. Give this envelope to him, he will understand. And take care of yourself. ***Khuda Hafiz***." Ibadat passed on a closed envelope and got up to bid adieu.

"Tell me all that you know." Jamilla demanded.

"And keep this box. It's for you. But open in the presence of brother Harfan."

"What's in it?"

"A surprise gift. ***Bhabiji*** you all are dear to me, for reasons I can't explain here. I'm like your brother. Tell Harfan to see me immediately. It's better if he leaves Pakistan for sometime."

"You aren't coming out clean." She insisted.

"I can reveal only this much for now," Ibadat turned towards the door and suddenly wheeled back, "I think it would be better if you come down to Jhumra. Better be by his side."

"How can I help?"

"He needs your help. You know what I'm hesitating to tell you. Brother Harfan is in danger and you alone can help. He's very alone."

Ibadat said ***adaab*** and closed the door behind him.

Jamilla followed and bolted the latch.

She walked over to the window, looked up at the minarets of the mosque and kneeled down in prayer.

"***Bismillah-ar-Rehman-ur-Rahim. Rasul Salla'llah Alaih***," She continued to pray, "Save him and the child from all evils. I shall observe complete ***roza*** (Ramadan fast), and offer the best sacrifice in your name."

Jamilla concentrated on the faces of Harfan and Parvez and focussed her will force to the united-field around the aura of the ***Allah***. She prayed for their safety. No, she wouldn't allow either the Indian or Pakistani evil machines to harm them. The benediction of the ***Allah***, the wonderful benign Supreme Being, would save them.

Harfan was her man. A very wronged person and she wouldn't allow the political butchers to harm him. There was space for them beyond the soils of India and Pakistan—two foolish countries bleeding each other. The hangmen of distorted history couldn't choke their life force off.

Chapter 57

The Lady of the Light, Athena Air Line's Boeing 707 dropped altitude to 25,000 feet, as it crossed the skies over Karachi. It followed the Indus, which appeared, in the golden fading light, like a fluttering blue ribbon on a naughty maiden's head, just swept free by the wild westerly wind. The river's vast winding course was girdled by a flood of yellow and grey hues; yellow of the first flush of flowering mustard plants and the golden grey of the almost mature, ready to harvest paddy fields.

Voodoorume followed ATC instructions, banked right and took a north easterly course from Muzaffargarh.

Harfan, seated behind the pilot, peered down the front windshield. Dera Ghazi Khan's faint lights on the left were blooming up in ones and twos, and some faint clusters of lights in Multan were glistening and pulsating like distant galactic debris.

"Anxious for Jamilla!" Voodoorume asked while levelling the plane.

"Voodoo, you know the causes of my anxiety," Harfan spoke in a hushed voice, "I'm doing my best to serve the country, you know it well. But some power hungry jackals don't want us to win this war against India. They think I'm an important cog in the CMLA juggernaut, close to the President. I smell a coup in the air."

"It's a pity. Hope I finish with this assignment before you people jump at each other's throat. I fly because it's my profession, not for war. That's your business."

Voodoorume again dropped altitude and aligned the plane to the railway track below, traversing north.

"I'm sick of this mission and want a break. I've flown to the naughtiest joints in Africa and South America, but your flunkies are real screwed up."

"Anyway," He shrugged, "I want to be with my kids before X Mas. How're your lovely wife and kid? You Muslims don't like to take your wives out of their veils! Isn't it?

"Don't be silly," Harfan helped himself to a cigarette, "Jami is a modern girl. We've been damn busy flying these horrible death machines. You must meet her this time."

"Pity I can't go to your town. My contract doesn't allow that."

"Why bother? I'll request her to come down to Bhagatanwala. It's not very far from my place at Jhumra."

"Why wait, call now. What's the exchange telephone number?"

"Yes. It's Lahore 9234786."

"What's the number of your wife?"

Harfan shared with him the number of Zahoor Chaudry.

Voodoorume picked up the handset, dialled and asked the operator to patch Zahoor Chaudry's number.

"That's not the procedure here. You can't access a private number" The operator objected.

"Hang your procedure. Bill the call to Israr Sharief and connect me to Lahore 9200430. It's a lightening call." Voodoorume bulldozed the operator.

"Who is it?" Jamilla's anxious voice sounded faint.

"It's me here Jami."

Jamilla took a fraction of a second to recognise Harfan's voice, slightly distorted by the noise of mechanical patching.

"Hi Jami, it's me. How are you? And Parvez?"

"Hai ***Rabba***! (Oh God)," Jamilla recovered her composure immediately, "Your voice is faint. Are you calling from Dacca?"

"No darling, just from the air, not far away from you. We're landing at Bhagatanwala. Can you come down there with Parvez? Perhaps, I won't be able to go down to Lahore this time. There's another job ahead."

"Sure. When do you expect me to be there?"

"Darling every minute is precious. I'm missing you a lot. Get at the wheel and you'll be there in two hours flat. Take a driver. Come straight to hotel Nishat."

Harfan's excitement infused a churning in Jamilla's surging emotions. She replied in the affirmative and brushed aside Sayeefa's protests and hit the road in fifteen minutes, with Parvez by her side.

What Jamilla hadn't expected and noticed was a Ford, which followed her at a safe distance with Ibadat at the wheels. Ibadat was intrigued by Jamilla's sudden move. He had expected her to drive straight to Jhumra. He was vexed when her car followed a different trail altogether towards Sargodha from Seikhupura.

What the hell was she up to? Was she in touch with Harfan? Were the Bukharis double-crossing him and escaping from Pakistan?

Ibadat almost lost control of his car, trying to keep track of the taillights of the car ahead. Her Toyota suddenly swerved from the main Sargodha road and headed towards Bhagatanwala town.

Was she going to meet Harfan? Had they kept him in the dark? Why not? He hadn't expected Harfan to trust him. A cornered pig didn't trust its own shadow.

Poor fellow! From day one, Harfan's biological and intellectual vibes hadn't clicked well with that of Alam. Two inflated egocentric individuals were in perpetual conflict with each other. Poor Delhi! Ibadat chuckled. All their meticulous calculations went haywire, simply because two minds didn't click.

Ibadat tried to make an intelligent guess. The mercenary flights operated from Bhagatanwala, Jhang Maghiana and Mianwali, under the supervision of the Air Traffic Control, Sargodha. These non-strategic airports were taken over by the Air Force and all civilian traffic was embargoed.

Was Harfan landing at Bhagatanwala this evening?

Ibadat's irritation squirmed up caustic juices in his guts. If Jamilla was going to meet Harfan, the ISI stool pigeons shouldn't be far behind.

They must be following her too. He adjusted the rear view mirror. No. There was no sign of any Mosur vehicle following him, not even the pockmarked face of Arman Ali Niazi. He accelerated, keeping pace with Jamilla's car. Her sudden change of course intrigued Ibadat. How could that sweet innocent girl play all those games of deception? It was perhaps foolish of him to have opened up all his cards before her. Ibadat steadied his steering wheel and adjusted his speed to maintain a steady hundred-meter distance from Jamilla's Toyota.

****

Voodoorume felt irritated and exhausted at the same time. Fatigue of non-stop flying from Colombo, all the way around the tip of India's Cape Comorin was writ large on his face. To top it all the Sargodha ATC just radioed, as he was on the descent mode, to hang on for a while. All air lanes in the vicinity were closed down.

He banked right, took a south-west tangent, leaving the Sargodha main base at far left, reduced speed, released the elevators and prepared for a landing.

"ATC Bhagatan, Lady of the Light here. I'm on the landing path."

"AAL 356, hang on for a while. Climb on to 14,000 ft. A VIP flight is scheduled at Sargodha in 10 minutes. All air lanes are embargoed." The ATC came in sharp in the Boeing's cockpit.

"Fucking hell! Why didn't you warn me?"

"Fly southward and approach after another fifteen minutes." The ATC, conversant with Voodoorume's tantrums, replied in a cool flat voice.

Voodoorume cursed the ATC supervisor and swerved down south and gained altitude. He swore using the choicest appellatives, which came in loud and clear in the tower terminals.

The foul up was due to an unscheduled landing of a presidential flight at Sargodha. Bad weather had resulted in closing down of the Rawalpindi airport. General Arif and his US Congressional guests, therefore, had decided to land at the strategic Air Force base, on their flight back from a forward base east of Lahore.

The CMLA's establishment was allergic to the idea of exposing Voodoorume's mercenary flight to the US lawmakers. Not all of them were enamoured with the occupant of the White House. A few Democrats in the delegation were highly critical of Islamabad's performance in East Pakistan. They had openly called for Sheikh Jainal's release from detention and the initiation of dialogues.

Voodoorume was blissfully ignorant of the complicated nerve wrecking games played by the sub-continental political players. He was neither concerned with the blatant US tilt nor the open Chinese interference in the Indo-Pakistan stand off. He flew the death machines for his keeps.

The ATC clearance came well after thirty minutes. Voodoo approached the runway from its southern funnel, following the course of a tributary of Jhelum. He released the under gear and asked Harfan to fasten his seat belt.

A red-light-flashing military police car guided Voodoo to a remote apron, camouflaged by well-landscaped curtains of vegetative growth from the rest of the airport

Voodoorume and his crew were driven down to hotel Nishat. Harfan followed them in a taxi. He braved the slight chill and waited behind the shadows of a jasmine vine. His eyes were riveted to the main approach, anticipating the arrival of Jamilla and Parvez. His knowledge of the working ethos and modus operandi of the intelligence organisations exacerbated his anxiety. His own company, the National Security India, was capable of bumping off its useless and estranged agents. The ISI bug was of immediate concern to him. General Hyder's dreaded company didn't bother about the rules of the game. Pushing Jamilla's car down the gorge was a kid game for his operatives. He wondered why Hyder's boys were playing coy! They should've picked him up by now. Was it because of his proximity to certain bigwigs in the arms bazaar and the top army brass? Or was it because of Malika Jahanara?

Whatever it was, he expected them to catch up with him, sooner than later.

Jamilla's car screeched to a halt under the portico of hotel Nishat, before Harfan could notice its passage through the main entrance. His eyes, though open, were lost in the imaginary gorge with Jamilla's gored body rolling down its slopes.

"Hi darling." Jamilla waved as she alighted.

Harfan opened the door and helped Jamilla pick up her night bag. Parvez giggled loudly and jumped into Harfan's hands.

Harfan asked the driver to move the car to a covered garage and park himself in a nearby low cost hotel.

Voodoorume ambushed them near the second floor landing.

"Hi prince charming," He waived out, "Now you can't escape me."

"Meet my wife Jamilla and our prince Parvez." Harfan introduced Voodoorume.

"Holy Christ! You are a lucky dog," The South African pilot whistled, "What do you say, ***namaste***, oh no! It must be ***salaam*** with you. Pardon me ma'am. You know, my parents were Hindu and I don't really know what I am."

"***Adaab***." Jamilla replied while covering her head with a white scarf.

"Be my guest for dinner." Voodoorume invited Jamilla with an expansive wave of his hand, like a banquet floor manager.

Dinner wasn't a big do, but the cuisine of the small hotel was characteristically Peshawari. Voodoorume added the romantic touch by producing a rare French champagne from his personal cellar.

"You must fly with me one of these days," He poured the frothy champagne for Jamilla, "Hope you've been in one of these jumbo crafts."

"Not really." Jamilla replied in a hushed voice.

"You must come. Bring her one of these days Harfan. It'll be my privilege to fly them." The South African pilot was in an expansive mood.

"My wife Janice, a German lady, is a pilot too."

"Is she from Germany proper?" Jamilla enquired.

"No, Austria. Her entire family, all Austrian Jews, were stuffed into a train and fed as fodder to Hitler's gas chamber. She alone survived the war in a concentration camp, serving the maniacal pureblooded Aryans and was rescued by the Allied forces. A brave lady indeed."

"Why don't you bring her down to Pakistan? She must be a tremendous person." Harfan intervened.

"She is. But you know Harfan I can't. My mission doesn't exist on the records, and she doesn't like, what I do for a living. Any way, bring Jamilla for one of the flights." Voodoorume cut short the personal topic.

A mercenary's life was definitely romantic, but there were not too many glorious tales to tell. His business was special, liked by a few and hated by many. People hired him, because he could deliver the merchandise of death even below the deathless God's palanquin.

"Please tell me more about Janice and your family." Jamilla demanded in a low voice.

"There's nothing great to tell. A coloured South African can't have much to say. Harfan knows the story. In simple language I was hounded out of the Air Force for pressing my children's right to study in an all white school." Voodoorume tried to cut short the dialogue.

"Please tell me more." Jamilla insisted.

"The inheritor of a bonded labourer can't protest in South Africa, even if you're married to a white woman. That in itself is a crime." Voodoo replied and continued...

"Janice, I mean my wife and Ralph and Ramie, our sons, live in Paris. She flies for a private aviation company. And my dear," Voodoo paused, "I want to retire and move to Paris, as soon as the boys finish their courses in medicine and engineering. That's the short story of a really long journey over three generations, from Ballia, an unknown corner in India. From a bonded labourer to a jet pilot, isn't it a big jump?"

Jamilla's liquid eyes drew Voodoo's attention.

"Oh dear!" He lifted Jamilla's wineglass by the stem and put it near her lips, "Don't weep. We've wept for generations. Now it's time to fight back. I can't be a Gandhi or a Mandela. But fight we must and fly to our freedom."

"I wish I could join in your fight. I've read a lot about Mandela."

Jamilla spoke in a hushed voice.

"Come to my flight to freedom."

"No captain, that's not possible," Harfan looked expectantly at Jamilla, breaking the momentary silence, "They won't allow civilians in your flight. The flight controller and the station commander won't agree."

"Leave it to me. It's my bird and I decide who should fly with me. Come on, be a sport."

Voodoorume picked up Parvez and put him on his lap, "My youngest one was just like him, cute and naughty. Bring him as well"

"Well Captain," Harfan added, "Don't insist too much. We may just accept your offer, one of these days."

Chapter 58

Harfan and Jamilla sat around a coffee table in the confines of their room.

"Did Ibadat say that Rama Bai died in an accidental fire?" Harfan asked.

"He didn't elaborate. All he said was that her death had something to do with your safety. He sounded nervous, edgy and hesitant. Better read the letter. He said it's urgent." Jamilla brought out Ibadat's letter and the small box from her night-bag.

Harfan opened the box first. The blue diamond shone tantalisingly under the fluorescent lamps of the room.

"What's this?" Jamilla looked intently at the gem.

Harfan picked up the stone and examined it against light. He could not make any sense out of it.

"Here is something." Jamilla picked up a chit from the box and started reading it.

"This rare blue diamond, ***Neel Kamal*** (Blue Lotus) is for the ***bahu*** (daughter in law) of my son and the son of the king of Jhumra. This is an heirloom of the Kaushal kings. Tradition says that this diamond belonged to the Pandavas of Hastinapur. A descendant of Nadir Shah, who had pillaged Delhi mercilessly, last possessed it. The second Kaushal king had retrieved the diamond in one of his campaigns, on behalf of the British, against the Afghan tribes in Kandahar region. Protect it."

"What's the meaning of this?" The short note baffled Jamilla.

Harfan opened the envelope rather hesitatingly.

Ibadat couldn't probably carry any message from Delhi. They never used this channel. Harfan nursed no illusions about it. To National Security India he was nothing more than an exposed and discarded agent. Nampoothiri's earlier message was clear; they had washed their hands off him with all the perfume of Kanauj (Indian town famous for perfumes). And his name was probably scratched off from their honour rolls.

Delhi would simply deny any knowledge of a person called Harfan, when confronted by the Pakistan foreign office. He wouldn't perhaps be treated even as a security prisoner, a bargaining chip, exchanged with Pakistani spies, at silly intervals. He was more of a poisonous thorn in Delhi's strategic concerns. They wanted him to clear out from their frontline secret war.

What was he doing in Pakistan even after the last message? He should have abandoned Jamilla and moved over to NSI's safe haven in London.

Harfan laughed. No mercy could be expected from Delhi. Had he reached, what the French called, fin de ligne, end of the line? Perhaps he ran too fast. Perhaps he had inherited the trait of hyper activity from his father. He had behaved like a fired arrow soon after he was stationed in Pakistan. Perhaps intelligence agents should behave like arrows in a quiver and remain passive observers.

What should he do?

What does an animal do when cornered by a dogged hunter?

Defend yourself fool! Harfan's soul screamed out.

The NSI must have given the order to eliminate him, Operation Elimination XXX. They would be more interested in salvaging their existing assets in Pakistan. They wouldn't care for retrieving a daredevil resident agent; who had been milked white with no juice left for the suckers in Delhi.

"What're you thinking about?" Jamilla brought Harfan back to his senses.

"Yah." He gingerly shelved the agonising thoughts and opened the envelope. He quickly glanced through the contents and looked up at Jamilla with an ashen pale face. Perspiration appeared in visible droplets on his forehead.

"Any problem? Are you okay?" Jamilla placed her hand on his forehead, "Hai ***Rabba***! You're absolutely cold."

"I'm fine, don't panic. Read this aloud."

He passed on the letters to Jamilla, placed his head on her lap and burst into loud sobs.

The first page was in Ibadat's hand:

"Brother Harfan. Or shall I salute the Prince of Jhumra! I don't recall the name given to you on the sixth day of your birth, according to Hindu rituals....

"By now you know that you're not a born Muslim, and I know that too. Perhaps Alam knows pretty well...

"Leave the preliminaries aside. You can't get back your kingdom. These small things in life aren't important. I wonder if you should consider such grandiose plans when you're inside the nutcracker....

"The most important truth in your life shouldn't frighten you. Face it bravely. Queen Kaushalya isn't your mother. She didn't bear you in her womb. She wasn't capable of bearing any child, because of an operation she had undergone soon after her marriage....

"Your father, in love with your mother, didn't like the idea of marrying again, at least not officially. He had no compunctions about taking occasional women, informally. Pardon me. The truth must be told...

"Rama Bai, the queen's companion, in fact her ***saheli*** (friend), by common consent and religious edict, nursed the seeds of your father in her womb and gave birth to you, behind the super-secret royal walls. It's an ancient Hindu practice, I'm told....

"Seconds after your birth, you were separated from your real mother and were brought up by the royal mother....

"Your both mothers were corresponding with each other. I've burnt all those letters, except four. Keep the rare photograph of your father and real mother snapped together. Read these carefully. You shall know how fortunate you've been to be blessed by two mothers and how they were concerned with your wild ways of life....

"Don't forget to tell Jamilla, how happy they were to know about your marriage to her. Rama Bai had recognised you and had blessed your wife in a peculiar Hindu way, when you had brought her to the palace for the first time. Remember that...

"The blue diamond is a gift from your ma to your wife...

"Coming back to business, I must tell you that the ISI has almost finished with their investigations. They hesitate because of your connections, and your frontline utility. You're the proverbial canary, taken down the mineshaft, for testing the carbon monoxide levels. You die, to save your masters....

"Alam has issued your neutralisation orders, that's what the Big Man has ordered me to do. I'm supposed to carry it out. As the son of your father's trusted ***khansama*** (cook), I must tell you one more truth. I can't execute his orders. I can't. Alam won't forgive me for this lapse, I know. Take care while on the road. His hands are long and we can't expose him....

"I've no more suggestions. Take care of yourself and sister Jamilla and Parvez. ***Allah*** willing, we shall meet somewhere, some day....

"Sorry for gate crashing the other day on Jamilla ***bhabi***. Perhaps we shall not meet again, hence this letter. Take care. ***Khuda Hafiz***."

Jamilla stopped. She was too stunned to speak. What a quirk of fate! She was just in the midst of a royal intrigue. She was caught in the crossfire of a sinister proxy war between India and Pakistan. And destiny had placed her in the arms of an Indian intelligence agent, son of a former king, now facing bullets from his supposed friends and foes. She had already reconciled with the fact of being the wife of a Hindu Indian spy. But the latest revelations were out of the scripts of an absurd Hollywood action movie.

She didn't know how to react.

"Read the other two letters too." Harfan, now more collected, requested Jamilla.

Jamilla silently went through the letters, one from Rama Bai and the other from Kaushalya. The contents confirmed in vivid detail her own visits to the former palace and the first meeting with Rama Bai. The unfortunate old lady was mighty glad to meet her! She had, in fact, accepted Jamilla as her daughter-in-law.

The poor old lady! She had lived a deprived life and had died unsung, for protecting her drop of blood, now blossomed as Harfan. So dignified, so self-effacing! Jamilla regretted the fact that on their first meeting she had rather rudely resented the rituals Rama Bai had forced on her. Poor soul! Jamilla burst into a loud sob.

No. She wouldn't allow the sacrifices of two mothers to be consumed by the fires of betrayal and hatred. She must preserve the old coins and the fabulous blue diamond, symbols of good luck and links with the legendary royal family. She must preserve the rare photograph.

Jamilla secured the letters and the diamond in her vanity case.

"Better destroy these by burning. These're solid evidence against us."

Harfan advised Jamilla.

"Destroy Ibadat's letter. I'll keep the others. ***Allah*** willing, I shall carry these with me."

Jamilla's voice sounded stubborn.

"Where do we go from here?"

"Don't despair dear. The closing of one window doesn't mean we're shut off from the world. If one closes another automatically opens up."

Jamilla replied in a buoyant mood.

Harfan didn't dare to contradict her. He silently burnt Ibadat's letter, poured the ashes into the toilet bowl and flushed it down. Gurgling water carried down some of his secrets to an unknown abyss. Emerging out from the toilet Harfan walked over to the window. His mind raced out to the red, blue and white beams of light from Bhagatanwala ATC tower, which pierced the dark night in lightening flashes.

What should he do now? Stay put for taking revenge? Avenge his father's assassination and the gruesome murder of his mother?

The thought bounced back from hollow crevices of his mind. He didn't get the correct replies, though his thoughts kept on flashing through the darkest alleys of his mind, like the ATC signal beams.

Jamilla kept on stirring the coffee she had just brewed. Tears rolled down her cheeks.

"What do we do now?" She asked.

Harfan lifted her head tenderly.

"Don't weep. My life is a wreck. Why don't you leave me? Let me surrender to the ISI. Let me face the consequences."

"No," Jamilla protested stoutly, "You won't do that. You can't desert Parvez and me. We'll do everything together, whether it is in life or in death."

"I'm not worthy of your affection."

"You alone can't take that decision. You can't allow the sacrifices of two mothers to be prematurely buried. You've a lot to pay back to them, to us and to yourself. You can't end up in front of an assassin's bullet."

Jamilla spoke in a firm and resolute voice.

"You don't understand Jami. Back in India they won't allow me to live in peace. The Indian NSI considers me a potential security risk, an embarrassment. We may not be safe there either." Harfan tried to argue out his point of view.

"India isn't the only place under the sun. The world is vast and we can start a new life, all of us together. And how do you know if Alam is acting on Delhi's advice? Your last instructions from Delhi were totally different." Jamilla surprised Harfan by her matter of fact argument.

Yes. He hadn't thought of that.

"There's a point Jami. The bastard must be acting by himself. But how do I verify it? The communication lines to Delhi are closed."

"Don't be afraid of life. Mummy used to say that life is like a flowing river. Every moment it assumes new character and new properties. Death isn't the final medicine for the problems of life. You can fight these ailments with your life force alone. Life has still many wonders to offer."

Jamilla moved closer and planted a light kiss on Harfan's lips.

Harfan suddenly felt a surge of energy flooding his entire existence. He clasped Jamilla firmly against his chest, returned her kiss, this time a hot and passionate one.

"You're correct, Jami. For a moment I had lost myself in the blind alleys of my own misdeeds and misadventures. I forgot that there is more to life than being a spy. I'm a son, a husband and a father too. Above all I'm alive and kicking. I can't be psychologically paralysed. Let's live together."

He guided Jamilla to the bed.

****

Around five in the morning, with the sun yet to cross the misty golden ribbon of the horizon, Harfan called Israr Sharief.

"Boss, sorry to call so early."

"No formality Harfan, when did you land?"

"Last night. There's a small problem boss."

"What's new? Hope the Indians aren't behaving too badly."

"It's not the Indians, boss. It's a minor problem of the heart."

Harfan narrated the romantic escapade of Jamilla driving down to Bhagatanwala and spending the night with him. He didn't want her to go back to Lahore. The next flight to Dacca should take off in another 24 hours, from Bhagatan itself.

"Can we spend a few hours together in your Bhagatan guesthouse?"

"Still the eternal love birds?" Israr asked indulgently, " No problem, you're welcome. Listen, I've an urgent piece of business. Come to my office, say around nine. It's a super secret task."

"Anything special?"

"Presume so. Naqi has a surprise packet for Dacca and Delhi."

"Fine boss. See you in the office."

Harfan disconnected and called Zahoor Chaudry to convey that, Jamilla was with him and she would stay on for another two days. They wanted privacy and no one should be given their address.

At day break Harfan walked down to the annexe building that housed the hotel staff and drivers. He called out Jamilla's driver.

"Salam Yazdan ***bhai*** ," He pushed a wad of notes in his hand, " Aren't you from Shukran village?"

"Yes sir. It's only 5 miles from this place."

"Have a holiday. Jami wouldn't require you for the next 48 hours. Report back here day after tomorrow. Have a nice time."

"But sir...."

"Come on Yazdan! Go home and spend some time with your ***begum*** (wife) and kids. Give me the keys."

Yazdan obliged hesitatingly. Harfan rushed back to the hotel. He vividly remembered the incident of bribing the college hostel guard before he assassinated Matang Singh. A flash smile rippled up and subsided immediately. Well! This time around he wasn't on a killing mission. This small deceit with the driver was necessary for saving his love and life.

By seven he kicked off the accelerator for Sangla, along the Grand Trunk Road. The nascent idea of escaping from Pakistan started rolling inside him. It started sprouting spontaneously. Moreover, the letters from his mothers helped in the magical growth of the beanstalk, the befuddled Jack that he was. Yes. He could climb that fragile beanstalk and disappear beyond the reaches of the NSI and the ISI. No. He had no desire to reach the other end of the world. He simply wanted a cosy, safe home for Jamilla and Parvez.

Yes. Voodoorume was his beanstalk and he could easily climb and vanish beyond the clouds.

For a while Harfan was lost in his thoughts. But he didn't fail to notice a car tailing him. He adjusted the rear view mirror and concentrated on the occupant of the car behind. He expected the pockmarked face of Arman Niazi.

There was a surprise in store for him. There was no mistake. It was Ibadat, following him at a safe distance. Was he there to pump in a few lethal bullets? Why should he follow him stealthily? He could have taken a pot shot at him long back and didn't require some lonely stretch of road to carry out Alam's orders.

Why was he tailing him?

Harfan took out a .38 colt with sawed off barrel from the inner pocket of his jacket and tucked it into his belt. He switched on Radio Pakistan broadcasting the morning bulletin, repeating an address to the nation delivered last night by the President.

General Arif spoke in chaste Urdu, blaming India, particularly its Prime Minister, for the warlike situation in East Pakistan. He assured his countrymen that he would be flying to Dacca tomorrow, for a one to one negotiation with the Peoples' League leaders. He assured the people of an ultimate victory for Pakistan. His speech reminded the Pakistanis of the historic support from China and US. They were not alone, he asserted. Islam would have a final victory over the ***jahilyya*** (non-believer) Hindu ***kafirs***; the President didn't fail to remind his countrymen.

Harfan changed the band and picked up All India Radio. The anchor harangued her listeners in chaste Urdu over the plight of the East Pakistan refugees. Her seductive voice vividly outlined the atrocities committed by the Pakistani army on the civilian population and exhorted all right thinking people to come to their aid. The broadcast was followed by an appeal from the self-styled Prime Minister of Bangladesh, for moral and material support in their just struggle.

Harfan switched off the radio in disgust. The foolish countries and their unfortunate people!

The leaders on either side of the border lost no opportunity to blame the neighbour for all conceivable ills; right from drought to flood and earthquake to plague. Not very infrequently, as a favourite past time, they used magnifying glasses, to unearth the unholy hands of the KGB and the CIA, the NSI and the ISI to justify their colossal failures. And there were veritable excuses like the El Nino or biological warfare.

Yesterday it was Kashmir; today the theatre of conflict had shifted to East Pakistan. Perhaps both the nations would mutually agree upon another new venue of conflict. That's what probably worked as an elixir on the systems of the politicians and their vested interests. They thrived on the blood of the innocent. Politics was the best bread earning and fortune hunting profession for the bloodhounds of the sub-continent. Harfan wondered if the mad men of India and Pakistan would ever see the light of sanity, and allow people, like him, gasping for breath, to live and love.

The emerging contours of Sangla and the sudden peeling off by Ibadat to a dirt road on his right made Harfan aware of the need for pressing the break, to avoid a head on collision with a truck.

Perhaps Ibadat wasn't the messenger of death, deputed by Alam. He liked to believe that Ibadat wouldn't betray him. If he were, where was the need for that lengthy sentimental letter? Why should he caution him? And why chaperone him in such a mother goose style?

Harfan heaved a sigh of relief, as he alighted from the vehicle. He could now coolly plan ahead. A new operation, the daring 'Operation Escape' was to be planned and executed. The time had arrived. The galactic watch ticking inside him kept on exciting his sixth sense.

It was time for the Jackal of Jhun Jhunu, or say Jhumra to borrow the wings of destiny and fly...

Well! Fly where? Into the uncertain blues? Would he be able to land with Jamilla and Parvez well tucked under his wings? He uttered a silent prayer. The power of love and life should enable him to make a perfect landing.

Where was he to land? Harfan smiled. The last gamble of the Knight of the Jackals was yet to be unfolded.

Chapter 59

Jamanat Ali stormed in, in double marching order, clicked his heels with a piercing sharp metallic sound and bowed in Japanese style. Brigadier Barqat looked up, anticipating another ecstatic outburst from the veteran sleuth. He must be bubbling to the brim with lots of information. The sharpest metallic sound ever produced by Jamanat's heels was indicative of the revelations to come. He appreciated Jamanat's tenacity. A near perfect counter-intelligence officer, who never said die, was in the habit of doggedly pursuing even the thinnest shred of evidence. Failures helped in honing up his spirit and determination.

Only a month away from superannuating, Jamanat espoused two pre-retirement ambitions; netting Harfan Bukhari, the Indian spy and ***Insha Allah***, a final visit to Phillaur, his alma mater and his maternal ***nana***'s (great grandpa) village near Fatehgarh Churian, both in Indian Punjab.

"***Janab, Allah meherban*** (God is merciful)." He spoke in a booming voice; "I've all the crucial evidence in my pocket."

"Evidence of what?"

"That bloody Harfan. He's an Indian spy. My evidence is incontrovertible." Jamanat took out a folder and placed it carefully before the Brigadier.

"Please read. There's everything in it."

"***Shukria*** (thanks) Jamanat sahib. Please sit down. Would you like to have some tea?"

"I wouldn't mind some sir."

Jamanat pulled out a corner chair and positioned himself a little away from the table. That was his way of maintaining a respectful distance from his senior. That's what William Burke, the British adjutant in Phillaur police training school had taught him.

The meticulously compiled report contained a complete profile of Harfan Bukhari, his family history in undivided India, the total annihilation of the lineage of Maqdoom Bukhari in communal riots, and his uncle Shamim Bukhari's migration to Karachi. Young Harfan Bukhari, according to the report, was hurled into a blazing infernal fire by the marauding Hindu-Sikh mob and burnt alive with his parents and two sisters.

His uncle had seen him last, a few days before the orgy of violence, when he was a five-year-old toddler, learning Urdu alphabets from the village ***madrasa*** (religious school).

Shamim's sister, married to a Delhi trader, died around 1952, two years after her husband was assassinated in another communal violence in 1950. Her husband's immediate family had migrated to Lahore.

"You mean this Harfan didn't live to grow up at all! He didn't exist!"

"A Harfan did exist till he was killed by the Hindu rioters. The Indian FIB picked up the name of the dead boy and retextured his family history in order to weave a cogent cover for their long-term resident agent. A good cover indeed, I must admit sir. The FIB and now the damn NSI has blistered our eyes and senses successfully." Jamanat sipped the tea with relish.

"That's a classic tradecraft strategy Jamanat."

"An excellent one at that; must be the handy work of Dutta sahib."

"Who is he?"

"The legendary Director of the Indian FIB sir, Rabindra Narayan Dutta. I've seen him functioning from close quarter."

Jamanat replied with an air of nostalgia.

"What about his documentation?"

"All forged. Some have been procured with the help of a Pakistani, who was in the employment of the Indian Mission in Karachi. And the rest were obtained by greasing the palms of Pakistani officials."

"Wait, wait," Barqat pleaded, "Not so fast. How did you get these materials? Our station in Delhi appears to be efficient."

"Pardon me sir." Jamanat spoke in an ingratiating voice," My man has done the job. The local station isn't involved at all."

"Your man? You're not authorised to run agents in India." Barqat quipped.

"No problem sir, I just gambled a little. You recall our Operation Aftab, the minister Ram Karan Prasad, who worked for the PIB and ISI for about 30 years and was killed in a blast!"

"Yes. I think so."

"Perhaps you recall our abandoned Project Magnet, developed by Col. Akram, the First Secretary, who was declared PNG."

"Yes. Now be quick."

"Sorry sir. I want to make sure that you link up the old threads. Raghu Chawla, the target in our Project Magnet, was tasked to enquire into the background of Harfan. He has done a thorough job. We have to pay him just Rupees five hundred thousand only, in Indian currency."

"I'm told by the PIB boss that his boys have collected valuable details."

"No problem sir. Their reports should corroborate our materials."

Jamanat tried to protect his subtle linkage with the PIB boss.

"Wonderful, Jamanat! Hope you'll be able to revive Magnet."

"Sorry sir, I'm retiring next month."

"Don't worry. I'll move the top brass for the extension of your tenure." Barqat again delved into the papers.

Fascinating! Jamanat had done a fabulous job. The devil had hooked two whales with one harpoon, busting the cover of Harfan Bukhari and reviving the prized Project Magnet. No doubt, Raghu Chawla should, in due course, replace Operation Aftab, Pakistan's most successful intelligence project.

Hai Rabba! How could he have overlooked the transparent evidence! Perhaps the bosses were too obsessed with that pugnacious two-bit courtesan, the supposed first lady. How could the ISI succumb to her fleshy whims! Jamanat was correct all the way.

"Sir, I'm not bothered about the extension of my tenure," Jamanat added, with an incandescent effusion lighting up his face, "I request you to scrutinise the mechanism, our enemy agencies have adopted to infiltrate and house this forward agent with almost a fool-proof cover."

"What do you mean by that?"

"We still don't know how he was infiltrated, who his Pakistani collaborators are! I've picked up Hassan Rathore of Umerkot, a notorious smuggler and partner of Aftab, a specialist in the narcotics and flesh trade."

"Was he responsible for Harfan's infiltration?"

"No sir. Amrik Singh, a front paw of Aftab had approached Rathore. But the Indian FIB didn't use that channel. We don't know why."

"Was that feudal Hindu chieftain of Ramsar involved in sheltering him?"

"No sir, we're yet to hit the correct tunnel."

Jamanat explained the role of the key dramatis personae, Irfan Cowasji, the Pakistani driver of the Indian Mission in Karachi. Now retired, the driver worked as a ***khidmatgar*** (voluntary worker) at the shrine of Abdullah Shah Ghazi, a ***Sufi*** temple above Clifton Viewpoint hilltop. He didn't require much persuasion. A few routine twists on his old bones had opened up the rusted reeds, and he revealed the fascinating details of induction and baptism of Harfan Bukhari in his treacherous trade inside Pakistan.

Shamim Bukhari, Jamanat explained, was a victim of his love and longing for the soils he had left behind. This was peculiar to all the ***muhajirs***. A little scratch often ripped open stored memories of the walled city of Delhi.

These people, explained Jamanat, the first generation migrants, were still living in a make believe world of self-deception. They physically lived in Pakistan; but all the while dreamt of their homes and hearths, which they had left behind in damn Hindustan.

No. Shamim Bukhari wasn't adamant. He came out clean and his wife, half his age, and two young brothers-in-law were more than co-operative. They blamed the old haggard for claiming a stranger as his nephew. Harfan was a fraud; they claimed and demanded his incarceration. What they didn't mention was that, they invoked the ***Allah*** in their daily ***namaz***, to call the old haggard to His services, at ***bahesht*** (heaven) or ***dozakh*** (hell); whatever slots His Angels had reserved for the fool.

The rest of Harfan's contacts came through open business connections, Jamanat opined. Jung Sher Khan, Alam Khan and Israr Sharief, all pure Pathans and Punjabis, weren't conscious players in the Indian drama. The wily fellow, this Harfan, was an efficient charmer and knew the tricks of climbing the correct ropes.

"What about his marriage?" Barqat asked.

"***Janab***, it appears to be a case of love at first sight. Jamilla's father, Zahoor Chaudry, an estuary tribal from a low caste delta fishing community, is an inferior Muslim. He married a nautch girl, not exactly a whore, but a famous ***mujrawali*** (professional singer) from Lucknow. Supposedly close to Malika Jahanara, she doesn't strictly believe in the tenets of Islam. Born of such parents, Jamilla isn't expected to be a puritan in her religious views. She's well educated and loves her husband."

No. She couldn't be called a committed Pakistani, but she wasn't a ***na-pak*** (impure) Pakistani either. She was one of those enlightened unislamic socialites, who impertinently questioned the wisdom behind several social practices prescribed by the ***Hadis*** and the ***Sharia***. Such blasphemous people should've no place in the land of the pure, Pakistan, Jamanat asserted forcefully.

He believed Jamilla wasn't a part of the spy game. She should, however, be picked up for interrogation. Were not men susceptible to divulging many secrets while in the arms of their beloved ones? She could reveal a lot.

"You've an iron cast case Jamanat. I'm fully convinced. But Zahoor is helping the government in a big way. Don't you think he would intercede on behalf of his son-in-law?"

"That's a valid point sir. But I don't think he would be delighted to know that his son-in-law is not even a Muslim."

"Let me think over the matter. Give a little time to plan out the operation. You have done a fine job."

Barqat complimented his junior colleague.

"We should pick him up, now. We've put our fingers in too many holes and the reptile must have been alarmed. And sir....," Jamanat hastened to add,"I doubt this fellow Ibadat as well. His behaviour is suspect. My foolish officers had trusted him in this stupid Rama Bai case and she died in a mysterious fire. And my reports say that, he's a limpet of this Indian spy, Harfan."

"I agree," Barqat advised his colleague, "But I must put the matter across to the chief and the Operations Appraisal Committee. And Jamanat, you know the sensitivity of this case. We surely don't want big names to be involved at this crucial stage."

"But, sir..." Jamanat fumed like a wounded bison.

"Keep your cool Jamanat. I'm with you. But a few more steps are essential. This time we aren't talking in the air. Our evidence is conclusive. Just give me two or three day's time. I'll take full responsibility. Let me prepare an executive summary for the chief and the PSO to the CMLA. Be in town for consultations."

"Hope we don't have to wait for a presidential consent." Jamanat was still not convinced that his immediate boss meant business.

"No Jamanat. It's an open and shut case, the biggest catch we have ever had so far. Let's play it cool. Our anxiety shouldn't betray our professional acumen."

Barqat tried to pacify his junior's ruffled feelings.

"The unmasking of the biggest Indian wizard, Jamanat, in fact, a single man operation, is entirely the story of a one-man ***jihad*** against India. You should be recommended for a top national honour, say the Nishan-e-Pakistan."

"I want no extension of service sir," Jamanat mumbled, "After forty years of slogging I want peace and time to remember the ***Allah***."

Jamanat stood up, again clicked his heels, bowed in Japanese style and made a smart about turn. He felt extremely happy today. His lifelong ambition of neutralising a top Indian resident agent in Pakistan was about to be crowned with success. He would prefer to have a deep sleep, only after bringing a few shining Pakistani heads under the chopper.

What better reward could a superannuating intelligence officer dream of!

****

Israr International's Bhagatanwala guesthouse was located on a midget sized hillock, locally known as Latuwali ***tikri***, a landmass that jutted into a tributary of the river Chenub. The river looped around the hillock isolating the small colonial bungalow, which once served as the official residence of the British agent to the nearby Shahpur Nawabdom. There was an old world charm to it.

Harfan selected the guesthouse not merely for its idyllic location and scenic beauty. The grand isolation of the bungalow had an added advantage. It was just about four kilometres away from the Bhagatan airbase. It had other strategic advantages as well.

The Chinese contingent, engaged in upgrading the instrument landing system and installing the advanced continuous-wave radar facility at the Bhagatanwala airbase were located at the far end of the township. The nearest army contingent, a Company of the Northern Light Infantry, which provided security to the airbase, had pitched tents at a distance of about 4 kilometres. Only a small mixed detachment of the military police and police guarded the control tower, the administrative buildings and the cargo holding area. The lax security ambience offered ample opportunities to Harfan, who like an accomplished wizard, was busy in giving the final touches to the plans to disappear from Pakistan.

Harfan wasn't asleep. His mind was hovering between the super and supra conscious levels of his cerebral cortex. Eyes closed, he was mixing, like an editor in the darkroom, forward, backward and multi-directional images of the immediate past events and rushes of probable forthcoming clips.

Israr Sharief's briefing floated on top of his mind. The next flight, he said, would carry a consignment of highly confidential load; nerve gas artillery shells. The deadly chemical weapons were procured from a delicate US source, connected with the Special Services Groups' commander, Major General Mukhtiar Ghori. Probably these were Vietnam surplus deadly chemical agents.

Harfan had protested on grounds of morality. How could he carry the deadly chemical weapons, which were meant for killing innocent millions in East Pakistan and probably India?

Israr overruled him. For him it was a simple business transaction. It did not matter to him if the junta killed innocent millions by conventional or chemical weapons. The orders were from the top, he added. And Harfan had no other option but to load the consignment all by himself. There would be no meddling by the Supply Corps personnel. General

Naqi had given specific instructions for safeguarding the secrecy of this particular flight. The CMLA and his small coterie of advisors did not want any leakage of the news of deployment of chemical weapons.

The very thought of carrying the blasted chemical weapons to Dacca had accelerated his heartbeats. Blood gushing into his head was about to blurt out in loud protest. Harfan breathed slowly, listened to Israr like a disciplined soldier and quickly ran over the scenarios hitting his psyche like accelerated neutron particles.

Yes. Why not? He visualised Jamilla's dream window opening up, through which he could fly to freedom, with Parvez and his love by his side.

Harfan rolled over in the bed...

His left hand was lightly resting on Jamilla's bosom. And the fingers of his right hand were locked with those of Parvez.

Their soul-vibes, Harfan wished to believe, were running through his blood stream and strengthening his determination. His own warmth and confidence, his steely-will to protect the family, Harfan imagined, were seeping into their existence. Impregnated impulses from their unified life forces created a unique protection field. It was a unique regeneration process, injecting driblets of strength in him with his own life force, transferring particles of hope and love into them.

Another elemental wave, however, was knocking into his supra conscious senses.

Dot-dot-dash, dot-dash-dot—

The Morse code sounds were hitting his trained eardrums in faint broken waves. Harfan's mind slowly started correlating the sound waves.

Yes. The pattern was clear.

I- B- A- D- A- T* O- P- E- N* U- R- G- E- N- T.

What the hell was the blighter doing here?

Harfan again listened to the faint sounds produced by the finger strokes on the door panel. He was left with no doubt that the mysterious visitor was generating the signals. What if someone had faked the signals? The ISI interrogators could have cracked Ibadat and he may have spilled the beans.

Perhaps Alam had hired a killer to execute him.

Nothing surprised him any more.

Harfan opened his eyes and tried to fathom the depth of darkness enveloping him. He gradually discerned the contours of the room. His glances traversed on the figures of Jamilla and Parvez.

Harfan removed his hands carefully and felt the loaded pistol under the pillow. Its warm metal gave him a feeling of confidence. He slithered out of bed, the warm colt in readiness, and stealthily stepped on the floor like a dragon lizard and proceeded towards the source of the signal. He held his breath and placed his right ear on the door panel. The Morse code was still piercing through the wooden barrier. He tried to sniff the smell of the stranger.

Damn! Harfan breathed out a curse.

Who could it be? The ISI would not have offered the courtesy of a wakeup call with sophisticated Morse signals. And Alam's killers could've broken in through one of the windows. Harfan collected his breath.

It could be Ibadat. He tiptoed to a side window that opened onto the balcony and climbed out. His gaze pierced the veil of darkness, and located the slight figure of Ibadat. Harfan hit his knee joints in a quick karate move, flooring and immobilising him.

"Let me off you fool. You'll wake up the entire guesthouse and your killers aren't far behind." Ibadat hissed out in anguish.

Harfan relaxed his grip and helped Ibadat stand up.

"Wait. Let me open the door."

Harfan slithered back into the room and opened the door. Ibadat squeezed past the opening and closed the panels behind.

"Why are you stalking us? I've seen you following me from Lahore. What's the game? Do you want to kill us?" Harfan asked, his pistol still aimed at Ibadat's head.

"Remove the gun and sit down. I'm not here to kill you. I need urgent consultations."

Ibadat pushed aside Harfan's loaded hand and made a move towards the sofa.

"I'm not stalking you Harfan. Don't mix up your reflexes. You're in a dark tunnel. Fly like a bat. Sharpen your radar. You require it now more than you ever did, in your walks on the razor's edge."

Their excited whispers ruined Jamilla's sleep. She carefully turned on her side and switched on the bed lamp.

"What's the matter?" She demanded an answer from Harfan.

"Put the light off. Nothing to worry about." Harfan whispered.

They sat around the coffee table, while Jamilla prepared black coffee.

"Pardon me, for disturbing you here at Latuwali," Ibadat sipped the invigorating brew." I'd no other option. I can't afford to be seen with you any more. Tell me what're your plans."

"What's this Alam up to? Why does he want me dead?"

"That's his problem,"Ibadat replied, "You know what the last instructions from Delhi are. It asks for a simple disengagement. The top boss wants you out and safe."

"Has Alam been sold to the Pakis?"

"Most unlikely. He's probably trying to insulate himself, by offering you as the sacrificial goat. He doesn't forgive, and I don't expect mercy from him as well."

"Why can't we expose him?"

"You won't do that, because I want you back in India, with Jamilla ***bhabi*** and Parvez. Another mother is waiting there for you. What's your plan?"

"Nothing in particular," Harfan replied, "I fly to Dacca in another couple of hours and Jamilla goes back to Lahore."

"Don't kid me. You know what I mean," Ibadat pushed the cup forward and requested another fill, "You're caught in a crossfire. This is no time to hedge."

"How near are we from death?"

Jamilla asked while pouring coffee, in the darkness, spilling some, her hands shaking slightly.

"Very near, in fact, in front of you." Ibadat took out a gun, tucked near the crevice of his spine.

"I've Alam's orders to eliminate Harfan. And if I don't do the job before the ISI catches up with brother Harfan, I get shot. It's as simple as that. The other fascinating way of executing Alam's order is to smother Harfan under the wheels of a speeding truck. Sounds charming! Doesn't it?"

"How can he give that order?" Jamilla asked.

"Don't ask me that ***bhabi***. Both of us are caught in the whirlpool of destiny. It's an inevitable journey to the core of a black hole. Most of the agents disappear that way."

"What's this darn job?"

"They call it espionage. One of the oldest trades, a refined form of knowing what cooks in the neighbours pot." Ibadat laughed heartily.

"Strange are the ways of politics." Jamilla commented.

"You know better. Politics and intelligence are the oldest bedmates. They're the hinge stones of the power structures that fashion our destiny." Ibadat heaved a philosophical sigh.

"Are you going to shoot?" Jamilla asked.

Ibadat placed his weapon on the table and pushed it in her direction.

"Keep it till I leave this room," He slipped back on the sofa, "Go to bed, relax and allow us to work out a strategy. We have to put to good use, whatever time we're allowed by the nutcracker closing its jaws in."

"Couldn't you save my real mother? Why did you not tell me the truth earlier?" Harfan asked Ibadat with a pain stricken voice.

"Believe me brother. I had no other option. The ISI would have killed her any way, perhaps after inflicting plenty of pain and humiliation. I faced the moment of truth much later. Perhaps you would've also offered her the grains of graceful poison, to save her from such indignity. The Hindu ladies are known for their valorous ***johar*** ceremony (mass suicide by poisoning to escape indignity)."

Ibadat embraced Harfan and tried to pacify his feelings.

"Destiny has played a cruel joke with me Ibadat. What a quirk of fate! I land up at Jhumra and fail to recognise my real mother! Did you find her nervous, afraid of dying?"

"On the contrary," Harfan tightened the embrace, "She welcomed death as a cure for all her sufferings."

"She really suffered, silently and nobody told me about it."

"Preserve these finer sentiments inside your chest, brother. Life isn't a programmed magic box. Take it as it comes. Your priority is to escape the ISI and Alam's dragnet, very fast. You don't have more than two days, before they pick you up."

"Why didn't you shoot me?" Harfan asked.

"I'm not a professional butcher and killing creates chain reactions. I kill you to protect Alam's secret. Probably the agents of the Indian intelligence and Alam will hire another goon to silence me. There is no end to it. You can't cover your bloody trail with blood alone."

Ibadat walked up and opened a window at the far corner of the room.

"Tell me, what's your plan?" Ibadat asked.

"Nothing whatsoever." Harfan wasn't ready yet to share his strategy, still half-baked, audacious and absurd, and the contours of which were still in its foetal form, in his imagination.

"As I was saying, you have precisely two days to dodge the ISI and Alam. My moles in the company say that Brigadier Barqat and Jamanat have pieced together all the missing links. Your full profile is now available with them. The only thing they don't know is the secret behind your birth."

"How good is your source inside the ISI?"

"Good, at the cutting edge level," Ibadat spoke cryptically, "And they'll give you only that much freedom, as essential to their operational needs with no extra bonus. Jamanat's people are everywhere, looking for you. I suggest you make for the Indian border."

"How can I? Every inch of the border is saturated with troops, on both the sides." Harfan added

"Escape to Kabul. Perhaps I can help." Ibadat suggested.

"It's too risky. I expect the ISI to cork up the Jalalabad and Quetta routes as well. The immigration sleuths must have been alerted to prevent me from boarding any domestic and international flight."

"Why don't you escape to Dacca in the next flight, which you're supposed to take today." Ibadat whispered, "They're not yet aware of your return and the CMLA hasn't restricted these special flights. General Naqi is very secretive too."

"That's the correct decision." Jamilla intervened.

"I agree Jami. But there are many imponderables in between." Harfan added.

"When do you fly next?" Asked Ibadat.

Harfan looked at his watch and smiled.

"It's three now. Just in another fifteen hours. We're supposed to take off at eighteen hundred. Loading should start at eleven hundred hours."

"Are you taking off from Sargodha?"

"No, from Bhagatan. Sargodha isn't used for these flights."

"That makes it easier, brother Harfan," Ibadat commented in a relaxed tone, "Bhagatan is a small place. Take the flight, if you've any chance of getting lost in Dacca. Crossing over to India from there won't be difficult."

"Thanks for the suggestion." Harfan looked up with a derisive smile, "I won't move out an inch, if I can't take Jami and Parvez with me."

"They can join you later. They can perhaps fly to London when the dust settles down."

"Yah! After they're peppered and salted and roasted by the ISI! I won't take any chance. Not any more. I've lost my mother and I would hate to leave them at the mercy of the vultures." Harfan replied with a tone of finality.

"I appreciate your sentiments," Ibadat replied, "You are entitled to fashion your destiny, but your approach will jeopardise the safety of Jamilla and Parvez. Learn to leave some aspects of your life to ***Allah***." Ibadat tried to convince Harfan with a persuasive smile.

"That's fine. But how do you guarantee our safety in India? Alam may have vitiated the air back there too."

"He must have. But once you land in India, the NSI will prefer to sweep the dust under its carpet. The intelligence agencies are too scared of publicity." Ibadat commented sarcastically.

"Calculate straight Harfan," Jamilla added, "What happens when we land in Dacca and cross over to India? Nothing. We can quietly go back to Jhun Jhunu and start afresh."

"How do I get you two out?"

"Talk to Voodoo, accept his invitation," Jamilla intervened forcefully; "I'm in favour of the gamble, if you can manage to put us in the flight."

"Wonderful," Ibadat jumped to his feet, "I like the idea. We can't wait for the ISI torture chambers and the final despatch to some insignificant jail. A security prisoner in Pakistan has no official recognition. They're left to rot and die in isolation. Most of them are injected with opium extracts, turning them insane."

A shiver ran down Harfan's spine. He lighted a cigarette and went over to the window and reflected on the daring suggestion. It wasn't Ibadat's unique brain wave. He had planned it out as the only viable alternative. Escaping the ISI noose was on top of his mind. He had lost all manoeuvrability in Pakistan, Harfan reasoned. His big contacts and friends at high places were likely to discard him like a piece of rotten melon. Malika Jahanara wouldn't even recognise the first alphabet of his name. Israr, a good friend, wouldn't dare to take a stand. And Nawab would perhaps be the first one to sauté him with plenty of hot Tabasco.

The magic mirror, he had assiduously crafted, had started cracking up. All his attempts to project a coherent collage of his thoughts had broken into uneven pieces. Perhaps Ibadat and Jamilla were correct. He was being unnecessarily emotional and cautious. He should take the plunge.

"Well, you're possibly correct," Harfan turned back, "Can you help me?"

"Brother Harfan, my veins carry the blood of a man who was loyal to the last drop of his blood. He died while defending his king. Tell me what can I do? I'll like you, Jamilla ***bhabi*** and Parvez to clear off, in another couple of hours." Ibadat spoke in an emotion-choked voice.

"I've a plan. Listen."

Harfan's scheme sounded simple, ridiculous and audacious. The absurd fellow and perpetual gambler had scripted a daring escape to Dacca, in the very next flight of Voodoorume. For him to disappear in Dacca and cross over to India wouldn't be a big deal. Ahsan Khondokar, the estranged Bengali officer of Pakistan Air Force and Major Anjum Mani had assured him a safe hideout, in their home village near Bhairab Bazaar, on the banks of the river Meghna. From there, a clandestine crossing over to India would be a cakewalk. The Tripura border was just 80 km away and highly porous. A few hundred bucks were good enough substitute for legal travel documents.

But the biggest catch was boarding the Lady of the Light. The ground staff, hoards of military police, the PIB and Special Branch sleuths wouldn't allow the boarding of any unauthorised passenger. He wouldn't have any chance of taking Jamilla beyond the VIP lounge. The

ISI, he reasoned, might not even allow him to board the flight. Perhaps these were his last few hours of freedom.

"I suggest you talk to the pilot. He may not have the tunnel vision, we're suffering from." Ibadat added.

"There is perhaps a way out," Harfan stood up in excitement, "Another cup of coffee, please Jami."

"What's that?" Jamilla asked.

Harfan narrated the story of his encounter with Israr the day earlier. They had discussed the airlifting of six special crates. Maj. General Mukhtiar Ghori brought this super secret hardware in a special flight from Oman. Israr was summoned by General Naqi to discuss the NODIS subject (not for distribution with other agency). His next charter flight was assigned to carry 60 nerve gas shells. The mercenary pilot, Naqi had warned, shouldn't be taken into confidence.

"What's special about these crates?" Asked Ibadat.

"These are lethal artillery shells, which can hit targets beyond 30 kilometres. The toxic gas can kill thousands in minutes. The warheads contain deadly nerve gas, called either VX aerosol or Sarin, may be Tabun. I'm not an expert on these weapons of mass killing." Harfan shrugged.

"You mean Pakistan is going to kill the Bengalis by toxic nerve gas shells!"

"I've no precise idea about the targets. They could be fellow Pakistani Bengalis or Indians as well. Who cares?" Harfan's comments sounded bitter and cynical.

"Are you going to carry these to the conflict zone?" Ibadat asked.

"Do I have any option? I don't care. These crates can help me out. The weapons of death for the unknown Bengalis and Indians can bring luck and life to me and my family, and even you."

Harfan explained his plan.

The loading of conventional military hardware would start by eleven in the morning. He would personally load the special crates around 1600 hrs. The doors would be armed for take off, precisely at 1750 hours. The kernel of his plan, Harfan explained, would be to put Jamilla and Parvez in one of the crates, minus the artillery shells. This would be the seventh crate, one extra than the packages delivered by General Ghori. The military police, he explained, had become lax over the last few weeks. They had left the boring task of loading the military hardware and preparation of the manifest and inventory to him. It wouldn't be difficult to hoodwink them. A few bottles of Scotch that he had saved from the last trip could seal their eyes and ears, till Voodoorume's bird was airborne.

Once out of the Pakistani airspace he would unpack Jamilla and Parvez. The other crewmembers, one Greek and the other a Cypriot could create a fuss. But Voodoorume was trustworthy and sympathetic. He would understand the intricacies and seriousness of the problem.

Once in Dacca, they could be passed off as Khondokar's Punjabi wife and child, visiting him from Lahore. Wives of the top army officers generally availed of special PAF carriers to visit their husbands. Khondokar's wife, related to a two-star General in the CMLA headquarters, was expected to receive preferential treatment in Dacca. The airbase security personnel weren't likely to lift her veil for an identification parade.

"It's an audacious plan Harfan. Do you seriously think it will work?" Asked Ibadat.

"Well, it's a gamble and let's hope we'll win," Harfan smiled enigmatically, "Can you give Parvez something to eat and administer half a tablet of barbiturate? That'll induce sleep for at least four hours and prevent detection by the security staff and ground crew." Harfan looked at Jamilla expectantly.

"Do you think it's safe to be packed like sardines for hours with those highly toxic shells? Won't it harm Parvez?" Jamilla looked pale and concerned.

"I'll take care to pack you two as comfortably as possible. I'll place soft foam padding. And there won't be any shell in the crate. It won't hurt you at all, except that you would be crammed in one position for at least three hours, till we cross the Pakistani airspace. Are you ready for the gamble? This is the only option left to us."

Harfan reassured Jamilla by placing his hands around her shoulder.

"Well! We'll at least live or die together, in a brave and dignified way. I'm game", She turned towards Ibadat, "Are you coming?"

"No ***bhabi***. I've to stay back. That's my fate. Get ready for the great escape. I shall be around. Don't panic."

The loud cock-a-doodle-doo of a rooster pierced the fading dark veils of the night. Ibadat stood up. He slowly lifted a corner of the curtain and tried to measure the intensity of the early morning light. The cover of darkness had started wilting, as the piercing arrows of light, travelling through the ethereal void, painted the waves and layers of clouds with indeterminate strokes.

Ibadat never claimed to be a devout Muslim, a believer in rituals. But the fast changing colours on the clouds, the chirping of birds and the soft aroma rising out of the soggy grounds enchanted him. He hadn't noticed before that the ***Allah's*** universe was so beautiful and full of love; unique love, exemplified by Harfan and Jamilla's desire to live and die together.

"I must go now. You go ahead. I'll pick up Jamilla and Parvez and join you at Bhagatan warehouse, well in time."

Ibadat embraced Harfan and briefly prayed by cupping his palms in the usual ***namaz*** format. He recited ***La Ilaha Illa'llah Muhammad-ur-Rasulullah***, and closed his eyes. Finally he said ***Khuda Hafiz*** and placed his caressing palms on sleeping Parvez.

Harfan cautiously opened the door, peeped out to survey the corridor. Ibadat slithered out and in a second disappeared in the morning mist.

"That's the only option left Jami. Get ready. Face the situation bravely. I know you can do that. At least it gives us a fair chance of living or dying together. I don't think they can bring down the flight once Voodoorume is airborne. I'll drop by Voodoo's hotel before meeting Israr sahib. I can't take the risk without his consent. The success of the scheme entirely depends on his concurrence."

"***Hai Rabba***! You've planned the great escape just like that!" Jamilla looked at Harfan with wide disbelief writ large in her eyes.

"I've been floating in the air of uncertainty all these years. ***Insha Allah***, Voodoo will help. You forget one thing, he's a big gambler himself."

"You're incorrigible Harfan, a born gambler."

"Perhaps it's in my blood. Have you seen one speciality in my palm?"

Harfan spread open both his palms and explained that, he was born with twin lifelines. It signified a tendency to live on the edge and survive inspite of it all.

"***Allah jane*** (God knows)," Jamilla threw up her hands, "Let me get the things lined up. Hope your gamble will pay off."

"It's time for me to report to Israr. I'd call you up, say in two hours time. Wait for Ibadat. If he fails to turn up, drive down yourself. Take the car inside the warehouse and park it at the rear. The gate-man won't stop. I've tackled him."

"Can we trust Israr?" Jamilla asked.

"No problem. He is totally depending on me for this operation. It's my show all the way. I've to load the crates, marked *UNICEF* EMERGENCY MEDICAL SUPPLIES**. That's how they've decided to deliver death to East Pakistan, or may be to India."

"Why you?"

"General Naqi doesn't want to involve the army regulars. It's a top-secret operation, involving, may be Washington and may be Peking. None of these peddlers of death would like to face embarrassing questions in the UN General Assembly."

"Are you sure about that?"

"I'm sure Jami. The defenders of the free world, I mean the Americans, wouldn't like to be seen as the perpetrators of a devastating chemical warfare in the sub-continent. They have once been stigmatised in the Vietnam."

Harfan planted a quick kiss on Jamilla's lips and on Parvez's forehead.

"Synchronise your watch. It's ten past six. You have to act in absolute precision. Don't get nervous."

He ran down the stairs, switched on the ignition and zoomed out of sight.

Chapter 60

Brigadier Barqat was busy giving the final touches to Operation Salamat, busting of a major Indian espionage network, spearheaded by Harfan Bukhari. Operations Briefing Room (OBR), the virtual heart of the India Counter-intelligence Section of the Joint Intelligence Miscellaneous was packed to the capacity. This holy corner, an exclusive preserve of the surveillance and enquiry cells of the 'S-I' Division, was solely devoted to cracking the Indian intelligence penetration in Pakistan.

Jamanat Ali lorded over the 'S-I' Division, which in its normal course didn't get involved in routine jobs. Crude surveillance of the Indian diplomatic premises and staff; stalking their family members, throwing obscene jokes and brushing past the bosoms and bottoms of the scared ladies were left to the 'S-III' Division.

Jamanat's boys, barring a few eggheads from the armed forces, were trained like sniffer dogs, in the art and science of rational investigation. Tradecraft methodologies were their forte.

The OBR walls were decorated with photographs of Indian agents neutralised during the last 10 years. A small paragraph below each photograph explained the essentials of each case study.

Photographs of the suspected Indian Federal Intelligence Bureau and National Security India agents, posted in Pakistan, under diplomatic cover, were displayed on another frame. Jamanat's boys regularly updated the data boards from the Indian civil list, departmental telephone directories, information obtained from friendly foreign agencies and Pakistan's own sources in embassies abroad.

Linear charts elaborated the connectivity between the Indian agents and their Pakistani contacts. The habitual trans-border smugglers and their Pakistani and Indian master handlers occupied another proud corner of the room. Each group was clubbed under the operational linkages of cartels on either side of the border. However, Jamanat wasn't allowed to display the names and identities of the drug barons and their collaborators in the Armed Forces. The holy camels of Pakistan were above the law.

The expectations of trapping a big catch had pushed up the ambience biological temperature by a few degrees.

Barqat, seated at the head table, addressed a group of 40 officers of the 'S-I' Division. This was a mandatory practice, before trained sleuths were deployed on sensitive operational tasks. It could be any task, from surveillance, breaking in, raids and agent interception to application of dirty tricks that often included assassination, bomb explosions and mass destruction in enemy territories.

Barqat switched on the slide projector. Harfan Bukhari's profiles from different angles were flashed on the screen at regular intervals of three minutes, allowing the agents to memorise the features.

"Memorise the photographs carefully," Barqat spoke in a commanding tone," His assumed Muslim name is Harfan Bukhari. We're not as yet not sure of his Hindu name."

He flicked the switch on. A full frame of Harfan standing on the stairs of the CMLA headquarters and talking to Capt. Ayoob flashed in. The clandestine photo, taken with a tele-lens captured the sharp frontal features of the suspect.

"Concentrate on the subject, ignore the Pakistani Captain. He's fighting the infidels at the war front. The Indian pigeon is 6 ft. plus, fair, with black backcombed hair and sports a thick growth of bushy beard. Look at his eyes. He doesn't have the features, either of a Punjabi or a Pathan. He looks like a Hindu Pundit."

Barqat spoke in studied short sentences, in chaste Punjabi.

"I'll now request Mian Jamanat Ali to brief you about the agent's activities and the task on hand."

Jamanat took the microphone and continued the briefing in chaste Urdu, often falling back on Punjabi, his mother tongue.

He expounded the importance of the task of physically apprehending Harfan Bukhari and his associates. He was, perhaps, the first Indian resident agent to penetrate deep inside the system, right into the core around the Presidency. He had caused tremendous damage to Pakistan by stealing super-sensitive secrets.

Jamanat, in his own brazen way, blamed the top brass for being gullible and trusting a foreign agent with the super-secret task of Pakistan's war preparations against India.

"Have you memorised the physical features of the spy?"

The officers nodded in silence. Jamanat continued in the same monotonous tone.

"I don't expect you to commit any mistake. Look at these photos, Harfan Bukhari without a beard and a moustache."

He clicked on the slide projector.

"We're deploying four teams. The Karachi team will act independently, raid his uncle Shamim Bukhari's house and search other places. One team headed by Osman Chistei will raid the house at Jhumra." Jamanat continued.

"The Lahore team, headed by Khaleq will leave immediately by a special flight and raid the suspect's in law's house in order to detain his wife. She'll require a thorough interrogation."

"What's your report from Lahore? I'm told your watchers haven't seen his wife for the last 38 hours. Hope she hasn't gone underground." Barqat intervened.

"You're correct sir. Enquiries with the servants of Zahoor indicate that the girl is suffering from fever and hasn't stepped out for two days," Replied Jamanat, " My men have rechecked and confirmed the report."

"As I was saying," Jamanat continued, "I'll lead a team to the Sangla complex of Israr Sharief. We have inside information, from sources close to the industrialist about his likely involvement with the Indian agency. The question is, why was Israr chosen by the Indian agency for housing their top agent? He must be involved too."

"Regarding Israr," Barqat intervened, "We have to take the allegations with a pinch of salt. Most of the information, I feel, has been fed by Nawab Sharief, his politically ambitious brother. These are political issues, better ignored."

"But sir...." Jamanat tried to contest the views of his senior.

"Are you sure that Harfan is at Sangla? I'm told by contacts in the CMLA's office that he'd gone over to Dacca with the special flight." Barqat enquired.

"Sir, that's our weak link. The CMLA's office and the office of General Naqi are too secretive about these flights. They refuse to share any information with us. Can't you do anything about it?"

"Well Jamanat," Barqat winked, "Let's talk about it later. Find out if the target is at Sangla."

"Fine sir." Jamanat took the hint and dialled a Sangla number, spoke briefly and turned to Barqat, "Sir, my contact says that Bukahri is returning this evening."

"Why don't we nab him at the airport itself?" Asked a junior officer.

"Sorry boy." Barqat replied, " We can't act rashly. Too many bigwigs are involved and we don't want any publicity. When he sings, many important heads will roll. We're not only trying to catch a spy, we're chasing a national scandal."

"We've placed surveillance teams at Sargodha, which is the normal operating terminal of these special flights. They'll ambush and lift Bukhari on his way home. No one should utter the name of the Company. The whole operation should be handled in total secrecy."

Jamanat added and explained the modalities of radio contact between different teams and the operations control room. There should be no use of firearms against the target, he warned. The subject would have to be captured alive, at any cost.

"We call this 'Operation Salamat'. Mosurs have been designated as Salamat 1, 2, etc. Your team captains have the details. Use codes during radio conversations. The call sign for the Ops Control Room is Badsha 1 and Badsha 2 for me. All teams barring the Lahore and Karachi ones will move simultaneously at 17.00 hrs today, four hours from now. Is that clear?"

Barqat watched the reactions of the team members and was pleased to see them tilting their heads in affirmation.

"Are we sure about the timings?" Arman Ali Niazi boomed out from a far corner of the room.

"Yes boy," Jamanat replied reassuringly, "We've tied up all the loose ends. We don't want to be late for the catch."

"One final point," Barqat said in a cool voice, "All teams have to ensure that no harm comes to the subject. I want him in one piece. There could be no leakage whatsoever to any other agency, be it the PIB or office of the CMLA. It's our exclusive operation. The top boss will break the news to the President. The suspect should be taken straight to location Badr. One of us will be there to receive him. Okay?"

Badr was the code name for the ISI's top-secret interrogation centre, located in the basement of 'Deeni Publications', a front company that published and marketed religious books. The establishment, located at an insignificant corner between Urdu Bazaar and Sarafa Bazaar, was equipped with modern and innovative interrogation facilities. Special rooms were fitted with hidden audio-video equipment and psychedelic lights. Observation rooms behind a one-way mirror acted as 'Truth Chambers', a euphemism for extracting a confession from the agency's targets and victims. The most fortunate ones rarely came out of the chambers with their sanity and soul intact.

In a floor below the interrogation centre was located the centrally air-conditioned, soundproof special treatment cell- ***Jannat 9*** (ninth heaven). It was headed by experts in the art and science of breaking physical and psychological barriers of their targets.

"Everybody has to keep his trap shut, understand!" Jamanat added.

"It's a controlled operation. No one takes any unauthorised initiative, no shooting from the hip." Barqat reminded the gathering.

"But sir, how do we tackle unforeseen developments?" Asked Arman Ali Niazi.

"Good question Arman," Barqat lifted a hand held VHF communication set, "Each unit will have these sets and standby batteries. You will simply ask for directions. Hope things are clear and there is no confusion."

Barqat wished them good luck and left the briefing room. He was expecting a call from Alam Khan, the most important cog in the complicated wheel. The PSO had indicated that the top arms hunter and peddler had returned from his foreign jaunt and was ready to help out the ISI. General Hyder had designated Brig. Barqat to debrief him. The level of interaction was pegged high, keeping in view the stature and connections of the man.

****

Alam Khan panicked.

The pow-wow with General Sarfaraz was a kid stuff. It wasn't difficult to sell dreams to the scheming Generals in Islamabad. Each one of them pretended to be the worthy successor to the gallant invading horsemen from the northwest, the Ghoris, the Lodhis, the Khans and the Mughals. Pakistan, the remnants of the past Islamic empire in India, they thought, was bequeathed to them by destiny. The men in uniform were licensed to plunder it.

But he was not keen to face a seasoned ISI officer. Brigadier Barqat wasn't a novice in the spy trade. And interrogation process, he knew for sure, was an endless labyrinth. Barqat's elegantly furnished front room could, in no time, lead to the dreaded basement bunkers of the Badr.

To add to his misery Ibadat had just disappeared. Hotel Royal Palace at Jhumra returned a stock reply. Ibadat was on short leave and didn't leave behind a forwarding address. He should be back in a couple of days.

Harfan Bukhari was still alive. That's what Israr Sharief had indicated on the phone. How could Qurban, the Double X asset, flout his orders?

Had this son of a cook ganged up with the prince charming? Had he overrated Ibadat? Was he playing the old loyalty tune? Perhaps he was.

Alam rued his decision to expose Ibadat to Harfan Bukhari. It wasn't a prudent move.

Well! Intelligence operations often required the generation of short-term intermediary cut outs. Some fuse somewhere was bound to blow up. It could never work in mathematical precision. There was nothing like a perfect game of wit between two inimical countries. Human beings played the intelligence game, and to err was only human.

Delhi had accepted Harfan as a trained zombie and expected him to dance to the commands of his masters, through the radio-control of his neuronal reflexes. But Jamilla the enchantress had injected him with strange chemicals. She had transformed his life, from a robot to a caring creature. Despite advance warnings, Nampoothiri had ruled against the physical neutralisation of the soured agent. This was one mistake; Alam thought that was definitely going to explode on Delhi's face.

To hell with Delhi!

It shouldn't explode on his face. That's what he prayed for, at that moment.

Alam's efforts to rationalise the situation generated more intellectual smog. The screw drilled deep down into his mind, inside the primordial chemical and electrical impulses of his brain. The serpent, hidden below his medulla started hissing.

No. He wasn't ready to face the ISI interrogators. He couldn't destroy his cover, built assiduously over the last 23 years. He had generated vital human intelligence assets in several target areas of Pakistan. He must prevent the ISI from destroying the super-structure crafted by him painstakingly, brick by brick.

How could he prevent visiting his nemesis, the ISI interrogator? What diversionary tactic could he adopt? He must invent some excuse to obfuscate the imminent urge of the ISI to interrogate and categorise him. His own survival was of cardinal importance. Delhi wouldn't be able to run its forward paws in Pakistan in his absence. His own exposure would spell disaster for his family too. The ISI was sure to get to his wife and kids in Switzerland, kidnap and liquidate them.

Alam burnt a couple of cigarettes and concluded that his foremost priority was to locate Harfan and Ibadat and destroy both of them. They couldn't be allowed the luxury of breathing freely. Their continued intake of oxygen could spew fire for him. And Ibadat had forfeited his right to live. A rogue agent deserved only a one-way journey to the mortuary.

Ibadat deserved the first shower of bullets. He knew more about him than Harfan did.

Alam picked up his mobile phone and called a Peshawar number and contacted Rayees, a Mengel tribal from Zhob, Baluchistan and a Dara Adam Khel based arms smuggler and hired killer.

"***Salaam*** brother Rayees, Mian Alam here."

"***Janab*** hearing from you after ages," The other end replied in effusive response, "What's the order?"

"There's a special job."

"***Janab***, business is dull. The Baluch ***sirdars*** have donned ***borkas***. It seems that they have lost the appetite for fighting. You haven't ordered new consignments for ages. Fresh supplies of Kalashnikovs from Mazar Tepe (Tajikistan) are expected in three days, with cheap spares."

"That's encouraging news Rayees ***bhai*** (brother). I'll require 5000 pieces. Organise a demo. But there's an urgent personal job here."

"***Janab*** order me and the job's done." Rayees replied in a genie-of the-lamp style.

Alam reverted back to dialogues better understood by hired killers like Rayees. The job was simple. A friend of his, Alam elaborated suffered from insomnia and required sleeping pills. Rayees, he said, should personally deliver it in the next 24 hours.

Yes, he was ready to pay the usual price. In dollars? Fine, no problem, he could take the entire amount in advance.

The dialogue over, Alam lighted a cigarette.

Well! Rayees was a sure shot. He never missed his target. That should take care of Ibadat.

Should he arrange Harfan's capture by tipping off his contacts in the CMLA and the ISI? Could that be self-defeating? What if Harfan betrayed him in turn? Would he sing like a pacific parrot? That was too risky.

Alam tossed the critical dilemma over in his mind while consuming liberal doses of cognac.

Yes. Harfan should be eliminated. For him the ISI shooters were the best executioners. The combination of Rayees for Ibadat and Hyder for Harfan sounded absolutely fine.

But he should provide Hyder with a steady target. And that required locating Harfan.

"Hello Israr sahib," He dialled Israr's Sangla office, "How have you been?"

"Where have you been?" Israr responded warmly, "There are lots of action around here."

"Where is my precious nephew?"

"Perpetually airborne. At Bhagatan today, busy loading the craft for a fresh sortie. He will be flying out tonight."

"Where's his angel, I mean my cute daughter Jamilla?"

"At Bhagatan only. Mian you've to see this couple to believe it. They're ideal lovers." Israr laughed loudly.

"A perfect match." Alam readily agreed and managed to add a faint laughter.

"Come down. There are some business discussions that you must be in on."

"May be tomorrow, ***Khuda Hafiz***."

Alam wasn't in a mood to listen to Israr's delirium. He seethed in anger and burnt in the churning fire of revenge. What was Jamilla doing at Bhagatan? The gambler must be planning something spectacular. Was he planning a quiet escape from Pakistan? Must be. Otherwise, why should his wife and child be at Bhagatan airbase?

No. He couldn't allow Harfan to escape.

Alam dialled Zahoor Chaudry's Lahore number and after exchanging meaningless small talk entered into a business like dialogue.

"How are darling Parvez and Jamilla?"

"Oh dear brother!" Zahoor replied in a jovial tone, "They are new generation kids. She has gone to spend a few days with Harfan at Sangla. She was missing him."

"I know, it's so cruel of us, all of us, to push nephew Harfan so hard. You know all about these special flights to East Pakistan." Alam feigned a genuine concern for Harfan.

"I know. In fact, the other day General Sarfaraz made a special mention of Harfan's valuable contribution to our defence preparedness. I'm proud of him." Zahoor replied.

"Me too. When do you expect her back?"

"Can't say, possibly by tomorrow."

"Sweet of you Zahoor sahib. I'd like to drive down, may be in another two days, for business talks and for looking up Parvez."

"Welcome Alam sahib. Jamilla and Sayeefa will be very happy to receive you." Zahoor extended a cordial invitation to Harfan's distant uncle

"My pleasure." Alam replied in a delightfully mechanical voice, "Convey my regards to ***mohtarma*** (madam) Sayeefa."

"My pleasure," Replied Zahoor, "Come over one of these days. Let's have a meal together."

"***Insha Allah*** !" Alam disconnected and immediately dialled the number of General Naqi.

"How're you General? ***Kaise mizaj*** (how is the mood)?" Alam asked General Naqi, who normally carried with him bags full of idiosyncrasies.

"Fine. Thanks for calling," Naqi replied, "Hearing from you after a long gap."

"Yes friend. I'd been to Amman and Riyadh. How're your flights? Hope there hasn't been any hiccup." Alam tried to prolong the dialogue.

"No problem. The President appreciated the exigencies. Your nephew's doing a fine job." Naqi added.

"Oh Naqi! He's not my nephew, by any stretch of imagination. I happen to know his uncle, and that's how he calls me uncle."

"Any way," Naqi replied, "He's doing a fine job."

"Where could I reach him?"

"He's at Israr's Bhagatan guest house. Here's his number." Naqi readily obliged Alam.

"What time does he take off?"

"Not sure." Naqi replied evasively. He didn't want to share the flight details of this special sortie.

"I want to talk to him urgently."

"Well! Try your luck. All that I know he takes off late tonight. Zia knows the details. But he is at Chak Lala in connection with the President's visit to Dacca."

"Thanks General. I'll try my luck." Alam replied curtly and hung up.

****

Alam smelt the vapour of burning cordite running through his intestines. He expected an explosion, a devastating one.

Harfan was definitely working on a super-secret escape plan. Should he allow him to clear out from Pakistan? Alam tossed over the idea for a while and discarded it. Liquidation of Harfan was the best prescription. He lifted the handset, dialled the Bhagatan guesthouse number and requested the operator to connect him to Jamilla Bukhari.

"Who's speaking?" The operator insisted on disclosure of the caller's identity.

"It's me brother, Harfan Bukhari." Alam replied closely faking Harfan's voice. The operator obliged.

"Hello, who's there?" Jamilla was surprised to hear Alam's voice.

"Hello dear Jamilla, Alam uncle this side. How're you, Parvez and dear nephew Harfan? Where is he?"

Jamilla hadn't expected the call. Alam wasn't supposed to be calling Harfan. Instead, she expected him visiting the mortuary, to see his frozen naked body. She gathered herself in seconds and replied haltingly.

"He's flying out late tonight uncle, at around two in the morning. He must be at Sangla."

"I am happy dear, that you've come down to give him company. The poor boy's really hard pressed for time."

"That's the problem with him uncle. He's totally wedded to his work, more than to me." She laughed, trying to prolong the talk and fathom Alam's intentions.

"I know dear Jami. It's in the family. He burns himself out. How can I get to him?"

"You may call Sangla," Jamilla answered, "He should be here around ten thirty for dinner. Call around that time. I intend to leave for Lahore as soon as he takes off. Come down to Lahore uncle. You haven't been with us for months."

Jamilla disconnected the line and called Harfan at the warehouse.

"I'm driving down now."

"Wait for Ibadat."

"No, I can't. Alam had called and I doubt his intentions. He's sure to get you killed. I didn't like his vibes."

"How did he get your number?"

"No idea. He must have sniffed us out. Receive me at the gate."

"Don't panic. Ibadat should call any time."

"Fine, but I won't wait indefinitely."

Jamilla disconnected and started packing Parvez's milk bottle and some foodstuffs.

Alam's trained mind could discern the fine mechanical strains in Jamilla's otherwise effervescent voice. An innocent girl, she always bubbled with life. Her untrained mind wasn't reacting spontaneously to his questions. She had hesitated for precious seconds, before spinning out the words. Alam admired her courage and presence of mind, but was convinced that the fairy queen of Harfan wasn't a good liar. The cordial invitation to Lahore and other shenanigans had convinced Alam that the chic couple were about to play a cute vanishing trick. The golden opportunity offered by Harfan should be used to maximum advantage. That should be his valid excuse to avoid appearing before the ISI Brigadier.

Yes. That was the easy way out.

Alam planned and executed another shrewd call.

"Pardon me Hyder sahib, I hope I haven't disturbed you." Alam's next call was to General Hyder Bux, the ISI chief.

"Sweet surprise! Where have you been all these days?"

"Mostly across the Atlantic, scouting for new supplies."

"What's cooking?"

"Hyder sahib, we must meet one of these days. The Pentagon corridors are abuzz with rumours that your friend, I mean, the boss in the CMLA's office is the hot favourite of the White House." Alam dangled the most attractive carrot in front of Hyder.

"You mean Sarfaraz! Alam sahib, I can assure you, that this nincompoop carries rotten balls between his thighs. How can he carry the country on his shoulders?" Hyder spat out venom against his rival.

"You're the fittest person General. You must lobby with the CIA and the Pentagon. I'm at your service, sir." Alam spoke in a seductive voice.

"I know. You're the only reliable bridge."

"Can I come down for some urgent talks? There's something wrong with this fellow, I mean Harfan Bukhari."

"I'm in a jam Alam sahib. I have to rush to Chak Lala Cantonment to accompany the President to Dacca. Be brief."

Alam breathed deeply, composed his thoughts and shared with the ISI chief, in chaste Punjabi, the most shocking piece of information. By the grace of ***Allah,*** Alam added, an American diplomat happened to narrate the story of a KGB agent neutralised by the MI6. The Russian spy had spilled the beans to CIA-MI6 interrogators, about the existence of a deep penetration Indian resident agent in Pakistan. He had, the interrogators revealed, learnt about this agent from his station chief in Delhi.

The sketch and accounts narrated to him by the US diplomat perfectly fitted Harfan Bukhari. It was the most shocking information, almost unbelievable. But the truth was always stranger than fiction. Wasn't it?

His American friends, Alam whispered, had burrowed tunnels into the pockets and conscience of some NSI operators. They had corroborated the basic ingredients of Harfan's cover story.

Alam's theatrics and general contours of the information struck the right chords in General Hyder Bux. He had gone through the Operation Salamat broadsheet, prepared by Barqat and Jamanat and had consciously decided to neutralise the Indian agent. Alam's controlled leak sounded highly feasible. The patriotic Pakistani, Hyder presumed had picked up the story correctly.

The spymaster however, paused for a few seconds. Should he seek corroboration from the CIA and MI6 liaison officers in Islamabad?

"Are you on the line Hyder sahib?"

"Are you sure that the story is reliable?"

"Sir," Alam modulated his voice to the sweetest possible decibel, "I'm hundred percent convinced. And I have a nasty feeling that Harfan is trying to escape from Pakistan."

"Well Alam sahib, I'm happy to know that the Americans have corroborated, what we already know. I'm just about to leave for the airport. Your story is fantastic. You had better rush to Barqat and tell him the details. See you on my return from Dacca."

"Right General."

"One more point Alam. Talk to your friends in Washington immediately. Time's running out."

"You're my only priority Hyder sahib. Your job will be done. You are surely the next occupant of the presidential palace. Kindly leave a message with Barqat, ***Khuda Hafiz***."

Hyder, in a hurry to reach the airport for joining the presidential entourage to Dacca, took a mental note of the urgency of an exclusive meeting with Alam after his return. This arms peddler was the right person to build bridges with the right quarters in Washington and London. The remote vision of the bridge, as spanned by Mian Alam Khan, had clouded up Hyder's earlier resolution to get the sensational information vetted by the Islamabad based CIA and the MI6 liaison officers. For a few precious moments the intelligence officer in him was overtaken by the vision of the ornate high chair in the presidential palace.

Alam disconnected the line rather hastily and climbed down the stairs in doubles and asked the driver to head for Brigadier Barqat's residence.

He quickly glossed over the turn of events. Well manoeuvred. Alam congratulated himself. God willing, Rayees should take care of Ibadat, and Harfan should be a piece of cold meat in another couple of hours. An obliged Barqat should be eager enough to strike the machete, straight at the jugular of the prize catch.

Alam laughed as he lighted another cigarette. The scenario wasn't as bleak as it had appeared a couple of hours back. He was shaken to his bones by the clever manoeuvres of Harfan, the crafty jackal. The young cub should have known that Alam had the infinite capability to turn and twist the events and personalities in Pakistan.

Nampoothiri was far removed from the ground to realise what had gone wrong with Triple X and Double X. He was sure to accept a plausible story dished out by his most trusted friend in Pakistan.

And Hyder, the scheming ISI chief, should continue to be beholden to him. Why not? His job was to build bridges. What was wrong if he helped in building bridges between General Hyder and the White House, the CIA and the Pentagon? Sarfaraz could wait for his turn. The planned coup by Hyder wouldn't be the last one. Pakistan was destined to witness many more military coups. Well! Let the Generals get bogged down in the intractable and unfordable marsh of power politics. Let them commit ***hara-kiri***; let them screw up the unfortunate people of Pakistan. That suited him, perhaps Delhi too.

At the end of the day, Alam chuckled; the bucks were well secured in his Swiss account.

But one unsolved mystery continued to haunt him. He was foxed by the mysterious chessboard moves of Harfan and Ibadat. The presence of Jamilla at Bhagatan was putting pressure on the mercury flow of his coronary barometer. He smelt a rat, a rotten one at that.

Harfan must have worked out an escape plan in one of the special flights. He knew the daredevil quite well. A born gambler, he would like to fly on the wings of hope and risk everything. He had been lucky all these years and could as well pull off one bigger gamble, the biggest in his life.

Barqat felt rather fidgety, to see Alam at the oddest possible hour, Hyder's call notwithstanding. He had wasted a good three hours of his precious time waiting for the celebrity arms peddler. He hadn't turned up at the appointed time. The ISI had been working on a tight time schedule for concluding 'Operation Salamat'. Alam's interrogation was expected to provide important inputs. But the big gun played truant.

Barqat glanced at his Swiss quartz, 17.25. It was time for him to drive to the airport, to show his face to the President and the CMLA, who was flying to Dacca, heading a high-powered team. The West Pakistani power brokers as well as the international observers had pinned high hopes on this visit, perhaps the final one by the head of the state. General Arif's failure to persuade the Bengali leaders to accept the compromise power-sharing formula designed by his team of experts would mean the end of the road. Pakistan's ugly civil war would explode into a disastrous fireball of conflict between India and Pakistan.

"Hello Alam sahib, anything urgent? I was expecting you a couple of hours ago. You didn't turn up for the cup of coffee you had promised to have with me." Barqat didn't hide his displeasure.

"I'm sorry for the delay Brigadier sahib." Alam apologised profusely, "Some unexpected events had held me up. I've something very explosive to reveal. It's a matter of state security, you can say. I didn't want to talk on the phone."

"Yes, the boss was telling me something to that effect. Jump into my car," Barqat boarded his Toyota and gestured Alam to ask his driver to follow.

What a bloody time to be disturbed! The drive to Chak Lala airport would take over 30 minutes. That would leave him with barely 5 minutes to seek out his slot in the bon voyage row. He would hate to miss the chance of showing his face to the President. The top man was scheduled to sign his promotion file, making him a Major General and assigning him the coveted post of the Director General SSG, replacing Gen. Mukhtiar Ghori.

"Speed up Basir." Barqat prodded his driver, "And Alam Sahib, tell me what's so important."

Alam opened up his treasure chest, exposing rare intelligence nuggets, concretising his suspicions about Harfan being an Indian spy. His sources of information, he added, were crucially placed in London, in the CIA and MI6.

"I'm told that this snake is a Hindu. He was given the cover of a Muslim from Ludhiana, and was infiltrated soon after the '65 war."

Alam released bits of information, from his treasure chest and convinced Barqat, that his story was genuine, which fitted into the mosaic already put together by the ISI.

"That's not all Barqat sahib. This viper has compromised the most sensitive military secrets to India. What a great chameleon he is! I wonder why this spy is still allowed to ferry weapons to the East."

"I believe you recommended him." Barqat quipped.

"That's an old story. Indeed I'd suggested his name, because General Naqi didn't want to deploy his regular reps."

Alam replied without batting an eyelid.

"Aren't you a little too late Alam?" Barqat retorted back, "You didn't reveal anything to the PSO."

"Nothing happens without it being willed by the ***Allah***," Alam raised his hands in prayer, "I was totally guided by the recommendations of Jung Sher Khan, a business associate of Shamim Bukhari, Harfan's uncle."

"When did you discover his seamy activities?" Barqat's voice seemed to be serious.

"Just 24 hrs ago. My London friends tipped me off and I took the first available flight. I just made two calls to ascertain Harfan's location and rushed to you."

"Why do you suspect him to fly out with his family?"

"She's lodged in a guesthouse near Bhagatan air base. It is really odd and adds up to the fact that they have hatched a plan to escape together. I have received a corroborative information from my MI6 friend in London."

Alam finished the sentence and breathed heavily, as if he was still gasping under a heavy shock, with the tragedy of betrayal by his close associate.

"As a loyal and patriotic Pakistani, I can't allow this scoundrel to endanger our national security." Alam added, "My London based CIA friends feel that Harfan is carrying some microfilms on our nuclear projects."

"I should be back from Chak Lala, as soon as the President's flight takes off. What time are they flying out tonight?"

"Probably late tonight, that's what Israr told me."

"Surprising!" Barqat muttered inaudibly.

"Are you surprised?"

"Not exactly. I was working on a different time schedule altogether."

"No Brigadier sahib, we've to act fast and get him at Bhagatan itself. That's a good three hours drive. Can you arrange a chopper for me? I can help in identifying the rascal."

Alam threw another bait and Barqat swallowed it, hook, line and sinker.

"Badsha 2 to Badsha 3." Barqat spoke into the handset.

Odd, damn odd! His static observers at Lahore were wrong. Jamilla wasn't confined to her bed. This damn Pakistani girl was mesmerised by the Indian spy.

"Badsha 3 here. Getting you fine, sir." Jamanat came on the air instantaneously.

"Badsha 3, your target is at Bhagatan, the old Political Agent's bungalow near Latuwali ***tikri***. Your bird is flying out late tonight with microfilms containing sensitive national secrets."

"If it's Bhagatan sir, I should be suffering about a 60 minutes handicap. I'm about to reach Sangla." Replied Jamanat.

"I know. Rush your teams to Bhagatan. Prevent him from boarding the flight. Listen, his wife and child should be in the guesthouse. Send out a separate team and arrest them. Shoot them, if it becomes absolutely necessary, only to immobilise Harfan. Don't kill. I want him alive. Keep Badsha 1 informed."

Barqat's orders were crisp and categorical.

"Roger, Badsha 2."

"Badsha 3, Listen. Mian Alam is flying down to Bhagatan in a chopper. He knows the details of the microfilms. Help him out."

"Roger sir. Ask him to team up with us at the Mangni-Bhagatan T-junction."

"Okay. Let ***Allah*** bless your mission. I'm on air and should be in my office in another 45 minutes. Over and out."

"Roger and out." Jamanat Ali switched on a reserve frequency and directed the Lahore team to rush to his aid. His own team took a sharp U-turn and accelerated for Bhagatan.

Alam thanked Barqat profusely and parted company short of Chak Lala Cantonment gate. His Mercedes followed a service road and drove straight to the heliport, three miles south of the airbase.

Chapter 61

Rayees Sikander was one of his kinds, who ran a parallel administration with the help of his vast following almost all over Pakistan. This shadow administration thrived on drug monopoly, trans-border smuggling and arms merchandise. The military administration normally winked at his activities as the genius like Rayees contributed significantly to the tottering economy of the country. Their forward and backward trading linkages brought in plenty of dollars from all conceivable nook and corner of the globe. The Army bosses used his services for engineering unrest, communal carnage and sectarian killings, in the absence of any other institutionalised arrangement. They preferred to follow, at that historical point of time, the Italian formula of running a second track administration. Rayees enjoyed his unique status in the putrid Pakistan of the day.

Rayees wasn't a magician, but he knew a few tricks to find his way out even in the dark back alleys of Lahore's Dabbi Bazaar. Jabbar Pathan, his Man Friday in Lahore, came up with confirmed information about Ibadat's whereabouts. He wasn't at Jhumra and hadn't visited his ancestral home at Mianwali for last six months.

"He can't disappear into thin air. What car does he use?" Exploded Rayees.

"A battered Ford, which carries a Mianwali number plate."

"He can't be far off. Alert our boys in Lahore, Karachi and Sargodha. He might team up with Harfan Bukhari." Rayees Sikander passed on the orders while removing a strand of hair from his nasal cavity, with great care and research.

A hopeful lead came from his scouts at Bhagatanwala. They had noticed Ibadat's Ford parked behind the bushy undergrowth, next to a Sikh ***Gurudwara*** (temple).

Gurudwara Bhagatan was a small affair. Once a bustling town mainly inhabited by Hindu and Sikh traders, Bhagatan boasted of a couple of temples and a Sikh shrine. Post-partition Bhagatan wore an affluent look, courtesy, a few medium-scale industries and a thriving Armed Forces' cantonment. The Second World War airstrip was expanded with Chinese assistance and renamed Quaid-e-Azam Airport, which worked as a standby to the main Air Force base at Sargodha.

Rayees jumped into his Volkswagen with five armed goons by his side.

The old Ford was there, parked behind assorted bushes. The advancing footsteps of nature overwhelmed what was once a pleasant garden, in the backyard of the Sikh temple. The trees and bushes, neglected for over two decades, had grown into giant proportions. The undergrowth had wiped out all vestiges of a human touch. Wild nature reoccupied with vengeance what was snatched away from her.

"Drag out the ***Granthi*** (priest)." Ordered Rayees.

His armed goons entered the dilapidated temple premises and literally dragged out its only occupant, an aged Sikh, who merged well with the wild nature around him.

"What's your bloody name?" Thundered Rayees.

"Sardar Kirpal Singh. I'm the chief priest of the Gurudwara."

"Where's that bastard Ibadat?"

"Who?"

"Ibadat-ud-Daula Khan, owner of the car, parked on your land."

"***Wahe Guru***," Replied the priest," I'm the only human soul, who lives here. The nearest human habitation is about 3 km away."

"How come the car is parked here?"

"***Janab***," Kirpal Singh added, "All sorts of animals, drug smugglers and criminals use the garden. I've no control on them."

Rayee wasn't convinced. He ransacked the temple premises and after a good one-hour was convinced that Kirpal was the only occupant of the deserted Sikh shrine.

"***Ustad*** (captain) shall we burn this ***kafir***'s temple?" Asked an accompanying goon.

"No. That won't help. Let's talk to the police chief. He should know what to do."

"It's a new place ***ustad***. Should we get involved with the local police?" Asked another goon.

"No harm done. Money speaks better than bullets. The local police should know if the joker has been moving the streets of this town." Rayees replied.

He wasn't far from the truth.

Ibadat had abandoned his car behind the bushy growth and hired a taxi for his local movement. He had anticipated the ISI sleuths to move into the area, following Jamilla's trail. And he didn't like the idea of carrying her and Parvez to the airport in his branded car, which was known to Arman Ali's Mosur teams.

The police officer, a rusty Punjabi, wasn't unaware of the name and fame of Rayees Sikander. Men of means and money, as well as the law enforcing agencies were painfully aware of the charismatic underworld don. He ran his own government from his Peshawar Fort capital, in addition to the one supposedly run by the men in uniform from Islamabad.

"What can I do for you sir?" The SHO (Station House Officer) asked with all the humility that he could muster.

"Have your men seen this character in town?" Rayees produced a photograph of Ibadat.

"Abdalla." Shouted the SHO.

Abdalla, a pot-bellied constable appeared gingerly as if from nowhere.

"Have you and your men seen this character in Bhagatan?"

Abdalla looked at the photo and looked back at his boss, simultaneously extending his palm.

"Stupid," Shouted the SHO, "Mr. Rayees is our honourable guest. Don't expect gratis from him."

"Look up hotel Aasman." Abdalla peevishly pulled back his palm and replied in a flat tone.

"Come with me. You'll be adequately compensated."

"Don't march up with the entire gang sir. Hotel Aasman is a small place, located in a crowded market place, next to a cinema hall. We don't want a big story in the morning's news papers." The discerning SHO advised.

"No problem. You all wait here," Rayees ordered his gang, "I should be back in half an hour. It's a small job."

Hotel Aasman, literally speaking hotel sky, offered a bird's eye view of the street that led to its stairs. Ibadat noticed the pot-bellied constable and Rayees from his first floor room. Rayees had in his hand a machine carbine.

Why should a potentate of law and an armed person, who could only be an ISI storm trooper, rush up to his hotel!

Ibadat collected his .9 mm Belgian pistol and spare magazines and climbed down a rain water pipe, which landed on an open gutter. He followed the drain and hailed a horse cart and ordered the driver to take him to the nearby mosque.

Rayees stormed up the stairs, the menacing machine carbine in his hand and kicked open the door. The hotel manager lodged a meek protest and was silenced by a burst from the carbine. Crowds from the nearby cinema hall and busy marketplace thronged the hotel approach. Abdalla, the policeman, waived his baton and made way for the frustrated and abusive Rayees and guided him back to the police station.

Ibadat performed the ritual ablutions and joined a gathering of ***namazis***. The prayers over he called the ***Imam*** to a corner.

"Can I use your phone? My mother is seriously ill."

"Sure. But you've to pay the charges."

"No problem." He pushed a ten-rupee note in Imam's palm.

Jamilla came alive on the line.

"Don't wait for me," Ibadat spoke in a collected voice, "There are problems here. Go by yourself. I shall be at your final destination."

"What's the problem? Is anything wrong with Harfan?"

"No. It's with me. Be on time. That's important. I shall be there."

"Alam had called." Jamilla spoke in a shaky voice.

"That's dangerous. Rush and board the flight."

"What about you?"

"I'll be there. Don't wait for me."

Ibadat thanked the ***Imam*** profusely and hurried down the stairs.

He did some quick thinking.

Back at hotel Aasman it wasn't the ISI. They didn't appear with a lone police pilot openly with arms in their hands.

Could the carbine-wielding man be Alam's hired executioner?

Must be.

Well, not bad! He could still make it to the airport and provide a buffer to Harfan and Jamilla, if the carbine-wielding goon was a part of Alam's private war. He wondered if Alam and the ISI were working in tandem.

Ibadat hailed a passing cab and zoomed for the airbase.

Chapter 62

Ibadat's call to Latuwala guesthouse and his inability to escort Jamilla triggered off Harfan's sensory alarms. Something was amiss. Perhaps the ISI and Alam were on hot pursuit of their prime catch and Ibadat had failed to befuddle the sniffer canines.

He hadn't expected to see Ibadat, of all places, at the special apron; restricted to authorised personnel and special flights like the one operated by Athena Air Lines. This exclusive part of the apron connected the parking bay to the arrays of over and underground hangers. The Army and Air Force police controlled access to the exclusive aprons with a massive drop-gate and galvanised iron sheet doors. The rest of the airport, both administrative and technical areas, were segregated by an eight feet high barbed wire fence, covered with a thick growth of assorted green creepers.

Ibadat had positioned himself behind a pile of containers, most of which were scribbled with Arabic and Chinese letters. Harfan had become familiar with these metal boxes that ferried arms and ammunition from destinations in China and the Middle East.

What was Ibadat up to? What was he doing there? Playing ducks and drakes!

He ruled out the possibility of Ibadat playing the last moment spoilsport. He had defied Alam's Operation Liquidation order twice. His own life might be in jeopardy. Alam wasn't known for oozing the milk of human kindness. He was a better killer than any other efficient deep-buried sleuth was.

Harfan was busy loading the last container on a forklift. Flight AAL-X-356, technically serviced, fuelled for a non-stop flight to Colombo and stocked with in-flight supplies was ready to take off at eighteen hundred hours sharp.

Voodoorume waited impatiently for the last crate to be loaded by Harfan. His chief steward and co-pilot, Antichopoulas, stood near the front door and waved at Harfan to speed up.

Two Air Force policemen inspected the cargo-crate meticulously and gave the thumbs up sign. Harfan heaved a sigh of relief. He had specially packed this very crate with lots of care and concern. His heart had started pounding erratically as the police duo drifted towards the main entry gate.

Thank God! The final barriers were crossed and it was just seconds before he fork lifted the most precious cargo to the fuselage of the aircraft. Two precious pieces of his life were inside that nondescript wood and metal packing.

The Air Traffic Control repeatedly reminded the pilot, amidst loud crackling and static noises that he had only ten minutes to take off. The tower wouldn't allow any craft to be airborne, half an hour before and after the scheduled VIP flight from Chak Lala. The air space over the landing and take-off approaches would be embargoed.

Harfan slowed down the forklift tractor.

"What the hell are you doing here?"

He stepped down from the forklift and asked Ibadat in an anguished voice.

Ibadat was all ears as his VHF set crackled loudly.

"Have you finished loading?" Ibadat asked, still listening to some agitated conversation on the handset.

"This is the last one. But, how did you manage entry into this bay? No civilian is allowed here."

Ibadat pointed his finger at a foxhole-sized gap in the fence, covered by ivy growth. He gestured at Harfan to listen to the loud exchange of messages, often interrupted by static and squelching noises.

"Have you put ***Bhabiji*** and Parvez in the plane?"

"They're just about to be loaded. Aren't you coming with us?"

"No. Be quick. Jamanat Ali and Alam are chasing you. Take off immediately."

"You come too."

"Don't be silly. Think of the safety of Jamilla and your son. Get going." Ibadat waved Harfan away.

"How far are you from Bhagatan Jamanat sahib?" Harfan could identify Alam's voice on Ibadat's handset.

"Just 40 km short. When are you landing?"

"***Insha Allah***, in another 10 minutes... The Indian agent is taking off anytime. That's what Chak Lala told me. He should be prevented from boarding the aircraft."

Alam's voice was distorted by static noise, caused by disruption of the line of sight contact by intervening hills.

"Order Bhagatan air traffic post to stop the 707 flight... surround the airport, your suspect is trying to escape." Alam's voice boomed in.

"So Alam is the double agent?" Harfan asked.

"No. He's trying to save his asshole more than securing Delhi's intelligence assets in Pakistan."

"At my cost, I presume. What if I expose him?" Harfan quipped back in anger.

"Dead men don't tell tales, brother Harfan. His order to me was to shoot you. And I don't think he'll play a hide and seek game with either of us. This jackal is more ferocious than his master, back in Delhi. Now run and take off."

"I regret that I can't pump bullets into Arman Ali's chest, the killer of my father."

"Leave that task to me. Alam's silence is necessary too, to protect India's network in Pakistan. The ISI won't take any time to turn the heat on him. His film of deception is really thin."

Ibadat spoke in a steely voice.

"You can't do that without Delhi's orders."
"Leave that to me. I know what I'm doing."

****

"**D**on't allow him to take off... That's the order of Brigadier Barqat and your chief.... Shoot him, if you can't take him alive." Alam's voice shrieked out from the set.

"Roger Alam sahib, be quick..." Jamanat's voice came in louder, indicating the fast approach of his chopper to Bhagatanwala.

"Has Sargodha directed Bhagatan TC to abort this flight?"

"No. There are some problems. My pilot says that Bhagatan tower has directed the flight to clear the skies in another few minutes." Alam conveyed in a nervous voice.

"Has there been a change in the schedule?"

"I can't say. It appears that we've been misinformed about the timings. There's some VIP movement from Chak Lala and they're keeping radio links to the minimum, to avoid interception by Indian airborne electronic ears and the SigInt station at Simla and Leh."

"Why don't you alert the port security people?"

"I can't. There's a frequency incompatibility. My pilot has radioed Sargodha to alert the Military Police."

"Oh hell! I'm rushing. I'll blow up the plane if need be."

Jamanat pressed hard on the accelerator.

"Don't waste time, rush and take off," Ibadat pushed Harfan towards the forklift tractor, "I'll take care of Jamanat and delay his entry into the tarmac."

Harfan embraced Ibadat, said ***Khuda Hafiz*** and turned the tractor towards the rear door of the fuselage.

"I leave with two regrets." Harfan said as he mounted the trolley, "I couldn't save my mother and kill this character Arman Ali, my father's killer."

"Accept things courageously that you can't change. Somewhere you have to concede defeat gracefully. Leave that serpent to my care. I've a score to settle with him. I've some personal wars to fight. Keep this letter. It's a report on Pakistan's plan for an Israeli-type air blitzkrieg on Indian airports, military installations and targets in Delhi. Call Delhi as soon as you make it to Dacca."

"Have the military bosses gone mad?"

"Read the letter leisurely. Run and take off..go..go..."

Ibadat almost pushed Harfan out. He crouched behind a massive container and took out the loaded pistol and eight spare magazines from his waistband.

The loading over, Harfan parked the tractor at a safe distance, climbed the ladder and signalled for the ground crew to peel off.

"Close and arm all doors for takeoff and fasten your seat belts." Voodoorume's voice boomed in from the intercom.

Antichopoulas and fellow Greek and Cypriot crew complied as Harfan took his seat next to the crates of cargo.

The Lady of the Light, a Boeing 707/C135A modified Stratolifter; all four Pratt & Whitney 157-PW-59W turbo jets revved up, wing flaps fully open, lurched towards the take off marker.

"AAL-X-356, ready to take off." Voodoorume aligned the plane along the mid-marker.

"ATC to AAL-X-356. You're cleared to take off. Bank west, avoid Chak Lala, and follow the charted ATR (Air Traffic Route). Climb to 15,000 ft, steer towards Lahore, climb 20,000 ft, bank right and expect instructions from Lahore ATC."

Bhagatanwala tower heaved a sigh of relief. These spooky flights usually scared them. It was especially bad today with Sargodha breathing fire down their neck. The VIP DC10 was ready to take off at 19.00, for a non-stop flight to Dacca.

The sleepy, puffy eyed and fatigued assistant air traffic controller, a northern tribal, was glued to the radar screen. He felt annoyed when the red hot-line phone rang sharply. What's the problem? The Air Headquarters and the Directorate of Civil Aviation Security rarely used that phone.

"Yes please, ATC Bhagatan here." He leisurely responded.

"Abort the Boeing 707 flight. It shouldn't take off under any circumstances." Shouted an angry voice.

"Who is it?"

"Jamanat Ali, Superintendent ISI. I order you, on the authority of the CMLA. Stop that flight."

"Sorry sir, the bird is already airborne," The ATC assistant replied, "I require orders from General Naqi's office to abort this special flight. I don't take orders from the ISI."

He switched on the desk tape recorder in disgust. How funny, he scowled! These police chaps had now turned to controlling air traffic too!

Jamanat shouted some expletives and screamed his head off, directing the ATC to abort the flight.

"Sorry sir, I don't take orders from the ISI. Please get the appropriate authority to call me. I'm under orders to clear this flight immediately."

"You traitor," Jamanat erupted on the phone, "You'll be hanged for betraying Pakistan."

"Sorry sir, I can't obey your orders. Sargodha has already cleared this priority flight. Talk to them or General Naqi's office."

Jamanat, now accompanied by Alam, in a last minute desperate move turned the wheels towards the wicket gate. The Air Force and Military Police, M-16 assault rifles slung on shoulder straps, stopped Jamanat and his cavalcade of mixed ISI and police officials.

"You can't get in. Show us your ID." The zombie faced security commander ordered Jamanat.

"To hell with you." Jamanat flaunted his ISI identity card.

"That's not valid for this airport. You require a yellow ID card from the Air Force."

"To hell with your red and yellow cards. I'm going in right now. Call Brigadier Barqat and get your damn orders." Jamanat pushed aside the guard commander and whizzed past the gate and turned the car towards the runway.

Alam picked up Jamanat's mobile phone, dialed Gen. Hyder Bux and hurriedly filed a situation report. He requested for the immediate aborting of flight 356.

"Alam, you've called at a critical moment. The President's cavalcade has just arrived, and I can't leave this place, you know that." General Hyder replied.

"But it's important to stop the Indian spy."

"What're you doing there? I suppose it's your baby. You abort it."

"He's not my baby. I've explained that to you General. An enemy of Pakistan is making good his escape. Please do something." Alam cried out in frustration.

"Are you sure you're on the right track? Where do you think he can take the plane?

"***Allah kasam*** (swear by the ***Allah***) Hyder sahib," Alam replied, "He's escaping with his family, to Delhi."

"Don't be silly. How can he take this aircraft to India? We can get him at Colombo, if not at Dacca. Why panic?"

"What prevents him from diverting the flight to India? The pilot is an Indian too. Why take a chance? Please order the Air Force to intercept the flight. It's carrying lots of Pakistani secrets." Pleaded Alam.

"Alam sahib," Hyder almost scolded the reputed arms peddler, "It's you who had hired these chartered flights. I had to ditch Nawab only for you. What's biting you?"

Hyder was surprised over Alam's choice of time for proclaiming an emergency. The smart guy, he thought, was acting rather funny. He decided against pushing the panic button and walked down to the ceremonial gate to receive President General Arif Khan. Alam or no Alam, he shouldn't be seen missing from the ceremonial celebrity gathering. His presence rather than his performance was important in the new dispensation.

Barqat, standing near the gate saluted smartly, as the chief approached him.

"Hey Barqat," He asked, "What's eating this character Alam?"

Barqat didn't expect Hyder to ask this awkward question, moments before the arrival of the President.

"We're concluding 'Operation Salamat', as you know sir."

"That's fine. But how does Alam figure in it?"

Barqat explained his eventful tryst with the celebrity arms peddler.

"Why the hell are you here then? Rush to the tower and stop the flight. Alam says, that bugger Harfan is escaping, with lots of national secrets. Hurry."

"Yes sir." Barqat rushed for the ATC tower, at a considerable distance from the ceremonial lounge. He cursed Alam for activating the live wire at an odd time.

General Hyder spotted General Mukhtiar Ghori puffing away frantically at a cigarette. An inveterate smoker, he wished, he could finish the fag before President Arif Khan arrived in his ceremonial cavalcade.

"Hi Ghori," Hyder spoke loudly, "There's an emergency. Talk to Barqat and ask your SSG boys to join my men at Bhagatan."

"What's the great problem?"

"Barqat," Hyder shouted, "Take Ghori with you. Tackle the situation. Keep in touch."

"AAL-X-356, abort your flight." General Ghori shouted at the pilot of the Boeing 707, "This is an order from the Director General SSG."

"What does it mean pal?" Voodoo replied in light voice.

"I'm the SSG chief. Obey my orders."

"Sorry, I can't abort my flight and land back. Sargodha has closed its airspace." Voodoorume ignored Ghori's orders, banked left and kept on ascending.

"Land at Lahore." Barqat shouted.

Voodoorume glanced back at Harfan standing near a crate and supporting it with a tender hand. He smiled, whistled out a tune and set the altimeter to 15000 and kept on climbing.

"What the hell's happening?" Voodoorume turned towards Harfan and asked.

"Sorry Captain," He replied, "As I told you earlier, we've accepted your invitation. My wife and child are your passengers."

"Really? Where are they? I don't see them."

"In this special crate." Harfan pointed his finger at the deadly consignment.

"ATC Lahore, this is the Lady of the Light. I'm facing turbulence and want to gain altitude. Suggest a safe cruising height."

"You blighter, return to the base." Shouted Barqat.

"Sorry pal." Voodoorume switched off the radio.

"What's the matter? Why have you packed your family like sardines?"

"Captain, you know the problem. Please don't abort the flight. They'll kill my family and me. The ISI blokes are after my blood. They suspect that I've leaked out vital information to India, about Islamabad's mad men ferrying nerve gas shells to Dacca, for another round of genocide."

"What? Did you say nerve gas shells? I wasn't told by Naqi's men."

"Sorry boss. There are 150 shells in these crates, enough to kill ten million."

"Holy Christ! I haven't carried such deadly weapons even to the primitive war zones in Africa. My wife and kids won't pardon me, specially my wife, after having survived Hitler's gas chambers."

"Well Captain, that's the truth for you. And that's why I'm hounded."

"Where have you packed your wife and child?"

"In this crate."

"Damn fool," Voodoorume shouted, "Don't you know that these shells emit toxic fumes. Hell of a guy you are! Take'm out, quick. Antico," He signalled at the co-pilot, " Help this rascal."

He grinned, whistled his favourite tune from The Sound of Music and notched the altimeter up to 25,000 ft.

****

Jamanat's men faced their first obstacle while negotiating a stationary array of gas tankers. The airport police shouted at them, for violating air-traffic security and speeding on the tarmac. Two security teams joined the fray with cars flashing red lights and blaring shrill hooters. A helicopter of the SSG head quarter detachment joined the cavalcade of the security staff. It flew dangerously low over his car as Jamanat shouted back in impotent rage and sped along the runway, sharply turning corners, which housed container stacks, barely missing an accidental impact.

Ibadat fired first, in short bursts and punctured two tyres of Jamanat's Toyota. The occupants jumped out, took positions behind a pile of containers and returned Ibadat's bullets.

Ibadat aimed at the fuel tank of the front car and set it ablaze. The occupants crawled out and took cover behind an array of containers.

Ibadat fired again, setting ablaze the second car.

He ignored the ISI and SSG contingent firing and inching forward to his position.

Ibadat crawled up behind a wall of containers as the helicopter flew in his direction. He sighted Alam and Jamanat through the firing sight of his pistol. They were advancing, inch-by-inch, on their knees and elbows. Arman Ali armed with an M-16 rifle covered their flanks.

He noticed, in the fading saffron light, the profile of Alam and shouted, "Alam sahib, ***Khuda Hafiz***."

Alam twisted his body to the right and saw Ibadat aiming at him from a cool range of 30 feet. Ibadat steadied his grip, aimed and fired, this time in the automatic mode, emptying the magazine. Alam's mouth gaped open in disbelief and terror and before he knew it Ibadat's bullets hit him on the chest. He slumped like an ice encapsulated frozen twig. Death came even before he hit the ground.

"***Allah kasam*** Arman," Ibadat shouted, "These bullets are for killing the king and my father. Jamanat sahib, take care. I'm coming for you, next."

Ibadat took calibrated aim and fired at Arman Ali Niazi, emptying an entire magazine. Ali's head cracked open with a loud sound and red and yellow matter splattered out of the bony cage.

Ibadat kept on firing at Jamanat, in raging fury, swaying between the dream of a martyr and the anger of an avenger. All his magazines empty, he shook the pistol with a luminescent smile on his face and stood firm like a sculpted figure.

Jamanat picked up Arman's M-16, took deliberate aim and perforated Ibadat's torso like a sieve.

Ibadat mumbled the name of his God, '***Bismillah***...' and collapsed.

Jamanat jumped over Alam's body, skirted past the burning cars and rushed towards the runway. He looked helplessly at the minuscule silhouette of the Boeing 707, now a disappearing saffron dot in the evening sky.

Someone fired from an M-16 in the direction of the distant dot.

"Stop it," Jamanat shouted, "The jackal has escaped."

Chapter 63

Voodoorume turned the radio on and adjusted the earphones. A new command came over with slowly punctuated precision.

"AAL-X-356. This is Air Vice-Marshal Rahim. I give you 2 minutes to descend to 10,000 ft. Prepare for a landing at Lahore."

The voice sounded cool and menacing.

"Don't talk rubbish. I'm at 28,000 ft, can't descend that fast like a dead bird." Voodoorume replied coolly.

"Look out, you've company in the sky."

Voodoorume leaned out towards the right first and left next. He wasn't really alone. Two F-104 Starfighters, their slim fuselage faintly gleaming in the saffron light of the setting sun, skimmed the skies at his flanks. The gleaming darts flew just 500 metres apart, maintaining a vulnerable distance.

Voodoorume wasn't a stranger to these deadly US multi-role fighter bombers, which carried 9 weapon stations under the fuselage and short-span thin wings; Sparrow and Sidewinder air-to-air missiles and a 20 mm M-61 Vulcan multi-barrel canon. These deadly flying machines supplied by the USA, through the Saudi conduit, constituted the striking fulcrum of the Pakistani Air Force.

So, this small adventurer Harfan was indeed a big guy! The Pakistani Air Force wouldn't have scrambled up its prestigious fighters just for saying bon voyage to a renegade salesman. They must be gunning for a big guy, Harfan.

Voodoorume looked out again. The F-104 formation was still escorting him. He imagined their grim faces and their fingers softly placed on the missile release buttons.

"Turn back, in two minutes." Crackled in the voice of one of the F-104 pilots.

"Sorry pal. Nice birds you guys fly. I wish I could fly one. But our times were different, flying those damn beautiful old dames." Voodoorume chuckled jokingly.

He signalled Harfan to make his wife and child comfortable in a passenger seat and directed one of the crew to serve them coffee and milk.

"There is no fun in suffocating them. The Pakis have in any case got scent of you skunk. Strange are the ways of you fellows. What are you? A spy? A big guy, defecting to the Indians?"

"Stop joking, you bloody shit. You've only a minute to descend," Came in the muffled voice of the F-104 fighter, "Come down to 10,000 ft and follow me."

"Sorry chum," Voodoorume replied, "I don't take orders from you." He set the altimeter at 30,000 ft and set the cruising course due east.

"I give you exactly thirty seconds, that's final." Air Vice-Marshal Rahim's voice came in sharply, "After that my boys have the orders to shoot you down."

"Sorry Marshal," Voodoorume replied, "You definitely won't do that, I know for sure. I'm carrying 150 nerve gas artillery shells, enough to kill the population of half of your Punjab province. The choice is yours."

"Don't bluff me," Rahim's voice sounded menacing in the cockpit, "I'll count up to 30 and you're responsible for the rest."

"Don't rush Marshal, talk to your bosses, I'm carrying these shells to Dacca, and these are of US origin. Instead of killing Bengalis and Indians, you'll be killing fellow Pakistanis. I propose to bring down the bird on the most crowded part of Lahore. What do you call it? The Fort market or Bazaar Anarkali?"

Voodoo's whistle irritated Rahim.

"Stop joking you bloody gunk. Be ready for the consequences."

"Don't rush Marshal. I suggest you call up your bosses. No doubt one of your indiscreet arrows'll kill me. But the entire world'll know that, you mad men in Pakistan, are dishing out death to the Bengalis and Indians, with American supplied nerve gas shells."

Voodoorume heaved a loud sigh and silently prayed that the gamble would pay off.

"Stop blackmailing me. We know how to evaporate you scum in the air." Rahamat threatened.

"Better ask your President, if he'd like to make the world wiser about his decision to resort to a unilateral chemical war on the defenceless Bengalis. Even your American friends had found the going tough in Vietnam. Remember Agent Orange?"

Air Vice Marshal Rahim's silence emboldened Voodoorume. He made the plane steady at 33,000 ft and asked Antichopoulas to chart out on air-route map to the nearby airports in India, capable of taking a Boeing 707 Stratolifter.

"We can land at Paattaankot (Pathankot) or Odaampore, (Udhampur), both have adequate ground facilities." Antichopoulas made a quick check of the air map and replied.

"Set me the bearing and contact the nearest tower." Voodoo directed his co-pilot.

"Are we going to land in India Cap?" Antichopoulas gasped in disbelief.

"What's wrong with that?"

"We aren't legal. The Indians won't roll out the red carpets for us."

"Who cares? I may be an angel of death, but I refuse to carry these Nazi weapons of mass murder. My life and time have suffered the ghastly perfidies of the mad men of the Third Reich. I can't be party to another Nazi crime against innocent people." Voodoorume grinned gingerly.

"The Indians will impound our bird and put us behind the bars, for war crime, Cap."

"Don't worry. Le'mme do the bargaining with the Indians. I'm carrying a surprise cache for them. They should thank their stars for it."

"What about Doug?"

"Antoc," Voodoorume replied, "Le'mme do the thinking. Have faith in me. I've been your Captain for ten years, I guess."

He leaned forward and looked out ahead.

The F-104 Starfighters gained speed, zoomed past ahead of the 707, climbed up vertically and peeled off. Their gas trails floated behind like spiralled white garlands.

"Do you get me Marshal?" Voodoorume addressed Lahore ATC, "What's your decision? Do I bring down my bird on Lahore?"

"You son of Satan," A faint voice cursed from Lahore end, "Get lost. We shall take care of you, anyway."

"Fine chum. It should be a pleasure doing business with you again, when you require to dump weapons of death in Sind or Baluchistan." Voodoorume spoke, punctuating his words with soft whistles in between.

"Cap, I've raised Odaampore. Please talk to them." Antichopoulas increased the volume.

"Hello Odaampore, This is Captain Voodoorume, flying the Lady of the Light, Boeing 707, a special flight from Bhagatanwala, destination Dacca. We want permission for an emergency landing."

"We've been reading you AAL 356, rather the Lady of the Darkness. You're already within 20 km. of Indian airspace." Boomed in a voice from Udhampur control room.

"Sorry pal. Hope you don't mind the infringement."

"Yes. We mind it. You have a funny name for your bird."

"It's the Lady of the Light. You know the lady who had brought hope to the hopeless victims of war."

"But you are carrying death."

"Not really. I bring hope and love to you."

"Stop the rhetoric. Your identification is inadequate. Please give us proper identification or turn back. A Pakistani aircraft isn't allowed to over fly the Indian airspace."

"I'm not flying the Pakistani flag," Voodoorume replied in his characteristic jovial voice, "I'm a flagless mercenary. Allow me to land at Paataankot or Odaampore."

"Captain, can I identify myself and request my boss to be at the airport?" Harfan interjected.

"Better help the crew and serve some coffee. Le'mme take care of the situation. Attend to Jamilla and Parvez." Voodoorume waived him off.

"AAL-X-356, descend to 20,000 ft and identify the flag you're flying." Udhampur Air Force Tower kept on tracking the mercenary flight.

"Squadron ZV-036 and squadron SS-001 do you get me?" A new voice came into the air.

Voodoorume adjusted his earphones.

"036 and 001 scramble two Gnats and two Maruts, level up with the intruder and wait for orders."

"A nice welcome team pal. Any way, guide me along the landing corridor. I'm carrying extra fuel." Voodoorume stretched his neck to locate the Gnats and Maruts.

He had encountered the Folland Gnats on the East Pakistan skies. These Amazonian mosquitoes gave him stomach cramps.

The Maruts, technically known as HF-24 Marut MK 1, were as deadly as any other aircraft flown by Pakistan. Each one of them carried four 30 mm Aden MK 2 canon, fifty 68 mm SNEB air-to-air rockets and four 1000 lb. bombs.

Voodoorume adjusted his on board radar screen to keep track of the climbing Indian fighters.

"Hello AAL-X-356," A voice from one of the Gnats came in, "I'm Wing Commander Blair of the Indian Air Force. Identify yourself and follow me. I'm 500 knots ahead of you at 23,000. You're flanked on all sides, follow instructions."

"Roger. This is AAL-X-356. I'm at 20,000 ft following your instructions. Guide me to the nearest airport." Voodoorume acknowledged the warning sounded by the Gnat pilot.

"Identify yourself. You've just got another two minutes." Udhampur ATC warned the pilot of the Boeing 707, "I've orders to shoot you down. Are you having a special bomb bay? What other weapons do you carry?"

"This is Captain Voodoorume here, formerly a Squadron Leader with the South African Air Force, now flying for Cyprus based Athena Air Lines, a chartered company."

"What the hell are you doing in Indian air space? You can't take this route to Dacca."

"The flight to Dacca is aborted. I'm carrying 30,000 Kgs of weapons, including deadly nerve gas shells."

"What're you doing over Indian air space?"

"I'm a hired mercenary flyer, now flying from Sarghoda to Dacca. I'm carrying, repeat, carrying VX nerve gas shells of US origin. I don't want to fly these Nazi weapons of mass killing. I want to terminate my flight in India. Require dumping of extra fuel before landing. Suggest location and direction."

Voodoorume explained the situation succinctly.

"This is Delhi ATC, elaborate weapons holding." Boomed in another new voice.

"Ditto as I said. Nothing new to add."

"Hang on."

Delhi ATC faded out.

Chapter 64

Voodoorume wasn't aware of the anxiety his flight had caused in Delhi. India's capital was in a spin mode. The riddle of flight AAL-X-356 was as formidable and earth shattering as the sighting of UFOs by a group of nutty stargazers.

The Joint Crisis Management Committee (JCMC) that drew members from three wings of the Armed Forces, Civil Aviation, FIB, NSI and other security outfits, were camping at Palam airport and monitoring the minute-to-minute developments. The Cabinet Secretary, India's topmost bureaucrat led the gang.

The new voice that sounded in Voodoorume's cockpit was from the Director of Military Intelligence, Major General Gandhi.

"I can't hang on indefinitely. We've plenty of time to talk. Allow me to land." Voodoorume replied.

"Avoid funny manoeuvres. Talk sense." The DMI shouted back.

"No tantrums friend," Voodoorume replied, "I hold 150 VX Aerosol nerve gas artillery shells, capable of killing a couple of million people. Guide me for offloading extra fuel and allow me to land. We can have a nice chat later. I don't mind sharing a coffee with you."

"Why do you seek emergency landing facility? Any technical problem?" Delhi asked.

"No technical problem, the problem is of the heart, my heart and the hearts of your son and daughter-in-law," Voodoorume chuckled, "And if you're information hungry, here it is. I repeat: it's an Athena Air Lines bird, a mercenary company, owned by a former Luftwaffe colonel. It's hired by Pakistan; CIA funded, and carrying Chinese weapons, including CIA supplied nerve gas shells. This is my thirteenth sortie to Dacca. Any more dope required?" Voodoorume chuckled on the microphone.

The JCMC huddled together and went into frantic consultations. The security luminaries threw about conflicting views on the unprecedented contingency. Some advised against the landing of the flight on Indian soil. That could invite a retaliatory attack from Pakistan. Finally they agreed on the formulation of a capsule executive summary for the Prime Minister, who was in constant touch over the UHF (Ultra High Frequency) radio channel, from her South Block office.

The Boeing 707, a mercenary chartered flight, the wise bureaucratic heads concluded, was flying weapons to Dacca, but for reasons unknown, diverted its course to the Indian airspace. They couldn't define the vague problem of the heart, as cryptically mentioned by the pilot. Some of them suggested the immediate mobilisation of a cardiac specialist at the port of landing. There wasn't any unanimity over the son and daughter-in-law riddle as well. Could it be a code? Could this be another dirty ploy by Pakistan?

"Hope you read me clear!" Voodoorume continued, "One more point. Please inform your NSI chief. He has a guest in the flight. He may like to receive him personally."

"Identify the guest." Delhi ATC demanded.

Voodoorume maintained silence.

"Speak up 356."

"Harfan. He has a very important message for the chief. Don't miss to inform him, it's vital for your national safety." Voodoorume replied in a commanding tone.

Delhi ATC came alive after a brief silence.

"Who's this bloody Harfan? Elaborate."

"Tell your NSI chief. He'll understand and I don't think you require further information."

The Joint Crisis Management Committee huddled their heads together again. Some of the members demanded an explanation from Balachandran Nampoothiri.

"Who's this character Balls?" Demanded the Cabinet Secretary.

"I'll explain later. Perhaps we can divert the plane for dumping excess fuel and consult the Prime Minister." The NSI chief made it clear that he wasn't willing to discuss Harfan with them.

"Is this pilot an agent of your company?" Asked a security expert.

"I refuse to comment. Please do as I say." Nampoothiri returned a curt reply.

The JCMC relapsed into silence.

"Hi friends," Voodoorume's voice came in, "I can't hang on indefinitely. What's your decision? Should I crash over Delhi?"

"Turn 12 o'clock, follow the Air Force birds, jettison extra fuel. Keep a reserve for two hours and follow landing instructions." The JCMC decision was conveyed by the ATC, after brief but hectic consultations.

Their decision was hastened by Nampoothiri's intervention. His argument was impeccable. Harfan was his liability and that wasn't going to rain death over Delhi. But the Aerosol VX nerve gas shells could; if the funny pilot decided against hanging over the Delhi skies or his bird developed some technical snag.

The Gnats banked right, signalled to the Boeing 707 to ascend to 30,000 ft and follow them for dumping extra fuel over the Himalayas.

The Delhi tower used a reserved digital channel to direct the Air Force to escort the Boeing 707 for landing at Hindon Airbase, about 70 kms north of Delhi. Two factors, the deadly weapons load and the presence of the mysterious passenger, a guest of the NSI, influenced the decision. Palam was too close to the capital and was easily accessible to the national and international media.

The Joint Crisis Management Committee, usually comfortable with bureaucratic indecision hustled up their acts, prodded by a call from the PMO. They flew in a MI8 chopper and landed on the green turf of the National Stadium, which stood at the end slope of the once imposing Raisina Hills, and now Lutyens' Viceregal palace, renamed Rashtrapati Bhavan after independence.

The Foreign Secretary, otherwise a docile happy-go-lucky diplomat, scurried in with his colleagues for a hurried meeting with the Prime Minister. Her South Block office was just at the other end of the elegant stretch of the Kings Way, renamed Raj Path.

The mercenary flight, he suspected could be part of a rogue intelligence operation by the National Security India. He had as much faith on Nampoothiri as fellow bureaucrats had on his diplomatic skill.

The Cabinet Secretary, when the chief foreign office mandarin whispered the suspicion into his ears, just managed to display a dry grin on his emaciated face. The very idea, his eyes conveyed, was ridiculous.

"Don't be silly." He managed to comment.

"It's real. It's copied from one of those CIA sting operations."

The Foreign Secretary insisted.

"Let's see. We'll take care of it."

****

Prime Minister Mandira seated behind the massive table, looked like an ivory sculpture. Her face looked stony and devoid of emotion. She was lost in the depth of unfathomable contemplation, dissecting the minute threads of the crisis.

Another war cloud was looming low and dark on the horizon. Was she guiding the country to another military stand off, like the one in 1965?

She glossed over the games she had played when her predecessor, Jung Bahadur had accepted the UN brokered peace deal, in the wake of the drawn 1965 war. It had been a child's play to instigate some ministers and members of parliament against that rustic hinterland leader.

But in less than 6 years, she had manoeuvred the country into the vortex of another whirlwind, another war. Had she pushed the country in the present eyeball-to-eyeball stand off?

No. Mandira shook her head. She hadn't.

Pakistan had bargained for this punishment by systematically and irrationally pursuing the so-called unfinished agenda of the Great Partition, twice in the Vale of Kashmir and with the ceaseless meddling in India's internal security concerns, by unleashing a proxy war in the Northeast.

Its misadventures and acts of genocide in East Pakistan had inundated India with a flood of human migration from the ravaged eastern wing of Pakistan. One way or the other India was sure to collapse, either by the onerous responsibilities of feeding and accommodating 16 million refugees, or by another round of war.

The war between India and Pakistan had become inevitable. In fact, an undeclared war was already raging in the eastern front. The war of attrition between the Pakistani forces and the combined forces of the Indian irregulars and the ***Mukti Bahini*** were ravaging the riverine rural East Pakistan.

Mandira was engrossed also, with a Cipher Bureau telegram from the Indian Mission in Kabul. It detailed a snap report about the alleged hijacking of a weapons laden Pakistani chartered aircraft by some unidentified Indian. The Mission had picked up the information from its Jalalabad listening post.

The chief of the Mission reported, quoting a sensitive source, about an armed skirmish between the SSG and unidentified Indian commandos, at an auxiliary airbase near Sargodha. Some diplomatic sources in Islamabad attributed the incident to a surreptitious commando attack on a defence radar formation by India's external intelligence agency, the National Security India.

It was indeed a queer development. She ruled out a rogue operation by her own intelligence agency. Nampoothiri, she shivered to think, would hasten up an Indo-Pak war by resorting to CIA and KGB type operations, without her clearance.

Could it be a Pakistani trick? It wasn't impossible. The dictator, back there, could throw up any smokescreen for mounting a blitzkrieg against India.

She must cripple this enfant terrible, the evil establishment of Pakistan, at least for another 50 years.

Her thought process short-circuited several strata of neuronal connectivity. The focus was shifted from macro overview to the micro crisis hanging over the Indian skies.

Was her decision correct in allowing the dangerous flight to land at Hindon airbase? What if something went wrong and the nerve gas shells exploded! Should she revoke the decision and ask the Air Force to direct the flight to a remote base in the Northeast! Say at Doomdooma or Jorhat! Any unfortunate explosion in remote Assam could be advertised as another Pakistani perfidy.

"Ma'am." Rajinder Singh Dewan rattled his throat cautiously to draw the PM out of her trance.

"Yes." She imperiously turned her neck, not really meeting the eyes of her aide.

"The JCMC members are here, they are requesting for an urgent audience. It has something to do with a Pakistani plane."

"Yes Dewan. What were they saying about a guest of the NSI being in the Pakistani flight?"

"Some Harfan, they said, was carrying important defence related information."

"Call in Nampoothiri first."

The NSI chief, tossed between unknown and half-known facts about his prized agents in Pakistan, briefly apprised the PM of the identity of Harfan Bukhari and the essentials of Operation Triple X.

He hastened to add that the events had taken him by total surprise. The NSI wasn't in a position to offer the Prime Minister a cogent and rational explanation of the events leading to an intrusion by the mercenary flight.

"I presume it's the same fellow who is giving us a running commentary of the weapon and armament induction in East Pakistan!"

"Yes ma'am."

"The same fellow who brought about the intelligence coup in Manipur!"

"Yes ma'am."

"I hope Balu," Mandira asked with a squinted look, "It's not one of your sting operations!"

"That's what Pakistan would like the world community to believe," Nampoothiri replied with a straight face, "Our sting operations too are closely monitored by the Security Advisor to the PM."

"I believe the pilot has about 150 nerve gas shells in his cargo bay. What are the security implications? Are we equipped to face a major chemical or biological attack by our enemy?"

"The implications are simple ma'am. The USA had used similar shells in Vietnam with devastating consequences. Our defence forces and the civil defence machineries have no contingency plan to cope with such attacks."

"I think your X fellow has done a great job. Take it easy. Talk to me before he is interrogated. Isolate him and other members of the crew. Now I have some nice X Mas gift for the White House."

A smile flashed over Mandira's face.

"Rajinder, call in others and order some coffee and some light eats."

She collected herself, looked down at her reflected image on the glass table top, combed back her unruly hair, shuffled her ***sari*** and asked Dewan to summon the Defence and External Affairs Ministers.

Seated around the table, the dozen seasoned bureaucrats, responsible for key areas in national life, stared blankly at the PM, as if they were disciples of Buddha, waiting for the message *of* ***nirvana***, under the Wisdom Tree.

"So, what's this drama in the skies?" Mandira asked, as if she wasn't aware of what acts were being unfolded in the sky.

The Cabinet Secretary, Chairman of the JCMC, narrated the story, in his Oxonian English, not forgetting to make a subtle dig at the NSI chief, for his stubborn refusal to elaborate on the identity of his guest.

Mandira, amazingly unruffled, offered coffee and snacks to the assembled officials and kept on surveying their faces.

"Anything else?" She asked.

"Ma'am," Balachandran Nampoothiri cleared his throat and reported in a low tone, "It's better if we keep my guest out of this discussion. We should be able to interrogate the other players in the drama in another few hours."

"Is it a case of hijacking?" The PM asked in an amused tone.

"It doesn't appear to be one." Nampoothiri replied peevishly.

A piqued and worried man, he wasn't in a position to share the details of the aborted Operation Triple X. He silently regretted Harfan's comet like appearance over the skies of Delhi.

"What's your assessment of the weapons being carried on the plane?" She asked the Military Intelligence chief.

"In fact ma'am," The fiercely moustached DMI responded in a squeaky voice, "We've been kept updated by the NSI and other sources, about the induction of conventional weapons to East Pakistan by some of these mercenary chartered aircrafts."

Mandira didn't respond. She kept on tossing a pencil on the glass top and moving her head gently. The people sitting across again went back to the yogic posture of receiving the ***nirvana*** message.

Finally she dropped the pencil with a deliberate wave of her hand.

"And Chief," She glanced at the Air Chief, "How do you expect Pakistan to react?"

"My intelligence and inputs from friendly sources indicate that, Pakistan has moved eight squadrons of advanced fighter bombers to Sargodha, Multan, Lahore and two other minor airbases. Their F-14 and Mirage squadrons are capable of striking at our strategic bases, at the shortest possible notice."

Replied the Air Chief.

"Thanks Chief. Natarajan...," She addressed the Cabinet Secretary, "Prepare a handout for a media briefing. It should state that a Pakistani mercenary cargo flight, carrying loads of dangerous weapons, including nerve gas artillery shells of Chinese origin has defected to India."

"US origin, ma'am, as the pilot says." The Cabinet Secretary mumbled.

"Make it 'probably Chinese origin'. I'd like to dangle the knot around Washington's neck at an appropriate time. And you," She turned to the Foreign Secretary, "Summon heads of the diplomatic corps and give them the same briefing. Collect additional materials from Nampoothiri, if necessary. However, no mention is to be made about the identity of the mercenary pilot, his crew and the guest of the NSI. Do I make myself clear?"

The wise men of Delhi nodded their heads in robotic synchronization.

"Dewan," She turned towards her secretary, "Connect me to Moscow, London, Washington, Paris and Tokyo, as soon as the flight lands."

"Yes ma'am."

"I'd like to meet the War Council, in another thirty minutes. And connect me to the ***Rashtrapatiji*** (the President). I'd like to call on him, after the War Council meeting."

"And Nampoothiri," She again picked up the pencil, "I hope you'll receive your guest suitably. There should be no conclusive action without my knowledge. And rush me the special message from him. I'm curious."

"Yes ma'am. I've positioned special communication posts both at your office and residence. They will keep you informed of the latest developments at Hindon" Nampoothiri bowed in compliance.

"I want an immediate assessment and appraisal of the information being carried by your guest, at your personal level. I don't want mindless meddling with the sensitive guests. Protect them well. Pakistan would surely try to bump them off."

"Yes ma'am."

Nampoothiri silently cursed Triple X for upstaging him in the most unexpected manner. He should have been in a London safe house by now. He wondered why Alam had failed to execute his last order and why he was dead silent for over 72 hours.

Well! He would require plenty of patience. Agent Triple X had indeed surprised him and India by delivering a dreaded consignment of nerve gas shells. There couldn't be a better birthday present for the PM, which was just three days hence, the nineteenth day of November.

The PM beckoned at the retreating hoard as the ministers and officials started dispersing.

"Examine the feasibility and probability of Pakistan launching pre-emptive air strikes. They would like to avenge the humiliation and bad publicity once our press handout is released. That man in Islamabad appears to be losing his shirt."

"We've made full preparations to meet all possible Pakistani threats." Replied the DMI.

"Are our radar formations capable of intercepting the aerial blitzkrieg by Pakistan?"

"Not really ma'am. Our radars can't detect tree-skimming aircraft. The Russian equipments are outdated and Pakistan has at least six squadrons of fighter bombers that can skim the tree tops." The Air Chief added.

"I'm not glad to hear that Chief," Mandira spoke with overt efforts to control the involuntary twitching of her right eyelid, "I want foolproof measures. I can't afford to send a message that Pakistan enjoys air superiority over us. Alert all your formations and order the air defence units to prepare for any eventuality."

"But we have an edge over Pakistan in missile technology. Our SAM batteries can take care of their advanced American fighter bombers." Added the Air Chief.

"That's your headache. I don't want their birds to penetrate our skies." Mandira dismissed the meeting.

"Dewan." She buzzed him on the intercom, "Are we ready for the War Council meeting?"

"Yes ma'am, they're waiting in the next room."

"Keep me informed of the developments at Hindon."

Mandira closed her eyes and switched back to the deep meditation posture. She tried to envision the proceedings of the next meeting, which she had summoned to take a momentous decision. War was finally knocking at the door and she had to have the stamp of the War Council so as to order the Indian troops to officially enter East Pakistan.

She smiled and pressed the button summoning Rajinder Singh Dewan.

"Call the War Council members in."

She looked into the glass top again and readied herself for the epoch making meeting. A mysterious smile lingered on her face as she greeted the senior cabinet colleagues and top brass of the Armed Forces.

****

Five shifting blinks gradually emerged brighter on the airport pulsed radar screens. The echo pulses, converted to video signals, indicated that the Gnats and the Maruts flying in a close V formation were chaperoning the Lady of the Light at 8000 ft.

"Approach from the southeast, runway at 2 o'clock. Do you get me 356?"

"Loud and clear." Voodoorume whistled and replied, "Hi pal, before you bundle me out to your prison, I hope, you'll allow me a visit to Ballia in Uttar Pradesh. My roots are there."

"Concentrate on your gears and instruments." The ATC mildly rebuked the pilot.

"Fine friend, be my guest for a nightcap, don't disappoint me. I hope you've alerted the emergency services and the fire tenders. I'm carrying volatile materials." Voodoorume advised Hindon ATC.

"That's our headache. Prepare for a touch down."

Voodoorume whistled for a while, before releasing the under carriage. He banked right, aligning the plane for a landing, his first on Indian soil.

"What's that fascinating tower pal?" He asked Harfan.

"That's the Qutub Minar Captain, a tower built by a Muslim ruler, on an old Hindu edifice."

"Hope I get to see this wonderful ancient place. Be my guide, if I'm not put behind the bars straight away."

Voodoorume shifted his eyes to the blinking panel consoles and the grounds below, which presented a dusty barren and battered look with ugly yawning mine holes dotting the carpet.

The Maruts whistled past the Boeing and disappeared into the horizon. The Gnats peeled off, climbed up vertically and proceeded to nearby Sarsawan base.

"Await for parking instructions at the special bay. Follow the blue light flashing pilot car." Delhi ATC, familiar with the dare devil voice by now, advised Voodoorume.

"We've a lady and a child in the flight, arrange a vehicle for them and a nice place for their stay."

Voodoorume came in, as the wheels screeched against bitumen and flared out tongues of fire and smoke.

"Who are they?"

"Your daughter-in-law and grand child." He giggled rather loudly.

"Take a right turn, follow the ground pilot." The ATC guided Voodoorume to a remote corner of the technical area.

"Did you say your daughter?"

"Mine yes, and yours too. Daughter-in-law of India."

"What? What nonsense are you talking about?" Asked the Cabinet Secretary.

"As I said daughter-in-law and a grand son too. Surprised?"

"Talk straight."

"Ask your NSI chief." Voodoorume whistled loudly and broke into a soft humming of his favourite song and brought the plane to a halt.

He looked out and was impressed by the motley reception crowd; a dozen vehicles of the armed forces, a phalanx of fire tenders, couple of ambulance vans and two white unmarked cars. Helicopter gunships whizzed past just a 1000 feet above the fuselage of the Boeing 707.

The distant silhouettes of truck-mounted ground to air missiles with mobile radar in tow didn't surprise him. Delhi wasn't taking any chances against the possible retaliatory air raid by the Pakistani fighter-bombers.

"Elaborate, about the lady and the child." Demanded a member of the Joint Crisis Management Committee.

"A big surprise pal! Wait. Hope you have ritual sweets to welcome her." Voodoorume laughed, as he applied the brakes.

"Don't talk rubbish."

"Ask your NSI chief, as I said. ATC, please order the ladder and requisite ground facilities. Advise a very delicate and expert handling of the volatile cargo, if you don't want a nasty accident."

He switched the powerful engines to idling position and asked the crew to disarm the doors.

Voodoorume wasn't aware of the other drama being enacted by the Indian Air Force and the crack contingents of 8th Grenadiers, a specialized force that handled emergencies like the one created by the landing of the Lady of the Light.

About half a dozen MIGs circled over the Hindon airbase for intercepting surprise intrusion by Pakistani aircrafts. A couple of MI8 gunships hovered over the flanks of the base with orders to shoot down intruders.

A few batteries of vehicle mounted SAM missiles, synchronized with the radar formations were positioned at Hindon and at several vulnerable places and installations in and around Delhi.

The Northern Air and Army Commands were put on the highest alert, ready to move against Pakistan in a few minute's notice.

Four columns of the Grenadier commandos rushed in and took positions under the fuselage and wings of the plane, as Voodoorume stepped out. Parvez Bukhari, wrapped up in white linen was on his lap. Jamilla followed him, a white scarf drawn on her head. Harfan trailed her shadow.

The South African pilot whistled a popular tune from The Sound of Music... Climb Ev'ry Mountain... as he trotted down the stairs. The haunting musical, portraying indomitable courage and a pining for freedom always excited the reeds of his mind.

It was indeed a flight to freedom, his final redemption from another bondage, at the end of a long journey through a dark winding tunnel. This was his final tryst with mercenary flights. He would fly back to Paris and join his wife and kids. The city of liberty, equality and freedom beckoned him. It was far removed from the daggers of Doug Chris and the jaundiced white skins of Johannesburg.

The merchants of death wouldn't be able to follow his furrow to the green pasture of peace. There wouldn't be any Pakistan, any India and any merchandise of death. Enough! He had seen enough of the deadly tangoing of the hungry marsh jackals, jumping at each other's throat over pieces of rotten flesh.

Voodoorume squeezed Harfan's shoulders and gently placed Parvez on Jamilla's lap.

"Thanks Captain." Harfan embraced Voodoorume tightly.

"Thank you pal. I'm indebted to you and baby Jamilla. You've taught me afresh, the meaning of life and love. No more plying of the ferry of death. I will rest on my oars. I too will go back home, to my wife and kids. I hope people in Delhi won't detain me here for the rest of my life."

Voodoorume walked straight into the waiting car, flanked by armed commandos.

Nampoothiri quietly walked past the JCMC members and approached Harfan, standing under the sprawling wing of the Boeing 707.

"Follow me. Come dear."

He cordially guided Jamilla and Ramendra Kaushal to an unmarked car. Her white scarf softly fluttered in the cool mid November breeze.

Parvez, enormously excited by the meaningless hustle and bustle around him, trailed his tiny hands about and giggled loudly, trying to capture the colourful beams of light from the control tower that momentarily lighted up his bewildered face and imagination in multicoloured hues.

– The End –

Index